Effective Literacy Instruction for Learners with Complex Support Needs

Second Edition

edited by

Susan R. Copeland, Ph.D., BCBA-D

and

Elizabeth B. Keefe, Ph.D.

University of New Mexico
Albuquerque

with invited contributors

·P A U L·H·
BROOKES
PUBLISHING CO.®

Baltimore • London • Sydney

Paul H. Brookes Publishing Co.
Post Office Box 10624
Baltimore, Maryland 21285-0624
USA

www.brookespublishing.com

Typeset by Absolute Service Inc., Towson, Maryland.
Manufactured in the United States of America by
Sheridan Books, Chelsea, Michigan.

Library of Congress Cataloging-in-Publication Data

Names: Copeland, Susan R., editor. | Keefe, Elizabeth B., editor.
Title: Effective literacy instruction for learners with complex support needs /edited by Susan R. Copeland, Ph.D., BCBA-D, University of New Mexico and Elizabeth B. Keefe, Ph.D., University of New Mexico, with invited contributors.
Description: Second Edition. | Baltimore, Maryland : Paul H. Brookes Publishing Co., [2018] | 2007 edition title: Effective literacy instruction for students with moderate or severe disabilities. | Includes bibliographical references and index.
Identifiers: LCCN 2017037606 (print) | LCCN 2017040611 (ebook) | ISBN 9781681250793 (epub) | ISBN 9781681250816 (pdf) | ISBN 9781681250595 (Paper : alk. paper)
Subjects: LCSH: Students with disabilities—Education—United States. | Language arts—Remedial teaching—United States.
Classification: LCC LC4028 (ebook) | LCC LC4028 .C66 2018 (print) | DDC 372.43—dc23
LC record available at https://lccn.loc.gov/2017037606

British Library Cataloguing in Publication data are available from the British Library.

2022   2021   2020   2019   2018

10   9   8   7   6   5   4   3   2   1

Contents

About the Forms

Purchasers of this book may download, print, and/or photocopy the handouts and forms for educational use. These materials are included with the print book and are also available at **www.brookespublishing.com/copeland/materials** for both print and e-book buyers.

About the Editors

Susan R. Copeland, Ph.D., BCBA-D, Regents' Professor, University of New Mexico, Albuquerque, New Mexico 87131

Dr. Copeland's research interests include developing strategies that allow individuals with disabilities to provide their own supports, direct their own lives, and enhance their active participation in their families, schools, and communities. She has published numerous research articles, book chapters, and two books in areas such as examining how teachers are prepared to teach reading/literacy to students with severe disabilities, and self-management instruction for individuals with complex needs for support.

Elizabeth B. Keefe, Ph.D., University of New Mexico, Albuquerque, New Mexico 87131

Dr. Keefe is an emeritus professor in the special education program at the University of New Mexico. She is committed to working with schools, school districts, community agencies, self-advocates, and families to implement effective literacy practices for all students. Her research interests center on inclusive practices and literacy. Dr. Keefe has published numerous journal articles, chapters, and books on effective instruction for students with complex support needs in the least restrictive environment.

About the Contributors

Turki S. Alzahraney, M.Ed., University of North Carolina at Greensboro, 1400 Spring Garden Street, Greensboro, North Carolina 27412

Dr. Alzahraney is a lecturer at the University of Jeddah in Saudi Arabia, with specific expertise in teacher education for students with high-incidence disabilities. He has taught college/university courses in two institutions of higher learning. His research interests include teaching instructional methods for improving reading outcomes for students with or at risk for learning disabilities to special education preservice teachers, and the effect of teaching vocabulary to students with learning disabilities using technology.

Kristie Asaro-Saddler, Ph.D., University at Albany, 1400 Washington Avenue, Albany, New York 12222

Dr. Asaro-Saddler is an assistant professor in the Division of Special Education at the University at Albany. Her research interests focus on writing and self-regulatory strategies, specifically for students with autism spectrum disorders (ASD). She has published in special education journals, including the *Journal of Special Education* and *Exceptional Children,* and has presented at national and international conferences in the area of writing. Prior to joining the faculty at the University at Albany, she was a special education teacher for children with ASD and developmental disabilities in self-contained classrooms.

Michael Burdge, M.Ed., Sp.Ed., OTL Education Solutions, 10526 Reeds Landing Circle, Burke, Virginia 22015

Dr. Burdge has facilitated and managed several full-inclusion programs for students with disabilities, including those with extensive support needs. He currently provides workshop-based trainings and consultation with several states and school districts on topics such as assessment, standards-based instruction, universal design for learning, and inclusion. Dr. Burdge has authored numerous book chapters, journal articles, and other publications related to the education of students with extensive support needs.

Christina R. Carnahan, Ed.D., University of Cincinnati, 2610 McMicken Circle, Cincinnati, Ohio 45222

Dr. Carnahan is an associate professor of special education and Director of Advancement and Transition Services at the University of Cincinnati. Her research interests include literacy instruction for individuals with autism and other significant support needs across the lifespan. Dr. Carnahan has published in journals such as *Exceptional Children, Focus on Autism and Developmental Disabilities,* and *Journal of Special Education.*

Tammy Day, M.Ed., Vanderbilt University, 230 Appleton Place, Nashville, Tennessee 37230

Teaching people to grow self-confidence by learning to think for themselves has been Ms. Day's main focus as an educator. She taught students of all ages for 18 years as a classroom special education teacher before serving as a transition coordinator for a county system in Tennessee. Since 2009, Ms. Day has been the inaugural director of an inclusive postsecondary education program on the Vanderbilt University campus, Next Steps at Vanderbilt.

Heather DiLuzio, M.A., Albuquerque Public Schools, P.O. Box 25704, Albuquerque, New Mexico 87125

Ms. DiLuzio is currently a doctoral student in special education at the University of New Mexico and is also pursuing her certification to become a Board-Certified Behavior Analyst (BCBA). For 11 years, she was a classroom teacher specializing in working with students with autism spectrum disorder (ASD). Ms. DiLuzio is currently a resource teacher for the Albuquerque Public Schools, specializing in supporting students with ASD and their teachers.

Megan H. Foster, Ph.D., Utica College, 1600 Burrstone Road, Utica, New York 13501

Dr. Foster believes that all students, regardless of disability, have the right to access the general education content and context. She is currently a professor at Utica College where she teaches both undergraduate and graduate courses in special education. Her research interests include policy, curriculum, assistive technology, and literacy as they relate to increasing access for students with extensive support needs.

Megan M. Griffin, Ph.D., University of New Mexico, 1 University of New Mexico, Albuquerque, New Mexico 87131

Dr. Griffin received her doctoral degree in special education from Vanderbilt University. She is currently an assistant professor of special education at the University of New Mexico. Her teaching and research activities focus on individuals with intellectual and developmental disabilities, particularly in the transition to adulthood, and on interventions based in applied behavior analysis (ABA) to support individuals with disabilities.

Sharon L. Head, M.A., University of New Mexico, 1 University of New Mexico, Albuquerque, New Mexico 87131

Ms. Head is a doctoral student and special educator who lives and works in rural New Mexico. Her current work focuses on helping teachers to find practical ways to broaden definitions of literacy as a means to empower all students. She is also exploring the ways in which teachers' personal/spiritual stories shape educational practice.

Jeongae Kang, M.S., University of North Carolina at Greensboro, 1300 Spring Garden Street, Greensboro, North Carolina 27412

Ms. Kang is a doctoral candidate in the Department of Specialized Education Services in the School of Education at the University of North Carolina at Greensboro. Her research interests are in teacher preparation, students with autism spectrum disorders, and literacy instruction for students with disabilities.

Laurel Lane, Ph.D., University of New Mexico, 1 University of New Mexico, Albuquerque, New Mexico 87131

Dr. Lane is currently employed full-time by the Albuquerque Public Schools as a middle school instructor in the Social and Emotional Support (SES1) program. She also holds regular adjunct professor positions at the University of New Mexico, Albuquerque. Dr. Lane infuses her teaching with engaging and rich reading, the arts, and life skills that help to enhance academic, social, and functional life skills.

Ruth Luckasson, J.D., University of New Mexico, 1 University of New Mexico, Albuquerque, New Mexico 87131

Professor Luckasson is a distinguished professor of special education at the University of New Mexico, where she has been the chair of the Department of Special Education for 14 years. She is a past president of the American Association on Intellectual and Developmental Disabilities (AAIDD). She currently serves on The Arc of the United States–Policy and Positions Committee and as Chair of its Legal Advocacy and Human Rights Subcommittee. Professor Luckasson has published widely in the following areas: definition, classification, and systems of supports for people with intellectual disability (ID); clinical judgment and professionalism; special education; legal and human rights; criminal justice of victims and defendants with ID; and community living of individuals with disabilities.

Jessica Apgar McCord, Ph.D., Central New Mexico Community College, 525 Buena Vista Drive SE, Albuquerque, New Mexico 87106

Dr. McCord spent 8 years as an elementary general and special educator where she worked toward ensuring equitable access to high-quality literacy learning opportunities for *all* students. She continues this work at the Central New Mexico Community College, University of New Mexico, and the University of North Carolina at Greensboro where she teaches preservice and in-service general and special educators.

Elise McMillan, J.D., Vanderbilt University, 230 Appleton Place, Nashville, Tennessee 37023

Elisa McMillan has more than 25 years of experience leading programs and projects that support individuals with intellectual and developmental disabilities and their families. She is an attorney and senior associate in the VUMC Department of Psychiatry and Behavioral Sciences. She holds leadership roles with Tennessee Works Partnership, Next Steps at Vanderbilt, and Tennessee Disability Pathfinder.

Stephanie Nieto, M.A., Maggie Cordova Elementary, 1500 Veranda Road SE, Rio Rancho, New Mexico 87124

Ms. Nieto has been working with students with disabilities her entire teaching career. Her areas of interest are in bilingualism and disability, literacy, universal design for learning, and leadership. Currently, she is an assistant principal for the Rio Rancho School District at Maggie Cordova Elementary.

Ann-Marie Orlando, Ph.D., University of Florida, 2046 NE Gainesville, Florida 32609

Dr. Orlando is a research assistant professor at the University of Florida Center for Autism and Related Disabilities (CARD). She provides community outreach services and professional development related to autism and related disabilities. A certified speech-language pathologist, Dr. Orlando's research activities focus on inclusive education, literacy, and the use of augmentative and alternative communication for individuals with autism and related disabilities. She has published journal articles and book chapters, and taught courses on these and related topics. Through her work at the University of Florida, Dr. Orlando has coordinated agency-funded grants focused on promoting communication for individuals with autism and related disabilities, as well as federal- and state-funded grants focused on teacher preparation, doctoral/postdoctoral preparation, and research in inclusive education for students with autism and other developmental disabilities. Dr. Orlando is a member of the American Speech-Language-Hearing Association and TASH.

Karen M. Potter, Ph.D., New Mexico State University, P.O. Box 30001, Las Cruces, New Mexico 88003

Dr. Potter's primary research interests include disability studies in education (how the multiple aspects of disability studies affect classroom experiences), teacher preparation to support inclusive practices, and literacy for students with complex support needs. She teaches undergraduate and graduate teacher preparation courses that tie research to practice and are informed by her 16 years as a middle school and elementary school general and special education teacher.

Phyllis M. Robertson, Ph.D., Texas A&M University Corpus Christi, 6300 Ocean Drive, Corpus Christi, Texas 78412

Dr. Robertson is a faculty member in special education at Texas A&M University Corpus Christi. She is an experienced teacher-educator, has obtained and administered federal research and training grants, and has provided professional development for local, state, and national organizations. Her research focuses on preparing teachers to provide culturally and linguistically responsive instruction, early intervention, and special education services in public school environments.

Andrea L. Ruppar, Ph.D., University of Wisconsin–Madison, 1000 Bascom Mall, Madison, Wisconsin 53706

Dr. Ruppar is an assistant professor of special education at University of Wisconsin–Madison and a former K–12 special educator. Her research focuses on factors influencing teachers' decisions about curriculum and instruction for students with complex support needs, including teachers' preparation and knowledge, self-efficacy, expectations, and the social context of the teaching environment. She has also developed and validated instructional strategies for enhancing students' membership and participation in inclusive high school general education English language arts classes. She teaches courses on applied behavior analysis and on individuals with complex support needs.

Diane Ryndak, Ph.D., University of North Carolina at Greensboro, P.O. Box 26170, 444 School of Education Building, Greensboro, North Carolina 27402

Dr. Ryndak is the chair of the Department of Specialized Education Services and a professor in special education for students with extensive support needs. Her expertise and experience is focused both nationally and internationally on inclusive education for students with extensive support needs, advocating with families for inclusive education services and changes in policies, and systemic school reform.

Julia Scherba de Valenzuela, Ph.D., University of New Mexico, 1 University of New Mexico, Albuquerque, New Mexico 87131

Dr. Scherba de Valenzuela is an associate professor of special education at the University of New Mexico. Her research assumes the perspective of disability as a social construction. Her research focuses on issues of educational equity for culturally and linguistically diverse learners, such as disproportionate representation and access of students with complex support needs to native language instruction.

Deborah A. Taub, Ph.D., University of North Carolina at Greensboro, 1300 Spring Garden Street, Greensboro, North Carolina, 27412

Dr. Taub believes strongly that all students deserve equal opportunities to learn and grow, and she has been actively involved in supporting best practices for all students internationally and at the federal, state, district, school, classroom, and student levels. Currently, Dr. Taub is a visiting professor at the University of North Carolina at Greensboro and has her own consulting company, OTL Education Solutions, specializing in transforming opportunities to learn for students with disabilities. Dr. Taub has provided research and professional development assistance around universal design for learning, standards-aligned instruction, collaborative teaching, systems change, and other topics that support transforming opportunities to learn for all students.

Pamela Williamson, Ph.D., University of North Carolina at Greensboro, 1300 Spring Garden Street, Greensboro, North Carolina 27412

Dr. Williamson is an associate professor at the University of North Carolina at Greensboro. She has experience working with individuals with autism and their teachers in the area of reading intervention and instruction. She has published numerous peer-reviewed articles related to reading and autism in journals such as *Exceptional Children* and *TEACHING Exceptional Children.* In addition, she is the coeditor of an award-winning textbook, *Quality Literacy Instruction for Students with Autism Spectrum Disorders,* and has educated in-service educators, related service personnel, and families on this topic across the United States.

Acknowledgments

We would like to acknowledge the wonderful teachers who we have had in our courses whose creativity and dedication to their students have inspired our thinking about how to provide quality literacy instruction for all students. They took our initial ideas and expanded and improved upon them in ways we would never have imagined. They have generously shared their work with us, and that work has enriched this new edition of our book in many ways. We thank them for their caring and commitment to providing the best literacy learning opportunities possible to their students.

We also thank the families who have been so generous to share with us their stories and experiences of literacy in their lives. In particular, our grateful thanks go to Magdalena Avilia and Lauro Silva and their amazing daughter, Milagro, and to Jill and Noah Tatz.

Special thanks also go to Diane Ryndak. Her persistent advocacy for individuals with complex support needs and generous support of new scholars in this area of study have created a remarkable change in how our field thinks about and implements literacy instruction for all students. Ashley Kruger provided much help in locating research studies and tracking down information crucial to developing the book. We give her our grateful thanks for all of her hard work.

We also thank the amazing group of Project PRAIS (Preparing Researchers in Assistive Technology Application in Inclusive General Education Contexts for Students with Significant Disabilities) scholars who have inspired, supported, and contributed to this book. In particular we acknowledge the support of Jessica Apgar McCord, Ann-Marie Orlando, Andrea Ruppar, Debbie Taub, and Megan Foster in the conceptualization and development of this book. Ruth Luckasson and Julia Scherba de Valenzuela also deserve special thanks for their ongoing support and encouragement of our work and their unfailing commitment to quality literacy instruction for all students.

Last but not least, we acknowledge the patience and support of our wonderful families who have been living through this project with us for the past 2 years.

Introduction

The purpose of this book is to provide the most current information on effective literacy instruction for individuals with complex support needs across the life span, based on sound research and respect for the human rights of people with disabilities. Much has been learned about this crucial topic since we last published a text on literacy instruction (Copeland & Keefe, 2007). The number and quality of research studies in this area has grown tremendously, and acknowledgment of the rights of students with complex support needs has become more widespread. This book is intended to provide up-to-date information for preservice and in-service practitioners in schools and community settings (e.g., teachers, speech–language pathologists, educational psychologists, direct support staff, administrators), individuals interested in pursuing more effective literacy instruction for themselves, and families wanting to learn more about effectively supporting their family member with a disability in literacy activities. It is also intended to serve as a resource for scholars in the field. Perhaps most important, this book also intends to address and dispel the numerous myths that many people still hold about literacy and individuals with complex support needs. (See Myths and Facts in the Supplementary Materials at the end of the book.)

Each of the following chapters describes assessment and instructional practices that have a solid research foundation. The authors, each expert practitioners and researchers in this field of study, provide examples of how these practices can be used to develop engaging, effective instruction for students of varying ages and across a range of skill levels. Each chapter includes learning objectives, reflection questions, and suggested resources for readers who want to do further study on their own. There are also detailed case studies included in the Supplementary Materials that instructors can use to create application assignments for students.

These additional resources make the text ideal for teacher preparation courses or for school or adult program-based learning communities of practitioners in schools or adult educational programs who want to improve literacy instruction for their students.

SECTION I: CHAPTERS 1–5

This section presents a foundation for literacy access and instruction as a human right for all people. Chapters address critical issues that affect the opportunities and access to high-quality literacy instruction that students with complex support needs are given. The first chapter lays out the history and legal basis for providing literacy instruction for individuals with complex support needs. The remaining chapters in this section address language as the foundation for literacy, considerations for instruction for students who are culturally or linguistically diverse, and the role of college- and career-ready standards in literacy instruction planning and implementation.

SECTION II: CHAPTERS 6–11

In this section, chapters focus on how to organize and implement high-quality comprehensive literacy instruction for students with complex support needs. Each chapter in this section describes how components of literacy instruction can be appropriately and meaningfully applied with age groups across the life span. Chapters include multiple examples of meaningful instruction for individuals with complex support needs who have a range of knowledge and skills, including older individuals who may be emergent literacy learners. Reflection questions are included in each chapter, as well as a list of print-based and Web-based additional resources for each instructional area.

SECTION III: CHAPTERS 12–15

Chapters in this section address literacy instruction beyond the traditional pre-K–12 school curriculum. These chapters provide a broad discussion of the importance of opportunity and access to literacy instruction for individuals of all ages and skill levels. Chapter 12 describes how and why practitioners and parents can adapt books and other reading materials in creative ways to provide access to learners with unique challenges. Chapter 13 explains how to incorporate literacy instruction into the arts as a way of motivating students and enhancing their learning. Chapter 14 describes the importance of continuing literacy education into adulthood.

The final chapter synthesizes the overarching ideas across the book and describes implications for future research and practice.

REFERENCE

Copeland, S.R., & Keefe, E.B. (2007). *Effective literacy instruction for students with moderate or severe disabilities.* Baltimore, MD: Paul. H. Brookes Publishing Co.

To my husband, Jim, without whose support this book would not have
been written and in memory of Maxine and Rob Spooner who showed me what is possible. (SC)

For Mike, Meg, Andrew, Rebecca, Andrea, and Brenna and
in loving memory of George and Mavis Barker and Margaret and John Keefe (EK)

The Foundations of Literacy as a Human Right

CHAPTER 1

Literacy for All

Susan R. Copeland, Elizabeth B. Keefe, and Ruth Luckasson

LEARNING OBJECTIVES

By the end of this chapter, readers will

1. Understand the basis of literacy instruction as a human right.
2. Learn the importance of, and implications for, how literacy is defined.
3. Be able to describe the legal mandates undergirding literacy instruction for students with complex support needs.
4. Be able to describe and critique the historical models of literacy instruction for students with complex support needs.
5. Be able to describe how literacy enhances opportunities for individuals with complex support needs.

The United Nations (U.N.) Convention on the Rights of Persons with Disabilities (CRPD; U.N. General Assembly, 2006) states that education is a human right for everyone, regardless of disability status. The purpose of education is to equip students with knowledge and skills that will lead to increased opportunities, choices, and autonomy, with literacy being a critical part of learning. As a crucial component of education, literacy is valued by and is, in fact, required for full participation in all societies. All individuals have a right to receive high-quality literacy instruction as part of their education.

Teaching literacy skills to any student, regardless of ability levels and support needs, is a complex process. For the student populations described in this book, who need various supports, teaching literacy skills requires particular dedication, expertise, sensitivity, and creativity from all members of the educational team. This book provides research-based information and strategies on how to deliver high-quality literacy instruction to students with complex support needs and equips educators with the skill set they need to bring literacy to all. This first chapter will define literacy, discuss how acquiring literacy skills empowers individuals to live fuller lives, advocate for literacy as a human right, and introduce literacy instruction for learners with complex support needs.

WHAT IS LITERACY?

Research, conceptual frameworks, and teaching methods related to literacy are often referenced without ever defining what is actually meant by the term *literacy* (Keefe & Copeland, 2011). Think for a minute about how you would define this term. Why is how you define literacy so important? You might think that defining literacy should be simple, but Knoblauch (1990) cautioned that "Literacy is one of those mischievous concepts, like virtuousness and craftsmanship, that appear to denote capacities but that actually convey value judgments" (p. 74). According to Knoblauch, we must be aware of the sociocultural aspects of definitions that are based on assumptions, ideological dispositions, and political influences. We agree. We believe the way in which we define literacy specifically communicates assumptions we make regarding the learning potential of students with complex needs for support.

Defining Literacy

Traditional skill-centered, functional, and individually focused definitions of literacy have dominated the educational landscape (Katims, 1994; Kliewer & Biklen, 2007; Mirenda, 2003). As discussed later in this chapter, these definitions have resulted in literacy programs built on readiness models and in functional approaches for students with complex needs for supports. Although some of these students can acquire conventional literacy skills with appropriate intensive instruction, others find themselves unable to reach the first rung of the metaphorical "ladder to literacy" as described by Kliewer et al. (2004, p. 378). Kliewer and Biklen (2007) described the unfortunate circular logic by which many students with complex needs for supports are deemed incapable of developing literacy skills and, often, placed in segregated classroom settings where they are not provided opportunities to develop literacy skills. The fact that these students do not develop literacy skills is then used as evidence that these students are indeed incapable.

It is clear that definitions are powerful and affect the classroom instruction, community services, and literacy opportunities offered to individuals with complex needs for support. Scribner noted the critical impact of definitions on educators: "Definitions of literacy shape our perceptions of individuals who fall on either side of the standard (what a 'literate' or 'nonliterate' is like) and thus in a deep way affect both the substance and style of educational programs" (1984, p. 6). We go further and reject definitions of literacy based on the assumption that only some people can be literate—there is no dichotomy of literate and illiterate individuals (Downing, 2005; Kliewer & Biklen, 2007; Koppenhaver, Pierce, & Yoder, 1995).

Taking all of the prior discussion into account, it is clear that no single definition of literacy will hold true for all times and places (Kliewer et al., 2004) and that literacy exists on a continuum and develops across an individual's lifetime (Koppenhaver et al., 1995). We propose five core definitional principles to broaden the ways we conceptualize literacy:

1. All people are capable of acquiring literacy.

2. Literacy is a human right and is a fundamental part of the human experience.

3. Literacy is not a trait that is isolated in the individual person. *It is an ever-developing interactive tool and status for mutual engagement between a person and a community and its people, knowledge, and ideas; literacy requires and creates connections (relationships) with others.*

4. Literacy includes observation, communication, social contact, internal connection and incorporation, and the expectation for interaction with all individuals and ideas; *literacy leads to enhanced empowerment.*

5. Acquiring literacy is an individual responsibility of each member of a community as well as a collective responsibility of the whole community; *that is, ensure that every person develops meaning-making with all human modes of communication* in order to exercise his or her personal and communal responsibilities and opportunities and to transmit and receive information and ideas.

These core literacy definitional principles underlie our discussion of literacy throughout this text and serve as important guidelines for providing quality literacy instruction. For a more in-depth discussion of each principle, we refer you to Keefe and Copeland (2011). We hope you agree that individuals with complex support needs must be welcomed as full and active participants into the literate community.

REFLECTION QUESTION 1

How do the ways we define literacy and the assumptions we hold affect educational opportunities for individuals with complex support needs?

Literacy in America: Historical and Legal Landscapes

Over the centuries, American law and legislation have been intimately tied to literacy. These ties between law and literacy illustrate how important literacy is in a society, and the ways in which its power is viewed and used by governments. Literacy's perceived and actual power to increase employability, enhance democratic participation, and limit or enhance human rights can all be seen in different types of laws. For example, law was used to prevent access to literacy, as in the slave laws forbidding the teaching of reading to slaves. Literacy was frequently denied women to "protect" them or limit their public participation. Literacy also serves as a strong legal tool for political purposes, such as excluding immigrants or preventing access to democratic voting.

Lunsford, Moglen, and Slevin stated that for all people, "literacy is a right and not a privilege: A right that has been denied an extraordinary number of our citizens" (1990, p. 2). Unfortunately, in the United States, certain groups have historically been denied access to literacy, including people of color, women, and the poor. Because they were denied literacy, few first-person accounts exist that describe the deprivation. But Asante described his understanding in his moving memoir: "Now I see why reading was illegal for black people during slavery. I discover that I think in words. The more words I know, the more things I can think about. Reading was illegal because if you limit someone's vocab, you limit their thoughts. They can't even think of freedom because they don't have the language to" (2014, p. 229).

Furthermore, attempting to analyze the importance of reading in the lives of women, Acocella explained the meaning of the harsh punishment of the young heroine caught with a book at the beginning of the novel Jane Eyre, "A nineteenth-century reader would have understood, as a twentieth-century reader might not, that Jane's crime was made especially serious by the fact that it involved a book. In the history of women, there is probably no matter, apart from contraception, more important than literacy" (2012, p. 88).

Keefe and Copeland noted, "People with extensive needs for support represent the last group of people routinely denied opportunities for literacy instruction" (2011, p. 92). Furthermore, in their excellent examination of the history of literacy opportunities for students with intellectual disability (ID), Kliewer, Biklen, and Kasa-Hendrickson concluded that much of the history of literacy for people with complex needs for support has been characterized by a "narrative of pessimism" (2006, p. 175). As a consequence, literacy instruction has often either been denied them or provided in ways that did not meet their learning needs.

More recently, law has also been used to attempt to increase access to literacy instruction for students, as in the reading mandates of the Individuals with Disabilities Education Improvement Act (IDEA) of 2004 (PL 108-446) and the No Child Left Behind (NCLB) Act of 2001 (PL 107-110); and to shape certain aspects of public education, such as in the use of students' reading test scores to "evaluate" teachers' suitability for continued employment; or as a requirement for a "real" high school diploma. Most recently, NCLB has been reauthorized as the Every Student Succeeds Act (ESSA) of 2015 (S. 1177), which continues the focus on reading instruction as a critical component of college and career readiness for all students. (See Chapter 4 for more about academic standards related to college and career readiness.)

The historical and routine denial of literacy instruction to students and adults with disabilities is rooted in this conflicted legal history as well as in the ongoing exclusionary practices that keep people with disabilities out of rigorous educational opportunities and literate environments. The push and pull of historically restricting access in order to control certain populations, and now mandating access in order to make up for lost opportunities, is currently playing out in educational policy and practices. Future directions in literacy for people with disabilities will be informed by past restrictions, current and future law, and contemporary research and practices. Understanding the context set by this legal history and the current legal landscape can provide a strong foundation for understanding the absolutely critical nature of literacy in the lives of people with disabilities, improving literacy legal policies and practices, ensuring effective advocacy for literacy for all, and enhancing the literacy rights of people with disabilities.

Literacy Is a Human Right

Luckasson explained that the human right to inclusive educational opportunities for individuals with extensive needs for supports is the same as for individuals without disabilities. She further noted that these rights are non-negotiable and are "aspects of being human that the social contract must respect" (2006, p. 12). At the national level, literacy is a vital part of inclusive education and is essential for full participation in society. Similarly, at the international level, reading and literacy are viewed as critical human rights and development tools for all people. On International Literacy Day in 1997, then U.N. Secretary General Kofi Annan stated:

> Literacy is a bridge from misery to hope. It is a tool for daily life in modern society. It is a bulwark against poverty and a building block of development, an essential complement to investments in roads, dams, clinics and factories.
>
> Literacy is a platform for democratization, and a vehicle for the promotion of cultural and national identity. Especially for girls and women, it is an agent of family health and nutrition. For everyone, everywhere, literacy is, along with education in general, a basic human right. (Annan, 1997)

In terms of international law, the U.N. CRPD, Article 24, contains this powerful obligation for education:

1. States Parties recognize the right of persons with disabilities to education. With a view to realizing this right without discrimination and on the basis of equal opportunity, States Parties shall ensure an inclusive education system at all levels and lifelong learning directed to:

    a. The full development of human potential and sense of dignity and self-worth, and the strengthening of respect for human rights, fundamental freedoms and human diversity;

    b. The development by persons with disabilities of their personality, talents and creativity, as well as their mental and physical abilities, to their fullest potential;

    c. Enabling persons with disabilities to participate effectively in a free society. (U.N. General Assembly, 2006)

Thus, literacy must be an essential part of CRPD's call for the development of fullest human potential of all people with disabilities.

Twenty years ago, Yoder, Erickson, and Koppenhaver (1997) recognized the critical right of all people to literacy instruction when they wrote the Literacy Bill of Rights (see Figure 1.1). A Literacy Bill of Rights, written by three pioneers in the field of literacy instruction for students with complex support needs, not only proclaims that literacy is a human right regardless of disability, but it explains the nature of this right in detail, describing the specific literacy opportunities that should be afforded each person and emphasizing the importance of high-quality literacy instruction. This document is a strong foundation on which to build literacy instruction for your students.

All persons, regardless of the extent or severity of their disabilities, have the basic right to use print. Beyond this general right are certain literacy rights that should be assured for all persons. These basic rights are

1. The right to an *opportunity to learn* to read and write. Opportunity involves engagement in active participation in tasks performed with high success.

2. The right to have *accessible,* clear, meaningful, culturally and linguistically appropriate texts at all time. *Texts,* broadly defined, range from picture books to newspapers, novels, cereal boxes, and electronic documents.

3. The right to *interact with others* while reading, writing, or listening to text. *Interaction* involves questions, comments, discussions, and other communications about or related to text.

4. The right to *life choices* made available through reading and writing competencies. *Life choices* include but are not limited to employment and employment changes, independence, community participation, and self-advocacy.

5. The right to *lifelong educational opportunities* incorporating literacy instruction and use. Literacy *educational opportunities,* regardless of when they are provided, have the potential to provide power that cannot be taken away.

6. The right to have teachers and *other service providers who are knowledgeable* about literacy instruction methods and principles. *Methods* include but are not limited to instruction, assessment, and the technologies required to make literacy accessible to individuals with disabilities. *Principles* include but are not limited to the belief that literacy is learned across places and time and that no person is too disabled to benefit from literacy learning opportunities.

7. The right to live and learn in *environments* that provide varied models of print use. Models are demonstrations of purposeful print use such as reading a recipe, paying bills, sharing a joke, or writing a letter.

8. The right to live and learn in environments that maintain the *expectations and attitudes* that all *individuals are literacy learners.*

Figure 1.1.   A literacy bill of rights. (From Yoder, D.E., Erickson, K.A., and Koppenhaver, D.A. [1997]. *A literacy bill of rights.* Chapel Hill: University of North Carolina at Chapel Hill, Center for Literacy and Disability Studies.)

THE POWER OF LITERACY

High-quality literacy instruction makes a real difference in people's lives. Acquiring even basic literacy skills can create opportunities to participate more fully in one's community, be less dependent on others, and make individual choices about what one wants to do or learn. In other words, literacy skills contribute to a more engaged, satisfying life. For instance, literacy facilitates participating as an active citizen in the democratic process and increases opportunities for communicating one's ideas, thoughts, and intentions (e.g., deFur & Runnels, 2014; Reichenberg & Lofgren, 2013). Acquiring literacy skills expands educational and employment opportunities and thereby promotes economic stability (e.g., Vaccarino, Culligan, Comrie, & Sligo, 2006). Improved safety, health, and well-being are also associated with basic literacy skills (Taggart & McKendry, 2009). Literacy skills create access to a greater variety of recreation and leisure activities and can boost self-confidence (van Kraayenoord, 1994) and support enhanced social interaction and relatedness (e.g., Forts & Luckasson, 2011). Take a moment to read about the ways in which literacy affects the lives of two young people with complex support needs, Milagro and Noah, in the "How Literacy Enriches Lives" textbox. Milagro and Noah have different interests, abilities, and backgrounds, yet their literate citizenship (Kliewer, 2008) enriches their lives in a multitude of ways, not the least of which is bringing them joy and personal satisfaction (see Figure 1.2 for an example of Noah's literacy journey).

HOW LITERACY ENRICHES LIVES: Milagro and Noah

Magdalena, Milagro's mom, says:

Our daughter, born August 7, 1998, was given the name Milagro Tonantzin, which means "miracle of mother Earth" in our native Spanish and Nahuatl language. As parents, we had no idea that our journey from the onset of her arrival would result in a constellation of unique outcomes that would provide a homegrown literacy-based framework. From the moment Milagro was born and suffered severe brain trauma, we were told by medical experts to expect the worst. Her initial medical diagnosis was hypoxic encephalopathy due an insufficiency of oxygen at childbirth, which resulted in a traumatic brain injury. She is now referred to as having cerebral palsy and is unable to swallow, blink, sit, or stand. She has seizures, cardiac hypertrophy, high blood pressure, and severe muscle spasticity with scoliosis. She breathes through a trach and is on oxygen 24/7, with severe intellectual impairment.

Initially, we were in shock because of the unexpected medical crisis. When we first saw Milagro, she was wrapped in wires, probes, and life-sustaining equipment. At that first moment of contact with our daughter, we touched her, looked at each other, and knew we had been presented with an extreme challenge. Creating a home environment for a medically fragile child, one completely predicated on her needs that would adapt and evolve over time, seemed insurmountable. We started to read and research to educate ourselves on children with traumatic brain injuries. The focus of our visits to the neonatal intensive care unit in those early days was talking to Milagro; touching her to stimulate her; and studying her every movement to learn every inch of her and her body responses, what she liked, and what she didn't like. These interactions became the first foundational actions of our parent-based literacy explanatory model. Creating literacy is an action-based process, and this was the first step.

Even when our daughter was at her most vulnerable due to her medical condition, she was still capable of learning through stimulation. As a newly made family, we were all three system outliers; we no longer fit into a "typical family" norm. My husband and I realized that whereas our daughter might be perceived by others as incapable, *we* perceived her as "capable with the potential to learn." It was we, as Milagro's parents, who held the ability to empower our daughter and to change the societal expectations and limitations that would be imposed on her because of her severe medical constraints. We supported her potential to become literate as defined by different norms, and we aided her learning as her capacity to learn was expressed in a series of nonverbal and later semivocal guttural responses and sound intonations. Milagro's form of communication is now the third language in our multicultural household. She challenges to us to understand it at every turn.

Every moment with Milagro became an opportunity to create an environment for learning. Lauro, her dad, excelled at coming up with story after story as he held her—even I became spellbound at his storytelling! Sound was the means of reinforcing Milagro's learning that she was important, that she mattered, and that we expected her to interact. She responded by smiling, cooing, engaging with her eyes, and creating repeated actions—her own self-developed forms of communication, to which we ascribed meaning. Gradually, we have changed her room from looking like a mini acute-care center to a place bright with color and alive with stimulating music, audio books, aromatherapy, and a collection of award-winning bilingual and bicultural books we read to her.

We also use music to create literacy and meaningful stimulation. We dance with her: slow dancing music so she gets a feel for the movement and rhythm of the body; fast dancing music to give her a feel for vibrant body movements. We are rewarded with smiles and eyes alive with joy, interest, and focus. We put her hands on our faces so she can feel and not just see our faces. We put her hands to our lips so she can feel the vibration of sound emanating from our mouths. We repeat her sounds as a way of affirming that what she says is important. Verbal and eye communication, in addition to touch, provide critical seeds of Milagro's literacy and are essential for building the bridge to her developing self-worth and self-esteem. We insist that everyone coming into our home introduce themselves to Milagro and speak *to* her, not *at* her. We strongly recommend that people new to her

Noah's Notes

Best Bud Brad

Noah Tatz | Features

Brad and I pose at "the wall".

My bowling buddy Brad Harvey loves to bowl. That is how I met him. I've known him for about two years. I bowl for Special Olympics. Brad cheers for me and helps me bowl better.

Brad is a senior at La Cueva High School. Brad is amazing and awesome because he is friendly to me. He always says hi, and we talk about bowling.

Brad started working at Silva Lanes bowling alley his freshman year. He does everything there! Brad helps with bowling, the front desk, and the snack bar. Basically he helps with anything and everything.

Brad works many hours at Silva Lanes. He gets tired sometimes, but he still has time for some fun. Brad gets to bowl for free when he's at work. That's good! He also likes to hang out with his friends.

On August twenty-second Brad and his identical twin brother Zach were born. Zach is older than Brad. His parents are Russ and Bari. Brad and Zach and his dad love to race cars on the asphalt track. At home he has two pets: a dog named Bear and a turtle.

Brad is in orchestra at LCHS. He plays the viola. He is really good at it. At age five he began to play the violin with a private teacher.

About 6 years ago his teacher asked him to try the viola. Brad likes the viola a lot because it is soothing and calming. So Brad has played twelve years! His orchestra has won two state championships. I think he is so happy and proud about it.

After high school Brad is going to do some more bowling and then college. He wants to go to West Texas A&M to become a special education teacher.

Brad plays the viola in orchestra class.

Figure 1.2. Noah's Notes.

read to her as the primary way of introduction, so she gets exposed to their voices and becomes familiar with them.

In August 2013, Milagro celebrated her 15th birthday. She is a calm, confident, loving child who knows she matters in this world. She watches PBS with her dad and listens to NPR with her mom. She is read to often, and she listens to books as well: bilingual and bicultural audio books that soothe her mind and continue to strengthen her world of literacy. Our assumption is that she can learn, and she does not disappoint. She is always listening and watching out of the corners of her eyes. In our eyes, she is a stellar student, an honor student of home-based literacy, and she fully participates and engages. She is an excellent communicator. Milagro has met our expectations and is an intelligent and literate child whose eyes tell all.

Jill, Noah's mom, says:

When Noah was in third grade, the teacher told us (bluntly!) that he was never going to learn to read. She was wrong. Noah was already reading, just not the way they were trying to teach him in school. Noah recognized lots of environmental print. He always knew when we passed McDonald's or Toys"R"Us. He loved to listen to the stories read to him every night. He started finishing the sentences and picking out familiar words.

Noah is now 21 and loves to read. He reads at a fifth-grade level, with excellent sight word skills and good comprehension, when he is given time to process. According to Noah, "Reading makes you smart. Reading is very important. Reading makes you effective. I love reading to kids."

Reading has enhanced Noah's quality of life. He loves to read books, magazines, and newspapers. Noah is fulfilled by the world around him. He is able to work on a computer, write for his school newspaper, and read to younger children. He can read a menu and order in a restaurant. Noah will tell you that reading is fun. We believe that Noah's ability to read enhances his life every day and continues to develop his great potential as an important participant in the world around him.

We believe that the need to be able to access and use information across all aspects of our lives is greater now than ever before. Everyone should be given the opportunity to gain these essential skills.

LITERACY FOR LEARNERS WITH COMPLEX SUPPORT NEEDS

We think it is more useful to consider individuals with disabilities in terms of the supports they need to be active participants in their families, schools, communities, and places of employment rather than considering them simply in terms of an educational label or medical diagnosis. A diagnosis or label is helpful for many purposes (e.g., providing access to resources or services), but this alone does not convey all the information an educator wants and needs—for example, what a student's strengths and interests are—or provide information on how to design instruction to meet individual learning needs. When teaching literacy skills, it is critical also to consider an individual's need for supports, defined as "resources and strategies that aim to promote the development, education, interests, and personal well-being of a person and that enhance individual functioning" (Schalock et al., 2010, p. 224). Supports come in many forms: some formal supports, some generic services that are available to anyone, some specialized paid services, and some natural supports from friends or family.

Using a supports–needs model to consider disability calls our attention to the fit between a given individual's current abilities and skills and the demands of the environments in which that person participates. Supports act as a "bridge between 'what is' (i.e., a state of incongruence due to a mismatch between personal ability and environmental demands) and 'what can be' (a life with meaningful activities and positive personal outcomes)" (Thompson et al., 2009, p. 136). This paradigm is based on the fundamental recognition that all humans require supports, and receiving appropriate supports improves our ability to function. Some may require more intense support or supports in more areas of their lives than others, but everyone needs some level of support at one time or another.

Defining Complex Support Needs

Individuals with complex support needs have varied, often overlapping needs for supports across multiple domains (e.g., academic skills, home living skills) and time. Their need for supports will likely be lifelong, although provision of appropriate supports creates a positive interaction between supports and functioning, improves life functioning, and may change the intensities and types of needed supports across time and circumstances (Schalock et al., 2010). Individuals with diagnoses such as ID, autism spectrum disorder, or multiple disabilities frequently have complex support needs, although individuals with other disability labels might also fit into this category. Although it is beyond the scope of this book to provide detailed information about how best to provide literacy instruction to individuals with every configuration of support needs, the guidelines, teaching methods, and examples provided throughout can be adapted for use with learners with many different types of support needs. Where applicable, we discuss research findings and recommendations pertaining to specific types of complex support needs an individual learner might have.

Using the supports–needs paradigm has the potential to positively affect the way in which education, health care, and other services are provided to individuals with disabilities. It requires that we take into account the demands of a given context and or environment and the individual's strengths and limitations in that context or environment when planning the supports that will allow the individual to be an active participant and acquire new skills to diminish the "gap" between demands and current skill performance (Thompson, Wehmeyer, & Hughes, 2010). This approach makes it far more likely that the instruction and services provided will be individualized, age-appropriate, and aligned with the individual's goals, interests, and preferences, in contrast with a medical model approach of focusing solely on an individual's deficits.

Consider, for example, how this supports–needs conceptualization of disability might affect provision of literacy instruction for Terri, a student with complex support needs. Rather than selecting an instructional program based on Terri's disability label (e.g., selecting a manualized sight word program because she has autism), the educational team—that includes Terri—considers her current performance level across the multiple components of literacy; her age; the curriculum standards for her grade level; her communication and language skills; and finally, and just as important, her interests (currently Japanese manga). Based on this information, the team selects goals that align with curriculum standards and plans instruction that takes advantage of Terri's strengths and interests while also building new skills in her areas of weakness. The outcomes of considering disability in this way are that Terri attends a world literature class with her general education peers while receiving individualized support and literacy instruction within the class. Her support is sometimes provided by a teacher or paraeducator, and sometimes it is provided more informally by her peers. Terri is engaged and motivated in her classes and has friends she sees in and out of school settings. Meanwhile, she is acquiring skills that will be critical for her success in the postsecondary program she wants to attend in a nearby university, where her older brother also goes to school.

REFLECTION QUESTION 2

What is the rationale for providing comprehensive literacy instruction for individuals with complex support needs?

Core Principles for Literacy Instruction

The closely related principles of *least dangerous assumption* and *presumed capability* are essential to opening the doors to effective literacy instruction for students with complex needs for support. The criterion of the least dangerous assumption was first proposed by Donnellan (1984) and can be summed up as assuming that all individuals, regardless of label or diagnosis, are capable of learning. Jorgensen noted that one outcome of the least dangerous assumption was that "Students are seen as capable of learning; educators do not predict that certain students will never acquire certain knowledge or skills" (2005, p. 4). Closely related to the least dangerous assumption is the presumed capability of students regardless of their label or diagnosis. This presumption of capability could be considered the most basic form of the least dangerous assumption. Low expectations based on an IQ score or label can have a negative impact on educational opportunities and outcomes for students with complex needs for support (Jorgensen, 2005).

This book is based on the least dangerous assumption that all people are presumed capable of acquiring literacy. The remaining sections of this chapter will lay a foundation to support the efforts of educators, policy makers, and individuals with disabilities and their families to support and uphold this assumption and enact the tenets of the Literacy Bill of Rights.

Literacy Instruction Models

It is particularly important that schools provide literacy instruction for individuals with complex support needs that will enable them to have access to the important benefits associated with literacy. Too often, as noted previously in this chapter, educational systems have either denied literacy instruction to these students, viewed them as incapable of learning, or offered instruction that is inadequate or ineffective (Kliewer et al., 2006). Such lowered expectations have resulted in poorer outcomes for many people with disabilities. For example, students with complex support needs have higher rates of postschool unemployment or employment in low-wage jobs, which results in lowered status and greater social isolation compared to typically developing peers or peers with high-incidence disabilities (Newman et al., 2011). Keeping this in mind, we will briefly examine the history of literacy instruction for students with complex support needs, addressing the implications, limitations, and strengths of different models used.

Readiness Model   For many years, educational programs for students with complex support needs used a readiness model. This model required students first to master sequential subskills considered to be prerequisites for more advanced literacy skills. Failing a subskill meant not being allowed to progress or being denied the opportunity to continue literacy instruction (Mirenda, 2003). For example, children might be expected to learn and name all of the letters of the alphabet in order before being taught to read their names. Unfortunately, many of these subskills were taught in a decontextualized, disconnected manner, which made it very difficult for learners with complex support needs to master them or use them in meaningful ways. Skills learned were not connected to authentic purposes, which limited students' generalization of what they learned. This resulted in students not using them outside of school or intervention settings or using them only in limited ways. This instructional model often placed students in the vicious cycle previously mentioned: They frequently failed to master low-level skills taught in a decontextualized manner, which resulted in educators not providing higher-level literacy instruction—such as comprehension—because the students were not considered "ready," which resulted in students not progressing, and so forth. Furthermore, this model frequently resulted in age-inappropriate instruction that had little real value to motivate students or address their interests. In classrooms using this model, for instance, it was not uncommon to see 17-year-olds still singing the alphabet song or being drilled on color words, a situation that engendered further stigma and devaluation by peers and teachers.

Functional Skills Model   Beginning in the mid- to late 1970s, the curriculum focus for students with complex support needs changed to functional skills (Browder et al., 2004). In terms of literacy instruction, this meant that educators taught students sight words considered necessary for survival in their schools and communities (Conners, 1992; Katims, 2000). Students receiving functional literacy instruction might spend time learning words like *exit* and *poison* or learning to write the words needed to complete job applications. In many ways, this instructional approach was an improvement over the readiness model. Students learned to read words that they could use immediately in their schools, job settings, and communities, which decreased their dependence on others. However, although functional literacy instruction has benefits, it also limits the range of literacy skills students can acquire and, therefore, their opportunities for full participation in their families, schools, and communities. This approach does not teach students skills that might allow a broader, richer range of literacy experiences, such as reading for pleasure, learning vocabulary terms that create access to science content, or writing an e-mail to a friend.

Comprehensive Instructional Model The National Reading Panel (NRP) identified components of effective reading instruction for typically developing students (Armbruster, Lehr, & Osborn, 2001) (see Figure 1.3). We assert that students with complex support needs benefit from literacy instruction that goes beyond a readiness or a functional skills approach to incorporate all the areas identified by the NRP and more. Functional skills, such as financial literacy, are important and should be a part of every student's educational experience. However, recent research examining literacy instruction for individuals with complex support needs has

---

The following are the components of effective reading instruction identified by the National Reading Panel (2000) with the addition of oral language.

Oral Language: Language forms the basis for literacy. Understanding the sound system of a language (its phonology), the rules for how words can be combined to create different meanings (its grammar and syntax), how to use language in social contexts (pragmatics), and word meanings (semantics) all influence development of literacy skills.

Phonological Awareness: Phonological awareness is the ability to recognize and manipulate the units that make up spoken language. It involves recognition that sentences are made up of words, words of syllables, and syllables of individual sounds or phonemes. *Phonemic awareness* is particularly important for developing reading skills. It entails detecting and manipulating the individual sounds in spoken words.

Phonics: Phonics is knowledge of the relationship between letters (graphemes) and their associated sounds (phonemes). Phonics knowledge allows children to map spoken language (speech) onto letters. This knowledge can be applied to decode unknown words or used to spell words when creating text (encoding).

Fluency: This is the ability to read text accurately and at a reasonably rapid, smooth pace. To be a fluent reader, a child must recognize words automatically without having to slow down to decode each word in a text. Fluent reading allows the child to concentrate on the meaning of what is being read instead of concentrating on each letter sound. Fluent readers can comprehend what they are reading more easily than readers who read slowly or in a choppy manner.

Vocabulary: A child's vocabulary is comprised of the words a child understands and uses in listening, speaking, reading, and writing. *Listening* vocabulary consists of words a child understands when she or he hears them spoken; it includes words that the child understands but may not use in his or her everyday conversation. *Speaking* vocabulary consists of words students understand and routinely use when speaking. *Reading* vocabulary consists of the words a child can read and understand. *Writing* vocabulary consists of words a child understands and can use when composing text. Having a well-developed vocabulary is important for beginning readers because to read a word in print requires having that word in your vocabulary. For example, decoding a word that you have never heard won't be very useful to you because you have no point of reference to understand its meaning.

Text Comprehension: Text comprehension is understanding the meaning of printed text, or, in other words, making sense out of what you read. It is the point of reading! Text comprehension can range from understanding the meaning of a single word ("Stop!") to understanding the nuances of meaning found in a Shakespeare sonnet. Effective comprehension requires several skills including efficient word recognition, a well-developed vocabulary, fluent reading, and adequate background knowledge ("knowledge of the world").

Figure 1.3. Components of effective reading instruction. (From Armbruster, B.B., Lehr, F., & Osborn, J. [2001]. *Put reading first: The research building blocks for teaching children to read: Kindergarten through grade 3.* Washington, DC: The Partnership for Reading.)

shown how important it is not to underestimate these students or inadvertently limit their skill development (Allor, Mathes, Roberts, Cheatham, & Al Otaiba, 2014; Conners, 2003). Although not all students will become conventional readers or writers, educators can no longer come to that conclusion merely by looking at students' disability labels. Instead, practitioners must give students the opportunity to develop a broad range of literacy skills while taking into account their individual needs for supports. This begins by viewing *all* students as readers and writers, having high expectations for what they can learn, and providing appropriate, sustained literacy instruction in meaningful ways that will allow students to develop their skills and interests to the fullest extent possible.

Research conducted within the past 10 years has demonstrated positive student outcomes associated with providing what we term comprehensive literacy instruction (e.g., Allor et al., 2014). We define a comprehensive literacy instructional model as integrated instruction that teaches all the components of reading concurrently: early literacy skills, such as concepts about print; language development and vocabulary skills; word recognition skills that include both sight word and phonics knowledge; listening and reading comprehension skills; fluency; and writing. This model is in contrast to the decontextualized instruction of the past that sought to teach discrete skills (Browder, Ahlgrim-Delzell, Courtade, Gibbs, & Flowers, 2008). Figure 1.4 graphically illustrates how using this approach to literacy assessment and instructional planning looks. This diagram can be a useful tool when planning instruction. Figure 1.5 shows how Laura White, an early intervention therapist, used comprehensive literacy instruction to create an overall literacy instructional plan individualized for a young child with ID who was at the emergent literacy level. The plan addressed all aspects of literacy and served to organize the individual lessons Ms. White provided. (This student is now a conventional reader and writer who uses her literacy skills to enhance her active participation in school, family, and community activities.)

Although we have necessarily addressed various components of literacy in separate chapters within this book, we encourage practitioners to plan lessons that reflect this model of comprehensive literacy instruction and include instruction on multiple components within lessons. (See, for example, the tools and sample lessons in Chapters 5 and 11.) Creating lessons in this manner will help students with complex support needs make meaning, which in turn will support maintenance and transfer of skills beyond the teaching or intervention settings.

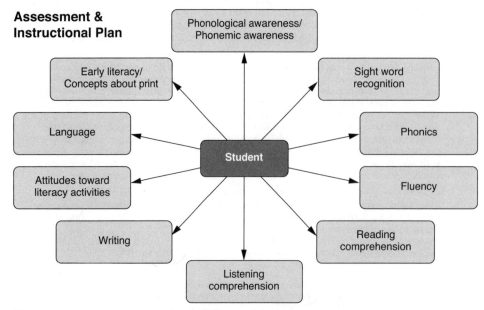

Figure 1.4. Components of a comprehensive literacy model.

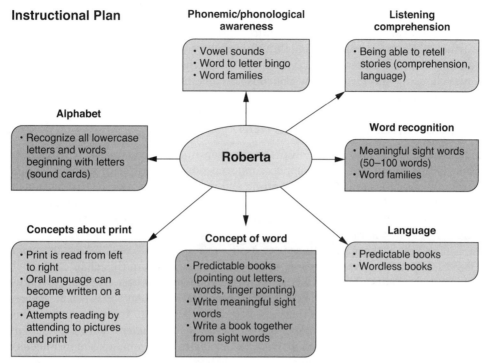

Instructional Plan

Phonemic/phonological awareness
- Vowel sounds
- Word to letter bingo
- Word families

Listening comprehension
- Being able to retell stories (comprehension, language)

Alphabet
- Recognize all lowercase letters and words beginning with letters (sound cards)

Roberta

Word recognition
- Meaningful sight words (50–100 words)
- Word families

Concepts about print
- Print is read from left to right
- Oral language can become written on a page
- Attempts reading by attending to pictures and print

Concept of word
- Predictable books (pointing out letters, words, finger pointing)
- Write meaningful sight words
- Write a book together from sight words

Language
- Predictable books
- Wordless books

Figure 1.5. Example of an individualized comprehensive instructional plan for a young emergent literacy learner.

Renewed Focus on Literacy Instruction for Individuals With Complex Support Needs

In recent years in the United States, several legislative mandates, accumulating research findings, and advocacy actions by parents and individuals with complex support needs have contributed to renewed attention to the creation of effective literacy instruction for this population. Increased accountability for the teaching and learning of these students was a by-product of NCLB (recently reauthorized as ESSA) and the most recent reauthorizations of the Individuals with Disabilities Education Act (IDEA) in 1997 (PL 105-17) and 2004 (PL 108-446). IDEA 2004 mandated authentic access to the general curriculum for all students and required that students' progress toward meeting grade-level standards be monitored. These mandates also required educators to implement evidence-based instruction with students with disabilities. Teachers must now prepare students to meet more rigorous curriculum standards that require higher-level literacy skills and focus on standards for college and career readiness. This, in turn, necessitates that schools critically reexamine the models and types of instruction they currently use. A curriculum based solely on learning safety words, for example, will not be sufficient for students to meet more rigorous academic standards.

Another recent development affecting literacy instruction for students with complex support needs is the reauthorization of the Higher Education Opportunity Act of 2008 (PL 100-315). This reauthorization created more opportunities for these individuals to attend postsecondary programs by providing ways for families to secure financial support to pay for these programs. As a result, the number of students attending postsecondary programs has increased. The students in these programs need stronger academic preparation to be successful (Grigal, Hart, & Weir, 2014), further raising the expectations of parents and students themselves that effective literacy instruction be provided.

Still another development affecting practices in literacy instruction is a growing awareness that individuals with complex support needs, like their typically developing peers, have the capability to be lifelong learners (Moni & Jobling, 2014). Much more is known about effective reading instruction for children and adolescents with complex support needs, but increasingly, researchers are now examining reading instruction for adults (Copeland, McCord, & Kruger, 2016). The available research with adults shows that learning does not stop when students leave formal school programs. Individuals with complex support needs, like many typically developing adults, may have increased motivation and focus when pursuing learning opportunities of their own choosing and for their own purposes. Thus, literacy instruction should be available for adults who wish to expand their skills.

GUIDELINES FOR LITERACY INSTRUCTION

Our own research and our review of the research and practitioner literature examining literacy instruction for students with complex support needs has resulted in our developing several overarching guidelines to use when planning and implementing literacy instruction for this group of individuals. Keep these in mind as you read each chapter. Each guideline arises from careful consideration of research findings and from the many years of advocacy by individuals with disabilities and their families.

The first of these guidelines is to *begin instruction with, and maintain, high expectations for students with complex support needs.* As you have read in this chapter, the beliefs we hold about our students' abilities and the definition and nature of literacy strongly influence what we choose to teach; how we teach it; and, as a consequence, student outcomes. Research simply does not support the outdated idea that we can know what a given student can learn based solely on a disability label. Second, *combine high expectations for students with provision of individualized, systematic, and sustained instruction.* Students with complex support needs benefit from well-planned, consistent instruction across their years of schooling (e.g., Allor et al., 2014). In the past, educators often discontinued instruction when students did not make rapid progress, not recognizing that they continue to learn when given high-quality, sustained instruction.

The third guideline is to *provide language and communication interventions and support from the earliest years of a child's life.* Language is the foundation on which later literacy develops, so it is crucial to support its development beginning at birth (see Chapter 2). Children use words to develop important conceptual understandings; language "drives cognitive development" (Neuman, n.d.), so we must give every child the opportunity to develop his or her language and communication abilities. We must also pay attention and consider a child's home language when planning language/communication and literacy intervention. (See Chapter 3 for a thorough discussion of the issues related to children whose home language is not English.) Related to this, the fourth guideline is to *begin structured, developmentally appropriate literacy instruction during the preschool years and continue instruction across a student's formal schooling.* Many individuals with complex support needs also choose to attend postsecondary programs (see Chapter 14 for more information) or adult education programs where they may choose to continue their literacy instruction.

Fifth, *create comprehensive literacy instruction that includes concurrent instruction in all the core components of reading*; this type of instruction is most effective for individuals with complex support needs (e.g., Allor et al., 2014; Browder et al., 2008; Browder, Ahlgrim-Delzell, Flowers, & Baker, 2012). Practitioner preparation programs have a responsibility to teach their students to move beyond highly scripted intervention programs focused narrowly on only one component of literacy and instead provide instruction across skill areas using engaging materials and activities. This leads to a sixth guideline: *Students with complex support needs learn to read in a manner similar to their typically developing peers and alongside those peers* (e.g., Wise, Sevcik, Romski, & Morris, 2010). Having students receive their instruction alongside typically developing peers utilizes the natural supports, motivation, and incidental learning opportunities this arrangement provides. Researchers and practitioners have documented that the intensive, individualized instruction required for students with complex support needs can be successfully provided within general education contexts (Hudson, Browder, & Wood, 2013; Ryndak, Moore, Orlando, & Delano, 2008/2009; Ryndak, Morrison, & Sommerstein, 1999). Researchers such as de Graaf and van Hove (2015), for example, found that students with ID who received literacy instruction in general education classrooms, regardless of their cognitive abilities, acquired higher levels of reading skills than students with similar cognitive abilities educated in segregated classrooms. Findings such as this lead to recognition that preservice practitioners should have coursework and field-work related to planning and implementing high-quality, comprehensive literacy instruction for students with complex support needs within general education settings. Teacher preparation program content must address universal design for learning lesson design, use of technology, and up-to-date literacy instructional practices. We hope that our book will prove useful to all those who want to provide effective literacy instruction to individuals with complex support needs.

REFLECTION QUESTION 3

Think about the importance of literacy in your own life. How can you use the guidelines in this chapter to help individuals with complex support needs become members of the literate community?

SUMMARY

The potential consequences of not providing effective literacy instruction for individuals with complex support needs are too serious to ignore. Michael Bach's statement on the importance of literacy, as cited by Ewing (2000), illustrates the critical need for appropriate instruction and support:

> No longer viewed as a set of particular skills, literacy refers to a status that accords people the opportunities and supports to communicate, given the skills and capacities they have and can develop. To be literate is to have status, respect, and accommodation from others; to have skills in communication (verbal, written, sign, gestural, or other language); and to have access to the information and technologies that make possible self-determined participation in the communication processes of one's communities and broader society (p. 1).

Providing effective, high-quality literacy instruction for individuals with complex support needs is the responsibility of all of us—educators, policy makers, researchers, families, and adult service providers. Society is strengthened when all members have the opportunity for the "literate citizenship" Kliewer (2008) described. However, making these opportunities a reality requires change—specifically, substantial adjustments in how teachers and other practitioners are prepared and in how supports for this group of learners are conceptualized, implemented, and funded across the lifespan. As the remainder of this book demonstrates, considerable knowledge now exists within the field about how to provide effective, comprehensive literacy instruction for students with complex support needs. Although additional research will continue to inform our practice, individuals with complex needs for support cannot afford for us to delay making changes. *Now* is the time to embrace the challenge and ensure that *all* individuals have opportunities for effective, lifelong literacy instruction.

REFERENCES

Acocella, J. (2012, October 15). Turning the page: How women became readers. *The New Yorker,* pp. 88–93.

Allor, J.H., Mathes, P.G., Roberts, J.K., Cheatham, J.P., & Al Otaiba, S. (2014). Is scientifically based reading instruction effective for students with below-average IQs? *Exceptional Children, 80*(3), 287–306.

Annan, K. (1997, September 4). Secretary-General stresses need for political will and resources to meet challenge of fight against illiteracy. Retrieved from http://www.un.org/press/en/1997/19970904 .SGSM6316.html

Armbruster, B.B., Lehr, F., & Osborn, J. (2001). *Put reading first: The research building blocks for teaching children to read: Kindergarten through grade 3.* Washington, DC: The Partnership for Reading.

Asante, M.K. (2014). *Buck: A memoir.* New York, NY: Random House/Spiegel & Grau.

Browder, D.M., Ahlgrim-Delzell, L., Courtade, G., Gibbs, S.L., & Flowers, C. (2008). Evaluation of the effectiveness of an early literacy program for students with significant developmental disabilities. *Exceptional Children, 75*(1), 33–52.

Browder, D.M., Ahlgrim-Delzell, L., Flowers, C., & Baker, J. (2012). An evaluation of a multicomponent early literacy program for students with severe developmental disabilities. *Remedial and Special Education, 33*(4), 237–246.

Browder, D.M., Flowers, C., Ahlgrim-Delzell, L., Karvonen, M., Spooner, F., & Algozzine, R. (2004). The alignment of alternate assessment content with academic and functional curricula. *The Journal of Special Education, 37*(4), 211–223.

Conners, F.A. (1992). Reading instruction for students with moderate mental retardation: Review and analysis of research. *American Journal on Mental Retardation, 96,* 577–597.

Conners, F.A. (2003). Reading skills and cognitive abilities of individuals with mental retardation. *International Review of Research in Mental Retardation, 27*(1), 191–229.

Copeland, S.R., McCord, J.A., & Kruger, A. (2016). Literacy instruction for adults with extensive needs for supports: A review of the intervention literature. *Journal of Adolescent and Adult Literacy, 60*(2), 173–184.

deFur, S.H., & Runnells, M.M. (2014). Validation of the adolescent literacy and academic behavior self-efficacy scale. *Journal of Vocational Rehabilitation, 40,* 255–266.

de Graaf, G., & van Hove, G. (2015). Learning to read in regular and special schools: A follow-up study of students with Down syndrome. *Life Span and Disability, 1,* 7–39.

Donnellan, A.M. (1984). The criterion of the least dangerous assumption. *Behavioral Disorders, 9,* 141–150.

Downing, J.E. (2005). *Teaching literacy to students with significant disabilities.* Thousand Oaks, CA: Corwin Press.

Every Student Succeeds Act of 2015, S.1177. Retrieved from https://www.congress.gov/bill/114th-congress/senate-bill/1177/text

Ewing, G. (2000). Update from the executive director. In *Metro Toronto Movement for Literacy Newsletter.* Retrieved January 12, 2005, from http://www.mtml.ca/newslet/july00/page1.htm

Forts, A.M., & Luckasson, R. (2011). Reading, writing, and friendship: Adult implications of effective literacy instruction for students with intellectual disability. *Research and Practice for Persons with Severe Disabilities (RPSD), 36*(3–4), 121–125.

Grigal, M., Hart, D., & Weir, C. (2014). Postsecondary education for students with intellectual disabilities. In M. Agran, F. Brown, C. Hughes, C. Quirk, & D. Ryndak (Eds.), *Equity and full participation for individuals with severe disabilities: A vision for the future* (pp. 275–298). Baltimore, MD: Paul H. Brookes Publishing Co.

Higher Education Opportunity Act of 2008, PL 110-315, 20 U.S.C. §§ 1001 *et seq.*

Hudson, M.E., Browder, D.M., & Wood, L.A. (2013). Review of experimental research on academic learning by students with moderate and severe intellectual disability in general education. *Research and Practice for Persons with Severe Disabilities, 38*(1), 17–29.

Individuals with Disabilities Education Act Amendments (IDEA) of 1997, PL 105-17, 20 U.S.C. §§ 1400 *et seq.*

Individuals with Disabilities Education Improvement Act (IDEA) of 2004, PL 108-446, 20 U.S.C. §§ 1400 *et seq.*

Jorgensen, C. (2005). The least dangerous assumption. *Disability Solutions, 6*(3), 1–9.

Katims, D.S. (1994). Emergence of literacy in preschool children with disabilities. *Learning Disability Quarterly, 17,* 58–69.

Katims, D.S. (2000). *The quest for literacy: Curriculum and instructional procedures for teaching reading and writing to students with mental retardation and developmental disabilities.* Reston, VA: Council for Exceptional Children.

Keefe, E.B., & Copeland, S.R. (2011). What is literacy? The power of a definition. *Research and Practice for Persons with Severe Disabilities (RPSD), 36*(3–4), 92–99.

Kliewer, C. (2008). *Seeing all kids as readers.* Baltimore, MD: Paul H. Brookes Publishing Co.

Kliewer, C., & Biklen, D. (2007). Enacting literacy: Local understanding, significant disability, and a new frame for educational opportunity. *Teachers College Record, 109,* 2579–2600.

Kliewer, C., Biklen, D., & Kasa-Hendrickson, C. (2006). Who may be literate? Disability and resistance to the cultural denial of competence. *American Educational Research Journal, 2,* 163–192.

Kliewer, C., Fitzgerald, L.M., Meyer-Mork, J., Hartman, P., English-Sand, P., & Raschke, D. (2004). Citizenship for all in the literate community: An ethnography of young children with significant disabilities in inclusive early childhood settings. *Harvard Educational Review, 74,* 373–403.

Knoblauch, C.H. (1990). Literacy and the politics of education. In A.A. Lumsford, H. Moglen, & J. Slevin (Eds.), *The right to literacy* (pp. 74–80). New York, NY: The Modern Language Association of America.

Koppenhaver, D.A., Pierce, P.L., & Yoder, D.E. (1995). AAC, FC, and the ABCs: Issues and relationships. *American Journal of Speech-Language Pathology, 4,* 5–14.

Luckasson, R. (2006). The human rights basis for personal empowerment in education. In E.B. Keefe, V.M. Moore, & F.R. Duff (Eds.), *Listening to the experts* (pp. 11–20). Baltimore, MD: Paul H. Brookes Publishing Co.

Lunsford, A.A., Moglen, H., & Slevin, J. (1990). *The right to literacy.* New York, NY: The Modern Language Association of America.

Mirenda, P. (2003). "He's not really a reader…": Perspectives on supporting literacy instruction in individuals with autism. *Topics in Language Disorders, 23,* 271–282.

Moni, K.B., & Jobling, A. (2014). Challenging literate invisibility: Continuing literacy education for young adults and adults with Down syndrome. In R. Faragher & B. Clarke (Eds.), *Educating learners with Down syndrome: Research, theory, and practice with children and adolescents* (pp. 221–237). New York, NY: Routledge.

Neuman, S.B. (n.d.). How to help children build a rich vocabulary day by day. *Early Literacy: Speak Up!* Retrieved January 5, 2017, from http://www.scholastic.com/teachers/article/early-literacy-speak

Newman, L., Wagner, M., Knokey, A.-M., Marder, C., Nagle, K., Shaver, D., . . . Schwarting, M. (2011). *The post-high school outcomes of young adults with disabilities up to 8 years after high school. A report from the National Longitudinal Transition Study-2 (NLTS2)*. Menlo Park, CA: SRI International.

No Child Left Behind (NCLB) Act of 2001, PL 107-110, 115 Stat. 1425, 20 U.S.C. §§ 6301 *et seq.*

Reichenberg, M., & Lofgren, K. (2013). The social practice of reading and writing instruction in schools for intellectually disabled pupils. *Psychological and Pedagogical Survey, 14*(3–4), 43–60.

Ryndak, D.L., Moore, M.A., Orlando, A.M., & Delano, M. (2008/2009). Access to general education: The mandate and role of context in research-based practices for students with extensive support needs. *Research and Practice for Persons with Severe Disabilities, 33–34,* 199–213.

Ryndak, D., Morrison, A., & Sommerstein, L. (1999). Literacy before and after inclusion in general education settings. *The Journal of the Association for Persons with Severe Handicaps, 24,* 5–22.

Schalock, R.L., Borthwick-Duffy, S., Bradley, V.J., Buntinx, W.H.E., Coulter, D.L., Craig, E.M., . . . Yeager, M.H. (2010). *Intellectual disability: Definition, classification, and systems of supports* (11th ed.). Washington, DC: American Association on Intellectual and Developmental Disabilities.

Scribner, S. (1984). Literacy in three metaphors. *American Journal of Education, 93,* 6–21.

Taggart, L., & McKendry, L. (2009). Developing a mental health promotion booklet for young people with learning disabilities. *Learning Disability Practice, 12*(10), 27–32.

Thompson, J.R., Bradley, V.J., Buntix, W.H.E., Schalock, R.L., Shogren, K.A., Snell, M.E., . . . Yeager, M.H. (2009). Conceptualizing supports and the support needs of people with intellectual disability. *Intellectual and Developmental Disabilities, 47*(2), 135–146.

Thompson, J.R., Wehmeyer, M.L., & Hughes, C. (2010). Mind the gap! Implications of a person-environment fit model of intellectual disability for students, educators, and schools. *Exceptionality, 18,* 168–181. doi:10.1080/09362835.2010.513919

United Nations General Assembly. (2006). *Convention on the rights of persons with disabilities.* A/RES/61/106, Annex 1. Retrieved from http://www.refworld.org/docid/4680cd212.html

Vaccarino, F., Culligan, N., Comrie, M., & Sligo, F. (2006). School to work transition: Incorporating workplace literacy in the curriculum for individuals with disabilities in New Zealand. *International Journal of Learning, 13*(8), 69–81.

van Kraayenoord, C.E. (1994). Literacy for adults with an intellectual disability in Australia. *Journal of Reading, 37*(7), 608–610.

Wise, J.C., Sevcik, R.A., Romski, M.A., & Morris, R.D. (2010). The relationship between phonological processing skills and word and nonword identification performance in children with mild intellectual disabilities. *Research in Developmental Disabilities, 31,* 1170–1175.

Yoder, D.E., Erickson, K.A., & Koppenhaver, D.A. (1997). *A literacy bill of rights.* Chapel Hill: University of North Carolina at Chapel Hill, Center for Literacy and Disability Studies.

CHAPTER 2

Developing Language and Communication

Ann-Marie Orlando and Julia Scherba de Valenzuela

LEARNING OBJECTIVES

By the end of this chapter, readers will

1. Understand major concepts related to the development of early communication, language, and literacy.
2. Understand the range of cognitive and communicative abilities that fall within the boundaries of the common descriptor, "nonverbal."
3. Identify the ways communication development (e.g., intentional, conventional, symbolic, linguistic) impacts decisions about assessment and intervention.
4. Examine the definition of literacy from the perspective of individuals with complex communication needs.

This chapter will describe the link between literacy, language, and communication skills. We begin by defining communication and discussing ways to promote the development of language and communication skills for children and adults with complex communication support needs. Next, we discuss communication opportunities embedded in everyday activities at home and in the classroom. Finally, we explore ways to build language to support literacy learning. Throughout, we provide concrete examples of ways to build language and communication skills and situations that provide opportunities to do so.

LEARNING TO COMMUNICATE: Monica

Monica is 16 years old and attends her local high school. When Monica was two, she and her family moved to the southeastern United States from Puerto Rico. She lives at home with her parents and older brother. Everyone in the family speaks both English and Spanish; at home, they fluently switch between the two according to the conversation topic and who is participating, as do many bilingual families and communities. Monica's mother, who is more proficient in Spanish and more comfortable speaking it, typically speaks Spanish but often code-switches into English vocabulary for common items. Many individuals in Monica's community, as well as her extended family and friends, also use both languages. Therefore, it is important for Monica to continue to learn and use both English and Spanish.

Monica is a vivacious teen with a variety of interests she enjoys sharing. She likes polishing her nails and collecting empty boxes of her favorite foods, such as pasta and snack cakes. She also uses Internet search engines to learn details about these preferred items, such as all the available shades of a particular brand of nail polish or all available flavors for a particular brand of cookies.

To communicate, Monica uses a text-to-speech applet on her iPad (Apple, Inc.) to type messages. She also uses some sign language approximations, vocalizations, beginning word sounds, and a small board with printed letters. Monica is learning to put together three- and four-word utterances with appropriate semantic structure—that is, agent-action-object ("I ate cookies") and agent-action-location ("I went home").

With a primary exceptionality of autism spectrum disorder (ASD), Monica receives special education services in segregated classes for small-group instruction in all academic areas. She also attends a general education home economics class with peers of the same age. Throughout the school day, Monica uses a printed schedule with words and pictures to assist with transitions. With the help of a paraprofessional, Monica is learning to navigate the school independently as she changes class. To help Monica continue to learn both English and Spanish, all visual supports contain words in both languages. However, she only uses English on her iPad. With the support of her family and a personal care attendant, Monica is learning to become more independent at home in completing tasks such as laundry and cooking. She follows a visual schedule of individual tasks to help her.

NAVIGATING LITERACY IN MULTIPLE FORMS

In our society, not only is literacy highly valued, but so is the ability to navigate literacy in its multiple forms. This ability has important implications for education, employment, and interaction in social contexts. Because literacy skills are linked to language and communication, students like Monica need extra support if they are to develop these highly valued literacy skills.

That our society highly values literacy abilities is evident in educational legislation and research. The passage of education legislation that supports the development of learning standards for language and literacy—such as the No Child Left Behind (NCLB) Act of 2001 (PL 107-110), recently reauthorized as the Every Student Succeeds Act (ESSA) of 2015 (S. 1177)—demonstrates the level of importance placed on reading and writing across all academic subjects. In addition, a number of federally funded projects have supported research on effective practices for literacy instruction (i.e., National Early Reading Panel, National Reading Panel). This legislative support for literacy development, together with the extant research literature, means educators have available a great deal of information about evidence-based practices to teach language and literacy to all students.

Available literature also indicates that the ability to navigate literacy in multiple forms significantly affects participation in education, employment, and social life. Use of various forms of communication can have an impact on employment opportunities. According to the National Commission on Writing (2004), those who communicate effectively through literacy activities such as writing have more opportunities for salaried employment (Barton, 2000). Because language forms the basis for literacy, providers must address ways that individuals with complex communication support needs can learn language and literacy so they too can participate in education, employment, and social life.

This broad goal—helping individuals with complex communication support needs learn the skills necessary to participate fully in society—informs Chapter 2 of this book. In the sections below, we will explore the link between communication, language, and literacy. We will begin by defining communication and concepts critical to understanding the development of early communication skills. Then, we define language as a distinct form of communication and as the most sophisticated and conventional. Knowledge of these concepts is necessary to understanding the link between language and literacy.

WHAT IS COMMUNICATION?

Language and communication are not synonymous terms. Although language is only one of the many ways people can communicate, it is one of the most critical for developing academic skills. However, one *can* communicate without language.

The National Joint Committee for the Communicative Needs of Persons with Severe Disabilities (1992) defines communication as follows:

> Communication is any act by which one person gives to or receives from another person information about that person's needs, desires, perceptions, knowledge, or effective [sic] states. Communication may be intentional or unintentional, may involve conventional or unconventional signals, may take linguistic or nonlinguistic forms, and may occur through spoken or other modes. (p. 3)

This definition emphasizes that all people, regardless of the perceived severity of their disability, their educational background, or their access to supports, can and do communicate. We carry this fundamental assumption throughout this chapter. Because we assume this, we assign considerable responsibility to the typically developing communication partners of people with complex communication support needs: the responsibility to recognize, value, and support the ongoing communication. We also take from this definition the importance of communicating not only about needs or wants, but also feelings, likes and dislikes, actions, observations, and thoughts.

Functions of Communication

People communicate with one another for many different reasons: to answer questions and make requests; to convey emotions; to engage in joking, teasing, or other forms of verbal play; to indicate rapport with others, as when we use social niceties like "thank you" and "please"; to express important aspects of personal identity such as cultural background, religious affiliation, or social interests; to interact with technology; to think through ideas; and to record information for future use (Crystal, 2006). We call these different *functions* of communication. What is important to understand about functions of communication is that just as people without communication difficulties enjoy sharing with friends and family what they did on their weekend, talking about other people in their lives, and tossing around plans for the future, individuals with complex communication support needs also want to communicate with others about their lives. Therefore, it is imperative that interventionists, teachers, and other service providers create opportunities for real and meaningful communication for their constituents who have complex communication support needs, regardless of an individual's level of communication or language development.

Forms of Communication

In addition to different functions of communication, it is also important to recognize different *forms* of communication. These include spoken, signed, and written language; gestures; graphic and tactile representations; body language; facial expressions; eye gaze; vocalizations; and changes in state (e.g., respiration, muscle tone). Most individuals use a wide variety of communication modes throughout their day, starting in early childhood. For example, many children reach for or point to a desired item while vocalizing as they begin communicating intentionally. This tendency to combine communication forms often continues as they progress to more complex forms, such as combining words with gestures or signs. For example, a toddler might point to a bag of snacks and say "more." Alternatively, a child who is learning to sign and speak might sign MORE while saying "cookie." There is no evidence that using gestures or augmentative and alternative communication (AAC) systems delays children's oral language development. In fact, it may help it.

Augmentative and Alternative Communication   We introduce the concept of AAC here because it has to do with the form(s) of communication people use. AAC often is considered an intervention or a piece of technology provided to an individual. However, the American Speech-Language-Hearing Association (ASHA) emphasizes that AAC be thought of a system by defining it as "an integrated group of components used to enhance communication" (ASHA, n.d.-b, AAC Systems section, para 1). We agree with ASHA's broad definition of AAC as including "all forms of communication (other than oral speech) that are used to express thoughts, needs, wants, and ideas" (n.d.-a, para 1). We find this definition useful because it encompasses a wide variety of means to assist individuals with complex communication support needs. These means might include gestures, vocalizations, miniatures and partial objects, pictures, written words on a page or a screen, and a host of other options that can be characterized as no-tech (e.g., sign language), low-tech (e.g., eye gaze communication board), or high-tech (e.g., iPad with communication applet). When describing the type(s) of AAC used with an individual, it is often useful to categorize them as *aided* or *unaided.* ASHA explains the distinction: "Whereas aided symbols require some type of transmission device, unaided symbols require only the body to produce" (2002, definition section, para. 2).

It is also important to recognize that AAC is not something used only at a particular stage of communication development—all individuals with a need to augment current forms or use an alternative form of communication, regardless of their level of communication development, might benefit from AAC. Indeed, ASHA suggests that "we all use AAC when we make facial expressions or gestures, use symbols or pictures, or write" (n.d.-a, para 1), thereby recognizing the reliance on the multiple communication forms naturally available to most communicators. We emphasize here that there are no prerequisites for AAC use and that it can be used throughout the lifespan. Therefore, the range of individuals who might use or benefit from AAC is very wide, from beginning communicators to those who have developed complex language. For example, people in early stages of communication development might use real or miniature objects to understand transitions to different activities, such as using a toothbrush to indicate that it is time to brush one's teeth. Others might use speech recognition software (such as Dragon Speech Recognition Software [2015]) to compose extended written text, as Julia did when writing this chapter.

For individuals with complex communication support needs, AAC systems are an essential component of intervention. The definition of communication previously presented emphasizes that all individuals can communicate, even those who are at a pre-intentional level of communication (defined below). Thus, AAC systems are important for individuals with complex communication needs "because all persons, regardless of the extent or severity of their disabilities, have a basic right to affect, through communication, the conditions of their own existence" (National Joint Committee, 1992, p. 3). Another important understanding is that AAC is not, in and of itself, an intervention. Rather, as a system of accessible forms of communication, AAC can be used with any strategy that addresses increasing communication, language, and literacy abilities.

REFLECTION QUESTION 1

What are important considerations in facilitating the communication of students using AAC with peers and family members? In your experience, how have these considerations been taken into account when developing and using AAC systems with students who have complex communication support needs?

LEVELS OF COMMUNICATION DEVELOPMENT

Various authors (e.g., Brady et al., 2012; Rowland & Schweigert, 1989; Rowland & Stremel-Campbell, 1987; Siegel & Cress, 2002; Wetherby, Reichle, & Pierce, 1998) have recognized several important watermarks in the development of communication, such as the development of *intentional communication, symbolic communication,* and *language.* These are particular abilities or clusters of skills that, as they emerge, may be significant for both assessment and intervention. We suggest that describing an individual's emerging communication abilities in terms of these specific communicative abilities is more precise than using the term *nonverbal.* We find *nonverbal* to be neither adequately descriptive nor useful for planning interventions, because individuals identified this way display a wide range of communication skill levels. Instead of focusing on what a student cannot do, we find it more worthwhile to describe the specific abilities the student has developed so that we can build upon them in intervention and instruction.

When we describe an individual's emerging communication, it is also important to recognize that the first forms of communication used might be *unconventional,* or *idiosyncratic,* forms of communication. Conventional forms are those generally accepted and used within a social group/community, such as using a *thumbs-up* gesture to indicate agreement or approval; they are not necessarily "standard" or "vetted" (e.g., only words found in a dictionary) but should be forms that are not restricted to a few people. For example, *ain't,* although not considered correct in the prestige dialect of English, is common in other dialects and is therefore conventional. Many emerging communicators initially might use idiosyncratic forms. For example, before Monica had developed symbolic communication (defined below), she often would open and close the door to the classroom microwave while looking at the teacher to indicate that she wanted a snack.

Individuals with complex communication support needs at all levels of communication development might use idiosyncratic forms or attach unique meanings to conventional forms. For example, although Monica knew many different signs, she came up with her own gesture to request to be taken to the store—tapping her fist against her chest. Some individuals with ASD who have developed language might use conventional words and phrases in an unconventional manner, such as repeating movie dialogue. For example, Monica often uses her iPad to say "Cap'n Crunch" or other phrases related to grocery items when she is anxious, especially about schedule changes.

Such unconventional forms are important in communication development and therefore should be recognized and responded to as legitimate. Interventionists can then use principles of applied behavior analysis (ABA) to shape these idiosyncratic forms into more conventional ones that will be understood by a wider number of potential communication partners. ABA's components include modeling, a system of least-to-most prompting, and reinforcement of correct responses. Interventions that focus on emerging communication development and use ABA principles include prelinguistic milieu teaching and responsivity education (Warren et al., 2008). In both of these interventions, communication partners learn to recognize communicative attempts and facilitate interactions.

Pre-intentional, Beginning Communication

At beginning stages of communication development, individuals might communicate their physical or emotional states through changes in respiration, muscle tone, and movements. When caregivers respond to the individual, it gives meaning to these changes in state. To promote this emerging communication, it is important for caregivers to provide opportunities for communication with *responsive* communication partners during predictable routines, opportunities to interact with others, opportunities for choice-making, and appropriate responses to choices. At this developmental level, it is critical that an individual's communication partners respond to communication attempts, regardless of whether or not they believe the individual is communicating intentionally, and do so in a consistent manner.

It can be challenging for all communication partners to be familiar with the changes in an individual's physical and emotional states and their potential meanings. To build this familiarity, it can be helpful to document the multiple ways in which an individual communicates needs, wants, feelings, and preferences and to share this documentation with members of the individual's natural support network and collaborative team. This type of *communication dictionary* should be readily available and updated on a regular basis. A well-developed communication dictionary can provide guidance for the development of augmented forms of communication, especially when an individual's functional verbal communication is not sufficient for all of his or her communication needs.

For example, Monica's team initially identified that she communicated frustration with an activity by wrapping her hair around her left index finger, hunching forward, biting at her bottom lip, and vocalizing. After brainstorming communication aids and strategies that might provide Monica with a more functional means of communicating her frustration, her team decided to teach her a more conventional replacement, such as signing ALL DONE or pointing to a task card to request a break. This is an example of an ABA-based intervention known as *functional communication training,* which has been found to be effective for individuals with severe disabilities who have limited verbal communication. It was developed as a method to teach individuals to use socially appropriate communicative responses to meet their needs rather than engage in challenging behaviors (Carr & Durand, 1985).

Intentional Communication

Bates defined intentional communication as "signaling behavior in which the sender is aware a priori of the effect that the signal will have on his listener, and he persists in that behavior until the effect is obtained or failure is clearly indicated" (1979, p. 36). Intentional communication, therefore, has a precursor: intentional behavior. According to Lifter and Bloom, "intentional behaviors are specifically purposeful and volitional. They are activities in the service of some goal, and they are observable" (1998, p. 165). These include voluntarily reaching for an object, interacting with a favorite toy, or engaging in an activity without prompting. Intentional behavior does not require the presence of or interaction with another person. However, through repeated and predictable interactions with others, intentional communication can develop from a base of intentional behaviors, such as grabbing for or orienting to desired objects.

Typically developing children develop intentional communication around 9 months of age (Bates, 1979). It may emerge much later for individuals with complex communication support needs. According to Lifter and Bloom, intentional communication "first appears with gestures and prelinguistic vocalizations and later with language" (1998, p. 170). When assessing whether an individual has developed intentional communication, it is important to recognize that intentionality is "not all or none"; it develops over time.

Wetherby and Prizant suggested the following stages in the development of communicative intentionality:

1. Absence of awareness of a goal

2. Awareness of the goal

3. Simple plan to achieve the goal

4. Coordinated plan to achieve the goal

5. Alternative plan to achieve the goal

6. Metapragmatic awareness of the plan to achieve the goal. (1989, p. 79)

Therefore, interventionists should recognize when early communicators are demonstrating emerging intentional communication and foster its development. Wetherby and Prizant proposed seven indicators that may help identify this important watermark:

1. Alternating eye gaze between goal and listener

2. Persistent signaling until a goal is accomplished or failure is indicated

3. Waiting for a response from a listener

4. Changing the signal quality until the goal has been met

5. Ritualizing or conventionalizing communicative forms

6. Ceasing signal production when the goal is met

7. Displaying satisfaction when the goal is met and dissatisfaction when the goal is not met (1989, p. 78)

Even considering these indicators, it can be difficult to determine whether an individual has developed intentional communication, especially with individuals with multiple disabilities, visual impairments, physical disabilities, or ASD who either do not use eye gaze as their partners expect or have limited physical movements. Therefore, we argue that when unsure, it is important to respond as if the behavior is an intentional act of communication. This is an example of a least dangerous assumption (Donnellan, 1984); assuming incompetence and not responding to a potentially communicative act may be more harmful than incorrectly assuming competence.

Facilitating Intentional Communication Joint attention is a type of intentional behavior that is a critical bridge to developing intentional communication and occurs when both communication partners are focused on the same object or topic of interest, such as a toy. Many individuals indicate joint attention through eye gaze, as described in the indicators of intentional communication proposed by Wetherby and Prizant (1989). However, Bruce and Vargas argued that "it is common for joint attention to be established or maintained without eye contact" (2007, p. 302). For example, individuals might interact with an object by touching, manipulating, holding out, pushing away, or physically orienting toward the object. Or, they might demonstrate another response, such as stiffening or stilling their movement, that indicates they are attending to a topic, activity, or object also attended to by their communication partner. Initially, the partner might scaffold joint attention by attending to the object or activity the individual is focused on or by using a highly stimulating object, such as bubbles, a small fan, or something that makes noise, to attract the individual's attention.

Gestures are also important to the development of intentional communication. Therefore, to promote its development, communication partners must be highly responsive to these earliest communication attempts, even if nonintentional, particularly within predictable routines. Modeling, encouraging, and responding to gestures are important strategies to encourage early development of communication, because intentional communication is a precursor to the development of symbolic communication. However, it is important to recognize that while some individuals, such as those with physical impairments, may not be able to produce gestures, this does not mean that they will not be able to develop more advanced forms of communication. Rather, their communication partners will need to find other ways through which they can express needs, wants, emotions, and other social goals.

Finally, for individuals with emerging intentional communication, language production probably is not the most appropriate target of intervention. Instead, tangible representations such as real objects, miniature objects, and partial objects (Rowland & Schweigert, 2000) may be used to facilitate communication at this stage. These objects can be linked to a speech-generating device and used to associate the object (i.e., goal) with language that can be interpreted by the communication partner. For example, a small carton of milk, similar in shape and size to the one the individual receives during lunchtime, can be used to request milk.

Symbolic Communication

Individuals who have developed intentional communication may progress to developing symbolic communication—including language. To understand what this means, it is important to define and distinguish among the terms *symbol, representation, referent,* and *icon.* Take a moment to review the definitions provided in "Communicating About Communication: Common Terms."

COMMUNICATING ABOUT COMMUNICATION

COMMON TERMS

Accurately evaluating communication development relies on professionals thoroughly understanding the concepts related to symbolic communication: *symbol, representation, referent,* and *icon.*

Very generally, a symbol is anything (e.g., a gesture, a picture, an object) that represents, or stands for, something else (Beukelman & Mirenda, 2013). However, in the fields of linguistics and child language development, the term *symbol* has a more precise definition. We will use *representation* as a general term for something that stands for something else and *symbol* when there is an arbitrary and abstract relationship between representations and their referents (Bates, 1979)—with *referents* meaning the thing the representation stands for. Furthermore, symbols are conventional (Peirce, 1998) and their meaning can be generalized beyond the context in which they were originally learned. According to Bruce, "the achievement of symbolism is significant because it is necessary to linguistic expression and it supports higher cognitive development" (2005, p. 233). Therefore, it is important to identify when an individual has begun using symbols, in the arbitrary and abstract sense we reference here.

Consistent with the definition above, words (oral, signed, and written) are symbols. They are considered such because there is not a direct and obvious relationship between words and their referents. Some might argue that some signs are not truly symbols because the relationship between the representation and the referent is obvious, such as *milk,* where one makes a fist and squeezes it. However, unless a child grows up on a dairy farm where cows are milked by hand, the origin of this sign is not obvious. This is also true for many other signs that adults might see as more directly representational of some feature of the referent than most children would, due to their wider life experience. Besides words and signs, other types of representations, such as pictures and objects, can also be symbols if they are arbitrary and abstract.

In contrast to a symbol, an *icon* has a concrete and perceptible relationship to its referent. In general, highly representational icons are easier to comprehend and learn than very abstract symbols. However, this depends on the relationship between the representation and the referent for the individual—what the intended or understood meaning is *for that person.* For example, if a picture of an apple is used to represent an apple, it is an icon, because the relationship between the two is concrete and easy to perceive. If the same picture of an apple is used to represent New York City, it is a symbol; the relationship is not concrete and obvious but instead depends on one's awareness that New York is nicknamed "The Big Apple."

Symbols, representations, icons—what do all of these things mean for fostering communication development? There are several principles to keep in mind. First, as individuals demonstrate comprehension and use of icons, it is important to provide them with increasing opportunities to comprehend and use symbolic representations. For example, if an individual understands that a picture card showing an apple is a representation of an apple, a teacher could add the written word for apple to this picture card. The eventual goal would be for the student to comprehend the word alone, without the picture support.

In addition, be aware that when individuals first begin to use a particular type of representation, such as gestures or picture cards, they may do so only within a specific context and may have difficulty generalizing its use outside of the context in which they initially learned it. To foster the development of symbolic communication, encourage individuals to use the representations they have been taught to communicate in a variety of contexts and for a variety of purposes. This means providing individuals with communication opportunities that go far beyond making requests and selecting from among forced choices. For example, recall that Monica uses a gesture to indicate her desire to go to the store. To foster her use of this gesture as symbolic communication, we would encourage her to use it and would use it with her after we returned from the store, to talk about this experience. We might also try to expand the gesture's meaning to encompass going to other places as well. By teaching Monica to use the gesture for a variety of purposes, she not only learns it as a more symbolic form of communication but also begins to use it for more communicative functions (i.e., commenting). In addition, strategies such as following the individual's lead, setting up routines and then varying them, arranging the environment to provide more opportunities to communicate across contexts, and responding to communicative attempts result in more authentic communication that might lead to the development of language.

Some ABA-based interventions, such as Pivotal Response Treatment, target behaviors that, when treated, increase other behaviors that are not the target of the treatment (Verschuur, Didden, Lang, Sigafoos, & Huskens, 2014). These targeted behaviors, therefore, are considered pivotal. In Monica's case, teaching her to use more symbolic forms of communication would be a pivotal skill.

Having defined the levels of communication an individual with complex support needs may have reached—pre-intentional, intentional, and symbolic—we will now turn to a particular type of symbolic communication—language—and begin to explore its relationship with literacy.

REFLECTION QUESTION 2

How does the student's level of communication development affect your approach to intervention? Why is it important to figure out whether an individual is using symbolic communication (e.g., abstract, decontextualized representations)? Is it enough to know whether the student is using any kind of representation (e.g., pictures)? If not, what else do you need to know about this individual?

WHAT IS LANGUAGE?

Language and *communication* are not synonymous terms; neither are *language* and *literacy*. However, language and literacy are inextricably connected, particularly given the current and broad definition of literacy. Both are critical for developing academic skills. ASHA defines language as "a complex and dynamic system of conventional symbols that is used in various modes for thought and communication" (1982, sec. Definition of Language). Important to this definition is the idea that language is a system that includes rules for how its different aspects, such as syntax and morphology, are combined. Another way language differs from other forms of communication is that it uses conventional symbols. Therefore, once an individual has developed a conventional use of symbols in complex, rule-governed combinations, the individual has developed or is close to developing language. Modes of language include oral, written, and signed. Additional modes of communication, such as the use of gestures and pictures, are not considered language in and of themselves.

Components of Language

The previously cited ASHA definition further elaborates that

- Language evolves within specific historical, social, and cultural contexts

- Language, as rule-governed behavior, is described by at least five parameters—phonologic, morphologic, syntactic, semantic, and pragmatic

- Language learning and use are determined by the interaction of biological, cognitive, psychosocial, and environmental factors

- Effective use of language for communication requires a broad understanding of human interaction including such associated factors as nonverbal cues, motivation, and sociocultural roles (1982, sec. Definition of Language)

In the following sections, we expand on each of the five components of language provided in this definition.

Phonology   *Phonology* refers to the study of the sound system of a spoken language. Human beings can produce many closely related speech sounds, including the consonants and vowels we are familiar with in English and other types of sounds not used in English, such as trilled and click consonants and nasal vowels; the smallest meaningful units of speech sound are called *phonemes*. For speakers to learn and use a language effectively, they must know the inventory of sounds used in a meaningful way in that language and how these sounds are sequenced. Within any one language, not all possible differences between related sounds are meaningful. For example, /l/ and /r/ are related sounds, both considered liquid consonants. In English, they are distinct phonemes because changing just this sound gives a word a different meaning (e.g., *lamb* vs. *ram*). Within a few months after birth, typically developing children can perceive differences between closely related sounds, regardless of whether these differences are meaningful in their language (Curtin & Hufnagle, 2009). However, before the end of their first year, they have identified most of the differences between phonemes that are meaningful in their language and stop paying attention to those are not (Gervain & Mehler, 2010). In addition, children learn what sounds can go together in their language. For example, words cannot start with the consonant cluster /mb/ in English, but consonant clusters like /str/ and /fl/ are allowed.

Morphology   *Morphology* examines the smallest meaningful units of words (morphemes) and how they are combined. For example, the word *dogs* has two morphemes, /dog/ and the plural /-s/. Speakers can draw on the knowledge of morphological rules as they learn new words. Therefore, when children who already know how to make words plural learn the name of a new object, they are able to form its plural without being taught. Morphology, like syntax, differs across languages. For example, English uses morphemes called *suffixes* at the ends of words and morphemes called *prefixes* at the beginning. In other languages, morphemes might occur elsewhere within a word. Therefore, if an individual with complex communication support needs has a background in a language other than English, it may be helpful to involve a professional specializing in teaching English as a second language (ESL).

Syntax   Although syntax is sometimes—incorrectly—equated with grammar, it is actually one aspect of grammar. Grammar includes both how words are put together (morphology) and how sentences are put together (syntax). As children begin to form sentences, they learn syntax: the expected order of words according to their grammatical classes (e.g., nouns, verbs, adjectives, adverbs). Syntactic rules vary across languages. For example, in English, adjectives precede nouns, while Spanish typically reverses this order (e.g., "the red car" vs. "el carro rojo"). Therefore, English language learners (ELLs) may use a word order (syntax) that differs from what is considered correct in English. This could be due to an influence (interference) of the home language rather than to a language disorder. This can be true as well for students who speak different varieties of English, such as African American English (also known as Ebonics), Chicano English, or Appalachian English.

Semantics   *Semantics* is the study of meanings, both of single words and words in sentences. It goes beyond the idea of vocabulary, to include understanding word meanings within the context of a phrase or sentence. As an example, Lessow-Hurley (2000, p. 29) provides the sentence "they were hunting dogs"; to understand which of the two possible meanings is intended, one needs to understand the relationship between the words. When thinking about semantic development for an individual who has a home language other than English, it is important to remember that words are often inexact translations; subtle differences in meanings can exist even between people who assume they are speaking the same language variety. Therefore, when interacting with speakers of a language variety other than your own, it is critical to understand what *they* mean when they say something, rather than assuming they are using words the exact same way you might.

Pragmatics   This aspect of language is important because it governs the "choice of language in social interaction and the effects of our choice on others" (Crystal, 2006, p. 275). Individuals with complex communication support needs, particularly those with ASD, might have difficulty with pragmatics—for example, difficulty either in using language appropriately to express an intended social meaning or incorrectly interpreting the social meaning of others' communication. Correctly conveying or interpreting subtle shades of meaning, such as sarcasm, politeness, respect, teasing, and compliments, requires the development of pragmatics. Therefore, intervention targeting the use of language across a variety of social contexts might be a relevant part of a language intervention program. In addition, as will be described in Chapter 3, wide differences in language use might exist between different language communities, such as differences in the use of turn-taking, interruptions, volume, rate, eye gaze, gestures, repetition, silence/pauses, discourse structures, and context cues. Therefore, as with the previously defined aspects of language, it is also important to attempt to differentiate language differences from impaired language in the area of pragmatics.

Expressive Versus Receptive Language

It is also important to differentiate between *expressive language* and *receptive language*. Expressive language is also known as *language production*—the ability to use language to produce a message. In contrast, receptive language is *language comprehension*—the ability to receive and understand a message. Although language comprehension often precedes expression developmentally, children frequently do repeat things they do not fully understand, as when they recite the Pledge of Allegiance by rote. Although they may have some general idea of the pledge's meaning, it is also possible they just stand up and recite it every morning, either without knowing the specific meaning of individual words or understanding them very differently than an adult would. The form, function, and use of expressive language are determined by both internal and external factors. Internal factors include the speaker's knowledge and the purpose of the communication. External factors include those associated with the listener, such as responsivity or ability to scaffold language production, and the context of the interaction.

The Link Between Language and Literacy

Literacy is a form of language because, as with other forms, it uses conventional symbols to represent ideas and is rule governed. As with other forms of language, children need pervasive, systematic instruction and consistent exposure to a rich literacy environment.

The National Reading Panel (NRP) describes five critical aspects of reading: vocabulary, phonological awareness, phonics, comprehension, and fluency (NRP, 2000). However, literacy includes more than just reading. At a minimum, it also includes writing; depending on the definition, it may include still more. The emergent literacy perspective defines literacy more broadly as acts of reading, writing, listening, and speaking that develop concurrently and interrelatedly (Koppenhaver, Pierce, Steelman, & Yoder, 1995). Early knowledge of literacy reflects emerging concepts about print, alphabet knowledge, phonological awareness, vocabulary knowledge, letter naming, and word manipulation (Bus, van IJzendoorn, & Pellegrini, 1995; National Early Literacy Panel [NELP], 2008).

With this broader definition of literacy, the group of individuals who can be described as "readers" increases, and so does the number of ways readers can engage in literacy activities. Specifically, the broad definition increases the ways that communicators who have not yet developed symbolic communication can engage in literacy. These might include alternative forms to written language, such as tactile or tangible representations (e.g., miniature or partial objects, textures, shapes, and other three-dimensional items that convey meaning through their tactile/physical properties); other forms of graphic communication, such as two-dimensional symbols (e.g., Picture Communication Symbols [PCS], Mayer-Johnson, Inc.) and icons (e.g., photographs of real objects); and spoken text. Our conceptualization of literacy also includes alternative permanent products (e.g., audio recordings, drawings) as well as more transient products such as oral texts.

This evolution of the definition of literacy can be seen in the work of Marie Clay (1966), who described the behaviors and knowledge that children bring to their interactions with books long before they can read and write in the conventional sense. This evolution continued with Teale and Sulzby's (1986) work on emergent literacy. These expanded ways of thinking about literacy make it clear that individuals can engage in literacy activities in multiple ways. For example, if during a shared book reading activity, a person uses a BIGmack switch with a symbol or object representing the message adhered to the top to say a repeated line in a book, then we might surmise that the person is demonstrating emergent literacy skills and intentional communication. Alternatively, if a student differentiates between one switch programmed to say the repeated line of a book and another switch to say, "turn the page," then we might surmise that the person is demonstrating symbolic communication skills, language, and emergent literacy. Therefore, the skills developed by emerging communicators through participation in communication activities are useful and foundational to literacy.

REFLECTION QUESTION 3

Consider your standpoint on different definitions of literacy. For example, must an individual be able to read and write alphabetic text to be considered literate? Is literacy a form of language, which therefore adheres to all components of the definition of language cited in this chapter (e.g., symbolic, conventional)? What does your personal definition of literacy imply regarding how you will approach literacy instruction for individuals with complex communication support needs?

CHALLENGES IN DEVELOPING COMMUNICATION, LANGUAGE, AND LITERACY

Before we address potential challenges in developing communication, language, and literacy for individuals with complex support needs, be aware that descriptions of these individuals often address skill deficits and the assistance individuals need to complete tasks. However, focusing on skill deficits does little to describe the individual beyond his or her disability or to inform support teams about the contexts in which the individual lives, works, and socializes. For example, many individuals have a home language other than or in addition to English; support teams do not always recognize that continued development of that language significantly affects the individual's ability to communicate with family and community. Descriptions based solely on deficits and skills that are important within the dominant culture also can result in functional limitations brought about by low expectations and environmental barriers. In this section, we discuss the characteristics of the population addressed in this text and the ways expectations and environment can impact the development of communication, language, and literacy.

Consider Characteristics of the Population—and the Individual

Individuals with complex support needs that include communication are a heterogeneous population with an array of skills and support needs. This population possesses certain general learning characteristics (discussed in Chapter 1), and there are general ways to support them in developing communication, language, and literacy. However, specific characteristics—individual traits, features of the disability that both challenge and facilitate learning, language background, culture, educational history, and family and student priorities and preferences—should dictate the supports and strategies used.

Monica, described previously, has characteristics consistent with individuals with complex support needs: She learns slowly and therefore learns less, and she has difficulty maintaining skills; generalizing skills across settings, materials, and people; and putting together skills learned in isolation (Westling, Fox, & Carter, 2014). She also demonstrates core features of ASD: difficulty showing interest in others' conversations, a limited range of unusually intense interests, and rigid adherence to routines. For example, for some time, Monica had an intense focus on obtaining all colors of a specific brand of nail polish and had difficulty transitioning when there was any change in her daily schedule, such as attending an assembly at school instead of her usual reading class.

However, when we describe Monica, characteristics other than features of her disability also matter. She has extended family who live nearby, and they socialize often. Within her family, she can communicate without using her AAC device because family members are familiar with her communication style and use of sign language approximations. She also integrates eye gaze and gestures to request nearby objects. Monica enjoys cooking traditional dishes with her family and can complete some tasks independently in the context of family routines. The family would like her to become more independent with tasks she enjoys, such as cooking, laundry, and creating shopping lists.

Monica's characteristics, communication skills, culture, and family preferences both facilitate and challenge her development of communication, language, and literacy. First, her characteristics can limit the amount learned but also can provide a context in which to develop skills. For instance, her interest in nail polish can be used to engage her in communication interactions and increase her use of language; it can also be incorporated into literacy instruction. Second, her language background suggests that she might have less knowledge of English words than Spanish. Therefore, the educational team would need to ensure that Monica has access to words in both languages to increase her understanding and use of language related to specific topics. In addition, they might find it helpful to teach new concepts in Spanish first and then teach the associated English words; helping her learn in the language she speaks better might be less frustrating, more effective, and more time efficient. Finally, the family's ability to understand Monica's use of a variety of communication forms might influence her development of communication, language, and literacy. For example, because the family can understand her use of various communication forms, they might not require her to practice the use of more sophisticated communication forms, such as using her AAC device to produce longer utterances across contexts.

Consider the Importance of Contexts

The contexts in which an individual spends time learning, working, and socializing can influence the development of communication, language, and literacy. Context includes the location, communication partners, instructional materials, communicative supports, topics, instructional configuration, discourse patterns, and assumptions about communication made by all participants in the exchange. When working to develop an individual's communication skills, consider the contexts that provide opportunities to learn and practice.

Because of their learning characteristics, individuals with complex communication support needs might find it difficult to generalize a learned skill to a different context if the skill was learned in isolation from other skills required for the task or if it was learned outside of the natural context in which it is used (Brady et al., 2016). For example, speech-language therapy often is delivered within a therapy room. If social communication skills are learned and practiced only within that context, it might be challenging for a student to become proficient in using social communication in a different context, such as the playground, particularly if the student has difficulty generalizing.

In addition, segregated settings present few or no opportunities for students to learn from same-age peers without disabilities. Although teachers, paraprofessionals, and related service personnel can be good communication partners for students with complex communication support needs, they provide only adult models of communication, language, and literacy use. Our students require examples of these skills in student-to-student, teacher–student, and teacher–teacher interactions. Segregated settings can limit the opportunities to observe and participate in age-appropriate communication, language, and literacy activities because other students in the class are likely also to have limited use of the skills involved and therefore cannot provide the frequent modeling and opportunities for students to improve their skills.

The limited opportunities for communication, language, and literacy available in segregated settings provide a strong argument for including students with complex communication support needs in classes with their peers without disabilities. The development of communication, language, and literacy has implications in education, employment, and social contexts (Barton, 2000). Therefore, the opportunity to learn these skills should be paramount in decisions about where educational services are provided for students with complex communication support needs. For all of these reasons, arguably the optimal language-learning environment for such students is the general education classroom. Moreover, when those students have a primary home language other than English, the most appropriate general education setting might be the bilingual education classroom. All of the services and programs available to ELLs who are typically developing *must* also be available to students with disabilities.

Consider Our Expectations, Assumptions, and Limitations

Most people approach a situation with certain expectations or assumptions about the outcome, grounded in their own knowledge and experiences. However, teachers, related service personnel, and paraprofessionals must set aside their biases; preconceived notions about another person can lead to low expectations of and limitations for that individual. Based on professional knowledge and experiences, educators and interventionists can make informed decisions about appropriate instructional strategies and ways of helping individuals meet their own goals. Reflection and collaboration with other team members to examine how biases might influence instructional strategies should be a frequent practice (Downing & Ryndak, 2015). Through reflection and collaboration, educators and interventionists also strive to balance opportunities to practice learned skills with instruction on more complex skills.

For example, Monica has limited fine motor skills, so she often uses either magnetic letters or a portable word processor to spell target words (e.g., *can, wait, sign*) selected by the teacher during word instruction at school. However, during this instruction, Monica often does not spell the target words and instead spells words related to her interests, such as her favorite nail polish colors. Adults working with her often thought she was perseverating and could not spell the target words. However, at home, Monica often used the target words when searching the Internet for media about her favorite topics, including sign language videos and pictures of nail polish and preferred food. Monica's mother revealed this at the individualized education program (IEP) meeting, explaining that Monica could indeed spell the words and providing the team with multiple examples of times she had. In this scenario, Monica was limited because her support team assumed she could not spell the target words; collaboration with the parent brought to light the conditions under which Monica was more likely do so. This kind of collaboration with families can help teams develop IEP goals that allow for the multiple contexts in which students like Monica demonstrate skills.

PROMOTING COMMUNICATION, LANGUAGE, AND LITERACY

How can educators work with individuals with complex support needs—including those who need complex communication supports—to promote communication, language, and literacy? One approach to curriculum development used by educators is *backward design* (Wiggins & McTighe, 2011), which consists of three stages: determining goals and objectives for intervention, which Wiggins and McTighe term *desired results*; deciding how to assess progress toward goals; and planning interventions to meet the goals and objectives. Although backward design was not originally designed with students with complex support needs in mind, it has been applied in a number of contexts and is compatible with current philosophies underlying best practices for curriculum development for these students (de Valenzuela, Green, & Hall, 2010). Guides for each stage of backward design are provided in the sections that follow.

Determining Goals and Objectives

Determination of learning goals and objectives, and modes of communication, must be grounded in a rich understanding of the individual's current abilities, priorities, needs, and preferences. Team members must collaborate to set goals that are meaningful, relevant, and active. For example, consider this goal: "During interactive small group lessons with peers, the student will construct two- and three-word utterances with a mobile technology over two to three communication turns, with scaffolding from adult and peer supporters." It is *meaningful* because it has a purpose for the individual and leads to other goals for longer communication sequences. It is *relevant* because it is important for the individual and applies within the contexts of both school and home. It is *active* because it describes the actions the student must perform. In contrast, in the goal, "The student will listen to large group instruction," the student's behavior is passive and it would be difficult for observers to reliably measure whether or not the student was actually listening. In addition to considering these three criteria, teams should plan for maintenance and generalization of goals by identifying opportunities for practice in natural contexts throughout the day with adults and peers. An infused skills grid can be used for this planning process (Ryndak & Alper, 2003). (See Chapter 11 for more about using this tool.) Teams can also plan instructional strategies that will support goal acquisition, such as shaping, fading, and scaffolding, and include these in the goal.

In planning goals, it is also important for practitioners to be aware of how their own perspectives affect goal setting. Teachers, therapists, and interventionists might have one of two perspectives when working with students with complex communication needs—one that suggests we can "fix" the individual, or one that suggests we can also work with the environment to support the use of the communication skills the student has at that time. "Fixing" means that if the individual has impairments that cannot be fixed, intervention is futile. From a social interactionist perspective, however, there is always something that can be improved, modified, taught, or supported—with intervention focusing on the individual, the environment (including people), or both. Therefore, when determining goals and objectives, teams should consider intervention targets aimed at increasing both the student's skill repertoire and the responsiveness of people with whom the student interacts frequently. Reviewing current goals and objectives, and prioritizing grade-level standards that support involvement in and progress toward state standards, contribute to the determination of desired outcomes.

Planning for Assessment

Once the team has determined the desired outcomes, they next must determine acceptable evidence of progress toward goals (Wiggins & McTighe, 2011). Evidence is gathered through assessment activities, which must be well documented and designed around meaningful, relevant goals and objectives. Information gleaned from these should influence instruction and intervention. Approaches to assessment vary and are guided by underlying principles. Selecting a given approach means that a conscious decision has been made to plan for assessment, because this is not an ad hoc procedure.

Assessment must take into consideration how an individual currently communicates across contexts. Therefore, teams must gather information about the individual's and family's preferences and about ways the individual communicates across daily activities and routines; in education, work, and community settings; and during activities with various communication partners, including peers. A range of methods can be used to collect evidence and document learning in terms of the scope, time frame, context, and structure (Wiggins & McTighe, 2011). These methods range from simple to complex assessments designed to measure short- or long-term achievement of contextualized or decontextualized material within structured and unstructured activities.

Because individuals requiring extensive support tend to have complex needs, such that no one discipline has sufficient expertise to address all needs of this population, it is imperative to use a team approach to assessment for these individuals (Ryndak & Alper, 2003). Collaborative teams should include professionals with expertise in a variety of disciplines, including educators, speech-language pathologists, occupational therapists, physical therapists, nurses, paraprofessionals, guidance counselors, and agency personnel, as well as caregivers and others who are important to and knowledgeable about the individual being assessed. Individuals with complex communication support needs may be ELLs; if so, their collaborative team *must* include bilingual educators or experts in teaching ESL.

Formal Assessment Strategies   Formal assessments typically include standardized, commercially available assessment tools. However, because few include normative data representative of individuals with complex communication support needs, professionals often must either adapt available assessment tools (designed for individuals without disabilities) or develop their own. Possible adaptions include changing the amount of response time given, the response mode, the materials used, and the feedback provided. For example, pictures can be enlarged and separated so that a student can view them with ease or respond through eye gaze instead of pointing. For multiple-choice responses, the choice array can be decreased. The collaborative team should determine and document well the type of adaptations used (Proctor & Zangari, 2009). Results of adapted forms of commercially available assessments need to be interpreted with caution because if assessments are not conducted with fidelity and/or with the intended population, results may lack reliability and validity. In addition, when published tests are administered in ways that differ from the standardized protocol, the use of the normative sample for comparison purposes is no longer appropriate. Nevertheless, information gleaned from standardized assessments about an individual's understanding and use of communication, language, and literacy can be useful in terms of suggesting what skills a student may or may not be able to demonstrate in a one-on-one educational setting.

For assessment of individuals with complex communication needs, several available formal assessment protocols rely on gestural responses (i.e., pointing to an array of choices) rather than verbal ones, or they rely on observation and caregiver reporting. For example, the Communication and Symbolic Behavior Scales, Developmental Profile (CSBS DP; Wetherby & Prizant, 2002) can be used to measure early communication for children 8 to 24 months old, or up to 72 months old if developmental delays are present. The Communication Matrix by Rowland and Fried-Oken (2010) can be used to measure presymbolic communication for children with severe and multiple disabilities. The Checklist of Communicative Competence (Triple C; Iacono, West, Bloomberg, & Johnson, 2009) is designed to assess pre-intentional to early symbolic communication skills of adults with severe and multiple disabilities. The Communication Complexity Scale (Brady et al., 2012) can be used with both children and adults who have limited symbolic communication.

Informal Assessment Strategies   Various types of informal assessment strategies can be used to gather evidence of an individual's current communication use and progress toward desired outcomes. This section provides a basic framework.

Language Sampling   A language sample is designed to gather information about an individual's use of expressive communication within natural contexts; it is essential for assessing expressive language skills. The procedure involves recording audio and video of an individual during a communication interaction to measure the mean length of utterance and the number of different words used. It typically requires 100 utterances and a duration of at least 30 minutes for an adequate range and number of utterances (Tager-Flusberg et al., 2009). Note that gathering this quantity of utterances might be difficult when assessing individuals with limited use of verbal communication. Also, samples gathered in natural settings with familiar communication partners and during authentic activities and routines are more likely to be representative of an individual's communication interactions (Kasari, Brady, Lord, & Tager-Flusberg, 2013).

Interviews   Interviewing a variety of people in an individual's life can provide a more holistic view of the individual's communicative repertoire. For example, previous teachers and therapists can provide valuable information regarding previous assessments as well as both successful and unsuccessful strategies for promoting communication, language, and literacy. Peers can provide information about age-appropriate topics and activities on which to focus conversation.

Caregivers are an especially rich repository of information about an individual's understanding and use of communication, language, and literacy across a variety of contexts. It is therefore imperative to interview them about how the individual communicates for various purposes across settings, people, and activities. Our own interviews with Monica's mother and brother revealed that she used both sign language approximations and a portable word processor to say "I love you" to family members. This information later served to help her team devise a strategy for increasing the number of different words she used to communicate. Through modeling, they elicited from Monica information about other items she "loved." They modeled using both sign language and her word processor to say, "I love ice cream," or "I love painting." Monica soon imitated these sentence structures. In addition, the team used information from interviews with family and other caregivers (i.e., personal care attendants, service providers) to add to Monica's repertoire of signed and written words for other preferred items and activities.

Observation   Because formal assessments provide useful information but might not give a complete picture, relevant information can also be gleaned through observation of the individual. Observers must have a clear purpose and focus from the outset. Observations that are well documented and systematic and rely on objective reporting provide useful information.

Observations can be documented in various ways, including the use of narrative recordings (i.e., running records, anecdotal records), collection of quantitative data (i.e., frequency counts, time sampling), criterion-referenced recordings (i.e., rating scales, checklists), and portfolios (McLean, Wolery, & Bailey, 2004). Care must be taken to administer these informal assessments with consistency and reliability so that results can be interpreted with accuracy. In addition, the developer of these tools must know the purpose of the assessment, the skills being assessed, and the individual's strengths and challenges (Proctor & Zangari, 2009).

REFLECTION QUESTION 4

Discuss ways that communicative competence of individuals with complex communication support needs can be assessed. What different components are needed in a thorough assessment plan?

Planning for Intervention

The final phase of backward design is to plan instruction and intervention activities that will provide opportunities for individuals to learn and practice skills. After identifying the individual's communicative intentionality, ability to use and understand symbols, and language use, the team plans for intervention. This should be provided within natural contexts, with real communication partners, and in a way consistent with research-based practices. According to Downing, "experts in communication intervention stress the value of teaching communication skills in general education classrooms, where students with severe disabilities have the support of their peer role models" (2005, p. 67). Professionals and caregivers must foster consistent, intensive opportunities for relevant and meaningful interactions with peers across a variety of learning contexts, and provide supports across those contexts (i.e., home, school, work, recreation).

When planning for intervention, teams should first consider which mode(s) of communication will be emphasized. Then, they must decide which AAC intervention approach will be used to facilitate the individual's communication across contexts. To be effective, AAC systems must function within a variety of environments; an AAC system's portability and functionality across multiple contexts should be primary factors in its selection. AAC systems should be used during naturally occurring social interactions, especially with peers and family. Interventions designed to teach their use must be implemented during real and meaningful interactions to promote generalization.

AAC systems should also be selected with consideration of the individual's level of communication development (i.e., pre-intentional, intentional, symbolic, linguistic), be congruent with family and individual preferences, and respect local norms (i.e., language, culture, religion). For instance, the use of an AAC system with symbolic representations will be most effective if the individual already has developed prerequisite communication skills, such as intentional communication, turn-taking, and joint attention. In our experience, some educators and interventionists select targets for intervention that are either far beyond or far below the individual's current level of communication development. This can lead the individual and potential or actual communication partners to become frustrated with or abandon the AAC system. Individuals with complex communication support needs can exhibit frustration in ways that are interpreted as challenging or inappropriate, although they actually might be logical, justifiable responses to demands to use communication forms outside one's current repertoire.

There are many different types of graphic or tangible representations that can be used with AAC systems, such as real objects, miniature objects, partial objects, black-and-white or color photographs of real objects, black-and-white line drawings (i.e., PCS), color drawings, or abstract symbols (including print). AAC systems can be added to individuals' current communication repertoires because no one mode can meet all needs in all environments. A variety of strategies (e.g., Picture Exchange Communication System; Bondy & Frost, 1994) have proved successful with individuals who have specific disabilities (e.g., ASD) and with particular AAC systems. Selecting the best intervention requires a clinician first to select the most appropriate strategy for the skill being taught and for the individual's level of communication development. Next, a clinician selects the intervention that has the most convincing evidence for the population and skills targeted, social validity, and fidelity.

Perhaps the most compelling evidence in the field for supporting communication intervention for individuals with complex communication needs is a systematic literature review conducted by Snell et al. (2010). The review shows that individuals with severe disabilities had immediate and positive responses to the interventions used. Many of the studies reviewed measured multiple forms of communication used by the participants, with the majority focused on improving expressive communication and language skills. Moreover, this evidence indicated that when systematic instructional strategies (i.e., prompting, time delay) were used, participants learned a variety of communicative forms, including both speech and AAC. Although the review focused on the quality and quantity of research in the area, a variety of interventions were reported to have positive effects on communication, language, and literacy skills.

REFLECTION QUESTION 5

In Chapter 3, you will learn about providing literacy instruction to individuals with complex support needs who also come from culturally and linguistically diverse backgrounds. Review your responses to Reflection Questions 1–4. How might your responses differ when considering a student from a culturally and linguistically diverse background? How might your own background influence your approach to assessment and intervention?

SUMMARY

In this chapter, we discussed ways to promote the development of communication and language skills for both children and adults with complex communication support needs, including the impact of the context on performance and learning. Context consists of not only the environment, activity, people, and materials but also the underlying assumptions about practice and the shared understanding of the communication partner. The information we provided reinforces the premise that communication opportunities should be embedded throughout everyday home and community activities to build language and support literacy learning. Understanding an individual's current level of communication development while acknowledging individual interests, preferences, and cultural practices are key to developing goals, assessing progress, and planning for interventions that build language to support literacy learning for individuals with complex communication support needs. *To do any less diminishes the opportunities individuals with complex communication needs have to freedom of expression, which is one of the most fundamental human rights to which all people are entitled.* Taking into consideration this population's support needs, we define this important human right as the right to communicate with others, to be supported in that communication, and to have that communication be acknowledged by communication partners.

RESOURCES

Organizations

- **The American Association on Intellectual and Developmental Disabilities (AAIDD)** (aaidd.org) promotes policies, research, evidence-based practices, and human rights of individuals with intellectual and developmental disabilities.

- **The American Speech-Language-Hearing Association (ASHA)** (asha.org) is the national professional, scientific, and credentialing association for audiologists; speech-language pathologists; speech, language, and hearing scientists; audiology and speech-language pathology support personnel; and student members.

- **The International Association for the Scientific Study of Intellectual and Developmental Disabilities (IASSIDD)** (iassidd.org) promotes research and information dissemination on intellectual disabilities.

- **The International Society for Augmentative and Alternative Communication (ISAAC)** (isaac-online.org) works to improve the lives of individuals with complex communication needs.

- **The National Center and State Collaborative (NCSC)** (ncscpartners.org) is a partnership that ensures students with the most significant cognitive disabilities achieve increasingly higher academic outcomes and leave high school ready for postsecondary options.

- **The National Joint Committee for the Communication Needs of Persons with Severe Disabilities** (asha.org/NJC) is focused on research, policy, and education; this eight-member organization advocates for individuals with complex communication support needs.

- **TASH** (tash.org) advocates for inclusive work, school, and community environments.

- **The United States Society for Augmentative and Alternative Communication (USSAAC)** (ussaac.org) is the United States chapter of the International Society for Augmentative and Alternative Communication (ISAAC).

Professional Development

- **IRIS Modules** (iris.peabody.vanderbilt.edu/iris-resource-locator/?term=assistive-technology) provide resources and materials on evidence-based practices for all students.

- **Modules Addressing Special Education and Teacher Education (MAST)** (http://mast.ecu.edu) provides special education professional development activities for teachers.

- **The National Professional Development Center on Autism Spectrum Disorder (NPDC)** (autismpdc.fpg.unc.edu) provides resources for and promotes the use of evidence-based practices for students with ASD.

- **Project IDEAL** (http://www.projectidealonline.org/) was created by the Texas Department of Developmental Disabilities as part of a professional preparation program to support teachers of students with disabilities.

- **Quality Indicators for Assistive Technology** (http://www.qiat.org) is a grassroots organization providing support and guidance for the provision of assistive technology services in schools.

Resources for Individuals Using Assistive Technology

- **AAC Language Lab** (aaclanguagelab.com) provides resources for language learning.

- **Center for Literacy and Disability Studies** (med.unc.edu/ahs/clds) addresses the literacy of individuals with disabilities across all ages.

- **Closing the Gap** (closingthegap.com) describes the latest assistive technology news, how-tos, and ever-changing technologies and implementation strategies.

- **CogLink** (coglink.com) is a supported e-mail program usable by people with significant impairments in attention, memory, and organization.

- **Creative Communicating** (creativecommunicating.com) has products for children with disabilities, including users of AAC.

- **PrAACtical AAC** (praacticalaac.org) has resources for professionals and families to support communication and literacy abilities of people with significant communication difficulties.

- **Spectronics** (https://www.spectronics.com.au/iphoneipad-apps-for-aac) provides a list and description of AAC apps for the iPod, iPhone, and iPad.

REFERENCES

American Speech-Language-Hearing Association. (n.d.-a). *Augmentative and alternative communication (AAC).* Retrieved from http://www.asha.org/public/speech/disorders/AAC

American Speech-Language-Hearing Association. (n.d.-b). *Augmentative and alternative communication: Key issues.* Retrieved from http://www.asha.org/PRPSpecificTopic.aspx?folderid=8589942773&section=Key_Issues

American Speech-Language-Hearing Association. (1982). *Language* [Relevant Paper]. Available from www.asha.org/policy. doi:10.1044/policy.RP1982-00125

American Speech-Language-Hearing Association. (2002). *Augmentative and alternative communication: Knowledge and skills for service delivery* [Knowledge and Skills]. Available from www.asha.org/policy. doi:10.1044/policy.KS2002-00067

Barton, P.E. (2000). *What jobs require: Literacy, education, and training, 1940–2006. Policy information report.* Princeton, NJ: Educational Testing Service.

Bates, E. (1979). *The emergence of symbols: Cognition and communication in infancy.* New York, NY: Academic Press.

Beukelman, D.R., & Mirenda, P. (2013). *Augmentative and alternative communication: Supporting children and adults with complex communication needs* (4th ed.). Baltimore, MD: Paul H. Brookes Publishing Co.

Bondy, A.S., & Frost, L.A. (1994). The Picture Exchange Communication System. *Focus on Autism and Other Developmental Disabilities, 9*(3), 1–19. doi:10.1177/108835769400900301

Brady, N.C., Bruce, S., Goldman, A., Erickson, K., Mineo, B., Ogletree, B.T., … Schoonover, J. (2016). Communication services and supports for individuals with severe disabilities: Guidance for assessment and intervention. *American Journal on Intellectual and Developmental Disabilities, 121*(2), 121–138. doi:10.1352/1944-7558-121.2.121

Brady, N.C., Fleming, K., Thiemann-Bourque, K., Olswang, L., Dowden, P., Saunders, M.D., & Marquis, J. (2012). Development of the communication complexity scale. *American Journal of Speech-Language Pathology, 21*(1), 16–28. doi:10.1044/2015_AJSLP-14-0093

Bruce, S.M. (2005). The impact of congenital deafblindness on the struggle to symbolism. *International Journal of Disability, Development and Education, 52*(3), 233–251.

Bruce, S.M., & Vargas, C. (2007). Communication acts expressed by children with severe disabilities in high-rate contexts. *Augmentative and Alternative Communication, 23*(4), 300–311.

Bus, A.G., van IJzendoorn, M.H., & Pellegrini, A.D. (1995). Joint book reading makes for success in learning to read: A meta-analysis on intergenerational transmission of literacy. *Review of Educational Research, 65*(1), 1–21. doi:10.3102/00346543065001001

Carr, E.G., & Durand, V.M. (1985). Reducing behavior problems through functional communication training. *Journal of Applied Behavior Analysis, 18*(2), 111–126. doi:10.1901/jaba.1985.18-111

Clay, M.M. (1966). *Emergent reading behaviour* (Doctoral dissertation, University of Auckland). Retrieved from http://hdl.handle.net/2292/778

Crystal, D. (2006). *How language works: How babies babble, words change meaning, and languages live or die.* Woodstock, NY: The Overlook Press.

Curtin, S., & Hufnagle, D. (2009). Speech perception. In E.L. Bavin (Ed.), *The Cambridge handbook of child language* (pp. 107–123). Cambridge, NY: Cambridge University Press.

de Valenzuela, J.S., Green, J., & Hall, J. (2010). Universal design: A reflective description of its application in the university classroom. In R. Hernández Castañeda & J. Gacel-Ávila (Eds.), *Innocación e internacionalización de la educación* (pp. 188–227). Guadalajara, México: Universidad de Guadalajara Press.

Donnellan, A.M. (1984). The criterion of the least dangerous assumption. *Behavioral Disorders, 9*(2), 141–150.

Downing, J.E. (2005). *Teaching communication skills to students with severe disabilities* (2nd ed.). Baltimore, MD: Paul H. Brookes Publishing Co.

Downing, J.E., & Ryndak, D.L. (2015). Integrating team expertise to support communication. In J.E. Downing, A. Hanreddy, & K.D. Peckham-Hardin (Eds.), *Teaching communication skills to students with severe disabilities* (3rd ed., pp. 21–50). Baltimore, MD: Paul H. Brookes Publishing Co.

Dragon Speech Recognition Software [Computer Software]. (2015). Retrieved from http://www.nuance.com/dragon/index.htm

Every Student Succeeds Act of 2015, S.1177. Retrieved from: https://www.congress.gov/bill/114th-congress/senate-bill/1177/text

Gervain, J., & Mehler, J. (2010). Speech perception and language acquisition in the first year of life. *Annual Review of Psychology, 61,* 191–218.

Iacono, T., West, D., Bloomberg, K., & Johnson, H. (2009). Reliability and validity of the revised Triple C: Checklist of Communicative Competencies for adults with severe and multiple disabilities. *Journal of Intellectual Disability Research, 53*(1), 44–53. doi:10.1111/j.1365-2788.2008.01121.x

Kasari, C., Brady, N., Lord, C., & Tager-Flusberg, H. (2013). Assessing the minimally verbal school-aged child with autism spectrum disorder. *Autism Research, 6*(6), 479–493. doi:10.1044/2015_AJSLP-14-0093

Koppenhaver, D.A., Pierce, P., Steelman, J.D., & Yoder, D.E. (1995). Contexts of early literacy intervention for children with developmental disabilities. *Language intervention: Preschool through the elementary years, 5,* 241–274.

Lessow-Hurley, J. (2000). *The foundations of dual language instruction* (3rd ed.). New York, NY: Longman.

Lifter, K., & Bloom, L. (1998). Intentionality and the role of play in the transition to language. In A.M. Wetherby, S.F. Warren, & J. Reichle (Eds.), *Transitions in prelinguistic communication* (pp. 161–195). Baltimore, MD: Paul H. Brookes Publishing Co.

McLean, M., Wolery, M., & Bailey, D.B. (2004). *Assessing infants and preschoolers with special needs* (3rd ed.). Columbus, OH: Pearson.

National Commission on Writing. (2004, September). *Writing: A ticket to work . . . or a ticket out: A survey of business leaders.* Retrieved from http://www.collegeboard.com/prod_downloads/writingcom/writing-ticket-to-work.pdf

National Early Literacy Panel. (2008). *Developing early literacy: Report of the National Early Literacy Panel.* Washington, DC: National Institute for Literacy. Retrieved from http://files.eric.ed.gov/fulltext/ED508381.pdf

National Joint Committee for the Communicative Needs of Persons with Severe Disabilities. (1992, March). Guidelines for meeting the communication needs of persons with severe disabilities [electronic version]. *ASHA, 34*(Suppl. 7), 1–8.

National Reading Panel. (2000). *Report of the National Reading Panel: Teaching children to read: An evidence-based assessment of the scientific research literature on reading and its implications for reading instruction: Reports of the subgroups.* Washington, DC: National Institute of Child Health and Human Development, National Institutes of Health.

No Child Left Behind (NCLB) Act of 2001, PL 107-110, 115 Stat. 1425, 20 U.S.C. §§ 6301 *et seq.*

Peirce, C.S. (1998). What is a sign? In The Peirce Edition Project (Ed.), *The essential Peirce: Selected philosophical writings, volume 2 (1893–1913)* (pp. 4–10). Bloomington, IN: Indiana University Press.

Proctor, L.A., & Zangari, C. (2009). Language assessment for students who use AAC. In G. Soto & C. Zangari (Eds.), *Practically speaking: Language, literacy, and academic development for students with AAC needs* (pp. 47–70). Baltimore, MD: Paul H. Brookes Publishing Co.

Rowland, C., & Fried-Oken, M. (2010). Communication Matrix: A clinical and research assessment tool targeting children with severe communication disorders. *Journal of Pediatric Rehabilitation Medicine: An Interdisciplinary Approach, 3*(4), 319–329. doi:10.3233/PRM20100144

Rowland, C., & Schweigert, P. (1989). Tangible symbols: Symbolic communication for individuals with multisensory impairments. *Augmentative and Alternative Communication, 5*(4), 226–234. doi:10.1080/07434618912331275276

Rowland, C., & Schweigert, P. (2000). Tangible symbols, tangible outcomes. *Augmentative and Alternative Communication, 16*(2), 61–78.

Rowland, C., & Stremel-Campbell, K. (1987). Share and share alike: Conventional gestures through emergent language. In D. Guess, L. Goetz, & K. Stremel-Campbell (Eds.), *Innovative program design for individuals with sensory impairments* (pp. 49–75). Baltimore, MD: Paul H. Brookes Publishing Co.

Ryndak, D.L., & Alper, S.K. (2003). *Curriculum and instruction for students with significant disabilities in inclusive settings.* Boston, MA: Allyn & Bacon.

Siegel, E.B., & Cress, C.J. (2002). Overview of the emergence of early AAC behaviors: Progression from communicative to symbolic skills. In J. Reichle, D.R. Beukelman, & J.C. Light (Eds.), *Exemplary practices for beginning communicators: Implications for AAC* (pp. 25–57). Baltimore, MD: Paul H. Brookes Publishing Co.

Snell, M.E., Brady, N., McLean, L., Ogletree, B.T., Siegel, E., Sylvester, L., . . . Sevcik, R. (2010). Twenty years of communication intervention research with individuals who have severe intellectual and developmental disabilities. *American Journal on Intellectual and Developmental Disabilities, 115*(5), 364–380. doi:10.1352/1944-7558-115-5.364

Tager-Flusberg, H., Rogers, S., Cooper, J., Landa, R., Lord, C., Paul, R., . . . Yoder, P. (2009). Defining spoken language benchmarks and selecting measures of expressive language development for young children with autism spectrum disorders. *Journal of Speech, Language, and Hearing Research, 52*(3), 643. doi:10.1044/1092-4388(2009/08-0136)

Teale, W.H., & Sulzby, E. (1986). *Emergent literacy: Writing and reading. Writing research: Multidisciplinary inquiries into the nature of writing series.* Norwood, NJ: Ablex.

Verschuur, R., Didden, R., Lang, R., Sigafoos, J., & Huskens, B. (2014). Pivotal response treatment for children with autism spectrum disorders: A systematic review. *Review Journal of Autism and Developmental Disorders, 1*(1), 34–61. doi:10.1007/s40489-013-0008-z

Warren, S.F., Fey, M.E., Finestack, L.H., Brady, N.C., Bredin-Oja, S.L., & Fleming, K.K. (2008). A randomized trial of longitudinal effects of low-intensity responsivity education/prelinguistic milieu teaching. *Journal of Speech, Language, and Hearing Research, 51*(2), 451–470. doi:10.1044/1092-4388(2008/033)

Westling, D.L., Fox, L., & Carter, E. (2014). *Teaching students with severe disabilities* (5th ed.). Upper Saddle River, NJ: Pearson.

Wetherby, A.M., & Prizant, B.M. (1989). The expression of communicative intent: Assessment guidelines. *Seminars in Speech and Language, 10*(1), 77–91.

Wetherby, A.M., & Prizant, B. (2002). *Communication and Symbolic Behavior Scales Developmental Profile™ (CSBS DP™)–First normed edition.* Baltimore, MD: Paul H. Brookes Publishing Co.

Wetherby, A.M., Reichle, J., & Pierce, P.L. (1998). The transition to symbolic communication. In A.M. Wetherby, S.F. Warren, & J. Reichle (Eds.), *Transitions in prelinguistic communication* (pp. 197–230). Baltimore, MD: Paul H. Brookes Publishing Co.

Wiggins, G., & McTighe, J. (2011). *Understanding by design* (2nd ed.). Upper Saddle River, NJ: Pearson.

CHAPTER 3

Addressing Cultural and Linguistic Diversity in Language and Literacy Instruction

Julia Scherba de Valenzuela

LEARNING OBJECTIVES

By the end of this chapter, readers will

1. Recognize the need to pay attention to their students' cultural and linguistic backgrounds.

2. Understand why it is important to involve educators with expertise in the following areas in planning and delivering literacy instruction for English language learners (ELLs) with complex support needs: first and second language development, methods of teaching English as a second language (ESL), and/or bilingual education.

3. Become knowledgeable about (a) common models for delivering English language support services to ELLs and (b) important considerations for making choices about how to support the language development needs of ELLs with complex support needs.

Bilingualism is a normal part of the human condition—many people speak multiple language or multiple varieties of a language. Appropriate education for culturally and linguistically diverse (CLD) students must include language supports. In this chapter, I describe the normal language variation that we encounter across the United States, define different populations of students who are recognized as linguistically diverse, and explore how bilingual development affects cognitive development and social relationships over the lifespan. Models and general principles for providing native language support will be provided, along with examples of effective instructional practices and supports.

A TRUE 21st-CENTURY CHILD: Vicente

When I first met Vicente, a very social young man, he was 2 years old and very interested in technology. He was quite capable of turning on an old cell phone his mother, Ana, kept for him, opening programs, and swiping through his favorite photo folders.

While Vicente was born and raised in the United States, his parents are from northern Mexico and still stay in touch with relatives there through the telephone and Skype. Vicente especially enjoys being on camera when a nearby older cousin makes a video call to his grandmother in Mexico. His engaging personality and ready smile make him an integral part of his family and community life.

Vicente's parents and older brother, Francisco, speak with him primarily in Spanish at home. However, when Vicente plays with his younger sister, Carolina, and several cousins who live in the same neighborhood, they often code-switch into English. With his family, Vicente communicates primarily in two- to three-word utterances. His articulation is quite poor, and people who do not know him well often have trouble understanding him, especially if they do not know whether he is speaking Spanish or English.

Diagnosed with Down syndrome at birth, Vicente began receiving early intervention through a community service provider when he was quite young. However, while his parents speak Spanish predominantly, the majority of his early interventionists and medical professionals spoke only English. Therefore, even though Ana wanted to foster her son's early cognitive and language development, she found it hard to converse in depth with the service providers about how to extend their interventions to her family's typical activities at home and in the community. For example, Ana wanted not just to repeat the one-to-one activities the early interventionist demonstrated but also to extend these techniques to social interactions during outings to the park with other families—which she saw as natural learning opportunities. In addition, she considered using family routines, such as bath time or meals, to foster Vicente's language development, but she wasn't sure exactly how.

Vincente is now in upper elementary school, in a segregated program designed for students with complex support needs, and receives a number of pull-out services, including speech-language intervention and physical therapy. Most students in his classroom have diagnoses of intellectual disability or autism spectrum disorder. At school, Vincente communicates using gestures, vocalizations, verbal output characterized primarily as "gibberish" by his current teacher, and picture cards. There are visual labels (made using Boardmaker software; Mayer-Johnson/Tobii Dynavox, Pittsburgh, PA) for many objects in the classroom, as well as a visual schedule using these pictures. Some of the pictures also include the written English word for the object. Both the classroom teacher and the speech-language pathologist work with Vicente using the Picture Exchange Communication System (Bondy & Frost, 1994), a commonly used augmentative and alternative communication intervention program. Inclusion is primarily fostered through eating lunch in the school cafeteria and going on community outings. His class regularly visits the zoo and a nearby nature center and goes swimming at a local community center every week.

Of the eight students in Vincente's classroom, four have Spanish as their primary home language, two are from homes where both English and Spanish are frequently spoken, and two are from English-speaking homes. Vincente's current special educator, like all of his previous teachers and service providers, speaks only English. His current classroom usually has two educational assistants (EAs).

Much of Vicente's verbal output is echolalic and considered unintelligible by most of his educational staff. Recently, by happenstance, a Spanish-speaking EA took a position in his classroom. She recognized that Vicente was attempting to produce short sentences in Spanish and that he followed requests more readily when she spoke to him in Spanish.

LANGUAGE VARIATION IS A NORMAL PART OF THE HUMAN CONDITION

Bilingualism is present in practically every country of the world, in all classes of society, and in all age groups. In fact it is difficult to find a society that is genuinely monolingual. Not only is bilingualism worldwide, it is a phenomenon that has existed since the beginning of language in human history. It is probably true that no language group has ever existed in isolation from other language groups, and the history of languages is replete with examples of language contact leading to some form of bilingualism. (Grosjean, 1982, p. 2)

Many people in the United States and in other countries use more than one language during the course of their daily lives. In fact, Cook suggested that "monolinguals are probably in a minority of the world as a whole" (2003, p. 488) and Romaine stated that bilingualism is "a normal and unremarkable necessity for the majority of the world's population" (2003, p. 512).

Some are bilingual because they enjoy learning and speaking other languages and actively seek out opportunities to speak different languages. For example, some people take classes to learn a foreign language so they can communicate with native speakers during a visit to another country. We call these kinds of second language learners *elective bilinguals* because learning a second language is a choice, rather than a necessity, for them. However, other people must speak more than one language in order to communicate with family and friends, people at work, and others in the wider community. Speaking more than one language, at least to some extent, is a requirement for participation in their daily lives. We call these people *circumstantial bilinguals,* because speaking more than one language is required by the circumstances of their lives.

In addition, many native English speakers use English in different ways from middle-class, white Americans because of their cultural or ethnic backgrounds. For example, many people in the United States speak African American English (also known as Ebonics), Chicano English, Hawaiian Pidgin, or Appalachian English. In addition to pronunciation, grammar, or vocabulary differences, language varieties can differ in how language is used. These differences, such as in eye gaze, body language, gestures, loudness, and the use and meaning of silence, are real and can be the source of miscommunication between students and teachers and can have an impact on the learning environment. In addition, some of these language varieties, especially those associated with historically discriminated populations, do not receive the same level of respect as others. For example, some people look down on the type of English spoken by people in rural areas or in particular regions, such as in the South, and look at it as "broken" or as incorrect. The lack of understanding that, from an objective linguistic perspective, all language varieties are equally valid, useful, and correct can also cause educational difficulties for students who come from these backgrounds.

Students who come from diverse cultural and linguistic backgrounds may have rich home and community experiences that can provide a strong foundation for teachers and other educational professionals to draw on if they are open to integrating these experiences into the curriculum. However, because these experiences might be different from those of middle-class families, educational materials might not be an accurate reflection of these children's home lives. Also, educators might not have enough knowledge about their students' home and community practices to incorporate them into the curriculum. Extra effort is needed for teachers to become familiar with the diverse cultures within the community so that their instructional activities are culturally relevant and go beyond trivial coverage of "heroes and holidays" and "foods, festivals, and folk tales."

For many students, like Vicente, bilingualism is often a necessity, not a choice. It develops when there is a social need for it. Even in the United States, where the majority of people speak English, many also speak another language. The U.S. Census Bureau collects information on what languages are spoken at home. Of thousands of languages spoken worldwide, the U.S. Census Bureau has identified 382 non-English languages and language families commonly spoken in the United States (U.S. Census Bureau, 2015). Data for the years 2006–2008 on languages spoken at home by individuals ages 5 years and over suggests that almost 20% of the population, more than 55 million, speak a language other than English at home (U.S. Census Bureau, 2010)—a larger proportion than those shown in the previous two decennial censuses: 11% in 1980 and 14% in 1990. Of those 55 million, 62% (>34 million) spoke Spanish. The next most commonly spoken language was Chinese, with almost 2.5 million home language speakers of multiple dialects; other languages with more than a million home language speakers reported during this period were, in order of number of speakers, Tagalog, French, Vietnamese, German, and Korean (U.S. Census Bureau, 2010).

Although a significant percentage of the U.S. population speaks a home language other than English, and the number is rising, most intervention research with students with disabilities— and, in particular, with those who have complex support needs—is conducted with monolingual native English speakers. Therefore, there is little information available for practitioners to guide the development of educational programs for English language learners (ELLs) with complex support needs. Recent research suggests that when confronted with students who require educational services resulting both from special education and ELL needs, professionals prioritize special education services and exclude students from second language support services (de Valenzuela et al., 2016). Conducting an in-depth comparison of ELLs who were and were not receiving special education services, Romero (2014) found that a significantly higher percent of typically developing ELLs received English as a second language (ESL) or bilingual education services than ELLs who were identified as having special needs. In particular, bilingual education was available to only a few students identified with mild disabilities (other health impairment, learning disability, or speech-language impairment). No students with complex support needs in that school district had access to a systematic program of instruction delivered in their home language.

Regardless of insufficient information about appropriate educational programs, research confirms that individuals with disabilities can be bilingual, to the extent that they are able to develop language in general. There is also evidence that bilingualism does not hinder language development. This chapter contains a review of some of this research in later sections. In addition, there are clear federal mandates to address barriers to instruction resulting from lack of proficiency in English. These mandates, as described later in this chapter, pertain to children with disabilities as well as those who are typically developing. Information from the fields of ESL and bilingual education, which have a long and rich history in U.S. education, is therefore pertinent when considering the development of instruction of ELLs with disabilities, including those with complex support needs. This chapter contains descriptions of key principles and important considerations for determining when and how to provide instruction. First, however, we will review some basic concepts and information related to first and second language development.

REFLECTION QUESTION 1

What types of language variation is represented in the people with whom you interact frequently? How might those differences influence your perceptions of them as individuals? Or, what sorts of reactions to these types of language variation have you heard?

TERMS USED TO DESCRIBE DIFFERENT GROUPS OF STUDENTS

A number of terms are commonly used to talk about the student population addressed in this chapter: "culturally and linguistically diverse students," "students with a primary home language other than English," "English language learners," and "bilingual individuals." Not all professionals use these terms the same way, and they may also have different meanings in different settings, such as the legal system, health care, and education. Therefore, it is important to understand what is meant when these terms are used to describe particular groups of students.

Culturally and Linguistically Diverse Students

Sometimes, people want to refer a broader category of students, not all of whom were raised with a non-English home language. This larger group of students may have been raised with two or more languages in the home or only non-English language. Or, they may be native English speakers but use a variety that is different from that expected in school. In the special education literature, we use *culturally and linguistically diverse* (CLD) to emphasize that in addition to having a language background that is different from monolingual standard-English speakers, these students also come from diverse cultural, ethnic, and/or racial backgrounds. This very general term does not have a precise definition or diagnostic criteria. It is useful, though, in capturing the largest group of students whose cultural and linguistic backgrounds need to be considered when developing educational programs.

Students With a "Primary Home Language Other Than English"

It is often important to identify those students who have a home language other than English because this is the first step in identifying students who need English language development support. Because students may be exposed to more than one language at home, it is sometimes useful to determine which students have a *primary home language other than English* (PHLOTE). Inserting the word *primary* emphasizes the difference between students who may have a family member, such as a grandmother, who speaks to the child in a language other than English versus those whose families speak a non-English language most of the time. The word *primary* also recognizes that within the United States, it is rare for students to not be exposed to English at home, at least some of the time. This is because English is the dominant language by far in our country, and siblings, other family members and friends, visitors, and even technology (e.g., television, radio, cell phones, tablets, laptops) bring this language into most homes, at least to some minor extent.

It is also important to recognize that students may have more than one non-English home language. For instance, families from indigenous backgrounds from Latin America may speak Spanish as a second language and English as their third language. For example, Yaqui and Tarahumara are spoken in communities in Northern Mexico, and Quechua is one of the two official languages of Peru. Therefore, it is important to get careful information from families about the languages their student has been exposed to at home and in the community and not make assumptions based on surnames, national origins, or hearing parents speak a particular language.

Students who have been exposed to a non-English language at home and/or have a primary home language other than English are typically identified based on a home language survey administered when students are first registered for school. Although not a specific federal requirement, home language surveys are used in virtually all U.S. states in order to identify those students who *might* require second language development support. Their exact format, the number and type of questions they ask, and their use of terminology all vary across states and districts. Some use the acronym *PHLOTE,* while others use *ELLs* or *English learners* (ELs); the latter two terms may also be used specifically for students with a home language other than English who also require English support services. Still other terms used in home language surveys include *language minority students* and *minority-language speakers.*

English Language Learners

The term *English language learner* or *ELL* is sometimes used when, for program planning purposes, it is important to differentiate between students who have a non-English home language but do not need second language development support and those who do. Identifying these students and assessing their proficiency in English poses particular challenges when the students also have complex support needs.

Challenges in Assessing Proficiency in English   Typically, students who need second language instructional assistance are identified via a language proficiency test. Although many such tests are available, 38 states currently use the ACCESS for ELLs test (WIDA, 2015). Because typically developing students are not expected to have language delays or deficits, test developers can set standards for what it means to be "proficient" in English; if they are identified as not yet proficient, it is assumed they will eventually become proficient with appropriate support.

Assessing English proficiency in students with complex support needs is far more difficult. An alternate version of the ACCESS for ELLs assessment has been developed for students with "significant cognitive difficulties" (WIDA, 2015–2016, p. 6). This alternate assessment provides levels of language proficiency that are linked to a set of English language development standards, as required by current federal guidelines, and skills the test developers identified as critical to English language proficiency development (WIDA, 2015–2016). It was first field tested in 2010. Because the test is relatively new, it is unknown how well it assesses the English language proficiency of such a heterogeneous group. Students with complex support needs may have widely varying levels of communication development, from those who have not yet developed intentional communication to those with relatively advanced language skills. (See Chapter 2 for a description of levels of communication development among these students.)

Developing and using an alternate language proficiency assessment for students with complex support needs therefore poses several challenges:

- It is difficult to define what language proficiency means.

- It is difficult, when interpreting students' scores, to separate the effect of their emerging development of English from the effect of their cognitive impairments.

- Because this instrument is administered only in English, students with limited communication development, who are relatively proficient in English, may be inaccurately identified as ELLs.

- Students who continue to demonstrate limitations in communication or language skills over time may continue to be identified as ELLs, regardless of their progress in learning English.

Therefore, great caution should be used when interpreting language proficiency scores for students with complex support needs. Much more in-depth information on home language use and students' communication abilities across contexts is needed to develop appropriate instructional programs.

Alternative Terms Used to Refer to English Language Learners   In the past, students were usually identified according to their level of English language proficiency using these terms: *non-English proficient (NEP), limited English proficient (LEP),* and *fluent English proficient (FEP).* Although no longer as common, they are still used in some areas. Currently, students who qualify for English language development programs are often identified as ELLs or ELs. According to the Office for Civil Rights (OCR; U.S. Department of Education, 2015), the term ELL "is often preferred over limited-English-proficient (LEP) as it highlights accomplishments rather than deficits" (para. 6). Consistent with current terminology in federal guidelines, in this chapter, I use *ELL* to refer to students who have a primary home language other than English *and* whose proficiency in English is still limited in relation to the development of their home language.

Bilingual Individuals

There are many different ways to define the term *bilingual.* This term, unlike *PHLOTE* or *ELL,* does not have an educational definition. And unlike *CLD, bilingual* does indicate that the individual knows, speaks, and/or uses two (or more) languages, at least to some extent. Some may assume that in order to be bilingual, one must speak two languages with equal proficiency. An alternate definition is proposed by Grosjean, who asserted that "bilinguals are those who use two or more languages (or dialects) in their everyday lives" (2012, p. 4). This definition gets to the notion that bilingualism is defined more by function than by levels of proficiency. Similarly, Valdés and Figueroa defined bilinguals as those with the ability to "function at some level in more than one language" (1994, p. 8). Both of these definitions are useful when considering students, such as Vicente, who have complex support needs.

Equal proficiency in both languages should not be used as a standard for bilingualism. Most people who use two or more languages in their daily lives are not equally proficient; rather, they regularly use two languages for different reasons and in different contexts. Romaine argued that "individuals are rarely equally fluent in the languages they know. Indeed, a society which produced such individuals would soon cease to be multilingual since no community uses two or more languages for the same set of functions" (2003, p. 512). Grosjean echoed this notion, applying it to individual speakers, when he reasoned that "levels of fluency in a language will depend on the need for that language and will be extremely domain specific" (1985, p. 471). For students with complex support needs, it is important to consider the need they will have for their different languages in different contexts (e.g., with different family members, in different activities in the community). They will likely have a lifelong need to use their home language. In addition, research suggests that many CLD families will not seek out-of-home placement for their children with disabilities after school-based services end at age 22 (McDonnell, Hardman, & McDonnell, 2003; Rueda & Martinez, 1992). Therefore, because individuals with complex support needs will most likely maintain sustained contact with and require support from family and community members across the lifespan, continued maintenance and development of their home language is vital. At the same time, they can and should be given opportunities to develop and use other languages.

Vicente is a good example of a person who uses different languages for different functions in different settings. Spanish is the primary language used during most of his interactions with his parents and with family members living in Mexico. He learns terms for family relationships (e.g., aunt, uncle, grandmother, grandfather, godparent) and family activities in Spanish. Vincente attends church on Sundays with his family and the service is in Spanish—he can repeat common short prayers and benedictions in Spanish. Vicente enjoys spending time with his father and older brother when doing chores—he learns words for common household tools (e.g., hammer, broom, shovel) in Spanish, as well as how to follow one- and two-step directions using those items (e.g., "bring me the hammer," "sweep up the dirt and empty the dustpan in the trash can").

During afterschool and weekend play activities, Vicente's family and friends speak mainly Spanish, but they use English for certain words and phrases, especially those related to pop culture such as movies and music. By going to the store with his mother, Vicente has learned to use greetings and polite phrases, such as "thank you" and "please" in English. At school, he uses English, although he often switches to Spanish when his teachers cannot understand his speech based on context alone. He has learned English words like "book," "scissors," "desk," and "cafeteria" in English, along with mathematical verbs such as "count" and "add." In short, Vicente is much like many other bilingual individuals, who do not use both languages in the same ways, in the same contexts, with the same people, and therefore, do not have identical competencies in both languages.

Like Vicente, many people who clearly are more proficient in one language than the other may be more comfortable in the language they consider weaker in some contexts, such as education, family, religion, or certain community settings, or in particular language domains (e.g., reading, writing, speaking, listening). For example, when students are only provided literacy instruction in English, they may be limited in their ability to read and write in their home language, even if their oral language skills overall are stronger in their home language. Therefore, educators need to recognize that a determination that a student is more proficient in one language than another many miss important subtleties that might have instructional importance.

REFLECTION QUESTION 2

What different terms have you heard that describe different groups of students from different linguistic backgrounds? How are they similar to or different from the terms defined previously?

DIFFERENT AVENUES TO BILINGUAL DEVELOPMENT

The experiences through which students develop more than one language vary. Some are raised with more than one language in the home. Many ELLs can be described as *simultaneous* bilinguals—that is, individuals exposed to both their first and second languages before age 3 years. Some ELLs learn both languages together as their first language, even though for educational purposes the minority (non-English) language is often designated as their first language and English their second. In contrast, *sequential* bilinguals are exposed to their second language after age 3 years. Many sequential bilinguals in the United States are first exposed to English on a regular and extensive basis upon entering school. It is important for teachers and other educational professionals to know what languages students have been exposed to, in what settings, and at what ages, because this may have an impact on educational programming.

In assessing students' language development, it is also important for teachers to recognize that not all bilingual students have the opportunity to become literate in both languages. In large part, this depends on whether students have access to literacy instruction in their native language at school. Although many families do engage in relevant home literacy activities together—reading magazines, books, and the Bible; coloring their names and practicing writing their names; making shopping lists—it is not reasonable to place on families the full responsibility of developing and delivering a literacy program in their home language. Opportunities to develop literacy also depend on the reading material available in each language. Although books and other media in languages other than English have become much more readily available in the United States over the past several decades, especially with the growth of online booksellers, families need sufficient disposable income to purchase these materials; purchasing online requires a credit card. Local libraries may not have an extensive selection of children's books in languages other than English—if they have any. Therefore, families need resources and support to foster literacy practices in the home language, if these are not available at school. Even then, bilingual students may have relatively lower proficiency in the home language than in English in the domains of reading and writing.

Understanding language development is even more complex for students with complex support needs. Because it is extremely difficult to determine their English language proficiency objectively, it may be more useful to determine when the student was first exposed to English, assess relative proficiency across different domains in the home language versus English, and develop a profile of typical language use across different settings and with different people. Grosjean suggests taking a holistic view of bilingualism, where a bilingual is seen as "an integrated whole which cannot easily be decomposed into two separate parts" (1985, p. 471). When taking this perspective, we don't simply compare bilingual students to monolingual students in both languages. Rather, we attempt to understand the entirety of an individual's knowledge within and across both or all languages used, and to understand the relationship between those languages. Informal assessment tools may be useful for obtaining this type of information. For example, Mattes and Saldaña-Illingworth (2009) provide a set of informal assessment tools, including interview questionnaires, criterion-referenced assessment, and observation protocols.

It is also important to recognize that the relationship between an individual's languages may shift over time. For example, many bilingual youth begin as monolingual speakers of a minority (non-English) language. Over time, children may bring English home, speaking it increasingly, often with their peers and siblings. The change may be due, in part, to messages children receive about different languages' relative worth once they begin school (Lutz, 2007/2008)—messages they relate to their self-identity. As a result, bilingual individuals may, over time, become increasingly dominant in English (Anderson, 2012). This phenomenon, common among bilinguals in the United States, is sometimes referred to as *first language loss* or *first language attrition.*

To explore this phenomenon with students with complex support needs, my colleague Susan Copeland and I analyzed parent responses to home language survey questions related to home language use, comparing responses from parents of students identified with an intellectual disability (ID) to responses from parents of students identified with other disabilities (de Valenzuela, Copeland, & Mayette, 2010). We also examined the relative frequency of language proficiency test administration and scores for these two groups. The data were provided by a large urban school district with a high percentage of CLD students. We found that similar percentages of students in both groups had a non-English primary home language. Yet, significantly more students with ID were reported to have a language other than English as their *first* language and as their *primary* language than their special education peers with other disabilities. They were also significantly more likely to be reported as monolingual *speakers* of a language other than English, although they were not any more likely to *understand* only one language. In short, although parents reported similar percentages of non-English home languages for both groups, significantly higher percentages of students with ID were reported to use the language-minority home language as their first, primary, and only spoken language. These results suggest that students with complex support needs may be less likely to demonstrate a language shift from a minority language to English. However, more research is needed to confirm these findings and explore possible reasons for such a difference.

In addition, we found that students with an ID were administered a language proficiency test significantly less frequently than students with other disabilities. However, of those who were, a much higher percentage were identified as ELLs, compared to students with other disabilities, suggesting that the correct identification of language proficiency of students with complex support needs is indeed a complex and problematic endeavor. These results are only preliminary. Yet, if supported by further research, they could further emphasize the importance of several factors: (a) instruction in the native language to support learning; (b) explicit instructional support to foster transfer of knowledge and skills from the home language to English; (c) thorough assessment of students' abilities across both home and school languages, including expressive and receptive language; and (d) careful attention by education professionals to make sure that augmentative and alternative communication systems can be used in both languages because students may continue to use the minority language at home and in the community.

Important Differences Between Bilinguals and Monolinguals

Bilinguals do not function exactly the same as monolinguals with respect to language development and use. Grosjean recognized that "the bilingual is NOT the sum of two complete or incomplete monolinguals; rather, he or she has a unique and specific linguistic configuration" (1985, p. 471). This is partly because using two languages requires additional skills not needed by monolinguals. For example, monolingual children do not need to learn to pay attention to what language others around them typically speak. Bilinguals do. Bilingual children who know particular speakers can anticipate what language others will speak; if they do not, they can make educated guesses based on the context or other cues. For example, Vicente knows he can run up to his mother and ask for a juice box in Spanish—he does not need to wait to hear what language she uses each time. But at school, he tries to use English for greetings, counting, and so on, because he has learned that the teachers and most staff do not understand him when he speaks Spanish. Research suggests that typically developing simultaneous bilingual children, by the time they are between 2 and 3 years of age, are aware of the differences between their languages, which they can indicate by stating what languages they speak (e.g., "I speak Chinese") or switching languages according to the speaker (Paradis, 2012).

Code-Switching In addition, bilingual speakers learn to identify other bilingual speakers—those with whom they can speak both languages—and when two people who speak the same languages interact, they commonly use a combination of those languages, a phenomenon called *code-switching*. MacSwan defined code-switching as "the alternate use of two (or more) languages within the same utterance" (2013, p. 323). Code-switching is normal and natural, and it does not mean that the speakers are unable to separate the different languages. Instead, because they have access to a wide range of language forms across two languages, they can make choices that best fit the interaction and social setting, as well as provide special emphasis or meaning. These choices are not random, and people who code-switch do not speak a "corrupt" version of one language or the other. Bilingual students who are just beginning to use language may sometimes mix languages—for example, by substituting a Spanish word for an English one—when they do not know to say something in one language or the other. However, according to Kohnert, "very young children do not speak the 'wrong' language or switch between languages with monolingual communication partners" (2013, p. 105). As Paradis (2012) reported, children learn to associate language with people by age 2 to 3. So when students with complex support needs use Spanish words—for example, during classroom interactions—it very well may indicate that their English language development is still insufficient to meet all of their communication needs. If this occurs, it may be useful for the classroom personnel to learn what those words mean in the child's home language so that they can respond appropriately and, in time, teach the student how to say those words in English. In addition, it is important to understand that languages differ in many ways, including their social aspects; learning a language is more than just learning a different word for the same thing, such as using *perro* for *dog* in Spanish.

Differences in Language Use (Pragmatics)
    It is common knowledge that people use different words, grammatical forms, and pronunciations across languages. What may be less well understood is that the ways that people *use* language can also differ greatly. This component of language, known as *pragmatics,* can vary considerably across languages—which affects how bilinguals develop overall communication skills. (See Chapter 2 for a discussion of the five components of language: phonology, syntax, morphology, semantics, and pragmatics.)

Pragmatics can vary significantly cross-linguistically. For example, some languages differ considerably in how they are used *by* and *to* male versus female speakers. Another difference is how loudly or softly people typically speak, and what a loud voice means—for example, anger or emphasis. Across language communities, differences in people's speech also include rate (speaking speed), pitch (higher or lower), intonation (variation in pitch), and the use of pauses, silence, and interruptions or overlapping speech. For example, in many Native American communities, when one person is speaking and another interjects, it is considered very rude, an indication that the other person wants to take over the conversation. Yet, in other language communities, listeners are expected to interject to indicate that they are paying attention.

According to Valdés and Figueroa, "knowing a language and knowing how to use a language involves a mastery and control of a large number of interdependent components and elements that interact with one another and that are affected *by the nature of the situation in which the communication takes place*" [emphasis added] (1994, p. 36). Similarly, Ochs argued that "one critical area of social competence a child must acquire is the ability to recognize/interpret what social event is taking place and to speak and act in ways that are sensitive to the context" (1986, p. 3). These quotes emphasize that understanding the situational nature of language use, in each language, is critical. Thus, in addition to linguistic competence, speakers of different languages need to develop *communicative competence* in each. Saville-Troike defined communicative competence as including

> both knowledge and expectation of who may or may not speak in certain settings, when to speak and when to remain silent, to whom one may speak, how one may speak to persons of different statuses and roles, what nonverbal behaviors are appropriate in various contexts, what the routines for turn-taking are in conversation, how to ask for and give information, how to request, how to offer or decline assistance or cooperation, how to give commands, how to enforce discipline, and the like — in short, everything involving the use of language and other communication dimensions in particular social settings. (2002, p. 18)

So, for instance, not only will speakers of different languages use different phrases and words during social routines, they will also vary greatly in how they accomplish these social routines. Consider how we greet people. It is not just a matter of knowing how to say "hello" and "goodbye" in another language; we also must know how to accompany that verbal greeting with appropriate gestures or physical contact, such as a hug, a kiss (or kisses) on the cheek, a handshake, a hand wave, or a nod. Communicative competence also means knowing that greetings can differ depending on the age, gender, and social status of the people involved, as well as the setting.

Some aspects of social communication develop very early. Research suggests that infants from different cultural groups begin to display differences in social communication, such as patterns of eye gaze and smiling, during the first months of life, even before they have demonstrated development of intentional communication. For example, Wörmann, Holodynski,

Kärtner, and Keller (2012), studying mothers and their infants in Cameroon and Germany, found differences in smiling between babies from each country by the time the children were 12 weeks old. This suggests that, even for students at beginning stages of communication, we need to pay attention to home language and cultural differences. Although students with complex support needs from CLD homes may not yet have developed language, they likely will have acquired a wealth of early communication skills, which may differ from those of children from the dominant culture. We cannot assume that because a student does not talk, the student is a blank slate and the language spoken to that student at home does not matter. Failing to address home–school language differences may hamper the student's educational progress.

REFLECTION QUESTION 3

Consider whether you have known or worked with any students with complex support needs from diverse language backgrounds. To what extent, if any, were their home languages taken into consideration at school? If so, how?

THE CASE FOR SUPPORTING BILINGUALISM FOR STUDENTS WITH COMPLEX SUPPORT NEEDS

Some people, recognizing how difficult it is for many individuals with complex support needs to develop language, reason that these students would find it much easier if they only had to learn one language—a belief that is erroneous. As a result, some well-meaning professionals suggest that parents stop speaking a non-English home language so their children can learn English more quickly (Marinova-Todd et al., 2016). However, this well-intentioned advice can have negative consequences, discussed below. In addition, it is grounded on two assumptions—that students with complex support needs cannot become bilingual and that exposure to more than one language will hinder their overall language development. Neither assumption is correct. Furthermore, it is possible that learning more than one language gives the bilingual individual cognitive and social advantages.

Effects of Bilingualism on Language and Cognitive Development

The available research suggests that bilingualism is possible for students with complex support needs. Recent reviews of research in the areas of autism spectrum disorder (Marinova-Todd & Mirenda, 2016), Down syndrome (Kay-Raining Bird, 2016) and developmental disorders (Kay-Raining Bird, Genesee, & Verhoeven, 2016) provide consistent evidence that children with complex support needs can become bilingual and that exposure to more than one language does not hamper their overall language development—nor does it hamper cognitive development. Rueda (1983) and Whitaker, Rueda, and Prieto (1985) found no evidence of bilingualism having negative effects on the cognitive development of individuals with ID. Limiting a child to one language, however, may.

Considering the opposite side of the bilingual equation, Kay-Raining Bird argued that "there can be severe negative consequences for children and their families that result from limiting language input to a single language in a society that is increasingly diverse" (2006, p. 249). Language-minority parents who are told that they should use only English at home may not be able to provide a rich language model in English. Or, if they have insufficient knowledge of English and are afraid that speaking with their child in their native language may be harmful, they may speak less. Even when parents are sufficiently proficient in English to avoid these problems, switching to English-only within the home may limit siblings' opportunities to develop the home language; limit all of their children's ability to maintain relationships with extended family, especially those living in other countries, who may not speak English; and limit the family's opportunities to participate in community activities conducted in the home language.

Research spanning more than 50 years examines the possible positive effects of bilingualism on cognitive development and functioning (see Kohnert, 2013, for an in-depth review of recent research). Kohnert reported that one effect of bilingualism appears to be a delay in the onset of memory problems in older bilingual adults. Because the research examining this phenomenon examined adults who were proficient in two languages, it is not known whether the protective effect of bilingualism in the area of memory would extent to bilinguals with complex support needs, who might have language deficits in both languages. Researchers have also examined the effect of language selection (e.g., choosing when to speak in which language) on executive functioning. Executive control includes "the activation, selection, inhibition, and organization of information during, for example, problem solving or planning" (Paradis, Genesee, & Crago, 2011, p. 51). A recent study (Olulade et al., 2016) found that adults who spoke two oral languages—English and Spanish—had a greater volume of grey matter in the areas of the brain related to executive control than monolinguals. Interestingly, they did not find differences between bilinguals who used English and American Sign Language and monolinguals. Oral language bilinguals cannot use both languages simultaneously and must select between languages when communicating. In contrast, signed language users can speak and sign at the same time and therefore do not need to choose between languages. Selectively activating or inhibiting languages to avoid interference requires increased cognitive effort (Kohnert, 2013). The research by Olulade et al. research suggests that this helps foster increased executive control and is possibly an important cognitive benefit of bilingualism.

Individuals with complex support needs have not been included in these research studies. However, even without confirmation that bilingualism conveys cognitive advantages for bilinguals with complex support needs, there are other important reasons to foster continued bilingual development in students who have a home language other than English. Perhaps the most important reasons stem from the reality of students' bilingual lives.

The Need to Be Bilingual

As illustrated by the demographics discussed previously, Spanish is by far the most commonly spoken language in the United States, after English, with Spanish-speaking communities in all U.S. states. Other language minority groups, although far less common, are also found in many regions. In addition, immigrants often settle in areas that include other residents from their home countries so that they can provide support to one another and engage in important cultural and religious practices. For bilingual students, continued development of the home language, alongside English, facilitates greater ability to participate in the entire repertoire of experiences, settings, and activities available outside of school. Indeed, one important purpose of schooling is to foster students' ability to engage in personal, social, community, and occupational activities *outside* of school. For bilingual students, many of those activities will be conducted in the home language. Furthermore, as mentioned earlier, students with complex support needs will most likely continue to need the support of family members, and others in the community, throughout their lives. Although service providers such as early interventionists, speech-language pathologists, and special educators are, all too often, monolingual English speakers, this may not be the case for direct care staff who come into frequent contact with individuals with complex support needs. For example, in New Mexico, where I work, and especially in more rural communities, support staff at group homes are often recent immigrants and more comfortable speaking Spanish than English. Therefore, bilingual adults with complex support needs will likely continue to need to use both languages across their lifespan.

Legal Requirements for Second Language Support Services

In addition to federal requirements for provision of special education services for students identified with a disability, there are equally compelling federal requirements to provide English language development services for ELLs. These services are sometimes also called *alternative language services.* Educational support for ELLs, both with and without disabilities, derives from the equal educational opportunity movement and is grounded in litigation and legislation such as *Brown v. Board of Education* in 1954 and the 1964 Civil Rights Act (Weinberg & Weinberg, 1990), as well as the Equal Educational Opportunities Act of 1974 (Welner, 2006). OCR has issued several documents that clarify school districts' responsibilities for educating language minority students, the most recent of which was released in 2015. The first of these documents, referred to as the "1970 memorandum" (U.S. Department of Education, 1970), explained that Title VI of the Civil Rights Act is violated when "students are excluded from effective participation in school because of their inability to speak and understand the language of instruction" and when "national-origin minority students are misassigned to classes for the mentally retarded because of their lack of English skills" (U.S. Department of Education, 2000, para. 9). This interpretation was upheld by the U.S. Supreme Court in *Lau v. Nichols* (1974).

This Supreme Court decision found that equal treatment of non–English-speaking students—for instance, providing the same textbooks, curriculum, and teachers made available to English speakers—did not, in itself, constitute equal education opportunity. This ruling provided a legal requirement for school districts to explicitly address the language needs of ELLs in educational planning. However, federal regulations do not specify the specific methods for providing alternative language services:

> OCR allows school districts broad discretion concerning how to ensure equal education opportunity for LEP students. OCR does not prescribe a specific intervention strategy or type of program that a school district must adopt to serve LEP students, nor does OCR require school districts to teach students in their primary language. Educational approaches that are recognized as sound by some experts in the field may reasonably be expected to ensure the effective participation of LEP students in the total education program. (U.S. Department of Education, 2000, para. 16)

These requirements have applied to students identified with disabilities since they were first established. Even so, Klingner and Bianco concluded that "services for English language learners with disabilities appear to be inadequate" (2006, p. 37). In addition, there are concerns, such as those raised by Romero's (2014) research (cited previously), that students with disabilities and those with complex support needs in particular may have less access to second language support services than their typically developing peers. The most recent guidance from OCR (U.S. Department of Education, 2015) is the most explicit with regard to the responsibilities of educational agencies toward students with disabilities. Take a moment to review some of the obligations specified in this memo provided in the textbox, "Legal Obligations to Ensure Equal Educational Access for ELLs."

LEGAL OBLIGATIONS TO ENSURE EQUAL EDUCATIONAL ACCESS FOR ENGLISH LANGUAGE LEARNERS

Following are some of the stipulations from the most recent OCR guidelines (U.S. Department of Education, 2015):

- "School districts can choose among programs designed for instructing EL students provided the program is instructionally sound in theory and effective in practice" (p. 1).

- "School districts must have qualified EL teachers, staff, and administrators to effectively implement their EL program, and must provide supplemental training when necessary" (p. 1).

- "EL students with disabilities must be provided *both* the language assistance and disability-related services to which they are entitled under Federal law" (p. 2).

- "To ensure that an individualized plan for providing special education or disability-related services addresses the language-related needs of an EL student with a disability, it is important that the team designing the plan include participants knowledgeable about that student's language needs" (p. 3).

- "School districts may not recommend that parents opt out for any reason. Parents are entitled to guidance in a language that they can understand about their child's rights, the range of EL services that their child could receive, and the benefits of such services. School districts should appropriately document that the parent made a voluntary, informed decision to opt their child out" (p. 3).

- "A school district must still take steps to provide opted-out EL students with access to its educational programs, monitor their progress, and offer EL services again if a student is struggling" (p. 3).

- "Districts must annually administer a valid and reliable English language proficiency (ELP) assessment, in reading, writing, listening and speaking, that is aligned to State ELP [English language proficiency] standards" (p. 3).

- "An EL student must not be exited from EL programs, services, or status until he or she demonstrates English proficiency on an ELP assessment in speaking, listening, reading, and writing" (p. 3).

- "School districts must monitor the academic progress of former EL students for at least two years" (p. 3).

These obligations make clear that students with a home language background other than English cannot be summarily exempted from the federal requirements to assess, monitor, and provide language assistance services. This includes students with complex support needs. It may be challenging to schedule both language support services and special education services. However, schools cannot recommend to parents that they choose between them or suggest that one is more important; instead, schools must clearly indicate that they will provide all of the services to which students are entitled. The OCR guidelines make clear that when students need both language support and special education services, neither takes priority over the other—students are entitled to both, and schools *must* provide both.

REFLECTION QUESTION 4

Given the complexities of scheduling special education and related services for students with complex support needs, what rationale could you provide to colleagues for involving ESL and/or bilingual education specialists and services?

PLANNING INSTRUCTION FOR ENGLISH LANGUAGE LEARNERS WITH COMPLEX SUPPORT NEEDS

As described previously, federal regulations do not specify exactly what type of alternative language services must be provided. Instead, states and districts develop policies and describe the instructional programs that comply with the federal guidelines. These programs can be provided wholly in English, or partly in students' native language (bilingual education); if the latter, bilingual education programs necessarily include a component of English language instruction. In the following sections, I describe several of the most common types of programs designed to meet federal requirements.

In addition to ensuring that students with disabilities receive required alternative language services, special educators and related service providers may decide to use students' home language while providing special education services. Several principles of bilingual education, discussed below, may be useful for determining how to integrate home language supports and providing examples of how to do so. It is important to emphasize, however, that providing native language supports during special education instruction or related services, by itself, will not fulfill federal requirements for alternative language services. As the most recent OCR guidelines make clear, ELLs are entitled to a district-designed program delivered by teachers who are qualified in the area of second language development. Ad hoc instruction for a particular student that does not follow district guidelines, regardless of how thoughtful or successful it is, will not fulfill language service requirements; ELLs with disabilities still need access to district-designed ESL or bilingual education programs. This is especially true if the other native language supports a student receives are implemented by EAs because they speak the student's home language, as they are not qualified teachers. However, even if these supports do not fulfill the English language development program requirements, they can be an important part of a student's instructional program.

Models of Alternative Language Services

The sections that follow describe several common models of alternative language services. Please note that the purpose here is not to provide a standard set of terms or common definitions because this would conflict with the terminology used within many state and district documents—terminology that may change over time and across different areas of legislation and regulations, even at the federal level. All education professionals working with ELLs have a responsibility to be knowledgeable about district and state policies and programs related to ESL services, and to get to know specialists within the school or district with whom they can collaborate. Larger districts typically have a dedicated ELL services department or unit, as well as staff who oversee compliance with federal requirements.

English as a Second Language Instruction There are a variety of ways to provide instruction *in English to teach English*—and, consequently, a need for a general term that captures all of these programs. I use *ESL* this way because of its long-standing history in the field. In contrast, some states and districts use *English language development* (ELD) or *English for speakers of other languages* (ESOL). All three terms may also be used in some contexts to refer to a specific instructional program.

There are a number of different types of ESL that might be available within a school or district. These might include Sheltered Instruction, Sheltered English, Structured English Immersion, Content Based ESL, Pull-out ESL, Specially Designed Academic Instruction in English (SDAIE), or Sheltered Instruction Observation Protocol (SIOP), among others. What each of these models looks like can vary greatly, even SIOP (http://siop.pearson.com), which has eight specified program components.

ESL instruction must be delivered by qualified teachers. What their specialized certification is called and what requirements it entails vary across states. For example, in New Mexico, general and special educators can hold an endorsement in Teaching English as a Second Language (TESOL). In California, all teachers must obtain a Crosscultural, Language, and Academic Development (CLAD) certificate. Florida teachers working with ELLs hold an endorsement in ESOL, and New York teachers hold a certificate in ESOL. In Arizona, all general and special educators must hold either a Structured English Immersion (SEI) or full ESL endorsement. These state-by-state variations mean that depending on the state, not all licensed special educators will have the necessary qualifications to provide ESL services. Even when they do, it is important for them to ensure that the ESL instruction that ELLs with special needs receive meets state and district guidelines as to how frequently these services are provided, how much time is regularly allotted for them (e.g., number of minutes), what methodologies are used, and which students are grouped together to receive them. For example, ESL, which is specially designed for ELLs, should not be provided to mixed groups of ELLs and non-ELLs. Instead, grouping ELLs together during ESL instruction ensures that teachers do not simply provide "sheltered instruction" to all students in the class without specifically addressing the unique language development needs of ELLs.

Bilingual Education Bilingual education programs differ in terms of their goals and the home language backgrounds of students they enroll. *Transitional bilingual education* programs are designed to assist students in learning grade-level content while they are developing English. The purpose is to provide content instruction in the home language so that students will not fall behind overall when they do not yet know enough English to perform academically in that language. Transitional bilingual education programs typically phase out within a few years; their duration depends on the school or district, with most ending by the end of elementary school. These programs initially provide most instruction in the home language, gradually shifting to English, so that instruction is primarily in English in the final years of the program. Literacy instruction in the home language is often not included.

In contrast, there are several different kinds of *developmental bilingual education* programs. Some include only students who have the same non-English home language; they foster continued development of the home language, as well as literacy in both the home language and English. These are often termed *maintenance bilingual education* programs because their goal is for students to maintain their home language as they develop English. Implementing these programs requires sufficient numbers of students across grade levels who all speak the same home language, and qualified teachers at every grade level who can speak, read, and write it. These programs are most common in the elementary grades; in higher grades, it can be difficult to find enough students or enough qualified teachers.

Another common developmental bilingual education model is *Dual Language Immersion* (DLI). DLI programs bring together native English-speaking students and students who speak a particular non-English home language. In most developmental bilingual education programs, most instruction is provided in the home language for the first few years. In later grades, these programs continue to use both languages a significant percentage of the time, with careful attention to continuing to build academic language skills (including advanced vocabulary and grammar) and literacy in both languages.

Native English speakers with complex support needs can be enrolled in DLI if development of a second language is important to the family. As discussed previously, there is no evidence that learning two languages is any more problematic for students with complex support needs than learning one, or that learning two languages is harmful. Bilingualism under these conditions may be more difficult for these language-majority students, unless educators pay careful attention to fostering social relationships with classmates so these students have extensive and consistent opportunities for communication and language learning in natural settings. As discussed previously, people become bilingual because they have a need for two or more languages. Therefore, a real need for both must be present, along with plentiful opportunities to use both.

REFLECTION QUESTION 5

Many students with complex support needs are still developing basic communication and language skills. Special education services address these emerging skills. Therefore, why would ELLs with complex support needs benefit from or require English language development services from ESL teachers or bilingual educators?

Principles for Providing Native Language Support

Several core principles are important to keep in mind for providing native language support to students who speak a language other than English:

- Providing *comprehensible input* is fundamental to second language pedagogy.

- *Knowledge transfer* means that knowledge learned in one language can transfer to another.

- Whenever educators use different languages during instruction, they should have a strong rationale for doing so, a principle termed *strategic language planning*.

Each of these core principles has significant implications, discussed in the following sections, for how best to instruct culturally and linguistically diverse students who also have complex support needs.

Provide Comprehensible Input   A fundamental principle of bilingual education is that *students learn content most quickly in a language they understand.* Imagine visiting an archaeological site in Greece and hearing a lecture on its history. If the tour guide speaks only Greek and you do not, you probably will not understand most of the details, or even the main ideas, very well. As an adult, you might use your background knowledge to make educated guesses. But the more the language used differs from yours, and the newer the content is, the harder it will be to do this. Making educated guesses is even more difficult for students with complex support needs. They are just beginning to learn the academic content being presented, they have a less comprehensive language basis from which to make assumptions, and many find it difficult to generalize information across contexts. Thus, ELLs with complex support needs struggle to make assumptions about meaning across languages, far more than you might struggle during that hypothetical lecture at the Acropolis. This idea underlies the emphasis in second language pedagogy on *comprehensible input.* Existing ESL literature provides a wealth of strategies to make input in English comprehensible, such as using simplified language, gestures, and pictures. Special educators use similar strategies to make their communication more understandable to students with complex support needs.

Because students must understand what they are being taught, it is vital for teachers of ELLs with complex support needs to figure out whether their students have stronger comprehension in English or in the home language. If the latter, instruction in that language will be more effective. For example, when these students move into a new instructional setting, an orientation to the classroom and typical instructional activities might be more useful if provided in their home language. This orientation might involve having parents or other adult relatives spend some time in the classroom, learning about the routine and providing support for the student. A teacher who plans ahead could audio record one-step directions in the home language for use during classroom activities. It is also critical to develop a dictionary of common ways the student expresses needs and wants. For example, it would be much quicker for the teaching staff to learn how a student might say "bathroom" in Farsi or Hindi than for the student to learn to say that in English. By learning a few phrases, staff may avoid, in the short term, behavioral difficulties that might occur when a legitimate request expressed in another language is ignored.

To provide native language support more consistently, special educators may need to collaborate with bilingual educators, if available, to determine how they could support students to be included in a bilingual education program. If a bilingual placement is not possible, an EA who speaks the student's home language might be assigned to the student's classroom. For ELLs with complex support needs, finding these EAs would be invaluable, at least for the first few years. However, the education of ELLs should never be simply given up to assistants. Rather, at specific times or for specific activities, the EA would teach the same lesson as the special educator to individual students or small groups who would benefit from instruction in their native language. Lesson design and curriculum development are the classroom teacher's responsibilities. It would be highly unethical to turn these responsibilities, or full responsibility for instruction, over to an EA for one group while another group benefited from a qualified teacher's advanced training and expertise.

Facilitate Knowledge Transfer   Related to the principle of comprehensible input is the understanding that *knowledge learned in one language can transfer to another.* For example, suppose students learn, in their home language, how plants grow—that they need water and light to do so, and so forth. Although they will need to learn the English vocabulary associated with those concepts, the knowledge of how plants grow will transfer across languages. Therefore, it may be most efficient to first teach the content knowledge in the home language and then, once students understand it, teach an ESL lesson covering the same material but targeting English vocabulary. In this way, teachers are explicitly teaching for transfer of concepts across languages, just as teachers of students with complex support needs must explicitly teach students to transfer academic skills across settings.

One bilingual education strategy that takes advantage of knowledge transfer is *preview–review*. In this strategy, small-group instruction in the home language is provided first, emphasizing key vocabulary and concepts that will be covered in the main, whole-group lesson conducted in English. Then, following the whole-group lesson, another small-group activity in the home language is used to reinforce the main ideas, clarify understanding, and assess how well students learned the underlying concepts. This is especially useful when a class includes both ELL and non-ELL students or students with different home languages.

Similarly, some literacy concepts can transfer across languages, such as book-handling skills and the understanding that print corresponds to spoken language and pictures often relate to the text. However, the two languages' similarity will influence what aspects of literacy can transfer. For example, students whose home language is Arabic or Hebrew might have been exposed at home to books and other print media that read from right to left. At school, students from those language backgrounds will therefore need to be explicitly taught that when reading English, they will read from left to right. Another aspect of literacy that may not transfer perfectly across languages is understanding of sound–symbol correspondences. Even when two languages use the same written alphabet, they often differ with respect to these correspondences. For example, in English, the letter *i* usually sounds like /ih/ (as in "bit") or /eye/ (as in "bite"), but in Spanish it sounds like /ee/ (as in "easy").

The question about what language(s) to provide literacy instruction in depends on students' knowledge of the home language and English, the availability of educational staff who *proficiently* speak the home language, and the ability of the special education staff to foster positive relationships with parents and collaborate on activities to foster literacy at home (in the home language) and at school (in English).

The first point is important because if exposure to English has just begun for a student, literacy instruction in English would be ineffective. Students would have next to no understanding of the teacher's spoken words or the words they are being taught to read. For example, if students are learning to read sight words, it would be important to make sure they understand these words in the language in which they are being taught. Regarding the second point, it is important to recognize that, although educational staff can easily learn to understand a few important words and phrases in a student's home language, such as when they indicate they need to take a break or are hungry, it is much harder to learn another language's speech sounds or phonology. Considerable knowledge of another language is needed to teach phonemic awareness in that language. Teachers who are not proficient in a language are all too likely to mispronounce words or use them in improbable or inappropriate ways.

However, even when staff cannot deliver a systematic program of literacy instruction in a language other than English, they can still find ways to support home language literacy efforts. For example, Vicente has been involved in some small construction projects around the home with his father and older brother. Most recently, they built a chicken coop for some chickens a neighbor gave them. The Spanish-speaking EA in Vicente's classroom learned this from Vicente's mother and told the classroom teacher, who asked Vicente's parents to take pictures of the project at different stages and send them to her. She then used MS PowerPoint to assemble the pictures and create a predictable book—that is, a book that uses repetitive language patterns, thus making the text somewhat "predictable" for readers. She had the EA write and narrate the accompanying Spanish text. The teacher then sent the electronic file to Vicente's parents, who kept it on their cell phone and also uploaded it to the family iPad. Vicente read this book with his parents, with and without the sound, and read it by himself, playing with the sound. Teachers can develop similar predictable books about common activities, such as trips to the animal park, lunch in the cafeteria, and playground games, that can be written and narrated in English or their home language and read to and by people who speak either language.

Engage in Strategic Language Planning

The third core principle for providing native language support is that *it is important for educators to have specific, well-thought-out reasons for using different languages during instruction*. Even if they are monolingual English speakers, they must have a plan in place, ahead of time, for use of each language. Some helpful questions for planning include the following:

- What instructional content and vocabulary would it be helpful to introduce and reinforce in the home language?

- What language and literacy concepts will transfer across languages, and which need to be explicitly taught in each language?

- Who could assist with developing/translating materials and providing this instruction?

Because resources for native language instruction or support may be limited, it is vital that educators, including professionals knowledgeable about ESL and/or bilingual education methods and cross-linguistics differences, work together to prioritize instructional needs. For instance, if a student already understands certain instructions or vocabulary in English, the student might not need native language support for similar activities; however, this support might be helpful or necessary for introducing a new activity or setting.

Suppose Vicente's class was planning its first outing to the community center to go swimming. The special educator might ask Vicente's parents whether he has been to a community center or similar place before and whether he has ever gone swimming. Other questions might include the following: What materials (e.g., swimsuit, towel) will be needed during the activity that are not commonly used at school? How do his parents say these words in Spanish? Does he understand these words in Spanish? In English? Can he name them in either language? The teacher could help prepare all students in the class, regardless of their language background, for the outing by visiting the location ahead of time and taking photos to use as visual support during lessons, explaining in each student's home language what will happen and what students will be expected to do. If such language support is not available at school, information can be sent home, including the photographs to be used as visual supports, so families can review the activity with their children. Readily available technology, such as the OneNote app, can be used on a phone or tablet to develop a visual schedule, along with an audio recording of key vocabulary or instructions in the home language as needed.

Strategic language planning involves careful decision making. When making these decisions, educators must understand that it is not considered best practice to mix languages during instruction. Although proficient bilinguals often code-switch, a teacher would need to have a clear rationale for doing so during instruction and establish very clear criteria for what to say in each language.

Why is this understanding so critical? An important goal for bilingual students is to help them develop proficiency in each language and understand when and with whom they can speak each one. This is especially important for emerging communicators who may not yet fully understand that they are learning and being spoken to in two different languages and need to make choices about which to use with different people.

In addition, it is a more complex cognitive task when the teacher speaks one language (e.g., giving instructions in the home language) and requires the student to respond in a different language (e.g., naming pictures or reading sight words in English), as was done in three of the few studies examining whether intervention in the home language would be more effective than intervention in English (Rivera, Spooner, & Hicks, 2013; Rivera, Wood, & Spooner, 2012; Rohena, Jitendra, & Browder, 2002). As discussed previously, suppressing one language while activating another involves executive control; it is much more natural for people to respond in the language spoken to them if they can. Therefore, it is more appropriate for teachers to allow students to either respond in the same language or respond in whatever language is more comfortable for them. When the objective is to teach vocabulary in the home language, instruction should be in the home language as well; when it is time to teach vocabulary in English, the instruction should be in English—preferably after first establishing the instructional routine in the home language. If the student does not yet know enough English to understand certain directions, such as "show me," "tell me," or "point to the X," their meaning in English should be taught to the student using vocabulary the student *already knows in English*. Once the student understands the English instructions, additional vocabulary can be taught in English, preferably words the student already knows in the home language. Beginning English vocabulary can also be taught using pictures and real objects with nonverbal instructions.

In some bilingual programs, teachers switch languages by day or week; for example, using English one week and Spanish the next. However, for all students, but especially for those with complex support needs, it is important that the reasons and/or contexts for using each language are clearly differentiated. For example, different people might use different languages. Or, different languages might be used for different activities or at different times during specific routines, such as preview–review lessons. Teachers can highlight the language of the interaction by using a particular antecedent for use of each language, such as "Now we're going to be speaking English." Providing clear contexts for use of each language fosters students' metalinguistic knowledge so they learn to make appropriate language choices in different situations.

REFLECTION QUESTION 4

How would you decide what language(s) to use during instruction with ELLs with complex support needs?

SUMMARY

The Community Imperative (Center on Human Policy, 1979) states that a fundamental human right "is the right to community living" (para. 1). Eidelman, Pietrangelo, Gardner, Jesien, and Croser (2003) argued that this is a civil rights issue. For ELLs with complex support needs, maintenance of the home language is critical for real community membership and participation. More generally, to develop communication and language skills to the utmost of their abilities, all students with complex support needs require ample opportunities to interact with peers who have well-developed language skills. They are most likely to have these opportunities in the general education classroom (Downing, 2005). In addition to opportunities for interaction with peers, these students require teachers who know how to provide instruction that meets their unique learning needs. Although all students with complex support needs benefit from teachers who are knowledgeable about special education interventions, ELLs also need access to teachers who are knowledgeable about cultural and linguistic diversity and first and second language development. However, the results of a survey of teachers of students with moderate and severe disabilities (Mueller, Singer, & Carranza, 2006) raised concerns about their preparation and practices related to ELLs. These researchers reported that most of the teachers surveyed did not have formal preparation in working with language minority students. They also found teachers frequently failed to consult parents regarding the language to be used for expressive and receptive language instruction, and that the vast majority of their respondents primarily used English with their students who were ELLs.

Unfortunately, many students with complex support needs are educated in segregated classrooms. Such environments may fail to provide these students with either the peer communication opportunities necessary for language development or teachers who are knowledgeable about their cultural or linguistic needs. Therefore, when available, inclusive bilingual classrooms may be more appropriate than segregated special education settings. When bilingual programs are not available, special educators should still find ways to support students' language development and academic progress through the avenue of native language support, in conjunction with district-approved ESL services. Examples of how this can be done were provided in this chapter, along with a rationale for such services. As the U.S. population of individuals speaking a language other than English at home continues to grow, addressing the educational issues unique to ELLs with complex support needs will become imperative for the special education community. We hope that our field will take this issue seriously. Indeed, it is a matter of civil rights and social justice.

RESOURCES

- **Academic Communication Associates** (www.acadcom.com) provides a variety of intervention and informal materials in the area of speech-language pathology and special education, many of which are available in English, as well as other languages.

- **Colorín Colorado** (http://www.colorincolorado.org) provides a wealth of resources and information to educators and parents of ELLs.

- **François Grosjean,** a well-known expert in the area of bilingualism and bilingual development, maintains a web site with a wealth of educator- and parent-friendly information: http://www.francoisgrosjean.ch/index.html

- **The National Association for Bilingual Education (NABE)** (http://www.nabe.org/) is a national organization of educator, parents, and policy makers that advocates for bilingualism and biliteracy. There is typically a bilingual special education strand at the national conference.

- **The Teaching Diverse Learners** web site (https://www.brown.edu/academics/education-alliance/teaching-diverse-learners/) at Brown University "provides access to information—publications, educational materials, and the work of experts in the field—that promotes high achievement for ELLs."

- **Teaching Tolerance** (www.tolerance.org) is a clearinghouse of information about anti-bias programs and activities being implemented in schools across the country. The organization provides a wealth of free educational materials.

- **Teachers of English to Speakers of Other Languages (TESOL)** (www.tesol.org) is an international professional organization dedicated to a wide range of issues related to individuals learning English as a second, additional, or foreign language. Aspects of the work of organization members pertain to K–12 students, whereas other aspects relate to adult learners.

REFERENCES

Anderson, R.T. (2012). First language loss in Spanish-speaking children: Patterns of loss and implications for clinical practices. In B.A. Goldstein (Ed.), *Bilingual language development and disorders in Spanish–English speakers* (2nd ed., pp. 193–212). Baltimore, MD: Paul H. Brookes Publishing Co.

Bondy, A.S., & Frost, L.A. (1994). The Picture Exchange Communication System. *Focus on Autism and Other Developmental Disabilities, 9*(3), 1–19. doi:10.1177/108835769400900301

Center on Human Policy, Syracuse University. (1979). *The community imperative: A refutation of all arguments in support of institutionalizing anybody because of mental retardation.* Retrieved from http://thechp.syr.edu/adimper.htm

Cook, V. (2003). Linguistics and second-language acquisition: One person with two languages. In M. Arnoff & J. Rees-Miller (Eds.), *The handbook of linguistics* (pp. 488–511). Malden, MA: Blackwell.

de Valenzuela, J.S., Copeland, S.R., & Mayette, A.M. (2010, October 20). Linguistic diversity of students with ID from language minority homes. In J.S. de Valenzuela (Chair), *Bilingualism and intellectual disability.* Symposium conducted at the 3rd IASSID-Europe conference, Rome, Italy.

de Valenzuela, J.S., Kay-Raining Bird, E., Parkington, K., Mirenda, P., Cain, K., . . . Segers, E. (2016). Access to opportunities for bilingualism for individuals with developmental disabilities. *Journal of Communication Disorders, 63,* 32–46. http://dx.doi.org/10.1016/j.jcomdis.2016.05.005

Downing, J.E. (2005). *Teaching communication skills to students with severe disabilities* (2nd ed.). Baltimore, MD: Paul H. Brookes Publishing Co.

Eidelman, S.M., Pietrangelo, R., Gardner, J.F., Jesien, G., & Croser, M.D. (2003). Let's focus on the real issues. *Mental Retardation, 41*(2), 126–129.

Grosjean, F. (1982). *Life with two languages: An introduction to bilingualism.* Cambridge, MA: Harvard University Press.

Grosjean, F. (1985). The bilingual as a competent but specific speaker-hearer. *Journal of Multilingual and Multicultural Development, 6,* 467–477.

Grosjean, F. (2012). *Bilingual life and reality.* Boston, MA; Harvard University Press.

Kay-Raining Bird, E. (2006). The case for bilingualism in children with Down syndrome. In R. Paul (Ed.), *Language disorders from a developmental perspective: Essays in honor of Robin S. Chapman* (pp. 249–275). Mahwah, NJ: Lawrence Erlbaum Associates.

Kay-Raining Bird, E. (2016). Bilingualism and children with Down syndrome. In J.L. Patterson & B.L. Rodríguez (Eds.), *Multilingual perspectives on child language development* (pp. 49–73). Bristol, England: Multilingual Matters.

Kay-Raining Bird, E., Genesee, F., & Verhoeven, L. (2016). Bilingualism in children with developmental disorders: A narrative review. *Journal of Communication Disorders, 63,* 1–14. http://dx.doi.org/10.1016/j.jcomdis.2016.07.003

Klingner, J., & Bianco, M. (2006). What is special about special education for English language learners? In B.G. Cook & B.R. Schirmer (Eds.), *What is special about special education? Examining the role of evidence-based practices* (pp. 37–53). Austin, TX: PRO-ED.

Kohnert, K. (2013). *Language disorders in bilingual children and adults* (2nd ed.). San Diego, CA: Plural.

Lau v. Nichols, 414 U.S. 563 (1974).

Lutz, A. (2007/2008). Negotiating home language: Spanish maintenance and loss in Latino families. *Latino(a) Research Review, 6*(3), 37–64.

MacSwan, J. (2013). Code switching and grammatical theory. In T.K. Bhatia & W.C. Ritchie (Eds.), *The handbook of bilingualism* (2nd ed., pp. 323–350). Malden, MA: Blackwell.

Marinova-Todd, S.H., Colozzo, P., Mirenda, P., Stahl, H., Kay-Raining Bird, E., ... Genesee, F. (2016). Professional practices and opinions about services available to bilingual children with developmental disabilities: An international study. *Journal of Communication Disorders, 63,* 47–62. http://dx.doi.org/10.1016/j.jcomdis.2016.05.004

Marinova-Todd, S., & Mirenda, P. (2016). Language and communication abilities of bilingual children with autism spectrum disorders. In J.L. Patterson & B.L. Rodríguez (Eds.), *Multilingual perspectives on child language development* (pp. 31–48). Bristol, England: Multilingual Matters.

Mattes, L.J., & Saldaña-Illingworth, C. (2009). *Bilingual communication assessment resource: Tools for assessing speech, language, and learning.* Oceanside, CA: Academic Communication Associates.

McDonnell, J.J., Hardman, M.L., & McDonnell, A.P. (2003). *An introduction to persons with moderate and severe disabilities.* Boston, MA: Allyn & Bacon.

Mueller, T.G., Singer, G.H.S., & Carranza, F.D. (2006). A national survey of the educational planning and language instruction practices for students with moderate to severe disabilities who are English language learners. *Research and Practice for Persons with Severe Disabilities, 31*(3), 242–254.

Ochs, E. (1986). Introduction. In B.B. Schieffelin & E. Ochs (Eds.), *Language socialization across cultures* (pp. 1–13). Cambridge, England: Cambridge University Press.

Olulade, O.A., Jamal, N.I., Koo, D.S., Perfetti, C.A., LaSasso, C., & Eden, G.F. (2016). Neuroanatomical evidence in support of the bilingual advantage theory. *Cerebral Cortex, 26,* 3196–3204.

Paradis, J. (2012). Cross-linguistic influence and code-switching. In B.A. Goldstein (Ed.), *Bilingual language development and disorders in Spanish–English speakers* (2nd ed., pp. 73–91). Baltimore, MD: Paul H. Brookes Publishing Co.

Paradis, J., Genesee, F., & Crago, M.A. (2011). *Dual language development and disorders: A handbook on bilingualism and second language learning* (2nd ed.). Baltimore, MD: Paul H. Brookes Publishing Co.

Rivera, C., Spooner, F., & Hicks, S. (2013). Multimedia shared stories for diverse learners with moderate intellectual disability. *Journal of Special Education Technology, 28*(4), 53–68.

Rivera, C., Wood, C., & Spooner, F. (2012). Comparative effects of Spanish and English vocabulary instruction for English language learners with moderate intellectual disability. *Multiple Voices for Ethnically Diverse Exceptional Learners, 13*(1), 42–55.

Rohena, E., Jitendra, A., & Browder, D. (2002). Comparison of the effects of Spanish and English constant time delay instruction on sight word reading by Hispanic learners with mental retardation. *The Journal of Special Education, 36*(3), 171–186.

Romaine, S. (2003). Multilingualism. In M. Arnoff & J. Rees-Miller (Eds.), *The handbook of linguistics* (pp. 512–532). Malden, MA: Blackwell.

Romero, C. (2014). *An investigation of alternative language services (ALS) received by English language learners (ELLs) identified with a disability* (Unpublished doctoral dissertation, The University of New Mexico). Retrieved from http://digitalrepository.unm.edu/educ_spcd_etds/17

Rueda, R. (1983). Metalinguistic awareness in monolingual and bilingual mildly retarded children. *NABE Journal, 8*(1), 55–67.

Rueda, R., & Martinez, I. (1992). Fiesta Educativa: One community's approach to parent training developmental disabilities for Latino families. *Journal of the Association for Persons with Severe Handicaps, 17*(2), 95–103.

Saville-Troike, M. (2002). *The ethnography of communication: An introduction* (3rd ed.). Malden, MA: Blackwell.

United States Census Bureau. (2010). *Detailed language spoken at home and ability to speak English for the population 5 years and older by states: 2006–2008.* Retrieved from http://www.census.gov/data/tables/2008/demo/2006-2008-lang-tables.html

United States Census Bureau. (2015). *Language use.* Retrieved from http://www.census.gov/topics/population/language-use/about.html

United States Department of Education, Office for Civil Rights. (1970, May 25). *Identification of discrimination and denial of services on the basis of national origin.* Retrieved from http://www2.ed.gov/about/offices/list/ocr/docs/lau1970.html

United States Department of Education, Office for Civil Rights. (2000, August). *The provision of an equal education opportunity to limited-English proficient students.* Retrieved from http://www2.ed.gov/about/offices/list/ocr/eeolep/index.html

United States Department of Education, Office for Civil Rights. (2015). *Developing programs for English language learners: Glossary.* Retrieved from http://www2.ed.gov/about/offices/list/ocr/ell/glossary.html

Valdés, G., & Figueroa, R. (1994). *Bilingualism and testing: A special case of bias.* Norwood, NJ: Ablex.

Weinberg, C., & Weinberg, L. (1990). Equal opportunity for bilingual handicapped students: A legal historical perspective. *NABE Journal, 14*(1–3), 17–40.

Welner, K. (2006). *Legal rights: The overrepresentation of culturally and linguistically diverse students in special education.* Denver, CO: National Center for Culturally Responsive Educational Systems. Retrieved from http://www.nccrest.org/Briefs/Legal_Brief.pdf

Whitaker, J.H., Rueda, R.S., & Prieto, A.G. (1985). Cognitive performance as a function of bilingualism in students with mental retardation. *Mental Retardation, 23*(6), 302–307.

WIDA. (2015). *ACCESS for ELLs* [Language proficiency assessment]. Retrieved from https://www.wida.us/assessment/ACCESS20.aspx

WIDA. (2015–2016). *Alternate ACCESS for ELLs: Test administration manual.* Retrieved from https://www.wida.us/accesstraining/alternatemodule/Alternate%20ACCESS%20for%20ELLs%20Test%20Administration%20Manual%202015-16.pdf

Wörmann, V., Holodynski, M., Kärtner, J., & Keller, H. (2012). A cross-cultural comparison of the development of the social smile: A longitudinal study of maternal and infant imitation in 6- and 12-week-old infants. *Infant Behavior and Development, 35*(3), 335–347. doi:10.1016/j.infbeh.2012.03.002

CHAPTER 4

Inclusive Literacy Instruction

State and National Standards and Beyond

Deborah A. Taub, Jessica Apgar McCord, and Michael Burdge

LEARNING OBJECTIVES

By the end of this chapter, readers will

1. Articulate how an educator's approach to literacy instruction communicates the educator's beliefs about the purpose of school.

2. Identify the dimensions of opportunity to learn (curriculum, instruction, assessment).

3. Describe and articulate the importance of aligning literacy instruction to standards and how this impacts students' opportunities to learn.

4. Identify components of good literacy instruction in typical settings when designed universally to meet the needs of all students.

5. Describe and create standards aligned individualized education programs to complement instruction and provide opportunities to learn that reflect high expectations for all students.

This chapter will address how the adoption of college- and career-ready (CCR) standards has changed the landscape of literacy teaching and learning and how all students can and should be engaged in standards-aligned literacy instruction. We will describe what literacy instruction looks like in general education settings that include individuals of all skill levels. Specific examples of how to align standards, individualized education program (IEP) goals, and instruction will be provided.

HIGH EXPECTATIONS FOR ALL STUDENTS

The landscape of education has changed tremendously since the inception of the No Child Left Behind (NCLB) Act of 2001 (PL 107-110), which was recently reauthorized as the Every Student Succeeds Act (ESSA) of 2015 (S. 1177). NCLB brought about sweeping changes to the roles standards and related accountability systems play in public schools. The requirements that all students participate in testing and that schools disaggregate data to ensure attention to the achievement of subgroups of students (e.g., students with disabilities) were put into place to ensure high expectations for the achievement of all students, especially those who have been historically marginalized and not previously given access to a high-quality, standards-based education. These goals remain with the authorization of ESSA, which specifically requires CCR standards as a major priority. Every state has adopted some form of CCR standards that identify rigorous academic content for all students.

This shift to CCR standards has signaled a change in emphasis from memorization and rote skills to critical thinking, problem solving, and real-world application of knowledge from prekindergarten through 16. It reflects the current reality that acquiring skills and knowing facts are no longer sufficient to keep up with fast-paced changes in technology and the resulting changes in the ways we complete daily routines and navigate through our world. Our discussion will focus on K–12 English Language Arts (ELA) standards as they relate to what is expected of all students, including those with complex support needs, and the opportunities students have to learn grade level, standards-aligned content.

As discussed previously, NCLB represented a commitment to "leave no child behind" through requirements to report disaggregated annual data about all students' achievement of state standards; ESSA maintains this commitment. Similarly, the Individuals with Disabilities Education Act (IDEA) of 2004 (PL 108-446) requires that all students have access to and make progress in the general curriculum as represented by the state adopted standards. Prior to NCLB and the Individuals with Disabilities Education Act Amendments (IDEA) of 1997 (PL 105-17) and IDEA 2004, expectations for students with complex support needs might only have been that they learn daily living and functional skills or be included in general education for the sole purpose of acquiring social skills. These previously narrowly conceptualized purposes of school for this population have left many students with complex support needs with dismal post-school outcomes. For example, 75% of adults with cognitive disabilities are unemployed or are not in the work force at all (U.S. Census Bureau, 2014). This corresponds with the national data reporting high numbers of individuals with cognitive and severe disabilities who live in poverty (American Psychological Association, n.d.). In addition, Morningstar (2010) analyzed data from the National Longitudinal Transition Study 2 and found a significant decrease in the percentage of students with intellectual and multiple disabilities who participated in the community after graduation; this finding is an important red flag indicating a decreasing quality of life for those individuals. We must expand our thinking about the purpose of school so that students with complex support needs have opportunities to learn that are meaningful and lead to a high quality of life after school. Teachers have an important role in redefining the purpose of school for this group by aligning expectations and instruction with federal guidance that continues to focus on equity and college and career readiness for all. Doing so will help ensure that students have opportunities to receive high-quality, standards-aligned instruction that represents a presumption of competence and a commitment to high expectations.

An equitable, excellent education for all students can be a reality, but schools and teachers must make a commitment to understanding how educational standards should drive planning, instruction, and assessment, including the development of IEPs for students with complex support needs. The general curriculum for students with complex support needs is intended to be based on the same CCR standards all students are expected to achieve (see ESSA, IDEA 2004, and NCLB). This communicates that the purpose of schools is to ensure that all students have the critical-thinking and problem-solving skills necessary to apply their knowledge in real-world settings that will promote individual choice and self-determination beyond formal schooling. When teachers implement high-quality instruction, it communicates a belief that all students, including those with the most complex support needs, can learn and that they deserve equitable learning opportunities. Lastly, a commitment to academic standards serves to communicate the purpose of school because it communicates that teachers are dedicated to meeting the needs of all students to ensure learning and progress. This is no small feat, but it can be attained. This chapter begins to build the foundation of understanding that teachers must provide excellent opportunities to learn for their students with complex support needs.

THE PURPOSE OF EDUCATION—OR, WHAT DO YOU BELIEVE AND WHY DOES IT MATTER?

Both pre- and in-service teachers are often asked why they chose the teaching profession and are asked to reflect on their teaching philosophy. Few are asked, however, what they think is the purpose of school for their students. We will begin by asking you to consider what you believe to be the purpose of school and how that purpose can and should be inextricably related to what you do every day in your classroom. Further consider how this translates into what you believe to be your role in fulfilling that purpose.

Teaching Philosophies

We often ask preservice teachers, at the beginning of their literacy methods courses, to write about their teaching philosophy. This is one way we present the assignment:

Parker J. Palmer (2007) says that "you teach who you are." Think about your strongest beliefs and how they will affect you as a teacher. What do you believe your role is in the lives of your students? How will your personality and beliefs shape what your classroom looks and feels like? What experiences did you have in school that impacted your choice to become an educator? What is your philosophy about being sure each learner's needs are met?

We ask these questions of our pre- and in-service teachers because their beliefs matter and impact every interaction with their students. Their beliefs also represent their background knowledge, experience, and preconceived notions, and what and how they choose to do in their classrooms.

REFLECTION QUESTION 1

Stop reading! Take a few minutes to jot down your own answers to Palmer's questions.

Did you take a minute to write down some of your own thoughts? If you have not, you should! Stop reading and think about your own personal beliefs and experiences and what deeply motivates you to be an educator before continuing.

Now that you have spent a bit of time thinking about your purpose as a teacher, your role in the lives of your students, and how your own personal beliefs and experiences will affect what your classroom looks and feels like, let's look at some responses we have seen from teachers we have worked with and explore how these responses translate to establishing a purpose of school for their students.

The excerpts in Figure 4.1 represent a composite of some of the most powerful responses we have seen from teachers when we asked them about their beliefs. Though communicated in different ways, several common themes emerge consistently: teachers want to ensure that all students are held to high expectations; they are committed to doing what is best for their students and not what is easiest for them as the teacher; they want to be advocates for presuming competence of all students; and they want to do what it takes to make sure their students feel safe, valued, and achieve their highest potential. How do these responses compare to yours? We imagine they are very similar. Most people become teachers because they want to inspire, motivate, and support their students to love learning and they want this learning to have meaningful outcomes in students' lives.

Implications

What does any of this discussion of teacher beliefs have to do with standards-based literacy instruction? A great deal, actually. If we want to make a genuine difference in our students' lives and ensure we are supporting them to achieve their very best every day, ultimately resulting in a meaningful education that leads to whatever opportunities they want to pursue, then we cannot limit their opportunities by deciding to hold them to a completely different set of expectations than we have for students without complex support needs or disabilities. In the past, more predictable, simple skills have been needed in the workforce—sorting papers in an office, answering phones, using a price gun to mark groceries, and the like; these skills often drove the expected

Teaching Philosophy Excerpts
"I believe that each and every child, regardless of his or her weakness, label, disability, or diagnosis, has unique strengths, gifts, and intelligence. I will make it my aim to uncover and display these abilities for all to see. This perspective causes me to have high expectations for all of my students. My belief in their abilities and celebration of their successes will challenge them to surmount even greater obstacles. I will also expect that others hold these same high expectations for my students."
"I want to create an inclusive community of learners who construct knowledge together by drawing from their individual experiences, backgrounds, cultures, beliefs, personalities, and perspectives. I believe it is important for me to provide relevant learning experiences that connect to real life and my students' prior knowledge. I will view them as scientists, explorers, problem solvers, community helpers, reporters, and children who love to have fun. My goal is to enable them to see themselves as all of these things as well." K. Winston, UNM Dual License Student
"I pledge to provide each of my students with the necessary resources and tools to maximize their learning potential and embrace their individuality. I will be there for my students. I will listen to them, advocate for them, and learn from them. I pledge to always remember that *they* are my priority." L. Galbraith, UNM Dual License Student

Figure 4.1. Teaching philosophy excerpts.

outcomes for individuals with complex needs. Times have changed, and the skills needed to be CCR are more complex and fluid in an increasingly fast-paced world. CCR standards are intended to support students' critical-thinking and problem-solving skills so they can navigate the innovative and ever-changing world we live in today. Most teachers would never consciously decide to take away their students' hope and inspiration for what they can accomplish in their lives, but that is ultimately what happens when we say, "My student can't/won't/shouldn't learn these standards."

Educators want students to feel capable and to feel that the instruction they provide is genuinely meaningful and inspiring to both the students and the teachers. But when educators decide that students with complex support needs should or can learn only certain kinds of skills, different than those expected of everyone else, they are communicating a very different purpose for themselves as the teacher and, more important, for their students. When teachers say, "Johnny doesn't communicate using oral speech and will therefore never be able to express himself in writing" or "Maria hasn't learned how to read yet and it's sixth grade, so *The Hobbit* is too difficult to give to her"; or when they choose to focus only on functional skills such as tying shoes, brushing teeth, and matching colors instead of integrating those skills (if necessary) into age-appropriate literacy instruction, they are communicating a powerful message about their students' potential and their own understanding of the teacher's role. Specifically, they communicate that it is the teacher's role to put limitations and restrictions on students' educational opportunities, which will ultimately affect what interests students can and cannot pursue throughout their education and the types of employment opportunities they will have as adults.

The teaching philosophies we shared in Figure 4.1, and those you have written and reflected upon yourself, most certainly communicate the very opposite of this statement. One of the most powerful ways you can put your philosophy into action in your teaching career is to embrace high expectations, represented by a commitment to providing an accessible, standards-aligned education to all students. To your students, this commitment says: "Your educational outcomes matter, I believe in you, and I will do whatever it takes to empower you to have opportunities to learn and be in charge of your own future."

Now, let's put *that* philosophy into action!

UNDERSTANDING THE STANDARDS

Before discussing how to implement standards-based instruction, it is important to ensure that there is a common understanding of standards. Standards are generally state-adopted guidelines for what students in particular grades should know and be able to do. Each content area, such as math and ELA, has its own set of standards.

For the purposes of illustration, we will use the Common Core State Standards (CCSS) throughout this chapter. (See http://www.corestandards.org for more information on CCSS.) Your state may use a different set, but the structure and content of standards is typically similar across different standards documents. In the CCSS, English Language Arts (ELA)/Literacy is divided into similar strands across K–5 and 6–12: Reading, Writing, Speaking, and Listening. In addition, Grades 6–12 have a section on Literacy in History/Social Studies, Science, & Technical Subjects, which works together with College and Career Readiness anchor standards. The anchor standards remain the same across all grades and content areas to help teachers see how instruction should cut across content areas (e.g., science and ELA). The CCSS are written to indicate clearly the content area, strand, grade, and standard level for each (see Table 4.1).

It is particularly important to focus on the grade level and the strand when choosing standards. All students should be doing work aligned to their assigned grade level. If a student is enrolled in an ungraded program, then the teacher would choose the grade that the student uses for large-scale assessments. If that information is not available, the teacher should use the student's chronological age to determine what grade-level standards to use. IDEA and ESSA both require that students use the assigned grade level as the basis of their curriculum. It is important to note that the IEP is in place to support a student's access to and ability to make progress in the grade-level curriculum. *The IEP is not intended to be the student's curriculum.*

Focusing on the strand is important because it provides additional information about the intent and context of the standard. It is possible to have standards in Reading Informational Text similar to those in Reading Literature; however, the strand clarifies the type of text the student should be using to learn that standard. For instance, both CCSS.ELA-Literacy.RI.5.1 and CCSS.ELA-Literacy.RL.5.1 state, "Quote accurately from a text when explaining what the text says explicitly and when drawing inferences from the text" (Common Core State Standards Initiative, n.d.). However, one is focused on informational text and the other on literary texts. The process of reading a science article and drawing inferences has some nuanced differences from that of reading *Bud, Not Buddy* and making inferences. Both skills are helpful for students to learn but will require different texts and background knowledge and, possibly, different teaching strategies and supports. To truly give students opportunities to learn to their full potential, it is important that teachers work in teams to understand the intent and big ideas within and across standards.

Table 4.1. How to read Common Core State Standards

CCSS.ELA-Literacy.RI.5.1			
Content area	Strand	Grade level	Standard number
English Language Arts (ELA-Literacy)	Reading Informational Text (RI)	5	1. Quote accurately from a text when explaining what the text says explicitly and when drawing inferences from the text.

Key: CCSS, Common Core State Standards; ELA, English language arts.

IMPLEMENTING STANDARDS: OPPORTUNITY TO LEARN

Opportunity to learn (OTL) is generally conceptualized as providing students with a unified and aligned curriculum that links together state-identified standards, instruction, and assessment into a single system. Typically, OTL is described as having three elements: the intended curriculum, the enacted curriculum, and the assessed curriculum. The intended curriculum is made up of the state identified standards. The enacted curriculum is what is taught, and the assessed curriculum consists of the tests and evaluations students are given (see Figure 4.2). Providing students with a valid OTL requires that all three curricula are present.

Universal Design for Learning as the Foundation for Opportunity to Learn Curricula

One typical assumption found in the OTL literature is that each element of the three curricula will be accessible for students (Taub, McCord, & Ryndak, 2017). This is not a fair assumption for students with complex support needs who may need additional adjustments to the curricula to experience authentic engagement. OTL needs to begin by ensuring that the intended, enacted, and assessed curricula are designed with the principles of universal design for learning (UDL) in mind and that they are further supported by meeting the individualized supports and accommodations needed to provide a specific student with true access to the three curricula. UDL is a framework designed to increase student success by breaking down environmental and curricular barriers to instruction (Rose, Meyer, & Hitchcock, 2005); Chapter 5 will provide more in-depth information on UDL and how it is applied in lesson and unit planning. For now, let's use the CCSS to illustrate what UDL means for instruction. The CCSS were designed to be open to UDL in that unless a specific skill is required, they allow the teacher to make determinations about how a student will access and demonstrate knowledge.

For instance, standard CCSS ELA-Literacy.W.5.7 is a fifth-grade writing standard. It states that students should be able to "Conduct short research projects that use several sources to build knowledge through investigation of different aspects of a topic" (Common Core State Standards Initiative, n.d.). In this case, the standard focuses on conducting research projects through investigation. It does not highlight a specific means to achieving that goal, such as using a computer search, reading books, or viewing documentaries. Thus, instruction should focus on the process of conducting research and then analyzing and compiling information from several sources. Teachers can make decisions about how to help students conduct that research without changing anything about the standard itself. For example, students could have texts read aloud to them, use nonprint media rather than print materials, present findings in a blog or PowerPoint, choose a high-interest topic, or have a graphic organizer to help them organize their research. These various ways to conduct research are all encompassed by the construct of this standard while addressing the three

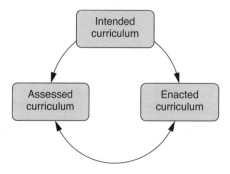

Figure 4.2. Opportunity to learn.

main principles of UDL—provide students with multiple means of representation, action and expression, and engagement:

- To provide *multiple means of representation* means to ensure that students can receive and interact with information in a variety of ways.

- To provide *multiple means of action and expression* means to ensure that students with different modes of communication have opportunities to demonstrate their learning.

- To provide *multiple means of engagement* means to capture and maintain student interest, preference, and background knowledge. Engagement encompasses strategies for activating background knowledge and garnering student interests, such as providing student choice. It also includes self-regulation strategies, such as using a timer or tactile materials to help elicit student focus.

Teachers' ability to use UDL principles to develop lessons and materials without changing the standard's intent in any way makes it much easier for students with complex support needs to be a part of the enacted curriculum without requiring retrofitting to make the curriculum accessible. However, given the complexity of some students' support needs, it is likely that many of these students will require additional supports to receive authentic opportunities to learn. Chapters throughout this book provide resources to help educators organize for universally designed, differentiated literacy instruction that will ensure that students are able to engage in, respond to, and communicate about the content.

Intended Curriculum: What to Teach

The intended curriculum is generally defined as the content, materials, and instruction present in a typical classroom for students without disabilities. Currently, the content is typically considered the state adopted content standards. IDEA 2004 states that all students should have access to and involvement in the general curriculum and make progress within it—that is, the same curriculum that is provided to students who do not have a disability. In addition, NCLB further clarified that *all* students be included in the general curriculum. One way NCLB and the proposed guidance for ESSA further established the idea that all students learn the general curriculum was by requiring that all students, including those with the most significant cognitive disabilities, be assessed on grade-level standards for the purpose of calculating adequate yearly progress.

Enacted Curriculum: What Instruction Looks Like

The enacted curriculum is generally defined as including time spent on learning, high-quality instructional practices, and content that is aligned to the intended curriculum (e.g., standards). It is up to teachers and schools to provide time for students to learn the content. The remainder of this text will explore high-quality instructional practices. This chapter addresses how to align classroom instruction with academic standards and what this process ultimately means for student achievement.

Align to Standards—Not Individualized Education Program Goals   What do we mean by "alignment"? Webb defines alignment as "the degree to which expectations and assessments are in agreement and serve in conjunction with one another to guide the system toward students learning what is expected" (2002, p. 3). The skills and concepts that are assessed should be directly linked to the targeted grade-level standard, and instruction should bridge the gap between the two. Imagine being in a class where the teacher spent weeks teaching French and then gave a final exam in Japanese. The exam would not be a valid measure of the students' understanding of the French skills and concepts taught in the course. A true OTL would not be present because the measure of the learning is invalid.

Many special education teachers are quite adept at seeing connections between instructional activities and skills that a student may need that are specified in the IEP, such as self-determination and social skills; this ability is just one reason they are such valuable members of the educational team. However, when it comes to planning academic lessons, sometimes this ability is extended too far. When teachers begin planning lessons from an IEP goal rather than the general education expectations set forth in the standards and general curriculum, the result is often a misalignment between the intended and enacted curriculum.

Consider the misalignment that occurred when two special educators tried to plan a literacy lesson on the standard CCSS.ELA-Literacy.W.5.3.a, "Orient the reader by establishing a situation and introducing a narrator and/or characters; organize an event sequence that unfolds naturally." The teachers also wanted to include instruction on student IEP goals in the lesson. They were working on creating lessons that would be accessible for their whole class, including some fifth graders who were reading sight words and some who were emergent literacy learners.

"I really think that the sequencing mentioned in the standard should be concrete actions, something we could show with picture cards as well as words."

"Oh yes! And think of the IEP goals we could embed in this instruction!"

"You are right. Oh, I know! We could do a lesson on tying shoes. We could have sequence cards that show how to start and then how to make the loops..."

"And we could do one for washing hands!"

"That is a great idea. So our targeted skill will be: 'student will sequence events that unfold naturally.'"

Did you notice that although these teachers have created a targeted skill that directly includes language from the standard, tying your shoes does not directly lead the student to be a better writer? Carefully constructing targeted skills, which are the skills and understandings the teacher plans for the student to demonstrate in a lesson or activity, is critically important. In this example, the teachers lost sight of the intent of the standard—to improve writing—and instead focused solely on IEP goals they wanted to address. Yet, it is easy to see how the teachers started to go astray in this case by focusing too narrowly on one small piece of the standard and by prioritizing IEP goals rather than the standard itself.

It is important to begin unit and lesson planning and assessment with the grade-level standard and the expectations for typical students. Staying grounded in these understandings reduces the likelihood of straying too far from the standard. Had the teachers above begun by considering what is expected for a typical fifth grader working toward the writing standard, they might have talked about developing situation and character outlines, mapping out plot events, or even following one character's actions across an already developed plot to examine character motivation. There is little chance that starting from these expectations would have led to a student sequencing pictures of tying his shoes or washing his hands.

Even with the standards as a starting point, it is still possible to go astray and develop misaligned lessons or assessments. Figure 4.3 presents five questions teachers can ask to evaluate the alignment of instructional or assessment plans with academic standards.

Use the Five Questions to Align Planning and Standards
Each of the five questions in Figure 4.3 is crucial for creating lessons, curricula, and assessments that align with academic standards. With this in mind, let's look more closely at how each question might be applied during planning.

1. Is the targeted skill academic?
If you are creating a lesson that is standards based, the first question in Figure 4.3, *Is the targeted skill academic?* should always be answered with a

The following criteria have been adapted from work developed by the National Alternate Assessment Center for checking whether or not instruction is aligned (adapted by D. Taub and M. Burdge, 2015). Use these questions to evaluate the alignment of assessment and instructional plans:

1. Is the targeted skill academic?
2. Would a content specialist be able to immediately see how it LEADS to and IS NECESSARY for demonstrating understanding of the standard?
3. Is the targeted skill a skill/concept that a student who is 2 years older or younger than the focus student would work toward?
4. Does the targeted skill maintain performance centrality with the grade-level standard?
5. Would a student without disabilities be embarrassed to walk through the halls with the materials or work product from this lesson?

Figure 4.3. Criteria for evaluating instructional alignment. (From Flowers, C., Wakeman, S., Browder, D., & Karvonen, M. [2007]. *Links for academic learning: An alignment protocol for alternate assessment based on alternate achievement standards.* Charlotte, NC: University of North Carolina at Charlotte. Reprinted with permission.)

"yes." Academic skills may include reading, writing, or performing mathematics calculations, among others. Nonacademic skills might include self-help skills such as feeding oneself or tying one's shoes. These nonacademic skills, which might be vital for students with complex support needs, should be embedded within lessons rather than being the primary targeted skill.

2. Would a content specialist be able to immediately see how the targeted skill LEADS to and IS NECESSARY for demonstrating understanding of the standard? The second question might require that you collaborate with a general educator or a content specialist—for example, an expert in social studies. A teacher well versed in the standards and content area can help you evaluate whether the targeted skill truly leads to a student's demonstrated understanding of the important skills and concepts embedded within a particular standard. A good rule of thumb is that the content specialist should be able to see the connection between the targeted skill and the standard without the educator explaining it. This step will help ensure that the content being taught is truly aligned to grade-level standards.

Sometimes, it is tempting to rationalize connections to standards that a content specialist might view as indirect or even tenuous. Consider this analogy: If we regard the standard as a frog, then we would expect targeted skills to be like tadpoles—a little smaller than the frog and probably not yet fully developed, but something that will become a frog and has some characteristics of frogs. A lily pad, on the other hand, is associated with frogs but will never become a frog. If any targeted skill requires rationalization, or if a content specialist would not immediately see how it leads to understanding of the standard, it is a lily pad. It should not be used as the targeted skill for instruction.

REFLECTION QUESTION 2

Consider the examples in Table 4.2. Would these targeted activities directly lead to understanding the grade-level standard or not? Are they tadpoles or lily pads?

3. Is the targeted skill a skill/concept that a student who is 2 years older or younger than the focus student would work toward? The content specialist can also help determine whether the targeted skill for a particular student is appropriate for a student who is in the same grade or who is two grades higher or lower. (Remember to review the process in "Understanding the Standards" for identifying a student's grade level if the student is in an ungraded program.) Across grade levels, the curriculum for a particular content area should be vertically aligned; *vertical alignment* is defined as a "logical, consistent order for teaching content in a subject area from one grade to the next" (Case & Zucker, 2005). Several organizations and states have resources such as vertical alignment documents and learning progression frameworks. These might be very

Table 4.2. Tadpole and lily pad example

Standard	Targeted skill	Tadpole/lily pad
CCSS.ELA-Literacy.RL.5.3 Compare and contrast two or more characters, settings, or events in a story or drama, drawing on specific details in the text (e.g., how characters interact).	Students will complete a graphic organizer (e.g., Venn diagram) to compare and contrast how two characters behave.	Tadpole This skill is clearly aligned to the standard and supports students' understanding of the standard. This activity could be completed in many different ways, such as by having the student use pictures of the characters to represent acting in different ways.
CCSS.ELA-Literacy.W.11-12.1.b Develop claim(s) and counterclaims fairly and thoroughly, supplying the most relevant evidence for each while pointing out the strengths and limitations of both in a manner that anticipates the audience's knowledge level, concerns, values, and possible biases.	Student will choose the best set of directions to take a bus to the store and identify one reason why it is the best choice.	Lily pad It is easy to see how this targeted skill could be rationalized: It involves the student making meaning and choosing an appropriate argument. However, the intent of this standard is to focus on "substantive topics or texts." A content specialist would not likely consider a bus schedule to fit this intent.
CCSS.ELA-Literacy.RL.3.9 Compare and contrast the themes, settings, and plots of stories written by the same author about the same or similar characters (e.g., in books from a series).	Students will identify the author of a story by pointing to the author's name on the cover.	Lily pad If this skill involved the student using knowledge about the author's themes, settings, plots, or word choices to identify the author, then this might align. However, the ability to locate the author's name is not going to directly lead to comparing and contrasting writing voice. It may, however, be an important embedded skill to include in the lesson.

Key: CCSS, Common Core State Standards; ELA, English language arts.

helpful for evaluating Question 3 and Question 4 related to *performance centrality*—meaning the level of agreement between the standard's expected level of performance and the targeted skill's expected level of performance. In addition, resources from the two national alternate assessment consortia, referenced in the Resources section at the end of this chapter, break the standards down into smaller skills and targeted skills and illustrate how they are connected. (Follow the links to the Essential Elements and Core Content Connector documents under Dynamic Learning Maps in the Resource section of this chapter.) Although these resources are not perfect, they outline how standards, skills, and concepts develop from year to year and allow the teacher to focus on the portions of the skills and concepts that are more grade-level appropriate.

4. Does the targeted skill maintain performance centrality with the grade-level standard? The fourth alignment question is related to performance centrality: the level of agreement between the standard's expected level of performance and the targeted skill's expected level of performance. Performance expectations are often thought of as the degrees of complexity with which the student is expected to demonstrate understanding. Two common, helpful models for conceptualizing performance centrality are Bloom's taxonomy and Webb's (2002) depth of knowledge. Both provide a hierarchy for understanding how skills move from less complex to more complex. (For instance, the lowest levels of Bloom's [1956] taxonomy are knowledge/remembering and recall, whereas the higher levels include synthesis and analysis; for a more complete discussion of Bloom's taxonomy, refer to Chapter 5.)

It is important to remember that complexity is not the same as difficulty. You might have a task that is not very complex but is still quite difficult. Consider the difference between memorizing a scale and memorizing Beethoven's *Moonlight Sonata*. Both tasks are at the lowest performance levels of Bloom's taxonomy (knowledge/remembering and recall), so they are not complex. Yet, one task is clearly much less difficult. Because complexity exists apart from difficulty, thoughtful teachers can adjust the latter without watering down the former. If the objective is for the student to demonstrate an ability to memorize, then a simple scale may be appropriate for some students, whereas for a more advanced student, memorizing an entire sonata may be more appropriate. Academically, the same construct applies. Adding supports and making modifications to a targeted task, such as using an adapted text or providing graphic organizers, should not and need not change the complexity level, only the difficulty level. These supports and modifications allow students with complex support needs to do work aligned to grade-level standards in a way that is accessible and adapted for their needs. For instance, all of the students may be reading Homer's *Odyssey*; however, two students may be reading the unabridged version and using notetaking skills; several other students may be reading a slightly abridged version (e.g., SparkNotes, CliffsNotes) and using notetaking skills; and another student may be reading a modified version that is no more than one page long, has less difficult vocabulary, and is using graphic organizers or sentence stems to support notetaking. All students are still able to experience the complex relationships and adventures within the *Odyssey*, although the difficulty of the reading level may differ. *Ultimately,* as a teacher, you want a mix of performance expectations at different degrees of complexity, remembering that modeling skills and using "think-alouds" to demonstrate how to work through more complex performance expectations are good strategies for helping students practice.

REFLECTION QUESTION 3

Using this targeted skill, "Student will identify the main idea," how might you make it more difficult? How might you make it more complex?

One way to make that targeted skill more difficult is to have the student practice it using multiple texts. Some ways to make it more complex are to require students to include supporting details to justify why they identified that main idea, or to use a text with multiple main ideas.

5. Would a general education student without disabilities be embarrassed to walk through the halls with the materials or work product from this lesson? This criterion is less of an academic question about alignment and more one of perception. Picture a typically developing student walking down the hall with the materials or resulting work product from the day's lesson. Would that student be embarrassed because the texts were "too babyish" or the pictures used as supports were inappropriate for someone in that grade? Experts indicate that instructional materials should be as close to a typical student's materials as possible, differing only as much as necessary to help the student access, engage with, and respond to the materials (Janney & Snell, 2006). In other words, materials and targeted tasks should be age appropriate.

Sometimes, students are truly, deeply engaged by a particular topic or interest area, so using these topics as a part of instruction can help to ensure that we have the student's attention. If, for example, a kindergarten student loves Thomas the Tank Engine, we can take advantage of this interest in age-appropriate ways, such as using a Thomas sticker to focus the student's attention on the page or even using Thomas as a character of a story he is reading. However, Thomas the Tank Engine is not age appropriate for a high school student. If a teenager nonetheless displays this specific interest, the IEP team should work on moving the student toward related, more age-appropriate topics within the same area of special interest, such as using photographs of real trains within instruction to engage the student. This transition incorporates the student's interests but maintains age appropriateness. By using age-appropriate academic materials, we are also helping students to connect socially with their same-age peers. It is a win–win situation.

Another consideration when selecting age-appropriate materials is the type of text. Many texts for beginning readers, written at a very simple level of text complexity, do not allow a student in middle or high school to work toward grade-level academic standards. For example, a beginning-level text such as *Big Dog, Little Dog* offers little for a teacher to work with when trying to teach how to identify key themes or examine character motivations. It is much easier to maintain alignment and performance centrality with grade-level standards if you start with grade-level texts when planning lessons. Throughout this book, chapter authors give examples of ways to modify or adapt grade-level texts, choose complex texts at basic reading levels, and provide supports that help make grade-level texts accessible.

Deconstruct a Standard   Even though you now have the pieces for understanding alignment, looking at a standard and determining how to deconstruct it into an aligned and useful targeted skill may still seem daunting. Collaboration with a content specialist is invaluable here. However, even if the content area is not your strongest suit, you can begin the process by considering what the student should be able to know and do to demonstrate the standard's intent. One concrete starting point is to identify the nouns/noun phrases and the verbs/verb phrases in the standard. In general (this is not a hard-and-fast rule), the *nouns* represent *what the student should know* and the *verbs* represent *what the student should be able to do*. This type of analysis does not replace the need for working with a content specialist, but it does help you break the standard down into target skills more quickly. Let's look at an example (see Figure 4.4) using the ninth-grade literacy standard CCSS.ELA-Literacy.RI.9-10.2, which states that students should "determine a central idea of a text and analyze its development over the course of the text, including how it emerges and is shaped and refined by specific details; provide an objective summary of the text" (Common Core State Standards Initiative, n.d.).

The key components of this standard are that students should be able to (a) determine the central idea of a text, (b) analyze the development of the central idea using details, and (c) provide a summary. Using these three different skill areas, next consider what specific targeted skill would allow students to demonstrate their understanding of these three key areas. In choosing the appropriate targeted skill, first examine how the standard progresses across the grades (a vertical alignment resource can be helpful here). If elementary school students are also expected to create summaries of a text, then it may be better when working with this ninth-grade standard to focus on skills that are more aligned to upper grades, such as analyzing central ideas. You may still include embedded instruction on summarizing texts, but summarization should not be the primary targeted skill of standards-aligned instruction because it is too far removed from a skill at the Grade 9–10 level.

Even though you may not be a content expert, it is important to understand thoroughly the academic standards we use as the basis for creating instruction. The information from the initial deconstruction can help you identify content vocabulary or concepts in which you may need a "refresher." To support your understanding of a standard, it may be helpful to think about how you would use the related concept or skill in everyday life. If you cannot think of a way to make it "real world," consider consulting www.Khanacademy.com or NCSC Curriculum Resources, or talking with a content specialist, to learn how that concept or skill applies to daily life.

Standard: CCSS.ELA-Literacy.RI.9-10.2 *Determine a central idea of a text and analyze its development over the course of the text, including how it emerges and is shaped and refined by specific details; provide an objective summary of the text.*

Nouns (know)	Verbs (do)
central idea of the text specific details objective summary	determine analyze development (emerges, shaped, and refined) provide

Figure 4.4. Deconstructing a standard by identifying key noun and verb phrases. *Key:* CCSS, Common Core State Standards; ELA, English language arts. (© Copyright 2010. National Governors Association Center for Best Practices and Council of Chief State School Officers. All rights reserved.)

REFLECTION QUESTION 4

Visit the Common Core State Standards Initiative web site at http://www.corestandards.org/ and choose one or two of the standards. Practice deconstructing them by finding the nouns (what students should know) and the verbs (what they should be able to do) used in the standard. Create a chart and identify (a) What should students know? (b) What should students be able to do? and (c) How would you use this in daily life?

Assessed Curriculum: What Learning Is Measured, and How

The third component of OTL is the assessed curriculum. Typically, discussions of assessed curriculum seem to focus on end-of-year or large-scale assessments. Students with the most significant disabilities often participate in alternate assessments based on alternate achievement standards. These alternate achievement standards are based on the same grade-level content used with typically developing students; it is just their degree of complexity and difficulty that may be modified. As noted previously, these alternate assessments are still aligned to the grade-level state-adopted standards; the process for judging alignment between assessment and standards is similar to the process detailed in the previous section.

More important for instructional purposes, however, are the formative and interim assessments that teachers should be conducting on a regular basis. It is these assessments that should inform and help teachers plan for daily instruction. Assessment across areas of literacy instruction is discussed throughout this book, so we will not address specific methods of assessment in detail here. However, we provide an example below of literacy instruction in a general education classroom for the sake of establishing a common foundation for thinking about where to start when teaching students with complex instructional needs.

TYPICAL LITERACY INSTRUCTION WITH UNIVERSAL DESIGN FOR LEARNING

To ensure that students have true opportunities to learn the general curriculum, let's consider what instruction might look like in a typical general education classroom where the principles of UDL are applied and all students are included.

Staying Focused on the Standards: Learning Goals, Assessment, and Universal Design for Learning

In a general education classroom, the teacher plans instruction using the intended curriculum. Teachers use standards and district or school curriculum guidance documents, such as curriculum maps, to determine what their students need to know and be able to do as a result of their instruction. In making this standards-based determination, teachers then set goals for instruction that also provide a universally designed target for classroom assessment.

The example discussed earlier in this chapter indicated how the CCSS incorporate principles of UDL by emphasizing learning concepts and skills that can be accessed and demonstrated in multiple ways. The learning goals and objectives a teacher decides on for a specific lesson ultimately determine how universally designed their instruction will be. Consider this learning goal from a typical general education lesson plan: *Students will analyze the theme of a story and cite evidence.* This example represents a universally designed learning goal because it allows the teacher to identify criteria for understanding the theme of a story and using textual evidence without specifying the mode in which students demonstrate that understanding.

Typically, a general education teacher thinks about the criteria necessary for students to meet a learning goal *before* planning instruction. Once the teacher has a plan for assessing student learning at the end of the unit or lesson (summative assessment), the teacher can plan formative assessments to inform the introduction, continued practice, and achievement of the learning goal(s). Suppose that, as part of students' understanding of theme, the teacher is looking at students' ability to identify major events in the story and determine if/how the main characters change. As a *summative* assessment for this overarching learning goal, the teacher might ask the students to convey what they think the author's view of the world is (the theme the author conveys in the text) and identify three supporting details. *Formative* assessments for the learning goal may then involve identifying three major events and identifying and analyzing related key words, phrases, or symbols to determine how they represent the underlying meaning of the text. For example, a student might demonstrate analysis of the theme and incorporate evidence from the story by designing a video collage of images and recorded text that represents a deep understanding of the text's underlying meaning. Other students might demonstrate understanding by describing three major events in writing and then summarizing how they illustrate the theme. Students might choose to take turns leading and participating in a small-group discussion to discuss major events and construct a description of the story's theme in the form of a poem or skit.

Each of these options illustrates how to apply the principles of UDL to both summative and formative assessment before planning for instruction. By ensuring that assessment will be accessible to students and incorporate *multiple means of engagement* to capture student interest, preference, and background knowledge; *multiple means of action and expression* that ensure students with different modes of communication have opportunities to demonstrate their learning; and *multiple means of representation* that ensure students can receive and interact with information in a variety of ways, teachers can then plan backward to design accessible instruction that supports student achievement of the standards-aligned learning goal. Standards-aligned planning processes and resources are included in Chapter 11.

Now that we have identified what a standards-aligned, universally designed learning goal and formative and summative assessment might look like in a general education classroom, let us consider what we would see if we walked into the classroom where initial instruction for this learning goal was taking place.

What Universally Designed Instruction Looks Like

Picture a sixth-grade ELA classroom with 25 students. The teacher has planned instruction to ensure that she is facilitating learning experiences that provide accessible opportunities to learn about themes in a story while citing evidence from the text. The class begins with a short lesson in which the teacher leads a discussion, providing examples and guided practice using a shared text, *Bud, Not Buddy,* which is the last book she read aloud to the class. Before the lesson begins, she communicates the learning goal both orally and in writing on the board to ensure that she is representing information her students need in multiple formats.

Today, we are going to practice identifying and analyzing the theme in fictional stories and using evidence to back up our answers. We can define theme as the underlying meaning of a story or the author's message. Sometimes, the author is really obvious about communicating the theme, but often we have to think about inferences and clues that help us identify and analyze the main idea and the underlying meaning and message in the text.

When the class finished the read-aloud of *Bud, Not Buddy,* they had created posters using text, symbols, and pictures to describe the main character; these are now posted on the classroom walls. They provide an engaging visual reminder of their shared experience with a text, which the teacher now uses to activate prior knowledge.

The teacher shares an example of theme, or underlying meaning, by giving a brief example from *Bud, Not Buddy.* To provide students with guided practice, she asks them to take 7 minutes to engage in a "think-pair-share" activity to exchange ideas with a partner and then further contribute to her example, focusing on events, words, phrases, or symbols that describe the underlying meaning of the text. She has provided students with the following: (a) index cards with words that describe different story events and words commonly used to describe a "theme" as prompts that pairs can choose to use if needed, (b) blank index cards for students to generate their own ideas, and (c) pictures from magazines and clip art students can use to represent underlying meaning visually. The students know they have these resources available because the teacher has ensured that choice-making is a classroom routine. The student pairs quickly make decisions about how to approach and complete this short task. Some groups take the stack of teacher-made index cards and start sorting words they think describe events and theme in *Bud, Not Buddy.* Other groups write words or paste pictures on index cards to contribute to the list. At the end of the "think-pair-share," the teacher asks students to place their index cards on the board to create an interactive visual resource that helps describe the underlying meaning of a text. The teacher uses this activity to transition from guided practice to the independent practice activity students will complete during this lesson. (Note that "independent practice" refers not to students doing an activity alone but to the scaffolded experience students have with less teacher guidance and direction.)

For this independent practice activity, the teacher has decided to use a video clip from a popular children's movie, *Holes,* to continue engaging student interest. She has a notes page available with key screen shots for any student who would like to use it. To set the stage for viewing the video clip, she asks students to think about the discussion they just had about *Bud, Not Buddy* and the words and ideas that represented its theme. She lets the students know that after viewing this short video clip, they will have the option to work independently, in pairs, or in groups of three to identify and analyze the theme represented in *Holes* and that they will need to support their response by providing evidence from the movie clip either in writing (in sentences or symbols/pictures) or orally (speaking or acting out). She directs students to remember the choice of materials available for completing the task (teacher-made index cards with preselected words, blank index cards, and magazines/clip art for symbols or visuals).

After watching the video clip, the students work in their chosen arrangement, with their choice of materials, to communicate their understanding of the theme illustrated in what they saw in the video clip. The teacher circulates, providing additional prompting, questions, resources, or supports as needed. She has graphic organizers on hand with spaces for key words and ideas and for listing supporting evidence. She has the video clip set up in a place where students can view it again, if needed, as they work.

Some students have read the book *Holes,* some have seen the movie, and others have no experience with the story at all. As the students present their responses to their classmates, the depth of their inferences varies, but because of the accessible learning experiences the teacher has provided, they are all able to demonstrate their understanding of theme using evidence from the clip to support their answers. For this activity, there is not a "correct" response; instead, the teacher has observed, throughout the students' interactions in guided and independent practice, the skills and learning behaviors that relate to the universally designed learning objective. The students were expected to work toward identifying three events, key words, and/or ideas that illustrate the theme, and all students have done this by either selecting events and descriptive words from a list, generating their own words and ideas, or finding pictures or symbols that represent their event and describing words. They have selected evidence from the video to support their responses by either acting out their response, writing their response using words or symbols, or orally describing their reasoning.

How a Universal Design for Learning Classroom Supports Students With Complex Support Needs

The previous section described what a typical universally designed general education classroom looks like. Let's take a moment to think about how this type of classroom would provide an accessible learning experience for a student with complex support needs.

Consider Matthew, a fifth-grade student with autism. Matthew uses a combination of verbal utterances and an augmentative and alternative communication (AAC) device to communicate. Matthew's AAC device is an iPad with a touchscreen that he uses to generate responses on his own using picture symbols and spelling some words. He independently reads at a second-grade level and is at the beginning stages of writing in complete sentences.

In a general education classroom like the one described previously, many of Matthew's needs would be met through the implementation of universally designed, differentiated instruction. Even though he might still require additional accommodations, the application of UDL supports for all students helps to ensure that Matthew's accommodations are truly individualized and only as specialized as necessary (Janney & Snell, 2006; Kurth & Keegan, 2012).

Because Matthew needs support to access grade-level texts, the teacher's presentation of *Bud, Not Buddy* as a class read-aloud and *Holes* as a video clip provide a way for Matthew to interact with the texts. Small-group activities help Matthew and other students to process and comprehend the text. The posters with pictures, symbols, and text, displayed to aid additional activities for comprehension, are resources that help Matthew think about the text and generate responses. During the guided practice activity, the teacher provides choices with varying levels of support by making available blank index cards, pre-made index cards, and pictures and symbols that students may use to practice applying what they are learning about theme. By providing these processing options, the teacher has addressed the needs of students who benefit from interacting with visual information while also ensuring that Matthew has an effective way to communicate his ideas. She has maximized the value of this activity for all students and made the inclusion of pictures and symbols "business as usual" instead of something specialized just for Matthew. Finally, the teacher assesses students' learning of theme by providing them the option to write, act out, or orally present their responses. If the teacher had required written responses, Matthew might have a difficult time expressing what he has learned. Including other options supports Matthew and other students who best demonstrate their learning using different modalities.

Look at Chapter 11, which further explores organizing for literacy instruction using universally designed routines and differentiated instruction, and Chapters 2, 5, and 12, which address aspects of creating an accessible literacy environment. These chapters will help you think about how you can design your classroom and instruction to benefit all learners while meeting the needs of students like Matthew. The following section will describe the important role of the IEP in addressing needs of students with complex support needs.

BUT WHAT ABOUT THE INDIVIDUALIZED EDUCATION PROGRAM?

It might seem strange not to have started this chapter with IEPs. Now that you know more about standards, why do you think we waited until the end of the chapter to discuss IEPs? Think about what you have learned so far about what is involved in aligning learning goals, instruction, and assessment to content standards, and how much priority teachers should give to IEP goals during this alignment process.

REFLECTION QUESTION 5

Think back to the lily pad activity in Table 4.2. What would have happened if you started with an IEP goal and tried to retrofit the goal into a standard? Would it be aligned? Would you be able to answer all five alignment questions in Figure 4.3 positively?

What role *does* the IEP play in all of this? We have met many teachers who believe, especially for students with complex support needs, that the IEP is the curriculum for students with disabilities. This misconception has been clearly addressed since the reauthorization of

IDEA in 1997: "The IEP must include annual goals to enable the child to be involved in and make progress in the general education curriculum" (300.320 a). New guidance from the Office of Special Education and Rehabilitative Services (OSERS; 2015) specifically outlines the importance of standards-aligned IEPs and the role the IEP should play in a student's education. Definitively, the IEP is developed to support the student's access to and progress in the general curriculum, which is the same for *all* students. Even though standards-based IEPs are not required by IDEA 1997 and 2004, NCLB, or ESSA, most states and territories have policies that guide, or even require, IEPs to have standards-based goals and objectives.

Unfortunately, there is a paucity of literature, training, and examples to guide IEP teams in developing meaningful IEP goals and objectives grounded in grade-level academic standards. Taub and Burdge (2017) systematically describe how IEP teams might develop IEP goals that are meaningfully based in grade-level standards and that promote access to and progress in the general curriculum. They define three different types of possible standards-based IEP goals:

1. Those that relate directly to grade-level standards

2. Those that relate directly to content-area foundational skills that can be embedded into grade-level standards

3. Those ecologically determined individualized goals that address communication, social, and behavioral skills that facilitate participation in general education instruction based on the general education curriculum and other inclusive activities and environments. To determine ecologically appropriate individualized goals, the IEP team should identify the naturally occurring settings the student will be in (e.g., the general education classroom, physical education) and identify which skills help the student access and fully support participation in that context.

The process Taub and Burdge (2017) describe is closely connected to that described in *A Seven-Step Process to Creating Standards-based IEPs* (Holbrook, 2007); however, Taub and Burdge (2017) contextualize those steps within a framework for each of the three types of goals they describe (see Figure 4.5). We will present this framework here to demonstrate how it may help IEP teams develop standards-based IEPs that are linked to meaningful, effective instruction.

Goal Type 1: Grade-Level Academic Skills

Educators' work with Thomas, an eighth grader with significant cognitive disabilities, provides an example of how we can develop Type 1 goals. His IEP team first looked at the general curriculum to determine which skills and concepts were emphasized in that grade level and which ones would best help Thomas make progress in the general curriculum. In this example, the team selected "Analyze how particular lines of dialogue or incidents in a story or drama propel the action, reveal aspects of a character, or provoke a decision" (CCSS.RL.8.3, 2010). They next used a series of steps to move from the standard to an appropriate, meaningful IEP goal (see Figure 4.5).

• *Step A. Break the construct(s) of the standard into smaller chunks.*

As part of accessing the general curriculum, Thomas will still receive instruction on everything contained in the standard, but the entire standard is too large a concept to address and measure as an IEP goal. In addition, some standards may have one concept or skill that is more important than another. The standard we are using for this example comprises several skills and concepts:

1. Analyze how particular lines of dialogue in a story or drama propel the action.

2. Analyze how particular lines of dialogue in a story or drama reveal aspects of a character.

3. Analyze how particular lines of dialogue in a story or drama provoke a decision.

4. Analyze how incidents in a story or drama propel the action.

5. Analyze how incidents in a story or drama reveal aspects of a character.

6. Analyze how incidents in a story or drama provoke a decision.

- *Step B. Decide which chunk(s) should be prioritized for the student.*

The team determined that, of all the specific skills included in the standard, Thomas should focus on understanding how dialogue reveals aspects of a character.

- *Step C. Determine how the student will perform the skill or demonstrate understanding of the concept.*

When considering this step, it is best to focus on the student's communication preferences and strengths. Remember, we want to assess what Thomas knows about this standard, not his ability to use a communication system that is new to him. Thomas's IEP team knew he does best when picture symbols are combined with text to support his access to printed materials; he also can choose from an array of three options. Thomas also does best when working with chunked information—that is, information presented in small, easily digested "chunks" rather than all at once—and when working with choices presented visually, rather than working from memory. Thus, his IEP team determined that he could best demonstrate understanding by selecting from visual choices. The team's first part of drafting an IEP goal, based on the standard, looked like this: "Thomas will verbally select the line of dialogue that best illustrates a character's personality trait."

- *Step D. Specify under what criteria the goal should be demonstrated to be considered "achieved."*

The team also decided that to achieve this goal, Thomas would need to show an accurate performance on five out of six trials. The team's final goal looked like this: "Given three choices represented by pictures and text, Thomas will verbally select the line of dialogue that best illustrates a character's personality trait, 5 out of 6 times."

    This goal is open-ended enough that it can be worked on throughout various literacy activities in the general education classroom that involve characters, including novels, plays, sagas, or other types of texts. In addition, Thomas may be assessed on this skill after reading each chapter, as he encounters key plot points in his reading, or after he reaches the end of a text.

Steps for Creating Type 1 Goals
A. Break the construct(s) of the standard into smaller chunks. B. Decide which chunk(s) should be prioritized for the student. C. Determine how the student will perform the skill or demonstrate understanding of the concept. D. Specify under what criteria the goal should be demonstrated to be considered "achieved."
Steps for Creating Type 2 Goals
A. Break the construct(s) of the standard into smaller chunks. B. Identify foundational skills important to one or more of the chunks. C. Prioritize foundational skills for the student to achieve. D. Determine how the student will perform the skill or demonstrate understanding of the concept. E. Specify under what criteria the goal should be demonstrated to be considered "achieved."
Steps for Creating Type 3 Goals
A. Identify activities that occur throughout the school day and select skills that will increase participation in the general curriculum. B. Determine how the student will perform the skill or demonstrate understanding of the concept. C. Specify under what criteria the goal should be demonstrated to be considered "achieved."

Figure 4.5. Creating standards-based IEP goals.

Goal Type 2: Academically Embedded Foundational Skills

Let's look at an example of this second type of goal using the practical, standards-based IEP process developed by Taub and Burdge (2017). Rochelle is another eighth-grade student who has significant cognitive disabilities. Rochelle's communication system includes vocalizations, eye gaze, body movement and changes in muscle tone, and a single-switch communication device. She recognizes some sight words but primarily is using an AAC system to indicate pictures paired with text. Rochelle's team selected the same standard identified by Thomas's team: "Analyze how particular lines of dialogue or incidents in a story or drama propel the action, reveal aspects of a character, or provoke a decision" (CCSS RL.8.3). To develop a Type 2 goal, Step A remains the same as for Type 1 goals: break the construct of the standard into smaller chunks. The rest of the process, however, differs from that used to develop a Type 1 goal (see Figure 4.5).

- *Step B. Identify foundational skills important to one or more of the chunks.*

Rochelle's team examined the chunks from the standard, looking for foundational skills that would be helpful for demonstrating achievement of the concepts and skills therein. Foundational skills include core skills that would support a robust understanding of the content. In this case, some of the foundational skills the team identified were to read; to identify character traits, dialogue, and plot points (e.g., events in the story); to determine cause and effect; and to discern point of view. Clearly, not all of these are required to demonstrate achievement on this standard, so the next step in the process is to select critical skills for the particular student to acquire.

- *Step C. Prioritize foundational skills for the student to achieve.*

The IEP team examined all of the foundational skills included in this standard and determined which ones would be most generalizable, would best support learning future standards, and were most important for Rochelle's goals and preferences. Although understanding cause and effect is a vital skill, at this point it was more important for Rochelle to focus on identifying plot points (events), a skill that could be generalized to other parts of her day, such as her daily schedule. The goal the team developed at this point was "Rochelle will identify events that occurred in each chapter of a novel."

- *Step D. Determine how the student will perform the skill or demonstrate understanding of the concept.*

To determine how Rochelle would perform the skill, the team needed to consider how information would be presented to her and how she would respond to it. To support Rochelle's understanding of events, she was provided with an adapted text that included fewer events in each chapter than the unabridged novel used by the rest of the class. In addition, to increase accessibility, the print was instructionally enhanced using iconic symbols. Knowing that Rochelle could express her responses best if she used her communication system, the team determined that she would have a choice of at least three events, visually represented in the form of symbols; the choices would include one to two that happened in a particular chapter and one to two that did not. Rochelle would then use her communication system to choose the correct event for each chapter. Furthermore, to better support alignment with the standard, the team prioritized for instruction events that are particularly important for character development. The IEP statement now looked like this: "Given a choice of iconic symbols that represent events, Rochelle will use her communication system to identify key events that occurred in each chapter of a novel."

- *Step E. Specify under what criteria the goal should be demonstrated to be considered "achieved."*

The IEP team determined that proficiency would be obtained if Rochelle responded correctly 75% of the time. The final IEP goal looked like this: "Given a choice of iconic symbols that represent events, Rochelle will use her communication system to correctly identify key events that occurred in each chapter of a novel 75% of the time."

Goal Type 3: Ecologically Determined Individualized Goals

Jeremy, another eighth grader who has autism spectrum disorder, provides a good example to illustrate Taub and Burdge's (2017) process for creating Type 3 goals. The types of skills included in Type 3 goals may be necessary for students with a wide range of academic achievement levels, not just those with complex support needs. Type 3 goals focus on the context of the activities the student engages in when involved in content area instruction, rather than focusing on the content itself. In this case, Jeremy reads close to grade level and needs few academic supports. His team used the following steps to create Type 3 IEP goals.

- *Step A. Identify activities that occur throughout school day and select skills that will increase participation in the general curriculum.*

Activities may include instructional activities such as small-group work, lecture, research, independent work, and projects (independent or group). When Jeremy's IEP team looked at his academic school day, it readily determined several skill areas that Jeremy could improve to increase his participation in these activities. Specifically, he would need to improve his appropriate manipulation of materials and his interactive skills with teachers and typical peers. In other words, Jeremy needed to use materials without ripping them and to keep his hands to himself. The team decided that for now, keeping his hands to himself was the priority. The IEP goal they began to draft looked like this: "Jeremy will appropriately keep his hands to himself."

- *Step B. Determine how the student will perform the skill or demonstrate understanding of the concept.*

The initial draft of Jeremy's goal was too broad to be measurable. For instance, does it count as one opportunity to keep his hands to himself if he makes it through an entire reading class without touching anyone, or is that 1,000 opportunities? Jeremy's team decided that they would focus the IEP goal on his performance during small group, when he was in close proximity to others and, according to behavioral data, was having the most trouble with this skill. This is not to say that Jeremy was allowed to do what he wanted with his hands the rest of the time but that small group would be the setting used to collect data on his performance of this skill. With this addition, the goal read, "During participation in small-group activities, Jeremy will appropriately keep his hands to himself."

- *Step C. Specify under what criteria the goal should be demonstrated to be considered "achieved."*

The team determined that they would break the 20-minute small-group time into 5-minute increments, meaning that to achieve 80% success, Jeremy had to keep his hands to himself for four of the five blocks of time. The team also decided that Jeremy would continue to benefit from verbal or gestural cues to achieve this goal. The final IEP goal looked like this: "During participation in small-group activities, Jeremy will appropriately keep his hands to himself 80% of the time. with verbal and/or gestural cues."

No single type of standards-based IEP goal is preferable over the other two. In fact, it may be that each one might be appropriate for every student, resulting in IEPs that have a combination of two or three goal types. The important takeaway is that IEP teams need explicit and direct guidance to develop IEP goals that are truly standards based and that guide instruction to fully realize "access to and progress in the general curriculum" (ESSA, 2015). Chapter 11 offers further support for organizing effective literacy instruction and ensuring IEP goals are addressed through tools such as the Program-at-a-Glance and Infused Skills Grid.

SUMMARY

Orelove (1995) cautioned that if a student goal can be done by a potato, it should not be on the IEP! Low expectations can result in "potato goals" for students with complex support needs—that is, goals where the student need not even be breathing to "achieve." (See Chapter 8 for more on this topic.)

We hope this chapter has provided a foundation to help you understand why deficit-oriented instruction should be replaced with standards-based instructional planning. This chapter explored how to deconstruct and align standards as critical steps for providing students with complex support needs the OTL. We have given many examples of how standards-based literacy instruction can be implemented in general education classrooms using UDL. Finally, we demonstrated how to design and apply standards-based IEP goals to provide all students with complex support needs access to differentiated literacy instruction. We highly recommend that you revisit this chapter and your reflection question responses as you explore the remaining chapters in this book.

RESOURCES

- **The Common Core State Standards Initiative** (http://www.corestandards.org) provides more information on CCSS.

- **Dynamic Learning Maps** (http://dynamiclearningmaps.org/) and the National Center and State Collaborative (NCSC) (http://www.ncscpartners.org/) provide information on some possible ways to break down standards and vertical alignment across grades. See resources to support understanding the standards at these links:

  - https://wiki.ncscpartners.org/index.php/Curriculum_Resources

  - http://dynamiclearningmaps.org/content/essential-elements

REFERENCES

American Psychological Association. (n.d.). *Disability and socioeconomic status.* Retrieved September 21, 2017 from http://www.apa.org/pi/ses/resources/publications/disability.aspx

Bloom, B.S. (1956). *Taxonomy of educational objectives, Handbook I: The cognitive domain.* New York, NY: David McKay Company, Inc.

Case, B., & Zucker, S. (2005, July). *Horizontal and vertical alignment.* San Antonio, TX: Pearson Education.

Common Core State Standards Initiative. (n.d.). Available at http://www.corestandards.org/

Every Student Succeeds Act of 2015, PL 114-95, 129 Stat. 1802, 20 U.S.C. §§ 6301 *et seq.*

Flowers, C., Wakeman, S., Browder, D., & Karvonen, M. (2007). *Links for academic learning: An alignment protocol for alternate assessment based on alternate achievement standards.* Charlotte, NC: University of North Carolina at Charlotte.

Holbrook, M.D. (2007). *A seven-step process to creating standards-based IEPs.* Retrieved from https://education.ohio.gov/getattachment/Topics/Special-Education/Federal-and-State-Requirements/Federal-Resources/7StepProcesstoCreatingStandards-basedIEPs.pdf.aspx

Individuals with Disabilities Education Act Amendments (IDEA) of 1997, PL 105-17, 20 U.S.C. §§ 1400 *et seq.*

Individuals with Disabilities Education Improvement Act (IDEA) of 2004, PL 108-446, 20 U.S.C. §§ 1400 *et seq.*

Janney, R.E., & Snell, M.E. (2006). Modifying schoolwork in inclusive classrooms. *Theory into Practice, 45*(3), 215–223.

Kurth, J.A., & Keegan, L. (2012). Development and use of curricular adaptations for students receiving special education services. *The Journal of Special Education, 48*(3), 191–203.

Land, L. (2010, September). *Is it mathematics?* (Common Core Version). Retrieved from http://www.naacpartners.org/presentations.aspx

Morningstar, M. (2010). *What does the future hold? Making the transition to supported adulthood.* Presentation at TASH Annual Conference. Retrieved from http://www.transitioncoalition.org/wp-content/originalSiteAssets/files/docs/What_does_Future_HoldTASH2010a1291785663.pdf

No Child Left Behind (NCLB) Act of 2001, PL 107-110, 115 Stat. 1425, 20 U.S.C. §§ 6301 *et seq.*

Office of Special Education and Rehabilitative Services (OSERS). (2015). *Dear colleague letter: Significant guidance on free and appropriate public education (FAPE).* Retrieved from https://www2.ed.gov/policy/speced/guid/idea/memosdcltrs/guidance-on-fape-11-17-2015.pdf

Orelove, F. (1995, February). Consider the potato. *Newsletter of the Severe Disabilities Technical Assistance Center, 10*(5).

Palmer, P.J. (2007). *The courage to teach.* Hoboken, NJ: Wiley.

Rose, D.H., Meyer, A., & Hitchcock, C. (2005). *The universally designed classroom: Accessible curriculum and digital technologies.* Cambridge, MA: Harvard Education Press.

Taub, D & Burdge, M. (2015) Presentation to South Dakota Community of Practice.

Taub, D. & Burdge, M. (Spring 2017). Standards Based IEPs—Are They Important and What Should Be In Them?TASH Connections 42: 1. Pp. 29-32.

Taub, D., McCord, J., & Ryndak, D.L. (2017, March 6). Opportunities to learn for students with extensive support needs: A context of research-supported practices for all in general education classrooms. *Journal of Special Education.* Advance online publication. https://doi.org/10,1177/0022466917696263

United States Census Bureau. (2014). *American Community Survey—1 year estimates.* Retrieved from http://factfinder.census.gov/faces/tableservices/jsf/pages/productview.xhtml?pid=ACS_14_1YR_B18120&prodType=table

Webb N. L. (2002). *Alignment Study in Language Arts, Mathematics, Science, and Social Studies of State Standards and Assessments for Four States.* Washington, DC: Council of Chief State School Officers, September 21, 2017; http://citeseerx.ist.psu.edu/viewdoc/download?doi=10.1.1.507.4349&rep=rep1&type=pdf

CHAPTER 5

Creating Accessible, Rich, and Engaging Literacy Environments

Jessica Apgar McCord, Ann-Marie Orlando, Elizabeth B. Keefe, and Stephanie Nieto

LEARNING OBJECTIVES

By the end of this chapter, readers will

1. Understand the application of universal design for learning principles to create an accessible, rich, and engaging classroom environment.

2. Understand the importance of the classroom environment and its impact on students' abilities to process information.

3. Identify specific strategies and resources to implement to enrich the classroom environment and enhance literacy learning opportunities.

4. Review research findings about how the brain learns and stores new information and examine the implication of these findings for literacy instruction.

This chapter will discuss how the principles of universal design for learning (UDL) can be used to create accessible, rich, engaging literacy environments. We will begin with an overview of the history of UDL and its application to literacy instruction for learners with complex support needs. Next, we will explore how to apply UDL principles to create the best possible classroom learning environments for these learners, providing specific examples of ways the teacher might make the environment more accessible. Finally, we will review available research about how the brain processes and stores new information—that is, how people learn—and what implications this research has for how we teach literacy skills to learners with complex support needs.

TWO CLASSROOMS

Picture a room with bare walls, flickering fluorescent lights, wobbly chairs, gum stuck beneath the tables, and trash on the floor. Electrical cords crisscross the floor to a pot percolating fresh coffee all over a countertop and to a computer haphazardly perched on a table in the front of the room. Papers and pencils are strewn about on the tables and floor. Students enter the room and toss their backpacks in the corner in a growing pile. Desks and chairs are so close to each other that students can barely move without bumping into each other. A poster hangs on the wall with the encouraging phrase, "You can do it!" A thick layer of dust rests atop a random assortment of books on a shelf.

Now picture this. You enter a classroom that is well-organized and intentionally staged for student learning. The walls are not bare; designated spaces announce school events, display student work samples, detail class procedures, and emphasize the vocabulary on interactive word walls. Books are organized by genre on a clean bookshelf with a small rug in front of it, where students are welcome to browse. The room arrangement also takes into consideration that students will move around and interact with each other. Clear aisles and walkways are established for both safety and physical accessibility, and the teacher has labeled the locations for supplies like paper, pencils, textbooks, and the like so that students can find all needed materials easily. The teacher can use the computer for instruction, but it is also available for student use. Easy-to-reach hooks allow students access to their backpacks, further ensuring that the space is safe and free of clutter.

Which environment do you think is more conducive to active and engaged learning experiences? We have shared these brief contrasting examples up front to help you begin thinking about the impact of decisions you will make about your classroom environment. Think about how each example made you feel and in which type of environment you would rather spend your time—whether for an hour-long, secondary-level class period or a full day in an elementary school. Which environment provides a better starting point for productive learning? Which is more academically and socially accessible for students?

In this chapter, we will discuss the idea that being well-planned and well-organized, and making intentional choices about the environment, supports high-quality literacy instruction and maximizes opportunities to learn literacy (Keefe, Copeland, & DiLuzio, 2010). (Chapter 11 will build on this concept by describing the importance of organizing for literacy instruction and providing helpful tools and resources for making that happen.) We begin by emphasizing the importance of two big ideas to help you create accessible, rich, and engaging literacy environments to support all students' learning. First, we will discuss the importance of applying UDL principles in the classroom. Second, we will explore the impact of the classroom environment and instructional practices on information processing. We will then describe specific tools and strategies you can use to enhance your classroom environment in ways consistent with these big ideas.

OVERVIEW: UNIVERSAL DESIGN FOR LEARNING

Rooted in neuroscience, UDL is a framework that increases student success by breaking down barriers found within the environment and within the curriculum that often restrict access to instruction (Rose, Meyer, & Hitchcock, 2005). Before we talk about ways to apply UDL principles to enrich the classroom environment specifically, however, it is important to discuss UDL from a broader perspective to understand its impact on all components of the curriculum, such as goals, instruction, materials, and assessment. UDL is more than a set of principles to apply. It provides a framework for developing a mindset that can guide your approach to all aspects of teaching, learning, and assessment. In this section we will consider the history of UDL, its origins in the universal design (UD) movement, and the legislation that has made UDL the standard for instructional design. Let's take a moment to consider an example of its powerful nature.

The History of Universal Design

An early application of UDL occurred years before UD officially came into existence, when publishing companies changed the size and weight of books to make them more accessible to soldiers during World War II. This was done as part of efforts by the Council on Books in Wartime, which had been formed in the wake of the German book burnings of the 1930s. The Council was an organization made up of literary professionals focused on boosting morale and encouraging soldiers to read more (Scutts, 2014). Its first efforts included encouraging the public to donate books for soldiers. However, most were children's books and hardcover books, which were too heavy for the men to carry with them while deployed. The Council then decided to publish smaller editions, bound with lighter paper, on topics of interest to soldiers. Because these Armed Services Editions could fit into a soldier's breast pocket or the back pocket of his pants, they became more accessible. These editions included titles like *The Great Gatsby* and *A Tree Grows in Brooklyn,* which owe much of their enduring popularity to their widespread distribution to soldiers during this time. The Council's attention to making the books accessible to soldiers is significant for two main reasons. First, the focus on ensuring American soldiers' access to literature was intended to send a powerful message about the importance of literacy and its role in a free society. Second, it illustrates the significance of making texts more accessible for individuals in different environments. This powerful example of UD to ensure access to text demonstrates the impact of making modifications to traditional formats.

The 1950s saw the emergence of another aspect of UDL: the barrier-free movement, which began as veterans with disabilities returned from war. This movement gradually improved people's access to a wide range of structures and technologies. National standards for barrier-free buildings were developed in the early 1960s; by the late 1960s, federal legislation began to lay the groundwork for Uniform Federal Accessibility Standards (see https://www.access-board.gov/guidelines-and-standards/buildings-and-sites/about-the-aba-standards/ufas). Subsequent federal legislation has continued to support access for all with Section 504 of The Rehabilitation Act of 1973 (PL 93-112), which prohibited discrimination against individuals based on their disabilities. The provision of access for all to public facilities was mandated by the Americans with Disabilities Act (ADA) of 1990 (PL 101-336). Section 255 of the Telecommunications Act of 1996 (PL 104-104) mandated consumer accessibility for all telecommunication devices.

These legislative mandates for accessibility led to the retrofitting of existing structures to support access for all; however, this can be expensive and unattractive. Built-in solutions for accessibility have far better cost savings, appearance, and functionality than retrofitting. The need for these built-in solutions has been addressed by the architectural movement of UD, developed by Ron Mace, which relied on architectural principles with the purpose of creating inclusive physical environments with built-in accessibility for all (Rose & Meyer, 2002). These principles led to modern architectural design elements that assist not only those with disabilities but also anyone who needs support, such as a person pushing a baby carriage or carrying boxes. Elements such as ramps, curb cuts, automatic doors, closed captioning on televisions, and tools with grip handles make the environment more accessible for everyone.

Applying Universal Design to Learning

These principles of UD were carried over to education in 1995, when CAST (Center for Applied Special Technology) began a new approach to apply UD principles to learning (CAST.org), coining the term *universal design for learning.* The focus of UDL was to change or redesign goals, materials, instruction, and assessment, but not the student. The new approach led to new assumptions about teaching students with disabilities, including students with complex support needs. These assumptions are that changes to teaching strategies help all students; curriculum and materials must be flexible, varied, and diverse; and all teachers plan curriculum (Rose & Meyer, 2002).

UDL has become part of the educational landscape as laws have been enacted to support access to curriculum, instruction, and materials for all. The reauthorization of the Individuals with Disabilities Education Improvement Act (IDEA) of 2004 (PL 108-446) mandated access to curriculum for all students. However, it was the Higher Education Opportunity Act of 2008 (PL 110-315) that defined UDL for the first time in federal education law and set the stage for UDL to be an integral part of the Every Student Succeeds Act (ESSA) of 2015 (PL 114-95).

These federal mandates (i.e., IDEA 2004, ESSA) require all students to be involved and make progress in the general curriculum. Expectations for student achievement are high, and measures of teacher accountability often are based on high-stakes testing. These increased expectations come at a time when classrooms are more diverse than ever. To meet the needs of these diverse learners, teachers need information about various instructional strategies and tools. The general curriculum that has, historically, been used—print-based and designed for a homogeneous group of students—is not flexible enough to meet the needs of diverse learners. UDL increases opportunities for diverse learners to be involved and make progress in the general curriculum.

Research indicates that, compared with typical peers, students with complex support needs might engage differently in academic instruction; therefore, goals, instruction, materials, and assessment should be universally designed. For example, Dalton, Morocco, Tivnan, and Mead (1997) indicated that students with disabilities participating in science learning activities frequently have limited prior knowledge, are reluctant to pose questions, are less likely to have a plan for solving problems, struggle to implement teacher recommendations, and have difficulty with inductive and deductive reasoning, and they seldom show generalization of their new knowledge. Thus, providing additional ways for these students to engage in these activities might increase their participation. To achieve this, teachers can provide multiple means of representation, expression, and engagement:

- To provide *multiple means of representation* means to ensure that students can receive and interact with information in a variety of ways.

- To provide *multiple means of action and expression* means to ensure that students with different modes of communication have opportunities to demonstrate their learning.

- To provide *multiple means of engagement* means to capture and maintain student interest, preference, and background knowledge. Engagement encompasses strategies for activating background knowledge and garnering student interests, such as providing student choice. It also includes self-regulation strategies, such as using a timer or tactile materials to help elicit student focus.

Additional examples of how teachers can provide these options in the classroom include the use of various means such as closed-captioned videos, multisensory demonstrations of concepts, and the use of word processing software with writing features such as spelling and grammar tools, or word prediction. In addition, incorporating technology tools (e.g., iPads, books, movies, software) can enhance students' knowledge of curriculum content and cognitive skills.

With these principles in mind, let's examine what specific tools help teachers implement UDL in literacy instruction. A variety of tools and resources are available to support the implementation of UDL in your classroom to make the learning environment optimally accessible.

ACCESSIBLE LITERACY TOOLS

Technology tools can provide access to text in a variety of ways. In this section, we describe various tools and provide some examples. (Note that it is important to be cognizant of copyright laws when providing alternate means of accessing text.)

Tools for Making Text More Accessible

Numerous forms of accessible text provide alternatives to traditional print-based curricula. For example, textbook companies often provide digital access codes so that consumers can access text and supplemental materials in electronic formats. These formats allow text to be altered to meet the learner's needs—for instance, by enlarging it, changing its color to contrast with the background, or having it read aloud using accessibility features (these may be part of the device operating system or separately purchased software and applications). Texts that are not available through the publisher, such as out-of-print books, can be accessed in digital formats through other resources, described in the following sections.

Accessible Text Available Online   The American Printing House for the Blind provides texts in accessible formats such as braille and large-print texts, audio texts, and computer files. Free demonstration versions of text accessibility software also are available through the web site. Another organization, Learning Ally, previously known as Recording for the Blind and

Dyslexic, provides largest available collection of audio recordings of textbooks and literature to its members. Print materials also can be accessed through online providers giving limitless access to the public via digital collections libraries. Links to these sources are provided in the Resources section at the end of this chapter.

Sources for online texts such as the Library of Congress, the New York Public Library, or Internet Archive offer a variety of accessible media including print. Other web sites, such as Project Gutenberg, offer free e-books that can be read online or downloaded and read aloud using device software. A number of web sites offer time-limited access to e-books in a variety of formats—a few include the World Public Library, Open Library, and Overdrive, which provide distribution and management services to local libraries for the purpose of providing e-book access. In addition, Bookshare, the largest accessible online library for individuals with print disabilities, is free to individuals with a documented disability and offers organizational membership. Links to these sources are provided in the Resources section at the end of this chapter.

Text-to-Speech Programs Text-to-speech (TTS) programs make traditional print available for a wide variety of students. Although we advocate that TTS software and applications be available for all, we especially emphasize their value in creating a rich and accessible literacy environment for students with complex support needs. If all students know that they may use TTS, this option becomes embedded in classroom expectations and routines instead of being "something we do for Tommy because he has a disability." Students without disabilities who learn better when information is provided in an auditory format or in multiple modes will benefit from having TTS available. For students who have disabilities such as vision impairments, intellectual disability, specific learning disabilities, or dyslexia, providing the option for TTS can mean the difference between academic success and failure. It is our job as teachers to remove the barriers to traditional print; using TTS is one way to make that happen.

Many digital texts are offered through platforms that automatically offer TTS functionality. Several platforms that might provide viable options—depending on school subscriptions, personal devices that students use, and so forth—are Kindle (Amazon, Inc.), NOOK (Barnes & Noble), and Scholastic Storia e-books, links for which are provided in the Resources section at the end of this chapter. Many textbook publishers now have either CD or online options for texts that also provide the TTS option.

If these options are not available, you will need to create digital text to be used in TTS software for your students. You can do that by either downloading digital text or by scanning text to the computer and then using software or accessibility features to read the digital text aloud. Some excellent online resources to explore so you can offer the best options for your students are ReadPlease, NaturalReader, Kurzweil, and Read&Write. (See this chapter's Resources section for links.)

Tools for Making Writing More Accessible

Traditional forms of writing often present many barriers for students with complex support needs. Students might have some or all of the following characteristics that make traditional forms of writing difficult:

- Challenges with fine or gross motor skills that prevent them from using traditional pen and paper or using a standard keyboard for word processing

- Challenges in gathering and/or organizing information or ideas to plan for writing

- Limited prior knowledge or instruction in writing, because these and other barriers have not been previously addressed by other teachers

In the following sections, we will discuss several categories of writing tools, why they are important to consider when creating a rich and engaging literacy environment, and what resources are available to help you begin using them. (See Chapter 10 for further examples of accessibility in writing instruction.)

Graphic Organizers   A convincing research base exists to support the use of graphic or "advanced" organizers with all students but especially those with disabilities (Kim, Vaughn, Wanzek, & Wei, 2004; Knight, Spooner, Browder, Smith, & Wood, 2013; Pashler et al., 2007). In addition, they were recommended for use in supporting text comprehension and vocabulary development by the National Reading Panel (2000). Graphic organizers, also discussed in subsequent chapters, typically assist with the following:

- Help students organize large amounts of information

- Allow students to visually represent information using colors, shapes, symbols, or links

- Help to show relationships between learned concepts such as cause and effect, compare and contrast, problems and solutions, or main ideas and supporting details

- Support vocabulary development

Research has further demonstrated the importance of using systematic instruction with graphic organizers to ensure that the purpose of the organizer is clearly communicated, along with supportive instruction and modeling that helps students understand how to best use the organizer to support both reading and writing instruction and practice.

Graphic organizers come in many shapes and sizes. From traditional, teacher-provided paper-and-pencil graphic organizers to general organizers such as a brainstorming web that students can draw themselves when needed, computer-generated graphic organizers provide additional options for accessibility. The Kidspiration Maps and Teachnology web sites provide graphic organizers you might use in your classroom to support rich and engaging literacy instruction. (See this chapter's Resources section for links.)

Speech-to-Text Programs   Ensuring that students have a way to document their thinking, learning, and ideas is essential. Speech-to-text (STT) software and applications are one means of doing so. In today's technology-rich world, there is no reason why students must "write" only by putting pencil to paper. Students who have fine or gross motor challenges may find it difficult to complete handwritten assignments; although it is sometimes important for them to work on building manual strength and dexterity, this work should be balanced with the use of other modes that allow them to communicate their message more easily. Furthermore, some students may have no movement of their arms or hands and therefore will not be able to use a word processor or traditional pencil and paper. None of these challenges means that a student cannot and should not be considered "a writer." We simply need to identify and remove barriers to support them as writers.

These programs should be available for all students but should especially be considered for students with complex support needs. STT applications allow the student to dictate a message and have it translated to text in a word processing document. Many software programs have additional features like auto playback and punctuation support. You can decide what features are best for your student and personalize the program. Note that the responsiveness and usability of certain free STT software and apps can vary greatly, particularly when students have difficulty with articulation. Our favorites include Dragon Anywhere and Chrome Voice Recognition. (See this chapter's Resources section for links.)

Word Processing Features   Most classrooms have access to computers with basic word processing applications already installed. We've become so accustomed to these common tools that we might not consider just what amazing resources they provide in terms of making our classrooms accessible and universally designed. In the following sections, we describe how various features can support all students' access to reading and writing instruction, activities, and assignments; all students, regardless of disability label, can benefit from mini-lessons or review lessons on the use of these features. Remember the importance of review and modeling; be sure to explicitly introduce and teach all of your students about the accessibility features and supports discussed in this chapter. Students cannot use something if they do not know it is available, know how to use it, and know your expectations!

Spell Check   Spell check can be a tremendously helpful resource in providing students with accessible opportunities to express themselves more independently. Students do not have to be conventional spellers for spell check to be a useful feature, but they do need a beginning understanding of what letters make particular sounds—for example, *c* says /k/ or *k* says /k/. (In the next section, we discuss some helpful word prediction add-ons that can further support students.) If used with the computer's TTS accessibility feature turned on, spell check can allow students to listen to the list of suggested options and select the word they need. If, however, you find that the red squiggly lines in the word processing document distract your student, this feature can be turned off so students can focus on drafting their message before using spell check to edit it.

Similarly, the autocorrect feature can be introduced to students; however, it is important to monitor its use to ensure that it enhances accessibility and does not create additional barriers. (Anyone who has ever sent a text message knows how incredibly frustrating autocorrect can be.)

Autotext   Autotext, or macros, a feature you might be less familiar with, can be a lifesaver in making writing accessible for students. Creating macros allows you to program shortcuts for text; for example, a macro could be set up to ensure that every time the letters *bc* are typed, the word processor will automatically fill in the word *because*. You can imagine how helpful this might be for many students, especially in this age of shorthand acronyms that are becoming mainstream like *ttyl* ("talk to you later") and *lol* ("laugh out loud"). The teacher could discuss these common acronyms in relation to macros so students understand how macros can be used— while also learning that these acronyms are not appropriate in certain forms of writing, such as school assignments and formal letters; this is why a computer without macros enabled converts them for you. (This feature combines accessibility with teachable moments!)

Grammar Check   Again, many adults use the grammar check feature routinely without necessarily considering how it can provide accessibility for students. Grammar check can indicate faulty sentences; the student might highlight the text and activate the TTS feature so they can hear what their text sounds like and think about what to change to make it grammatically correct. (Because grammar check sometimes flags sentences that are perfectly fine, use this feature with caution.)

Readability Statistics   Word processing software often includes, as an optional function within its spelling and grammar checks, a feature called *readability statistics*. This feature is helpful for teachers to use with digital texts or texts that have been converted from print to digital format using a word processing document. Readability statistics provide the usual word, paragraph, and line counts, but what is really useful is that they provide two different metrics for determining the selected text's grade level. Thus, teachers creating an adapted text (as described in Chapter 12) or creating a digital text from scanned print materials can use this feature to check its reading level to determine whether additional modifications should be made for a particular student.

Autosummarize   This feature, standard in versions of Word before 2010, may still be included in the word processing software you have available, so it is worth exploring. Macintosh computers allow users to turn on *Summarize* as a feature for the entire computer so that any text from any program can be highlighted and summarized. Certain free web sites, such as www.splitbrain.org, allow users to input text via cut-and-paste and then summarize this text. These autosummarize tools are useful because they can help teachers determine the most salient parts of the text when making adaptations. These tools also provide a helpful means for students to have digital text summarized to reinforce the main ideas; this can help ensure students can access the important points when reading lengthier texts. With autosummarize as with other accessibility tools, keep in mind the importance of teaching your students how to use these features and what expectations you have for their use. These expectations might vary across activities, so students must be familiar with different purposes for using the resource.

Templates and Outlines   All word processing programs include a variety of templates for taking notes and for creating brochures, newsletters, research papers, and so forth. In addition, many applications also allow users to import additional templates chosen from the wealth of options available online. Templates can impact student engagement because they are often novel and interesting to work with; what's more, they provide structure for students' writing projects. Because so many templates exist to choose from, this is an easy feature to introduce so all students know templates are available for them to use anytime.

Highlighting   All word processing software includes the option to highlight text, which can be useful when student writers need to emphasize particular words, phrases, or concepts. As a teacher, you might also use highlighting to draw students' attention to particular items within any electronic text you have imported into word processing software. Similarly, if students are using a template or outline to guide their writing process, you can highlight particular components to ensure students focus on specific items. In addition, highlighting can be used to color code—often a helpful strategy for increasing accessibility by helping students to distinguish between different types of information. This can be effective for various purposes, as long as students understand the different color codes used; a key can be inserted in the footer of the Word document.

Word Prediction   Word prediction options are available to individuals with disabilities through several programs, such as Applied Human Factors, Co:Writer, Read&Write, and WordQ. (To access these programs online, see the links in the Resources section at the end of this chapter.) Many of these programs were designed for individuals who have physical impairments as a way to reduce the number of keystrokes necessary to type words and to increase accuracy (Tumlin & Heller, 2004). Word prediction software suggests a list of possible intended words based on the beginning letter selected, the words used in the preceding string of text, and the frequency of other words used by the author (MacArthur, 2009). For individuals with reading and writing challenges, these programs provide options within their settings that also can increase spelling accuracy and support composition. More recently, word prediction has become a built-in feature on portable phones and tablets such as iPhones and iPads. Many apps and software programs can be purchased to work alongside other programs. For example, Co:Writer (Don Johnston) works with Write:OutLoud (Don Johnston) or Microsoft Word to assist in the writing process.

REFLECTION QUESTION 1

Take a moment to turn to the end of this chapter and look over the Resources section provided, which includes links to the various online resources mentioned previously. Visit the links to get a sense of what these resources provide. What are two web sites that you would like to use to make your classroom more accessible for students with complex support needs? Describe why you chose those particular web sites and how you might use them to increase accessibility for students.

A Final Word About Assistive Technology

As described in this book, UDL is about carefully designing learning environments from the beginning of the curriculum and instructional planning process in order to address student variability and provide access to academic and social communities. In the past, many of these technologies we have described were provided only for students designated under IDEA 2004 as having disabilities; for these students, based on assessment, the technologies were considered essential. Today, the literacy tools mentioned are accessible within popular technology and commonly used by students with and without disabilities. Students with complex support needs, however, may need more specialized assistive technology (AT) devices or services as well. In the textbox, "Assistive Technology Under IDEA," we delineate the right to AT devices and services under IDEA 2004. We include this here because it is important to be knowledgeable about services and resources that may be available and will help you provide accessible learning environments for students with complex support needs.

ASSISTIVE TECHNOLOGY UNDER IDEA

Through the individualized education program (IEP) process, the provision of AT can provide additional funding for schools to meet the needs of students with complex needs for support. Assistive technology tools are designed to compensate for a disability that limits a person's functional capabilities. IDEA 2004 differentiates between AT devices and services.

Assistive technology device means any item, piece of equipment, or product system, whether acquired commercially off the shelf, modified, or customized, that is used to increase, maintain, or improve the functional capabilities of a child with a disability. (IDEA 2004, 20 U.S.C. § 1401 [1])

Assistive technology service means any service that directly assists a child with a disability in the selection, acquisition, or use of an AT device. This term includes:

(A) the evaluation of the needs of a child with a disability, including a functional evaluation of the child in the child's customary environment

(B) purchasing, leasing, or otherwise providing for the acquisition of assistive technology devices by children with disabilities

(C) selecting, designing, fitting, customizing, adapting, applying, maintaining, repairing, or replacing assistive technology devices

(D) coordinating and using other therapies, interventions, or services with assistive technology devices, such as those associated with existing education and rehabilitation plans and programs

(E) training or technical assistance for a child with a disability or, where appropriate, the family of such child

(F) training or technical assistance for professionals (including individuals providing education or rehabilitation services), employers, or other individuals who provide services to, employ, or are otherwise substantially involved in the major life functions of such child. (IDEA 2004, 20 U.S.C. § 1401 [2])

INFORMATION PROCESSING IN CLASSROOM ENVIRONMENTS

Thus far, we have discussed UDL as it relates to the external learning environment; we turn now to internal factors that are equally important in ensuring students can access learning. Together with providing environments consistent with UDL principles, we also need to consider how students process information. Researchers can now examine the brain's functioning in unprecedented detail thanks to advances in imaging technologies such as magnetic resonance imaging (MRI), functional magnetic resonance imaging (fMRI), and positron emission tomography (PET). Classic studies in educational psychology focused on external observation of human behavior as the basis for intuiting how brains functioned. In contrast, these imaging technologies provide a window into the real-time neuronal activity associated with how our brains perceive environmental stimuli, process sensory input, and store information in memory—in other words, how brains learn. The knowledge gained from studies using these technologies, combined with results from classic educational psychology research, has produced a new level of understanding concerning the learning process—information that can guide educators interested in maximizing the impact of instruction (Tomlinson & Imbeau, 2010).

It is important to recognize the functioning of the brain is both highly complex and integrated across all of its parts in both hemispheres. Attempting to isolate a single part of the brain and *teach* it leads to educational fads such as the right brain–left brain hoopla in vogue some years ago, in which lessons were designed to accommodate either left-brained individuals, said to be more verbal and analytical, or right-brained individuals, said to be more artistic and emotional. In truth, both halves of the brain are actively engaged at all times during all activities, either analytic or creative, so the notion of left- or right-brained teaching strategies may be misguided. Nevertheless, it is a valid enterprise to work to make instruction more effective based on a more sophisticated understanding of how brains learn. That goal may be achieved more fruitfully by looking at the brain not structurally, but functionally. Keeping this in mind, let's examine how our brains process and store information.

The Information Processing Model

The information processing model (Gagne & Driscol, 1988; see Figure 5.1) describes the functions of the brain responsible for learning while ignoring the specific biological structures underlying those functions. In this model, the first thing that happens is that the environment generates a variety of stimuli that activate the body's sensory receptors. So, light enters the eye and triggers neurons on the retina, sound enters the ears and triggers neurons in the inner ear, particles enter the nose or mouth and trigger neurons associated with smell or taste, and stimulation of the skin triggers neurons associated with pressure, temperature, or pain.

Next, neurons transmit these stimuli to the brain, where they enter the sensory register, which is responsible for perceiving the stimuli's prominent features through a process of pattern recognition. For example, when you look at the letter *X,* it generates a visual stimulus that your brain's sensory register recognizes as two crossed lines—a familiar pattern. This process takes the merest fraction of a second before the information is transferred to the short-term or conscious memory, where it is coded into a meaningful concept (i.e., the crossed line pattern is associated with a stored memory of the letter *X,* retrieved from long-term memory). The consciousness is now aware that the letter *X* has been seen. This information will reside in short-term or conscious memory for a few seconds at most unless it is actively dealt with. Conscious memory might actively consider some aspect of the *X* or its meaning as part of a word within a sentence, which would result in the information being retained for a longer period. If the information in conscious memory is to be remembered, it is sent to the long-term memory, where it is stored for later retrieval.

You may be wondering how this functional description of the brain relates to improving student literacy. Good question. To answer it, we need to examine both conscious or short-term memory and long-term memory more deeply.

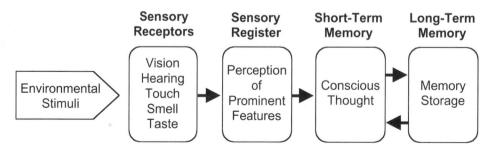

Figure 5.1. The information processing model (From Gagne, R.M., & Driscol, M.P. [1988]. *Essentials of learning for instruction* [2nd ed., p. 13]. Englewood Cliffs, NJ: Prentice Hall.)

Short-Term Memory

Short-term memory is constantly bombarded with incoming stimuli, far more than can be consciously dealt with. For example, right now, neurons are sending messages to your brain about the feel of your clothes against your skin and the pressure of your body against your chair, as well as ambient sounds; yet, until you read this sentence, you weren't consciously aware of any of those things. Instead, you've focused your attention on reading this book. Although people can consciously focus their attention for a period of time, choosing what to pay attention to is most often an unconscious process. As Patricia Wolfe (2001), author and consultant on brain-based teaching, suggests, children may be criticized for not paying attention, but in truth, everyone is always paying attention to something; it's just that students may not pay attention to what teachers would like. Most teachers would probably agree that students might learn more if they paid more attention to instructional tasks. Research offers clues as to what factors influence short-term memory in deciding where learners' attention will be focused: novelty, intensity, meaning, emotions, and the limited number of separate "bits" of information we can keep in short-term memory at any given time.

Novelty People pay more attention to what is new or different. Something as simple as putting up a new bulletin board or rearranging classroom desks will foster greater attention in a classroom. So will varying instructional styles, such as whole-class versus small-group; or delivery methods, such as overheads, lectures, videos, MS PowerPoint presentations, or manipulatives. Fisher and Frey (2003) discussed the importance of getting students' attention in order to teach literacy skills more effectively. They suggested that this can be done through demonstrations, discrepant events, visual displays, and/or thought-provoking questions. Similarly, many lesson plan formats include an anticipatory set as a critical element intended to gain student attention and interest before instruction. The anticipatory set is a short activity at the beginning of the lesson that connects to prior learning, focuses the students' attention, and prepares them to learn.

Intensity Students typically pay greater attention to more intense stimuli. Therefore, stimuli that are louder, faster, or more colorful than other competing stimuli are more likely to attract attention. Teachers make use of this fact when they use their "teacher voice" or incorporate colorful illustrations into instructional materials. Movement also affects where short-term memory focuses its attention, so teachers who act out story events or use props while reading aloud will command greater attention than those who sit passively in a chair.

Meaning Meaning also influences attention. For example, if we are in a group that spontaneously begins speaking Spanish and we speak only English, the meaning of the conversation vanishes and our attention begins to wander. It's no different for a child when instruction is unclear, disorganized, presented in too-broad steps, or riddled with unfamiliar words. Under such circumstances, students' attention will invariably wander.

Emotions Robert Sylwester, emeritus professor of education at the University of Oregon, is well known for his assertion that emotion drives attention, and attention drives learning (1995). A study conducted by Larry Cahill and James McGaugh (1995) at the University of California at Irvine demonstrates the point. Study participants were split into two groups, with each group viewing a slide show and listening to an accompanying story. Both stories used the same images of what appeared to be an accident scene, including images of a victim's badly mangled legs. One story indicated that no one had actually been injured because the accident scene was a staged disaster drill; a slide explained that make-up had been used on the legs of the "victim" to simulate injury and make the drill realistic. The other story, intended to engage listeners' emotions more, indicated that the images showed the scene of a real accident in which real people had been badly hurt; in this story, the young victim's legs were severed from his body and surgeons later struggled to reattach them. Two weeks later, the participants were tested to see how well they remembered specific story details. Those who were told that the accident scene was real remembered significantly more than those told it was staged (Cahill & McGaugh, 1995). What this and similar studies demonstrate is that people are more likely to remember things that engage their emotions.

As teachers, we can increase our students' emotional engagement in learning in many ways. One is to allow the students to pick their own topics of interest to study. For example, rather than being assigned a poem to analyze, or an animal to write about, the students can suggest questions they'd like to answer through science experiments. Another strategy is to pique students' curiosity by presenting a conundrum or puzzle as the lead-in to a lesson—another good example of an anticipatory set. Allowing students to work in groups can raise their emotional engagement. So can tying instruction to real-world questions and issues facing society; for example, students could investigate the plight of an endangered animal or write a state legislator and present an argument or proposal concerning a local issue. Letting students know that certain information will be covered on a test will also increase emotional engagement, although too much negative emotion in the form of anxiety or stress can be detrimental to learning.

We've discussed how novelty, intensity, meaning, and emotion all influence our capacity to pay attention. An example is the design of the children's television show *Sesame Street,* which is research-based; when we think about it, the elements influencing attention are obvious. Consider Big Bird. A giant, talking bird is certainly novel; his coloration is intense; he moves a lot as he walks and talks; he interacts with children on a meaningful level—and, if you've ever seen children with a *Sesame Street* fixation, they are definitely emotionally engaged! However, even when the factors discussed above are consciously used to influence attention, short-term memory nevertheless has limits.

Limited Capacity, or the "Miller Seven"   Another important characteristic of short-term memory for teachers to consider is its limited capacity. Research by George Miller, psychology professor emeritus at Princeton University, demonstrated that at most an adult's short-term memory can hold seven elements, plus or minus two, at any given time—the number of discrete elements of information within a telephone number, or perhaps a brief grocery list. For children, the limits are lower. At age 7, the limit is two; at 9, the limit is four; at 11, it is five; and at 13, it is six (Miller, 1956). It is important to remember that students with complex support needs may have even lower limits.

Teachers see evidence of these limits every day. Consider a student reading aloud who comes to an unfamiliar word, stops, and then starts sounding out the word letter by letter. After several seconds, she manages to piece it together, but she now has forgotten what the sentence was about, so she jumps back to the beginning of the sentence and starts over. This example illustrates how reading is a complex task requiring the decoding of letters and a given word while maintaining a memory of the preceding words and the sentence's overall meaning. Stumbling over an unfamiliar word and having to stop and sound it out letter by letter consumes the entire capacity of short-term memory, with the result that the meaning of the whole sentence is lost.

REFLECTION QUESTION 2

Given what we know about information processing and short-term memory, what can we learn from the success of commercials in persuading us to buy their products?

General Instructional Strategies to Support Short-Term Memory

What practical steps can teachers take to help students overcome the limited capacity of short-term memory? There are many.

Segment and Sequence Instruction   First and foremost, instructional materials should segment and sequence what is to be learned into manageable, logical steps. When each learning step is small and steps are ordered logically, students are able to follow the instruction without overwhelming their limited short-term memory in attempts to make sense of the instruction. A task analysis is used to break complex tasks into a sequence of smaller steps or actions. This is a good example of an instructional strategy using segmentation and sequencing that is particularly effective with students who have complex support needs. During instruction, teachers should also ensure that students aren't lost by checking for understanding—and by basing these checks on specific questions that require students to demonstrate their understanding by answering, not simply asking if students understand or have questions of their own. Students who are nonverbal can show through gestures, signs, or demonstration that they understand the instruction.

Provide Clear and Explicit Instructions   Another strategy for limiting cognitive load is to provide clear, explicit instructions as well as examples. If students are confused about what they should be doing to complete an assignment, figuring this out becomes the focus of attention, usurping short-term memory capacity that would be better used to focus on learning from the activity. Providing examples, such as completed sample items on a test or worksheet, can help clarify what is to be done, thereby allowing students to focus mental resources on the activity at hand.

Provide Scaffolds   Scaffolds are supports teachers use to help students by reducing the amount of information they need to hold in short-term memory while completing tasks. Examples of scaffolds used in literacy instruction include ABC charts posted in the room or on a student's desk, nametags on desks for quick reference, word walls, graphic organizers, and prompt questions for comprehension. These supports could be individualized or made available to the whole class through a bulletin board, chalkboard, handouts, manipulatives, or classroom wall space. Scaffolds are not meant as long-term supports but rather as temporary supports to students' thinking while they learn new information or processes. Mentally juggling a lot of information at once is a burden; by removing some of that burden for kids who are trying to complete a task, teachers can help ensure that their short-term memory limitations aren't exceeded. Some students with complex support needs may continue to need individual scaffolds to complete tasks independently.

Use Images and Graphics   Another strategy for reducing the demands on short-term memory during instruction is the use of images and graphics. We've all heard the saying "A picture is worth a thousand words." But why is this so? Insights were revealed through a series of studies—conducted by Ray Kulhavey in association with various graduate students at Arizona State University—which suggested that an entire image is processed as a single entity in short-term memory, so all the information in the image (spatial and otherwise) can be conveyed as just one of the roughly seven elements available during mental processing (Kulhavey, Stock, Verdi, Rittschof, & Savanye, 1993). That is, an image can convey a great deal of information as just one element; the same information presented in another format might be taken in as multiple elements, quickly using up our short-term memory's capacity to hold only seven (plus or minus two) elements. Embodying all of this information as a single entity reduces the impact on short-term memory. Therefore, using any type of graphic, such as pictures, diagrams, flow charts, timelines, or graphs, to support instruction will help prevent overburdening short-term memory capacity.

Many of the strategies useful for reducing demands on short-term memory also support students' ability to use long-term memory for storing and retrieving information. And it is through an understanding of how brains store and organize information in long-term memory that teachers can find the greatest insight into specific strategies for supporting student learning.

Long-Term Memory

Long-term memory is tasked with both storing everything a person learns and making it available for future recall on demand. How is this possible, given the vast quantity of information a person acquires over a lifetime and the limited number of neurons available for storage? People used to think the brain organized information like a filing cabinet, with the file folders made up of neurons. This theory supposed that a given localized group of neurons was responsible for storing a given piece of information, such as the concept of an apple.

However, brain imaging technologies show that when a person thinks of an apple, areas all over the brain are activated, including parts of the occipital lobes responsible for vision, parts of the temporal lobes responsible for hearing, and many other areas. Thinking of an apple activates all of those parts of the brain responsible for processing the incoming stimuli that you associate with experiencing an apple: seeing its round shape and red color, smelling its scent, hearing its crunch when it is bitten, feeling its texture when held, and experiencing its feel and taste in the mouth. Researchers realized the concept of the apple wasn't stored in a single location by a dedicated set of neurons but rather is stored as a spiderweb-like pattern of neuronal activation throughout the brain. If a person is asked to think of a banana, a different pattern of neuronal activation in each of the brain's processing areas will result. It is these differing spider-web patterns of activation that represent stored learning and memory; this is highly efficient because any given neuron can play a part in many different memories.

These complex spiderweb patterns are called *schemes*. You have one scheme for an apple, and another for a banana, and yet another for a Ford Mustang. But the schemes are not limited to these items' physical properties. Each scheme also includes any other related pieces of information. In the case of the apple, the scheme links to the concept of stories involving apples, and from there, to specific details of stories such as the biblical story of Adam and Eve or the fairy tale of Snow White. The scheme also links to the different types of apples, their colors and tastes, and the varied dishes made from apples. The scheme might include links to historical information about the spread of apple trees and Johnny Appleseed, as well as links to information about apple cultivation in orchards, or ways in which apples are propagated and harvested or crushed for their juice. The links within the scheme keep expanding, tying together more and more information. Recalling any given specific piece of information requires accessing that part of the scheme where it lies, and this recall can be accomplished by following any series of links within the scheme that lead to it.

General Instructional Strategies to Support Long-Term Memory

Once you understand that a scheme is a complex pattern of informational nodes connected by links, and that recalling specific information you have learned is a process of following those links back to the appropriate node, you have a powerful insight into how to make instruction more effective. Suppose you want your students to learn something such as how the letter *c* can make the sound /k/ or /s/. You know that this phonics fact represents a node that will be linked to other information as part of a scheme and that recalling this fact later will require following links back to the original information node. How can you increase the probability that a student will be able to do that?

One way is to create as many links as possible to the newly learned fact. Poorly defined schemes with few links make accessing a given information node more difficult; more robust, better developed schemes, with more links to a given piece of information, make this access easier. The reason for this is simple: more links allow for more "paths" back to any given piece of information. With a greater number of well-developed links, if the student isn't successful recalling the information following one set of links, he or she could access it another way. In contrast, when using a scheme with only a few tenuous links, the student has few options for recall. If the first attempt doesn't work, there may be no other options to try, with the result that the information can't be accessed.

Create Links Through Multiple Senses How can teachers support students in creating multiple links to a given concept or fact? Recall that brain scans of people thinking of an apple showed activity in all areas of the brain associated with the sensory experience of an apple. With that in mind, consider how to teach that *c* makes the sound /k/ or /s/. If you can associate a student's learning with multiple senses, each sense will contribute its own links to the scheme, resulting in more available links the student can use to get back to the learning. These multisensory approaches are used in many reading programs (e.g., Wilson Reading Program, Animated Literacy, Patterns for Success). Accordingly, you could have students use manipulatives to show different representations of the letter *c* in the beginning, middle, and end of words; this would use sight and touch. You could recite words and rhymes using the letter *c*, which involves speaking and hearing. Students could form the letter *c* with their bodies or draw it in shaving cream, thereby using sight, touch, and kinesthetics. Many creative teachers have known for years that engaging multiple senses in instruction results in better learning. But other factors also contribute to the creation of more robust schemes with more links that connect new learning to what is already known.

Connect to Prior Learning

Research done in the 1880s graphically demonstrated how difficult it can be to learn information if it has few or no links to previous learning. German researcher Hermann Ebbinghaus investigated how people learn in the absence of the previous knowledge, learning, and experiences that are normally available. He memorized random lists of nonsense syllables such as *doj* or *geb*—thus ensuring that there was essentially no connection between the syllables and any prior knowledge he might have. Although he memorized them well enough that he could confidently repeat each list when given the first syllable, the memory was short-lived. He discovered that after 24 hours, he could recall fewer than 50% of the syllables, and after 48 hours, only 35% (Ebbinghaus, 1913). This clearly suggests that rote memorization as a learning strategy—the learning of isolated facts not tied to an existing scheme—is far from successful.

As teachers, we can do much to support students in linking new learning to existing schemes. When designing instruction, we can begin lessons by connecting that day's topic to prior lessons or learning. Thus, a teacher might begin a lesson on the Incas' stepped pyramids by asking students to think about what they know about Egyptian pyramids. Connecting to prior learning represents the first step in most systematic lesson design models—for example, Madeline Hunter's (1994) seven-step model, taught in preservice teaching programs.

Teachers can also help students forge links during lessons by relating new content to prior learning. One way is to use metaphors, similes, and analogies, each of which compares something new with something known. During a lesson on Incan pyramids, the teacher could use metaphor, simile, or analogy to link a new concept—thousands of workers cooperating to construct the pyramids—to a familiar one, bees working to construct a hive. This link would help students better understand the Incan workers' organization and cooperation.

Engage Students at Higher Levels of Bloom's Taxonomy

Another way to forge more links within a scheme is to engage students on a deeper mental level during learning. Benjamin Bloom (1956) created a taxonomy describing different levels of thinking, the lowest levels of which are *knowledge* and *comprehension*. Knowledge and comprehension represent the type of thinking required to memorize and regurgitate facts—for example, recognizing the symbol *M* and knowing the sound it stands for. Above these two levels is *application*, the level where knowledge is used to solve real-world problems—for example, applying knowledge of letter sounds to read. Above the application level are *analysis, synthesis,* and *evaluation,* each a successively deeper level of thought and engagement. Analysis, an assessment of meaning, would be reflected in finding the theme of a poem or the pattern in a set of data. Synthesis, the creation of something new, might involve rewriting *Goldilocks and the Three Bears* from the perspective of the bears. Evaluation, the judging of something by a set of criteria, would be reflected in the critique of a novel or painting.

Instruction that engages students in deeper levels of thinking, as represented by Bloom's taxonomy, results in the development of a more complex conceptual scheme whose information nodes and associated links are greater in number and complexity. Such instruction is the exact opposite of the rote memorization investigated by Ebbinghaus. Although Ebbinghaus rapidly lost the ability to recall nonsense syllables, research demonstrates that instruction engaging students at higher levels of Bloom's taxonomy results in greater recall, in both the short and long term.

Bring Recall to the Level of Automaticity

So far, the strategies we have discussed for supporting long-term memory have focused on increasing the number and complexity of links within a scheme as a way to increase a learner's likelihood of accessing and understanding a given fact or memory. Another means for supporting the recall of information from long-term memory is to strengthen the links leading to it—in fact, to make them as strong as possible. This is analogous to following a path through a forest: It's easier to follow a well-worn path than one used less often. In the same way, it's easier to follow a well-worn path of links in the brain.

How does this translate to classroom teaching? There are certain types of learning that we want students to know to the point where they can access and use the learning automatically. This is called bringing learning to a point of automaticity. Skills teachers would want students to master at this level include sound–symbol relationships, sight words, and writing conventions (e.g., capitalization, punctuation). Because these skills are so basic, we want students to access and use them without conscious thought. The way to achieve that is through practice. Each time a student decodes *c* as /k/ or /s/, the link to that fact is reinforced. With sufficient repetition, the neuronal links within the scheme become so strong that accessing that information becomes fast and automatic. With no conscious thought required to recall the information, there is no imposition on short-term memory limits, allowing conscious memory to engage in more meaningful pursuits.

What does this mean for learning, based on the examples given previously? When basic sound–symbol relationships are each a level of automaticity during decoding, short-term or conscious memory can focus fully on the process of comprehension. When teaching basic writing conventions like capitalization and punctuation, requiring students to use them for all curricular areas and assignments will result in their use becoming automatic over time. Therefore, teachers can move beyond expecting students to use complete sentences in writing assignments. They can also embed spelling words into complete sentences, with students responsible for writing the entire sentence on their papers, or have students write complete sentences in response to short-answer questions on a science test. Through repetition, use of correct writing conventions will be raised to a level of automaticity, freeing short-term memory resources to focus on the writing's content.

In the following sections, we explore how these understandings of information processing influence the environments we create for our students. If teachers develop their classroom environments intentionally, they can maximize the benefits of what is known about short- and long-term memory. This supports universally designed instruction that is accessible to all students. The rest of the chapter will describe and discuss specific instructional tools and strategies that lead to the creation of rich literacy learning environments.

SPECIFIC INSTRUCTIONAL EXAMPLES

This section will include concrete examples of instruction consistent with the two big ideas to consider in instructional planning: UDL and information processing. Please see other chapters throughout the book for additional concrete examples of unit plans, lesson plans, strategies, and resources consistent with the provision of accessible, rich literacy environments.

Using Environmental Print

In general, a print-rich environment is characterized by easy access to the printed word in multiple formats and genres, together with ways to engage actively with the printed word (Keefe et al., 2010). The concept of print richness should not be confined to the classroom or school environment. Naturally occurring environmental print is a great source of vocabulary instruction for students, particularly students with complex support needs, as will be discussed in Chapter 9. Environmental print consists of high-frequency print found in the home and community environments, such as common signs (e.g., STOP, EXIT, IN, OUT), business signs (e.g., Kmart, Wendy's, Car Wash), and product packaging (e.g., Coke, Pepsi, Fruit Loops, Starburst). It has many advantages in that it is readily available, cheap, highly motivating, and age appropriate. Because environmental print naturally builds upon students' prior knowledge about the world around them and their ability to associate symbols consistently with an object, it can be used to develop skills in all areas of literacy:

- *Oral language.* Preschool and elementary school students can "show and tell" their favorite food, drink, and toy. Middle school students can use environmental print from magazines, newspaper, web sites, and other media to support a discussion of what they would buy if they won the lottery. High school students can use similar media to talk about a current political or sporting event, such as an election.

- *Letter recognition.* Students can use environmental print to make books or posters showing objects that begin with target letters, or to compose acrostic poems using the letters of their name.

- *Phonemic awareness/phonics.* Environmental print could be used to enhance a word wall to help elementary students identify the initial, medial, and final sounds in a word and/or the letters in these positions. Cards using environmental print could support students in learning word families (e.g., *man, can, plan*). Students can demonstrate phonics knowledge by sorting words in environmental print items by the words' initial, medial, and final sounds. Environmental print cards can act as signal words to help students remember sound–symbol relationships (e.g., *Cheerios* for the digraph /ch/).

- *Vocabulary.* One way to use environmental print to support vocabulary development is to have students classify and sort environmental print words and pictures—for instance, words or pictures representing foods that need to be refrigerated and those that do not, clothing items for different seasons, or different emotions. Many more examples of using environmental print to support vocabulary development, such as reading the room, can be found in Chapter 8.

- *Fluency.* One fun way to work on fluency using environmental print is to have a "readers theater" focused on presenting advertisements in magazines or other media. Another is repeated reading of favorite magazine articles or comics. Teachers can also conduct read-alouds using newspapers, magazines, or other media. Finally, note that fluency includes fluent silent reading, which students can practice using environmental print media such as magazines.

- *Comprehension.* Students can complete sentences by choosing environmental print words ("On my birthday, I like to eat [*cake, ice cream, elephant, iPad*]") so that the sentence makes sense—or create new sentences this way. Other ways environmental print could be incorporated are to retell a field trip experience using photographs, sort items named in environmental print into categories (e.g., *alive* and *not alive*), or compare and contrast advertisements for competing brands of items such as cars, phones, or mascara.

- *Writing.* Students can create stories or poems using environmental print as a writing prompt, or they can use environmental print to create a teen magazine or write a commercial for an item such as car, phone, or restaurant. Teachers can use environmental print to facilitate language experience activities (see Chapter 6) or create MadLibs-style compositions with blanks for students to complete using environmental print words.

Many of these ideas address multiple areas of literacy instruction. Environmental print can also be used to supplement or augment other strategies such as semantic feature analysis, language experience, time-delay sight-word instruction, making words, spelling programs, and so forth.

REFLECTION QUESTION 3

How might the use of environmental print connect home, community, and school environments?

Creating Anchor Charts

Just as an anchor holds and keeps something in place, such as a boat, an anchor chart provides students with clear, precise expectations that will help "anchor" their learning. Simply put, an anchor chart is a tool used largely to support instruction and to move the student toward achieving success within the classroom. Anchor charts are created during instruction with students. The teacher states the purpose of the activity and models the lesson, concept, or new strategy. Then, the teacher guides the students through a classroom discussion on the topic. Next, the teacher records their co-constructed ideas from the discussion on chart paper, which becomes the anchor chart. The anchor chart itself can be a piece of construction paper, butcher paper, or chart paper, or it can even be constructed in a table using MS PowerPoint or other word processing software, so long as available classroom technology allows you to project the chart on the wall so that students can actively engage with it as it is being developed. (See Figure 5.2 for an example of an anchor chart used for a nonfiction author study.) In this example, the teacher is using a table in a MS PowerPoint document to construct the anchor chart with the students. The teacher would have the table headings created ahead of time: *title, text features, examples, and how they helped us*. The teacher selects the text features that are the focus of the lesson and works through at least one example with the whole class before asking students to identify these text features on their own. When teaching older students, a teacher might construct a class anchor chart but also have students document the chart in their journals to refer to independently in the future—for example, by copying and writing it on their own, writing on a teacher-provided template, or pasting a printed electronic version. In this way, the teacher ensures that students have the chart easily accessible.

Once the chart is complete, the teacher displays it strategically where the students can easily refer to it as a resource. Students can also add ideas as they apply new learning (Dorn & Soffos, 2005). Teachers and students can add to these charts by recording important facts, useful strategies, steps in a process, or quality criteria (Dorn & Soffos, 2005). In addition, an anchor chart provides the same expectations for all students, regardless of their ability. In turn, it can provide access to students who struggle with complex concepts. It is especially helpful for students who are visual learners.

Because the students and teacher actively work together to create an anchor chart, these charts are instructional artifacts that are *co-constructed* by a teacher and students. An anchor

Our nonfiction author study of Seymour Simon			
Title	Text features	Examples	How they helped us...
Mountains	*Pictures/photographs*	*Photo of Mount Everest*	*Ask questions about the text, such as* ❑ *What is the weather like on the mountain?* ❑ *Who has climbed the mountain; what are their stories?*
	Descriptive words and phrases	*Old, worn mountains*	*Visualize and make comparisons* ❑ *How mountains wear down over time like the knees on an old pair of jeans*

Figure 5.2. Sample anchor chart for an author study: Seymour Simon, Mountains.

chart within a classroom community provides students access and security to their learning by providing them a co-constructed reference (Dorn & Soffos, 2005). They can also provide an important way to introduce new concepts and ideas. Because they are co-constructed, they provide students with opportunities to have enriched discussions, and students can learn how to use the information on the chart as needed throughout a lesson or school year. An anchor chart not only makes learning accessible for all students, but it can also be used to teach many literacy components. According to Dorn and Soffos, anchor charts are commonly used to teach literacy concepts based on the needs of the students. Dorn and Soffos stated that teachers traditionally teach discrete skills, but the authors believed that the focus should be on creating opportunities for students to become problem solvers who have a deeper understanding of knowledge. An anchor chart can be used to create literacy-rich classroom conditions, which can help activate students' thinking processes because it is a tangible resource on the classroom walls to which both teachers and students can refer often. For example, an anchor chart could be helpful to use in teaching guided reading guidelines for writer's workshop (see Figure 5.3), expectations for centers/rotations, and guidelines for peer discussions (Dorn & Soffos, 2005). Additionally, a teacher may use an anchor chart to teach other skills such as figurative language, the use of conversational moves (specific phrases used to keep a discussion moving, such as "I agree with...," "I would like to add to the conversation by...," etc.) during a literature discussion, examples of punctuation (see Figure 5.4), how to pick a "just right" book, and genre and author studies (Dorn & Soffos, 2005).

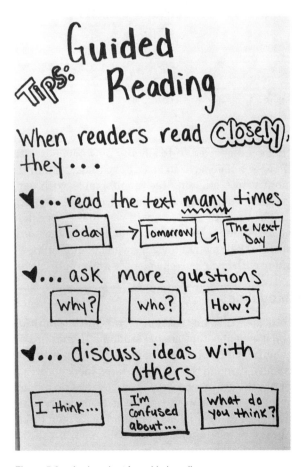

Figure 5.3. Anchor chart for guided reading.

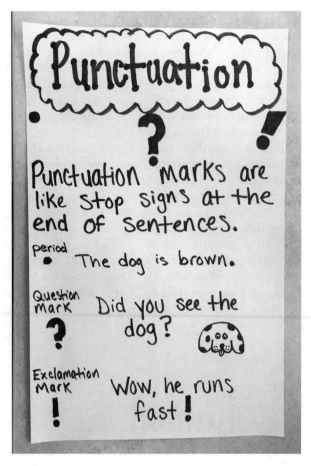

Figure 5.4.　Anchor chart for punctuation.

An anchor chart can be used to teach *any* new concept within a classroom. It requires a marker, a piece of paper, a teacher who has a deep understanding of the needs of their students, and an environment where students feel comfortable with expressing and discussing their thoughts. Easier said than done, right? Wrong! If you have high expectations for all students and start using anchor charts, your students will rise to the occasion and you will be successfully providing them access to more complex concepts and higher-order thinking skills. When students are co-creators of their own knowledge, you not only empower them to be critical thinkers but also provide them with enriched experiences and create a love for learning.

Incorporating Multiple Modalities

Schema theory indicates that instruction incorporating multiple modalities (or senses) will result in more robust schemes that enable students to more easily recall learned information. For example, presenting the alphabet visually, on a poster, incorporates one modality—sight; presenting it musically, through the alphabet song, incorporates a different modality—hearing; drawing the letters in the air incorporates the kinesthetic modality; and making letters out of sandpaper or shaving foam incorporates the tactile modality. This occurs as each different modality used during the learning process contributes its own links within a conceptual scheme, with each new link serving as a potential means for recalling the information. Teaching by using multiple modalities helps all students learn, but it can be particularly important for those who have complex support needs.

Multiple Modalities and the Theory of Multiple Intelligences   Howard Gardner (1983) popularized teaching using multiple modalities or senses through his theory of multiple intelligences (MI). This theory questions the narrow definition of *intelligence* embodied in traditional intelligence and achievement tests that educators use. Gardner proposed that there are at least seven intelligences: logical–mathematical, linguistic, spatial or visual, musical, kinesthetic (involving body movement), interpersonal, and intrapersonal (involving self-knowledge). Gardner was concerned that many students are not viewed as intelligent because they cannot perform well on tests designed to measure logical–mathematical and linguistic abilities only. Note that MI theory does not suggest that there are seven *types* of people, rather that all people possess and can develop each intelligence; moreover, these multiple intelligences are not mutually exclusive and often work together. The importance of MI theory is that students are acknowledged for their intelligences and allowed to use all intelligences to increase their learning. Armstrong (2000) proposed many ways in which Gardner's theory could be used to design classroom instruction that would enable a diverse group of learners to be successful.

An Example of Multiple Intelligences in the Classroom   Suppose students are studying World War I in a 10th-grade world history class. Competencies to be addressed include the ability to describe and discuss the war's causes and its impact on different countries' economic, political, and social development. In addition, students will be demonstrating reading, writing, and oral-language skills and their ability to use varied sources to research a topic. This history class includes Karen, a 16-year-old girl who has multiple disabilities, including intellectual and physical disabilities. Karen's individual goals include using an augmentative and alternative communication (AAC) device for communication and for improving her receptive language and sight-word reading skills, maintaining her range of motion in limbs, and improving her fine motor skills through grasping objects. Instructional strategies and activities for the unit include the following elements, which address different modalities and intelligences:

- Lectures (linguistic)

- Advance organizers, overhead transparencies, and videos (spatial)

- Discussion and group work (interpersonal)

- Journals and letter writing (intrapersonal)

- Music from the 1914–1918 era (musical)

- Reenactment of life in the trenches (kinesthetic)

- Debate on the causes of the war and factors leading to victory (logical)

- Graphs of the casualties and population change in participating nations (logical, spatial)

- Museum exhibit for the school library exploring various aspects of the war and its aftermath (linguistic, logical, spatial, and interpersonal)

These instructional strategies and activities enable Karen to participate meaningfully by listening and answering questions, using her communication device to join the discussion, learning sight words connected to the unit, using the computer to research information, and using gross and fine motor skills to help make the museum display. These multimodal activities create more links within her information scheme, and the increased links, in turn, increase the likelihood that she will successfully recall the information when desired.

Cooperative Learning

Research has demonstrated that cooperative learning benefits students with and without disabilities (Johnson & Johnson, 1989; Putnam, 1998; Sapon-Shevin, Ayres, & Duncan, 2002).

Cooperative learning is structured group work designed to incorporate five major elements (Johnson, Johnson, & Holubec, 1993):

1. *Positive interdependence,* which requires that there be a reason for students to work together. Students with complex support needs can have meaningful roles in the group.

2. *Individual accountability,* which requires that students be held accountable for their learning within the group. Goals can be adapted to the individual needs of students with moderate or severe disabilities.

3. *Cooperative skills,* which must be taught as part of cooperative learning; teachers cannot assume students will know how to work together effectively. Cooperative learning groups provide an opportunity for students with complex support needs to learn and practice social skills.

4. *Face-to-face interaction,* which is important to ensure interaction among group members

5. *Group processing,* which is important in evaluating the effectiveness of the group. Students will often have better ideas than adults about how to modify the cooperative group structures for students with complex support needs.

When students with complex support needs are included in general education classrooms, cooperative learning is an effective way to facilitate meaningful participation and interaction with peers.

Cooperative learning can be used in many ways in classroom instruction and can benefit students with a range of needs. For example, Barbara is a student with Down syndrome in a second-grade classroom. Barbara is an emergent literacy learner who has not yet developed conventional reading and writing skills. Barbara can communicate using short sentences, gestures, and pictures. Her class is working in cooperative groups to create a model of their small rural town; each group has chosen one building to recreate. Students work in groups of four to build their structures (face-to-face interaction). Group members must share materials (positive interdependence and cooperative skills). Each student must tell the class about which part of the building he or she created (individual accountability). Students talk to the teacher about how well their group was able to share materials and work together (group processing). Because this activity does not involve reading and writing, Barbara needs no special modifications for this lesson. It also gives her a natural opportunity to work on her social interaction and communication skills.

Another student, Michael, is a sixth grader with complex support needs; he does not speak and has extremely limited movement. As a cooperative group activity in his science class, students are measuring the pH of various foods. Michael is the materials manager during this activity, providing a place on his wheelchair tray for the materials students will use (positive interdependence). When the students pick up their materials, they interact verbally with Michael and note whether he makes eye contact and smiles at them (individual accountability, cooperative skills, and face-to-face interaction). After the group activity, the students are asked to evaluate their interactions and to suggest ways in which Michael could better participate in the future (group processing).

Another student with complex support needs, Celeste, is a ninth grader with a diagnosis of autism. Students in her classroom are doing a cooperative math activity that involves developing a budget for a simulated career and living situation. Celeste plays the role of fact checker, using her calculator to make sure her group's checkbook calculations are correct (positive interdependence and individual accountability). She is working on physically staying within her group during the activity (face-to-face interaction and cooperative skills). Celeste and the other students in the group later complete a self-evaluation about how well they each contributed to their group (group processing).

PUTTING IT ALL TOGETHER TO CREATE A UNIVERSAL DESIGN FOR LEARNING CLASSROOM

Now that you are more familiar with UDL and have some great ideas for resources and strategies that you can use in your classroom, we would like to share a checklist you can use to evaluate your classroom environment (see Figure 5.5). You can use this periodically throughout the year to ensure that you are implementing UDL in ways that make your classroom accessible to all students and to address areas you think might need improvement. Remember, UDL is about proactively removing barriers to learning for your students, and the climate you create in your classroom is vital to ensuring accessibility.

Each section of the checklist aligns to UDL principles and is consistent with supporting information processing. In the next section, we will describe what each of these items might look like in your classroom.

Examining the Environment for Multiple Means of Representation (Presentation)

Adhering to the following guidelines helps ensure that your classroom environment allows for multiple means of representation.

1. Classroom resources are organized and displayed clearly throughout the room. As discussed at the beginning of this chapter, the importance of the environment cannot be overstated; it should therefore be intentionally constructed to best support student learning. The first part of the UDL checklist addresses two points: what is represented in the classroom environment and how that supports the presentation of content and instruction. Enter a classroom for students of any age and subject and it will undoubtedly have "things" on the wall—potentially useful resources. For example, we have talked about what a powerful resource anchor charts can be when used purposefully and co-constructed. When thinking about the charts' actual content, and the content of other posted classroom resources such as lists of rules and procedures, consider how to make them accessible to all learners. Ask yourself: Is the print large (and legible) enough for students to read? Do students know how to locate relevant anchor charts, rules, and procedures and how to use them? Have you included visuals along with the text? These could take the form of magazine cutouts to represent key vocabulary, pictures of procedures to illustrate each step of a process, or drawings constructed by you or the students. How about considering tactile representations? We do not often think about how to make things we post on our classroom walls kinesthetically accessible, but this can be done quite easily.

Consider the author study example from the "Creating Anchor Charts" section, for instance. To help students access and engage with the content, we used puffy paint to outline the first letter of the title of each book. In other anchor charts, we have paired vocabulary, such as words for character traits, with a texture students could associate with the word (e.g., sandpaper for the word *gruff*). If students in your classroom will frequently be expected to follow important procedures, such as procedures for small-group activities, you could take pictures of your students performing each step (e.g., gather materials, move desks together) and paste them next to the text. Small recording devices, such as might be found in Build-a-Bear stores, can be used to record the text; these can then be attached to the wall with a push pin so students can play the audio that accompanies the anchor chart. We have included some essentials in the checklist.

2. Distractions are minimized. Most classrooms include posters with inspirational quotes, and posters or charts with content-specific information such as the periodic table, multiplication facts, descriptions of literature genres, and so forth. Although it is definitely necessary to post a few such resources, having too many can be visually distracting or even overwhelming, especially if they are not used on a regular basis. We like to post a couple of favorites at the beginning of the year, but as the school year progresses, we focus instead on anchor charts and other meaningful, purposeful resources created with students. This helps to minimize distractions and ensure

Presentation/Representation

❏ Classroom resources (rules, anchor charts) are organized and displayed clearly throughout the room.
   ❏ Print is large enough to read.
   ❏ Students know how to locate resources and what they are used for.
   ❏ Visuals are presented with text.
   ❏ Tactile representations are available with text.
   ❏ Important procedures are posted with visual, tactile, and audio support.
   ❏ Checklists, graphic organizers, and sticky notes are available for student use.
❏ Distractions are minimized (e.g., classroom displays are purposeful and not overwhelming; background noise is dampened).

❏ Instructional areas are clearly defined.
   ❏ Classroom library (if applicable)
   ❏ Supplies are organized and labeled.
   ❏ Student work spaces are defined.
   ❏ Technology is accessible and organized.
   ❏ Instructional presentation occurs in a place accessible for all students.
   ❏ Visually accessible
   ❏ Auditorily accessible
   ❏ Physically accessible

❏ Options are present for interacting with instruction and materials (e.g., content is auditorily, visually, and kinesthetically accessible during all phases of instruction).

Expression

❏ Students have opportunities to make choices about
   ❏ Seating
   ❏ Supplies available for use
   ❏ Instructional materials

❏ Communication needs are addressed.
   ❏ Computers/tablets are accessible and available.
   ❏ Students' personal communication devices interface with instructional delivery and materials.
   ❏ Manipulatives are accessible and available (e.g., magnetic letters, letter cards, word cards).
   ❏ Resources and materials are available in different modes.
   ❏ Audio texts/books are available.
   ❏ Materials are available in other languages as needed.

❏ Classroom displays support student expression and interaction with instructional objectives.

Engagement

❏ Room arrangement allows for different instructional configurations.
   ❏ Space for whole-group instruction
   ❏ Conducive to independent work (e.g., quiet spaces with room to work)
   ❏ Options for small-group collaboration (e.g., tables, easily moved desks, floor space)

❏ Classroom is physically accessible.
   ❏ Walkways are clear.
   ❏ Supplies and resources are easy to reach.

❏ Background noise is dampened.
❏ Classroom sound-field amplification system is used.
❏ Student work is displayed in an organized space in room.
❏ Students can choose from a variety of materials.

Figure 5.5. Universal design for learning checklist based on the work of CAST (http://www.cast.org).

that displays are relevant and supportive. As we have emphasized, when used well, co-creating classroom displays can be a powerful way to enhance the accessibility of the content you present.

When considering the accessibility of instruction you present, it is important also to think about how to dampen background noise to maximize students' ability to interact with learning experiences. If you have a noisy hallway nearby, consider setting up student desks and whole-group instructional areas well away from the door so students can focus on what they are learning instead of having to discriminate between two sources of auditory input: your teaching and the outside noise. Noise generated within the classroom (e.g., by small-group discussions) should also be considered when planning the location of small-group or individual work spaces.

3. Instructional areas are clearly defined.
No matter what type of classroom you have, you will need to think about how to use the space for instruction and related activities. Will you have a classroom library? If so, how will you ensure that it is organized, labeled, and accessible for your students? How will you organize and label available supplies? Where will students do independent or group work, and where will you provide whole-group instruction? Where will you set up computers, interactive white boards, document cameras, tablet stations, laptops, and playback devices for audio recordings and books? How will you ensure that any classroom technology is readily available and accessible for both your use and students' use? When thinking about the different features of student accessibility, consider how all of these elements will be visually, auditorily, and physically accessible.

4. Options are present for interacting with instruction and materials.
This UDL checklist item emphasizes the importance of ensuring that you consider how to use multiple means of presentation to deliver content instruction and provide students with modeling and opportunities for guided practice. (See the lesson plan examples in Chapter 11.) If the interactive whiteboard at the front of your classroom serves more as a coat rack than an instructional tool, or if your students are rarely provided options for how to interact with your instruction and related materials, you might need to revisit this checklist item and change your environment and instruction to ensure accessibility. Allowing students choices about how to respond to content presented might include the use of sticky notes to write responses to questions you ask as you guide them through new material, or the use of a PowerPoint presentation that is also uploaded to a computer or tablet for an individual student to access and take notes with. Students also benefit from being provided options for accessing related instructional materials. For example, if you are conducting an interactive read-aloud in which you present a book to the class and expect students to listen for particular information such as the setting, author's purpose, or character traits, you might provide a graphic organizer that helps students focus on the elements you've identified, a laminated copy of the text for following along, or an adapted version of the text (see Chapter 12) that allows students to process what you are reading aloud in a more accessible manner.

Examining the Environment for Multiple Means of Expression

Following these guidelines helps ensure that your classroom environment allows for multiple means of expression.

1. Students have opportunities to make choices.
It is essential to consider how your students best express their learning and knowledge. Students should have choices about the way they interact with the instructional content (as discussed previously in the section on presentation) as well as how they communicate their learning and knowledge. (See Chapter 2 for more on this topic.) To promote multiple means of expression, provide students with choices about their seating arrangements. Do they learn best when standing or when sitting? Do they need a wiggle seat or an exercise ball? Are barriers to student expression removed (e.g., have communication devices been programmed with the vocabulary needed to participate in discussion; have needed symbols been added to a communication board; are there options for both written and

verbal response), both when they have their own defined individual learning space and when they are seated in groups?

Beyond seating arrangements, do students know what materials they will use to communicate their learning and will they have the opportunity to choose among different materials? For example, if you have asked students to take notes during whole-group instruction, can they choose to use index cards, sticky notes, or notebook paper? Are computers, laptops, and tablets available as options, and do students know how to use them? What about instructional materials? If the class is examining the impact of setting in literature, do students have a choice about what book they will read to apply this knowledge? Is the literature available in audio and text format and can students choose how they will read the text? These are just a few specific examples of ways students should be able to make choices about instructional materials they use to demonstrate their own learning.

2. Communication needs are addressed.

If students have no way to communicate, they do not have access to instruction and have no real opportunity to learn (Kleinert et al., 2015). Students' communication needs should be at the forefront of environmental and instructional considerations for any grade, age, or perceived ability level. (See Chapter 2 for more information.) Students must have the means to communicate; it is our role as educators to ensure that their needs are addressed—period. In our technologically advanced age, this means that computers and tablets should be available for student use at all times. If students have personal communication devices like GoTalk, BIGmack, or NovaPro, you should ensure that they interface with instructional delivery and materials in a way that allows students full access to the learning experiences you facilitate. That might mean additional planning and preparation on your part, but communication is a universal right. It should therefore be addressed in a way that it is embedded throughout both the classroom environment and instruction.

In addition, manipulatives should be accessible and available for all students to use. Resources and materials should be available in multiple modes (visual, auditory, kinesthetic/tactile), just as we present instruction in multiple modes. Audio texts and resources should be available for students. If you work in a school where particular languages, such as Spanish or American Sign Language, are prevalent, having materials available in these languages, and using these languages to interact with students, must occur as a universally designed consideration instead of as an individualized accommodation.

3. Classroom displays support student expression and interaction with instructional objectives.

As discussed in the previous section on presentation, classroom displays should be intentional, supportive, and accessible. Anchor charts, class procedures, and other displays in the environment should be relevant to learning objectives and provide scaffolding and support that help students to interact with instruction and demonstrate their own learning. A great example of this is the use of co-constructed anchor charts that illustrate procedures or provide examples related to a particular instructional objective.

Examining the Environment for Multiple Means of Engagement

The guidelines below help ensure that your classroom environment allows for multiple means of engagement.

1. Room arrangement allows for different instructional configurations.

Much of what we have previously discussed applies also to ensuring accessibility by addressing multiple means of engagement. You will also see this item reflected in the universally designed differentiated instruction (UD-DI) checklist included within the lesson plan format in Chapter 11. You will want to make sure that your classroom has a defined space for whole-group instruction, along with spaces where students can work independently and be free from auditory and visual distractions. Additionally, it is important to promote small-group work by ensuring that your classroom space can be easily used for classmates to gather with each other and with you to complete learning activities. There will undoubtedly be times when you have students working in multiple configurations, especially if you provide students the choice of working in the arrangement most conducive to their own learning and processing style. To support those who will work independently while others work together, you might make noise-cancelling headphones available for student use and place study carrels in corners or spaces with few distractions. To communicate clearly your expectations for working in different configurations, you can create accessible anchor charts with your students to which they can easily refer. (See the previous section on creating physically accessible spaces.)

2. *Classroom is physically accessible.* As we discuss accessibility of curriculum, instruction, and assessment, let's not forget about physical accessibility as an essential component of accessing learning opportunities. Students must be able to make their way through the room to spaces or resources they need. That means you must minimize clutter and ensure that walkways are clear, and clearly label supplies and resources that are easy to reach.

3. *Auditory accessibility is ensured.* The next two items in on the UDL checklist both involve removing auditory barriers to ensure that students can engage with instructional experiences. Background noise should be dampened as much as possible. If your classroom is near a busy, noisy hallway, make sure you can close your door and situate whole-group instruction in the part of the room farthest from the source of noise and distraction. In addition, many classrooms are now being equipped with sound amplification systems, which usually have several speakers installed in the ceiling to amplify the voice of whoever is using the microphone. (The microphone itself is usually on a lanyard for easy, hands-free use.) If your school doesn't yet have this technology installed as a standard classroom feature, you might speak with your administration about the possibility of making that happen schoolwide; you might also discuss this during student IEP meetings as an AT need for your classroom.

4. *Student work is displayed in an organized space in the classroom.* Just as anchor charts and other resources should be displayed with purpose, so should student work. This is an easy way to engage students, provide models and exemplars, and promote a strong and welcoming classroom climate.

5. *Students can choose from a variety of materials.* Choice is an important aspect of any universally designed classroom, as indicated in many of the items we have discussed. Do you have a variety of materials for students to choose from? Providing students with a choice of using a pencil or a pen, a word processor or a notebook, sticky notes or mailing labels, and so forth can make a world of difference in how they engage with the quality instruction and learning opportunities you provide in your classroom.

REFLECTION QUESTION 4

How could you start a conversation with educators at your school about using the UDL checklist to ensure that all students have access to literacy instruction?

SUMMARY

Our least dangerous assumption is that we should provide a rich learning environment for all students by using instructional strategies consistent with what we know about UDL and information processing. Educators need to be thoughtful about how they organize their classroom; how they provide access to language, to print resources, and to other literacy materials; and how they present information in ways that make the information easier for students to process and store—that is, to learn. In this chapter, we have discussed the history and core principles underlying UDL; we have also reviewed available research on how the brain processes and stores information and what implications these research findings have for educators. Throughout, we have emphasized the importance of considering UDL and information processing prior to setting up learning environments and designing learning opportunities. We shared ideas for general and specific resources and strategies that ensure access, support information processing, and help teachers to design instruction. Finally, we have provided the UDL checklist, a tool that ties all of these ideas together and has the potential to enhance the planning of any teacher or educational team.

RESOURCES

Accessible Text Online

The following web sites are great sources of online texts; they offer a variety of accessible media including print:

- **The Library of Congress** (http://www.loc.gov)
- **The New York Public Library** (http://www.nypl.org/research/collections/digital-collections/public-domain)
- **Internet Archive** (https://archive.org)
- **Project Gutenberg** (https://www.gutenberg.org). This site offers free e-books that can be read online or downloaded and read aloud using device software.
- **The American Printing House for the Blind** (http://www.aph.org). This site provides texts in accessible formats such as braille and large-print texts, audio texts, and computer files.
- **Learning Ally** (http://www.learningally.org), previously known as Recording for the Blind and Dyslexic. This site provides the largest available collection of audio recordings of textbooks and literature to its members.

These sites offer time-limited access to e-books in a variety of formats:

- **The World Public Library** (http://www.worldlibrary.org)
- **Open Library** (https://openlibrary.org/borrow)
- **OverDrive** (https://www.overdrive.com); OverDrive also provides distribution and management services to local libraries to provide e-book access.
- **Bookshare** (https://www.bookshare.org), the largest accessible online library for individuals with print disabilities, is free to individuals with a documented disability and offers organizational membership.

Text-to-Speech Programs

These resources allow for conversion of existing print texts to speech:

- The **Kindle app** for Mac/PC is available from the Amazon store (https://www.amazon.com/gp/digital/fiona/kcp-landing-page). You can also import PDF documents to Kindle applications and use the TTS options.
- **NOOK** is available for download from Barnes & Noble (http://nook.barnesandnoble.com).
- **Scholastic Storia** (http://www.scholastic.com/storia%2Dschool) e-books are available by subscription.

If a given text is not available through these resources, you may visit these sites to create digital text to be used in TTS software for your students.

- **ReadPlease** (http://readplease.en.softonic.com)
- **NaturalReader** (http://www.naturalreaders.com/index.html)
- **Kurzweil** (https://www.kurzweiledu.com/products/products.html)
- **PDFaloud** (https://www.texthelp.com/en-us/products/-read-write)

Graphic Organizers

These sites are useful resources for finding and creating graphic organizers of all kinds:

- **Kidspiration Maps** (http://www.inspiration.com/go/kidsmaps) is available online or as a download for an iPad.
- **Teachnology** (http://www.teach-nology.com/web_tools/graphic_org) provides a collection of additional links to different types of graphic organizers.

Speech-to-Text Programs

These sites are useful resources for STT programs:

- **Dragon Anywhere** (http://www.nuance.com/dragon/index.htm) is a free download from mobile app stores, but software for other devices must be purchased.
- **Chrome Voice Recognition** (https://dictation.io/) is available from the Chrome Web Store.

Word Prediction

These sites are useful resources for obtaining word prediction software:

- **Applied Human Factors** (http://www.ahf-net.com)
- **Co:Writer** (http://donjohnston.com/cowriter)
- **Read&Write** (https://www.texthelp.com/en-us/products/read-write)
- **WordQ** (http://www.goqsoftware.com)

Additional Resources

- **National Center on Accessible Educational Materials** (http://aem.cast.org). This center provides resources and technical assistance for educators related to making materials and technologies accessible across the widest range of individual variability.
- ***Accommodations Manual: How to Select, Administer, and Evaluate Use of Accommodations for Instruction and Assessment of Students with Disabilities* (2nd ed.) by Sandra J. Thompson, Amanda B. Morse, Michael Sharpe, & Sharon Hall, 2005** (https://www.osepideasthatwork.org/node/109). This resource includes an overview of best practices that should be considered when selecting and implementing accommodations for students with disabilities. It includes fact sheets for different types of accommodations (presentation, response, setting, timing and scheduling) along with other helpful topics (what to do and not to do when selecting accommodations, guidelines for administering particular accommodations). Teacher tools are also available for topics such as helping construct an accommodation plan and keeping an accommodation journal to track effectiveness for particular students.

- **AEM Navigator** (http://aem.cast.org/navigating/aem-navigator.html#.WKVBErGZP_Q). This is an interactive tool that helps make decisions about specialized formats of print instructional materials for individual students.

- **Accessibility for iPad** (http://www.apple.com/education/special-education/ios/#learning). This web site provides an overview of accessibility functions available on iPads with examples of how they support students with disabilities.

REFERENCES

Americans with Disabilities Act (ADA) of 1990, PL 101-336, 42 U.S.C. §§ 12101 *et seq.*

Armstrong, T. (2000). *Multiple intelligences in the classroom.* Alexandria, VA: Association for Supervision and Curriculum Development.

Assistive Technology Act of 1998, PL 108-364, 112 Stat. 3627, § 2432.

Bloom, B.S. (1956). *Taxonomy of educational objectives, Handbook I: The cognitive domain.* New York, NY: David McKay.

Cahill, L., & McGaugh, J.L. (1995). A novel demonstration of enhanced memory associated with emotional arousal. *Consciousness and Cognition, 4,* 410–421.

Center for Applied Special Technology (CAST): Home. (n.d.). http://www.cast.org

Dalton, B., Morocco, C.C., Tivnan, T., & Mead, P.L.R. (1997). Supported inquiry science teaching for conceptual change in urban and suburban science classrooms. *Journal of Learning Disabilities, 30*(6), 670–684.

Dorn, L.J., & Soffos, C. (2005). *Teaching for deep comprehension.* Portland, ME: Stenhouse.

Ebbinghaus, H. (1913). *A contribution to experimental psychology.* New York, NY: Teachers College, Columbia University.

Every Student Succeeds Act (ESSA) of 2015, PL 114-95, 129 Stat. 1802, 20 U.S.C. §§ 6301 *et seq.*

Fisher, D., & Frey, N. (2003). *Improving adolescent literacy: Strategies at work.* Upper Saddle River, NJ: Merrill/Prentice Hall.

Gagne, R.M., & Driscol, M.P. (1988). *Essentials of learning for instruction* (2nd ed.). Englewood Cliffs, NJ: Prentice Hall.

Gardner, H. (1983). *Frames of mind.* New York, NY: Basic Books.

Higher Education Opportunity Act of 2008, PL 110-315, 20 U.S.C. §§ 1001 *et seq.*

Hunter, M. (1994). *Enhancing teaching.* New York, NY: Macmillan College Publishing.

Individuals with Disabilities Education Improvement Act (IDEA) of 2004, PL 108-446, 20 U.S.C. §§ 1400 *et seq.*

Johnson, D.W., & Johnson, R.T. (1989). *Cooperation and competition: Theory and research.* Edina, MN: Interaction Book Company.

Johnson, D.W., Johnson, R.T., & Holubec, E. (1993). *Circles of learning.* Edina, MN: Interaction Book Company.

Keefe, E.B., Copeland, S.R., & DiLuzio, M.A. (2010). Creating print-rich environments to support literacy instruction. In C. Carnahan & P. Williamson (Eds.), *Quality literacy instruction for students with autism spectrum disorders* (pp. 161–187). Lenexa, KS: AAPC Publishing.

Kim, A., Vaughn, S., Wanzek, J., & Wei, S. (2004). Graphic organizers and their effects on the reading comprehension of students with LD: A synthesis of research. *Journal of Learning Disabilities, 37*(2), 105–118.

Kleinert, H., Towles-Reeves, E., Quenemoen, R., Thurlow, M., Fluegge, L., Weseman, L., & Kerbel, A. (2015). Where students with the most significant disabilities are taught: Implications for general curriculum access. *Exceptional Children, 81*(3), 312–328.

Knight, V.F., Spooner, F., Browder, D.M., Smith, B.R., & Wood, C.L. (2013). Using systematic instruction and graphic organizers to teach science concepts to students with autism spectrum disorders and intellectual disability. *Focus on Autism and Other Developmental Disabilities, 28*(2), 115–126.

Kulhavey, R.W., Stock, W.A., Verdi, M.P., Rittschof, K.A., & Savanye, W. (1993). Why maps improve memory for text: The influence of structural information on working memory operations. *European Journal of Cognitive Psychology, 5*(4), 375–392.

MacArthur, C.A. (2009). Reflections on research on writing and technology for struggling writers. *Learning Disabilities Research & Practice, 24*(2), 93–103.

Miller, G. (1956). The magical number seven, plus or minus two: Some limits on our capacity for processing information. *The Psychological Review, 63,* 81–97.

National Reading Panel (NRP). (2000). *Report of the National Reading Panel: Teaching children to read. Reports of the subgroups* (NIH Publication 00-4754). Washington, DC: National Institute of Child Health and Human Development.

Pashler, H., Bain, P., Bottge, B., Graesser, A., Koedinger, K., McDaniel, M., & Metcalfe, J. (2007). *Organizing instruction and study to improve student learning (NCER 2007-2004).* Washington, DC: National Center for Education Research, Institute of Education Sciences, U.S. Department of Education.

Putnam, J.W. (1998). *Cooperative learning and strategies for inclusion.* Baltimore, MD: Paul H. Brookes Publishing Co.

Rehabilitation Act of 1973, PL 93-112, 29 U.S.C. §§ 701 *et seq.*

Rose, D.H., & Meyer, A. (2002). *Teaching every student in the digital age: Universal design for learning.* Alexandria VA: Association for Supervision and Curriculum Development

Rose, D.H., Meyer, A., & Hitchcock, C. (2005). *The universally designed classroom: Accessible curriculum and digital technologies.* Cambridge, MA: Harvard Education Press.

Sapon-Shevin, M., Ayres, B.A., & Duncan, J. (2002). Cooperative learning and inclusion. In J.S. Thousand, R.A. Villa, & A.I. Nevin (Eds.), *Creativity and collaborative learning* (2nd ed., pp. 209–222). Baltimore, MD: Paul H. Brookes Publishing Co.

Scutts, J. (2014, December 22). How books became a critical part of the fight to win World War II. *Smithsonian.* Retrieved from http://www.smithsonianmag.com/history/how-books-became-critical-part-fight-win-world-war-ii-180953689/#3iTBomaAD0hzdLJV.99

Sylwester, R. (1995). *A celebration of neurons: An educator's guide to the human brain.* Alexandria, VA: Association for Supervision and Curriculum Development.

Telecommunications Act of 1996, PL 104-104, 110 Stat. 56 (1996).

Tomlinson, C.A., & Imbeau, M.B. (2010). *Leading and managing a differentiated classroom.* Alexandria, VA: Association for Supervision and Curriculum Development.

Tumlin, J., & Heller, K.W. (2004). Using word prediction software to increase typing fluency with students with physical disabilities. *Journal of Special Education Technology, 19*(3), 5–14.

Wolfe, P. (2001). *Brain matters: Translating research into classroom practice.* Alexandria, VA: Association for Supervision and Curriculum Development.

Evidence-Based Comprehensive Literacy Instruction

CHAPTER 6

Getting the Point

Comprehension Instruction

Susan R. Copeland, Sharon L. Head, and Heather DiLuzio

LEARNING OBJECTIVES

By the end of this chapter, readers will

1. Know the definitions of listening and reading comprehension.

2. Learn how the component skills of reading influence listening and reading comprehension and identify specific factors that affect these skills in students with complex support needs.

3. Learn strategies to assess listening and reading comprehension, including how to adjust assessment for students who use augmentative and alternative communication (AAC) systems.

4. Learn strategies to improve listening and reading comprehension and how to adjust these strategies for learners with complex support needs.

This chapter will discuss the role of reading and listening comprehension in literacy instruction for individuals with complex support needs. We will begin by defining comprehension and exploring the relationship between comprehension and other processes and skills involved in reading. Next, we will discuss factors that might adversely affect comprehension. We will then discuss methods of assessing comprehension, general principles for comprehension instruction, and specific strategies to use before, during, and after reading, all grounded in research.

WHAT IS READING COMPREHENSION?

The primary goal of learning to read written language is to make meaning out of text. We read and listen for the sake of gaining information (learning), for enjoyment and exploration of our interests (e.g., reading about a favorite music group), and for connection with family, friends, and the larger community (Forts & Luckasson, 2011). Reading comprehension—that is, making meaning out of a text—is an active, not passive, process that is deeply complex. The reader has to recognize the words, reflect on them, and use them in some way to make meaning. This complex comprehension process requires all the other components of reading to function together if meaning-making is to occur. Simply being able to recognize words or even to provide a word's meaning, for example, does not guarantee that a student can comprehend an entire story (van Wingerden, Segers, van Balkom, & Verhoeven, 2014).

Comprehension includes both reading and listening (or linguistic) comprehension. Duke and Carlisle define comprehension as "the listener or reader's understanding of the message expressed by the speaker or writer" (2011, p. 200). Therefore, comprehension involves "accessing the meaning of a message communicated by someone else" (p. 200), be it in written or oral form. *Reading* comprehension requires the recognition of words in written form and the extraction of meaning from this format. It requires students to have (a) the ability to fluently decode words; (b) adequate language comprehension (i.e., skills in grammar, syntax, and pragmatics as well as ample vocabulary); (c) familiarity with varied text structures (narrative and expository); and (d) working memory, planning, organizing, and monitoring skills—that is, executive function skills (Sesma, Mahone, Levine, Eason, & Cutting, 2009). *Listening* comprehension involves hearing spoken words and deriving meaning from what is heard.

Educators must build their students' skills in both types of comprehension—reading and listening—if students are to access meaning from oral and written language. This can, of course, also include gaining meaning from signed language (e.g., American Sign Language) and AAC systems as well as gaining meaning from pictures and symbols. Keep this focus on both types of comprehension in mind as you read about the various types of comprehension instruction described in this chapter. We can involve all learners in comprehension activities. The activities we highlight are useful for students who are conventional readers and for those who are still developing their understanding of written language. The use of just a few adaptations will build listening comprehension for developing readers and support their emerging ability to comprehend written symbols and/or text.

Understanding the Comprehension Process

Scarborough's (2001) diagram (see Figure 6.1) illustrates how all of the component skills of reading must work together for comprehension (skilled reading) to take place. The impact of each of these factors on comprehension changes over time as students acquire skills (Ouellette & Beers, 2010). Word recognition, for example, is more strongly linked to reading comprehension

The Many Strands that Are Woven into Skilled Reading
(Scarborough, 2001)

LANGUAGE COMPREHENSION

BACKGROUND KNOWLEDGE
(facts, concepts, etc.)

VOCABULARY
(breadth, precision, links, etc.)

LANGUAGE STRUCTURES
(syntax, semantics, etc.)

VERBAL REASONING
(inference, metaphor, etc.)

LITERACY KNOWLEDGE

(print concepts, genres, etc.)

WORD RECOGNITION

PHONOLOGICAL AWARENESS
(syllables, phonemes, etc.)

DECODING (alphabetic principle,
spelling-sound correspondences)

SIGHT RECOGNITION
(of familiar words)

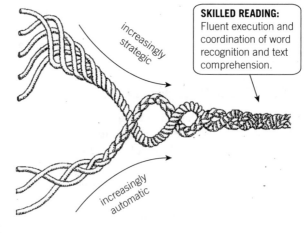

increasingly strategic

SKILLED READING:
Fluent execution and coordination of word recognition and text comprehension.

increasingly automatic

Figure 6.1.   Scarborough's reading rope: an illustration of the many strands that are woven together in skilled reading. (From Scarborough, H. [2001]. Connecting early language and literacy to later reading [dis]abilities: Evidence, theory, and practice. In S.B. Neuman & D.K. Dickinson [Eds.], *Handbook of early literacy* [pp. 97–110]. New York, NY: Guilford Press. Reprinted with permission of Guilford Press.)

in early readers, whereas oral language abilities are more strongly linked to comprehension in more skilled readers. This makes sense when you consider that beginning readers put most of their effort into recognizing words (e.g., decoding) and are typically reading simple texts. These processes become more automatic as a student's word recognition and reading fluency improve over time. Moreover, as readers encounter different kinds of texts over time, the texts' degree of complexity also increases. More complex texts make a greater demand on language skills such as vocabulary and understanding of syntax; as a result, listening (linguistic) comprehension plays a larger role in reading comprehension (Hogan, Adolf, & Alonzo, 2014).

For advanced texts, good comprehension requires the additional complexity of understanding both the *explicit* meaning (e.g., "Who were the characters in *Romeo and Juliet*?") and the *implicit* meaning (e.g., "What issues from *Romeo and Juliet* are relevant today?"). This requires making a mental model or representation of what one is reading in order to understand it (Hogan et al., 2014). Kendeou and colleagues called this model "a coherent representation or picture of what the text is about in the reader's mind" (2005, p. 92). In other words, the reader makes links between events or ideas in the text and these, combined with the reader's prior knowledge of the text's content, allow him or her to go beyond what is actually written in the text to understand broader or deeper meanings of the text (Hogan et al., 2014). Making inferences can be difficult for any student and may be particularly challenging for students with complex support needs.

Another related comprehension skill readers must constantly employ is to monitor their understanding as they read, continually adjusting that understanding as they notice something that does not make sense. Some students—for example, some who have autism spectrum disorder (ASD)—may have more difficulty doing this, compared to typically developing students, because they struggle with making shifts in their thinking, or mental representations, about a text as they encounter new information (Carnahan & Williamson, 2010). These students may also have more trouble seeing how all the pieces of information in connected text, such as in a science text, fit together to create a whole structure (Carnahan & Williamson, 2013).

Factors Affecting Reading Comprehension

Reading comprehension levels of individuals with complex support needs vary widely (Jones, Long, & Finlay, 2006). This group of learners often struggles with comprehension due to a number of factors. For example, although this is still an understudied area, the research that has examined reading comprehension in individuals with intellectual disability (ID) has shown that these individuals typically display lower nonverbal reasoning, decoding, and language comprehension skills than their typically developing peers (van Wingerden et al., 2014). All of these skills are necessary for reading comprehension and, consequently, affect students' abilities in this area. Remember, however, that research also shows that when teachers take into account these challenges, students can improve their comprehension abilities.

There is one factor that affects reading comprehension levels in students with complex support needs that educators and parents can address immediately and definitely. Put simply, it is that, historically, these students may have had limited systematic reading comprehension instruction, or none, due to teachers' low expectations of their literacy potential (e.g., Lundberg & Reichenberg, 2013). This factor can be corrected for when educators provide appropriate, sustained, and systematic comprehension instruction (e.g., Allor, Mathes, Roberts, Cheatham, & Al Otaiba, 2014). It is important to presume competence and use the least dangerous assumption when planning instruction—core principles referenced throughout this book and discussed in detail in Chapter 1.

To implement these principles, what other factors do we need to consider because of their potential effect on reading comprehension in students with complex support needs? Bear in mind that these students may have less experiential knowledge to apply when reading text because they have had more limited life experiences. For example, if all or most of their education has taken place within segregated settings, they may have missed out on opportunities to participate in many typical academic and social experiences that their peers experience in and out of school settings. This restricts the background knowledge they have available when trying to make meaningful connections between stories or educational materials they are reading and their prior knowledge and experience. Additionally, teachers' low expectations of these students' literacy abilities may have resulted in less exposure to important content knowledge and concepts and less experience working with various types of texts (e.g., narrative vs. expository). All of these factors combine to contribute to difficulties in successfully comprehending reading material and accessing curriculum in settings with typically developing peers.

Given the multiple, layered skills necessary for successful reading comprehension, it is easy to see that the process can break down in several ways. It is also apparent that there is seldom a single cause of reading comprehension problems. Most often, multiple problems affect students' comprehension. Some of the most likely difficulties include underlying language impairments— such as difficulties with listening comprehension, semantics, vocabulary, or grammar—that interfere with understanding; problems integrating incoming information with prior knowledge; poor (nonfluent) decoding skills; limited automatic word recognition; attentional problems that interfere with monitoring comprehension; limited knowledge of text structures; poor short-term (working) memory; and restricted experiential (background) knowledge (Erickson, Hanser, Hatch, & Sanders, 2009; Lundberg & Reichenberg, 2013; Morgan, Moni, & Jobling, 2009; van Wingerden et al., 2014). Also, students who do not use speech may comprehend the text they have read but have very limited means to express their understanding, making it appear that they lack comprehension skills. Two factors that can contribute to this problem are teachers' low expectations of students' abilities and a lack of appropriate technology to support communication. (See Chapter 2 for a more thorough discussion of the effects of low expectations in the areas of language and communication.)

As with other aspects of literacy development, there have been relatively few research studies examining instructional approaches that have targeted reading comprehension for students with complex support needs, such as those with cognitive disabilities or autism (El Zein, Solis, Vaughn, & McCulley, 2014; Lundberg & Reichenberg, 2013). Fortunately, research examining reading comprehension instruction for students with other types of disabilities, such as learning disabilities, provides numerous instructional practices educators can use to assess, teach, and support the reading comprehension of their students with complex support needs. The remainder of this chapter will provide examples of these assessment and instructional strategies.

REFLECTION QUESTION 1

What factors affect listening and reading comprehension skills of students with complex support needs?

ASSESSING COMPREHENSION SKILLS

Assessment is the first step in designing effective comprehension instruction; before educators design instruction, it is critical that they have a clear understanding of their students' existing comprehension skills. This includes knowing which strategies, if any, their students are trying to apply in order to comprehend text. Only after learning their students' strengths and limitations with regard to comprehending what they read or hear can teachers design effective instruction.

There are many ways to assess comprehension. For some students with complex support needs, standardized tests such as the Woodcock Language Proficiency Battery–Revised (Woodcock, 1991) can be useful. Often, however, these standardized assessments may not be usable; students with more significant disabilities may not be able to perform at a level high enough to be assessed because individuals with these disabilities were not included in the norming sample for the assessment (Connor, Alberto, Compton, & O'Connor, 2014). In this case, informal reading inventories, or classroom-based assessments that use the reading material students are working with in their classrooms, can be used to assess comprehension. One comprehensive literacy assessment that is unique in having been designed specifically for individuals with complex support needs is the Nonverbal Literacy Assessment (Ahlgrim-Delzell, Browder, Flowers, & Baker, 2008–2009). It assesses six literacy areas, including comprehension, vocabulary, and listening comprehension, and includes ways to assess comprehension through nonverbal means, such as having the individual use eye gaze or point to responses.

For some students with complex support needs, simply changing the format of the assessment can provide access to demonstrate their understanding of a passage. One simple example is to provide a student with multiple written choices from which to select an answer for comprehension questions about a reading passage. The multiple-choice format provides support for a student with memory challenges while still assessing understanding of what was read. For a student who does not speak, possible answers can be affixed to an eye-gaze board or preprogrammed into the student's AAC device. For example, the teacher writes the multiple-choice items for a comprehension question on separate cards and tapes one card in each of the four quadrants of an eye-gaze board. The teacher asks the student the comprehension question, holds up the eye-gaze board, and watches to see which item the student selects with his or her eyes.

Regardless of a particular student's perceived strengths or challenges, using several different types of assessment tasks provides a more complete picture of that student's current comprehension abilities and permits the teacher to pinpoint areas of need more closely (Carlisle & Rice, 2004). As mentioned previously, it is rare that students have just one problem area affecting their comprehension. The more information collected about students' comprehension skills, the more likely it is that educators can develop an effective, comprehensive instructional plan to improve their ability to read and listen for meaning. With this in mind, we will explore several means of assessing comprehension.

Running Records

If students have sufficient skill to read a short passage, even at a very low reading level, a simple running record provides much useful information about reading comprehension. Running records also have the advantage of being completed quickly—usually in 5 to 10 minutes—and requiring no special materials, making them something that can be easily repeated at regular intervals to monitor student progress.

This type of assessment requires that students read aloud a short passage at their instructional reading level—that is, the level at which they can read the words in the text with 90%–95% accuracy and comprehend with 90% accuracy with teacher support—while the teacher notes any errors, substitutions, or self-corrections. This allows the teacher to determine what types of decoding errors a student is making and provides a direct assessment of the student's understanding of the text. The running record pinpoints whether decoding errors are impeding comprehension.

After a student completes the reading, the passage is put away, and the teacher asks the student comprehension questions about the passage or asks the student to retell it. Depending on the type of text that was read, the teacher can score the retelling by counting the number of content words the student used in it or by counting the number and type of ideas therein, or the teacher can evaluate it for correctly sequenced events, important information about characters, main ideas, key details, or evidence of making inferences. To adjust the comprehension portion of the assessment, a teacher can let the student keep the passage when answering questions or supply pictures or objects for the student to use to support retelling.

Figure 6.2 is a story grammar retelling assessment—that is, an assessment that measures students' understanding of basic story elements such as characters, setting, a problem or conflict that must be resolved, and plot events. (A simpler form of this assessment is to have students simply retell what happens at the beginning, middle, and end of the story.) This assessment can be used across the school year to track students' progress in reading or listening comprehension. This tool includes a section to indicate the supports a student used during the retelling.

Story Grammar Oral (Expressive) Retelling Assessment

Student: _____   Date: _____

Text: _____

Assessor: _____

Instructional level: _____

Format: Reading _____   Listening _____

Story grammar element	Unaided retelling	Retelling with prompting questions	Retelling with picture and/or tactile prompts
Character(s)			
Setting(s)			
Problem (or conflict or challenge)			
Event(s)			
Resolution (or moral)			

Figure 6.2.   Story Grammar Oral (Expressive) Retelling Assessment.

Figure 6.2. *(continued)*

Story Grammar Oral (Expressive) Retelling Assessment

Student: _____   Date: _____

Text: _____

Assessor: _____

Instructional level: _____

Format: Reading _____   Listening _____

Story grammar element	Unaided retelling	Retelling with prompting questions	Retelling with picture and/or tactile prompts
Beginning			
Middle			
End			

Maze and Cloze Assessments

A maze is another common assessment to examine students' reading comprehension skills. To employ the maze method, a teacher creates or selects a short passage at the student's instructional reading level and gives it to the student with one word removed at regular intervals throughout the text (e.g., every fifth word is removed). At each of these intervals, the teacher inserts three words from which the student can choose one word to complete each sentence. For example:

Jim went to the zoo.

He went through a big (car / gate / door) *to get into the zoo.*

Jim saw many (books / it / animals) *at the zoo.*

Maze assessments may be timed if this would be useful, as a measure of fluency, and scored by measuring the number of correct words selected. They can also be adapted to assess listening comprehension by having a student read the passage and answer choices aloud and giving the student the opportunity to select answers verbally.

Cloze tasks are similar to maze tasks but are more difficult. The passage the student is given has a certain number of words omitted at regular intervals, but it does not include word choices the student can use to fill in the blanks; instead, the student is asked to insert a word that makes sense into each blank. This more difficult task would not be an effective measure for students with very low reading skills. It can also be adapted to measure listening comprehension by reading the text aloud, pausing at the blanks, and having students provide the words.

Picture Cards

Using picture cards as a part of reading comprehension assessment reduces the load placed on students' expressive and receptive language skills. This can be especially important when assessing students with less well-developed language skills as well as those who do not use speech. Picture cards allow students to demonstrate their understanding of a text's meaning even when they cannot express their ideas completely using speech. They also act as memory support. As mentioned previously, many students with complex support needs have difficulty holding information in working memory; a picture card can cue memory of the information read, allowing a student to demonstrate understanding. Picture cards can also be used easily in conjunction with maze or cloze tasks to assess listening comprehension. The teacher simply reads the text aloud and proceeds with the maze or cloze assessment as planned using the picture cards (i.e., the teacher provides an array of pictures and the student selects one to fill in the blank for the close or maze task).

Picture cards can be used in several other ways to allow students to demonstrate understanding. For example, the teacher can ask the student to read a sentence or short passage and select from an array of pictures the one that best represents the main idea of the text or best illustrates answers to specific comprehension questions (see Figure 6.3 for an example). To assess students' knowledge of narrative, the teacher can give them a set of cards illustrating key story events and ask that they put them in the order in which they took place. To assess prediction skills, the teacher can have students read or listen to a portion of a passage, then provide an array of pictures and ask, "What do you think will happen next?" and prompt students to choose the picture that best represents their prediction. If possible, students can supplement picture selection by explaining why that prediction was made. Alternatively, students can be asked to draw a picture(s) to retell the passage that was read, if appropriate for that student.

The disadvantage of using picture cards is that they do not allow evaluation of how a student comprehends abstract ideas in the text. Vocabulary or content that cannot be easily illustrated cannot be assessed in this way. Using picture cards may also require extensive preparation of

This chapter was about:

During World War II, many Japanese Americans were put in:

Figure 6.3. Example of using pictures to assess reading or listening comprehension. Students can point to or circle the picture that answers the comprehension question.

materials prior to the assessment. This disadvantage may be outweighed, however, by the quality of information provided about a student's understanding of text, valuable information that might be lost using a more traditional comprehension assessment.

Role-Playing Answers

Another way of assessing comprehension that decreases the load on expressive language is to ask students to act out, or role-play, the meaning of a sentence or longer text selection. For example, a student can be asked to read the sentence, "Put the red ball in the blue box" and then demonstrate what it means. This can be especially helpful in assessing reading comprehension in learners who are beginning to read connected text and do not yet have sufficient skill to read a passage consisting of several sentences. This assessment task is easily incorporated into a game-like format, making it more motivating than traditional testing materials for students. For example, Ms. Brawley, an elementary school teacher, used this method as a motivating, creative way to assess the comprehension of her young students with ASD. She placed individual sentences from a simple story on a series of cards. She and her students took turns selecting a card and role-playing the sentences on it using objects and props found in the classroom. The sentences incorporated silly or unexpected actions such as "I put the hat on the dog." Students were responsible for checking the accuracy of each student's role play of the targeted sentence in addition to reading and acting out their own sentences.

With these methods of assessment in mind, let's turn now to the question of how best to provide comprehension instruction.

REFLECTION QUESTION 2

Describe at least three ways to assess listening and/or reading comprehension. How would you adapt the assessment tool and process for a student who does not use speech to communicate?

GENERAL PRINCIPLES OF READING COMPREHENSION INSTRUCTION

Several key guidelines should be kept in mind when planning comprehension instruction for students with complex support needs: it should begin as early as possible; should be individualized to meet individual students' needs, based on information gathered from assessment data; and should use texts that relate to students' particular interests. In addition, it is helpful to organize instructional activities around skills that readers employ before, during, and after reading; we will discuss specific activities in the next section.

Provide Comprehension Instruction to Beginning Readers

When developing instruction for beginning readers, an important consideration is to include comprehension activities from the very beginning. In other words, incorporate comprehension instruction into instruction on word recognition and fluency, rather than waiting until students have developed the latter skills. (See Chapter 9 for more information on why this is important.) Duke and Carlisle describe this process as teaching skills "synergistically" (2011, p. 217). Waiting for students to have well-developed word recognition skills before teaching comprehension wastes precious time that can be used creatively to build language and vocabulary skills. Also, waiting to build reading/listening comprehension may make it more difficult for students with complex support needs to understand the purpose for learning to read. (See Chapter 1 for more about the importance of teaching skills within meaningful contexts.)

Comprehension instruction is critical even for students who are able to read only single words or very short connected text. Begin instruction for learners in this stage by using only a short sentence ("Stand up") and gradually build to longer sentences or to several sentences within a passage as students gain skill and confidence. Using even one short sentence at a time offers numerous possibilities for a student to develop comprehension skills. For example, use *wh-* question words to facilitate comprehension development, as described in the following section. Ask the student to role-play the sentence (as Ms. Brawley's class did) or to draw a picture illustrating it. Give students cut-apart sentences and have them reassemble the sentences so they make sense. (See the textbox, "In the Classroom," for an example of how to adapt comprehension instruction for a child who does not speak.) The key point is that reading comprehension should be a part of every lesson, whether a student is working at the single-word level or is reading chapter books.

IN THE CLASSROOM

TEACHING COMPREHENSION USING ALTERNATIVE COMMUNICATION FORMATS

Maria, a 7-year-old first grader with ASD, uses single spoken words to request preferred tangible items and activities. Maria entered the first grade independently using Picture Exchange Communication System (PECS; Bondy & Frost, 1994) at Phase V. Her educational team moved Maria to a speech-generating device (SGD) soon after entering first grade. She currently uses her SGD across all school environments with some prompting and modeling from staff.

Maria's first-grade teacher uses a systematic sequence of instructional steps when working on reading and listening comprehension with new texts during literacy instruction. In Step 1, she introduces the new book using visual supports to familiarize Maria with the topics in the text. In Step 2, the teacher uses a *picture walk* (i.e., the teacher shows the book to the student and together they examine the illustrations; the teacher asks a variety of *wh-* questions while they look at the pictures and models new vocabulary on the student's SGD to present and model new vocabulary from the selected book. She uses Maria's communication system to model how to access and use the new words. The teacher makes sure to provide multiple examples of new vocabulary words using pictures, objects, or video to ensure deep understanding of each new word or concept. In Step 3, the teacher reinforces new vocabulary by asking Maria to match identical/nonidentical pictures connected to key vocabulary words from the text, being sure to provide multiple examples of each new word. After reading the story, she completes Step 4 by asking Maria to sequence pictures from the story to support Maria's comprehension of the sequence of story events. Finally, as Step 5, she integrates *wh-* comprehension questions into instruction, providing visual supports and prompts to teach Maria how to answer or where to look for answers in the text.

Maria's teacher used this sequence of steps when beginning instruction for Maria on a new book, *Bananas Sometimes* (www.Readinga-z.com). She first discussed with Maria what the book might be about, encouraging her to make predictions. Then, together, they examined the pictures on each page of the book. The teacher used one to two words to describe each picture. She actively engaged Maria in the activity by asking her to point to various parts of the illustrations as they worked through the book. For example, the teacher asked Maria to point to the picture of *bananas* and modeled doing so. After Maria pointed to the correct picture, the teacher then modeled selecting the word *banana* on Maria's SGD. Finally, a paraprofessional prompted Maria to find the word *banana* on her device in response to the teacher's question, "What is this?" Maria's teacher added the SGD sequence for the word *banana* to the page of the book that featured a picture of a banana. This gave Maria an additional visual support to use when working with the book. The teacher followed this same procedure with all the key vocabulary identified in the book. The teacher then read the book aloud to Maria. She asked *wh-* questions after the read-aloud to assess Maria's comprehension of the story and provided pictures relevant to actions in the story in an array. Maria could select an answer to *wh-* questions using the array so that she did not have to construct a reply verbally or by using her SGD. As they read and reread the book across time, Maria began to rely less on the pictures and to use her SGD to answer the comprehension questions.

REFLECTION QUESTION 3

How would you explain to parents and other educators the importance of teaching for comprehension from the very beginning of literacy instruction?

Tailor Comprehension Instruction to Individual Needs

As noted previously, many factors affect an individual's ability to understand the meaning of text. Successful reading comprehension instruction not only teaches specific comprehension strategies but also must include intervention in related areas that affect a student's ability to comprehend what is read. Designing effective comprehension instruction requires teachers to carefully consider student assessment information and create an individualized, multifaceted intervention approach that not only addresses comprehension instruction specifically but also addresses other areas affecting comprehension. If a student has limited decoding skills, for example, reading comprehension will likely be affected because the student must put so much effort and attention into decoding that he or she cannot devote sufficient attention to understanding what is being read. Therefore, instruction for such a student would necessarily include explicit instruction in decoding skills as one component. If language and vocabulary skills are weak, then an effective instructional plan will target these areas in addition to specific comprehension instruction. Because various areas related to reading comprehension, such as word recognition and language skills, are addressed in other chapters in this book, we will focus here on strategies specifically for comprehension instruction.

Tailor Comprehension Instruction to Individual Interests

It is crucial for students to understand that reading is meaningful and enjoyable, not merely an exercise in solving a puzzle (i.e., decoding letter patterns). Thus, when designing instruction for a student with complex support needs, it is important to consider carefully the student's interests and select related texts. Students will not make the highly motivating connection of reading for pleasure and function if instruction uses reading material they cannot relate to at all or introduces reading material on new topics in a way that prevents students from relating unfamiliar information to previous experiences.

It is up to educators to help all students make the connections between what they are reading and their own experiences. One way to ensure that this occurs is to spend time surveying students' interests and then locating a selection of reading materials, in various formats and on various reading levels, on these high-interest topics. Materials should include both fiction (narrative text) and nonfiction (expository text) so students can learn how to work with a variety of text structures. Instructional materials must also take students' age into account. In designing instruction for adults, for example, we must consider their interests, prior life experiences, and the ways in which they want to use literacy in their daily lives.

If appropriate books are not easily available, teachers can also use digital images to create personal books for students about family, friends, and hobbies. The "In the Classroom" examples in the following textbox illustrate teaching methods that embody these crucial components of effective comprehension instruction. The first example describes how Leanora Mariano created a personalized book for a young child with multiple disabilities. The second example describes the process Rosalia Pacheco used for an adult with complex support needs.

IN THE CLASSROOM

CREATING PERSONAL BOOKS USING DIGITAL IMAGES
For a First Grader: Learning About Neighborhoods

At Leanora Mariano's school, a particular book was used with all the children in first grade to teach the concept of *neighborhoods*; Ms. Mariano adapted this book for one of her first-grade students with complex support needs. The original book included drawings from a large city to illustrate vocabulary related to the idea of *neighborhood*. Because Ms. Mariano teaches in a small community, she knew the examples and pictures might not be meaningful to her student(s). Her student also had significant cognitive and behavioral challenges that made it difficult for him to learn abstract concepts or to focus on and retain new information. She adapted the book in several ways to enhance comprehension and to allow her student access to the concepts being taught therein. For example, she added photographs of the student's friends to reinforce the vocabulary word *pals* and included photos of other people in his neighborhood who had important roles in the community, such as the person who baked bread for everyone (see Figure 6.4).

Ms. Mariano also highlighted key vocabulary within sentences in the book and drew lines connecting these highlighted words to pictures in the text. These visual supports (i.e., scaffolding) helped the student remember word meanings as they read the story together. She also created a map of the community, labeling places important to the student and to family members, including photographs of these places on the map (see Figure 6.4).

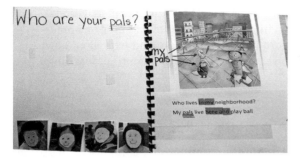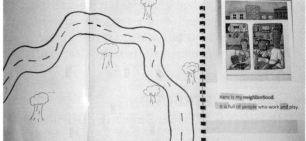

Figure 6.4. Creating personal books.

Ms. Mariano attached the photos with Velcro so that the student could practice matching the photos to the words on the map. For example, there was a photo of the community store to be matched to the word *Store* on the map. Adapting the book and creating interactive lessons around it allowed Ms. Mariano's student to learn important vocabulary and provided authentic access to the same curriculum that all first-grade students at his school were expected to learn.

For an Adult Learner: Learning About Music

Rosalia Pacheco, a local teacher, created literacy instruction for an adult with ID that beautifully demonstrated the power of centering instruction on a student's interests. Ms. Pacheco and her student began instruction by visiting a bookstore and exploring topics the student was interested in learning more about. The student wanted to learn about music, so she and Ms. Pacheco worked together to adapt a basic music theory text written for adults (see Figure 6.5). They used pictures and simplified text to bring the reading level of the book down without altering the content. Ms. Pacheco took time to preteach key vocabulary before each lesson. (See Chapter 8 for more about the types of preteaching strategies teachers can use.) She used questions to activate the student's prior knowledge about music, and then she used repeated readings of the text and discussions of its content to enhance comprehension. She and the student even used latch hook,

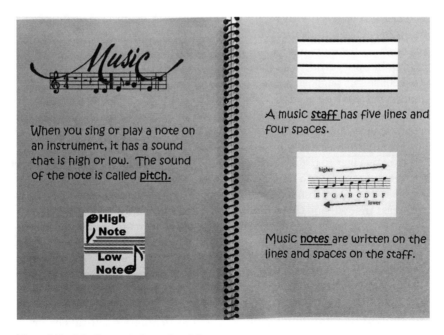

Figure 6.5. Adapting music theory for adults.

one of the student's favorite leisure activities, to create an art project around this instructional theme. At the end of the project, the student's scores on informal measures of listening and reading comprehension showed excellent growth, and, more important, the student expressed how much more confident she felt about learning to read and how excited she was to continue learning.

PLANNING INSTRUCTION: STRATEGIES TO USE BEFORE, DURING, AND AFTER READING

It is helpful to plan reading comprehension instruction by organizing teaching strategies to use *before, during,* and *after* reading. Competent readers automatically do several things at each of these points in the reading process that help them make sense of what they read. Research supports teaching these specific things to students struggling with comprehension. This will improve their understanding of what they are reading (e.g., Howorth, Lopata, Thomeer, & Rodgers, 2016; Whalon & Hanline, 2008). The following sections describe several strategies that students can use at each point in the reading process to improve comprehension.

Before Reading

Skilled readers do several things before reading a story or informational passage that assist their comprehension of the text. They think about several things: their goal for reading the selection (setting a purpose), any previous knowledge or experience they may have that relates to the passage (activating prior knowledge), and what might happen in the story or what the passage might be about (prediction). Readers with complex support needs or other students struggling with comprehension do not do these things routinely and will likely need to be taught specific strategies to accomplish these actions.

Set a Purpose for Reading   Students can improve their comprehension by learning to set a goal or purpose for reading. For example, ask yourself why you are reading this textbook. What is it you want to know or find out by reading? Are you reading for fun, or to discover some specific information such as how to more effectively teach comprehension strategies to students with complex support needs? Chances are that you deliberately selected this text for a specific reason—one that you constantly reflect on as you read through each chapter and that guides your understanding of the information you find.

Although it may seem obvious to you, a skilled reader, that reading is done with a specific purpose in mind, poor readers often do not realize why they are being asked to read or how reading with a conscious purpose might be helpful to them. As a consequence, they do not focus on critical information in the text that will lead to understanding what they have read. At the end of a reading, they may have successfully decoded the words but they cannot express the key ideas or concepts. These students need explicit instruction in determining the purpose of a particular reading activity and how that purpose can be useful to them.

One effective way to teach setting a purpose for reading is to use a think-aloud to model the process. Deciding the reason for reading prior to actually reading a passage helps students activate any prior knowledge related to that purpose, and it alerts them to key information or ideas within the text that will aid their understanding of the passage.

To get started, discuss with students possible reasons for reading different kinds of texts. Select a particular type of text and think out loud about why you are reading that selection. Model the kinds of self-talk to use to set a goal. For example, using a set of directions to the store, you might say, "I need to go to the store to buy my groceries. The words tell me how to get to the store. I need to pay attention to the names of the streets as I read, and the way I should turn on each street. That way, I won't get lost. Reading this carefully will help me walk to the store by myself." After modeling think-alouds, ask the students to practice self-talk before reading a similar type of passage, coaching them as they practice the process.

To be most effective, explicitly link the reading purpose to a follow-up activity done after reading. For example, if students previously set a purpose for reading directions, a follow-up activity might be to provide a set of directions to a mystery location in the school and ask students to read and follow the directions to the site, where they find a surprise such as bag of goodies to share with the class. This activity (finding a mystery site) is clearly linked to the purpose set for reading (following directions). It requires students' active involvement in an enjoyable, meaningful way that helps them understand the usefulness of setting a reading purpose.

Repeat the think-aloud activity frequently with students, using different kinds of texts on topics that students will find interesting and personally relevant, such as stories, content-area texts (e.g., social studies text), sets of directions (e.g., recipes), or other informational texts (e.g., a web site with facts about a favorite sports team). Experience with many different types of texts helps students understand that reading can be done for numerous, important reasons.

Preview Text Structure and Text Features

Another before-reading activity that facilitates comprehension is to help students become familiar with the structural organization and common features of different kinds of texts. We saw this vividly illustrated when conducting a research project that included students with complex support needs in a local high school. These students, who had received most of their education within segregated self-contained classrooms that focused primarily on functional academics and life skills, were now taking some general education courses in elective and content areas. It quickly became clear that they had very little experience working with textbooks and were unfamiliar with the typical organizational structures used therein. This made it difficult for them to successfully complete typical assignments such as answering chapter review questions. Unlike their classmates, who could complete assignments by using headings, diagrams, and other characteristic text structures to locate the information they needed, these students flipped randomly through chapters. Part of our intervention then became teaching them to locate some key features, such as headings and bolded vocabulary words, that are found in texts with this structure. This improved their participation in and understanding of the class assignments. Another simple support is using sticky notes to mark key locations in the text.

Preteach New Vocabulary and Concepts

Preteaching new vocabulary and concepts is another effective strategy to apply before reading. Teachers can preteach text-specific vocabulary that students must know to fully understand a reading selection. Preteaching can take place during individual or small-group instruction sessions prior to attending a general education class, or it can be done within the classroom before work begins on a new text.

Vocabulary can be taught in many different ways; these will be discussed more thoroughly in Chapter 8. Use of a word wall, for example, is a common and effective strategy. To work with a word wall, conduct a variety of activities with students to help them learn the meanings of words they will encounter in a new reading selection. Have them write these words on large cards or strips of chart paper, adding a drawing, photo, or even an object to illustrate each word's meaning. Then display the cards on the word wall, referring to them frequently as students work on the new text. Use games such as Vocabulary Jeopardy to continually practice word recognition and associated meanings. You can also have students put these words and their illustrations on small cards that are placed on a metal ring (Fisher & Frey, 2003), which becomes an individualized, portable dictionary students can refer to as needed when they are reading the assigned text.

Use Anticipation Guides to Activate Prior Knowledge and Make Predictions

Two other key "before-reading" components in skilled reading comprehension are activating students' prior knowledge that is relevant to the passage and teaching students to predict what the passage may be about. These components are included in a teaching tool called an *anticipation guide* (which can also function as an after-reading strategy to boost comprehension) (Kozen, Murray, & Windell, 2006). Anticipation guides also can build students' interest in reading a particular passage and help them set a purpose.

Anticipation guides consist of teacher-created statements about a passage. Simple *yes/no* statements should be avoided; teachers should write statements that might challenge students' thinking. Before reading or listening to the passage, students respond to these statements by agreeing or disagreeing; afterward, they revisit their responses. These guides work well for narratives, informational texts, and even content-area texts, such as math textbooks. They are effectively used with videos, too. Ask students to complete a guide before watching a video that illustrates or is related to a particular academic topic (e.g., a video on how ants communicate when studying social insects in biology) and then revisit the guide afterward to analyze their predictions and assumptions.

Teachers can create anticipation guides based on the type of passage the class will be studying, students' current literacy skill levels, and their understandings of the topic. (Figure 6.6 shows an example of a guide used with Lois Lowry's [1993] *The Giver.*) To teach students how to work with them, use modeling and prompting. Before reading, give students a written copy of the guide, project a copy onto the whiteboard so everyone can see it, and model its use by reading each statement in turn and thinking aloud about whether you agree or disagree with it. Encourage students to think about each statement and mark on their own paper whether they agree or disagree. Prompt them to explain their decisions by reflecting on what they already know about the topic of the passage and by predicting what they think the passage will describe.

The next step is to read the selected passage aloud, stopping at strategic points to allow the students to think about their initial answers in the anticipation guide. Students can change their agreement/disagreement marking but have to support their change using an idea or quote from the text. This active engagement with the text (e.g., altering predictions, if needed) offers another opportunity for students to support their understanding of it. It also helps build higher order thinking skills, and the use of ideas and quotes creates a language-rich classroom environment, all of which facilitate improved comprehension.

Do you agree or disagree with each statement? Check the box for how you think. After you read or listen to the story, go back and look at what you chose. Change any answers you want to. Be ready to say what in the text made you change your choice

(*The Giver* by Lois Lowry, 1993)

Statement	Before reading		After reading	
	I agree	**I disagree**	**I agree**	**I disagree**
1. Having lots of rules to live by is a good idea.				
2. It is best when everyone in a community acts and thinks in the same way.				
3. It is OK to tell a lie.				
4. Jonas's parents love him.				
5. It is OK to feel sad sometimes.				

Figure 6.6. Example of an anticipation guide used as a pre- and post-reading comprehension activity.

Once students learn how to use anticipation guides, they can do so individually, in pairs, or in small groups. The key is to have students think about and explain why they agreed or disagreed with a statement and use the text to justify their choice. This can generate a rich, active discussion that builds vocabulary and comprehension and teaches higher level thinking skills (Kozen et al., 2006).

Anticipation guides are easily adapted for students with low reading skills by simplifying the wording of statements or adding pictures to them. Another adaptation is to have students listen to the teacher or a peer read aloud the statements and the passage or story, or to create the guide on a laptop computer or tablet and have the device read the statements aloud. Students indicate agreement or disagreement using a touch screen or mouse. Statements can also be programmed into a student's AAC device to allow for opportunities to read aloud and respond.

Use Question Words to Activate Prior Knowledge and Make Predictions   Another effective strategy to help students make predictions and activate relevant prior knowledge is to use question words. This helps students with complex support needs remember information they know, or experiences they have had, that relate to the topic of the readings. After introducing question words, the teacher previews the text with the students, looking at the title, the first few sentences, and any pictures or graphics. Next, students make predictions about the passage topic; to help them do so, the teacher uses question words the students worked with previously: "*Who* do you think the story is about?" "*Where* do you go to buy a fishing license?" "*What* do you think will happen in the story?" "*Why* do you think the story will be about a dog?" Student predictions are listed on one side of a whiteboard or piece of chart paper. Or, the students record their predictions about the passage using some type of graphic organizer (e.g., Morgan, Moni, & Jobling, 2004; Nation & Norbury, 2005). (They can revisit the graphic organizer after reading or listening to discuss why their predictions were or were not correct.) In addition, the teacher uses the question words to activate any prior experiences students may have that are relevant to the predicted topic. All of this gets them ready to do the actual reading.

This before-reading strategy must be used carefully when teaching students who have complex needs for support. Before assuming they know what *wh-* questions are asking, it is vital to know that research related to this very skill shows that these students may have trouble with this type of questioning. Michelle Morgan and her colleagues (2009) have discovered that many individuals with complex support needs may have special difficulty understanding the meaning of question words, especially those that ask about time (*when*). This lack of understanding makes it difficult to accurately assess a student's comprehension using *wh-* questions, and they can easily get confused when reading or listening to a text. Students who struggle to understand what the question words mean need extra instruction to develop a clear understanding of these question types before they apply them to reading stories or other texts.

Morgan et al. (2009) recommend beginning question-word instruction by teaching the *who, what,* and *where* questions using explicit, engaging instruction with lots of hands-on activities. They used modeling and think-alouds in their work with adults with complex support needs to explain what the *wh-* questions mean. They also used what they called "tell-about" words to explain how to answer questions beginning with the question words. For example, a tell about word that matches with *who* is *people* (or the name of a person); to answer a *who* question, a student must tell about a person or people. Students in this study practiced by creating charts with pictures of items (e.g., photographs of people from magazines) that were examples of each type of *wh-* question and matched tell-about words with *wh-* questions. For example, finding and creating charts that included pictures of a variety of people helped the adults understand and remember the underlying meaning of *who* and what *who* refers to. This knowledge increased their ability to answer *who* questions and thus improved their comprehension. After this type of practice, they applied their growing understanding of the *wh-* questions to a familiar story.

These researchers (Morgan et al., 2009) taught the *when* question separately, making sure to give lots of different examples of what this concept meant. They used pictures as visual support for developing the students' understanding of *when* and asked students to talk about their prior experiences, emphasizing *when* their experiences had taken place. For example, they showed students pictures of holiday experiences and asked them when different things students associated with the holiday had occurred, such as "When did you open presents with your family at Christmas?"

After teaching *when,* Morgan et al. (2009) taught *how* and *why* questions using strategies similar to those previously described. They gave students simple sentences and asked them to identify key words in each sentence that answered one of the *wh-* questions. For example, "If the question word is *where* and *where* asks about a place, what are the words in the text that tell us about the place?" (2009, p. 183). Students matched these key words to a question card. Next, students learned to use highlighters to mark key words in short sentences that answered the questions. The students used these words to write answers to questions related to the sentences.

The whole instructional process for teaching the *wh-* questions took about 6 weeks. But at the end of that time, the students truly understood the meaning of the *wh-* questions and could apply them to what they were reading.

Use a Language Experience Approach   Another unique type of prereading activity is the language experience approach (LEA) to teaching reading, a powerful tool that is used with learners of all ability levels. There are many ways to use the LEA, but there are three overarching component steps when using this approach. First, students engage in an activity or experience, preferably a shared one. After the activity, the teacher elicits and writes down student-generated language about the activity. Students can, for example, give a temporal sequence of what they did, or they can give personal opinions about the activity. The teacher then uses a shared writing structure to support students to create some type of text based on their descriptions. You can read about how one teacher did this in the "In the Classroom" feature in the textbox.

IN THE CLASSROOM

A LANGUAGE EXPERIENCE ACTIVITY FOR SEVENTH-GRADE SOCIAL STUDIES

Mr. Baca, a special educator, decided to use an LEA activity to build his seventh-grade students' comprehension skills. Mr. Baca worked with Ms. Alexander, a general educator, to co-teach a social studies class that included students with a wide range of literacy abilities, from emergent learners to conventional readers without disabilities. Mr. Baca wanted to develop an activity that would be useful for all the students in the class and that would have a strong focus on building the comprehension skills of his students with complex support needs.

Because Mr. Baca knew that it was important to use students' actual experiences as the basis for creating texts, he and Ms. Alexander began the process by scheduling a field trip to a local history museum. The museum was hosting an exhibit on the Japanese internment camp that had been established in that state during World War II. Before visiting the museum, the teachers did some shared reading activities with the whole class, using both fiction and nonfiction young adult books on the topic. They used pictures and artifacts to support all students' understanding of the content. They also pretaught vocabulary that all students needed to know, such as what *camp* meant in the context of the internment camps.

After visiting the museum, Mr. Baca and Ms. Alexander held several whole-class discussions with students about what they had seen and learned. They recorded students' comments and thoughts on chart paper. As a class, and using shared writing, they supported the students in turning this into an article for the school's parent newsletter. The teachers helped the students brainstorm the key information they wanted to include in the articles. Next, they used small-group activities to have students generate text to communicate those ideas. The teachers took the text generated from these groups and compiled it into one document. They led a whole-class activity to edit the draft. Some students created artwork or used photographs they found on a history web site to illustrate the article. Other students incorporated the text edits. When this process was completed, the teachers projected the finished product on a screen and read it aloud for final approval before submitting it to the newsletter.

Students next worked either individually or in small groups to create fictional stories, informational text, or art projects that illustrated what they had learned about the internment camps and the treatment of U.S. citizens of Japanese descent during World War II. Mr. Baca made sure that each student with complex support needs worked with him or with a peer buddy who could support participation in these activities. To help these students create a written product, Mr. Baca used questions, photos he had taken during the field trip, and other pictures and artifacts to elicit students' words about their field-trip experience. He recorded their words on chart paper, asking questions occasionally to clarify something or to prompt the students for more explanation of what they had learned or experienced on the field trip. Using this process over several class sessions, Mr. Baca gradually shaped students' responses into a coherent text. The examples in Figure 6.7 show the types of texts created. (As indicated by the italicized text, some students were working on learning key vocabulary, whereas others were working on learning to read consonant blends like /tr/.)

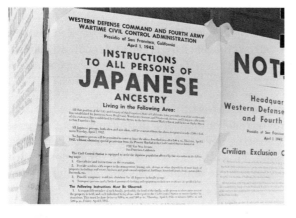

The *government* said we were bad people.

My family had to leave our *home*.

We packed up our things. We had to *travel* on *trains* and *trucks*.

I was scared. I missed my *friends*.

Figure 6.7. A language experience activity.

Once the text was created, the students with complex support needs practiced reading what they had written; Mr. Baca and the students' peer buddies worked with them to practice this. Practice included echo reading for some students and, for others, independent reading. Students (or their peer buddies) typed up the students' texts and drew or found pictures to illustrate what they had written.

LEA incorporates thinking, listening, reading, and writing, and so it is truly a comprehensive instructional approach. This method targets all aspects of reading, including comprehension. Figure 6.8 illustrates just how many components of literacy that LEA involves. It can be used with individuals, a small group, or an entire class. Although it is often used with younger readers, it can be an effective strategy with older emergent readers for whom it is difficult to find age-appropriate reading materials. It can be particularly effective for students with complex support needs because literacy instruction is linked to students' own experiences and uses their words (language). Because LEA uses students' oral (expressive) language and experiences as the text for study, it provides a scaffold for developing literacy skills. The teacher writes down what the students say verbatim, thus making the link between spoken words and print very explicit. For more ideas about how to build students' skills this way, see the resources on LEA provided at the end of this chapter.

During Reading

Reading comprehension, as we have seen, is an active process. During reading, skilled readers constantly monitor their comprehension of a passage and go back to reread and repair any breakdowns in understanding. Students with complex support needs may not know to engage in this self-monitoring behavior and benefit greatly from strategies that teach them to do this.

Reciprocal Teaching   Reciprocal teaching can address this need (e.g., Whalon & Hanline, 2008). Reciprocal teaching involves the student and teacher (or peers) taking turns reading portions of a text. They take turns predicting, generating questions, summarizing, or clarifying something in the text to help their comprehension. This strategy works well for students with poor independent reading skills who have listening comprehension skills at a level higher than their current reading skills.

Strategy Instruction   There is strong evidence that teaching students with disabilities to use specific comprehension strategies increases their comprehension abilities (e.g., Mason, 2013). This has not been studied widely with students with complex support needs, but there have been promising demonstrations that at least some of these learners can benefit from comprehension strategy instruction. Van den Bos, Nakken, Nicolay, and van Houten (2007), for example, taught adults with ID to use four reading strategies while reading (summarizing, questioning, predicting, and clarifying) to improve comprehension of written texts. They compared

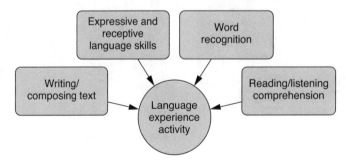

Figure 6.8.   LEA components of literacy.

two experimental conditions (i.e., two ways of providing intervention to these adults with ID) to each other and also compared them to a control group of adults with ID that received no intervention. In the first condition, researchers used direct instruction to teach the strategies one to one; in the second, they provided strategy instruction in small groups using elements of reciprocal teaching. Results showed that although both groups that received interventions performed better than the control group, there were no significant differences in strategy performance between adults who received strategy instruction in small groups and those who received it one-to-one. Participants in both groups acquired the strategies and demonstrated improved reading comprehension, maintained across 3 months.

Explicit instruction in a strategy called Reread-Adapt and Answer-Comprehend (RAAC) also helped young adults with ID and ASD improve their skill in understanding informational and narrative texts (e.g., Hua, Hendrickson et al., 2012; Hua, Therrein et al., 2012). The researchers broke the strategy into steps and taught undergraduate tutors how to teach their peers with ID or ASD to use the strategy, using explicit instruction. In the first step, tutors asked students with disabilities to read *wh-* questions related to the story (*who, where, what, when, why,* and *how* questions) and reminded them to think about the questions as they read the story. The students read the passages three times. The tutors provided feedback and error instruction for any misread words, along with feedback on overall reading performance. Next, the students orally answered the *wh-* questions they had reviewed before reading. The tutors prompted the students to find the answers in the text if any questions were missed. All of the students in this study increased their fluency and comprehension after learning the RAAC strategy.

Anaphoric Cuing
Students with poor comprehension often have difficulty understanding to whom pronouns refer within a reading passage. Even if they are not clear about a pronoun's referent, they continue reading instead of going back to clarify this relationship. Confusion about the correct referents can easily break down their comprehension of events within any given passage.

Anaphoric cuing (O'Connor & Klein, 2004) is a strategy that can be used to remind students to monitor their comprehension and to go back and reread in order to clarify any breakdowns in their understanding. To teach this strategy, give students a passage with the pronouns underlined. List three possible referents under each underlined pronoun: one that is not appropriate, one that fits the sentence but not the story, and one that fits both the sentence and the story (see Figure 6.9). Students then read the passage and mark the appropriate referent under each

---

The bus driver walked to his bus. <u>He</u> opened the door and walked up the steps.
  police officer
  Carlos
  bus driver

The bus's two-way radio made a loud noise. The driver picked <u>it</u> up. He said, "Hello, this is Mike. What do you need?"
  two-way radio
  key
  cup

The two-way radio operator said, "There is some road work on Main Street. <u>You</u> will need to leave soon, or you will be late picking up passengers.
  cab driver
  Mike
  Steve

Figure 6.9. Text adapted for the anaphoric cuing strategy.

pronoun as they read. (Alternatively, a peer or teacher can read the sentence and choices aloud and a student can indicate the referent.) The list of possible referents seems to act as an anteced-ent cue for students to go back and reread to clarify any misunderstandings about what they have read. This rereading helps them better understand the meaning of what they read.

After Reading

Effective comprehension instruction also includes postreading activities students engage in that support them in making meaning of what they have read. These after-reading instructional activities, described in the following sections, may take many forms, but all facilitate students' understanding of what they have read and help them organize and synthesize new information.

Graphic Organizers: Cooperative Story Mapping

A small but growing number of studies show that teaching students with complex support needs to use various types of graphic organizers during and after reading strengthens comprehension abilities (e.g., Carnahan & Williamson, 2013). Organizers can be used at either point in the reading process as an instruc-tional strategy (and/or as an assessment). One good example of using graphic organizers to help students with complex support needs improve their comprehension is to teach story mapping. Story mapping addresses the similar structural components found in most narratives, which are called *story grammar* elements: one or more characters, a setting, a problem the character(s) must solve, details of attempts to solve the problem, and its resolution. Narratives may also include a moral or theme.

Students struggling with comprehension are often unaware of these story grammar elements. This lack of awareness negatively affects their understanding of what they have read. Research supports explicitly teaching story grammar to students with and without dis-abilities to improve reading comprehension (e.g., Mathes & Fuchs, 1997; Whalon & Hanline, 2008). Teaching students to construct story maps is one way to assist them in learning this concept.

Story maps are visual representations that show each story grammar element in a given story. They not only help students identify and make connections between key elements of a story but also cue students to formulate questions to ask themselves as they read.

Story mapping can be done individually, but working in cooperative, mixed-ability groups allows students to work with peers to expand and deepen comprehension of a given text (Whalon & Hanline, 2008). A small-group format is often more motivating to students and provides them with multiple models of how to think about and apply comprehension strategies. Mathes and Fuchs (1997) described an effective cooperative story mapping pro-cedure they used to improve the comprehension of students with and without disabilities. We have adapted it here.

The first step is to introduce and teach story grammar elements. For this initial teaching, select a story with a clear story grammar structure. Fairy tales or fables often have most or all of these elements; however, it is important to remember to select age-appropriate materials when working with older learners. This can present difficulties; many stories for older individuals are too complex for the initial learning of story grammar elements. However, even older readers enjoy some of the alternative versions of well-known fairy tales and fables available today (e.g., *The True Story of the Three Little Pigs*), so it is possible to use one of these simple, familiar stories in an age-appropriate manner as the initial teaching example.

After selecting an appropriate book, use a shared reading activity to introduce the concept of story grammar. First, set the purpose for reading. Explain that most stories have the same key components (story grammar) and identifying them helps readers better understand what is hap-pening in the story. Instruct students to be on the lookout for each component as they read: main character, setting, problem, major events, resolution, and, possibly, a moral or theme. Read aloud while students follow along using a copy of the text, or project the text onto a screen so that all the students can see it. (See Chapter 9 for more information on read-alouds.)

After reading, work with students using a story map to identify and record each story grammar element. This part of the lesson is highly interactive. The students must give their opinions about why they selected particular events or details as key story grammar components and then go back to the story to find the text or quote that supports their opinions. Once students have had several opportunities to practice story mapping with you, move on to cooperative story mapping with small groups.

Begin cooperative story mapping with a story that has very clear story grammar elements, written at a level that allows most of the class to work with the text independently. Ideally, this activity is done in mixed-ability groups that include students with disabilities and their typically developing peers. Students read the story independently or with a buddy. When engaging in buddy reading, each reader takes turns reading and summarizing sections of the text. They clarify questions each may have, provide support in decoding difficult words, and take turns predicting what will happen next. (Please note that if the class includes students who are not conventional readers, a peer buddy or an adult can read the story to the student, or the student can listen to a recording. This allows the student to participate in the story grammar group work and benefit from the group interaction, discussion, and modeling of comprehension strategies.)

On a subsequent day, have students work in cooperative groups of four. Ask them to quickly reread the assigned story together. As they begin to read, instruct them to think about the major elements of the story and where to find information about these elements in the text. After rereading, have the group members discuss each of the story's important elements.

Based on their work, Mathes and Fuchs (1997) suggested that each group member take on the role of discussion leader for one story element and one major event. Thus, one student is in charge of the discussion of the main character and an important event, another leads the discussion for the setting and an important event, another leads discussion for the major problem and an important event, and the fourth student leads discussion for the story resolution and an important event. (If the story has a moral or theme, another student role could be added.) As part of this process, the students rotate jobs routinely so they gain experience with all story elements.

Mathes and Fuchs (1997) recommended a five-step procedure to help leaders perform their roles. Leaders are responsible for doing the following:

1. *Telling:* They share with their group their answer about the story element for which they are responsible and why they think this answer is correct.

2. *Asking:* They ask their group members what answers they came up with for this story element and ask them to support their opinions using details from the text.

3. *Discussing:* They discuss the various answers with their group, trying to help them come to an agreement about the answer. If the group cannot reach a consensus, the leader's answer becomes the final answer.

4. *Recording:* They record the group's answer for that story element on a story map.

5. *Reporting:* They report to the whole class their group's answer for that story element.

The final step in cooperative story mapping requires that all groups come back together for a whole-class discussion. One group reports on a story element—for example, a main character—and states the group's answer. If they found a different answer, other groups should be given the opportunity to share. Any disagreements that arise are opportunities for additional discussion about how groups arrived at different, yet correct, answers. (Groups must be able to support their answers by going back to the text for supporting details.) Such discussions can deepen students' understanding of the story and demonstrate how others can arrive at different conclusions when reading the same text. After all story grammar elements have been discussed, summarize the story grammar for the assigned story and review the ways that understanding story grammar is helpful in "growing" comprehension skills.

Story Retellings   Another effective method of enhancing comprehension after reading is to have students engage in story retellings. Students can retell stories in many different ways. Colasent and Griffith (1998) described a project in which they successfully used a variation of story retelling to improve the comprehension skills of three students with autism and cognitive disabilities. This approach uses many of the strategies we have described in this section.

To teach students this strategy, first provide information about the theme or topic that is going to be studied. This helps to activate prior knowledge about the topics of stories students will be reading. Next, read several different stories on this theme. (Colasent & Griffith [1998], for example, read stories about rabbits.) Stop at various points during reading to ask students to predict what might happen next in the stories, and use visuals such as pictures, objects, or even short video clips to foster understanding and build interest and engagement (much as Maria's teacher did with her, as described previously in this chapter).

After reading each story, work with the students to retell the story. Ask questions, refer back to pictures in the story, and record students' responses on chart paper. Including pictures or objects on the retelling chart can further support students' understanding and cue recall of additional details. One teacher we know collects small objects related to stories; she uses these with students while they read and allows the students to use them when they are retelling stories they have heard or read themselves. Asking students to draw their own pictures of major events is another way to support retellings. Another possible approach is to use an interview format, as Colasent and Griffith (1998) did; they asked the students in their study a series of questions to cue their memories of the stories they had read. The students pretended to be interviewed by a radio station and responded to the authors' questions using a microphone.

Story Retellings Using Reader's Theater   Reader's theater is another variation of story retelling that can be used with narratives, poetry, or even picture books to boost comprehension. To use this strategy after reading a selection, work with students to develop a script based on the reading that they will then act out for others. Incorporate main ideas, dialogue, and events into the script so that the meaning of the piece is clearly illustrated.

Reader's theater is ideal for groups of students with mixed literacy abilities because of its versatility. Students can read directly from the script the group has developed while performing reader's theater, or they can act out roles that do not require verbalization but that illustrate important events or ideas from the selection. Students who use SGDs can use their device to speak their part; or parts can be prerecorded on devices like the AbleNet Step-by-Step communicators. This strategy facilitates comprehension for all students and offers active involvement and opportunities to develop additional literacy skills such as fluency. (More information about reader's theater activities is provided in the discussion of fluency instruction in Chapter 7.)

Combining Wh- Questions With Graphic Organizers   Graphic organizers, described above as a strategy for organizing story elements, can also be combined effectively with *wh-* questions as an after-reading strategy for informational text. Wood and her colleagues (2015) conducted a study that demonstrates how teaching *wh-* questions in combination with graphic organizers can be used to improve listening comprehension and to support students' access to the general education curriculum. Researchers used these two strategies to help middle school students with ID acquire social studies content in their general education class; these students needed access to the content but were not able to read the grade-level social studies text independently. Their special education teachers used systematic instruction (i.e., system of least prompts) combined with a graphic organizer to teach them the *wh-* questions and to practice asking relevant questions about sections of the social studies text. Teachers read passages from the social studies text aloud and wrote student-generated questions on the graphic organizer. The graphic organizer included pictures representing types of *wh-* questions that could be asked as reminders to the students and checkboxes for students to mark whether answers to questions they asked about the text were in the book, not in the book, or if they didn't know.

When they had mastered asking questions, the students began working in cooperative learning groups with their general education peers in the social studies classroom, with five to seven students per group. The general education teacher taught all the students to use three cooperative learning roles, which were rotated each day. The Picture Person read chapter headings and led discussion of pictures in the chapter. The Question Asker prompted group members to ask questions about the text and record questions and answers in their journals. Finally, the Answer Person prompted group members to say whether they had been able to answer the questions they had asked by listening to the section of the text they were studying. The students with ID took turns fulfilling these roles, just as other group members did. Groups earned points for asking and answering questions they could use to play content-related games. After learning this strategy using *why* questions, all the students with ID increased the number of questions that they asked and answered, and all agreed that they liked using the strategy and liked the cooperative learning groups. The general education peers also commented that they had enjoyed the activity and believed it helped them as well.

REFLECTION QUESTION 4

Develop a lesson plan to teach a specific comprehension skill (e.g., sequence) to a group of students with mixed abilities. Describe how you would adjust instruction to ensure active participation in the lesson of a student with complex support needs. Remember to include a description of how you would assess student learning for *all* of the students in the group.

SUMMARY

Comprehension is a complex process that requires active participation by the listener or reader and involves many reading subskills working in tandem. There are many effective ways to build the comprehension skills of individuals with complex support needs and to help them to understand and enjoy the reading process; moreover, comprehension instruction can be provided even for individuals who read at a very low level or who are not yet conventional readers. Formal or informal assessments of an individual's existing skills should be used as a tool in planning instruction. An important key to successful comprehension instruction is giving learners opportunities to work with a variety of texts within authentic literacy activities, and teaching them specific strategies to apply before, during, and after reading. Including typically developing peers in these activities can be especially helpful, as research has shown, by providing models of successful application of comprehension strategies. All students (with and without complex support needs) can learn valuable comprehension skills and connect with each other around written and spoken text as humans have for millennia.

RESOURCES

Web Sites

- **News 2 You** (http://www.n2y.com) requires a yearly paid subscription to access Unique Learning System and other products with built-in adaptations for students with complex support needs; this site provides tools that help with word recognition and comprehension; age-appropriate, differentiated texts for all learners; and built-in assessment.

- **ReadWorks** (http://www.readworks.org) offers users a free subscription; the site provides reading passages organized by Lexile and/or grade level and provides comprehension activities. One example of how to use the site is to find alternate texts for social studies and science topics.

- **Reading A–Z** (http://www.readinga-z.com) requires a yearly paid, but relatively inexpensive, subscription to access materials that are generally based on the Fountas and Pinnell leveling system; the site provides useful tools like readers theater scripts and books on the same topic that range across multiple levels.

Books

- Carnahan, C. R., & Williamson, P. (Eds.). (2010). *Quality literacy instruction for students with autism spectrum disorders.* Lenexa, KS: AAPC Publishing. This text addresses all aspects of a comprehensive literacy program. It includes the evidence base for instructional practices and gives practical ideas for implementing the strategies with students with ASD across a range of functioning levels.

- Porter, J. (2011). *Autism & reading comprehension: Ready-to-use lessons for teachers.* Arlington, TX: Future Horizons. These practical lessons provide structured, engaging comprehension lessons for students with ASD or other complex support needs. The lessons include links to web sites and lists of books on related topics to extend and build students' interest and comprehension skills.

Assessment Tools

- **OWLS-II** (Oral and Written Language Scales, Second Edition; http://www.pearsonclinical .com/language/products/100000293/owls-ii-lcoe-and-rcweoral-and-written-language-scales-second-edition-owls-ii.html) provides more detailed assessment information than many other tools. It is especially useful as a formative assessment for some students with complex support needs. It includes reading and listening comprehension subtests. If you cannot find a copy, ask the speech-language pathologist assigned to your school; many speech-language pathologists use this on a regular basis.

- **Center for Literacy and Disability Studies: Resources** (https://www.med.unc.edu/ahs/ clds/resources) has myriad assessment and instructional resources for teaching literacy to students across the lifespan. Take advantage of the videos, informational MS PowerPoint presentations, and informal assessment tools when planning instruction.

REFERENCES

Ahlgrim-Delzell, L., Browder, D., Flowers, C., & Baker, J. (2008–2009). *Nonverbal literacy assessment.* Charlotte, NC: University of North Carolina.

Allor, J., Mathes, P.G., Roberts, J.K., Cheatham, J.P., & Al Otaiba, S. (2014). Is scientifically based reading instruction effective for students with below-average IQs? *Exceptional Children, 80*(3), 287–306.

Bondy, A.S., & Frost, L.A. (1994). The Picture Exchange Communication System. *Focus on Autism and Other Developmental Disabilities, 9*(3), 1–19. doi:10.1177/108835769400900301

Carlisle, J.F., & Rice, M.S. (2004). Assessment of reading comprehension. In C.A. Stone, E. Silliman, B.J. Ehren, & K. Apel (Eds.), *Handbook of language and literacy: Development and disorders* (pp. 521–540). New York, NY: Guilford Press.

Carnahan, C., & Williamson, P. (Eds.). (2010). Autism, cognition, and reading. In *Quality literacy instruction for students with autism spectrum disorders* (pp. 21–44). Lenexa, KS: AAPC Publishing.

Carnahan, C., & Williamson, P. (2013). Does compare-contrast text structure help students with autism spectrum disorder comprehend science text? *Exceptional Children, 79*(3), 347–363.

Colasent, R., & Griffith, P.L. (1998). Autism and literacy: Looking into the classroom with rabbit stories. *The Reading Teacher, 51,* 414–420.

Connor, C.M., Alberto, P.A., Compton, D.L., & O'Connor, R.E. (2014). *Improving reading outcomes for students with or at risk for reading disabilities: A synthesis of the contributions from the Institute of Education Sciences Research Centers* (NCSER 2014-3000). Washington, DC: National Center for Special Education Research, Institute of Education Sciences, U.S. Department of Education.

Duke, N.K., & Carlisle, J. (2011). The development of comprehension. In M.L. Kamil, P.D. Pearson, E.B. Moji, & P.P. Afflerbach (Eds.), *Handbook of reading research: Volume IV* (pp. 199–228). New York, NY: Routledge.

El Zein, F., Solis, M., Vaughn, S., & McCulley, L. (2014). Reading comprehension interventions for students with autism spectrum disorders: A synthesis of research. *Journal of Autism and Developmental Disorders, 44,* 1303–1322.

Erickson, K., Hanser, G., Hatch, P., & Sanders, E. (2009). *Research-based practices for creating access to the general curriculum in reading and literacy for students with significant intellectual disabilities.* Chapel Hill, NC: Center for Literacy and Disability Studies.

Fisher, D., & Frey, N. (2003). *Improving adolescent literacy: Strategies at work.* Upper Saddle River, NJ: Merrill/Prentice Hall.

Forts, A.M., & Luckasson, R. (2011). Reading, writing, and friendship: Adult implications of effective literacy instruction for students with intellectual disability. *Research and Practice for Persons with Severe Disabilities, 36*(3–4), 121–125.

Hogan, T.P., Adolf, S.M., & Alonzo, C.N. (2014). On the importance of listening comprehension. *International Journal of Speech-Language Pathology, 16*(3), 199–207.

Howorth, S., Lopata, C., Thomeer, M., & Rodgers, J. (2016). Effects of the TWA strategy on expository reading of comprehension of students with autism. *British Journal of Special Education, 43*(1), 40–59.

Hua, Y., Hendrickson, J.M., Therrien, W.J., Woods-Groves, S., Rice, P.S., & Shaw, J.J. (2012). Effects of combined reading and question generation on reading fluency and comprehension of three young adults with autism and intellectual disability. *Focus on Autism and Other Developmental Disabilities, 27*(3), 135–146.

Hua, Y., Therrien, W.J., Hendrickson, J.M., Woods-Groves, S., Ries, P.S., & Shaw, J.W. (2012). Effects of combined repeated reading and question generation intervention on young adults with cognitive disabilities. *Education and Training in Autism and Developmental Disabilities, 47*(1), 72–83.

Jones, F.W., Long, K., & Finlay, W.M. (2006). Assessing the reading comprehension of adults with learning disabilities. *Journal of Intellectual Disability Research, 50*(6), 410–418.

Kendeou, P., Lynch, J.S., van den Broek, P., Espin, C.A., White, M.J., & Kremer, K.E. (2005). Developing successful readers: Building early comprehension skills through television viewing and listening. *Early Childhood Education Journal, 33*(2), 91–98. doi:10.1007/s1064-005-0030-6

Kozen, A.A., Murray, R.K., & Windell, I. (2006). Increasing all students' chance to achieve: Using and adapting anticipation guides with middle school learners. *Intervention in School and Clinic, 41*(4), 195–200.

Lundberg, I., & Reichenberg, M. (2013). Developing reading comprehension among students with mild intellectual disabilities: An intervention study. *Scandinavian Journal of Educational Research, 57*(1), 89–100.

Lowry, L. (1993). *The giver.* New York, NY: Houghton Mifflin Books for Children.

Mason, L.H. (2013). Teaching students who struggle with learning to think before, while, and after reading: Effects of self-regulated strategy development instruction. *Reading & Writing Quarterly, 29,* 124–144.

Mathes, P.G., & Fuchs, D. (1997). Cooperative story mapping. *Remedial & Special Education, 18,* 20–28.

Morgan, M., Moni, K.B., & Jobling, A. (2004). What's it all about? Investigating reading comprehension strategies in young adults with Down syndrome. *Down Syndrome Research and Practice, 9,* 37–44.

Morgan, M., Moni, K. B., & Jobling, A. (2009). Who? Where? What? When? Why? How? Question words— What do they mean? *British Journal of Learning Disabilities, 37,* 178–185.

Nation, K., & Norbury, C.F. (2005). Why reading comprehension fails: Insights from developmental disabilities. *Topics in Language Disorders, 25,* 21–32.

O'Connor, I.M., & Klein, P.D. (2004). Exploration of strategies for facilitating the reading comprehension of high-functioning students with autism spectrum disorders. *Journal of Autism and Developmental Disorders, 34,* 115–126.

Ouellette, G., & Beers, A. (2010). A not-so-simple view of reading: How oral vocabulary and visual-word recognition complicate the story. *Reading & Writing, 23,* 189–208.

Reading A–Z. (n.d.). Retrieved May 15, 2016, from http://www.readinga-z.com/

Scarborough, H. (2001). Connecting early language and literacy to later reading (dis)abilities: Evidence, theory, and practice. In S.B. Neuman & D.K. Dickinson (Eds.), *Handbook of early literacy* (pp. 97–110). New York, NY: Guilford Press.

Sesma, H.W., Mahone, E.M., Levine, T., Eason, S.H., & Cutting, L.E. (2009). The contribution of executive skills to reading comprehension. *Child Neuropsychology, 15,* 232–246.

van den Bos, K.P., Nakken, H., Nicolay, P.G., & van Houten, E.J. (2007). Adults with mild intellectual disabilities: Can their reading comprehension ability be improved? *Journal of Intellectual Disability Research, 51*(Pt. 11), 835–849.

van Wingerden, W., Segers, E., van Balkom, H., & Verhoeven, L. (2014). Cognitive and linguistic predictors of reading comprehension in children with intellectual disabilities. *Research in Developmental Disabilities, 35,* 3139–3147.

Whalon, K., & Hanline, M.F. (2008). Effects of a reciprocal questioning intervention on the question generation and responding of children with autism spectrum disorder. *Education and Training in Developmental Disabilities, 43*(3), 367–387.

Woodcock, R.W. (1991). *Woodcock Language Proficiency Battery–Revised.* Chicago, IL: Riverside.

Wood, L., Browder, D.M., & Flynn, L. (2015). Teaching students with intellectual disability to use a self-questioning strategy to comprehend social studies text for an inclusive setting. *Research and Practice for Persons with Severe Disabilities, 40*(4), 275–293.

CHAPTER 7

A Broader Approach to Fluency

Pamela Williamson, Christina R. Carnahan, Jeongae Kang, and Turki S. Alzahraney

LEARNING OBJECTIVES

By the end of this chapter, readers will

1. Explain the role of fluency in comprehending text.
2. Name and describe the components of fluency and explain how each component contributes to overall fluency.
3. Describe several ways to assess fluency and design fluency instruction that takes into account the learning needs of students with complex support needs.

This chapter will discuss the role that reading fluency plays in comprehension. We will begin by defining fluency and exploring its components in depth. Next, we will discuss overarching goals in fluency instruction for students with complex support needs, along with recommendations for how best to assess fluency in this population. Finally, we will discuss general principles of effective fluency instruction and specific instructional techniques that promote fluency.

LEARNING TO READ: Emma

Emma is a 6-year-old first grade student who is learning to communicate using TouchChat (Saltillo Corp., 2012) on her iPad. Emma spends the majority of her school day in the general education classroom with support from various service professionals, including a special education teacher, speech-language pathologist (SLP), occupational therapist, and physical therapist. These related service professionals work with the general education teacher, Mrs. Perkin, to plan activities throughout the day, support Emma during academic instruction, and also provide one-on-one and small-group instruction outside of the classroom.

Mrs. Perkin is concerned about Emma's progress in expressive vocabulary and reading, so she has planned to meet with the special education teacher and the SLP to develop an instructional plan. Before the meeting, the team spoke with Emma's family to gather information about her likes and interests. Emma's father reported that she loves clothes, shoes, and accessories; watching movies about princesses; and playing outside.

Mrs. Perkin opens the team meeting by sharing important literacy assessment data. She describes Emma's strengths, which include her knowledge of books. For example, Emma differentiates between the front and back of a book and between the top and bottom, she turns pages, and she knows where to find information about the author. Her strengths also include awareness of some concepts of print: she knows the difference between the words on the page and the pictures and she tracks print from the beginning to the end of sentences. Emma also knows that one spoken word corresponds to one word on the page, and she has a growing list of sight words. Yet, Mrs. Perkin is concerned that despite these well-developed skills, Emma isn't making progress using simple, decodable texts. She explains that Emma often disengages or becomes frustrated when it is her turn to read—for example, pushing books away, closing her eyes, and often running to the corner of the classroom. Mrs. Perkin uses technology to provide opportunities for Emma to learn how to decode words, such as blending individual letter sounds and making words with phonograms, or word families (words with similar spelling patterns, such as *bat, mat,* and *flat*). However, she is unsure how to use a decodable text with Emma. She also wonders if teaching Emma a list of high-frequency words, such as the Dolch sight-word list, might be valuable.

The team discusses the importance of addressing concerns about reading decodable texts as part of comprehensive literacy instruction (Allor & Chard, 2011). Together, they develop Emma's reading fluency plan, which includes (a) reading decodable texts, (b) shared story reading, (c) read-alouds, and (d) independent practice. In addition, instead of focusing on Dolch words, the team decides to focus on core words to help develop Emma's communication *and* reading skills. The team also decides to continue the phonics instruction already in place because it focuses on blending sounds and working with phonograms, which are important to developing reading fluency (Hudson, Torgesen, Lane, & Turner, 2012).

At a subsequent meeting, the team reviews and selects texts aligned with Emma's interests, as identified by her family. The team understands that this is important to ensure Emma's motivation to practice reading (Allor & Chard, 2011). From these texts, the team identifies books for each of these purposes.

The team selects decodable books written at the preprimer level, which was Emma's independent reading level, or the level at which she can read with support from a teacher (Hudson, Lane, & Pullen, 2005). These books have few words on each page and follow an easy-to-discern pattern (e.g., "I wear *boots,*" "I wear *socks*"). They also have pictures that closely represent the text, such as a photograph of rain boots. The special education teacher develops a protocol for reading the decodable texts with Emma, which includes these steps:

1. The adult reads the text aloud and points to the words.

2. The adult rereads the book using the TouchChat app on Emma's iPad.

3. Emma and the adult read the book together as Emma uses TouchChat to find some words (e.g., core words) while the adult reads aloud other words (e.g., specific nouns).

The books identified for the shared story reading approach are narrative stories including *Fancy Nancy* (O'Conner, 2005) and *Not All Princesses Dress in Pink* (Yolen & Stemple, 2010). These narratives have characters, settings, and plots, which provide opportunities to work on *wh-* questions (e.g., *Who* is the story about?). Using these books, the team also identifies a list of core words in the books, including *I, mine, she, they, play,* and *wear,* that will be targeted during shared reading to continue to develop Emma's communication skills and sight-word vocabulary. (The protocol for shared reading is provided in Table 7.1.)

The team selects two additional books from the *Fancy Nancy* (O'Conner, 2005) series to use as read-alouds each day with Emma. They do so because they recognize the importance of providing Emma with oral language models to help her understand what fluent reading sounds like (Rasinski, 2003). Finally, to provide independent practice, the team also develops a teaching protocol for sustained silent reading sessions (Carnahan, Williamson, Clarke, & Sorenson, 2009). Peers and Emma's family will be asked to listen to Emma read aloud using TouchChat to encourage her to practice reading. The team decides to implement the new plan for 2 weeks. They plan to reconvene at the end of 1 week to resolve any problems that arise and to select new reading materials for the next 2 weeks.

WHAT IS READING FLUENCY AND WHY IS IT IMPORTANT?

What is "fluent" reading? We know what it means to say someone *speaks* a language fluently: it means that the person can easily express ideas through speech, without struggling

Table 7.1.　Teaching protocol for shared book reading

Teacher behavior	Student behavior	Contingency plans
1a. Say, "We are going to read a book together. When we read, our job is to understand what the author is telling us. Let's start with reviewing words the author will use in the story." Review core vocabulary cards (cards with picture representations and printed words) by placing cards on the table and selecting one at a time to discuss.	1a. Locate and select the word in TouchChat.	1a. If the student doesn't respond, say, "Let's see if we can find it together." Then, use a penlight to point to the location on the board where the student navigates to select the word. If there is still no response, touch the button.
1b. After the student selects the word in TouchChat, look in the book to find examples; talk about words in the book together. For example, say, "Yes, the word is *she*. Let's find pictures of this word in the book." Wait for the student to point to the picture.	1b. Point to pictures on the page in the book that correspond with the vocabulary word.	
Say, "That's it. Tell what the word is again."	Use TouchChat to again label the word.	
2. Read one page at a time aloud. Say, "Now we are going to read each page and summarize what we read. This helps us understand the story. Use your finger to read as I say the words aloud."	2. Look at pictures and use a finger to track print as the adult reads.	2. Entice the student to read by talking about the pictures. Use a gesture prompt and say, "Let's start here."
3a. At the end of each page, stop and model a summary statement using the core word. For example, on p. 2 of *Not All Princesses Dress in Pink* (Yolen & Stemple, 2010), say, "She plays ball. Let's use your device to say it with our words."	3a. Use TouchChat to either (a) repeat the teacher's statement OR (b) create your own sentence using the core words.	3a. If there is no response, say, "Let's do it together. We can use these words." Point to core vocabulary word cards. Build a sentence using vocabulary cards and then navigate to and select core words using TouchChat.
3b. During consecutive readings of the text, say, "You tell me about the story using your words."	3b. Navigate to and select buttons to describe what is happening using core words.	3b. If there is no response, initially provide encouragement ("You can do it!"). Wait 5 seconds and then use the penlight to provide a visual cue to indicate the appropriate core words. If there is still no response, use a physical prompt to indicate the appropriate words.
4. Repeat Step 3b for each page of text.		
5. After reading, select one page of the book (the page in which the student demonstrated greatest interest) and say, "Let's write about what we read. Tell me what happened."	5. Navigate to and select appropriate core words to create a sentence such as, "She play ball" or " She play rain."	If there is no response or an incorrect response, present the core word cards from the table that the student can use to make a sentence. Say, "Remember, you can use [insert words] to talk about this picture."
	Listen and watch as the teacher writes.	If there is no response, say, "Let's see if we can arrange these pictures to make a sentence." Use a gesture cue to prompt the student as necessary. After sequencing words, encourage the student to build a sentence in TouchChat.
After the student drafts a sentence, repeat it, write it, and model correcting and rereading it. For example, say, "Yes! She play rain" and write the sentence on a piece of paper. Then say, "We can also say, 'she plays in rain'" and add the extra words to the page in small print. Say, "Let's read it together." Point with the student to each word and read aloud.	Point to words as the teacher reads aloud.	Use a gesture prompt to indicate where to point.

to find the right words, to form sentences, or to articulate words and sentences. *Reading* fluency, however, is somewhat harder to define. What does it mean to say someone is a "fluent" reader, and why is it important for students to become fluent readers? How does fluency contribute to the achievement of our ultimate instructional goal for students—silent reading comprehension?

Defining Fluency

There are multiple definitions of *fluency*. These definitions address several aspects of how we read connected text:

- How automatically we read—that is, do we process words quickly without having to devote a great deal of conscious effort to figuring out what the text says?

- How accurately we read—that is, can we recognize and/or decode words correctly?

- How we employ prosody—that is, can we read with appropriate intonation that "sounds like" good reading?

Different definitions of fluency vary in how much importance they ascribe to each of these three components, which will be explored in greater depth later in this chapter.

There are at least five different definitions of *fluency* found in the literature (Kuhn, Schwanenflugel, & Meisinger, 2010). One definition particularly emphasizes elements also included in most other definitions: specifically, the importance of accurate and automatic word recognition, including rapid skills in phonemic awareness and letter–sound correspondence (Fletcher, Lyon, Fuchs, & Barnes, 2007; Good, Kaminski, Simmons, & Kame'enui, 2001). However, this definition does not explicitly address prosody. A second model of fluency emphasizes prosody while underemphasizing reading rate and accuracy (Daane, Campbell, Grigg, Goodman, & Oranje, 2005). Still another conceptualizes reading fluency as skilled reading (Samuels & Farstrup, 2006), but some experts have argued that skilled reading does not account for the complexities of comprehension (Kuhn et al., 2010). A fourth model from Chard and his colleagues (Chard et al., 2005; Chard, Pikulski, & McDonagh, 2006) defines reading fluency primarily as the oral language/word reading bridge to comprehension. Finally, Kuhn and her colleagues proposed a comprehensive definition of reading fluency suggesting, "fluency combines accuracy, automaticity, and oral reading prosody, which, taken together, facilitate the reader's construction of meaning" (2010, p. 240). Ultimately, while debates regarding the definition may seem theoretical or academic, or even challenging to apply when working with students with complex learning needs, how we define fluency has implications for assessment and instruction.

Why Fluency Matters

On to our second question: Why does fluency matter? You probably noticed that the different definitions of fluency above addresses accuracy, automaticity, and prosody but also comprehension. Silent reading comprehension is the goal of all reading instruction, and this requires the integration of multiple processes, including reading fluency (Allor & Chard, 2011; Allor, Mathes, Roberts, Cheatham, & Champlin, 2010; Kuhn et al., 2010).

Although it is easy to assume that "fluency problems lead to comprehension problems" (Allor & Chard, 2011, p. 1), the relationship between reading fluency and reading comprehension is not so straightforward. Growing evidence suggests that there may be a reciprocal relationship between comprehension and fluency (Allor & Chard, 2011; Kuhn et al., 2010). In other words, fluency doesn't just help comprehension; comprehension probably helps fluency. This suggests that for students to learn how to read, including students with complex learning needs, comprehensive literacy instruction that addresses all components is essential (Allor et al., 2010), and the center of instruction should be making meaning from the text. The purpose of this chapter is to develop current understandings of reading fluency informed by theory and research, fluency assessments, and comprehensive fluency instruction.

TOWARD A THEORY OF READING FLUENCY FOR STUDENTS WITH MODERATE AND SEVERE DISABILITIES

As noted previously, how we define fluency—and how we understand the relationship between fluency and comprehension—has implications for assessment and instruction, especially for individuals with complex support needs. These individuals may have specific challenges that affect different aspects of fluency and thereby affect comprehension. With this in mind, let's look more closely at the components of fluency and at how existing models of comprehension address the role of reading fluency.

Components of Fluency

Although debate continues regarding factors that influence fluency and reading comprehension, generally speaking, reading fluency occurs during the reading of connected text. Fluency includes aspects of accuracy, automaticity, and prosody (see, e.g., Hudson, Pullen, Lane, & Torgesen, 2008; Rasinski, Reutzel, Chard, & Linan-Thompson, 2011).

Accuracy and Automaticity　　How accurately we read affects how automatically we read. If our sight-word vocabulary and decoding skills are well developed enough for us to look at a text and process most words easily and correctly, we can read it fairly automatically without laboring to decode each word. This, in turn, affects comprehension. Conceptually, the big idea is that for comprehension to occur, words on the page must be processed rapidly enough to leave working memory available for readers to engage in comprehension processes (e.g., retrieving relevant background knowledge, pairing meanings of receptive vocabulary words with printed words). It may seem obvious, but when readers identify words accurately by sight instead of decoding words with phonics, they use less working memory to process the printed word. Thus, accuracy of word reading and automaticity are related.

That is why Emma's team concluded that the general education teacher should continue phonics and sight-word instruction, with a slight modification—core words would be taught instead of Dolch words. Being able to identify words automatically during the reading of connected text, such as sentences and passages, leaves more working memory for comprehension, and core words are useful for communication *and* reading. (See Grether & Pelatti, 2010, for more information on core words.) Furthermore, building flexibility with words—which includes the ability to read the words we use to communicate—is critical for students with complex learning needs.

What does automaticity look like as it develops in students like Emma? Logan (1997) suggests that automaticity includes four dimensions: speed, effortlessness, autonomy, and lack of conscious attention. Speed and accuracy emerge together as automaticity develops, but *developing speed is not the goal;* rather, the goal is to apprehend words quickly enough to provide ample time for other processes to take place, such as activating knowledge of the word's meaning. Furthermore, there is a limit as to how fast connected text should be read to support, rather than negatively affect, comprehension (Kuhn et al., 2010).

Ideally, word reading should be effortless and require little from working memory beyond retrieving information from long-term memory. When this happens, it is automatic and likely to occur without conscious effort or attention. The more experience students have with words in context, the greater automaticity they will have while reading. This is why it was essential for Emma's educational team to plan thematic instruction using connected texts. They chose to use books that would provide multiple exposures to words using shared book reading and read-alouds. They also provided multiple ways for her to interact with these words, including listening to the words and reading the words with TouchChat. Over time, these experiences help her to read the words with increasing accuracy and automaticity.

Prosody　　Imagine listening to a skilled reader reading a chapter aloud from your favorite book. They are reading with prosody. Prosody links the printed word to oral language (Kuhn & Stahl, 2003). It includes features found in oral language, such as stress, phrasing, and intonation. However, it is important to note that there are distinct features in both oral reading and oral speaking. For example, in oral speech, transitions between sentences might involve shorter pauses compared to transitions between sentences we read aloud. Also, prosody differs when we read an expository, rather than a narrative, text; the rhythm and phrasing are markedly different.

Finally, it is important to note that most reading is done silently, not orally. Thus, developing silent reading habits is critical. This is why Emma's team included silent reading as part of her comprehensive fluency development plan.

Fluency and Models of Reading Comprehension

Because silent reading comprehension is the goal of all reading instruction, we examine fluency as it relates to various models of comprehension. To achieve minimal comprehension, readers must translate letters and/or symbols on a page into the ideas they represent.

Many different models describe the process of reading comprehension. One model, developed by Hudson and her colleagues (2008), includes elements of decoding as contributors to reading fluency. They also included elements of reading comprehension (i.e., metacognition, knowledge, passage context, social context) in their model. When tested, phonogram fluency, or the ability to identify word families, predicted reading fluency. In addition, phonemic awareness and letter–sound fluency did not directly contribute to fluency, which is logical given that both skills are represented by higher level phonogram fluency. Thus, this model emphasizes the word-level skills contribution to overall fluency.

Another model, described by Allor and Chard, is a "deep construct view" of fluency (2011, p. 1). This model acknowledges the importance of decoding while also suggesting that oral language and listening comprehension contribute to word-reading skills. Specifically, this model connects the linguistic system (phonology, syntax, and morphology) and lexicon (i.e., subcomponents of vocabulary knowledge) to the reading process.

Thus, while Hudson et al.'s (2008) model emphasizes the contribution of word reading to fluency, and Allor and Chard's model (2011) emphasizes transfer of oral language processes to reading, a third model, the Simple View of Reading model, depicts reading as a two-path process that includes two components—decoding and linguistic competence—and suggests that weaknesses in either area will make skilled reading difficult (Gough & Tunmer, 1986). All three models recognize reading fluency as important for developing reading comprehension.

Surprisingly little research has been conducted to investigate the relationships among oral reading fluency (ORF), silent reading fluency, listening comprehension, and reading comprehension (Kim, Wagner, & Foster, 2011). Kim and her colleagues investigated relationships among these constructs with 316 first-grade students. They found that although ORF and silent reading fluency are related, they are distinctly different skills related to fluency. Generally, tasks related to word reading (e.g., reading word lists, ORF) were better predictors of reading comprehension for average readers, whereas tasks related to language processing better predicted the reading comprehension of skilled readers (e.g., silent reading comprehension, listening comprehension). Thus, the researchers concluded that the reading comprehension of average readers was constrained by decoding, which was not true for skilled readers; and thus, skilled readers profited more from oral language influences on reading comprehension. The authors could not conclude if their findings originated with reading development, acquisition of reading skills, or both.

REFLECTION QUESTION 1

Why is fluency an important component of comprehensive literacy instruction?

Fluency and Students With Complex Learning Needs

We have emphasized an essential idea that the ultimate goal of all reading instruction, including fluency, is silent reading comprehension. This is true for *all* students, including those with the most significant or complex learning needs. Although some of these learners may never develop typical oral speech, building instruction to support their overall reading comprehension is essential. To address the components of reading fluency for these students, it may be helpful to move away from traditional definitions of prosody, which can be challenging to apply for students with limited verbal language, and instead conceptualize reading prosody as something that occurs during silent reading as students apply what they know from oral language about semantics, syntax, and pragmatics (Williamson & Carnahan, 2010). (To review these components of language, refer to Chapter 2.) In addition, for students with complex learning needs, modeling prosodic features during read-alouds may make apparent these important linguistic markers for comprehension.

With this in mind, we will examine the role of fluency as part of a comprehensive literacy instruction program for students with complex support needs. We begin by discussing why fluency is assessed, and how and when to assess it, keeping in mind particular caveats about assessing fluency in this student population. Then, we will discuss instructional techniques for promoting fluency.

ASSESSMENT OF READING FLUENCY

Assessments of reading fluency have been used as proxies, or indicators, of comprehension. However, it is important to remember that there is likely a reciprocal relationship between fluency and comprehension (Allor & Chard, 2011; Kuhn et al., 2010). Although there is widespread agreement about the positive correlation between reading fluency and reading comprehension at lower reading levels, the relationship between the two weakens as students read more difficult text (Jenkins & Jewell, 1993; Shinn, Good, Knutson, Tilly, & Collins, 1992; Silberglitt, Burns, Madyun, & Lail, 2006). Furthermore, although reading fluency assessments might highlight potential reading problems, on the surface they lack diagnostic value because fluency problems may occur for any number of reasons, such as sight recognition issues, decoding problems, or lack of background knowledge about the topic. Furthermore, for students who are affected by communication challenges, the relationship between fluency and comprehension is likely compromised. For example, students with autism spectrum disorder (ASD) may have reading skills that are disassociated (Nation, Clarke, Wright, & Williams, 2006). They may be able to pronounce all the words in a text while not associating the words with meaning.

Ultimately, for students with complex learning needs, fluency assessments alone are insufficient for developing a true picture of a student's reading comprehension needs. Fluency assessments must be conducted as part of comprehensive literacy assessments that include multiple measures, especially related to comprehension and vocabulary. We discuss approaches for assessing reading fluency with the understanding that such assessments cannot occur in isolation or as a proxy for comprehension.

When, How, and Why Should Fluency Be Assessed?

ORF should be assessed periodically once students begin reading connected text (Hasbrouck & Tindal, 1992; 2006). For students without disabilities, the first time ORF is assessed is around the middle of first grade. ORF information can provide insight as to

- Whether students are generalizing what they are learning from phonics and sight-word instruction to the reading of connected text (i.e., accuracy)

- Whether they are reading at a comfortable pace that allows for comprehension (i.e., rate, which is one aspect of automaticity)

- How they are transferring intonation developed from oral language experiences to reading aloud (i.e., prosody)

There are many commercially available products that provide standardized measures of fluency (e.g., DIBELS, AIMSWEB), and informal measures of fluency (e.g., running records, curriculum-based measures, informal reading inventories). For students who are readers without speech, assessing silent reading fluency is an option.

ORF procedures generally include having students read two grade-level passages orally for one minute. The assessor records any deviations from the printed text, including mispronunciations, substituted words, omissions, rereading words, reversals, and insertions. The number of words per minute (WPM) is calculated as a proxy for automaticity, and the number of words correct per minute (WCPM) is calculated (i.e., WPM – errors = WCPM), as a measure of accuracy. These scores are averaged for the two passages and compared to norms (see the discussion of norms below). Prosody, the third aspect of reading fluency, is typically assessed qualitatively using a rubric.

The scores are then compared to norms—meaning, a comparison group, ideally of individuals from the same population. Some school districts develop and use local norms, while others use national norms provided by the assessment being used or established by large studies (e.g., Hasbrouck & Tindal, 2006). We present the fluency norms identified by Hasbrouck and Tindal in Table 7.2. Normative data were collected from gifted students, students with reading disabilities, and English language learners who were in general education classrooms. Not surprisingly, individuals with significant learning needs were not included, which should be considered when fluency data from these students are interpreted.

Norms for silent reading are not readily available for students reading texts written below fifth-grade level. As with ORF, students read two passages silently for 1 minute. Since students are not reading orally, words per minute cannot be calculated. Generally, however, we expect silent reading rates to be somewhat faster than oral reading rates. Leslie and Caldwell (2010) suggested that students read between about 73 and 175 words per minute, and those in sixth grade read between about 91 and 235 words per minute silently. In middle school, students read between about 119 and 233 words per minute in narrative text and between 105 and 189 in informational text. Silent reading ranges increase in variability once students reach high school, with students reading anywhere from 65 to 334 words per minute.

Interpreting Fluency Assessment Data: Deviations From Print

What can these assessment data tell us about an individual student? For ORF administrations, two different kinds of deviations from print are analyzed separately and can provide more information about how students approach the task of reading connected text. The two kinds of deviations are those related to the process of reading (i.e., rereading, omitting words or punctuation, transposing words) and miscued words (i.e., substituting one word for another, mispronouncing a word). Process errors and miscues are analyzed separately.

For process errors, the big idea is to consider what the error suggests about the reader's fluency. For example, an instance or two of rereading text might suggest that the student was monitoring their comprehension, whereas more than two occasions of rereading might indicate problems with tracking text across the page or problems with decoding. Additional assessments or instruction can be used to follow up on the assessor's interpretations. For example, if the student appears to have decoding problems, a diagnostic phonics assessment could confirm this. If a student has problems tracking text while reading, teaching a student to use a finger sweep under a line of text, or a piece of paper underneath each line of text, might remedy this problem.

Miscues analysis provides insight into which cues students attend to during reading when they are unsure of a word—that is, cues related to a word's letter–sound patterns, its grammatical function in a sentence, or its meaning. To conduct a miscue analysis, the word from the text is compared to what the student actually read and is analyzed to determine what both words have in common. Miscues can be similar to target words *graphophonetically, syntactically,* or *semantically.* Graphophonetic miscues share similar phonetic patterns at the beginning, middle, or end of words. For example, suppose the target word was *goat* and the student read *got.* These two words are graphophonetically similar because they share the same beginnings and endings but differ in their medial (middle) vowel sound. Words and miscues may also be syntactically similar, meaning they occupy the same grammatical function. *Goat* and *got* are not syntactically the same, because *goat* is a noun and *got* is a verb. Suppose the student read *coat* instead of *goat,* however—in this case, the target word and miscue are syntactically similar

Table 7.2. Oral reading fluency norms

| Grade | Percentile | WCPM | | |
		Fall	Winter	Spring
1	90		81	111
	75		47	82
	50		**23**	**53**
	25		12	28
	10		6	15
2	90	106	125	142
	75	79	100	117
	50	**51**	**72**	**89**
	25	25	42	61
	10	11	18	31
3	90	128	146	162
	75	99	120	137
	50	71	92	107
	25	44	62	78
	10	21	36	48
4	90	145	166	180
	75	119	139	152
	50	**94**	**112**	**123**
	25	68	87	98
	10	45	61	72
5	90	166	182	194
	75	139	156	168
	50	**110**	**127**	**139**
	25	85	99	109
	10	61	74	83
6	90	177	195	204
	75	153	167	177
	50	**127**	**140**	**150**
	25	98	111	122
	10	68	82	93
7	90	180	192	202
	75	156	165	177
	50	**128**	**136**	**150**
	25	102	109	123
	10	79	88	98
8	90	185	199	199
	75	161	173	177
	50	**133**	**146**	**151**
	25	106	115	124
	10	77	84	97

Key: WCPM, words correct per minute.

From Hasbrouck, J.E., & Tindal, G.A. (2006). Oral reading fluency norms: A valuable tool for reading teachers. *The Reading Teacher, 59*(7), 636–644.

because both are nouns. Finally, words can be similar semantically—meaning they have similar meanings. *Goat* and *got* are not similar semantically but *got* and *get* are.

Once each miscue has been analyzed, the percentage of similarities is calculated and interpreted. We include a miscue analysis form in Figure 7.1. To use this form, the assessor should

- Record the target word from the text in the Text column.

- In the Miscue column, record the word uttered by the student. (Include all miscues from text at the student's independent or instructional reading level.)

- Use the appropriate column under the Similar heading to record *yes* when the miscue has graphophonetic, syntactic, or semantic similarity to the target word from the text.

- In the Total row, count the number of target words from the text, the number of miscues (this should be the same), and the number of *yes* responses for each category of similarity.

- Finally, calculate the percentage of times words from the text were similar to miscues.

As with process deviations, miscues should be interpreted with frequency in mind. For example, if a large number of miscues are graphophonetically similar, and are not semantically similar, this may indicate an over-reliance on phonics during reading. On the other hand, if miscues are most frequently related semantically, and not graphophonetically, this might suggest that the student is underusing phonics. Leslie and Caldwell (2010) suggest drawing miscues from passages written at a student's independent and instructional levels, because miscues from overly difficult passages may involve little more than guessing. They also recommend analyzing no fewer than 15 miscues. The National Center on Intensive Intervention at the American Institutes for Research recommends analyzing the first 10 miscues (National Center on Intensive Intervention, n.d.).

Interpreting Fluency Assessments: Prosody

To assess prosody, a rubric is typically used. The assessor compares the student's oral reading to the rubric and judges the level. The most common prosody rubric, which we present in Table 7.3, was developed for the National Assessment of Educational Progress (NAEP; U.S. Department of Education, 1995). Given that students with complex learning needs have prosodic differences in their everyday speech, we would expect them to have differences in oral reading prosody.

In summary, reading fluency may be assessed orally or silently. Fluency assessments should be used when students are reading connected text and included as one aspect of comprehensive literacy assessment. Some evidence suggests that ORF and silent reading fluency are highly related but uniquely related to reading comprehension; silent reading fluency may be one useful assessment of reading abilities when working with students who do not have oral speech (Kim et al., 2011). Kim and her colleagues suggested that both ORF and silent reading fluency measures include direct measures of comprehension (e.g., present question and answer choices postreading).

REFLECTION QUESTION 2

Describe how you might adjust fluency assessment for a student who does not use speech. Consider each component of fluency in determining how to adjust the assessment.

FLUENCY INSTRUCTION

Because fluency is closely related to other component skills in literacy, it is worthwhile not only to assess fluency in readers with complex support needs but also to provide them with fluency instruction as part of a comprehensive literacy program. Research evidence supports the potential value of this instruction. Allor and her colleagues (2010) found that a comprehensive, consistent,

	Text word	Miscue	Similar		
			Graphophonetic	Syntactic	Semantics
1.					
2.					
3.					
4.					
5.					
6.					
7.					
8.					
9.					
10.					
Total					
Percentage					

Figure 7.1. Miscue analysis form.

Table 7.3. Prosody rubric

Level	Description
4	Reads primarily in larger, meaningful phrase groups. Although some regressions, repetitions, and deviations from text may be present, these do not appear to detract from the overall structure of the story. Preservation of the author's syntax is consistent. Some or most of the story is read with expressive interpretation.
3	Reads primarily in three- or four-word phrase groups. Some small groupings may be present. However, the majority of phrasing seems appropriate and preserves the syntax of the author.
2	Reads primarily in two-word phrases with some three- or four-word groupings. Some word-by-word reading may be present. Word groupings may seem awkward and unrelated to larger context of sentence or passage.
1	Reads primarily word by word. Occasional two- or three-word phrases may occur, but these are infrequent and/or they do not preserve meaningful syntax.

From U.S. Department of Education, National Center for Education Statistics. (1995). *Listening to children read aloud: Oral fluency.* Washington, DC: Author. Available at http://nces.ed.gov/pubs95/web/95762.asp

explicit reading intervention for students with intellectual disability (ID) produced improvements in phoneme segmentation, phonics, and ORF. In terms of reading fluency, more than 50% of these students, regardless of IQ, reached end-of-year benchmarks when reading first-grade passages after 2 or 3 years of instruction (Allor et al., 2010). Reading progress did not appear to be influenced by IQ scores. Allor and her colleagues emphasized that although progress was made, students with ID needed extremely intensive instruction. They also noted that students in their study had "difficulty transferring and applying skills, and required extensive instruction and motivation to develop and maintain appropriate behavior" (p. 464).

With this in mind, we drew upon suggestions from Allor and Chard (2011) and our own prior research (Williamson & Carnahan, 2010) to develop the following principles for effective fluency instruction.

Principles of Effective Fluency Instruction

For students with complex learning needs to become skilled readers, comprehensive literacy instruction is needed, with fluency as one component (Allor & Chard, 2011; Allor et al., 2010; Carnahan & Williamson, 2010). These principles should inform all aspects of fluency instruction from planning to implementation.

- *Promote motivation and meaning making using students' interests.* In the literature on Direct Instruction for reading, much has been written about using reinforcement to maintain students' attention (see, e.g., Carnine, Silbert, Kame'enui, & Tarver, 2010). At times when early reading instruction focuses on teaching discrete skills such as phonological awareness and phonics, we suggest embedding these skills within the broader context of a student's interests. For example, Emma's team found appropriate decodable texts related to one of Emma's interests—fashion. This context has the possibility of making certain tasks, such as learning to apply decoding skills and sight-word recognition, more interesting for Emma. Furthermore, using students' interests also promotes meaning-making. Emma already knows something about fashion, which may provide cognitive support for learning or enjoying new information she reads.

- *Promote attention to the task through its structure.* For students with complex learning needs, during instruction, various internal and external stimuli are constantly competing for the student's attention. For instruction to be successful, it is critical for teachers to provide appropriate structure (Allor & Chard, 2011; Carnahan et al., 2009). Structure includes not only systematically providing cues related to completing the task but also explicitly stating the purpose of the instruction. Bock and Erickson referred to this as "building cognitive clarity" for students (2015, p. 143). Teaching protocols, like the one we shared in Table 7.1, helps students better understand the purpose of shared reading. Verbally connecting discrete pieces of the reading with the whole is critical for students with intensive learning needs.

- *Promote high levels of accuracy during reading by managing task difficulty and building background knowledge.* To become fluent, readers must develop automatic word recognition, which is best achieved through practice (Kuhn et al., 2010). Although some scholars have suggested that fluency practice should occur in texts that students can read at the independent level (i.e., 97–100% of the words read correctly) (see, e.g., Hudson et al., 2005), others have suggested that fluency practice can also occur in texts written at students' instructional levels (i.e., 90–96% of the words read correctly) (Allor & Chard, 2011). Students with intellectual disability will likely require extensive practice (Allor et al., 2010). For learning to occur, teachers must develop tasks that are appropriately challenging and interesting. If the task is too hard or boring, the activity will likely not improve outcomes, even if taught for a longer time. These factors were considered by Emma's team when they selected related texts as part of her comprehensive fluency development plan. Decodable texts in Emma's plan were written at her instructional level, which is critical, and were related to topics of interest. The books used for shared story reading and read-alouds were written at her interest level (i.e., appropriate for first-grade students). Shared story reading texts were also identified for the specific vocabulary they included (i.e., core words), and read-alouds were written by the same author. This afforded Emma access to background knowledge about the characters and setting, developed through her shared reading experiences.

- *Provide appropriate intensity.* Educational research is only beginning to address and define intensity. Intensity is related to instructional time, task difficulty, group size, and within-student factors (e.g., attention, internal motivation). For students with complex needs, research suggests that they will need longer to develop literacy skills (Allor et al., 2010). Thus, teachers must be persistent, relentless purveyors of literacy instruction.

Finally, and perhaps most importantly, teachers must find ways to connect students' interests with other instructional topics (Carnahan & Williamson, 2010). We recognize that students with complex learning needs, just like other students, will not necessarily be interested in learning about all of the topics included in content standards. However, we have watched very clever teachers get children interested in a multitude of age-appropriate topics by relating novel topics to students' interests.

Instructional Techniques That Promote Reading Fluency

While keeping the above general principles in mind, we will address more discrete strategies found in the literature for specifically addressing reading fluency. Within a comprehensive literacy instructional plan, Williamson and Carnahan (2010) suggested that fluency instruction should include (a) repeated and wide reading, (b) assisted reading, (c) performance reading, and (d) explicit methods to address reading prosody (i.e., phrasing, intonation, stress, and inflection during oral reading). *Repeated* reading strategies have students reread the same text multiple times, whereas *wide* reading emphasizes student reading of a wide variety of texts. (The idea is that wide reading provides exposure to more vocabulary while providing opportunities to generalize word reading in many different texts.) *Assisted* reading strategies make use of a fluent model, such as a recording, peer, or other adult, whereas *performance reading* includes numerous methods such as reader's theater, newscasting, or sportscasting.

In a study comparing rereading and wide reading, Kuhn (2004) found that wide reading had a larger effect on reading comprehension; however, she concluded that both were helpful in improving students' reading comprehension. For students with intensive learning needs, it is important to note that rereading or wide reading alone is unlikely to help improve students' reading outcomes, but they may be helpful as part of comprehensive literacy instruction (Allor et al., 2010; Wexler, Vaughn, Roberts, & Denton, 2010).

How can these four techniques—repeated, wide, assisted, and performance reading—be implemented effectively? Typical *rereading* strategy implementation is to read the same book and chart improvements in reading rate. But, because of underlying language challenges, and new understandings about the potentially reciprocal nature of reading fluency and comprehension, repurposing books used during instruction might be more helpful for this student population. For example, decodable texts read for fluency practice could be read by Emma during silent reading, as could books that were used during shared book reading. As part of *wide reading*—implemented by providing reading practice across many different texts—Emma might watch a video about Jimmy Choo, a famous shoe designer, as he discusses traveling to Hong Kong. The video helps develop background knowledge for reading.

Assisted reading strategies that make use of a fluent model are helpful for students. For example, Dowhower (1987) found that pairing the rereading of text with an audio recording of the text improved students' prosody. For Emma, the team planned to provide models extensively to support her reading during shared reading and independent reading with family and peers.

The idea behind *performance reading* is that text is created by the teacher or by the students and the teacher and is rehearsed and eventually performed. For a student like Emma, who does not use spoken language, her device (e.g., TouchChat on iPad) would be used. Another useful form of performance reading is choral reading, in which students collectively read a piece of text aloud together, such as poetry or rap lyrics; almost any text can be read chorally.

Apart from the four techniques previously described, what explicit methods can be used to address reading prosody for students with complex support needs? Prosody may be challenging for these students because there are few visual cues (e.g., no punctuation to show which word is stressed) to alert readers to prosodic features in text (Rasinski, 1990). However, certain techniques can help teachers address aspects of prosody, such as phrasing and intonation. To improve phrasing in text reading, Hudson and her colleagues (2005) suggest using a forward slash mark (/) after each phrase and a double forward slash mark at the end of each sentence. Students are instructed to pause briefly (e.g., for 1 second) at a single forward slash and pause slightly longer (e.g., for 2 seconds) at a double forward slash. For example, a text would be marked as follows:

When John entered the gym,/ he saw/ the crowd looking for seats.// The section/ where the press sat/ looked orderly/ like a well-run office/ where each person attended/ to their assigned task.//

To work on intonation and to illustrate how punctuation influences meaning, students practice reading the same sentence with different punctuation. For example:

1. *It's hot out?* For this sentence, the end punctuation mark signifies a question, as does the voice's rising pitch at the end of the sentence.

2. *It's hot out.* The period at the end of this sentence signifies an exchange of information—a fact.

3. *It's hot out!* For this sentence, the end punctuation mark suggests that for some reason, the speaker is excited that it's hot.

Similarly, Hudson and her colleagues (2005) suggest an exercise to emphasize inflection, which can also change the meaning of the same sentence. Words in italics would be stressed, and the teacher should point out how these variations affect the sentence's meaning.

1. I love pizza.

2. I *love* pizza.

3. I love *pizza.*

In the first example, the speaker might be arguing with a friend about who likes pizza the most. In the second, the speaker is expressing genuine sentiment about pizza, whereas the third response is likely a response to someone else's question.

Use of these techniques can be paired with the use of voice output devices. For students who use these devices, prosodic features are embedded when sentences are put together and read aloud. It is also possible to program devices to practice saying phrases with particular intonation, and the teacher can then ask the student to pair the intonation with the speaker's intention.

REFLECTION QUESTION 3

Select two students in your class with differing communication and literacy skill levels. Design a fluency lesson that would allow both students to fully participate and work on one or more components of fluency.

SUMMARY

Literacy and communication are integrally related, and for students with the most complex learning needs, attending to both not only is essential for academic and life outcomes but is a basic human right (Keefe & Copeland, 2011). These learners deserve student-centered instruction that engages them in making meaning, and they benefit from such comprehensive approaches (Allor et al., 2010). Teachers' conceptualization of reading and instruction plays a critical role in students' lives (Bock & Erickson, 2015). Thus, developing literacy environments that address the components of reading, including fluency, is essential for promoting positive life outcomes for students with complex learning needs.

In this chapter, we have discussed the specific components of reading fluency and explored the link between fluency and comprehension. Throughout the chapter, we have emphasized that silent reading comprehension is the ultimate goal of fluency instruction; this is particularly important to keep in mind for students with complex support needs, some of whom may have limited oral speech. We have discussed when and how to assess fluency and how to interpret assessment results. This chapter also provided a detailed discussion of the principles of effective fluency instruction and how to implement these principles through specific teaching techniques grounded in educational research.

RESOURCES

- **PrAACtical AAC** (http://praacticalaac.org) has a toolbox that includes helpful resources, such as Boardmaker Core Words.

- **Penn State** (http://aacliteracy.psu.edu) maintains a web site with useful reading resources that include sample instructional materials.

- **Core Vocabulary for Students with Significant Cognitive Disabilities: Essential Tools, Teaching Strategies and Assessment Components** (by Lori Geist, Karen Erickson, and Penny Hatch, 2015; https://www.med.unc.edu/ahs/clds/files/conference-hand-outs/asha-2015-core). Geist and her colleagues have available a MS PowerPoint presentation that includes resources related to core word instruction.

- **The Center for Literacy and Disability Studies** (https://www.med.unc.edu/ahs/clds/resources/core-vocabulary) provides additional resources.

REFERENCES

Allor, J.H., & Chard, D.J. (2011). A comprehensive approach to improving reading fluency for students with disabilities. *Focus on Exceptional Children, 43*(5), 1–12.

Allor, J.H., Mathes, P.G., Roberts, J.K., Cheatham, J.P., & Champlin, T.M. (2010). Comprehensive reading instruction for students with intellectual disabilities: Findings from the first three years of a longitudinal study. *Psychology in the School, 47*(5), 445–466. doi:10.1002/pits.20482

Bock, A.K., & Erickson, K.A. (2015). The influence of teacher epistemology and practice on student engagement in literacy learning. *Research & Practice for Persons with Severe Disabilities, 40*(2), 138–153. doi:10.1177/1540796915591987

Carnahan, C., & Williamson, P. (2010). *Quality literacy instruction for students with autism.* Lenexa, KS: AAPC Publishing.

Carnahan, C., Williamson, P., Clarke, L., & Sorenson, R. (2009). A systematic approach for supporting paraeducators in educational settings. *TEACHING Exceptional Children, 41*(5), 34–43.

Carnine, D.W., Silbert, J., Kame'enui, E.J., & Tarver, S.G. (2010). *Direct instruction reading* (5th ed.). Boston, MA: Merrill.

Chard, D.J., Clarke, B., Baker, S., Otterstedt, J., Braun, D., & Katz, R. (2005). Using measures of number sense to screen for difficulties in mathematics: Preliminary findings. *Assessment for Effective Intervention, 30*(2), 3–14.

Chard, D.J., Pikulski, J.J.. & McDonagh. S.H. (2006). Fluency: The link between decoding and comprehension for struggling readers. In T. Rasinski, C. Blachowiez, & K. Lems (Eds.), *Fluency instruction: Research-based best practices* (pp. 39–61). New York. NY: Guilford Press.

Daane, M.C., Campbell, J.R., Grigg, W.S., Goodman, M.J., & Oranje, A. (2005). *Fourth-grade students reading aloud: NAEP 2002 special study of oral reading.* Washington, DC: National Center for Education Statistics, U.S. Department of Education.

Dowhower, S.L. (1987). Effects of repeated reading on second-grade transitional readers' fluency and comprehension. *Reading Research Quarterly, 22*(4), 389–406.

Fletcher, J.M., Lyon, G.R., Fuchs, L.S., & Barnes, M.A. (2007). *Learning disabilities from identification to intervention.* New York, NY: Guilford Press.

Good, R.H., Kaminski, R.A., Simmons, D., & Kame'enui, E.J. (2001). Using Dynamic Indicators of Basic Early Literacy Skills (DIBELS) in an outcomes driven model: Steps to reading outcomes. *OSSC Bulletin, 44*(1).

Gough, P.B., & Tunmer, W.E. (1986). Decoding, reading, and reading disability. *Remedial and Special Education, 7*(1), 6–10.

Grether, S., & Pelatti, C.Y. (2010). Linking communication and literacy. In C. Carnahan & P. Williamson (Eds.), *Quality literacy instruction for students with autism spectrum disorders* (pp. 287–320). Lenexa, KS: AAPC Publishing.

Hasbrouck, J.E., & Tindal, G.A. (1992). Curriculum-based oral reading fluency norms for students in grades 2 through 5. *TEACHING Exceptional Children, 24*(3), 41–44.

Hasbrouck, J.E., & Tindal, G.A. (2006). Oral reading fluency norms: A valuable assessment tool for reading teachers. *The Reading Teacher, 59*(7), 636–644. doi:10.1598/RT.59.7.3

Hudson, R.F., Lane, H.B., & Pullen, P.C. (2005). Reading fluency assessment and instruction: What, why, and how? *The Reading Teacher, 58*(8), 702–714. doi:10.1598/RT.58.8.1

Hudson, R.F., Pullen, P.C., Lane, H.B., & Torgesen, J.K. (2008). The complex nature of reading fluency: A multidimensional view. *Reading & Writing Quarterly, 25*(1), 4–32. doi:10.1080/10573560802491208

Hudson, R.F., Torgesen, J.K., Lane, H.B., & Turner, S.J. (2012). Relations among reading skills and sub-skills and text-level reading proficiency in developing readers. *Reading and Writing: An Interdisciplinary Journal, 25*(2), 483–507. doi:10.1007/s11145-010-9283-6

Jenkins, J.R., & Jewell, M. (1993). Examining the validity of two measures for formative teaching: Read aloud and maze. *Exceptional Children, 59*(5), 421–432.

Keefe, E.B., & Copeland, S.R. (2011). What is literacy? The power of a definition. *Research and Practice for Persons with Severe Disabilities, 36*(3–4), 92–99.

Kim, Y.S., Wagner, R.K., & Foster, E. (2011). Relations among oral reading fluency, silent reading fluency, and reading comprehension: A latent variable study of first-grade readers. *Scientific Studies of Reading, 15*(4), 338–362. doi:10.1080/10888438.2010.493964

Kuhn, M.R. (2004). Helping students become accurate, expressive readers: Fluency instruction for small groups. *The Reading Teacher, 58*(4), 338–344.

Kuhn, M.R., Schwanenflugel, P.J., & Meisinger, E.B. (2010). Aligning theory and assessment of reading fluency: Automaticity, prosody, and definitions of fluency. *Reading Research Quarterly, 45*(2), 230–251. doi:10.1598/RRQ.45.2.4

Kuhn, M.R., & Stahl, S.A. (2003). Fluency: A review of developmental and remedial practices. *Journal of Educational Psychology, 95*(1), 3–21. doi:10.1037/0022-0663.95.1.3

Leslie, L., & Caldwell, J. (2010). *Qualitative Reading Inventory: 5.* Boston, MA: Pearson Education.

Logan, G.D. (1997). Automaticity and reading: Perspectives from the instance theory of automatization. *Reading and Writing Quarterly: Overcoming Learning Difficulties, 13*(2), 123–146.

Nation, K., Clarke, P., Wright, B., & Williams, C. (2006). Patterns of reading ability in children with autism spectrum disorder. *Journal of Autism and Developmental Disorders, 36*, 911–919. doi:10.1007/s10803-006-0130-1

National Center on Intensive Intervention at American Institutes for Research. (n.d.). *Reading miscue analysis.* Retrieved from http://www.intensiveintervention.org/sites/default/files/Reading_Miscue_Analysis.pdf on February 17, 2017.

O'Conner, J. (2005). *Fancy Nancy*. New York, NY: HarperCollins.

Rasinski, T.V. (1990). Effects of repeated reading and listening-while-reading on reading fluency. *Journal of Educational Research, 83*(3), 147–150.

Rasinski, T.V. (2003). *The fluent reader: Oral reading strategies for building word recognition, fluency, and comprehension*. New York, NY: Scholastic.

Rasinski, T.V., Reutzel, D.R., Chard, D., & Linan-Thompson, S. (2011). Reading fluency, In M.L. Kamil, P.D. Pearson, E.B. Moje, & P.P. Afflerbach (Eds.), *Handbook of reading research* (Vol. IV, pp. 286–319). Philadelphia, PA: Routledge.

Saltillo Corporation (2012). TouchChat [Mobile application software]. Retrieved from https://touchchatapp .com/ on February 17, 2017.

Samuels, S.J., & Farstrup, A.E. (2006). *What research has to say about fluency* (6th ed.). Newark, DE: International Reading Association.

Shinn, M.R., Good, R.H., Knutson, N., Tilly, W.D., & Collins, V.L. (1992). Curriculum-based measurement of oral reading fluency: A confirmatory analysis of its relation to reading. *School Psychology Review, 21,* 459–479.

Silberglitt, B., Burns, M.K., Madyun, N.H., & Lail, K.E. (2006). Relationship of reading fluency assessment data with state accountability scores: A longitudinal comparison of grade levels. *Psychology in the Schools, 43*(5), 527–535. doi:10.1002/pits.20175

U.S. Department of Education. (1995). *Listening to children read aloud: Oral fluency*. Retrieved from https:// nces.ed.gov/pubs95/web/95762.asp

Wexler, J., Vaughn, S., Roberts, G., & Denton, C.A. (2010). The efficacy of repeated reading and wide reading practice for high school students with severe reading disabilities. *Learning Disabilities Research & Practice, 25*(1), 2–10. doi:10.1111/j.1540-5826.2009.00296.x

Williamson, P., & Carnahan, C. (2010). Building fluency. In C. Carnahan & P. Williamson (Eds.), *Quality literacy instruction for students with autism spectrum disorders* (pp. 287–320). Lenexa, KS: AAPC Publishing.

Yolen, J., & Stemple, H.E.Y. (2010). *Not all princesses dress in pink*. New York, NY: Simon & Schuster Books for Young Readers.

CHAPTER 8

Words, Glorious Words!

Elizabeth B. Keefe, Phyllis M. Robertson, and Karen M. Potter

LEARNING OBJECTIVES

By the end of this chapter, readers will

1. Articulate the rationale for including explicit vocabulary instruction as part of comprehensive literacy instruction for students with complex support needs.

2. Understand how to create print-rich environments to support vocabulary instruction.

3. Identify the ways in which structural analysis and morphology are related to vocabulary development.

4. Describe how to design and implement effective vocabulary instruction for students with complex support needs across all content areas, including life skills.

This chapter will discuss vocabulary as a crucial component of literacy instruction. We will begin by defining vocabulary and discussing different types of vocabulary. Next, we will summarize research findings on effective vocabulary instruction for students with complex support needs and discuss formal and informal means of assessing vocabulary knowledge. Finally, we will explore in-depth how to set goals for vocabulary instruction and choose target words as well as how to teach vocabulary using a variety of approaches, including approaches adapted from traditional instruction for typically developing learners.

THE IMPORTANCE OF VOCABULARY INSTRUCTION

The National Reading Panel (NRP, 2000) proposed that vocabulary instruction, historically viewed as a subset of comprehension, was one of the five critical components of reading instruction in its own right. Indeed, research has demonstrated that vocabulary development plays a prominent role in the reading process in general, and this has further supported consideration of vocabulary development as a critical area of literacy instruction in its own right (Beck, McKeown, & Kucan, 2013; Fisher & Frey, 2008; NRP, 2000; Reutzel & Cooter, 2012). Research indicates that effective literacy instruction for students with complex support needs must be comprehensive and include explicit vocabulary instruction (e.g., Allor, Mathes, Roberts, Cheatham, & Al Otaiba, 2014; Browder, Ahlgrim-Delzell, Flowers, & Baker, 2012). Vocabulary is most simply defined as the knowledge of words and word meanings. Vocabulary instruction can thus be defined as teaching words and word meanings (e.g., National Reading Technical Assistance Center, 2010; Reutzel & Cooter, 2012).

We believe that vocabulary development is of great importance to students with complex support needs. We also believe that best practices in vocabulary development for students without disabilities lend themselves particularly well to differentiation and modification for diverse learners. This chapter will discuss the various definitions and types of vocabulary, research on vocabulary learning, the assessment of vocabulary, and effective instructional approaches for improving the vocabulary development of students with complex support needs.

WHAT IS VOCABULARY?

There are generally four types of vocabulary recognized in the literature—listening, oral, reading, and writing. All are related, and all are important to the development of effective literacy skills for all students. Vocabulary can further be referred to as *receptive* or *expressive*. Receptive vocabulary is used to describe words that a person can comprehend and respond to, even if the person cannot produce those words. Expressive vocabulary is the ability to produce and use words to express oneself.

Listening Vocabulary

Listening vocabulary—the largest vocabulary an individual has—includes all words an individual can hear and understand, although he or she may not be able to use the words when communicating expressively. This definition of listening vocabulary also applies to individuals who receive words through signing or tactile input rather than hearing. Think of the infant who clearly understands many words before she or he is able to say or sign them, or people who learn a second language and are typically able to understand more vocabulary words than they can generate—an understanding that remains even when they have not taken instruction in the language for many years. Listening vocabulary functions as an information receiver and is categorized as receptive vocabulary (Cooter & Flynt, 1996).

Speaking Vocabulary

Speaking vocabulary is considered an expressive vocabulary and is typically an individual's second largest vocabulary. Speaking vocabulary includes all the words an individual can hear, understand, and use in speech. For students with sensory, physical, speech, and/or language impairments, this might include words the individual can understand and use in sign or through the use of augmentative and alternative communication (AAC). For most students, the gap between listening and speaking vocabularies is greatest at younger ages, with the gap narrowing as the student approaches adulthood. However, the gap may not narrow for students with complex support needs as they get older; in fact, the opposite may be true. Students with complex support needs may understand more and more words, but because of sensory, physical, speech, and/or language impairments, they may still not able to express their knowledge of vocabulary though oral language. For these students, speaking vocabulary may be their smallest vocabulary.

Reading Vocabulary

This vocabulary consists of all the words a student can read and understand. For students with vision impairments, this includes reading and understanding through the use of braille. As with listening vocabulary, reading vocabulary functions as a means to receive information and is categorized as receptive vocabulary. Sight-word recognition is an element of reading vocabulary and is addressed in detail in Chapter 9.

Writing Vocabulary

Writing vocabulary consists of all the words a student can understand and reproduce when writing. Typically an individual's smallest vocabulary, it includes written language produced through the use of assistive technology (AT) devices and word processing programs. Writing is categorized as expressive vocabulary.

Relationships Among the Four Vocabularies

For typically developing students, the four types of vocabulary described previously are considered subsets of one another. Speaking vocabulary is a subset of listening vocabulary, reading vocabulary is a subset of speaking and listening vocabularies, and writing vocabulary is a subset of speaking, listening, and reading vocabularies. However, this hierarchical conception does not work as well for many students with sensory, physical, speech, and/or language impairments. As a result, for students with complex support needs, this view of vocabulary is not necessarily accurate or useful. In order to provide appropriate literacy instruction, it is critical that the concept of *oral* vocabulary be broadened for students with complex support needs to *expressive vocabulary* to include sign language, gestures, symbols, objects, and AAC (Keefe & Copeland, 2011; Kliewer, 2008). In addition, students with complex support needs may have an expressive vocabulary that is smaller than their reading and/or writing vocabulary—due to physical or sensory challenges, for example. Instructional decisions in the area of reading for students with complex support needs should not be made based on the size of their expressive vocabulary because this can result in low expectations and lack of access to comprehensive literacy instruction.

We must be careful to remember the least dangerous assumption and presume that students are capable of learning. We must not deny individuals with complex support needs access to instruction in reading and writing vocabularies simply because some of them cannot demonstrate their true knowledge and ability through oral/expressive vocabulary.

RESEARCH ON VOCABULARY INSTRUCTION FOR STUDENTS WITH COMPLEX SUPPORT NEEDS

It is challenging that the term *vocabulary* is often not explicitly defined in literacy research in general. It is used interchangeably with *sight-word instruction* at times in the research relating to students with complex support needs (Browder, Wakeman, Spooner, Ahlgrim-Delzell, & Algozzine, 2006). In fact, within the past three decades, very little research has been done specifically addressing vocabulary development for students with complex needs for support. As will be discussed in Chapter 9, the majority of research in reading for these students has focused on word recognition, so it might be assumed that vocabulary has been sufficiently addressed therein. This assumption, however, would be wrong, because vocabulary instruction incorporates much more than being able to recognize a word. A narrow focus on sight-word instruction has led to a long history of teaching individuals with complex support needs limited vocabulary skills in a decontextualized manner (Browder et al., 2006; Copeland & Keefe, 2017; Keefe & Copeland, 2011). That is to say, instruction in vocabulary skills needs to be grounded in the contexts in which students will actually *use* those skills—such as reading a book, writing an e-mail message, or giving a speech. In the following sections, we sum up some general, research-based principles to keep in mind for vocabulary instruction and then discuss specific studies with particular relevance.

A Synthesis of Recommendations From the Literature

The NRP (2000) review of vocabulary research can provide guidance for teaching literacy to students with complex support needs. Its eight recommendations can be summarized as follows:

- Students should be provided direct instruction on vocabulary words.
- Effective instruction incorporates repetition and multiple exposure.
- Vocabulary words need to be useful in multiple contexts.
- Vocabulary tasks should be restructured as necessary.
- Vocabulary instruction should require active engagement and go beyond definition.
- Computer technology can be useful.
- Vocabulary can be acquired through incidental learning.
- Dependence on a single method will not optimize learning.

Although these findings were based on typical students, we believe they are consistent with the emerging research base about teaching vocabulary to students with complex support needs (Copeland & Keefe, 2017).

Johnson (2001) made the following general recommendations for teaching vocabulary to middle school students based on his review of the research:

- Set aside time for reading in the classroom and increase reading volume.

- Use direct instruction.

- Use methods that involve active learning by the students.

- Provide opportunities for repetition and repeated exposure to targeted vocabulary words.

- Encourage students to develop their own strategies to learn vocabulary.

Similarly, Fisher and Frey recommended four principles for effective vocabulary instruction for improving adolescent literacy instruction:

- Be actively involved in word learning.

- Make personal connections.

- Be immersed in vocabulary.

- Consolidate meaning through multiple information sources. (2008, p. 58)

Given the dearth of research into vocabulary instruction for students with complex support needs, we believe the least dangerous assumption is that if these approaches and principles are important for students generally, they may hold promise for students with complex support needs. It is clear that vocabulary instruction for these students must go beyond a narrow focus on sight-word instruction in decontextualized instructional contexts. To develop effective vocabulary instruction, educators who work with these individuals must be creative in integrating best general practices for teaching students with complex support needs together with best practices for teaching vocabulary. For example, strategies such as "reading the room" and using environmental print may not have a specific research base for students with complex support needs, but these activities build on the accepted practice of using ecological inventories to guide instructional planning (Brown et al., 1979; Downing, 2005). (Use of environmental print was discussed in Chapter 5, and "reading the room" involves labeling common objects in the classroom; both strategies will be discussed at length later in this chapter.) In addition, these practices are consistent with the recommendations previously mentioned for personal relevance, repeated exposure, and multiple sources and contexts.

With these general guidelines in mind, let's take a closer look at specific recommendations grounded in the available research on this topic.

Direct and Systematic Instruction

The use of direct and systematic (step-by-step) instruction is recommended for teaching vocabulary to students with complex needs for support. (This is similar to the findings for word recognition discussed in Chapter 9.) Interestingly, this parallels the recommendations that direct and explicit instruction in vocabulary constitutes evidence-based practice for typical students (e.g., NRP, 2000; NRTAC, 2010; Reutzel & Cooter, 2012). The form that such instruction takes will be more intensive for students with complex needs for support, as will be discussed later in this chapter. Specifically, strategies such as time delay, response prompting, differential reinforcement of responses, and systematic prompting have been used with these students to improve vocabulary in general (e.g., Allor et al., 2014; Browder et al., 2006, 2008, 2012), and in content areas such as science (Spooner, Knight, Browder, Jimenez, & DiBiase, 2011) and middle school language arts (Mims, Lee, Browder, Zakas, & Flynn, 2012), and in general education settings (Hudson, Browder, & Wood, 2013). Please refer to Chapter 9 for a more in-depth discussion of these strategies. Shared stories and comprehensive reading approaches are two research-based examples of how direct and systematic instruction can be implemented.

Shared Stories　　A review of the research on shared stories and reading indicates moderate evidence that this is a research-based practice to increase literacy skills, including vocabulary, for students with extensive support needs (Hudson & Test, 2011). An overview of the six single-case design research studies included in the review identifies the following common instructional practices:

- Shared reading of a text

- Systematic instruction

- Task analysis

- System of least prompts

- Adapted books and use of AAC/AT

Shared stories have been shown to increase vocabulary with typically developing students (e.g., NRTAC, 2010) and students with disabilities (e.g., Katims, 1994). Shared stories are a good example of a practice that embodies one of the most important recommendations for teaching vocabulary to all students: active engagement in vocabulary-rich environments where children have repeated exposure to words and word meanings (Beck et al., 2013; NRP, 2000; NRTAC, 2010; Reutzel & Cooter, 2012).

Comprehensive Reading Approaches　　Comprehensive or multicomponent approaches embed direct and systemic instruction and serve to combat the historical tendency to teach vocabulary through decontextualized sight-word approaches. These reading programs show promise for increasing the vocabulary skills of students with complex needs for support (Allor et al., 2014; Browder et al., 2012; Mims et al., 2012). Three studies of these approaches are described briefly in the following sections, specifically with regard to vocabulary instruction and outcomes. All three use systematic instruction, including time delay and system of least prompts, to build vocabulary knowledge. All three also include going beyond word recognition to understanding and applying word knowledge in connected text.

Allor et al. conducted a longitudinal study to examine the effectiveness of "comprehensive scientifically based reading instruction" (2014, p. 289) that had been effective with struggling readers. They compared the outcomes on an extensive battery of dependent measures covering basic reading skills for students with IQs between 40 and 80 randomly assigned to the treatment group ($n = 76$) using *Early Interventions in Reading* (Mathes & Torgeson, 2005 as cited in Allor et al., 2014), with the outcomes of a contrast group ($n = 65$) receiving the typical instruction provided at their school over one to four academic years, beginning in Grades 1–4. The dependent measures for vocabulary were The Peabody Picture Vocabulary Test–Third Edition (PPVT III; Dunn & Dunn, 1997) and Expressive Vocabulary Test (EVT; Williams 1997 as cited in Allor et al., 2014). Allor et al. (2014) described the ways in which vocabulary instruction occurred in their intervention. First, they targeted words and concepts that held meaning for the students. Second, the meaning of words was taught through pictures, conversation, and connected text. Third, puzzles and games were developed for independent and supported practice. Allor et al. reported moderate to high effect sizes for measures of vocabulary for the treatment group.

Browder et al. (2012) compared a multicomponent literacy curriculum they developed, the *Early Literacy Skills Builder* (ELSB), with a sight-word approach (Edmark; Austin & Boeckmann, 1990 as cited in Browder et al., 2012) across 3 years for students with severe developmental disabilities. The 93 participants were in grades K–4 and were randomly assigned to receive literacy instruction using the ELSB ($n = 46$) or Edmark ($n = 47$). The ELSB curriculum is described in Browder et al. (2008). The vocabulary objectives included reading vocabulary words, pointing to sight words to complete sentences to demonstrate comprehension, and pointing to pictures of spoken words by using a variety of pictures for the same word. These encompass all levels of word knowledge by building word recognition, definition, and conceptual understanding. Methods used to teach the vocabulary objectives included flash card drill with constant time delay and system of least prompts. Browder et al. (2012) used the PPVT III as the dependent measure for receptive vocabulary. Although the treatment group had significantly higher mean literacy scores over the control group, the smallest effect size was seen for receptive vocabulary when compared to the subtests measuring conventions of reading and phonics skills.

In a smaller-scale study, Mims et al. (2012) piloted the use of a multicomponent treatment package in self-contained middle school language arts classrooms serving 15 students with moderate to severe disabilities. The study used a one-group pre–posttest nonrandomized design. Organized around four themed units, the curriculum targeted skills in vocabulary, comprehension, story elements, and writing. Vocabulary words were assigned based on students' symbolic communication level and taught using flashcards, pictures, and time delay. Instruction occurred in groups, and the researchers encouraged incidental learning by having all students attend as their peers responded to the prompts. Students pointed to named words and found words or pictures that corresponded with definitions. This study's dependent measure was a pre- and posttest based on the scripted lessons for Unit 1 of the curriculum and on the middle school's English language arts target skills; the vocabulary assessment was 5–15 words and definitions. Students' most significant gains were found in vocabulary, compared with comprehension and writing measures.

These three studies demonstrate that vocabulary knowledge of students with complex support needs can be improved through systematic direct instruction in a comprehensive or multicomponent program. This provides support for including vocabulary instruction as part of comprehensive reading instruction for these students. However, it should be noted that all three studies reported improved growth across almost all areas of reading instruction. The reality is that these different areas are interrelated; no area should be taught in a decontextualized, isolated way. Vocabulary has been shown to be significantly related to word recognition, comprehension, and fluency for typical students (NRP, 2000). It should come as no surprise that the same is true for students with complex needs for support.

REFLECTION QUESTION 1

Think of three ways you could use targeted vocabulary words in connected text.

CONSIDERATIONS FOR ASSESSMENT: WHAT DOES IT MEAN TO "KNOW" A WORD?

This section will discuss formal and informal means of assessing vocabulary for students with complex needs for support. However, be aware that evaluating and discussing effective practices in vocabulary instruction is complicated by the challenge inherent in defining what it means to "know" a word. Beck et al. noted, "It is not the case that one either knows or does not know a word. In fact, word knowledge is a rather complex concept" (2013, p. 10). Beck et al. in general describe word knowledge as a continuum ranging from no knowledge of the word, to a general sense of the word meaning, to a narrow and context-based knowledge of the word, to a rich, decontextualized knowledge of the word. Thus, there are many ways in which to *know* a word. For example, Dale (1965) conceptualized word knowledge as passing through the following four stages:

1. Never saw it before

2. Heard it but doesn't know what it means

3. Recognize it in context as having something to do with _____

4. Know it well

As a result, assessing vocabulary for any student is difficult. As discussed previously, typical conceptions of vocabulary development may not be appropriate for individuals with complex support needs. When assessing students with complex needs for support, who may manifest sensory, physical, speech, and/or language impairments, the task of determining how well a student *knows* a word becomes even more challenging. Assessment of vocabulary can occur through formal and informal procedures.

Formal Testing

Gunning (2015) noted that additional testing specifically to measure vocabulary knowledge may not always be necessary. Some indication of an individual's vocabulary knowledge may be gained from previously administered formal testing. Students with disabilities have usually been given multiple tests to determine eligibility for special education services. Examples of formal assessments that might yield information about a student's vocabulary knowledge are the Peabody Picture Vocabulary Test, the vocabulary portions of IQ tests, the Diagnostic Assessments of Reading with Trial Teaching Strategies (DARTTS; Roswell & Chall, 1991), and the Stanford Diagnostic Reading Test (Karlsen, Madden, & Gardner, 1985). It is important to remember that, for many reasons, students with complex support needs may not perform to their ability in a formal testing situation, so results should be used as just one source of information about vocabulary knowledge, not the sole source.

In reviewing the research literature, we found two common dependent measures for students with complex support needs. The first is the PPVT III (e.g., Allor et al., 2014; Browder et al., 2012). The PPVT III measures receptive vocabulary by asking a student to point to a picture after the examiner presents the word orally. Second, Allor et al. (2014) used the EVT as a dependent measure for vocabulary. The EVT measures expressive vocabulary and word retrieval. Although both tests are useful assessments, it is important to recognize that both address the lower end of the word knowledge continuum, so they do not indicate a rich decontextualized understanding of the word.

In addition to using the tests previously described, teachers may gain insight into vocabulary words that cause difficulty for a student through assessments carried out for language, comprehension, fluency, and/or word recognition, as described in Chapters 2, 6, 7, and 9.

Informal Assessments

We believe the most reliable and common forms of assessing vocabulary knowledge are teacher observation and teacher-made assessments (Beck et al., 2013; NRP, 2000; Reutzel & Cooter, 2012).

Teacher Observation   Teacher observation involves paying attention to the vocabulary words the student seems able to understand and use in the classroom and other school environments. Anecdotal records can be used to document these observations. Gunning (2015) recommended recording anecdotal information on sticky notes and later transferring it to the student's file or a notebook.

Teacher-Created Assessments   Teacher-created assessments can include checklists, quizzes, or tests that document the student's mastery of target vocabulary words that may apply to literacy instruction and/or content areas.

Choosing Target Vocabulary for Informal Assessments

You might be wondering how to choose the target vocabulary words on which students are to be assessed. We will discuss this topic in greater depth later in the chapter, but for now, keep these general guidelines in mind. First, know that a number of word lists relating to beginning reading proficiency (e.g., Instant Words, Dolch words) can help teachers identify high-frequency reading

Book/author	Publisher	Vocabulary words	Alternate vocabulary words
Curious George Takes a Job By H.A. Rey	Houghton Mifflin	curious cozy mischief	big little yellow hat zoo bus monkey

Figure 8.1. Target vocabulary words from a storybook. (From Beck, I.L., McKeown, M.G., & Kucan, L. [2002]. *Bringing words to life.* New York, NY: Guilford Press.)

vocabulary words. Environmental print is also a great source of target vocabulary for young students and students with complex support needs.

Target vocabulary words can also be selected from stories, poetry, newspapers, textbooks, and/or any other text-based curriculum material. The selection and assessment of target vocabulary words can be individualized for students of differing abilities. For example, Beck, McKeown, & Kucan (2002) recommended vocabulary words to target for many books (see Figure 8.1). We have added the fourth column to demonstrate how simpler words could be selected as appropriate for students with complex needs for support. Teachers could select one or more of these words as vocabulary targets.

Content area textbooks often identify target vocabulary for teachers. For example, *The American Nation* (Davidson, 2005), a textbook used in eighth-grade social studies, identifies key terms for each section. Teachers can simplify these key terms or add other related section vocabulary appropriate for students with complex needs for support (see Figure 8.2).

This principle of simplifying vocabulary can be applied to any grade level and any content area. Figure 8.3 shows the way in which target vocabulary in a high school science lecture can be modified for students with complex needs for support.

Additional Considerations in Assessing Students With Complex Needs for Support

Ascertaining whether students with complex needs for support understand and can use vocabulary words may be difficult when students have physical, sensory, speech, and/or

Textbook/section	Publisher	Key terms	Alternate key terms
The American Nation Chapter 8, section 2	Prentice Hall	House of Representatives Senate bill electoral college appeal unconstitutional override impeach	president White House state country white house year two four six

Figure 8.2. Target vocabulary words from a textbook.

Subject area/ grade level	Lecture topic	Target vocabulary	Alternate target vocabulary
life science ninth grade	Structure of the Earth	geology atmosphere hydrosphere lithosphere crust mantle asthenosphere outer core inner core	Earth core mantle crust sun moon inside outside air

Figure 8.3. Target vocabulary words from a lecture.

language challenges. Some students can demonstrate their knowledge using braille, sign, AAC, or other AT devices. However, we frequently encounter teachers who suspect that one of their students with complex support needs is more capable than he or she has been given credit for; standardized or formal assessment methods do not fully reflect the student's capabilities. These teachers have to be very creative in figuring out how to individualize assessment for these students. For example, flashcards are a very common means of assessing vocabulary knowledge (Reutzel & Cooter, 2012); usually the student demonstrates knowledge by saying the word. The following are some simple suggestions for assessing vocabulary for students with physical, sensory, speech, and/or language challenges:

- Ask the student to point, gesture, or eye gaze to indicate the target vocabulary word. You can ask the student to choose from two or more words. It is important to vary the position of the target word and the distracters. For example, some students may have limited mobility, so it is easier for them to point, gesture, or gaze at a word using one side of their bodies; varying word positioning would be very important in this case.

- Give the student the definition of the target vocabulary word and ask him or her to point, gesture, or eye gaze to identify the correct word from a choice of two or more.

- Ask the student to physically match the printed target word to the printed definition.

- Ask the student to indicate *yes* or *no* when asked the definition of a vocabulary word or whether a vocabulary word is the correct choice to use in a sentence.

- Read a sentence with the target vocabulary word missing. Ask the student to select the appropriate word from a choice of two or more using pointing, gesturing, or eye gazing.

- Use iPads, tablets, and other widely available technology tools (described in Chapter 5) to provide pathways for students to demonstrate what they know about vocabulary.

- Work with related service providers to ensure AAC and AT devices have targeted vocabulary words included (see also Chapters 2 and 5).

These are just a few ways you can assess the vocabulary knowledge of students with physical, sensory, speech, and/or language challenges. Be aware that it often takes trial and error, along with creativity and persistence, to get an accurate picture of the true abilities and potential of students with complex support needs. Don't ever give up! You will be rewarded for your efforts as these students finally get access to engaging literacy instruction. (Remember, vocabulary instruction should be just one element of a comprehensive reading program and taught concurrently with other areas of literacy.)

The Importance of Collaboration

The previous sections on assessment demonstrate that teachers can identify various levels of vocabulary to assess their students' vocabulary knowledge to create opportunities for active participation. These multilevel assessments should occur with the collaboration of a general education teacher, a special education teacher, related services personnel, paraprofessionals, and family members, as appropriate. In addition, the assessments included in this section are just examples. Students with complex support needs often display unique combinations of characteristics that require creative thinking from the educational team. In addition, universal design for learning (UDL) principles—and, specifically, popular technology that is widely available—may provide ways for students with complex support needs to demonstrate their knowledge. (See Chapter 5 for an in-depth discussion of UDL and AT.)

Our lack of knowledge of how best to assess the understanding of students with complex support needs should not create an additional barrier to literacy for them; our challenge is to make sure we presume competence and find out what these students really know. To accomplish this goal, collaborating with other members of the educational team is essential.

INSTRUCTIONAL PRACTICES: SETTING GOALS AND CHOOSING WORDS

Vocabulary development is closely related to word recognition, reading fluency, and comprehension. As a result, many of the instructional strategies discussed throughout this book can also be used to increase vocabulary development (e.g., Making Words [Cunningham, 2009], word families, word banks, word sorts, shared book experiences, reader's theater, cloze exercises). Similarly, many strategies in this chapter, designed to increase vocabulary, will also help improve word recognition, reading fluency, and comprehension.

Effective vocabulary instruction has three major steps: setting instructional goals; selecting appropriate vocabulary words for instruction; and of course, teaching those words. In the next sections, we discuss how to set instructional goals and how to select appropriate vocabulary words; in addition, we explore specific instructional methods.

Setting Active Learning Goals

One of the most consistent recommendations from the research into vocabulary instruction is that it should be active and engaging. Unfortunately, the extent of a student's perceived *dis*ability can lead teachers to take a deficit approach and focus on the challenges rather than the possibilities. As a result, students with complex needs for support are often limited to passive participation in classrooms. Even worse, educators in both segregated and inclusive settings sometimes think it is okay for these students just to be present in a classroom.

Chapter 1 described the importance of presuming competence for students with complex support needs and having the least dangerous assumption with regard to literacy; Chapter 4 examined ways to align instruction and individualized education program (IEP) goals to provide meaningful access to standards-based education. We believe the first step in developing appropriate, engaging instruction for this student population is to apply the potato test to all learning goals we set for them (Orelove, 1995). The potato test is simple: If a *potato* can achieve a certain goal, then that should not be a student goal. For example, a potato can *sit* in class, but we should always be looking for active class participation from students. See Figure 8.4 for examples of common potato goals in vocabulary instruction and active student goal counterparts.

Time and again, we have seen students get so excited when they are finally able to show their knowledge actively and participate. As a result, teachers catch their students' excitement and are almost always surprised by what they *can* do instead of focusing on what they *cannot* do.

Choosing Words for Instruction

It does not matter how effective your instructional methods are if the choice of vocabulary words is flawed. This section will build on the previous discussion of targeting vocabulary words in different forms of instruction (see Figures 8.1–8.3).

Potato goals	Active goals
Student will listen to a story.	When asked a vocabulary question, student will choose the target word from a choice of three.
Student will sit in science class.	Student will match three target vocabulary words taken from their lecture to photographs or their definition.
Student will observe peers in language arts.	Student will participate in cooperative groups by indicating choice of words to include in group story.
Student will be placed in prone stander for 20 minutes.	Student will assist teacher in handing out materials to class from the stander.
	Student will use AAC device to greet each student and acknowledge each thank-you.

Figure 8.4. Potato versus active goals in vocabulary instruction. *Key*: AAC, augmentative and alternative communication.

Prioritizing Words by Tier   Although it may seem obvious, it is worth noting that we cannot teach every vocabulary word! Educators must therefore find ways to prioritize vocabulary words for instruction. Beck et al. proposed conceptualizing words in three tiers:

- Tier 1: The most basic words that rarely require attention to their meaning for most students (e.g., *clock, baby, happy, walk*)

- Tier 2: Words that occur at high frequency and are found across many domains (e.g., *coincidence, absurd, industrious, fortunate*)

- Tier 3: Words that occur with low frequency and are usually related to a specific discipline (e.g., *isotope, lathe, peninsula, refinery*) (2002, p. 8)

Beck et al. (2013) recommended a process to determine which words fit which tier for any specific text. The identification of words in each tier will vary by grade level and by the readiness of specific groups of students.

For students with complex support needs, we can use a similar conceptual framework while adjusting the scale to be appropriate for their vocabulary, which is typically more limited than that of other learners. This makes the choice of words for instruction even more critical. We offer the following three tiers for students with complex support needs:

- Tier 1: Basic words that occur with high frequency in the student's immediate environment (e.g., *home, school, community*). Attention may still need to be paid to the words' meaning for some students, but most will understand the words receptively (e.g., *Mom, Dad,* student's name; words like *Walgreens, Pepsi, chair, door, home, school*).

- Tier 2: Words that occur with high frequency across multiple environments and may facilitate access to, and meaningful participation in, home, school, and community life (e.g., the names of the teacher and therapist, subject areas, classmates' names; words like *push, pull, in, out, office, cafeteria, library, computer*). This tier may include some high-frequency sight words.

- Tier 3: Words with abstract meanings that are taught in academic settings but also can be used in home, school, and community environments, such as high-frequency sight words and target vocabulary from general education classes. (See Figures 8.1–8.3.)

The vocabulary words for the tiers described here will not be drawn solely from text; many words will be drawn from the home, school, and community environments. The challenge for educators is that these three tiers will vary from student to student; you will have to determine all three individually for each student on your caseload. Note that these tiers do not form a strict hierarchy. Vocabulary words will be chosen from all three, but the highest priority should be given to the words in Tiers 1 and 2.

Student: Meg Brown　　　　　　　Age: 10　　　　　Date of assessment: 8/30/17

Parent(s): Andrew Brown and Rachel Finley

Teachers: Maria Sandoval (special ed.), Peggy Alford (general ed.), Bill White (SLP)

Word(s)	School	Home	Community	Type*	Tier
Meg	X	X	X	L, S, R, W	1
Mom	X	X		L, S, R	1
Dad	X	X		L, S, R	1
Ms. Sandoval	X	X		L, S,	2
Ms. Alford	X	X		L, S	2
Days: Mon–Fri	X	X	X	L, S	2
A, and, the	X	X	X	R, W	2
Earth	X			L, S, R	3
Sun	X			L, S, R	3
Moon	X			L, S, R	3

*L: Listening, S: Speaking, R: Reading, W: Writing

Figure 8.5. Sample environmental vocabulary inventory. *Key:* SLP, speech-language pathologist.

Using Ecological Inventories　　One method to target appropriate tiers of vocabulary for students with complex support needs is to take into account their environmental contexts. Brown et al. (1979) suggested that teachers conduct *ecological inventories:* informal assessments of school, home, and community domains to identify functional skills on which to focus for individual students. Many experts in the field of complex support needs have built upon Brown et al.'s work, which remains a critical assessment and instructional planning tool (e.g., Downing, Eichinger, & Demchak, 2008; Ryndak & Alper, 2003; Snell & Brown, 2010). We suggest completing an environmental vocabulary inventory to help you identify appropriate Tier 1–3 vocabulary for students with complex support needs across home, school, and community environments. You will need to collaborate with other educators and family members to identify important words in your students' environments. You may also visit community settings such as the grocery store or restaurant a student visits the most, other recreational settings, and vocational settings.

　　The number of words selected for instruction for each student will be individualized. You will need to identify whether you are targeting each word as part of listening, speaking, reading, and/or written vocabulary (see Figure 8.5 for an example). The environmental vocabulary inventory should be a dynamic assessment, adjusted as needed depending on student progress and changing environments and curriculum.

REFLECTION QUESTION 2

Why is it important to make connections to home and community environments when teaching vocabulary as part of a comprehensive literacy program for students with complex support needs?

INSTRUCTIONAL PRACTICES: TEACHING VOCABULARY

Once you have set appropriately challenging goals and selected target vocabulary for each student, you can use a variety of strategies to teach it. These strategies, discussed in depth here, can be summarized as follows: create environments that are rich in print and language;

teach analysis of word structure and morphemes directly; modify traditional sight-word approaches to suit individual needs; and modify other traditional approaches to vocabulary instruction, used with typically developing students, for students with complex support needs.

Create Print- and Language-Rich Environments

Chapter 2 emphasized the critical importance of language-rich environments to the development of oral language skills for students with complex support needs. This rich language and print environment is also critical to the development of all four types of vocabulary from spoken to written (Allington, 2006; Beck et al., 2002; Reutzel & Cooter, 2012). In general, a print-rich environment is characterized by easy access to the printed word in multiple formats and genres, together with ways to engage actively with the printed word (Keefe, Copeland, & DiLuzio, 2010). This print-rich environment encourages incidental learning of vocabulary and can be used to support direct instruction in vocabulary.

Inadequate exposure to print is cited by Allington (2006) as one factor contributing to poor vocabulary development. We believe access to language- and print-rich environments is negatively affected by the segregation of students with complex support needs from their general education peers and settings. We have found that when these students are placed in community-based or intensive-support classrooms, their instruction tends to be limited to the deficit-based goals and objectives on their IEP. Because all students in the class have complex needs for support, they suffer from a lack of strong role models for speaking, reading, and writing. Furthermore, teachers' expectations for these students, often low, may lead to a dearth of high-quality, engaging, and challenging literacy materials.

Chapter 3 addressed the creation of a culturally responsive, language-rich environment; here, we will focus on the creation of print-rich environments in the classroom and school. Every classroom should have plenty of books, magazines, posters, and other printed material at various reading levels. Every classroom should also have literacy tools, including computers and other technology, so that students can make and interact with printed materials. These materials and tools should not be haphazardly assembled and organized. Teachers need to think carefully about the print in their classroom and organize the environment so that the students know how to access and use the materials (Reutzel & Cooter, 2010). This may require direct instruction about how to use specific equipment or learning centers. Finally, teachers need to think about ways in which the print in the classroom can reinforce target vocabulary and expose students to additional vocabulary in meaningful ways.

Reading the Classroom (or Other Environmental Setting)   One way to be strategic about print in the classroom environment is to label common objects in the room (e.g., chairs, doors, windows, computers, tables). This strategy, common in foreign language classrooms, can be used for both incidental and direct instruction. The idea is that the students will see these words frequently and associate them with the objects. For example, teachers can help students build vocabulary with environmental print in these ways:

- Provide sight-word instruction incorporating time delay and system of least prompts using the environmental words.

- After placing a Velcro or library pocket next to each classroom label, have the student match a set of sight words, symbols, or photographs to the labeled items. (This can also serve as an assessment; in addition, this activity builds in movement for students who have trouble sitting for instruction.)

- Make a book using the classroom words.

- Classify or sort the words into categories.

- Alphabetize the words.

- Complete sentences using the words; for example, "I sit on the *chair*." "I like to play Math Munchers on the *computer*."

- Match the words with pictures or definitions.

- Match targeted vocabulary to the daily agenda or learning objective; for example, in a secondary chemistry class, a student with complex support needs could select the word *mixture* and attach it to the daily agenda. The same student could match the word *mixture* in cooking class.

- Match numbers or letters for sequential steps in an activity during whole-class directions, in conjunction with the teacher's statement of "first," and so forth.

- Use a sentence frame with blanks and multiple targeted words available; for example, "Jaime gives *Amy* the *paper.*" The student can complete the action and may also demonstrate incidental learning that has occurred in the environment.

- As a student gains proficiency in using the word, enlist a peer or adult collaborator to create a simple sentence that does not make sense when using the target word in context, and ask the student to help fix the sentence.

Many of these same ideas could be done in other home, community, and vocational environmental settings.

One major challenge in vocabulary instruction is to make sure we go beyond simply identifying a word in isolation to using the vocabulary words in connected print. Often, words found in the classroom, such as *door, desk,* and *computer,* do not occur naturally in books very frequently. Teachers can achieve the goal of having students read the targeted classroom words in connected text using the sentence completion and sentence frame ideas described previously. One of our favorite ideas is to create books using the targeted classroom words. We'll expand on this here with an example:

Where Is Missing Millie Mouse?

Is Millie Mouse behind the door?

No, Millie Mouse is not behind the door.

Is Millie Mouse looking out of the window?

No, Millie Mouse is not looking out of the window.

Is Millie Mouse playing on the iPad?

No, Millie Mouse is not on the iPad.

Is Millie Mouse on the table?

No, she is not on the table.

Is Millie Mouse on the chair?

No, Millie Mouse is not on the chair.

Look under the chair.

Yes, here is silly Millie Mouse!

This story could be created by the class as a language experience story. A stuffed or plastic mouse could aid comprehension and be motivating. The story could also be created by a student with complex support needs with a peer. Or, the teacher could write the story for the students. Sample extension activities include the following:

- Make a book. Write each sentence on a page with illustrations. Put each page in a sheet protector and use book rings to connect the pages. This could also be done on large paper to make a big book or on a SMART Board (SMART Technologies, Calgary, Canada). Students can participate in making the book with peer or adult support as needed.

- Engage in shared reading of the story. Using a plastic or plush mouse, students could take turns looking for Millie Mouse while demonstrating comprehension of the sentence.

- Let the student take the story or book home and read it to his or her family.

- Complete sentences demonstrating comprehension of vocabulary; for example, "Millie Mouse was under the (chair, desk, window)."

- Cut out the sentences from the story and ask students to put them in the correct sequence.

The strategy of reading the room can expand to include labeling photographs, pictures, and posters around the classroom and school environment. Ultimately, the strategy can be coordinated with the word wall strategy common in elementary school classrooms (see Chapter 9). Although classroom-labeling is designed to help students with complex support needs, all students may benefit from the labeling and frequent exposure to common printed words—for example, English language learners (ELLs) or students who are poor spellers.

Working With Environmental Print   The goal of providing a print-rich environment should not be confined to the classroom or school. Naturally occurring environmental print is also a great source of vocabulary instruction for students, particularly for students with complex needs for support (Keefe et al., 2010). Environmental print consists of printed material frequently found in the school, home, and community environments. This may include common signs (e.g., *Stop, Exit, In, Out*), business signs (e.g., Kmart, Wendy's, car wash), and product labels (e.g., Coke, Pepsi, Froot Loops, Starburst). Using environmental print builds upon students' prior knowledge about the world around them and their ability to associate symbols consistently with objects. The following are ideas for activities using environmental print that you can use to increase students' vocabulary:

- Ask students to bring environment print from home that contains a targeted letter, sound, or topic.

- Include environmental print words on the word wall.

- Classify and sort environmental print words (e.g., for drinks, food, toys).

- Put environmental print words on flashcards to teach as sight words.

- Make sentences out of environmental print words.

- Finish sentences with environmental print words (e.g., "I like to drink Coke").

- Match environmental print to flashcards of the same word.

- Cut up the individual letters in environmental print words and ask the students to put the letters back in the correct order.

- Make word families out of the letters in environmental print.

- Make an alphabet chart with an environmental print vocabulary word for each letter.

- Use environmental print to help with instructions for class activities such as cooking.

- Create a booklet that includes selections from the multiple examples listed above, as well as separate pages for each word to add new examples; provide the opportunity for the student to read this book to other students or adults several times throughout the day, as well as including the book in the home–school communication folder to read and add examples from home.

- Allow the student with complex support needs to serve as an environmental print tour director, guiding another student or adult to places on campus to read target vocabulary.

Environmental print has potential beyond the classroom and can be used in the wider school environment, home, and community. By learning common signs such as *Stop, Poison,* and *Exit,* students increase their vocabulary and become personally safer and more independent.

REFLECTION QUESTION 3

How would you justify the need for a literacy rich environment to the family of a student with complex support needs?

Break It Down: Teach Analysis of Word Structure and Morphemes

In vocabulary instruction, morphemic or structural analysis involves breaking a complex word down into its smallest meaningful parts (morphemes) and using the meaning of those parts to determine the meaning of the entire word (Edwards, Font, Baumann, & Boland, 2004; Reed, 2008). Approximately 60% of new words students are exposed to can be broken down into meaningful word parts that provide important clues to their overall meaning (Nagy & Anderson, 1984). Because it is virtually impossible to teach students all of the words they will ever encounter in school, they need ways to analyze unfamiliar words. Morphemic analysis supports students in making connections among words with similar component parts and encourages them to apply their knowledge of how words work when they encounter new words. For this reason, one potentially important consideration when selecting targeted vocabulary across the tiers for students with complex support needs is using words that share roots, prefixes, and/or suffixes.

Beck, McKeown, and Kucan (2008) point out that the research on the effectiveness of vocabulary instruction in general, and morphemic analysis in particular, is not conclusive. However, available evidence indicates that teaching morphemic analysis can have a positive impact on the vocabulary development of students without disabilities (Bowers, Kirby, & Deacon, 2010), students who are acquiring English as a second or other language (Kieffer & Lesaux, 2008), students with learning disabilities (Goodwin & Ahn, 2010; Harris, Schumaker, & Deschler, 2011; Reed, 2008), and students with communication disorders (Good, Lance, & Rainey, 2015). Numerous authors, including Beck et al. (2008), suggest providing students information about morphemes as one component of robust language instruction. Although morphemic analysis has often been advised for students at the secondary level, Rasinski, Padak, Newton, and Newton (2008) recommend that such instruction begin at the elementary level. Given the need to ensure that students with complex support needs have access to the general curriculum, teachers must consider how to adapt and modify it in order to provide *all* students with effective instruction in morphemic analysis.

Free and Bound Morphemes

There are two types of morphemes that students will encounter, free and bound (Vaughn & Bos, 2015). Free morphemes stand alone; in and of themselves, they constitute words. *Happy, girl, walk,* and *cover* are all examples. Bound morphemes cannot stand alone; instead, they are word parts that must be linked to other morphemes and that affect those other morphemes' meaning. Affixes—that is, prefixes and suffixes—are bound morphemes. Consider this example: The free morpheme *cover* can stand alone but can also be combined with other bound morphemes such as the prefixes *un-* or *re-* and the suffixes *-ed* or *-ing.* This combining yields the following words: *uncover, recover, covered, covering, uncovered, uncovering, recovered,* and *recovering.* Breaking down these more complex words into their individual morphemes can provide students with important information regarding their meaning.

Our example illustrates how a free morpheme might be combined with bound morphemes; you can probably think of many other words that combine a free morpheme with one or more affixes this way, such as *preheat* or *played.* Some English words, however, consist entirely of bound morphemes that have been combined. These words combine word roots with each other, with prefixes or suffixes, or both.

Rasinski et al. describe a word root as "a word part that carries meaning . . . when a root appears inside a word it lends meaning to the word" (2008, p. 27). They go on to point out that words that share the same root also share aspects of meaning. Greek and Latin roots are common in the English language, and many are found in the vocabulary of the average elementary student (Greenwood, 2004). For example, the Latin root *mov-/mot-* means *to move,* and even very young children know words like *motor, motorcycle,* and *move;* this knowledge can later be applied when they encounter words like *promotion* and *motivate* (Padak, Bromley, Rasinski, & Newton, 2012). Content area texts, in particular, include many discipline-specific root words, and a knowledge of these roots directly influences students' ability to understand the vocabulary and benefit from content area instruction (Mountain, 2015).

General Guidelines for Teaching Structural Analysis   To apply morphemic or structural analysis, students must first understand that words can be broken down into component parts so that when they encounter an unfamiliar word, they think about whether they know any of its parts. Cunningham (2009), Rasinski et al. (2008), and others suggest beginning morphemic analysis with compound words, teaching the most common prefixes and suffixes next, and then exploring the meaning of various roots. It is generally recommended that morphemic analysis be paired with contextual analysis, particularly when emphasis is placed on the development of reading vocabulary. Ebbers and Denton recommend a strategy they describe as *outside-in:*

1. First, look outside the word at context clues in the neighboring words and sentences.

2. Then, look inside the word at the word parts (prefix, root, suffix).

3. Next, reread the section, keeping the meaningful word parts in mind. Make an inference: What do you think the word might mean? (2008, p. 98)

Certain cautions should be applied when teaching morphemic analysis to all students and particularly to students with complex support needs. First, it is not foolproof (Cunningham, 2009; Vaughn & Bos, 2015). Many words contain syllables that are spelled the same as common morphemes but don't carry the same meanings. For example, the common English prefix *in-* means *not* in words such as *incorrect* and *inappropriate,* but that meaning doesn't apply in words like *injury,* where *in* is simply the first syllable, or *inside,* where *in* functions as a prepositional free morpheme in a compound word. Second, as in all areas of vocabulary instruction, teachers must use assessment data in planning instruction for each student. For some students with complex support needs, exploring intricacies in morphemic analysis might be inappropriate; however, for others, particularly those whose reading and writing vocabulary is more extensive than their speaking vocabulary, understanding these intricacies may be critical.

Teaching Compound Words   The English language includes numerous compound words; determining their meaning by studying their component parts is among the least complex morphemic analysis tasks. Suggestions abound for activities that teach students about compound words. For example, students can be asked to identify compound words in materials they read or in those read aloud, they can match compound word parts to create new words, and they can break apart compound words into their two free morphemes. For students with complex support needs, consider beginning instruction with already familiar words—for example, words like *bedroom, bathroom,* and *classroom,* which students have likely encountered in home, school, and community environments. Note, also, that Rasinski et al. (2008) suggested beginning instruction with compound words using those composed of two monosyllabic word parts (e.g., *bedroom, birthday, backpack*) before exposing students to multisyllabic compound words (e.g., *dishwasher, mountaintop, Spider-man*). For familiar two-syllable compounds, students can segment and connect the individual morphemes using objects, pictures, symbols, or words to represent each part; they can be asked to point, gesture, or eye gaze to the appropriate morpheme. Students can be given a list of words and asked to use a programmed switch to distinguish between compounds and noncompounds. Using other AAC devices to work with compound words, students can identify specific activities that might occur in each room, or they can choose the correct compound from several choices to complete a sentence.

Teachers might use a variety of activities in the inclusive classroom to expose students to compound words, and students with a wide range of disabilities can easily be included in these activities. As mentioned previously, students can be asked to complete activities with symbols representing the component words, can be instructed with a subset of the words being used for classroom instruction, and/or may use a variety of response modes that can easily be incorporated into word study activities.

Teaching Prefixes and Suffixes

When teaching affixes, consider the frequency with which they occur in the curriculum and the regularity of their spellings. Instruction should begin with the most common and regular affixes. As students progress in the content areas, they can learn affixes that are particularly relevant to specific disciplines.

Learning prefixes is generally much simpler than learning suffixes (Gunning, 2015) because they can be easily identified at the beginning of the word and their spellings and meanings are fairly consistent (Ebbers & Denton, 2008). *Un-, re-, in-,* and *dis-* are the most commonly occurring English prefixes (Edwards et al., 2004) and these should be taught early in the instructional sequence. Begin by teaching students to recognize and separate the prefix from the rest of the word. This can be done by highlighting it; physically separating the two word parts; having the student gesture, point, or eye gaze to indicate where the word should be divided; or using an AAC. Next, discuss the meaning of the prefix and provide examples of familiar words that include it. Rasinski et al. (2008) recommend using words like *unwrap, unbutton, unzip,* and *unhappy* because they will be familiar to many students. For students with complex support needs, concrete objects can be used to demonstrate the difference between *button* and *unbutton* and *zip* and *unzip,* symbols can be used to represent the word parts, and students can use alternative response modes to identify the correct use of the words in context.

Teaching suffixes is somewhat more complex. There are two types of suffixes that students will encounter—inflectional and derivational. Inflectional suffixes serve primarily grammatical functions and have little influence on the meaning of the word (e.g., *-ed* changes a verb to past tense). Derivational suffixes can be more complex, abstract, and difficult to explain (Gunning, 2015), and often change the spelling of the root, which adds another level of complexity (Cunningham, 2009). For example, consider how the spelling of the base word *plenty* changes when the suffix *-ful* is added to form *plentiful.*

Although many students learn inflectional suffixes, such as *-s, -es, -ed,* and *-ing,* without direct instruction, this is not always the case, and students with more significant support needs may require instruction to appropriately use and understand these morphemes. Photographs can be used to help student distinguish between singular and plural nouns: *girl* and *girls, dog* and *dogs.* Video sequences can help students differentiate verb tenses: *jump, jumped,* and *jumping.* Once a student recognizes these differences, the student can be asked to select the appropriate word to complete a sentence. Again, a variety of response modes can be used.

When introducing derivational suffixes, begin with those that are the least complex and most regular before moving to those that are more abstract. The suffixes *-er* and *-est* in words like *big, bigger,* and *biggest* can be taught very concretely and are therefore a good starting point. Some agreement exists that *-ful, -less, -able,* and *-ible* are logical choices for teaching next (Cunningham, 2009; Rasinski et al., 2008).

Mountain (2015) advocates exposing students to discipline-specific affixes as they are exposed to increasingly complex content-area material. For example, *bi-, tri-,* and *quad-* can be particularly important in understanding mathematical concepts like *bisect, triangle,* and *quadrilateral.* Again, concrete objects, pictures, and symbols can help make these concepts accessible for students with complex support needs, and encouraging students to respond in the ways most appropriate for them can ensure that all students benefit from this instruction.

Familiarity with students and the curriculum is crucial in determining which affixes should be introduced and in what order, particularly the more abstract suffixes encountered in content area texts. For example, the suffix *-cracy* (a type of government or rule), which occurs with some frequency in words like *aristocracy, autocracy,* and *democracy,* can enhance understanding of social studies content (Mountain, 2015). Teachers must determine if and when it is appropriate to introduce these more abstract morphemes and use their ingenuity to ensure that their teaching methods address the needs of all students, including those with complex support needs. Remember, when operating from the perspective of the least dangerous assumption, every effort should be made to ensure that each learner has access to the general education curriculum.

Teaching Roots   Less agreement tends to be found in the research literature regarding the introduction and teaching of root words. Cunningham (2009) advocates using common root words like *work* and *play,* to which numerous affixes can be added, before introducing Greek and Latin roots. (That is, standalone English root words should be introduced first.) Graves (2006) cautions teachers to avoid systematic teaching of non-English roots, with the exception of incidental instruction for secondary-level students. Rasinski et al. (2008) strongly recommend directly teaching Greek and Latin roots beginning in elementary school, and these authors specify that in order to unlock meaning, students should be taught to remove the prefix and focus on the root first. Finally, Mountain (2015) suggests that the teaching of discipline-specific roots is critical to content area instruction, and Helman, Calhoun, and Kern (2015) concur, reporting that teaching Greek and Latin roots enhances the understanding of science vocabulary among secondary ELLs with learning disabilities.

The general teaching principles discussed for other aspects of morphemic analysis also apply to word roots: Introduce them systematically and provide plenty of opportunities for practice and reteaching. Start with the most concrete examples and progress to the more abstract, teaching those roots that occur most frequently in the content being taught (Edwards et al., 2004). Rasinski et al. (2008) provide an excellent example of using *realia* (concrete objects) to teach the meaning of the root *graph/gram.* The teacher begins by showing students a photo*graph,* a bio*graphy,* a tele*gram,* a cardio*gram,* and a holo*gram.* After encouraging classmates to discuss and identify each item, the teacher lists the words on the board and has students identify commonalities among them. Afterward, the teacher can use the realia to expand on students' understanding. Such a lesson can be easily adapted to address a variety of learning needs, with the objective for some students being to match the word associated with each object, and for others, to generate additional words with *graph/gram.*

At the secondary level, the power of knowing discipline-specific roots cannot be overstated. Consider, for example, the root *gen,* meaning *family* or *race,* in terms from biology such as *genus, genome,* and *genetics;* that same root is critical to understanding *genome, progeny,* and *genocide* when teaching history (Mountain, 2015). These terms typically represent what Beck et al. (2008) describe as Tier 3 words. However, as Rasinski, Padak, Newton, and Newton (2010) remind us, some discipline-specific vocabulary, including Greek and Latin roots, may become high-frequency (Tier 2) words for more mature language users. Remember, students' receptive and expressive vocabularies may vary considerably along with their oral and written vocabularies. Teach only those roots that will have the most "meaning power" for the individual student, and work collaboratively to develop creative ways to accommodate or modify materials, activities, and response modes to ensure that all students are active participants in instruction.

Additional Guidelines for Teaching Structural Analysis   Apart from the guidelines discussed previously for specific types of morphemes, certain general principles apply when teaching morphemic and structural analysis. First, introduce words in families; some roots—for example, the root *cycle* in *motorcycle, bicycle, tricycle, cyclist,* and so on—occur within potentially dozens of related words. Exposure to these word families gives students more opportunity to see semantic relationships and familiarizes them with the types of meaning changes that occur among related words (Edwards et al., 2004).

Second, build a classroom community of morphemic analyzers and word detectives. Word walls or word spokes—on which the students and/or the teacher record all the words students discover with the same component part—can be used to explore various morphemes. One suggestion is to add words to these walls or charts using index cards of two different colors to represent examples and nonexamples.

Third, support students in maintaining word study notebooks and affixionaries to organize and consolidate their knowledge of word parts.

Last, but hardly least, make word work fun! Use games, puzzles, and riddles to this end. Have students play Concentration to match compound word parts or match affixes with roots in a game of Go Fish, or provide crossword puzzles and word searches that incorporate particular morphemes. Create riddles and ask your students to create them—for example, "I have pedals, young children ride me, and I have three wheels" (Rasinski, Padak, Newton, et al., 2010, p. 6).

The Internet abounds with ideas for teaching students to look for and consider word parts in terms of both decoding and building understanding. Use all available resources to engage students as they explore words and their parts, and think creatively to ensure that all students have access to meaningful vocabulary instruction.

Use Modified Approaches to Traditional Sight-Word Instruction

Exposure to print-rich environments and systematic instruction in morphemic and structural analysis can help expand students' vocabulary; modified approaches to traditional sight-word instruction can also be valuable for students with complex support needs.

Stimulus Pairing and Fading   Sometimes, students have difficulty learning targeted vocabulary with traditional sight-word approaches. To enhance vocabulary acquisition and comprehension, we suggest pairing the new vocabulary word with something that is known by the student (e.g., an object, symbol, or photograph). When the purpose is teaching word recognition (see Chapter 9), it is important to fade the stimulus. When the purpose is teaching the meaning of words, students ideally will progress to learn the meaning of the word apart from the stimulus. This won't always be possible, but that does not mean that we should abandon vocabulary instruction if the student cannot understand the word apart from the stimulus. It is appropriate instruction to teach students to use words to refer to objects, people, and other items in their immediate environment.

If a student cannot understand a word in isolation, pair it with a more concrete stimulus and then gradually fade that stimulus. The sequence may proceed through the following stages:

- Stage 1: Vocabulary word paired with an object

- Stage 2: Vocabulary word paired with a specific photograph

- Stage 3: Vocabulary word paired with a generic picture

- Stage 4: Vocabulary word paired with an icon

- Stage 5: Vocabulary word paired with the written word

These stages can be used to teach target vocabulary that is identified for individual students in any content area. Some students with complex support needs may not need all of these stimulus prompts or even need any of them; others will consistently need the maximum level of prompting. The sequence can be adjusted so that all students will be participating meaningfully in classroom instruction and developing vocabulary at their own levels.

Word Sorts   Word sorts, which will be discussed further in Chapter 9 as a strategy to increase word recognition, can also aid in building vocabulary comprehension. In traditional phonics instruction, students may be asked to sort words by letter-sound patterns—for example, words that spell the long /a/ sound with *ai*, and those that spell it with *ay*. To use them for vocabulary instruction, the teacher simply varies the way in which the students are asked to sort or classify words. For example, they can sort by similarities or by opposites, determine which word in a set does not belong, sort by a feature (e.g., size, color, function), or sort words in the order in which they occur in a lecture or film. Word sorts are a good way to give students repeated exposure to words and help them develop a deeper understanding of meaning; this strategy can be used in conjunction with other approaches discussed in this chapter.

Word sorting activities can be used to reinforce vocabulary knowledge even as they also build knowledge or critical thinking skills within a content area. For example, in inclusive secondary language arts classes, students studying Shakespeare's *Julius Caesar* might use a chart like the one in Figure 8.6 to apply characterization and plot knowledge in a way that requires unexpected categorization: determining what each character would purchase in a particular store. A student with complex support needs in this class might sort a personal set of vocabulary

	Walmart	Petco	Home Depot	Post Office
What will Caesar buy at Walmart, and why? Support your answer with a quotation from the play or biographical excerpt.				
Caesar				*Stamps* because he needs to communicate with fellow Romans and countrymen.
Brutus	*Soap and stain remover* "And let us bathe our hands in Caesar's blood, Up to the elbows, and besmear our swords"			
Cassius				
Calpurnia				
Mark Antony				

Figure 8.6. Sample language arts word sort.

notecards by what one might purchase in each location and add this contribution to the group's chart. Sorting can be further aided by pictures, symbols, or prompts that can be faded as the student progresses in learning the vocabulary.

A second way this class might sort words would be to list the characters and sort premade character descriptors for each character; the student with a small set of target words could, instead, put one word with each character and then use the target word to generate a sensible sentence about the character. There are unlimited ways to complete word sorts; varied, carefully thought out use of this strategy maximizes results for the whole class.

Word sort activities can also be combined with organizing transitions from introductory and/or whole-class instruction to small-group instruction. For an example, see Figure 8.7. This chart can be used in an inclusive middle school science classroom in two ways: to reinforce what the class has been studying about taxonomy and then to organize teams, named for different animals, for a small-group activity. The chart headings name animals; all but one of the animals named are mammals. After looking at the headings, students can apply knowledge of classification by determining which animal does not belong. In this example, students must recall what they know about mammals to conclude that *turtle* does not belong; they may also have to investigate the meaning of *gnu;* the brief review requires them to consider examples and nonexamples of a science concept—mammals. A student with complex support needs can meaningfully participate in various individualized ways, such as physically matching one of the targeted vocabulary words in the headings to an object or picture. After students conduct the quick whole-class word sort, they move into the groups indicated by the team name for the planned small-group activity. Again, a student with complex support needs might meaningfully participate, for example, by selecting her name from one of four choices given or by indicating *yes* or *no* when asked if her name is Lee.

A similar word sort at the elementary or preschool level might target receptive vocabulary and require students to physically move into varied groups based on category. This may be picture supported, with each child given a different picture that fits in one of the categories; the teacher can provide additional guidance in switching groups as needed. Afterward, the teacher can print or upload a picture of the correctly completed sort to display in the classroom or in a personal book for review. For the student with complex support needs, the individual word used will match the targeted vocabulary.

Quiz Me Cards   Students can record and review words by using *quiz me cards,* made from index cards or cardstock and bound into a "book" with a string or binder ring. As students learn new vocabulary, they write the word and its definition on the front of the card and then draw five lines for five signatures on the back for later use in informal quizzing. In the example given by Fisher and Frey (2008), the music teacher introduces vocabulary words and their definitions. After the students record the information, they are required to ask five adults from outside their class to quiz them on the word and sign the back of the card if the student gets the definition correct. This provides students with an opportunity for meaningful practice of the vocabulary words; a bonus benefit is that it also encourages them to interact with adults around campus.

Quiz me cards are easily adapted by grade level, content area, and ability; not all students in the class need to have the same vocabulary words for this strategy to be successful. The activity can be adapted by having the students quiz one another in class and sign each other's cards or

Bat	Gnu	Leopard	Rabbit	Turtle	Whale
James	Amina	Luis	Lee	Meg	Makenzie
Martin	Robin	Kumi	Leslie	Delila	Sami
Teresa	Dion	Maria	Rayanne	Brayden	Lauren
Ashley	José	Rusty	Shane	Ty	Rae

Figure 8.7.   Sample science word sort.

gather signatures from family or community members. Quiz me cards can be used appropriately with students with and without disabilities and with ELLs, and they can be adapted for students with physical, sensory, speech, and language disabilities by using pointing, gesturing, eye gazing, braille, AT devices, and peer support.

Quiz You Cards　In this adaptation of Fisher and Frey's quiz me cards (2008), shown in Figure 8.8, a student with complex support needs carries an enlarged, laminated version of his cards throughout the day, with one word on each page. He periodically writes (stamps, tapes, etc.) the target word, *book,* in the blank and then asks another person to fill in the second blank and sign. The second person can read the completed sentence for the student's approval. This provides both repetition and opportunities to generalize the target words to other settings.

Vocabulary Cards　Fisher and Frey (2008) described the use of vocabulary cards to enhance understanding through visual representation and application; the basic idea is to help students come up with their own meaning of words rather than passively copying the teacher's definition. Fisher and Frey described asking students to draw lines dividing the index card into quadrants (see Figure 8.9) and then fill in the quadrants by writing the vocabulary word in the first quadrant, the definition in the student's own words (or a category classification) in the second quadrant, a graphic or picture to represent the word in the third quadrant, and a sentence using the word in the fourth quadrant. Students can later use the cards (hole-punched and bound) to practice words individually or with a partner.

It's important to note that students should not be required to find definitions in a dictionary with no guidance. Beck et al. (2002) shared research indicating that when students used dictionaries to find definitions of words, the definitions were frequently incorrect or incomplete. They suggested providing *student-friendly* explanations of words by giving examples of how the words are usually used in everyday language.

As with quiz me cards, this activity can be varied so the quadrants match the purpose of instruction for any grade or ability level and content area. For example, a student with complex support needs who has a goal of recognizing and using environmental words and differentiating between drink and food could use a card designed like the template shown in Figure 8.9. These environmental print vocabulary cards could then be used for word sorts and other practice activities. This activity can be used successfully for students with and without disabilities and ELLs, and it can be adapted for students with physical, sensory, speech, and language disabilities by using pointing, gesturing, eye gazing, braille, AT devices, and peer support. Different-sized index cards allow for the larger writing and drawing of younger children or children with disabilities.

Modify Traditional Approaches to Vocabulary Instruction

In this section, we will share a few examples of making traditional vocabulary instruction—that is, methods long used with typically developing students—accessible and meaningful for students with complex support needs. (See Chapter 12 for more ways to make text accessible.) These ideas can be applied to many literacy materials or to content area instruction.

Working With Synonyms　Fisher and Frey (2008) describe a "shades of meaning" strategy to help students differentiate degrees of meaning between synonyms: using paint color sample chips to order synonyms by the degree to which they share a feature. For example, students could order synonyms for the word *happy* (*glad, contented, joyful, ecstatic*) by degree; that is, by what intensity of happiness each word denotes. To reflect this order, the words are then written on the different shades on the paint chip. The paint chip can then be attached to a notebook page, with each word's definition to the side.

Rasinski, Padak, and Fawcett (2010) describe a similar strategy they term "vocabulary timelines," which are collaboratively created on a large sheet of paper, Smart Board, or other visual display. As an example, Rasinki, Padak, and Fawcett describe asking students to come

Target word	1. I want to read a *Book* about _____.
Book	*Signature* _____
	2. The best *Book* is _____.
	Signature _____
	3. May I please borrow a *Book* for _____?
	Signature _____
	4. My *Book* is under the _____.
	Signature _____
	5. Have you read a *Book* about _____?
	Signature _____

Figure 8.8.   Sample quiz me card.

Quadrant 1 Name of food or drink e.g., MILK	Quadrant 2 Definition/Classification e.g., DRINK
Quadrant 3 Paste word, icon, or picture from environmental print	Quadrant 4 Complete the sentence e.g., I LIKE TO DRINK MILK.

Figure 8.9. Vocabulary card activity using environmental print.

up with synonyms of the word *said*. The students write their synonyms on sticky notes, placing them on butcher paper in order of loudness, ultimately creating a vocabulary timeline ranging from soft to loud: *whisper, murmur, declare, shout, scream.*

Shades of meaning and vocabulary timelines can easily be modified to provide access for students with complex support needs. Here are just a few ideas:

- Photographs, other images, and/or tactile cues can supplement the words.

- Students can match pictures to the words, or pictures to pictures.

- Students can match picture/word to oral definition.

- Use Build-a-Bear voice box or other technology to read the word with cues for correct ordering (e.g., "whisper" would be whispered, "scream" would be yelled).

- Reduce the number of words to be ordered—paint color chips come in different sizes and number of colors.

- Reinforce target words on the timeline.

- Use environment print to order foods by preference or what time of day they would be eaten (breakfast to dinner).

- Use environmental print to order items by preference or cost.

- Use in content areas to order a critical feature of a topic; for example, fierceness of animals (mouse, cat, dog, wolf, lion).

Time delay and system of least prompts can be used in combination with any of these ideas. Figure 8.10 shows an example of some of these modifications used in a science unit on weather.

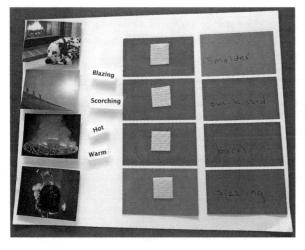 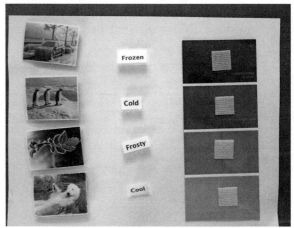

Figure 8.10. Example of modified shades of meaning in science.

Semantic Feature Analysis   The purpose of a semantic feature analysis (SFA) is to visually display critical features of interrelated concepts or a word class. SFA is particularly useful "to see connections from known vocabulary to the new and master important concepts" (Reutzel & Cooter, 2012, p. 534). One great advantage of this strategy is that it can be used in any content areas and for any age group. As noted by Rasinski, Padak, and Fawcett, "Animals, trees, types of clouds, simple machines, presidents, authors, book titles, months of the year, and parts of a car are examples of the general categories from which we have chosen words for SFA with students" (2010, p. 151).

The SFA is a grid that can be created on a page, butcher paper, Smart Board, computer, or other visual display. On its left side are listed words from the target group, which are related in some way (e.g., *apple, banana, orange, grape; football, tennis, swimming, golf; Alaska, Hawaii, California, New York*). Across the top of the grid are listed features of the word class (e.g., *color, sweetness, method of growth; equipment, length of game, scoring, professional teams; location, size, population, climate, major industries*). Students complete the grid by using + or – to indicate whether a specific feature applies to each word/concept (see Figure 8.11 to see an example in social studies).

Implementation of SFA is very flexible; it is easy to modify for students with complex support needs. For example, educators can have students complete the SFA individually, in pairs, with a peer tutor, in a small group, or as a whole class. The number of words or features in the SFA can be adapted for individual students' needs. The teacher can create the SFA using target vocabulary; alternatively, students can generate their own word class and/or their own list of features or create an SFA for another group to complete. As with other vocabulary activities, words can be supplemented with photographs or other images; students can match pictures to the words, match pictures to pictures, or match pictures or words to oral definition. Again, a Build-a-Bear voice box or other technology can be used to read the word and/or feature. See Figure 8.12 for an example of a modified SFA.

Photo Analysis   We discovered the value of photo analysis while team-teaching a general education social studies methods class with a special education reading class; our colleague, Dr. Rebecca Sanchez, used photo analysis to teach about Japanese internment camps. We immediately saw that this activity was an excellent way to provide wordless content for all students, including those with complex needs for support. Using photos of historical events is an excellent way to develop vocabulary and comprehension (Barton, n.d.).

Introductory activities can include having students looking at the photograph(s) individually, in pairs, in small groups or as a class, and answering teacher prompts—for example, "What do you see in the photo? What inferences or guesses can you make? What questions do you have?" To further develop content vocabulary and comprehension, you might have students label the photographs, match related visual images, or and/or match pictures to words. Working individually or with a partner or group, students can choose a photo and describe it with a word or

	Rule by one or minority	Leader elected	Inherited leadership	Absence of organized government	Totalitarian	Rule by majority
Autocracy	+	–	+/–	–	+	–
Anarchy	–	–	–	+	–	–
Democracy	–	+	–	–	–	+
Monarchy	+	–	+	–	+/–	–
Communism	One party	+?	–?	–	+	–

Figure 8.11. Sample semantic feature analysis in social studies.

sentence; another student, pair, or group then finds the photo described. Students can add dialogue to photos containing people or animals and add commentary to other photos; they can also complete sentence frames about the photos.

Work with photo analysis need not be limited to matching and describing activities. You can also ask students to sort or group the photos in some way; for example, placing them in chronological order along a timeline, or grouping photos evoking an emotional response, photos containing people, photos containing targeted vocabulary, and so on. Finally, students can use the photographs in conjunction with other tools or activities; for example, they can create related

	Alive	Not alive	Human	Not human
Penguin	✓			✓
Book		✓		✓
Children	✓		✓	
Dog	✓			✓

Figure 8.12. Sample of an adapted semantic feature analysis.

vocabulary or quiz me cards related to the photos, create graphic organizers to compare and contrast photos, or use the photos as the basis for creating language experience that can later be expanded into classroom books.

Although photos can also be used to develop all areas of literacy, they are especially valuable for developing vocabulary for students with complex support needs who may have more limited life experiences. Photo analysis can also be used in other content areas including science, health, fine arts, and life skills. Chapter 13 includes additional ideas for using photographs to build literacy skills.

REFLECTION QUESTION 4

What are the most important elements of vocabulary instruction for students with complex support needs?

SUMMARY

This chapter discussed the importance of vocabulary as a component of reading instruction for learners with complex support needs. Four types of vocabulary were defined, and the relationship among them explored: listening, speaking, reading, and writing vocabulary. We reviewed formal and informal means of assessing vocabulary knowledge, along with guidelines for setting learning goals and choosing target vocabulary for instruction. Finally, we discussed the design of effective instructional strategies to develop vocabulary for student with complex support needs. One of the most important elements of vocabulary instruction is that it needs to be active and engaging. We believe this makes vocabulary instruction one of the easiest areas of instruction to modify for students with complex support needs in general education. This chapter included specific strategies and examples to help teachers accomplish meaningful vocabulary instruction in any setting, including inclusive classroom and community settings. These strategies have the potential to benefit all students; with a little effort and creativity, vocabulary can become one of the most engaging aspects of your comprehensive literacy program.

RESOURCES

- **Dolch Word Activities** (http://www.gate.net/~labooks/xLPDolch.html). This web site contains numerous ideas for using Dolch words to facilitate student literacy.

- **Reading Rockets** (http://www.readingrockets.org). This web site contains classroom strategies, research, webcasts, videos, and blogs for parents and teachers.

- **A Pictures Worth—Analyzing Historical Photographs in the Elementary Grades** (http://www.socialstudies.org/sites/default/files/publications/se/6505/650503.html). This web site contains a lot of ideas for lesson planning using photographs.

- **Library of Congress Prints and Photographs Reading Room** (http://www.loc.gov/rr/print). This web site provides access to the Library of Congress archives, reference information, and activities.

- **All About Adolescent Literacy** (http://www.adlit.org). This web site contains resources for parents and teachers about research, books, articles, blogs, and video and webcasts on all topics related to adolescent reading instruction.

- **What Works Clearinghouse** (https://ies.ed.gov/ncee/wwc). This is the web site of the Institute of Education Sciences and a great source for evidence-based literacy strategies and programs. Intervention and practice guides can be found on all areas of literacy instruction.

REFERENCES

Allington, R.L. (2006). Fluency: Still waiting after all these years. In S.J. Samuels & A.E. Farstrup (Eds.), *What research has to say about fluency instruction* (pp. 94–105). Washington, DC: International Reading Association.

Allor, J.H., Mathes, P.G., Roberts, J.K., Cheatham, J.P., & Al Otaiba, S. (2014). Is scientifically based reading instruction effective for students with below-average IQs? *Exceptional Children, 80*(3), 287–306.

Austin, P., & Boeckmann, K. (1990). *Edmark functional word series.* Redmond, WA: Edmark.

Barton, K. (n.d.). *A picture's worth: Analyzing historical photographs in the elementary grades.* Retrieved July 28, 2016 from http://www.socialstudies.org/system/files/publications/se/6505/650503.html

Beck, I.L., McKeown, M.G., & Kucan, L. (2002). *Bringing words to life.* New York, NY: Guilford Press.

Beck, I.L., McKeown, M.G., & Kucan, L. (2008). *Creating robust vocabulary: Frequently asked questions and extended examples.* New York, NY: Guilford Press.

Beck, I.L., McKeown, M.G., & Kucan, L. (2013). *Bringing words to life* (2nd ed.). New York, NY: Guilford Press.

Bowers, P.N., Kirby, J.R., & Deacon, S.H. (2010). The effects of morphological instruction on literacy skills: A systematic review of the literature. *Review of Educational Research, 80*(2), 144–179.

Browder, D.M., Ahlgrim-Delzell, L., Courtade, G., Gibbs, S.L., & Flowers, C. (2008). Evaluation of the effectiveness of an early literacy program for students with significant developmental disabilities. *Exceptional Children, 75*(1), 33–52.

Browder, D.M., Ahlgrim-Delzell, L., Flowers, C., & Baker, J. (2012). An evaluation of a multicomponent early literacy program for students with severe developmental disabilities. *Remedial and Special Education, 33*(4), 237–246.

Browder, D.M., Wakeman, S.Y., Spooner, F., Ahlgrim-Delzell, L., & Algozzine, B. (2006). Research on reading instruction for individuals with significant cognitive disabilities. *Exceptional Children, 72*(4), 392–408.

Brown, L., Branston, M.B., Hamre-Nietupski, S., Pumpian, I., Certo, N., & Gruenewald, L. (1979). A strategy for developing chronological and age-appropriate and functional curricular content for severely handicapped adolescents and young adults. *Journal of Special Education, 13,* 81–90.

Cooter, R.B., & Flynt, E.S. (1996). *Teaching reading in the content areas: Developing content literacy for all students.* Columbus, OH: Merrill/Prentice Hall.

Copeland, S.C., & Keefe, E.B. (2017). Teaching reading and literacy skills to students with intellectual disability. In M.L. Wehmeyer & K.A. Shogren (Eds.), *Research-based practices for educating students with intellectual disability* (pp. 320–342). Philadelphia, PA: Routledge.

Cunningham, P.M. (2009). *What really matters in vocabulary: Research-based practices across the curriculum.* Boston, MA: Pearson.

Dale, E. (1965). Vocabulary measurement: Techniques and major findings. *Elementary English, 42*(8), 895–901.

Davidson, J.W. (2005). *The American nation: Beginnings through 1877.* Upper Saddle River, NJ: Pearson Education.

Downing, J.E. (2005). *Teaching literacy to students with significant disabilities: Strategies for the K–12 inclusive classroom.* Thousand Oaks, CA: Corwin Press.

Downing, J.E., Eichinger, J., & Demchak, M. (2008). *Including students with severe and multiple disabilities in typical classrooms: Practical strategies for teachers* (3rd ed.). Baltimore, MD: Paul H. Brookes Publishing Co.

Dunn, L.M., & Dunn, L.M. (1997). *Peabody Picture Vocabulary Test–Third Edition (PPVT-III).* Circle Pines, MN: American Guidance Service.

Ebbers, S.M., & Denton, C.A. (2008). A root awakening: Vocabulary instruction for older students with reading difficulties. *Learning Disabilities Research & Practice, 23,* 90–102.

Edwards, E.C., Font, G., Baumann, J.F., & Boland, E. (2004). Unlocking word meanings: Strategies and guidelines for teaching morphemic and contextual analysis. In J.F. Bauman & E.J. Kame'enui, (Eds.), *Vocabulary instruction: Research to practice* (pp. 159–176). New York, NY: Guilford Press.

Fisher, D., & Frey, N. (2008). *Improving adolescent literacy: Strategies at work* (2nd ed.). Upper Saddle River, NJ: Merrill/Prentice Hall.

Good, J.E., Lance, D.M., & Rainey, J. (2015). The effects of morphological awareness training on reading, spelling, and vocabulary skills. *Communication Disorders Quarterly, 36,* 142–151.

Goodwin, A., & Ahn, S. (2010). A meta-analysis of morphological interventions: Effects on literacy achievement of children with literacy difficulties. *Annals of Dyslexia, 60,* 183–208.

Graves, M.F. (2006). *The vocabulary book: Learning & instruction.* New York, NY: Teachers College Press.

Greenwood, S.C. (2004). *Words count: Effective vocabulary instruction in action.* Portsmouth, NH: Heinemann.

Gunning, T.G. (2015). *Creating literacy instruction for all students* (8th ed.). Boston, MA: Pearson.

Harris, M.L., Schumaker, J.D., & Deschler, D.D. (2011). The effects of strategic morphemic analysis instruction on the vocabulary performance of secondary students with and without disabilities. *Learning Disability Quarterly, 34*(1), 17–33.

Helman, A.L., Calhoun, M.B., & Kern, L. (2015). Improving science vocabulary of high school English language learners with reading disabilities. *Learning Disability Quarterly, 31*(1), 40–52.

Hudson, M.E., Browder, D.M., & Wood, L.A. (2013). Review of experimental research on academic learning by students with moderate and severe intellectual disability in general education. *Research and Practice for Persons with Severe Disabilities, 38*(1), 17–29.

Hudson, M.E., & Test, D.W. (2011). Evaluating the evidence base of shared story reading to promote literacy for students with extensive support needs. *Research and Practice for Persons with Severe Disabilities, 36*(1–2), 34–45.

Johnson, D. (2001). *Vocabulary in the elementary and middle school.* Boston, MA: Allyn & Bacon.

Karlsen, B., Madden, R., & Gardner, E.F. (1985). *Stanford Diagnostic Reading Test.* San Antonio, TX: Harcourt Assessment.

Katims, D.S. (1994). Emergence of literacy in preschool children with disabilities. *Learning Disability Quarterly, 17,* 100–111.

Keefe, E.B., & Copeland, S.R. (2011). What is literacy? The power of a definition. *Research and Practice for Persons with Severe Disabilities (RPSD), 36*(3–4), 92–99.

Keefe, E.B., Copeland, S.R., & DiLuzio, M.A. (2010). Creating print-rich environments to support literacy instruction. In C. Carnahan & P. Williamson (Eds.), *Quality literacy instruction for students with autism spectrum disorders* (pp. 161–187). Lenexa, KS: AAPC Textbooks.

Kieffer, M.J., & Lesaux, N.K. (2008). The role of derivational morphology in the reading comprehension of Spanish-speaking English language learners. *Reading and Writing, 21,* 783–804.

Kliewer, C. (2008). Joining the literacy flow: Fostering symbol and written language learning in young children with significant developmental disabilities through the four currents of literacy. *Research and Practice for Persons with Severe Disabilities, 33,* 103–121.

Mims, P.J., Lee, A., Browder, D.M., Zakas, T.L., & Flynn, S. (2012). Effects of a treatment package to facilitate English/Language Arts learning for middle school students with moderate to severe disabilities. *Education and Training in Autism and Developmental Disabilities, 47*(4), 414–425.

Mountain, L. (2015). Recurrent prefixes, roots, and suffixes: A morphemic approach to disciplinary literacy. *Journal of Adolescent & Adult Literacy, 58,* 561–567.

Nagy, W.E., & Anderson, R.C. (1984). How many words are there in printed school English? *Reading Research Quarterly, 19,* 303–330.

National Reading Panel (NRP). (2000). *Report of the National Reading Panel: Teaching children to read. Reports of the subgroups* (NIH Publication 00-4754). Washington, DC: National Institute of Child Health and Human Development.

National Reading Technical Assistance Center (NRTAC). (2010). *A review of the current research on vocabulary instruction.* Retrieved July 28, 2016 from http://www2.ed.gov/programs/readingfirst/support/rmcfinal1.pdf

Orelove, F. (1995, February). Consider the potato. *Newsletter of the Severe Disabilities Technical Assistance Center, 10*(5).

Padak, N., Bromley, K., Rasinski, T., & Newton, E. (2012). Vocabulary: Five common misconceptions. *Educational Leadership, 69.* Retrieved from http://www.ascd.org/publications/educational-leadership/summer12/vol69/num09/Vocabulary@-Five-Common-Misconceptions.aspx

Rasinski, T.V., Padak, N.D., & Fawcett, G. (2010). *Teaching children who find reading difficult* (4th ed.). Boston, MA: Allyn & Bacon.

Rasinski, T., Padak, N., Newton, R.M., & Newton, E. (2008). *Greek & Latin roots: Keys to building vocabulary.* Huntington Beach, CA: Shell Education.

Rasinski, T., Padak, N., Newton, R.M., & Newton, E. (2010). *Combine and create: A vocabulary learning routine for grades 1–11.* Chicago, IL: International Reading Association.

Reed, D.K. (2008). A synthesis of morphology interventions and effects on reading outcomes for students in grades K–12. *Learning Disabilities Research & Practice, 23*(1), 36–49.

Reutzel, D.R., & Cooter, R.B. (2010). *Strategies for reading assessment and instruction: Helping every child succeed* (4th ed.). Upper Saddle River, NJ: Pearson Education Inc.

Reutzel, D.R., & Cooter, R.B. (2012). *Teaching children to read: Putting the pieces together* (6th ed.). Upper Saddle River, NJ: Merrill/Prentice Hall.

Roswell, F.G., & Chall, J.S. (1991). *Diagnostic Assessment of Reading with Trial Teaching Strategies (DARTTS).* Itasca, IL: Riverside.

Ryndak, D.L., & Alper, S. (2003). *Curriculum and instruction for students with disabilities in inclusive settings* (4th ed.). Boston, MA: Allyn & Bacon.

Snell, M.E., & Brown, F. (2010). *Instruction of students with severe disabilities* (7th ed.). Upper Saddle River, NJ: Pearson Education Inc.

Spooner, F., Knight, V., Browder, D., Jimenez, B., & DiBiase, W. (2011). Evaluating evidence-based practice in teaching science content to students with severe developmental disabilities. *Research and Practice for Persons with Severe Disabilities, 36*(1–2), 62–75.

Vaughn, S.R., & Bos, C.S. (2015). *Strategies for teaching students with learning and behavior problems* (9th ed.). Boston, MA: Pearson.

CHAPTER 9

What's the Word?

Word Recognition Instruction

Susan R. Copeland, Sharon L. Head, and Heather DiLuzio

LEARNING OBJECTIVES

By the end of this chapter, readers will

1. Understand the two processes used to recognize words.
2. Know the particular challenges students with complex support needs face with word recognition.
3. Be able to define emergent literacy and describe two instructional strategies for students in this stage of literacy learning.
4. Understand how to select target sight words and be able to describe at least two strategies to teach sight words.
5. Be able to describe two strategies to teach phonics skills.

This chapter will address the processes involved in word recognition and the challenges it may pose for students with complex support needs. We will begin by discussing the mental processes involved in decoding and in sight-word recognition. Next, we will discuss the progression of skills involved in learning to read words, from emergent literacy skills, to phonological and phonemic awareness, to acquisition of the alphabetic principle and phonics skills. In our discussion, we will review research-based instructional practices and provide examples of engaging classroom activities and how to differentiate them for learners with complex support needs. The second half of the chapter will discuss how to provide sight-word instruction, again providing examples of effective classroom practices.

WORD RECOGNITION: A MEANS TO AN END

In this chapter, we will explore the processes involved in developing one aspect of literacy: word recognition, or the ability to read and process a word "automatically" when one sees it in print, without having to decode it laboriously, letter by letter. Words we can recognize this way are often called *sight words* because we know them on sight. Typically developing children begin developing a sight-word vocabulary when they are very young; educated, literate adults have a vast sight-word vocabulary. If you can read this paragraph easily, the process of word recognition has essentially become automatic for you. Because it is automatic, you can attend to other aspects of the text: shades of meaning, sentence structure, relationships among ideas, connections between this content and your prior knowledge and life experience, and so on.

Everyone should have the opportunity for these rich experiences engaging with a text—experiences that go far beyond simply recognizing words. Thus, word recognition, crucial as it is, is a means to an end; by no means is it the only skill appropriate to teach to students with complex support needs. However, for this population, word recognition often has been treated as an end goal, even when students are capable of developing far more advanced skills.

As mentioned in Chapter 1, educators have not always believed that students with complex support needs could acquire conventional literacy skills. Literacy instruction, if provided, often consisted only of learning functional sight words, such as environmental signs. Many practitioners did not think these students could learn phonics or other word analysis strategies, so they rarely taught students these skills. However, relying solely on a sight-word approach to identify words restricts students' opportunities to participate in literacy experiences. Students who are taught only sight words have to memorize words based on their appearance. They don't have many strategies to apply when trying to read a new word. Limiting a student's reading "toolkit" to just one skill, sight-word memorization, means limiting that student's reading vocabulary to the number of words the student can memorize.

This chapter will explore word recognition as one component of literacy. Recent research has shown that many students with complex support needs can and do acquire conventional reading skills (e.g., Lemons, Mrachko, Kostewicz, & Paterra, 2012). We will provide examples of ways to assess students' word recognition skills and describe some research-based practices educators can use to build these skills. However, even with this focus on teaching students to recognize individual words, keep in mind that these words should be put into connected text and used in interesting and meaningful activities as soon as possible (Foorman et al., 2016). Doing so helps students with complex support needs more quickly learn to apply (generalize) what they are learning across different contexts and settings.

WHAT HAPPENS WHEN WE RECOGNIZE A WORD IN PRINT?

What, then, is involved in word recognition? Readers identify words using two processes. One process involves recognizing words automatically by their visual properties (i.e., recognizing sight words). The other process involves using phonics knowledge to decode (sound out) words. Successfully recognizing a word requires using several different underlying skills that must all work together. Researchers have found that the following reading skills are all related to successful word recognition for both typically developing children and those with complex support needs, such as students with intellectual disability (ID):

- Phonological processing (phonological memory and phonological awareness—i.e., memory and awareness of speech sounds)

- Orthographic processing (recognition of visual patterns)

- Rapid automatized naming (being able to quickly name familiar items such as letters or numbers) (Channell, Loveall, & Conners, 2013; Wise, Sevcik, Romski, & Morris, 2010)

As discussed in Chapter 2, it is important to build strong language and vocabulary skills as a foundation for developing literacy. Having a well-developed vocabulary is positively associated with word recognition (e.g., Burgoyne et al., 2012). When students see a printed word for the first time, they will recognize it more easily if it is already in their listening or speaking vocabulary because they already have the pronunciation for the word in their mental lexicon or dictionary. (See Chapter 8 for more on the types of vocabularies we use.) Thus, word recognition skills are linked to oral language skills that begin developing before children learn to read.

EARLY READING SKILLS AND WORD RECOGNITION: TEACHING EMERGENT LITERACY LEARNERS

Young children develop their understanding of written and spoken language over time. Each time children engage in a language- or literacy-related activity—even when they do not yet fully understand written language—they build the foundational skills upon which conventional reading and writing skills can develop. As noted previously, word recognition is linked to many other reading skills, such as phonological processing and vocabulary, so activities that support early reading skills in general lay the groundwork for developing word recognition. The nursery rhymes children delight in learning are a good example. Simple, repetitive chants such as Pat-a-cake or "The Itsy-Bitsy Spider" teach important skills such as phonemic awareness, or awareness of the smallest units of speech sounds (e.g., rhyming), vocabulary (comprehending through gesture), and social aspects of language (pragmatics), such as shared attention and turn taking.

Children in this phase of literacy learning are often called *emergent literacy learners.* Although they cannot yet read and write conventionally, they are increasing their understanding of how written language works. Because children's early experiences with written and spoken language strongly influence their later literacy development, it is important for all children—those with and without disabilities—to have many opportunities, over time, to interact with spoken and written language in a variety of formats, to be read to by adults, and to explore using writing or other graphic means to represent spoken language (Ricci, 2011).

For typically developing children, this emergent literacy phase begins at birth and extends to about age 5. Individuals with complex support needs who are well beyond early childhood may also be emergent literacy learners, for several reasons. They may not have had the same types of early literacy experiences as their typically developing peers and, as a result, may not have acquired skills their peers learned at an early age. Also, their formal school experience may not have provided the sustained, systematic literacy instruction required for the acquisition of more conventional literacy skills (Browder et al., 2009). They may also have cognitive, sensory, or motor challenges that have affected their acquisition of language and literacy skills (Kaiser & Roberts, 2011). It is essential for educators to learn emergent literacy instructional practices since they may encounter individuals with complex support needs who are in this phase.

REFLECTION QUESTION 1

What are the two primary processes that individuals use to recognize words? What factors may affect the ability of students with complex support needs to use either of these processes?

In the following sections, we describe some early reading practices that support the development of important language and literacy skills that help to build word recognition. As you read and consider how you might use these practices, keep in mind that students with complex support needs learn and retain new information best when instruction occurs in meaningful contexts and for authentic purposes. Practices must also be adapted for older learners to ensure that the materials and methods are age appropriate. Finally, it is important to remember that emergent literacy is not the end goal. Ultimately, these practices are used with the goal of moving students to conventional reading and writing (Erickson, Hatch, & Clendon, 2010).

Shared Reading

As Breit-Smith and Justice point out, "Emergent literacy interventions are grounded in the notion that reading and writing knowledge is built through social interactions with others" (2010, p. 228). Shared reading (also called *read-alouds*), an effective practice adapted from reading instruction for typically developing students, capitalizes on the social nature of literacy. A few adjustments can make this practice, most often used with young children, effective for older learners in the emergent literacy phase. In fact, Hudson and Test (2011) found that shared reading was an evidence-based practice for students with complex support needs, including those who are older.

One way in which read-alouds support word recognition skills is by including a focus on print. Acquiring concepts about print is a foundational skill for literacy development (Shanahan & Lonigan, 2010). Thus, a focus on print during read-alouds provides many opportunities for students of all ages to increase their understanding of how print functions. For example, teachers can bring to the students' attention letter names, model that (in English) we read from left to right, and point out key features of words (Justice, McGinty, Piasta, Kaderavek, & Fan, 2010). Read-alouds should also focus on building listening comprehension and vocabulary. This can be done by carefully selecting both informational and narrative texts and providing explicit vocabulary instruction on keywords. Discussions of new words and how they relate to the book's theme or concept are also a part of the shared reading experience (e.g., Pollard-Durodola et al., 2010). (See Chapters 6 and 8 for more ideas and examples of how to do this.)

It is always important to set a purpose for the reading before beginning to read. This helps students understand how the read-aloud will fit in with what they already know or understand and how they will use the information. Another helpful tip is to have students follow along with their own copy of the text as the teacher reads aloud, or project the text onto a screen so that all the students can see it as the teacher reads and points out important aspects of the print, pictures, or story. Before beginning the activity, the teacher should point out the title and author and spend some time discussing the cover illustration. This helps students understand the context of the reading and will help them learn and remember words, ideas, or concepts that will be highlighted during the reading. Lane, Keefe, Copeland, and Kruger (2015) suggest asking students to name objects on the book's cover and label them with sticky notes. Students can later find those words in the book, either by matching the sticky note to the word in a line of text, or, for some students, by reading the word without matching.

Wordless Books

Read-alouds using wordless books are a variation of shared reading that can be especially useful for students with complex support needs (Katims, 2000). Wordless books use pictures to tell a story or communicate other information. Despite the lack of print, these books offer multiple ways to teach important literacy skills, including early reading skills that support word recognition. For example, students can learn important concepts about print, such as text features, and can learn to gain comprehension from pictures. A skilled teacher can also support vocabulary development by helping students connect images with prior knowledge.

Many people associate wordless books with young children, but there are numerous such books written for older students, including adults. For example, a wordless informational text, *The Arrival* (Tan, 2006), visually describes the experiences of immigrants and aligns nicely with the renewed focus on academic standards (see Chapter 4). The "In the Classroom" textbox describes how another wordless book, David Wiesner's *Flotsam* (2006), might be used for different types of early literacy activities—some that directly relate to word recognition and others that address other areas of literacy, such as comprehension and writing. Notice that these activities can be easily adapted to accommodate learners of different ages and with different language and communication abilities, from those who are emergent literacy learners to those with some conventional reading and writing skills. (Chapter 12 includes many more ideas about using wordless books to support literacy learning.)

IN THE CLASSROOM

USING WORDLESS BOOKS TO TEACH EARLY LITERACY SKILLS: *FLOTSAM*

Here are just a few of the ways David Wiesner's wordless book *Flotsam* (2006) might be used for emergent literacy activities addressing skills across a variety of literacy components.

ORAL LANGUAGE AND/OR FLUENCY

- Work as a group to generate a narrative for each page of the book. Jot these down on sticky notes and place them on each page. Have students type these into a single document to create that group's narrative for the whole book. After some practice, have individual students use a new wordless book to independently create their own storylines; as needed, provide help with scribing. Then, bring the students together in a small group and compare and contrast each student's unique storylines. Work on critical thinking by asking students to describe why they chose a particular narrative or perspective for an event or image in the book.

- Have students retell the story, or one page or event therein, by using an augmentative or alternative communication (AAC) device or visuals or by acting out an event using a reader's theater approach.

- Have students choose a favorite picture, page, or animal, and share with the group why this is their favorite using oral language or AAC.

- Take a field trip with students and take pictures of places in your local area. Support students to create a story of who (animals/people) lives there now and in the past. Ask them to describe what they saw and then imagine what animals or people might have lived there before. Write down their ideas, and use questions to extend their thinking to create the story.

- Select some word-wall words from the book (e.g., *sea, ocean, waves*) and create wall activities using oral language, sign language, graphics, or AAC.

VOCABULARY

- Connect word-wall words with the book by labeling objects, people, or animals therein. Use a combination of pictures, words, and objects for the word wall to increase the accessibility of the keywords.

- Have students identify targeted vocabulary on pages.

- Have students match pictures to words, pictures to pictures, or pictures to objects.

- Have students use targeted vocabulary in sentences.

- Have students make vocabulary cards and/or foldables defining words and using words in different ways.

- Link the book content with a science unit to work on words related to oceans and marine life.

- Choose categories of words on which to focus (e.g., describing words for colors, sounds, textures, size—*swoosh, slimey, cold, roaring, plopping, blue, orange*), and design lessons around these categories.

PHONEMIC AWARENESS/PHONICS

- Select pictures from the book, making sure each one can be described clearly in a word. Have students sort the pictures by the initial, medial, and final sounds in the word (e.g., /w/ for *wave*). For phonics activities, use the same pictures but ask students to say the sound (beginning, final, or medial) and select the letter(s) that represents that sound.

- Say a target sound and ask students to find a picture in the book of something whose name begins with that sound; alternatively, use final and medial sounds.

- Take words from the book, such as *fish,* and substitute initial sounds to make different words (real or nonsense words)—for example, "What happens when we change /f/ in *fish* to /t/?"

- Have students compare and contrast pictures of things whose names include long and short vowel sounds.

- Create an alphabet book using creatures from the book to illustrate each letter. Older learners can work on this to practice the alphabet and/or sounds and then read it and/or share it with students in a preschool or kindegarten class.

- Use a familiar, age-appropriate tune to create a song or rap that uses vocabulary from the book and rimes that students are learning.

COMPREHENSION

- Have students order photos according to where related topics and events are discussed in the book (e.g., beginning, middle, and end).

- Have students sequence photos within a page.

- Have students classify pictures into categories (e.g., *boy, girl, marine life, beach life*).

- Have students complete sentences using pictures, words, or AAC symbols to demonstrate comprehension (e.g., "The boy found the camera on the _____").

- Have students compare and contrast two pages using a Venn diagram. For example, what are the sea creatures doing in both pictures (pages) that is the same or different? What plants are the same or different in the two pictures?

WRITING

- Help the students make a PowerPoint book from photos taken on a field trip to a local nature site, such as a park, aquarium, or hiking trail. Give students the opportunity to show their strengths in narration, typing, drawing, organizing, and so forth, as appropriate. Scribe student's ideas if they are not conventional writers.

- Help students create a photo journal of an activity or field trip they took.

- Help students write sentences using words, photos, objects, or AAC symbols to accompany each picture or page of the book.

- Help students make a class book from favorite *Flotsam* sentences.

- Help student write "the next chapter" in the book; for example, "Where will the next child who finds the camera use it to take pictures?"

- Individual students or pairs of students can write their version of the story. Then groups/pairs print out their stories and meet to compare and contrast their stories.

PHONOLOGICAL AND PHONEMIC AWARENESS AND THE ALPHABETIC PRINCIPLE

Phonological awareness, another early reading skill, is an *oral* (spoken) and *aural* (heard) language skill. Simply put, it is the ability to perceive that sentences are made up of words, words are made up of syllables, and syllables are made up of individual sounds or phonemes (Armbruster, Lehr, & Osborn, 2001). (A phoneme is the smallest unit of sound in a language; e.g., the word *dish* has three phonemes: /d/, /i/, and /sh/. None of these sounds can be broken down further.) Phonological awareness begins to develop as young children acquire language and continues to grow throughout the elementary school years (Torgesen & Mathes, 1998; Troia, 2004). It is influenced both by heredity (i.e., the neurological basis for phonological processing) and by language and literacy experiences (Torgesen & Mathes, 2000). As mentioned previously, many of the word-play activities in which young children engage, such as reciting nursery rhymes or playing singing games like "Miss Mary Mack," actually build phonological awareness. These types of activities help children attend to the sound units that make up speech; developing this attention is at the heart of phonological awareness.

Phonological Awareness

How, you might wonder, does phonological awareness help children learn to read? Phonological awareness increases their recognition of the sound structure of language—recognition that helps them process written language more efficiently when they encounter it later on. Children typically develop these skills in sequence. First, they become aware that speech is made up of words. Then, they understand that words are made up of smaller units, syllables (Liberman, Shankweiler, Fischer, & Carter, 1974; Treiman, 1983). Next, they perceive the presence in words of onsets (the part of a syllable that includes the consonant sound[s] that comes before the vowel sound) and rimes (the portion of a syllable that includes the vowel sound and any consonant sounds that come after it) (Goswami, 2001; Treiman, 1985). Finally, children are able to detect that words are made up of individual sounds (phonemes) and can manipulate phonemes in words and sentences.

Phonemic Awareness

Phonemic awareness falls under the umbrella of phonological awareness and is especially important if one is to become a skilled reader (Ehri, 2005). A student who has developed phonemic awareness can, for example, notice that two spoken words differ by only one sound (e.g., *mat* and *bat* are the same except for their initial sounds) and can manipulate individual sounds within words (Yopp, 1992). Students with well-developed phonemic awareness can perform language tasks such as the following:

- Isolate individual sounds in words, or phoneme identification—for example, "What is the last sound in *pat*?" (/t/)

- Identify common sounds within words, or oddity tasks—for example, "What sound do the words *cat* and *cup* have in common?" (/k/ at the beginning)

- Segment sounds in words, or phoneme segmentation—for example, "How many sounds are in the word *fish*?" (three)

- Categorize sounds by recognizing which in a series of words does not have the same sound, or phoneme categorization—for example, "Which of these three words does not belong with the others: *cat, cot, tree*?" (*tree*)

- Delete sounds within words, or phoneme deletion—for example, "What word do you make when you remove the /d/ sound from *Dan*?" (*an*)

- Blend separately spoken sounds into words, or phoneme blending—for example, "What word do these sounds make: /l/ /o/ /g/?" (*log*)

- Substitute sounds within words, or phoneme manipulation—for example, "If I take the /sh/ out of *ship* and replace it with /l/, what word do I make?" (*lip*)

Phonemic awareness is important, as you can guess, because it is the foundation for applying letter–sound knowledge to sounding out, or decoding, new words. These skills, in turn, help students understand the *alphabetic principle*, an understanding that is crucial for learning to read (Torgesen & Mathes, 2000). This principle sounds simple: learning that the individual sounds in words (phonemes) can be represented by letters or letter combinations (graphemes). However, it takes time to develop, and because it is abstract, it can be difficult for individuals who have language and cognitive challenges.

Ehri's Phases and the Alphabetic Principle

Ehri (2005) described phases through which students progress in acquiring the alphabetic principle. This framework can be helpful in determining what an individual understands about letter–sound associations (see Table 9.1).

Students who have grasped the alphabetic principle realize that speech sounds can be represented by symbols (letters) and, as a result, written down and read by themselves and others. With this knowledge, they can decipher new words or spell words and create their own texts. Learning all the rules about how word sounds are represented by letters, however, takes time and many opportunities to practice. The English language, for example, is made of approximately 44 different sounds or phonemes. Each sound can be written down (spelled) using a letter or letter combination, or grapheme. What makes learning to read and spell in English so difficult is that the same sound often can be represented in multiple ways, particularly vowel sounds—in fact, there are more than 200 ways to spell the 44 sounds in English! For instance, the /ā/ sound in the word *baby* is represented with the letter *a*, but in *play*, this sound is represented by two letters, *ay*, whereas the same sound in *rain* is written as *ai*.

Figure 9.1 contains two examples of writing from individuals in different stages of acquiring the alphabetic principle. The first sample is a list of items to purchase from the grocery store; the second is an account of the student's trip to see the doctor. As you study these examples, think about which one demonstrates a clearer understanding of how letters represent speech sounds.

REFLECTION QUESTION 2

Think about what students know about the alphabet and the alphabetic principle in each of Ehri's phases as described in Table 9.1. Based on the writing samples shown in Figure 9.1, which of Ehri's phases has each of these students reached? Why do you think so? Where might you begin word recognition instruction for each student, given his or her current understandings of the alphabetic principle?

Table 9.1.   Phases in acquiring the alphabetic principle

Phase	Description	What it might look like: Reading	What it might look like: Writing
Prealphabetic	Students do not know that letters represent sounds.	Students might focus on the shape of a word to recognize it.	Students may scribble, use letters or letter strings, or even use shapes or numbers in their writing.
Partial alphabetic	Students have some, but very limited, understanding that a letter can represent a sound in a word.	Students might focus on either the beginning or ending letter when trying to read a word; they have some letter sounds but little understanding of how to use that knowledge.	Students can write some short words correctly (e.g., some CVC words) but often have only a few of the letters in a word in the correct order, such as the first two or three letters in longer words.
Full alphabetic	Students have most letter–sound correspondences mastered.	Students can use knowledge of letter sounds to sound out a new word.	Students are able to write many words correctly; they have mastered the letter-sound representations for most spellings.
Consolidated alphabetic	Students are more efficient readers. They can chunk parts of words and read words that are exceptions to the common phonics rules.	Students recognize larger letter units automatically, making them able to quickly read novel multisyllabic words.	Students have learned most spelling patterns (onsets, rimes, syllables).

Key: CVC, consonant–vowel–consonant.

From Ehri, L.C. (2005). Learning to read words: Theory, findings, and issues. *Scientific Studies of Reading, 9*(2), 167–188.

Figure 9.1.　Writing samples from two individuals in different stages of the alphabetic principle.

Using Ehri's Phases to Guide Instruction

Once we know what a student understands about the alphabetic principle, we can create lessons that build on that knowledge to help the student develop a deeper understanding of how written language works. Consider, for example, Rob, who is a 45-year-old man with ID. Rob knows the names of only a few letters, the ones in his name. He recognizes a few words by sight but doesn't associate any sounds with the letters in these words. He can read a wide range of environmental print such as logos and signs, especially the ones associated with his favorite restaurants and soft drinks.

Using Ehri's phases as a framework to consider Rob's skills, we can conclude that he is in the prealphabetic phase of learning. Knowing this is helpful for the speech-language pathologist (SLP) who wants to develop word recognition instruction for him. Because he has very incomplete knowledge of letters and sounds, this is a logical skill to build: He can learn the names of letters and the sounds they represent. The SLP knows that because Rob has significant cognitive challenges, lessons built around things he is familiar with and enjoys will be most successful. This approach increases the likelihood that Rob will retain and use what he learns. Because Rob is an adult, it is also critical to choose age-appropriate learning activities linked to his everyday life.

After talking with Rob and finding out more about what he wants to learn, the SLP begins by teaching the names of letters in the names of Rob's family members. The SLP ties this instruction, which could be very abstract and meaningless, to supporting Rob in writing short e-mails to his family using an adapted computer keyboard. Over time, Rob learns the letters in each person's name and types those names into the e-mail messages. The SLP routinely scribes the rest of the message Rob wants to send, stopping occasionally to have Rob identify or type letters he has learned that are part of a word he wants to use. Because the SLP has tied the abstract information about letter sounds to a meaningful and highly motivating activity, Rob can learn and remember the letters and use them in a highly functional way. This activity has the added value of increasing Rob's communication and interaction with his family.

Assessing Phonemic and Phonological Awareness

Phonological and phonemic awareness can be assessed in several ways, both formally and informally. Formal assessments include standardized tests that measure skills such as identification of rhymes and the isolation and manipulation of individual sounds within words, or phonological memory. There are many assessments available for this purpose, such as the Comprehensive Test of Phonological Processing (CTOPP; Wagner, Torgesen, & Rashotte, 1999). However, standardized assessments do not always capture accurate information about the skill levels of students with complex support needs due to the communication, motor, and sensory challenges experienced by many of these learners. In this situation, educators must turn to informal assessment tools.

Informal assessment is useful in determining students' phonological awareness skill levels and providing a practical way to monitor student progress in acquiring new skills. For students with complex support needs, it is important to think carefully about the type of assessment tasks selected. Be certain that you are evaluating the targeted skill (in this case, phonological awareness) and not inadvertently measuring a different skill such as the child's expressive speech ability or vocabulary knowledge. Using a difficult or unfamiliar task gives an inaccurate picture of students' phonological awareness abilities. For instance, assessment tasks that put a large demand on cognitive skills or memory or that use unfamiliar vocabulary may be so difficult that students do not really understand what is being asked of them. Their responses to these ambiguous tasks may not accurately reflect their phonological awareness and thus will not reveal much about their skill levels.

Fortunately, researchers and practitioners have developed phonological awareness measurement tasks that take into account some of the assessment problems practitioners may encounter with students who have intellectual or severe disabilities (e.g., Boudreau, 2002; Cupples & Iacono, 2000; Kennedy & Flynn, 2003). Some general suggestions from this work are to use assessment tasks that allow the child to respond nonverbally, use pictures to support auditory memory, use vocabulary that is familiar to the child, and use game-like assessment formats. It is also a good idea to keep assessment sessions short in order to maximize the student's attention to the tasks. The "Informal Assessment of Phonological Awareness Skills" textbox lists key phonological awareness assessment tasks used with all children and provides specific adaptations to these tasks, which will allow more accurate assessment of these skills with children with complex support needs.

INFORMAL ASSESSMENT OF PHONOLOGICAL AWARENESS SKILLS

For each task, be sure to use pictures or line drawings of words that are familiar to the student (i.e., in the student's listening vocabulary). Always model what you want the student to do, and offer several opportunities to practice the task before beginning the actual assessment. Some younger children may enjoy it and be motivated if you use a puppet to model the tasks and provide the directions.

Rhyme: recognition that two or more words end with the same sounds (e.g., *cat, hat*)

- *Matching:* Give the student two to four pictures or line drawings of objects, verbally labeling each one or asking the student to do so. Then, say a word and ask the student to indicate (e.g., point to) which picture rhymes with that word.

- *Oddity detection:* Give the student three pictures or line drawings and either verbally label each one or ask the student to do so. Then, ask the student to indicate (verbally or by pointing) which of the three pictures does *not* rhyme with the others.

- *Generation:* Give the student a picture or line drawing and either verbally label the picture or ask the student to do so. Then, ask the student to say a word that rhymes with the object depicted in the picture.

Alliteration: recognition that some words begin with the same sound (e.g., *hat, house*)

- Provide two or three pictures or line drawings of objects and either verbally label each picture or ask the student to do it.

- Say a word or phoneme and ask the student to point to the picture that begins with the same sound as the spoken word (or phoneme).

- Randomly change the position of the target picture on each trial to reduce the chance that the student will guess the correct answer.

- This activity can also be used to assess a student's awareness of ending or middle sounds by using the same format but asking the student to find the picture that *ends* with the same sound as the word spoken by the examiner, or find the picture that has the same *middle* sound as the world spoken by the examiner.

- Use the procedures previously described under "Rhyme" to also assess *oddity detection* and *generation* of alliteration ("Which picture does not have the same beginning sound as *house*?" or "Tell me a word that begins with the same sound as *house*").

Blending: putting together two or more sounds to say a word (e.g., /d/ /o/ /g/, *dog*)

- Show the student a picture or line drawing of a familiar item and ask him or her to listen while you say the name of the picture very slowly. (This is often called *word stretching* or *word rubber banding*. It may be helpful or motivating to the student for you to stretch out a large rubber band while modeling this task, or use your arms to show how you are stretching out the word.)

- Slowly say each individual sound of the word represented by the picture.

- Next, give the student two or three pictures or line drawings and say the name of one of the pictures slowly, phoneme by phoneme.

- Ask the student to point to the picture whose name you said.

- Begin the assessment with words made up of two or three phonemes (consonant–vowel [CV] or CVC); progress to longer words that require up to four phonemes (CVCV).

Segmentation: breaking words into individual sounds (e.g., *blue* /b/ /l/ /oo/). Keep in mind that this is the most difficult phonological task because it requires more memory than other tasks. Segmenting a word requires the student to hold the word in memory and, at the same time, break it down into separate sounds.

1. Syllable segmentation (e.g., *ta-ble*)

    - Show the student a familiar picture of a two-syllable word and say the first syllable of the word for him or her. Ask the student to supply the next syllable.

    - An alternative is to provide the student with a spoken one-, two-, or three-syllable word and ask him or her to clap or tap for each syllable heard.

2. Phoneme segmentation (e.g., *boy* /b/ /oi/)

    - Show the student a familiar picture (using a word that has only two or three phonemes) and ask the student to "say the sounds very slowly" (say each individual phoneme).

In summary, it is critical to present testing materials in a format students can access. Again, we want to ensure that students' phonological skills are being assessed, and to do so, we must eliminate any barriers that interfere with that process. Paying attention to factors such as the individual's seating position, placement of assessment materials, size of print, type of font, and so forth is critical to successful assessment. The print access checklist in Figure 9.2 is an excellent tool to use to evaluate any access issues that might interfere with assessment of skills that require students to process written text.

REFLECTION QUESTION 2

Consider one of your students with complex support needs. Describe how you would assess that student's word recognition abilities (e.g., assessment instrument[s], how the student would demonstrate responses to assessment items).

Student: _____ Age: _____

Teacher: _____ Date: _____

Assessed by: _____

Skill	Yes	No	Support needed
Maintains stable and comfortable body position to see print			
Visually discriminates print			
Focuses on printed text			
Tracks print from left to right			
Tracks print from top to bottom			
Manipulates reading material			

Other observations: _____

_____

_____

Figure 9.2. Print access checklist.

EFFECTIVE PHONICS INSTRUCTION

Phonics instruction teaches students to make the connections between phonemes (sounds) and the graphemes (letters) we use to represent these sounds. For all students, it is vital that reading intervention focus on this letter–sound correspondence in a systematic (step by step) and practical ("hands on") way (Harm, McCandliss, & Seidenberg, 2003). Once students acquire phonics knowledge, they can apply their knowledge of letter sounds to unfamiliar words to identify them or to spell words when creating written text.

We cannot stress enough that effective phonics instruction must be integrated within a comprehensive literacy program and should build on students' prior knowledge of print functions. We have described ways to build knowledge of how print "works" for students of all ages. Phonics instruction should be a part of that multicomponent approach to literacy.

Summary of Research Findings on Effective Phonics Instruction

Effective phonics instruction for students with complex support needs has several key characteristics. It should be based in phonemic awareness and should begin early. It should also be structured and explicit and be reinforced through reading and writing activities. Finally, for students with complex support needs, it should be intensive and sustained. A brief summary of research findings supporting these principles is provided here.

1. *Instruction is based in phonemic awareness.* Skill in sounding out or decoding a word requires phonemic awareness, as discussed previously, and phonological memory—the ability to hold and manipulate sounds in working memory to decode words. Researchers have found that individuals with complex support needs, such as ID, have weaker phonological memory than their typically developing peers (Channell et al., 2013). This does not mean that they don't need phonics instruction; research strongly supports providing phonemic awareness and phonics instruction for these students. Many years of research have shown that we cannot predict who will learn decoding skills based on an educational label or even an IQ (Allor, Mathes, Roberts, Cheatham, & Al Otaiba, 2014). Because of this, it is important that all children receive systematic, effective phonics instruction. If we do not provide instruction or sustained opportunities to learn, students definitely will not acquire these critical skills.

2. *Instruction begins early.* As we do for typically developing children, we should begin providing instruction in phonemic awareness and phonics early on for individuals with complex support needs so as to maximize learning outcomes. Burgoyne and her colleagues (2012), for example, conducted a random control trial study with young children with Down syndrome. They found that children who received instruction in a comprehensive reading program that included phonics instruction showed higher skill levels than those who began instruction later. This does not mean, however, that older individuals should be excluded from instruction. Moni, Jobling, Morgan, and Lloyd's (2011) work with adults with ID demonstrates that older students with complex support needs can and do continue to acquire phonics skills that increase their ability to read new words.

3. *Instruction is structured, explicit, and systematic.* Another characteristic of effective phonics instruction is that it is structured, explicit, and systematic. It is clear and carefully sequenced across time so that students learn and apply new skills in a logical manner and have opportunities to continue to practice previously learned skills. Students with complex support needs, in particular, need this type of instruction.

To provide structured, explicit, systematic phonics instruction, a teacher must first assess students' understandings of letter–sound relationships. Instruction begins by teaching letter–sound correspondences using clear, explicit models; it then moves to teaching students to apply their knowledge of these correspondences to actual words. Teaching should include clear instruction that focuses on how to apply letter–sound knowledge to words. For example, Lemons and Fuchs (2010) found that for students with Down syndrome, knowing letter sounds was not enough; these students needed explicit, systematic instruction in how to apply this knowledge to decodable words. Students practice these skills with single words and words in connected text (sentences). Over time, instruction focuses on increasingly complex phonemic patterns.

Teachers who are successful in teaching phonics use direct instruction to teach these skills, providing multiple opportunities for students to practice sound–letter knowledge so that they can apply it automatically to unfamiliar words (e.g., Fredrick, Davis, Alberto, & Waugh, 2013). Teachers carefully set a moderate pace that keeps students engaged but also allows them time to process. Sample instructional activities are provided in the next section.

4. *Instruction is reinforced through reading and writing activities.* Students taught by effective teachers also incorporate their growing sound–letter knowledge in writing for a variety of purposes. They also read target decodable words in connected text during every lesson. Many published programs such as Early Literacy Skills Builder (Browder, Gibbs, Ahlgrim-Delzell, Courtade, & Lee, 2016) or Early Interventions in Reading (Mathes, Torgesen, Menchetti, Wahl, & Grek, 2004) include specially created storybooks on age-appropriate topics that use targeted decodable and irregularly spelled (sight) words.

5. *Instruction is intensive and sustained.* Finally, researchers have found that students with complex support needs require intensive, sustained instruction (e.g., Allor, Champlin, Gifford, & Mathes, 2010; Burgoyne et al., 2012). Allor et al. (2014) found that students in their study required 40–50 minutes of daily instruction across 2–3 years to acquire a solid foundation of skills. We should not stop instruction if students do not make large gains within short time frames.

Engaging Activities for Phonics Instruction

Keeping in mind the core research-based principles previously described, let's turn to another aspect of effective phonics instruction: It should be fun! Good teachers devise engaging, active ways for students to practice applying their phonics knowledge—not worksheets! This includes activities such as games and puzzles that use words with targeted patterns.

In the following sections, we describe two activities that allow students to have fun and engage with each other socially while applying the phonics skills they have learned.

Word Sorts   A word-sort activity is a particular, active way to build phonics skills that has been used successfully with students with complex support needs (e.g., Joseph & McCachran, 2003). Students sort words by identifying common patterns among them. For example, they may sort by initial sounds or by a spelling pattern (e.g., grouping all the words with the rime *ot*). Engaging in word sorts helps students begin to identify patterns within words and become more aware of letter–sound relationships. Word sorts may be open (students define their own sorting categories) or closed (the teacher specifies the categories).

To conduct a word sort, the teacher can write the words to be sorted on cards or use one of many word-sort apps for an iPad or computer. The teacher explains the pattern students should look for and models the activity. Then, students manipulate the word cards to place them in the correct categories. This can be done as an individual activity, or students in a small group can take turns sorting words in a pocket chart that has each target category labeled. Students should read the words aloud, either as they are sorting them or after the sorting is completed. Another strategy is to ask questions such as "Why did you put those cards in that stack?" to get the students to focus on what patterns are present. If a student does make a mistake, ask the student about the mis-sorted word to determine why the mistake was made. The student might have misread the word or may be struggling with a particular spelling pattern. Asking yields information that helps to plan future instruction for that student.

Phonics Feely　　Morgan and Moni (2005) recommend a game called Phonics Feely. For this activity, students form teams; the teacher places familiar objects into a bag and asks a student to reach into the bag, feel the object without looking at it, and then name it. After naming it, the student identifies the first sound in the object's name and states what letter is associated with that sound. For example, if a student pulls out a pen from the bag, he or she would say, "/P/, *pen* begins with /p/. The letter *p* makes the sound /p/." This game can easily be differentiated for students who are in different stages of acquiring phonics skills, and also for those who are in different stages of acquiring language skills; see "In the Classroom" in the next textbox.

Phonics Instruction for Students Who Do Not Speak

You may have wondered how to provide phonics instruction for students who do not speak. Although less research is available for this group of learners, what is available indicates that they can benefit from systematic, explicit instruction just as their peers do. A key difference between instruction for students who use AAC systems and those who speak is how they respond. Teachers provide similar instructional opportunities, but they ask students to "say it in your head" and then point, eye gaze, or select a response on an AAC device to indicate understanding. For instance, Becky, a 12-year-old student, listens as her teacher sounds out a CVC word (/m/ /a/ /n/). She looks at the four word-cards the teacher has placed on the table and points to the printed word *man*. John, on the other hand, uses an AAC device. He responds by selecting the item on his device that shows the printed word *man*.

Like their peers, students who do not speak should receive phonics instruction that includes building phonemic awareness, learning letter–sound associations, blending, and reading connected text. Students should also practice using their phonics skills when writing for a variety of purposes. A small but growing number of published literacy curricula are available for students who use AAC. These curricula include explicit, systematic phonics instruction. The Accessible Literacy Learning (ALL) Reading Program (Light & McNaughton, n.d.) is one example. Keep in mind, however, that even if a teacher is using an electronic curriculum or app with a student, the teacher still must work directly with the student and use systematic instruction. A common mistake among teachers and parents is to sit a child down with an iPad or computer and expect the child to interact with the electronic device and learn independently. Although independent practice is a useful part of instruction, it should never take the place of effective, teacher-directed instruction.

IN THE CLASSROOM

USING GAMES FOR ENGAGING, DIFFERENTIATED PHONICS INSTRUCTION

In Mrs. Chavez's classroom, phonics instruction isn't based on dull drills and worksheets—students learn phonics while having fun. Mrs. Chavez has created teams of students and taught them to play a phonics game using familiar objects. Teams earn points for correct answers and can use those points toward earning time to play board games on Friday afternoon. (Mrs. Chavez has cleverly made sure that many of these board games also focus on literacy skills; she has created games such as a phonics bingo game and a Who Wants to Be a Millionaire?–style game that gives students practice with their vocabulary words! Students enjoy the social aspect of playing these games without realizing how they are also getting additional practice with their literacy skills.)

One of the students' favorite phonics learning activities was the Phonics Feely game (Morgan & Moni, 2005) described previously. Student teams play this game frequently; if a student is stumped while trying to name a letter, the student can ask a teammate for help (a "lifeline") and still earn the point. This keeps everyone engaged because they never know when they might need to help a teammate.

Because Mrs. Chavez's students are in different stages of acquiring phonics skills, she differentiates the activity by asking some students to identify ending or medial sounds and others to only identify initial sounds. One of her students, Rosa, does not speak, so Mrs. Chavez uses an eye-gaze board that allows Rosa to participate and practice her phonics skills. Mrs. Chavez places a sticky note on each quadrant of the board with a different letter printed on each note. The letters are ones for which Rosa is currently learning sound correspondences. When Rosa pulls out an object, she selects one of her teammates to name the object and say the beginning sound. Rosa then identifies the letter associated with that sound by gazing at the corresponding letter on her board.

BEYOND DECODING: LEARNING TO RECOGNIZE SIGHT WORDS

Thus far, this chapter has focused on how to foster emergent literacy skills, phonological and phonemic awareness, and, ultimately, the phonics skills students use to decode words. However, it's also crucial for teachers and other practitioners to become skilled at providing effective sight-word instruction—because, for a variety of reasons, decoding is not always the best strategy for word recognition. To begin with, some students with complex support needs will not acquire sufficient phonics skills to make decoding a practical strategy for identifying most novel words they encounter. Practitioners must teach these students other word recognition strategies as a part of a comprehensive literacy program. In addition, researchers have found that learning sight words seems to facilitate acquisition of other reading skills in children with ID (e.g., Lemons & Fuchs, 2010). Some students who begin formal literacy instruction by learning sight words may be able to build on these skills to learn phonics (decoding) strategies that will expand their reading abilities.

Furthermore, many high-frequency words with irregular spellings, such as *was, sight,* and *of,* are easier for students to learn by focusing on their visual properties rather than trying to apply decoding skills (e.g., *was, sight, of*). As a result, every comprehensive literacy program for beginning readers with and without disabilities includes instruction in both phonics and sight words so that students learn multiple approaches to word identification and gain proficiency in each.

REFLECTION QUESTION 3

How might you explain to parents or other educators your decision to teach young students with complex support needs both phonics and sight-word recognition skills?

EFFECTIVE SIGHT-WORD INSTRUCTION

Effective sight-word instruction has several key characteristics. First, it addresses not just recognition of a word but comprehension of that word. Second, the teacher must provide regular opportunities for students to apply their sight-word–reading skills across multiple contexts. In addition, the target words for the student to learn must be selected carefully. Finally, sight words must be taught, and students' knowledge of these words extended, through carefully chosen instructional activities. We discuss each of these points in depth here.

First, keep in mind that when teaching sight words, instruction must go beyond simply recognizing or naming a word; students must also comprehend the word. Teach comprehension of target words from the beginning. It is also critical that students practice recognizing and comprehending words in connected text, beyond the word or sentence level (Allor et al., 2010). This is certainly appropriate for high-frequency words such as *of, and,* or *that,* whose meanings are abstract outside of the context of a sentence. Even sight words encountered in the environment—for instance, safety words like a *Danger!* sign—are most effectively taught when students learn what the words mean and what the appropriate response is to these words.

Second, be aware that teachers can help improve students' ability to transfer their sight-word skills across settings and tasks by providing opportunities to practice reading target words in different types of contexts (e.g., in books, digital texts, or handwritten letters). Some school districts rely on computer-based sight-word instruction or boxed curricula marketed to teach sight words to students with complex support needs. Although these may be an effective means of learning to recognize a word, they are not usually sufficient if the intent is that students use these words in daily life. Such limited instruction may actually prevent students from achieving the levels of literacy of which they are capable (Copeland & Cosbey, 2008–2009). To support retention and use of sight words, students need extensive supplementary activities in which they use words in a range of contexts, for a variety of meaningful purposes.

With these two guiding principles in mind, let's examine how best to choose the sight words a student should learn, teach those words, and then extend students' understanding.

Strategies for Selecting Target Sight Words

Out of the tens of thousands of words available, which words should be targeted for sight-word instruction? This decision is especially important for students with the most complex needs for support. If a student is likely to master only a limited number of words, these words must be selected with care so that the student learns words that are most meaningful and useful to him or her. On the other hand, if a student is developing conventional reading and writing skills, it may be more important to learn high-frequency words (e.g., Instant Words [Fry, 1999], Dolch words) that will help the student move toward reading textbooks, stories, newspapers, social media, and so forth. (Note that some available sight-word assessments for high-frequency words can easily be adapted for students who use AAC systems. For example, the graded sight-word assessments found in developmental reading inventories or other formal assessments can be adapted by putting the assessment words on index cards, presenting them in arrays of three to four words, and asking students to point to a word instead of verbally naming it.)

General Guidelines   A general rule of thumb is to choose words for instruction that fit one or more of these categories:

- Words of interest to the student (e.g., TV words, car words)

- Words needed to increase participation in general education activities (e.g., classmates' and teachers' names, direction words, key content vocabulary such as science or social studies terms)

- Words found in the student's current environments (e.g., environmental print in the classroom or school)

- Words that are useful in staying safe (i.e., safety words such as *exit* or *fire extinguisher*)

- Words found in product labels (for older students)

- Words found in the student's employment site (for older students)

Of course, names of friends and family are also valuable for students to learn as sight words.

Using Ecological Assessments   One approach with a long history of effectiveness for students is to use ecological assessment to select target sight words. This systematic process has several steps. Survey the students' current environments to see what words they might need to know to be more successful in a general education setting. Consider future environments that students will be moving into—for example, words a student transitioning from middle to high school might need to know to function more independently. Most important, consult students and their families to generate a list of possible target words that will increase students' participation in home or community activities. (See Chapter 8 for more about using ecological inventories to select key vocabulary for instruction.)

Special Considerations for Bilingual Learners

Be aware that for many students, target sight words may need to include words from languages other than English. Because the school population includes more and more students with complex support needs whose home language is not English, students' home languages are an important instructional consideration. These students certainly need to learn English sight words but likely will also need a core of sight words in their home language. For example, you might want to find out about the environmental print found in a student's home community, such as signs written in languages other than English. It may be important to students and their families that they learn to recognize these community words; this would allow increased participation in community events and cultural celebrations and deepen connections with faith communities. Connect and consult with teachers who are bilingual or teachers of English as a second language in the school for ideas about the types of non-English sight words that would be important for a particular student. (Chapter 3 provides more information about this population of students and how to consider their instructional needs; see Chapter 10 for more ideas about working with environmental print.)

After determining which words to teach, arrange the words in sets for instruction (usually 4–10 words depending on the learning characteristics of the student). Decide whether to teach sight words in one-to-one or small-group arrangements. The next critical step will be to give students opportunities to practice their sight-word recognition in context, either within connected texts or for functional sight words, in natural settings in which the words are found. This facilitates skill generalization and aids in developing students' broader understanding of literacy. Students with more significant cognitive challenges and those with less well-developed language skills will need more instruction in the natural settings in which the target words are used. Some students may even require that all of their sight-word instruction take place within settings where word usage is most likely to occur, if it is to be effective.

REFLECTION QUESTION 4

Imagine that you have a student with complex support needs in your class whose home language is not English. What steps might you take to address this student's learning needs when planning word recognition instruction?

Instructional Strategies for Initially Teaching Words

In general, sight-word instruction involves directly teaching the association between the word and the thing or idea that the word represents. Teachers can select from several useful strategies for this kind of instruction. In the following sections, we will describe some of the instructional strategies that research and practice have identified as effective.

Systematic, Direct Instruction

One highly effective instructional method is using direct instruction to teach sight words. In this method, teachers use time delay and response prompts to teach students the association between the printed and spoken word. Diane Browder and her colleagues (2009) examined the research on sight-word instruction and concluded that time-delay instruction is an evidence-based method, meaning that if this instruction is presented correctly, it produces reliable, consistent learning for students with complex support needs.

To provide direct instruction using time delay and response prompts, the teacher begins by simultaneously showing and saying the target word and then asks the student to say the word. For example, the teacher shows the student the word *danger* while saying, "This word is *danger.*

Read *danger.*" (If the student does not use speech to communicate, ask the student to identify the target word by pointing, using eye gaze, or selecting it using an AAC device.) This strategy is called *simultaneous prompting* and is a form of errorless learning. It is helpful because the student is instantly provided with a model and knows exactly how to respond. It is especially effective for students who get upset when they make a mistake (Browder, 2001).

Once the student understands the process and is responding consistently, move on to the next step: insert a brief time delay between presenting the target word and prompting the student. Show the word, say, "Read the word," and then wait several seconds for the student to respond before giving a prompt. This time-delay strategy gives the student time to respond before receiving a cue from the instructor. When using time delay, you can wait a predetermined number of seconds on each trial (*constant time delay*) or vary the amount of time you wait within a teaching session (*progressive time delay*).

If the student doesn't respond during the delay or gives an incorrect answer, use response prompts to help the student respond correctly. Response prompts are any assistance or feedback the teacher gives a student that increases the likelihood that the student will respond correctly. Prompts may consist of verbal cues, gestures, modeling, or even full physical assistance.

See the "In the Classroom" textbox for an example of how this strategy might be used to teach a seventh-grade student with multiple disabilities to recognize science terms she will encounter in an upcoming unit in her general education class.

IN THE CLASSROOM

DIRECT INSTRUCTION WITH TIME DELAY AND RESPONSE PROMPTS

Mr. Markham, a special education teacher, works with Connie, a seventh grader with multiple disabilities. He collaborates with her general education teachers for each content area. Connie's general education science teacher let Mr. Markham know that the class would soon begin a unit focused on understanding how cells function. The science teacher worked with Mr. Markham to reviewed the key terms all students would learn in the unit. Together, they selected four terms for Connie to learn as sight words and as vocabulary words: *cell, cell wall, cytoplasm,* and *nucleus.* Mr. Markham created two sets of flash cards with the target words. He wrote a simple, clear definition of each word on the back of the card. He also borrowed some related photographs from the science teacher (photos the teacher planned to use on a word wall in the science classroom). Mr. Markham planned to use the photos to extend Connie's understanding of the target words.

Because Connie is very social (and competitive!), Mr. Markham decided to provide direct instruction to a small group that included Connie and a few of her peers. All of the students would learn target words to prepare for upcoming units in their general education classes; each student would have a different set of four target words. Because Connie doesn't speak, Mr. Markham planned to have her demonstrate her recognition of the words by pointing to a word in an array.

Mr. Markham began instruction by explaining the objective: students would learn to read some new words that would help them in their general education classes. He explained that everyone needed to pay attention and be prepared to respond whenever called upon; students would not know in advance when their turn was coming up.

Mr. Markham began instruction using simultaneous prompting with Connie. He put all four target-word cards on the table in front of her and said "Point to *cell. Cell* means the smallest unit of life." As he did so, he reached over and pointed to the card with the word *cell* printed on it. Connie looked at the cards, paused, and then pointed to the correct card. Mr. Markham then called on another student who does communicate using speech. This time Mr. Markham held up the card with that student's target word and said, "This word is *neuron.* A *neuron* is a special type of cell that connects the brain and other parts of the body. Read *neuron.*" The student repeated Mr. Markham's response and said "neuron." Mr. Markham continued this activity until each student had taken one turn, and then he repeated it until each student had been given

10 opportunities to practice each word. Throughout the activity, he deliberately varied the order in which he called on different students, so students were never sure when they would be called on next. This kept the students engaged and excited. Mr. Markham also used a moderate pace to ensure that Connie and the other students never had to wait too long between turns but did have enough time to process the instruction and respond when it was their turn.

Connie did well during the simultaneous prompting activity, correctly responding on 9 out of 10 trials for each word. Mr. Markham decided she was ready to practice sight words using a 3-second time-delay procedure. During the next day's instructional session, he put the target-word cards in front of Connie. This time, he said, "Find *cell*. A *cell* is the smallest unit of life." He provided a 3-second delay by silently counting *1, 2, 3* to himself. On this first trial, Connie moved her hand but didn't select the word *cell* during the delay period. Mr. Markham then touched the correct word, said "cell," and started the trial again. This time, Connie touched the correct word immediately after the instruction.

You probably noticed that Mr. Markham included the meaning of the words while teaching students to recognize them. This research-based strategy is especially helpful for students with complex support needs who often learn best when educators teach them words in a meaningful context rather than drilling single words repeatedly. Mr. Markham also made deliberate choices about pacing and turn-taking that kept the activity fun and engaging. Research shows that when students are taught sight words in small groups like this, they will learn their own words and some of their peers' words through engagement and observation (Gast, Doyle, Wolery, Ault, & Baklarz, 1991). Once students are able to recognize the target words, the teacher should put them into connected text (Alberto, Waugh, & Fredrick, 2010; Allor et al., 2010). This strategy supports students' generalizing the words to other materials and deepens understanding.

Using Stimulus Prompts

Another instructional strategy for teaching sight words is the use of *stimulus prompts*; this strategy may be modified for use with students who have complex support needs. *Stimulus prompts* are visual changes to, or accompaniments to, the appearance of a target word that help students recognize and remember the word. A set of words may be color coded, with, for example, *school* written in green, and *exit* in red. Or, a word may be placed within a picture that represents the same concept; alternatively, the picture may be placed within the word.

As a type of stimulus prompt, many teachers place a picture (the stimulus) next to a word, hoping students will learn the printed word associated with the picture that represents what the word means. Unfortunately, research findings comparing this procedure with other instructional strategies show that it is not very effective (Sheehy, 2002). Students with complex support needs tend to pay more attention to the picture than the word and learn to associate the picture with the spoken, rather than the printed, word. Because the picture "blocks" their attending sufficiently to the printed word sufficiently, they cannot identify the printed word once the picture stimulus is removed (Didden, Prinsen, & Sigafoos, 2000).

Researchers have found that certain variations of the picture–word method are more effective than merely placing a word and picture together. These strategies transfer stimulus control (i.e., performing a behavior in response to a stimulus) from the picture (the stimulus prompt) to the printed word. For example, a student learns that the printed word *cat* represents a cat just as a picture of a cat represents that animal. One variation is a form of *stimulus fading*. In behavioral psychology, to "fade" a stimulus means to gradually reduce it. For this type of sight-word instruction, stimulus "fading" is quite literal: over time, successively fainter versions of a picture are presented, with a word appearing within the picture (see Figure 9.3). After initially pairing a picture with a word during instruction—a clear image like the black-and-white line drawing in the first panel of Figure 9.3, the teacher next presents a fainter version of the same image, such as the dark gray line drawing in the second panel. As instruction progresses through subsequent sessions, successively lighter or fainter images are presented, until eventually, only the printed

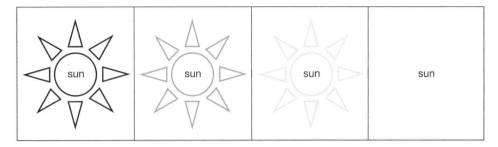

Figure 9.3. Example of using stimulus fading to teach sight-word recognition.

word remains. Embedding the word within the picture and then fading the picture seems to focus the student's attention more closely on the word instead of the picture, thus transferring stimulus control from the picture to the written word (Didden, de Graaff, Nelemans, Vooren, & Lancioni, 2006).

Research has shown that this strategy can be effective in teaching letter sounds and sight words to children with complex support needs (e.g., Sheehy, 2002) and to typically developing children (e.g., de Graaff, Verhoeven, Bosman, & Hasselman, 2007). It presents a challenge for teachers because preparing the required materials can be time consuming; the teacher must prepare multiple sets of words in which the picture has been reduced in size or intensity. However, the strategy is effective and may be just the approach a given student needs to begin acquiring sight words. The stimulus fading procedures discussed here are also sometimes referred to by other names, such as *embedded picture prompts, integrated picture mnemonics* (e.g., de Graaff et al., 2007), or *picture fading* (e.g., Didden et al., 2006).

Another, related strategy used to teach sight words to students with complex support needs is called *stimulus shaping;* this strategy helps students learn not only to recognize sight words, but also, over time, to differentiate among sight words they might easily confuse (e.g., words that begin with the same letter, such as *to* and *the*). Teachers using this strategy present the target word with distractor words; at first, the distractor words should be very different from the target word. For example, if the target sight word is *the,* the teacher might show this word with the distractor word *an* and ask the student to point to the word *the* and read it. Over time, the teacher gradually changes the number and type of distractor words in a way that requires students to make increasingly fine distinctions between words. For example, as the student continues working with the target sight word *the,* the teacher might show this target word with distractor words that are more similar in appearance, such as *to* and *then,* and may increase the number of distractor words shown. This instructional strategy of stimulus shaping is used in the Edmark Reading Program (n.d.), a published sight-word reading program.

The goal of these stimulus-based approaches, of course, is to help students build a vocabulary of sight words they can recognize easily. This process of learning to recognize printed words is inextricably tied to a fundamental understanding that is crucial for developing literacy: understanding that printed language is connected to spoken language (the alphabetic principle). Once students have grasped this principle, they may be able to benefit from instruction that provides a less significant level of support than these picture–word approaches provide and move on to more traditional instruction that does not involve extensive stimulus modification.

Instructional Strategies for Extending and Transferring Sight-Word Recognition

Students with complex support needs, like their typically developing peers, should be supported in using learned sight words in multiple contexts. Providing support is crucial because these students often have difficulty transferring knowledge learned in one context to another setting or task. There are several ways to provide support. A critical step is to give students opportunities to practice recognizing sight words in context, either within connected texts or, for functional sight words, in the natural settings in which the words occur. Having students use their growing sight-word vocabulary in writing, as in the "mailbox" activity described in the following section, is another way to help students maintain understanding of the words and generalize them to new contexts.

Word Walls

Word walls are also an engaging and effective way to support students' learning and use of sight words. Word walls can be used in many different ways and are meant to be interactive, not static displays. The idea is to display mastered words on a wall, bulletin board, or other surface in the classroom and to create ways for students to actively work with the words. Students can have their own individual word wall arranged on poster board, or the class can have a large word wall on which everyone participates. One enterprising teacher even created a word ceiling—but check school policies before trying this yourself.

Arrange the word wall using different formats based on the skills students are currently practicing. For example, words can be arranged alphabetically, grouped by parts of speech (nouns, verbs, adjectives, adverbs), or even organized by concepts related to specific content areas. For example, a high school science teacher might create a word wall using key terms for a unit on marine life and group the target words in categories such as plants, vertebrates, and invertebrates. Note that in addition to physically grouping words by category, you can also use color coding to categorize words—for example, writing nouns in red and verbs in blue.

Word walls are useful across grade levels. The most important thing is that the students actively practice using word-wall words. For example, students might use the word wall during writing as a handy reference to consult if they forget how to spell a word or need support choosing a word to use in a sentence.

As discussed previously, games are highly effective for getting students to apply word recognition skills in a context they find fun, meaningful, and socially engaging; the teacher can create games to practice words from the word wall. For example, a creative preschool teacher we know, who worked with children with autism, created a word wall about food groups. On it, he put up cards with food words, along with a picture of each food and a miniature object representing it. By including photographs and objects, this teacher created access for all the students, not just those who had learned to read the print. He also played games with the students using the word wall. For example, for students learning to recognize sight words, the teacher presented a card showing only the printed word and asked them to find the photo or object the word represented; students who selected the corresponding item correctly earned points for their team. Students who were not yet reading print could earn points by matching a printed word on a card to the printed word on the wall or by identifying a photo or object when the teacher presented the spoken word (e.g., "Find the orange").

Using Words in Social Contexts: The Mailbox Activity and Beyond

Another way to maintain and extend students' understanding of words they have learned is to provide opportunities for them to use these words in a social context—that is, to communicate with others. Consider, for example, Morgan and Moni's (2007) idea for a meaningful way to practice new sight words that motivates students by taking advantage of the social nature of literacy: the mailbox activity.

This activity uses social interaction to motivate students to learn sight words. The teacher places a mailbox in a corner of the classroom and writes short letters addressed to individual students, using the words each student is currently learning. Students can "check their mail" daily and write back to the teacher or write a letter to a classmate using the bank of words they are learning. This mailbox activity is far more motivating than simply drilling students on newly learned words because it allows students to apply their literacy skills in a highly motivating social context: reading and writing the new words in connected text used to communicate with people they knew well. This activity promotes fluency and maintenance of the words. It also takes advantage of the motivating, social nature of literacy to increase the likelihood that students will not only remember the new words but be able to use them in functional ways.

Teachers can extend the mailbox activity by including pen pals from other classes; creating an e-mail version of the activity to build digital literacy skills; or—if school policies allow a class Facebook page—allowing students to use their words in posts about interesting things they are studying or upcoming school events. This might be especially motivating for adolescent or adult learners who want to learn how to use social media. Another way for students to use sight words is to create, edit, and publish short articles in the high school newspaper—an activity one high school teacher in our local district used with students with complex support needs. This high-status activity provides an age-appropriate and socially motivating way for students to practice using their growing sight-word vocabularies.

REFLECTION QUESTION 6

Explain why it is especially important that students with complex support needs read connected text during literacy instruction, even if they are beginning readers. Design a lesson for a beginning reader with complex support needs that focuses on word recognition and includes activities to generalize learned words to different contexts, materials, and/or activities.

SUMMARY

Word recognition instruction for students with complex support needs should be a part of a comprehensive, multicomponent literacy program. Practitioners must consider both of the processes by which we identify words—decoding words using phonics skills, and recognizing sight words automatically—and address both in instruction. It is also important for practitioners to be aware of the role that other early literacy practices play in building a foundation for the word recognition skills students later develop.

Word recognition instruction should be systematic, explicit, and direct. It should encompass several approaches, as described in this chapter, so that students are equipped with multiple strategies when they encounter new words, and as a result, can make increasingly meaningful social and intellectual connections through access to text. Instructional decisions should not be based on a student's disability label or diagnosis—for instance, a student should not be denied the opportunity to learn basic phonics skills because of a belief that students with cognitive disabilities cannot benefit from such instruction. Instead, teachers and other practitioners must start with high expectations and provide quality instruction so that the students are not inadvertently limited in the literacy skills they acquire. They must monitor students' progress carefully and be flexible, changing or fine-tuning teaching strategies based on actual student progress. Finally, they must never stop giving students opportunities to apply newly learned skills within meaningful literacy activities, and while working with connected text, so students can develop a fuller understanding of what literacy is and how it can enrich their lives. As a teacher, be tireless in presuming that all students will have "competence" (Biklen & Burke, 2006) as literate human beings who have a fuller understanding of what literacy is and how it can enrich their lives.

RESOURCES

Web Sites

- **Down Syndrome Education Online** (http://www.down-syndrome.org) provides ideas for literacy education for young adults.

- **Literacy Instruction for Individuals with Autism, Cerebral Palsy, Down Syndrome and Other Disabilities** (http://aacliteracy.psu.edu) provides extensive resources and guidelines for teaching students with complex communication needs.

- **The Reading Rockets** web site (http://www.readingrockets.org) features videos, informational articles, research, and how-to articles on all aspects of reading instruction.

- **Teachers Pay Teachers** (https://www.teacherspayteachers.com). This web site allows teachers to share ideas and materials with each other; initial sign-up is free. The site features lessons, activities, games, center ideas and more for students of any age and any content ranging from free to approximately $75.00 for large sets of materials (most items range around $3.50).

Articles and Books

- Browder, D.M., & Spooner, F. (Eds.). (2014). *More language arts, math, and science for students with severe disabilities.* Baltimore, MD: Paul H. Brookes Publishing Co. This book provides extensive descriptions and examples of instructional strategies to use in each of these content areas.

- Morgan, M., & Moni, K.B. (2005). 20 ways to use phonics activities to motivate learners with difficulties. *Intervention in School and Clinic, 41*(1), 42–45. This short article is packed with specific games and activities to teach phonics skills to students in an engaging, fun manner.

- Schnorr, R.F. (2011). Intensive reading instruction for learners with developmental disabilities. *The Reading Teacher, 65*(1), 35–45. This short article explains how to use guided reading as a means of providing literacy instruction for students with complex support needs.

Assessment Instruments

- **Early Reading Screening Instrument** (ERSI; Morris, 1992). This assessment tool assesses alphabet knowledge, concept of word, phonemic awareness, and word recognition.

REFERENCES

Alberto, P.A., Waugh, R.E., & Fredrick, L.D. (2010). Teaching the reading of connected text through sight-word instruction to students with moderate intellectual disabilities. *Research in Developmental Disabilities, 31,* 1467–1474.

Allor, J.H., Champlin, T.M., Gifford, D.B., & Mathes, P.G. (2010). Methods for increasing the intensity of reading instruction for students with intellectual disabilities. *Education and Training in Autism and Developmental Disabilities, 45*(4), 500–511.

Allor, J.H., Mathes, P.G., Roberts, J.K., Cheatham, J.P., & Al Otaiba, S. (2014). Is scientifically based reading instruction effective for students with below-average IQs? *Exceptional Children, 80*(3), 287–306.

Armbruster, B.B., Lehr, F., & Osborn, J. (2001). *Put reading first: The research building blocks for teaching children to read—Kindergarten through grade 3.* Washington, DC: The Partnership for Reading.

Boudreau, D. (2002). Literacy skills in children and adolescents with Down syndrome. *Reading and Writing: An Interdisciplinary Journal, 15,* 497–525.

Breit-Smith, A., & Justice, L.M. (2010). Building emergent literacy skills. In C. Carnahan & P. Williamson (Eds.), *Quality literacy instruction for students with autism spectrum disorders* (pp. 161–187). Lenexa, KS: AAPC Publishing.

Browder, D.M. (2001). Functional reading. In B. Wilson & D.M. Browder (Eds.), *Curriculum and assessment for students with moderate and severe disabilities* (pp. 179–214). New York, NY: Guilford Press.

Browder, D.M., Gibbs, S., Ahlgrim-Delzell, L., Courtade, G.R., & Lee, A. (2016). *Early Literacy Skills Builder.* Verona, WI: Attainment Company.

Browder, D.M., Gibbs, S., Ahlgrim-Delzell, L., Courtade, G.R., Mraz, M., & Flowers, C. (2009). Literacy for students with severe developmental disabilities: What should we teach and what should we hope to achieve? *Remedial & Special Education, 30*(5), 269–282.

Burgoyne, K., Duff, F.J., Clarke, P.J., Buckley, S., Snowling, M.J., & Hulme, C. (2012). Efficacy of a reading and language intervention for children with Down syndrome: A randomized controlled trial. *Journal of Child Psychology and Psychiatry, 53*(10), 1044–1053.

Biklen, D., & Burke, J. (2006). Presuming competence. *Equity & Excellence in Education, 39,* 166–175.

Channell, M.M., Loveall, S.J., & Conners, F.A. (2013). Strengths and weaknesses in reading skills of youth with intellectual disabilities. *Research in Developmental Disabilities, 34,* 776–787.

Copeland, S.R., & Cosbey, J. (2008–2009). Making progress in the general curriculum: Rethinking effective instructional practices. *Research and Practice for Persons with Severe Disabilities, 33,* 214–227.

Cupples, L., & Iacono, T. (2000). Phonological awareness and oral reading skill in children with Down syndrome. *Journal of Speech, Language, and Hearing Research, 43,* 595–608.

de Graaff, S., Verhoeven, L., Bosman, A.M.T., & Hasselman, F. (2007). Integrated pictorial mnemonics and stimulus fading: Teaching kindergartners letter sounds. *British Journal of Educational Psychology, 77,* 519–539.

Didden, R., de Graaff, S., Nelemans, M., Vooren, M., & Lancioni, G. (2006). Teaching sight words to children with moderate to mild mental retardation: Comparison between instructional procedures. *American Journal on Mental Retardation, 111,* 357–365.

Didden, R., Prinsen, H., & Sigafoos, J. (2000). The blocking effect on pictorial prompts on sight-word reading. *Journal of Applied Behavioral Analysis, 33*(3), 317–320.

Edmark Reading Program. (n.d.). Austin, TX: PRO-ED.

Ehri, L.C. (2005). Learning to read words: Theory, findings, and issues. *Scientific Studies of Reading, 9*(2), 167–188.

Erickson, K.A., Hatch, P., & Clendon, S. (2010). Literacy, assistive technology, and students with significant disabilities. *Focus on Exceptional Children, 42*(5), 1–16.

Foorman, B., Beyler, N., Borradaile, K., Coyne, M., Denton, C.A., Dimino, J., . . ., Wissel, S. (2016). *Foundational skills to support reading for understanding in kindergarten through 3rd grade* (NCEE 2016-4008). Washington, DC: National Center for Education Evaluation and Regional Assistance (NCEE), Institute of Education Sciences, U.S. Department of Education. Retrieved from http://whatworks.ed.gov

Fredrick, L.D., Davis, D.H., Alberto, P.A., & Waugh, R.E. (2013). From initial phonics to functional phonics: Teaching word-analysis skills to students with moderate intellectual disability. *Education and Training in Autism and Developmental Disabilities, 48*(1), 49–66.

Fry, E. (1999). *1000 instant words.* Westminster, CA: Laguna Beach Educational Books.

Gast, D.L., Doyle, P.M., Wolery, M., Ault, M.J., & Baklarz, J.L. (1991). Acquisition of incidental information during small group instruction. *Education and Treatment of Children, 14*(1), 1–18.

Goswami, U. (2001). Early phonological development and the acquisition of literacy. In S. Neuman & D. Dickinson (Eds.), *Handbook of research in early literacy for the 21st century* (pp. 111–125). New York, NY: Guilford Press.

Harm, M.W., McCandliss, B.D., & Seidenberg, M.S. (2003). Modeling the successes and failures of interventions for disabled readers. *Scientific Studies of Reading, 7*(2), 155–182.

Hudson, M.E., & Test, D.W. (2011). Evaluating the evidence base of shared story reading to promote literacy for students with extensive support needs. *Research & Practice for Persons with Severe Disabilities, 36*(1–2), 34–45.

Joseph, L.M., & McCachran, M. (2003). Comparison of a word study phonics technique between students with moderate to mild mental retardation and struggling readers without disabilities. *Education and Training in Developmental Disabilities, 38,* 192–199.

Justice, L.M., McGinty, A.S., Piasta, S.B., Kaderavek, J.N., & Fan, X. (2010). Print-focused read-alouds in preschool classrooms: Intervention effectiveness and moderators of child outcomes. *Language, Speech, and Hearing Services in Schools, 41,* 504–520.

Kaiser, A.P., & Roberts, M.Y. (2011). Advances in early communication and language intervention. *Journal of Early Intervention, 33*(4), 298–303.

Katims, D.S. (2000). *The quest for literacy: Curriculum and instructional procedures for teaching reading and writing to students with mental retardation and developmental disabilities.* Reston, VA: Council for Exceptional Children.

Kennedy, E.J., & Flynn, M.C. (2003). Training phonological awareness skills in children with Down syndrome. *Research in Developmental Disabilities, 24,* 44–57.

Lane, L.A., Keefe, E.B., Copeland, S.R., & Kruger, A. (2015). *Literacy strategies for all students: Accessing the general education curriculum.* In B. Cole & W. Farone (Eds.), a publication of the Parent Education & Advocacy Leadership (PEAL) Center. Retrieved from http://pealcenter.org/wp-content/uploads/2017/05/Literacy_07-07-2015.pdf

Lemons, C.J., & Fuchs, D. (2010). Modeling response to reading intervention in children with Down syndrome: An examination of predictors of differential growth. *Reading Research Quarterly, 45*(2), 134–168.

Lemons, C.J., Mrachko, A.A., Kostewicz, D.E., & Paterra, M.F. (2012). Effectiveness of decoding and phonological awareness interventions for children with Down syndrome. *Exceptional Children, 79*(1), 67–90.

Liberman, I.Y., Shankweiler, D., Fischer, F.W., & Carter, B. (1974). Explicit syllable and phoneme segmentation in the young child. *Journal of Experimental Child Psychology, 18,* 201–212.

Light, J., & McNaughton, D. (n.d.). *Accessible Literacy Learning Reading Program.* Pittsburgh, PA: Mayer-Johnson.

Mathes, P.G., Torgesen, J.K., Menchetti, J.C., Wahl, M., & Grek, M.K. (2004). *Early Interventions in Reading:* Teacher guides, daily lessons materials, and student activity books for first-grade reading intervention. New York, NY: SRA/McGraw-Hill Education.

Moni, K.B., Jobling, A., Morgan, M., & Lloyd, J. (2011). Promoting literacy for adults with intellectual disabilities in a community-based service organisation. *Australian Journal of Adult Learning, 51*(3), 456–478.

Morgan, M., & Moni, K.B. (2005). 20 ways to use phonics activities to motivate learners with difficulties. *Intervention in School and Clinic, 41*(1), 42–45.

Morgan, M., & Moni, K.B. (2007). 20 ways to motivate students with disabilities using sight-vocabulary activities. *Intervention in School and Clinic, 42*(4), 229–223.

Morris, D. (1992). What constitutes at-risk: Screening children for first grade reading intervention. In W.A. Secord and J.S. Damico (Eds.), *Best practices in school speech language pathology* (pp. 43–51). Orlando, FL: Harcourt, Brace & Jovanovich.

Pollard-Durodola, S.D., Gonzalez, J., Simmons, D.C., Kwok, O., Taylor, A.B., Davis, M.J., . . ., Simmons, L. (2010). The effects of an intensive shared book-reading intervention for preschool children at-risk for vocabulary delay. *Exceptional Children, 77*(1), 1–23.

Ricci, L. (2011). Home literacy environments, interest in reading and emergent literacy skills of children with Down syndrome versus typical children. *Journal of Intellectual Disability Research, 55*(6), 596–609.

Shanahan, T., & Lonigan, C.J. (2010). The National Early Literacy Panel: A summary of the process and the report. *Educational Researcher, 39*(4), 279–285.

Sheehy, K. (2002). The effective use of symbols in teaching word recognition to children with severe learning difficulties: A comparison of word alone, integrated picture cueing and the handle technique. *International Journal of Disability, Development, and Education, 49*, 47–59.

Tan, S. (2006). *The arrival.* New York, NY: Arthur A. Levine Books/Scholastic.

Torgesen, J.K., & Mathes P.G. (1998). *What every teacher should know about phonological awareness.* Tallahassee, FL: Florida Department of Education Division of Public Schools and Community Education Bureau of Instructional Support and Community Services. Available at http://www.fldoe.org/core/fileparse.php/7690/urlt/0070133-phon9872.pdf

Torgesen, J.K., & Mathes, P.G. (2000). *A basic guide to understanding, assessing, and teaching phonological awareness.* Austin, TX: PRO-ED.

Treiman, R. (1983). The structure of spoken syllables: Evidence from novel word games. *Cognition, 15*, 49–74.

Treiman, R. (1985). Onsets and rimes as units of spoken syllables: Evidence from children. *Journal of Experimental Child Psychology, 39*, 161–181.

Troia, G.A. (2004). Phonological processing and its influence on literacy learning. In C.A. Stone, E.R. Silliman, B.J. Ehren, & K. Apel (Eds.), *Handbook of language and literacy: Development and disorders* (pp. 271–103). New York, NY: Guilford Press.

Wagner, R.K., Torgesen, J.K., & Rashotte, C. (1999). *Comprehensive Test of Phonological Processing (CTOPP).* Austin, TX: PRO-ED.

Wiesner, D. (2006). *Flotsam.* New York, NY: Clarion Books.

Wise, J.C., Sevcik, R.A., Romski, M.A., & Morris, R.D. (2010). The relationship between phonological processing skills and word and nonword identification performance in children with mild intellectual disabilities. *Research in Developmental Disabilities, 31*, 1170–1175.

Yopp, H.K. (1992). Developing phonemic awareness in young children. *The Reading Teacher, 45*(9), 696–703.

Conveying Your Message

Writing Instruction

Kristie Asaro-Saddler

LEARNING OBJECTIVES

By the end of this chapter, readers will

1. Define writing and explain evidence-based writing instruction and its application with students who have complex support needs.

2. Describe the writing considerations for students who have complex support needs.

3. Provide examples of instructional strategies, accommodations, and tools that can be used to promote social communication and writing development in students who have complex support needs.

Chapter 10 will address ways to provide effective writing instruction for individuals with complex support needs. I will begin by defining writing and discussing the importance of writing as a means of participating fully in a literate society. I will also explore the challenges involved in writing well—including the challenges faced by many typically developing students and those challenges that are particularly common among students with complex support needs. Specific, effective practices for providing writing instruction for these students, based in educational research, will be discussed in depth, along with effective means of assessing writing.

AN EMERGING WRITER: Danielle

Danielle is an 8-year-old student with autism spectrum disorder (ASD). She was diagnosed by a neurologist at age 2 years and has been receiving services ever since. She is enrolled in a self-contained class with eight students, one teacher, and four paraprofessionals.

Danielle uses minimal verbal language for communication. This includes some short phrases—mostly echolalia, such as phrases from movies or television shows—and some three-word requests such as "I want yogurt." Danielle does not yet use her language consistently; to express herself, she will often engage in tantrum behaviors instead: screaming, crying, flailing her arms, and dropping to the floor. When she does speak, she often uses inappropriate volume, ranging from low mumbling to shouting when she does not receive an immediate response.

In the past, Danielle has had some success communicating using Picture Exchange Communication System (PECS; Bondy & Frost, 1994). However, her use has been inconsistent; she will often perseverate on the pictures or swipe the book across the table. Her teachers have recently begun using an iPad loaded with Proloquo2Go (AssistiveWare), a symbol-supported, easily personalized communication application, as an alternative form of communication. Danielle's receptive language appears stronger than her expressive language, but her inattention to tasks and lack of motivation to respond often prevents her from responding to requests to complete a task or engage with others. She has few interactions with other students or adults in the classroom.

In terms of Danielle's literacy, she enjoys looking at books and has memorized a few to the point where she can "read" them aloud (e.g., *Brown Bear, Brown Bear, What Do You See?* [Martin & Carle, 1996]). She also enjoys singing along to books such as *The Wheels on the Bus* (Zelinsky, 1990). Her writing consists mainly of scribbling and random strings of letters, but she is beginning to put letters together to approximate words. She can write her name and has demonstrated an understanding of directionality—that is, that we write from left to right and from top to bottom. Danielle's occupational therapist is working with her to learn to hold a pencil appropriately because she has some fine motor difficulties and often does not use a pincer grip. Her team is also using technology—a word processor and an iPad—for writing. Danielle finds technology engaging and uses the iPad both for instructional purposes and for behavioral reinforcement. She enjoys music, arts and crafts, and ice cream. She also loves certain movies, like Disney's *Frozen* and Pixar's *Toy Story.* She can often be motivated to make requests for activities involving things she enjoys.

WHY TEACH STUDENTS TO WRITE?

Why does learning to write matter for a student like Danielle? Writing is an important skill needed for full participation in our highly literate society. Through written language, civilizations have retained their history, culture, identity, and literature via the transmission of information (Graham & Harris, 2005). Writing allows people to communicate from a distance. Author Stephen King has referred to writing as telepathy, because it can convey a message across space and time (King, 2000). Writing is also a means of expression, personal reflection, and self-discovery (Kluth & Chandler-Olcott, 2008).

Skill in written expression is also critical for school success. Beyond first grade, writing is the principal means by which students demonstrate their knowledge in school (Boucher & Oehler, 2013) and the major method by which teachers evaluate students' academic functioning (Graham & Harris, 2005). In school, students write for a variety of purposes and within different modes, including but not limited to informational writing, expressive writing, and opinion writing. They are expected to use their writing as a means both to communicate with others and to demonstrate their knowledge about the content areas (Common Core State Standards Initiative, 2014). Furthermore, once they leave school, students are expected to write well to achieve success professionally and to interact socially.

To be fully integrated into the classroom and, later, into society, students need to be skilled yet flexible writers, often using different forms of written communication in text messages, e-mail communications, and social media for interaction with others. Writing is particularly important for students with disabilities because it can aid in increased communication, socialization, and independence (Wollak & Koppenhaver, 2011). Writing can give them a voice, allow them to advocate for themselves, and help them participate more fully in society.

WHAT IS WRITING?

Writing is a process of communicating. Let's look at both keywords in that phrase. *Communicating* in writing involves communicating through a system of language using letter symbols that represent speech sounds. Writing involves the use of a vocabulary, along with a structured grammar and syntax, that is shared by people within a given society (Fromkin & Rodman, 1998). It is a holistic and authentic process used to make meaning (Sturm & Koppenhaver, 2000, p. 75): *holistic,* meaning that it involves a process of composing rather than distinct skills, and *authentic,* in that people write for real purposes that have personal meaning.

Writing is also a complex *process*. It entails a movement among the processes of planning, composing, revising, editing, and sharing (Flower & Hayes, 1987; Graves, 1983).

1. *Planning* involves setting goals, formulating ideas, and organizing thoughts to be shared with others; Flower and Hayes (1980) contend that planning is what separates immature from sophisticated writers.

2. *Composing* requires students to develop the ideas or material intended to be used in their paper into letters, words, sentences, and paragraphs (Bereiter & Scardamalia, 1987).

3. *Revising* is something conventional writers engage in to improve, transform, and clarify the text they produced while planning and crafting an initial draft (Bereiter & Scardamalia, 1987). At its most basic level, revision involves the author adding additional text (i.e., "saying more") for the reader. More sophisticated revision involves making changes to the overall meaning by revising word choice and vocabulary, grammar, sentence-to-sentence cohesion, and overall coherence across a text.

4. *Editing* involves review of writing for errors in surface-level skills, such as spelling and punctuation. Both revising and editing require that the writer has the ability to detect errors and modify the text to enhance meaning for the reader.

5. Finally, *sharing* is an integral part of the writing process because writing is a form of communicating with others. Writers can share drafts or final products aloud or have others read what they have produced.

The processes described—planning, composing, revising, editing, and sharing—do not necessarily occur in a perfectly linear way. For instance, planning both in advance and during composing is an essential element in the writing process. Although composing is distinct from planning, conventional writers will often write in a recursive cycle by generating text content, planning additional ideas, and returning to composing/text generation. When composing, a writer's goal is to produce text that matches his or her intent and the audience's needs; a writer may compose a few paragraphs, go back to revise them, and then move on to composing the next few paragraphs. Sharing text may occur as part of revision—it supports development of audience awareness, especially if the reader or listener provides feedback—and the writer may use this audience awareness to revise the overall text.

When composing, writers must also coordinate a range of higher order processes known as *executive functions* that relate to regulating one's behavior (Reid, Mason, & Asaro-Saddler, 2013), including skills such as organizing, planning, self-monitoring, and utilizing working memory. These complex cognitive demands must be accomplished while simultaneously managing the fine motor demands to produce a written or typed product (Boucher & Oehler, 2013). Thus, it is a challenging communication process that takes time and effort to learn.

LEARNING TO WRITE

It is challenging for anyone to master the skills previously described and to make the transition from "beginning writer" to "sophisticated writer." Before addressing specific challenges faced by individuals with complex support needs, we'll take a quick look at how typically developing students evolve as writers.

Beginning and Sophisticated Writers

Beginning writers are those who, regardless of age, are learning to use written language to express communicative intent by scribbling, drawing symbols, and making recurring marks on paper (Sturm, Cali, Nelson, & Staskowski, 2012). They may not yet understand the conventions of written language and may use inventive spelling (e.g., stringing letters together), but they demonstrate intentionality (Sturm et al., 2012). Beginning writers progress from scribbles, marks, and random letter patterns into early conventional writing in which they compose their first decipherable words. Later, they develop sophisticated conventional writing skills in which they begin to combine words into sentences and paragraphs.

Sophisticated conventional writers demonstrate competency across a variety of areas and are purposeful in their writing (Sturm & Koppenhaver, 2000)—writing which is understandable to a reader (Sturm et al., 2012). Their writing often consists of cohesive pieces that demonstrate an understanding of the audience's needs, with a clear beginning, middle, and end. These writers have competency or even automaticity in lower level components of writing, such as spelling and punctuation, and competency in higher level components, such as planning and generating content (Bereiter & Scardamalia, 1987). They are skilled in planning what to say and how to say it, generating content to translate plans into written text, and revising to improve text (Hayes & Flower, 1986). Their plans are tailored for the context—for example, writing personal e-mail or business letters; and the genre—for example, writing a persuasive essay or fictional narrative (Graham & Perin, 2007). Their plans are more organized and hierarchal as well, including goals and subgoals (Hayes & Flower, 1986). Sophisticated writers can also self-regulate their behaviors, independently monitoring, assessing, and reinforcing both the process and the products of their writing (Graham & Harris, 2005).

The Challenges of Writing Well

Given the range of sophisticated processes involved in writing, it is not surprising that many students, with and without disabilities, struggle to become skilled writers. Struggling writers may have difficulty coordinating the stages of the writing process. They tend to engage in little or no advance planning (Graham & Harris, 2003) and have difficulty generating content. When asked to revise, struggling writers may make surface-level edits to spelling or punctuation (Saddler, 2003) but be unable to execute more sophisticated revision. This difficulty often occurs because they struggle to identify what needs to be revised, or they lack the skills necessary to make the revision (Saddler, 2003). When the student is stuck, he or she may not persist, which may indicate a lack of motivation or a lack of both the content knowledge and the writing skills needed to continue (Graham & Harris, 2005). Students also may have trouble attending and focusing, which makes writing even more difficult given the numerous, concurrent mental and physical tasks involved in the execution of the writing processes (Graham & Harris, 2003).

Language impairments may also impact a student's writing ability (Wollak & Koppenhaver, 2011). According to Sturm and Clendon, language "is the cornerstone of literacy learning" (2004, p. 76). If students cannot access language the way typically developing peers can, they may be unable to manage the intricacies of reading and writing. Difficulties in acquiring and processing both expressive and receptive language can lead to shorter, disorganized texts containing poor sentence structure and fewer ideas (Dockrell, Lindsay, & Connelly, 2009). Even students without language impairments may have difficulty translating their oral language into written language (Graham & Harris, 2005). One reason may be their difficulty understanding the needs of an absent audience, because the support that they would typically receive from a conversational partner is removed (Bereiter & Scardamalia, 1987). Another may be lack of fluency in lower level writing processes, such as spelling and mechanics; attending to these drains their cognitive energy and does not allow them to focus on higher level writing skills (Bereiter & Scardamalia, 1987).

In addition, struggling writers often lack self-regulation skills in several executive function components, including planning, cognitive flexibility, inhibition, and self-monitoring, which impact their ability to write (Reid et al., 2013). They may also lack motivation, particularly when asked to write about a topic that is not personally meaningful (Boscolo, Gelati, & Galvan, 2012). Finally, students who have motor/coordination issues that affect handwriting or word processing are at a disadvantage when asked to produce written text.

CHALLENGES FOR WRITERS WITH COMPLEX SUPPORT NEEDS

Student writers with complex support needs may face particular challenges. These students are a heterogeneous group with diverse abilities and needs—for example, intellectual disability (ID), ASD, multiple disabilities (MD), and/or physical or sensory impairments. Our focus is on their individual needs for support rather than specific disability labels. Writers with complex support needs demonstrate a range of writing ability—beginning, sophisticated, and in-between—with multiple factors across a variety of domains impacting their writing. These factors may include language ability, motor ability, and social skills, along with external factors such as limited life experience, low academic expectations for these students, and a lack of instruction in writing skills.

Language ability may have a direct impact because lower levels of language, including less-developed oral language and vocabulary, as well as limited understanding of grammar, syntax, and pragmatics, may limit students' spelling, organization, and text diversity, or variation in the types and genres of texts they produce (Lewis, O'Donnell, Freebairn, & Taylor, 1998; Sturm et al., 2012; Sturm & Clendon, 2004). (See Chapter 2 for more information on the role of language in reading and writing.) Delays in pragmatics, syntax, phonology, and morphology can limit their ability to write well. Students with complex support needs often have limited experience in classroom discourse. In addition, they often have underdeveloped vocabulary that limits their ability to express themselves both orally and in writing (Sturm & Clendon, 2004). This may be a particular concern for students who use alternative and augmentative communication (AAC) devices (Sturm & Clendon, 2004).

Motor ability can have a direct correlation with the ability to write or type longer papers (Boucher & Oehler, 2013). Even if students have good ideas, they may have difficulty transferring those ideas to written form and as a result may produce brief writings that they are unwilling to develop because it is too difficult physically (Asaro-Saddler, 2014). Slower rates of writing may put more strain on short-term memory, an area of difficulty for many students with complex support needs (Westling, Fox, & Carter, 2015).

Social understanding may also affect the ability to write. Students who have better social awareness may write better narrative and persuasive pieces (Dray, Selman, & Schultz, 2009), so an inability to respond to social information or understand social conventions may well impact the writing of some students with complex support needs. Deficits in theory of mind, an ability to take another's perspective, may impact writing in that children with complex support needs may find it difficult to write for an absent audience (Hillock, 2011), because they may not understand that their writing will be read by someone who thinks differently than they do.

Writers with complex support needs may be affected by external barriers as well. Lack of life experiences may limit the background information or context a writer has available, making it difficult to generate ideas. Students with sensory disabilities may be particularly vulnerable in this area due to their limited exposure to visual or auditory stimuli (Wilson, 2010). Teachers', parents', or other caregivers' low expectations of these students may also limit writing opportunities, which limits opportunities to improve writing skills (Keefe & Copeland, 2011).

Another external barrier to these students' writing development is lack of instruction in higher level writing skills. Often, it is assumed that conventional writing is not possible for this population (Keefe & Copeland, 2011). As a result, they often are excluded from writing activities and are not exposed to quality writing instruction (Carnahan, Williamson, Hollingshead, & Israel, 2012). In a recent study exploring the literacy activities of students with severe disabilities, for example, writing occurred for only 11% of activities, and only one of four teachers was observed to include writing in class literacy activities (Ruppar, 2015). When beginning writers with complex support needs are provided with instruction, teachers usually focus on lower level skills such as tracing, spelling, and handwriting (Kluth & Chandler-Olcott, 2008). Although these skills are one aspect of writing, they involve surface details, not the higher level skills, such as vocabulary, syntax, and organization, that are at the core of this communication form.

Writing instruction for students with complex support needs often includes drill and practice and a focus on lower level or functional writing skills, and it often occurs through decontextualized writing opportunities (Wollak & Koppenhaver, 2011). For example, students may work on letter writing or punctuation worksheets rather than composing text. Unfortunately, when these students are taught writing in decontextualized environments, it does not support their ability to develop the skills necessary to become conventional writers.

Research has found, however, that when provided with effective, evidence-based instruction, students with complex support needs can develop higher level writing skills. A brief review of this research is provided in the next section, followed by a discussion of how best to implement specific effective practices in your classroom.

REFLECTION QUESTION 1

What factors can make it difficult for anyone—regardless of disability status—to learn to write well? What specific challenges can make it difficult for students with complex support needs to learn to write well?

REVIEW OF CURRENT RESEARCH ON TEACHING WRITING TO STUDENTS WITH COMPLEX SUPPORT NEEDS

Research has indicated that when provided with effective instruction, students with complex support needs can improve their writing skills. Pennington and Delano (2012) conducted a review of the literature to explore the effectiveness of writing interventions with students with ASD and found several writing interventions that were effective with this population, including strategy instruction, sentence construction skills, and technology. Since then, several additional studies have explored the effects of the self-regulated strategy development (SRSD) approach on students with ASD, which combines strategy instruction with prompts for self-regulation such as goal setting and self-monitoring, and found positive findings in persuasive writing and story writing (e.g., Asaro-Saddler, 2014; Asaro-Saddler & Bak, 2014). Other studies have highlighted the use of technology for students with ASD to write stories (e.g., Pennington, Collins, Stenhoff, Turner, & Gunselman, 2014; Schneider, Codding, & Tryon, 2013), write names (Moore et al., 2013), and check the spelling of words (e.g., Kagohara, Sigafoos, Achmadi, O'Reilly, & Lancioni, 2012).

There has been less research on students with other complex support needs. Joseph and Konrad (2009) conducted a review of the literature on writing interventions for students with intellectual and developmental disabilities, and they discovered few writing studies conducted with this population. Of the identified studies, strategy instruction was again the most commonly used approach to teaching writing. Other interventions that have been used with this population include technology to teach spelling (Purrazzella & Mechling, 2013) and text messaging (Pennington, Saadatzi, Welch, & Scott, 2014), as well as the use of specific software programs such as First Author (Don Johnston, Inc.) to improve the story writing of students with developmental disabilities (e.g., Asaro-Saddler, Muir-Knox, Meredith, & Akhmedjanova, 2015; Sturm & Knack, 2011). Skills such as paragraph writing (e.g., Konrad, Trela, & Test, 2006), essay writing (e.g., Woods-Groves et al., 2014), and cover letter writing (Pennington, Delano, & Scott, 2014) have also been examined.

Although research is scarce in the area of writing instruction for students with complex support needs, the recent increase in the number of empirical studies in the area is encouraging. Teachers and practitioners should continue to seek out research-based practices when designing their writing programs for students with complex support needs. With this in mind, we will explore effective practices in teaching and assessing writing and how these practices might be adapted for students with complex support needs.

EFFECTIVE INSTRUCTION FOR WRITERS WITH COMPLEX SUPPORT NEEDS

Effective writing instruction is guided by practices that are evidence-based, meaning they have been proven effective by empirical research studies. These practices should also be standards based, meaning that goals are targeted and instruction is provided based on the appropriate grade-level writing standards. This section will include a brief introduction to effective practices in writing for all students, with and without complex support needs, as recommended by various reviews of the literature and technical reports (e.g., Graham et al., 2012; Troia, 2014).

Practice 1: Make Writing an Important Part of the Day

Students should be writing every day, throughout the day, and for a variety of purposes. According to researchers, teachers should have a dedicated instructional time to directly teach the skills necessary to be effective writers (Graham et al., 2012). In addition to allocating this set time, teachers should also encourage students to write as part of work in other subject areas. Writing should be used for a variety of purposes in content area instruction, ranging from responding to comprehension questions in English language arts, to writing lab reports in science, to writing diary entries from a character's or historical figure's perspective. Students should also have free writing time when they can choose the genre and topic about which they would like to write (Sturm, 2012).

Implementation for Writers With Complex Support Needs   For all students, but particularly writers with complex support needs, teachers should have a set block of time when they focus on teaching basic skills necessary for writing. About 1 hour per day should be spent on writing, including both direct instruction and independent writing time (Graham et al., 2012), but this may vary depending on students' attentional needs. For example, in Danielle's class, the teacher gives a brief minilesson focusing on an important writing topic for that day, such as brainstorming or adding periods, and then has students engage in independent writing for as long as they wish. She has students write again later in the day in response to their science or social studies lesson. For instance, after a lesson about the seasons, Danielle's teacher provided a list of words and pictures of winter clothing and asked the students to write about which items they would wear in winter and why.

For students with complex support needs, writing instruction may include collaboration with the speech-language pathologist (SLP) to focus on increasing the written language, such as richer vocabulary and providing details, used while writing, or the occupational therapist to work on the fine motor skills necessary to write or type. For example, Danielle's occupational therapist will often provide in-classroom sessions during writing time to help Danielle learn to hold a pencil correctly or learn keyboarding. Her SLP will often work on writing during therapy sessions as well, encouraging Danielle to use her words in writing as a means of expressing her wants and needs.

Practice 2: Focus Instruction on Both the Process and the Product

Teachers should provide instructional support in the writing process, including planning and generating content, drafting, and then revising and editing the text, as appropriate to the student's ability level (Troia, 2014). This should be taught by explicitly modeling good writing behaviors, providing examples, scaffolding instruction, and then slowly releasing responsibility to the students (Graham et al., 2012). Writing should also be taught through strategy instruction, in which teachers explicitly teach a strategy for a given genre, such as story writing, along with techniques for self-regulating the writing process, such as goal setting, self-instruction, and self-monitoring (Graham & Harris, 2005). (See also Practice 6: Create Independent Writers on page 235.)

Teachers are also encouraged to focus on the students' products by helping them make these products more creative and enjoyable to a reader (Troia, 2014) and eventually teaching them proper conventions for writing. Depending on students' writing skills, this may include organizing their work at the word, sentence, or paragraph level. Vocabulary is an important part of the writing product and an area in which students with complex support needs may experience significant difficulty (see Chapter 9). Teachers should be sure to provide instruction in both topic- and genre-specific words to improve students' vocabulary use (Troia & Olinghouse, 2013).

Implementation for Writers With Complex Support Needs   Students with complex support needs who struggle with writing may require more scaffolding and explicit instruction in the writing process. Students such as Danielle may particularly benefit from visual aids to assist in this process. For example, Danielle's teacher often uses pictures as a visual support to help Danielle and her classmates generate ideas about which to write. Using these pictures provides recognizable images students can use to help them select topics and increase the diversity of topics they write about (Sturm, 2012). Danielle's teacher uses a variety of sources—including magazines, the Internet, and pictures sent from home or taken at school events or class trips—to select pictures on topics of interest to Danielle. She also uses basic graphic organizers, as well as cloze paragraphs, to help students formulate and organize ideas. For example, after a field trip to the zoo, Danielle's teacher presented her with the following paragraph: "We went on a field trip to _____. I saw _____ on our trip. I felt _____." When Danielle struggled to complete the blanks, her teacher provided a selection of pictures from which to choose. She then encouraged Danielle to write the word corresponding to the pictures she selected.

Practice 3: Use Technology in the Writing Process

Using technology has been shown to improve writing quality for students with and without disabilities (Graham & Perin, 2007). Technology tools may be considered "high-tech" or "low-tech." High-tech options may include technologies such as computers with writing-specific software programs and touchscreen keyboards, as well as more current technological applications such as handheld devices, cell phones, and social media platforms (Troia, 2014). Low-tech options, such as adapted pencils and communication boards, may also be used. Writing technology should be selected based on the individual student's interest and ability levels. For example, some writers may be highly motivated to use high-tech devices, such as an iPad, whereas others may be distracted by them or unable to manipulate the touchscreen features or hold a stylus (Reichle, 2011). As with all technology, students should be provided with training in the use of any specific writing technology; keyboarding, for example, should be explicitly taught and practiced before students are expected to use it to create written products (Graham et al., 2012). Teachers should model proper care and use of the technology system to support appropriate use and minimize potential damage (Graham et al., 2012).

Implementation for Writers With Complex Support Needs   Technology has become an essential means of education for some students with complex support needs (Reichle, 2011). The use of technology is an evidence-based practice for students with ASD (Wong et al., 2015) and has been recommended to support the writing process for students with other complex support needs (Wollak & Koppenhaver, 2011). Researchers who support using technology have asserted that computers and software programs can allow students with complex support needs to focus on the content of their written products, rather than use cognitive and physical energy to correctly form letters or spell words (Carnahan et al., 2012). Technology programs also can provide concrete, visual supports, which are especially helpful for these students (Kluth & Chandler-Olcott, 2008) and can allow students to work more independently without the need for additional personnel support (Carnahan et al., 2012). Finally, students with complex support needs may show higher levels of engagement and be more motivated to write when using technology (Wong et al., 2015).

Technology is a valuable way to help these students focus on both the writing process and the resulting product by allowing them to more easily add, rearrange, or delete words. Students with complex support needs can use software programs for organizing ideas; programs such as Draft:Builder (Don Johnston, Inc.), and Kidspiration and Inspiration (Inspiration Software, Inc.), can be used to create graphic organizers whose content can then be transferred into an outline of a first draft (Kluth & Chandler-Olcott, 2008). Specific supports, such as word prediction software, electronic graphic organizers or story webs, and programs that provide immediate feedback, may also be used. (See the Resources section at the end of this chapter for links to technological programs available online that can provide students with various kinds of valuable supports.)

Danielle's teacher uses the First Author curriculum and software in her class. First Author guides students through the writing process by providing the following:

- A planning screen, which supports topic selection by providing students with individualized photo images

- A composing screen, which offers vocabulary support through word banks that offer high-frequency, high-utility, and topic-specific words, along with a read-aloud feature and self-monitoring prompts

- A "publish and share" screen, in which the program provides a copy of the text in a book format that can be read aloud and printed (Sturm & Knack, 2011)

The First Author program's Teacher Central tool allows teachers to customize the features of each student's program. Danielle's teacher, for example, used it to individualize her program to include photos and word banks related to topics about which she was likely to write, such as the movies *Frozen* and *Toy Story*. Since using First Author, Danielle's writing has improved in both quantity and quality, and she appears to enjoy sharing it during the "author's chair" portion of the lesson.

A final note on technology: When selecting devices for students with complex support needs, it is important to consider whether the technology will ostracize them or make them stand out from their peers. More current technological devices commonly used by the general population, such as iPhones and tablets, may be more acceptable than assistive technology devices such as a Dynavox (Tobii Dynavox). In fact, according to John Elder Robison, an adult with ASD, these common mobile technologies "may help erase the disabilities (of people with ASD and other complex support needs) that might otherwise be visible and humiliating" (Robison, 2014, p. xxiv). Therefore, it is important to ensure that the device is socially acceptable in the eyes of the student and/or the student's family.

REFLECTION QUESTION 2

What are the most important considerations in selecting the best types of technology to use with your students with complex support needs?

Practice 4: Create a Supported and Engaged Community of Writers

Research indicates that teachers should help create a community in which writers feel supported by the teachers, comfortable expressing their ideas and choosing their own topics about which to write, and excited and motivated to write (Graham et al., 2012; Troia, 2014). It is important that students believe their teacher (and peers) are interested in what they have to write and supportive of their writing, regardless of whether they write at a basic or conventional level of competency. Teachers are encouraged to participate in this community through stressing writing's importance as a means of communication and expression, writing along with the students, and sharing their writing with the class (Graham et al., 2012). Other methods of supporting the community may include offering personally meaningful writing activities, arranging peer writing structures, providing frequent and meaningful feedback, and providing accommodations for individual students (Graham et al., 2012; Troia, 2014).

Implementation for Writers With Complex Support Needs   Creating a supportive writing community may require adaptations for some individuals with complex support needs for different aspects of the writing process. In addition to the technology and organizers previously mentioned, Danielle's teacher also adapts her writing instruction in several ways: shorter lessons spread throughout the day, adapted writing tools (including technology, pencils with a pencil grip, and dry-erase boards and markers), access to pictures or an alphabet board while composing, and a visual schedule that explains the steps of the process (e.g., minilesson, pick a picture). Occasionally, Danielle's teacher or another adult in the room will serve as a scribe as Danielle dictates what she would like to write. Danielle then copies what the adult has written, using handwriting or typing. She is encouraged to "say more" as she writes.

It is important for all teachers to allow students the opportunity to write about self-selected topics (Graham et al., 2012), but this may be particularly important for students with complex support needs to help increase their motivation and the likelihood they will have sufficient background knowledge to write. For example, research with students with ASD indicates that students were able to provide more details in oral narratives when writing about their special interest areas (SIAs; Winter-Messiers, 2007); although this has yet to be explored in written narratives, it is possible that the use of SIAs may similarly improve the motivation and quality of written texts of individuals with ASD like Danielle. Teachers should still, at times, assign topics, because it is important for students to learn how to write in response to a prompt (Graham et al., 2012); however, when trying to build motivation and writing skills, it is helpful to use students' interests.

Finally, teachers can help create an engaged community and build writing fluency for students with complex support needs by using the language experience approach. (See Chapter 6 for an example of using this approach for reading instruction.) With this approach, teachers engage students in a discussion about a shared experience such as a class trip or read-aloud, and then ask all students to make a contribution, which is written down. As each student contributes, the teacher adds to the product, reading it as he or she goes, and finally having the students read it aloud together, if possible (Kluth & Chandler-Olcott, 2008). In Danielle's case, she is able to contribute to the story by either verbalizing or using her Proloquo2Go.

REFLECTION QUESTION 3

Is your classroom a community that fosters writing? Is so, how? If not, how can you make it so?

Practice 5: Help Increase Fluency in Writing

Students need to develop fluency with basic writing skills such as handwriting or typing and spelling. When students gain this fluency, they can focus on higher level writing skills, such as developing their ideas, without being impeded by lower level skills, such as transcription (Graham et al., 2012). Sentence-level skills, such as sentence-combining instruction (Saddler, 2012), could also be taught to help increase students' writing fluency (Troia, 2014).

Implementation for Writers With Complex Support Needs   Students with complex support needs may have significant difficulty with basic writing skills. Given the physical components involved in writing, including sensory processing, muscle tone, posture, and motor skills, these students may require increased attention to their use of the pencil or keyboard

(Wollak & Koppenhaver, 2011). Therefore, it is crucial to provide direct instruction in the appropriate way to hold a pencil or type on a word processor (Graham et al., 2012). Alternative pencils, word processors, on-screen keyboards, or iPads, as appropriate to the individual student, should also be used.

Many students with complex support needs also need support in spelling. Because their linguistic development is delayed (Sturm & Clendon, 2004), they often struggle to use complex and varied vocabulary in their writing. They also may be less likely to use words they cannot spell (Graham et al., 2012). As a result, teaching students high-frequency words and words related to their interests and daily lives is crucial. Danielle's teacher, for example, posts index cards of high-frequency words around the classroom, but she also keeps an individualized word wall inside each student's writing folder. Danielle occasionally still needs prompting to remember to go to her word wall, but she has increased her independence with this task and asks the teacher for help much less often than before. Spelling can also be supported using the technological supports mentioned previously, such as word prediction software and word banks.

As students develop more complex writing, teachers may focus on grammar, usage, and mechanics (e.g., punctuation). Troia (2014) recommends that these strategies be taught through natural authentic writing tasks rather than decontextualized practice such as worksheets. At the sentence level, several technology programs for both computers and iPads help students focus on sentence construction. Sentence frames can be used to teach sentence structure; they can start simply ("I want _____") and gradually become more complex ("I _____ to the _____ because _____"). In Danielle's case, the teacher has to present each sentence one at a time so that she is not overwhelmed by the amount of text.

Sentence structure can also be taught through sentence expanding (Graham et al., 2012). For example, the teacher might start with a basic subject–verb sentence, "The cat ran," and then add an adjective and/or an adverb ("The black cat ran quickly"). Danielle's teacher often provides two choices of words for this activity—for example, she might provide two index cards with the words *fat* and *fluffy,* so Danielle can select and write in the word she wants to use to describe the cat. Finally, instruction in sentence combining (Saddler, 2012) can be adapted for these learners' needs by having the words of the sentences written on index cards and allowing the students to physically add, delete, or move the words around to combine the sentences. Such practice can allow students to improve sentence variety and style (Troia, 2014).

Practice 6: Create Independent Writers

An important goal for teachers is to create writers who can set their own writing goals and work to achieve them without the need for continued support. This involves directly modeling and teaching writing strategies and skills for self-regulation (Troia & Olinghouse, 2013). Goal setting, for example, could include a goal to increase the number of words written or to write about a different topic. The self-regulation skill of self-monitoring could be taught through the use of a self-monitoring chart that includes a certain number of boxes per task. For example, if the students should include a *who, when,* and *what* in their stories, the chart would include three boxes for them to fill in as they include each element (Graham & Harris, 2005; see Figure 10.1 for an example).

One example of strategy instruction that includes self-regulation components is the SRSD approach to teaching writing (Graham & Harris, 2005). SRSD has been demonstrated to improve writing outcomes for a variety of students with and without disabilities (Graham & Perin, 2007). With SRSD, students are explicitly taught specific writing strategies and procedures for regulating these strategies and the writing process, such as goal setting, self-monitoring, and self-talk (Graham & Harris, 2009). SRSD instruction is criterion based rather than time based, meaning students move through the lessons at their own pace; the level of support is meant to be adjusted depending on the individual's needs (Graham & Harris, 2005). Therefore, SRSD can be used effectively with students with a variety of cognitive, academic, and linguistic characteristics.

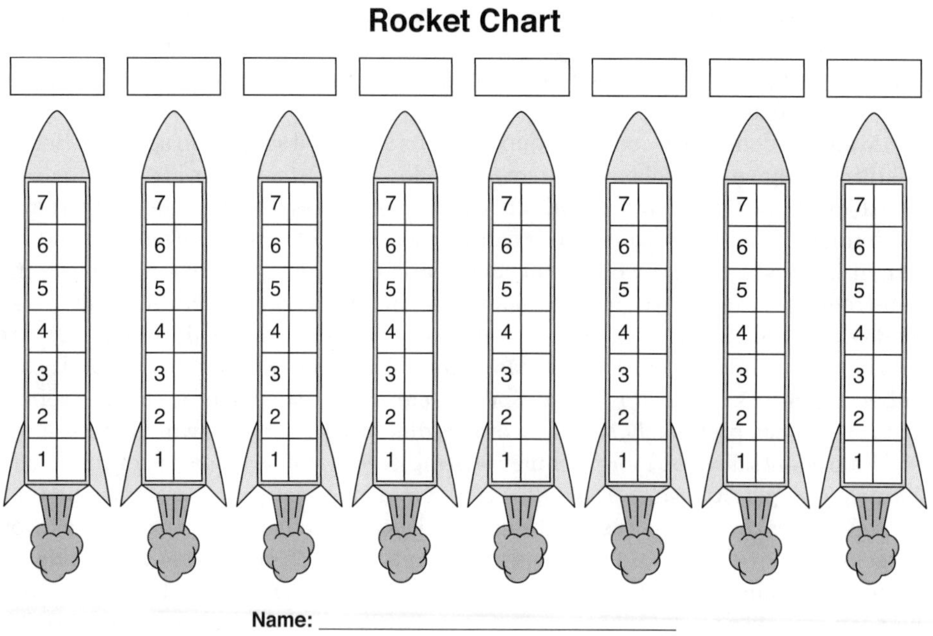

Rocket Chart

Name: _____

Figure 10.1. Self-monitoring rocket chart. (*Source:* Graham & Harris, 2005.)

Implementation for Writers With Complex Support Needs   As indicated previously, learning to write may be especially essential for students with disabilities to increase socialization and independence (Wollak & Koppenhaver, 2011) and allow them an avenue for self-expression. It is imperative for these students to gain independence so they are not reliant on adult support and can learn to advocate for themselves as they progress through school and reach adulthood (Westling et al., 2015). Teachers should provide direct instruction in self-regulation skills as appropriate to the students' individual strengths, needs, and interests. Danielle's teacher, for example, adapted a traditional self-monitoring rocket chart, using a chart that included an ice cream cone with five scoops for each of the five parts of a story she should include (*who, where, when, what* happened, and *how* the character felt). As Danielle completed each of the five steps of the task, Danielle was able to color each scoop a different color to represent her favorite flavors.

Another recommended practice, the use of technology, can also help create independent writers. For example, software programs such as First Author, word prediction, spelling check, and grammar check can help students draft and revise independently, without having to wait for a teacher or another adult to help them (Asaro-Saddler et al., 2015). When Danielle wanted to write about Disney's *Frozen,* for example, she could easily access words such as *queen, Elsa,* and *snowman,* so she did not have to ask how to spell them. When she finished her story, the text-to-speech function on First Author allowed her to share her work with her classmates and therapists without having to read the text orally, allowing her to fully participate in the literacy lesson.

ASSESSING THE WRITING OF WRITERS WITH COMPLEX SUPPORT NEEDS

The assessment of writing is important for teachers in determining whether students with complex support needs are responding to the teachers' instructional practices. Assessment could occur at the letter, word, sentence, paragraph, or text level (Olinghouse & Santangelo, 2010), depending on the student's writing ability and goals. Overall quality of an entire text or a paragraph can be scored using a rubric; rubrics can be based on holistic quality (the assessor's overall impression of the writing) or primary traits (a number of specific dimensions including ideas, organization, voice, word choice, sentence fluency, and conventions) (Olinghouse & Santangelo, 2010; Saddler & Asaro-Saddler, 2013). Teachers can use published rubrics or create their own; web sites such as Rubistar or Teachnology allow teachers to create rubrics based on the criteria they deem important. (See the Resources section at the end of this chapter for links to these web sites.) Holistic quality and primary trait rubrics may be less valuable, however, for beginning writers because the brevity of their texts may make validity a concern (McMaster & Espin, 2007). In other words, the assessment may not measure what it is intended to measure because the quantity of writing is not sufficient for determining quality.

Curriculum-based measurements (CBM; Deno, 1985) are frequently used with students both with and without disabilities to assess writing at the sentence, word, or letter level. CBM involves frequent administration of 3- to 5-minute probes, typically with students writing in response to a picture or story prompt (McMaster et al., 2011). Using CBM, writing may be assessed by measuring the number of words spelled correctly, correct letter sequences, and correct word sequences (i.e., two adjacent words that are correctly spelled, capitalized, and punctuated and that are grammatically and semantically acceptable) (McMaster et al., 2011; Saddler & Asaro-Saddler, 2013). Writing quantity may be assessed by counting the total number of words or letters written. Many of these measures may be more appropriate with students with complex support needs who have become sophisticated writers, but less so for beginning writers.

One difficulty with using typical assessment measures with beginning writers is that many of these tools are not sensitive enough to detect small changes in writing (Sturm et al., 2012). To address this challenge, Sturm and colleagues (2012) created a measure, called the Developmental Writing Scale, to be used specifically with beginning writers with and without complex support needs. This scale, developed to identify qualitative progression of beginning students' writing skills, includes 14 levels ranging from the lowest quality of writing (scribbles) to highest (well-organized samples with one coherent idea). It may be helpful for teachers because it can provide more information about students' conceptual understanding of complex writing skills than could an assessment such as words spelled correctly (Sturm et al., 2012). Other measures that may be useful for beginning writers with complex support needs are topic diversity (i.e., not repeatedly choosing the same topic about which to write) and text type diversity (i.e., writing using a variety of genres). Regarding quantity for students with complex support needs, the number of letters written, the number of intelligible words written (meaning those that could be understood by a reader), or the number of unique words (to measure vocabulary diversity) may be more helpful measures than the total number of words (Sturm, 2012).

REFLECTION QUESTION 4

Given the strengths, challenges, and needs of your particular students with complex support needs, how can you best support them in the writing process?

SUMMARY

Writing is a crucial skill to develop for many reasons; for students with complex support needs in particular, writing can be a means of expression, socialization, and independence. Communicating through writing is a complex, recursive process involving planning, composing, revising, editing, and sharing one's work. Learning to write well poses challenges for many students; students with complex support needs often face particular challenges such as limits in language abilities, motor abilities, and social understanding; limited life experience or lack of adequate instruction may also hold them back as writers. Use of research-based practice, perhaps with modifications, can help students with complex support needs develop into sophisticated writers.

Teachers and practitioners should familiarize themselves with the research base in writing instruction. They can use the evidence-based practices described in this chapter to design instruction targeted toward the Common Core State Standards to create an environment that fosters excited, engaged, and confident writers.

RESOURCES

The following technology programs can provide valuable supports for students with complex support needs:

- **Co:Writer Universal** (http://donjohnston.com/cowriter) is a grammar-smart word prediction software program with topic-specific dictionaries, spelling and grammar support, and built-in text-to-speech features.

- **FirstAuthor** (http://donjohnston.com/firstauthorsoftware) guides students through a three-step writing process of choosing a topic, selecting a picture prompt, and writing with the support of built-in accommodations such as word banks, on-screen keyboards, and self-regulation prompts.

- **Clicker** (http://www.cricksoft.com/us/products/clicker/home.aspx) provides supports such as a Clicker Board built-in planning tool for pictures and words, an on-screen keyboard, and text-to-speech software. It also works with eye-gaze systems and switches, and it is touchscreen friendly.

- **Dragon NaturallySpeaking** (http://www.nuance.com/for-individuals/by-product/dragon-for-pc/home-version/index.htm) is a speech-to-text software program that allows students to speak into a microphone and have their words typed into a word-processing program.

- **Write:OutLoud** (http://donjohnston.com/writeoutloud) is a text-to-speech software program that allows students to type into a word-processing program and have their words read aloud.

- **The SnapType** app (http://www.snaptypeapp.com) allows students to take a picture or import a worksheet from e-mail, photo library, or Google Drive and type or draw directly on the worksheet.

- **Inspiration** (http://www.inspiration.com/Inspiration) and **Kidspiration** (http://www.inspiration.com/Kidspiration) are outlining, brainstorming, and organizing tools that can be used to create graphic organizers.

These sites allow teachers to create rubrics based on the criteria they deem important:

- Rubistar (http://rubistar.4teachers.org/index.php)

- Teachnology (http://www.teach-nology.com/web_tools/rubrics/writing/)

REFERENCES

Asaro-Saddler, K. (2014). Self-regulated strategy development: Effects on writers with autism spectrum disorders. *Education and Training in Autism and Developmental Disabilities, 49,* 78–91.

Asaro-Saddler, K., & Bak, N. (2014). Persuasive writing and self-regulation training: Pairing writers with autism spectrum disorder. *Journal of Special Education, 48,* 92–105.

Asaro-Saddler, K., Muir-Knox, H., Meredith, H., & Akhmedjanova, D. (2015). Using technology to support students with autism spectrum disorders in the writing process. *Insights on Learning Disabilities, 12,* 103–119.

Bereiter, C., & Scardamalia, M. (1987). *The psychology of written composition.* Hillsdale, NJ: Lawrence Erlbaum.

Bondy, A.S., & Frost, L.A. (1994). The Picture Exchange Communication System. *Focus on Autism and Other Developmental Disabilities, 9*(3), 1–19. doi:10.1177/108835769400900301

Boscolo, P., Gelati, C., & Galvan, N. (2012). Teaching elementary school students to play with meanings and genre. *Reading and Writing Quarterly, 28,* 29–50.

Boucher, C., & Oehler, K. (2013). *I hate to write! Tips for helping students with autism spectrum and related disorders increase achievement, meet academic standards, and become happy, successful writers.* Lenexa, KS: AAPC Publishing.

Carnahan, C., Williamson, P., Hollingshead, A., & Israel, M. (2012). Using technology to support balanced literacy for students with significant disabilities. *TEACHING Exceptional Children, 45,* 20–29.

Common Core State Standards Initiative. (2014). *Key shifts in English language arts.* Retrieved from http://www.corestandards.org/other-resources/key-shifts-in-english-language-arts/

Deno, S.L. (1985). Curriculum-based measurement: The emerging alternative. *Exceptional Children, 52,* 219–232.

Dockrell, J.E., Lindsay, G., & Connelly, V. (2009). The impact of specific language impairment on adolescents' written text. *Exceptional Children, 75,* 427–446.

Dray, A.J., Selman, R.L., & Schultz, L.H. (2009). Communicating with intent: A study of social awareness and children's writing. *Journal of Applied Developmental Psychology, 30,* 116–128.

Flower, L.S., & Hayes, J.R. (1980). The cognition of discovery: Defining a rhetorical problem. *College Compositions and Communication, 31,* 21–32.

Flower, L.S., & Hayes, J.R. (1987). A cognitive process theory of writing. *College Compositions and Communication, 33,* 365–387.

Fromkin, V., & Rodman, R. (1998). *An introduction to language* (6th ed.). Orlando, FL: Harcourt Brace College Publishers.

Graham, S., Bollinger, A., Booth Olson, C., D'Aoust, C., MacArthur, C., McCutchen, D., & Olinghouse, N. (2012). *Teaching elementary school students to be effective writers: A practice guide* (NCEE 2012-4058). Washington, DC: National Center for Education Evaluation and Regional Assistance, Institute of Education Sciences, U.S. Department of Education. Retrieved from http://ies.ed.gov/ncee/wwc/publications_reviews.aspx#pubsearch

Graham. S., & Harris, K.R. (2003). Students with learning disabilities and the process of writing: A meta-analysis of SRSD studies. In L. Swanson, K.R. Harris, & S. Graham (Eds.), *Handbook of research on learning disabilities* (pp. 383–402). New York, NY: Guilford.

Graham, S., & Harris, K.R. (2005). *Writing better: Effective strategies for teaching students with learning difficulties.* Baltimore, MD: Paul H. Brookes Publishing Co.

Graham, S., & Harris, K.R. (2009). Almost 30 years of writing research: Making sense of it all with "The Wrath of Khan." *Learning Disabilities Research & Practice, 24,* 58–68.

Graham, S., & Perin, D. (2007). *Writing next: Effective strategies to improve writing of adolescents in middle and high schools—A report to Carnegie Corporation of New York.* Washington, DC: Alliance for Excellent Education.

Graves, D. (1983). *Writing: Teachers and children at work.* Exeter, NH: Heinemann Educational Books.

Hayes, J.R., & Flower, L.S. (1986). Writing research and the writer. *American Psychologist, 41,* 1106–1113.

Hillock, J. (2011). Written expression: Why is it difficult and what can be done? In K. McCoy (Ed.), *Autism from the teacher's perspective* (pp. 321–354). Denver, CO: Love Publishing.

Joseph, L.M., & Konrad, M. (2009). Teaching students with intellectual or developmental disabilities to write: A review of the literature. *Research in Developmental Disabilities, 30,* 1–19.

Kagohara, D.M., Sigafoos, J., Achmadi, D., O'Reilly, M., & Lancioni, G. (2012). Teaching children with autism spectrum disorders to check the spelling of words. *Research in Autism Spectrum Disorders, 6,* 304–310.

Keefe, E.B., & Copeland, S.R. (2011). What is literacy? The power of a definition. *Research and Practice for Persons with Severe Disabilities, 36,* 92–99.

King, S. (2000). *On writing: A memoir of the craft.* New York, NY: Scribner.

Kluth, P., & Chandler-Olcott, K. (2008). *A land we can share.* Baltimore, MD: Paul H. Brookes Publishing Co.

Konrad, M., Trela, K., & Test, D.W. (2006). Using IEP goals and objectives to teach paragraph writing to high school students with physical and cognitive disabilities. *Education and Training in Developmental Disabilities, 41,* 111–124.

Lewis, B.A., O'Donnell, B., Freebairn, L.A., & Taylor, H.G. (1998). Spoken language and written expression: Interplay of delays. *American Journal of Speech Language Pathology, 7,* 77–84.

Martin, B, Jr., & Carle, E. (1996). *Brown bear, brown bear, what do you see?* New York, NY: Henry Holt.

McMaster, K.L., Du, X., Yeo, S., Deno, S.L., Parker, D., & Ellis, T. (2011). Curriculum-based measures of beginning writing: Technical features of the slope. *Exceptional Children, 77,* 185–206.

McMaster, K., & Espin, C. (2007). Technical features of curriculum-based measurement in writing: A literature review. *Journal of Special Education, 41,* 68–84.

Moore, D.W., Anderson, A., Treccase, F., Deppeler, J., Furlonger, B., & Didden, R. (2013). A video-based package to teach a child with autism spectrum disorder to write her name. *Journal of Developmental and Physical Disabilities, 25,* 493–503.

Olinghouse, N.G., & Santangelo, T. (2010). Assessing the writing of struggling learners. *Focus on Exceptional Children, 43,* 1–27.

Pennington, R.C., Collins, B.C., Stenhoff, D.M., Turner, K., & Gunselman, K. (2014). Using simultaneous prompting to teach generative writing to students with autism. *Education and Training in Autism and Developmental Disabilities, 49,* 396–414.

Pennington, R.C., & Delano, M.D. (2012). Writing instruction for students with autism spectrum disorders: A review of literature. *Focus on Autism and Developmental Disabilities, 27,* 158–167.

Pennington, R.C., Delano, M., & Scott, R. (2014). An intervention for improving resume writing skills of students with intellectual disability. *Journal of Applied Behavior Analysis, 47,* 1–5.

Pennington, R.C., Saadatzi, M., Welch, K.C., & Scott, R. (2014). An investigation of robot delivered instruction to teach texting to students with intellectual disability. *Journal of Special Education Technology, 29,* 49–58.

Purrazzella, K., & Mechling, L.C. (2013). Evaluation of manual spelling, observational and incidental learning using computer-based instruction with a tablet PC, large screen projection, and a forward chaining procedure. *Education and Training in Autism and Developmental Disabilities, 48,* 218–235.

Reichle, J. (2011). Evaluating assistive technology in the education of persons with severe disabilities. *Journal of Behavioral Education, 20,* 77–85.

Reid, R., Mason, L., & Asaro-Saddler, K. (2013). Self-regulation strategies for students with autism spectrum disorder. In S. Goldstein & J. Naglieri (Eds.), *Interventions for autism spectrum disorders* (pp. 257–282). New York, NY: Springer.

Robison, J.E. (2014). Foreword. In K. Boser, M. Goodwin, & S. Wayland (Eds.), *Technology tools for students with autism* (pp. xxiii–xxvi). Baltimore, MD: Paul H. Brookes Publishing Co.

Ruppar, A.L. (2015). A preliminary study of the literacy experiences of adolescents with severe disabilities. *Remedial and Special Education, 36,* 235–245.

Saddler, B. (2003). "But teacher, I added a period!" Improving the revising ability of middle school students. *Voices from the Middle, 11,* 20–26.

Saddler, B. (2012). *Teacher's guide to effective sentence writing.* New York, NY: Guilford.

Saddler, B., & Asaro-Saddler, K. (2013). Response to intervention in writing: A suggested framework for screening, intervention, and progress monitoring. *Reading and Writing Quarterly, 29*(1), 20–43.

Schneider, A.B., Codding, R.S., & Tryon, G.S. (2013). Comparing and combining accommodation and remediation interventions to improve the written language performance of children with Asperger syndrome. *Focus on Autism and Other Developmental Disabilities, 28,* 101–114.

Sturm, J.M. (2012). An enriched writers' workshop for beginning writers with developmental disabilities. *Topics in Language Disorders, 32,* 335–360.

Sturm, J.M., Cali, K., Nelson, N.W., & Staskowski, M. (2012). The developmental writing scale: A new progress monitoring tool for beginning writers. *Topics in Language Disorders, 32,* 297–318.

Sturm, J.M., & Clendon, S.A. (2004). Augmentative and alternative communication, language, and literacy: Fostering the relationship. *Topics in Language Disorders, 24,* 76–91.

Sturm, J.M., & Knack, L. (2011, November). *First Author: A writing software tool for students with developmental disabilities.* Poster session presented at the American Speech-Language-Hearing Convention, San Diego, CA.

Sturm, J.M., & Koppenhaver, D.A. (2000). Supporting writing development in adolescents with developmental disabilities. *Topics in Language Disorders, 20,* 73–92.

Troia, G.A. (2014). *Evidence-based practices for writing instruction* (Document No. IC-5). University of Florida, Collaboration for Effective Educator Development, Accountability, and Reform Center. Retrieved from http://ceedar.education.ufl.edu/tools/innovation-configuration/

Troia, G.A., & Olinghouse, N.G. (2013). The Common Core State Standards and evidence-based educational practices: The case of writing. *School Psychology Review, 42,* 343–357.

Westling, D.L., Fox, L.L., & Carter, E.W. (2015). *Teaching students with severe disabilities* (5th ed.). Upper Saddle River, NJ: Prentice Hall.

Wilson, S. (2010). *Students with deafblindness: Literacy development for learners. Modules Addressing Special Education and Teacher Education (MAST).* Greenville, NC: East Carolina University. Available from http://mast.ecu.edu/modules/sb_1

Winter-Messiers, M.A. (2007). From tarantulas to toilet brushes: Understanding the special interest areas of children and youth with Asperger syndrome. *Remedial and Special Education, 28,* 140–152.

Wollak, B.A., & Koppenhaver, D.A. (2011). Developing technology-supported, evidence-based writing instruction for adolescents with significant writing disabilities. *Assistive Technology Outcomes and Benefits, 7,* 1–23.

Wong, C., Odom, S.L., Hume, K.A., Cox, C.W., Fettig, A., Kucharczyk, S., …, Schultz, T.R. (2015). Evidence-based practices for children, youth, and young adults with autism spectrum disorder: A comprehensive review. *Journal of Autism and Developmental Disorders, 45,* 1951–1966.

Woods-Groves, S., Hua, Y., Therrien, W.J., Kaldenberg, E.R., Hendrickson, J.M., Lucas, K.G., & McAninch, M.J. (2014). An investigation of strategic writing instruction for post-secondary students with developmental disabilities. *Education and Training in Autism and Developmental Disabilities, 49,* 248–262.

Zelinsky, P. O. (1990). *The wheels on the bus.* New York, NY: Dutton.

CHAPTER 11

Organizing Effective Literacy Instruction

A Framework for Planning

Megan H. Foster, Jessica Apgar McCord, and Elizabeth B. Keefe

LEARNING OBJECTIVES

1. Understand how to apply the principles of universal design for learning (UDL) to differentiate literacy instruction.
2. Understand how to organize routines and structures that promote access to robust literacy instruction.
3. Understand how to use authentic literature to plan for grade-level, standards-aligned instruction that promotes achievement for all students.

This chapter will focus on how to conceptualize and organize appropriate literacy instruction for all students that is differentiated and founded on the principles of universal design. As noted by Taub, McCord, and Burdge in Chapter 4, students with complex support needs are capable of mastering literacy skills if they are given appropriate and challenging opportunities to learn. For students to have opportunities to learn the core curriculum, teachers must know and use standards to plan and implement instruction. This chapter will address two major challenges. The first challenge is to break away from a hierarchical approach to literacy instruction while still addressing individualized education goals and objectives. The second challenge is to avoid retrofitting existing curriculum and lesson plans (Udvari-Solner, Villa, & Thousand, 2002) and instead find ways to plan for all students from the beginning of the planning process.

READY TO LEARN: Max

Max is a 12-year-old student with cerebral palsy and an intellectual disability. He is very friendly and hard working. He uses a power wheelchair for mobility, and he uses an iPad as his primary means of communication. He has limited use of his left arm and no use of his right.

Max is in an inclusive seventh-grade class with an educational assistant to help support him. He enjoys being at school and works well with his peers. This year, the middle school that Max attends implemented a peer supports program, pairing Max up with a same-age peer. The two attend classes together, and Max receives support from his peer rather than his aide. This program has increased Max's self-confidence and helped him become more involved in his classes. Without the aide next to him, Max has become more social, and his classmates report feeling more comfortable socializing with him.

Max is working on increasing his ability to identify and read sight words. He is currently able to read approximately 15 sight words, and his goal is to increase this number to 50. Max is also able to answer *who, what, where, when,* and *why* questions if a text is read aloud to him. He is working on increasing his comprehension skills to be able to answer higher level questions. When he writes, he can write one or two short sentences at a time, usually about three to four words each. Max is working on increasing the number and length of sentences he can write in one sitting.

As noted previously, Max enjoys being around his peers. He is respectful of his classmates and is a good listener. However, he rarely initiates conversation or responds to questions unless they are directed at him in one-on-one situations with peers or with the teacher. He is working with a speech-language pathologist twice per week to increase his expressive language skills.

MAXIMIZING OPPORTUNITIES TO LEARN

What kinds of opportunities to learn does a student like Max have, and how can a good teacher maximize these opportunities? The opportunities all students have to learn are directly impacted by the relationships among the adopted state standards, the way teachers interpret those standards to plan instruction, and the way this planning is implemented in the classroom. When these elements are aligned, students have the greatest opportunity to learn the core curriculum. To achieve this alignment, teachers must know and understand the literacy standards in which all students are expected to demonstrate progress for their grade level, as discussed in Chapter 4. Teachers then must interpret the standards to create learning goals and objectives that lead to the mastery of those standards. The Individuals with Disabilities Education Improvement Act (IDEA) of 2004 (PL 108-446) requires that all students be provided access to grade-level curriculum, and the new federal Every Student Succeeds Act (ESSA) of 2015 (S.1177) mandates the use of UDL for *all* students. To meet these requirements, all students must be provided accessible opportunities to learn standards-aligned content, and students with disabilities must also have individualized education programs (IEPs) that include goals and objectives aligned to grade-level standards.

A RATIONALE FOR UNIVERSALLY DESIGNED DIFFERENTIATED INSTRUCTION

To increase accessibility for all students, including those with complex support needs, teachers should organize their classrooms and plan instruction using the principles of UDL that were introduced in Chapter 4 and discussed in depth in Chapter 5. The application of UDL requires a shift in thinking. Educators often have the misconception that students or their abilities present barriers to learning, but teaching through the lens of UDL means that we instead evaluate barriers that are present within the curriculum, instruction, and materials and make adjustments to address those barriers so all students can learn. As discussed in Chapters 4 and 5, principles of UDL include embedding opportunities for multiple means of representation, engagement, and expression to meet the needs of a wide variety of students (CAST, 2011). This ensures that all students have an opportunity to meaningfully interact with the lesson, which can reduce the need for additional accommodations.

Incorporating the principles of UDL in classroom organization and instructional planning supports effective differentiated instruction. You have likely heard this term during the course of your training as an educator but may wonder exactly what it means. Differentiated instruction is a responsive approach to teaching that recognizes and respects the varying ways students interact with, and demonstrate knowledge of, the learning goals. Teachers provide scaffolding—supports that reduce the amount of information students need to hold in short-term memory while completing tasks—and other supports to address students' individual strengths and challenges. This differentiation occurs at three levels: content, process, and product (Tomlinson, 2001). Differentiating by content refers to offering options to access topics and materials according to student readiness, interest, or learning profile. This can be done through the purposeful selection of topics and materials that are interesting, engaging, and connect appropriately to the background knowledge and prior experiences students have had with the content you are teaching. Differentiating by process means providing multiple avenues for students to understand and master the content. This might include using both visual representations and verbal explanations of topics and skills in a lesson. Finally, differentiating by product ensures that students are provided with many ways to demonstrate their knowledge; for example, students often benefit from having a choice between traditional written responses and a verbal or visual presentation of their learning. Although differentiated instruction is not the same as UDL, because UDL considers how to create instruction that is accessible for all learners from the beginning, the UDL principles of multiple means of representation, action and expression, and engagement support the development of instruction that is differentiated to meet the individual needs of your students. In this chapter, we will focus on how to apply UDL to differentiate literacy instruction for all learners, including those with complex support needs. We refer to this as universally designed differentiated instruction (UD-DI). The application of UDL principles gives differentiated instruction limitless potential for ensuring that all students have high-quality opportunities to learn.

Although accessibility is a key component of ensuring that students with complex support needs are afforded opportunities to make progress in the general curriculum as required by IDEA 2004, teachers are often not prepared to provide accessible instruction. When we conducted an informal review of several methods textbooks that are currently used to prepare preservice teachers to deliver literacy instruction, we noted sections or chapters dedicated to organizing for instruction that tended to focus solely on traditional lesson planning without attention to differentiated instruction. When differentiation was included, attention was typically given only to flexible grouping and choice. These textbooks did not often include a focus on UDL and devoted little attention to the needs of learners with complex support needs. Yet, teachers responsible for literacy instruction must be prepared to meet the needs of all learners, regardless of disability or diversity of need.

When teachers are not prepared to meet the needs of this population of students, they often turn to the use of prepackaged curricula written specifically for students with complex support needs. These separate curricula often claim to be aligned to state standards or the Common Core State Standards (CCSS). In fact, preliminary findings from an alignment study of several curricula for this student population indicate that these curricula are poorly aligned to academic standards (Taub, McCord, Foster, & Ruppar, 2015). In addition, the use of these prepackaged curricula further limits opportunities to learn for students with complex support needs by requiring the teacher to pull them out of instruction in general education classrooms where instruction is more likely to be aligned to academic standards. To ensure that students have rich literacy learning opportunities, teachers must instead rely on their own professional knowledge and skills to plan and implement UD-DI.

By the end of this chapter, you should have a clear understanding of how to implement universally designed routines in your classroom that will facilitate differentiated instruction using authentic, high-quality literature. First, we discuss specific routines grounded in the principles of UDL to set the stage for incorporating these elements into planning for and implementing differentiated instruction. We call this UD-DI. The foundation of this concept is described in greater detail in Chapter 1.

PLANNING FOR INSTRUCTION: SETTING EXPECTATIONS

How teachers organize their classroom environment and enact instructional routines has an impact on how well their plans are translated into learning experiences that foster students' achievement within the core curriculum. Chapter 5 addressed organization of the physical classroom environment in depth, focusing on the best ways to create a rich, engaging literacy environment that is well organized and that makes the learning content accessible to all students. Here, we discuss considerations for the classroom's social climate and expectations. The section that follows will address classroom routines, emphasizing routines that apply UDL principles within the constructs of differentiated instruction (content, process, product) to support planning and, ultimately, support the implementation of UD-DI to maximize students' opportunities to learn the general education curriculum.

One of the most important ways teachers can plan for accessible literacy experiences is to consider in advance what expectations they will set and how they will create a welcoming and supportive classroom climate. Students thrive in an environment where they know exactly what is expected; this is especially true for students with complex support needs.

An excellent way to set the stage for accessible learning experiences is to establish class norms or rules (Marzano, Gaddy, & Foseid, 2006). We suggest beginning with four to five broad rules that will serve as a framework to lead a class discussion. Examples include *Be respectful, Be prepared, Be on time,* and *Be responsible,* but you can use any general rules or norms you would like. Keep in mind, studies indicate that keeping the number of rules to a maximum of five increases students' "buy-in" and teachers' ability to enforce the expectations.

Once you have introduced this general set of rules, you can lead a discussion with your students about what the rules mean to them and what they look like in action. Our sample rules would serve as the basis for a conversation about what specific actions demonstrate respect, preparedness, and responsibility. You will undoubtedly be surprised at the depth of the thoughts your students will share. Recently, in a conversation with students about what it means to be respectful in class, students decided that in their learning environment, they expected others to demonstrate open-minded behaviors. Further discussion about what that looks like revealed different perspectives but allowed us to come up with a set of guidelines about our common expectations, which included eye contact when speaking, asking clarifying questions, and not interrupting. This method ensures two things: that students' needs are valued as they contribute to defining expectations and that they have a clear understanding of the expectations in your classroom. To capture students' thoughts and ideas, it is important to document this collaborative conversation. The end-product of this documentation might serve as a "contract" posted in the room, with student and teacher signatures. For students in middle or high school who might have multiple teachers in multiple classrooms, this collaborative generation of rules and norms can easily be recorded on notebook paper or on a word processor, with signed copies placed in a binder or notebook. The signed agreement then represents a commitment from all members of the classroom to common expectations; it can be easily referenced throughout the year.

During the discussion to generate these rules, teachers should also incorporate conversation about consequences. Consequences for some behaviors, such as fighting or tardiness, might exist as unalterable school policies. For other infractions, you can enlist student support for the consequences you establish. For example, your class might decide that part of being responsible is turning in homework on time. You might elicit student feedback about what they think is a reasonable consequence for not following this rule. Students might suggest multiple options for the consequence, such as staying in for recess or an extra class period, or turning in their homework the next day and having points deducted from their grade. However you decide to discuss consequences, it is an essential conversation. All students do better when they know what is expected and what will happen if they do not meet these expectations.

Once classroom rules and norms have been agreed on, the teacher must ensure that they are applied fairly and consistently in all interactions between the teacher and students and between students and their peers. A set of classroom expectations, developed through collaborative, respectful discussion and implemented supportively throughout the year, is an important aspect of a productive, accessible learning climate. In this kind of classroom, students can take risks, and literacy learning and progress can occur. Once these general classroom norms are established, more specific classroom routines can be used to support UD-DI.

REFLECTION QUESTION 1

Think about and list four to five rules or norms you might use to facilitate a collaborative discussion with your students.

ROUTINES THAT SUPPORT UNIVERSALLY DESIGNED DIFFERENTIATED INSTRUCTION

Chapter 5 of this book addressed how UDL provides a useful, proactive structure that will help you remove barriers to learning for all your students. In Chapter 11, we have also touched upon how differentiating instruction ensures that you are meeting your students' needs in the literacy learning opportunities that you provide. In addition, routines you establish as a teacher are an essential component of an accessible classroom learning experience. Together, these concepts add up to UD-DI that results in robust instruction for all students.

This chapter focuses on essential routines that should be consistently embedded within the classroom environment and culture and therefore need to be considered in all planning. Most students, including students with complex support needs, benefit from predictable routines and structures that facilitate smooth transitions before, during, and after learning activities. These routines represent what students should expect from learning experiences in your classroom: know your students; teach them about choice; plan for accessibility; provide explicit, highly scaffolded instruction and modeling; understand the importance of background knowledge; engage learners as they process new information; and always remember that communication is key. Let's take a closer look at how you can establish these routines for yourself as an educator.

Know Your Students

The UDL principle of multiple means of engagement supports differentiating both the content of instruction and the processes used to teach concepts and skills. Recall that to provide multiple means of engagement means to capture student interest, preference, and background knowledge. To effectively engage students, you must get to know them, because students should understand that their interests, needs, and preferences are valued as an integral part of their learning. Although it is important to get to know your students at the beginning of a school year through more formal means, such as interviews or surveys, you should also be an intentional observer throughout the year to ensure that you know and respect your students' dynamic and ever-changing preferences and needs. Let's talk about how to get to know your students and how this helps you plan for instruction.

Many resources are available to give you ideas about the kinds of questions you might ask your students to learn about their particular interests, passions, and preferences—including information about multiple intelligences and learning styles. (See the links provided in the Resources section at the end of this chapter.) Although the resources could be printed out and delivered to students in a paper-and-pencil format, there are also many universally designed options for using them with your class. For example, you could have students interview each other with questions that they construct or that you provide. You could list questions in an electronic format, such as a Word document or PowerPoint presentation, so students can use the computer's text-to-speech option to dictate or record responses. Alternatively, you can program questions into students' communication devices for them to ask their peers, and ensure they have vocabulary programmed into the device so they are also able to respond to interview questions about what they like as well.

When collected early on, this information not only builds community but also gives important insight into what kinds of literature might grab student interest. In addition, it tells the teacher what kinds of materials should be available for both reading and writing projects, and it can also inform teachers about what topics and themes they should choose for units and lessons with high-quality literature (as described later in this chapter). Throughout the year, it is important to be keenly observant of student levels of engagement and aware of their changing interests and to take informal surveys after particular lessons or units to continue gathering information to inform planning.

Teach Students About Choice

Options and choice are central features of UD-DI. Although UDL is about providing a multitude of options to ensure accessibility of the curriculum, differentiating provides scaffolding and supports that serve as multiple pathways to the same learning goals. To maximize the benefit of the options you will provide, you must explicitly teach students how to make good choices about which options work best for them. It is important to remember that not all students will have prior experience making choices in their learning environment. For younger students, embed routines that explicitly teach about choice making and that scaffold this teaching through specific activities that allow you to model thinking processes that guide the selection of a particular choice over another. One example might be teaching students what questions to ask themselves when deciding to work independently, with a partner, or with a small group. Although additional scaffolding is necessary for younger students, provide structures and expectations for older students as well.

Students should have multiple options for learning activities, materials, topics or content, tools and supports, and ways to use their time. Every lesson should include multiple ways of representing the content—meaning multiple ways for students to receive and interact with information—as well as multiple ways of engaging students. These various representations serve two purposes: (a) to ensure that students have an opportunity to interact with the content in multiple ways; and (b) to clearly explain and model different approaches to the content, which can then can be provided as options when students engage in guided or independent practice.

For example, suppose that you intend to teach students to identify the ways powerful language in a text creates imagery for the reader. In your presentation of the concept and subsequent modeling of how to perform this skill, you might think aloud as you identify and respond to a powerful word or phrase in the text, and then show students how you would transfer your thoughts to a journal entry about the imagery it evoked for you. You could then also show students how you would transfer your thoughts by drawing of these image(s), or how you could choose pictures from magazines, web sites, and so forth to create a collage depicting the imagery you communicated in your think-aloud. By modeling the transfer of your thoughts to different modalities, you provide students with multiple opportunities to interact with the learning objective and with different ways of understanding the concept of imagery. You also model universally designed options they can choose from during guided or independent practice.

Finally, it is important to provide opportunities for students to make choices with your support and scaffolding. Giving them responsive feedback helps them take ownership of their own learning and choices, which ultimately builds problem-solving and critical-thinking skills and self-determination.

Plan for Accessibility

How will you support students to help them access the content and learning experiences you present in the classroom? It is important to consider how the application of multiple means of representation, engagement, and expression provide guidance for routines that should be in place to ensure accessible opportunities to learn from the start. This includes considering low- and high-tech supports. (See Chapters 5 and 12 for more on this topic.)

Among students with complex support needs, many students use augmentative and alternative communication (AAC) devices to communicate; many others are in the presymbolic or emerging phase of developing communication skills. (See Chapter 2 for an in-depth analysis of language and communication development.) Recall that communicating through language involves both producing it (expressive language) and comprehending it (receptive language); Students might have difficulty with either or both of these, which will require multimodal supports to make sure instruction is accessible. Regardless of communication style or level, all students must have a way to actively engage in learning. Let's look at a few ways that you can address these needs to benefit the diverse learners in your classroom.

When planning literacy lessons, it is essential to think about what digital materials and interfaces are available. Gaining access to electronic versions of texts, as discussed in Chapter 5, is something to consider for every text you use because it will reduce barriers for many students for whom traditional printed text is inaccessible. For example, if a student with low vision has difficulty tracking text on a page, providing electronic text would create options such as enlarging the text or using a text-to-speech function. Incredibly useful for students who have complex support needs, electronic texts also provide improved functionality for any student—for example, the ability to highlight text, to type notes, or to select a word to see its definition instantly.

Another means of enhancing accessibility is to consider ways that students can interact with texts and materials through touch or movement. As discussed in Chapter 5, multimodal approaches to learning create more links within the mental information schemes a student has for a given concept, and they also provide a range of ways students with varying needs can access the content. Thus, teachers should consider how to embed kinesthetic activities and tactile materials into literacy instruction whenever possible. For example, students might benefit from manipulating raised letters to construct words, or from using the feel of particular textured materials to understand the associated meaning of powerful words in a text (e.g., using sandpaper as a representation of the word *scuffle*). Teachers can be very creative when including these types of materials and activities in lessons. If students know they can expect tactile and kinesthetic materials and activities in your classroom, they may themselves offer a surprising number of suggestions about other materials to use and other tactile ways to adapt or enhance text. Chapter 12 describes many more ideas you can use to adapt a variety of texts for students with complex support needs.

It is also important to consider the physical actions involved in students' interactions with content and materials and to provide options whenever possible. For example, if you provide an e-book for a student, how will the student best interact with that electronic text? Can the student click a mouse, or is an alternative such as a touchpad needed? Does the student need a large screen like the one on a desktop computer for magnification, or would the student benefit most from a touchscreen like a tablet? Does your student use a switch (a device that can be preprogrammed with responses), necessitating that the electronic book be uploaded in a way that allows for using the switch to navigate the text by turning pages, highlighting, or dictating notes? When you do hands-on activities that require students to manipulate materials—for example, completing word sorts or creating posters—do you ensure that these activities are accessible for all of your students by checking that you have provided enough time and set appropriate expectations for physical movement? These are important questions to ask when considering the physical demands required of your lessons.

Support, Scaffold, and Be Explicit

All students, but especially those with complex support needs, benefit from multiple opportunities to interact with new information. Be prepared to clarify, support, scaffold, and provide multimodal demonstrations to help students understand a concept or text. Vocabulary and key terms should always be clarified and explicitly taught. To ensure that you are prepared to provide needed support, preview authentic texts prior to using them in your units and lessons; consider the structure of sentences and of whole texts. For example, the complicated syntax in Shakespeare's writing makes it challenging for many readers, including those with complex support needs. Teachers must be aware of such challenges and *proactively* plan ways to address them explicitly during instruction. Students who know they can expect scaffolding as a routine part of their learning experiences will be more comfortable taking risks and interacting with complex texts.

Understand the Importance of Background Knowledge

Chapter 5 discussed the value of helping students link new information to their existing information schemes. Thus, to effectively plan UD-DI, you must consistently find ways to support students' ability to make connections to prior and background knowledge. This can be done by highlighting patterns; emphasizing critical features and big ideas; guiding students' processing of information, visualization, and manipulation of new knowledge; and planning to maximize for transfer and generalization of learned content and skills (CAST, 2011). The use of high-quality graphic organizers, in print or electronic form, is an excellent strategy that helps to address many of these recommendations. For example, if you are teaching a lesson on character analysis, you might use a graphic organizer that includes categories students should consider when analyzing a character, such as traits, actions, influences, and relationships. The teacher can provide examples in each of these categories as necessary to increase scaffolding for students who need additional support. Considering what information you need to pre-teach, chunk, and provide cues and emphasis for are additional ways you can plan with a focus on accessibility. It is important to provide multiple opportunities (in multiple modes) for guided practice as students interact with learning objectives; this enhances instruction for all students.

Another way teachers can help students connect to prior learning is to consider ways to bridge concepts across disciplines and across units so students have opportunities to apply their knowledge in different scenarios. In addition, students should have opportunities to see newly learned concepts and skills applied as the teacher models making connections in the lessons presented. Planning for these instructional routines will have a tremendous impact on students' generalization and transfer of skills.

Engage Learners as They Process New Information

You can engage students by providing learning experiences that are clearly explained, varied, appropriately challenging, collaborative, and focused on building mastery of a concept or skill. To engage students fully, consider how you will do the following:

- Communicate clear goals and objectives.

- Vary the demands and resources used in instruction to provide appropriately challenging activities and experiences.

- Foster collaboration and communication during learning tasks.

- Ensure that your feedback is focused on mastery instead of comparison and competition between students.

You will find that considering these questions becomes habitual. They play an important role in your decisions about how to structure your classroom; considering these questions should be part of your routine for planning literacy instruction.

Clear goals and objectives that are aligned to grade-level standards were discussed in detail in Chapter 4. Here again, we emphasize the importance of creating goals and objectives that are not only universally designed but also student friendly and communicated in a variety of ways. For example, we recommend that when beginning a new unit, you verbally share the essential question—that is, the overarching question you want your students to be able to answer at the end of the unit—and the overall learning goals and objectives with students. As you do so, write them on the board or point to a poster where they are displayed. This allows students to refer back to learning expectations as you present daily lessons and helps them understand how each lesson's goals connect to the overarching purpose of the unit.

For students with complex support needs, you might communicate learning goals by pasting them in a notebook, having them programmed into a communication device, or representing them with symbols; these means ensure that the goals are easily accessible and presented in a mode the student can interact with fully. When you clearly communicate expectations to students in an accessible way, students can take a more active role in their learning. Moreover, with scaffolding and support, students can use the overarching unit or lesson goals and objectives to set their own personal goals, which promotes self-determination. All of these considerations help ensure that students are engaged and active participants in their own learning.

Remember That Communication Is Key

Kearns et al. note that "At the heart of all academic achievement is communication" (2011, p. 11). Communication is essential; it is the teacher's role to support students' communication skills throughout literacy instruction. Without adequate communication and a means to demonstrate what they know, students do not have a real opportunity to learn. Although you should always be focused on how to help students acquire effective communication skills, be aware that even students with limited communication abilities are able to participate in high-quality, standards-aligned literacy instruction; neither verbal nor proficient symbolic communication skills are a prerequisite. Students must be supported along the continuum of developing communication skills within the context of high-quality instruction; this, in turn, helps them generalize these skills to other situations. Contrary to historical and current trends in practice, working on communication skills by themselves instead of embedding them in academic instruction can be counterproductive (e.g., Calculator & Black, 2009). You must consider how you will ensure that you have removed barriers to student learning by providing multiple options for expression. Sometimes, removing these barriers will mean ensuring that content and materials are accessible for students who have a home language other than English (e.g., Spanish, American Sign Language). (See Chapter 3 for more information on how to consider students' home language in planning instruction.) It might also mean ensuring that students have communication devices with the language and supports necessary to interface with the content as you present your lessons.

We've highlighted universally designed routines that, if considered in advance, will support planning high-quality differentiated instruction that is accessible to all learners. Considering these factors as a matter of course develops good habits of mind in teachers; these habits of mind will ensure that you have addressed barriers within curriculum, content, materials, and instruction so that all students have an opportunity to learn.

REFLECTION QUESTION 2

What are two things you can do to ensure that UDL is considered right from the start of the planning process?

PLANNING FOR INSTRUCTION: KEY CONSIDERATIONS

Now that you've had a chance to think about important routines that should be embedded within your thought processes as you plan, we will talk about further organizing for instruction and planning your lessons. The planning process discussed below will ultimately result in universally designed differentiated lesson plans that align to standards; it will help create rich opportunities for all students to access, actively participate in, and make progress in the general curriculum.

Good instruction involves planning. Although it is important to be responsive to the ongoing needs of your students and to adjust instruction accordingly, you must be able to make these adjustments from a foundation of high-quality instruction that is carefully planned, not spur-of-the-moment. In this section, we discuss the importance of being clear about what you want students to know and how you will assess their progress. As you begin brainstorming and lesson planning, these key considerations will guide your thinking.

The first step to lesson planning is unit planning, which begins with creating big ideas aligned to grade-level standards. These big ideas help you formulate essential questions—that is, the overarching questions you want your students to be able to answer at the end of the unit. These essential questions should be differentiated to meet the needs of all your students, including students with complex support needs, students with and without IEPs, and students with gifts and talents. (See Figure 11.7 for an example of what this kind of unit planning looks like in practice.)

To determine the ideas that will shape a unit of instruction, ask yourself:

- *What information do all students need to know?* This initial level of questioning should represent "non-negotiable" ideas that all students should understand very well; all students will be expected to demonstrate a high level of understanding of these ideas and be able to answer related essential questions.

- *What information should some students know?* Some students may be able to extend learning beyond the initial essential question(s) and demonstrate more sophisticated understandings of the concepts; they can work with additional big ideas and related essential questions.

- *What material will a few students be able to understand?* A few students might demonstrate exceptional understanding of a concept, be able to work with related ideas and questions at a more advanced level, and be ready for more in-depth evaluation at the end of the unit.

This tiered system helps you create essential questions that represent a range of depths of knowledge and create a roadmap or foundation upon which to build your lesson plans.

After establishing your big idea(s) and essential questions, the next step is to write clear lesson goals and objectives that connect to them. These goals and objectives indicate your measure of success. It is important to make sure that the goals are broad and connect to the big ideas, and that the objectives contain measurable behaviors and criteria.

Next, you need to create meaningful assessments. Ask yourself, "How will I know if my students have mastered the lesson goals, objectives, and essential questions, and what will I use to assess this?" Give attention to what types of assessments will allow your students to best demonstrate their knowledge, ensuring that assessments match your goals and objectives. To align with the principles of UDL, give students multiple options for demonstrating their learning that include multiple means of expression. Once you have established the big ideas and essential questions, created goals and objectives, and determined the means of assessment, you can begin writing your teaching procedures and strategies.

At this stage in planning, there are several important considerations. The first is to ensure you are using evidence-based teaching strategies. This is required by ESSA and IDEA 2004, which mandate that scientifically based teaching strategies be used in all classrooms. (See Chapters 6 through 10 for evidence-based instruction in specific areas of comprehensive literacy instruction.) The next consideration is making sure that the principles of UDL are embedded throughout the lesson. In the previous sections, we discussed routines and habits of mind that should guide your lesson planning process; here, we reiterate that you should create lessons based in the principles of UDL, rather than retrofitting preexisting lessons that are not designed to meet all learners' needs. (See Chapter 5 to review UDL principles in greater detail.)

USING AUTHENTIC TEXT TO PLAN LITERACY UNITS

Many reading programs and prepackaged literacy curricula are not designed to meet the needs of students with complex support needs. As noted previously, the results from a recent alignment study done with popular literacy curricula for these students found that the majority of lessons in all curricula studied were not aligned to the core standards (Taub et al., 2015). To provide high-quality instruction and to comply with IDEA 2004 mandates, teachers will have to use supplementary planning tools to ensure that curriculum and instruction meet the needs of all students in their classrooms, regardless of ability level. The planning and implementation tools shared in the following section will help teachers attain that goal.

Unit and Lesson Planning: Choosing Activities and Texts

In the previous section, we described how the essential *concepts* in a particular unit of study should inform your unit and lesson planning. This planning must also involve thinking carefully about what literacy *skills* students will learn and apply and what texts they will work with. The planning templates and processes we provide below build upon structured brainstorming to support your use of authentic, grade-appropriate texts. The use of the literacy planning wheel (see Figure 11.1) and/or literacy planning matrix (see Figure 11.2) helps teachers avoid the decontextualized ladder to literacy, as described in Chapter 1, and facilitate approaching unit planning from a broad perspective using all of the components of literacy instruction. One advantage of these tools is that they can be used with any type of text at any grade level.

Literacy Planning Wheel

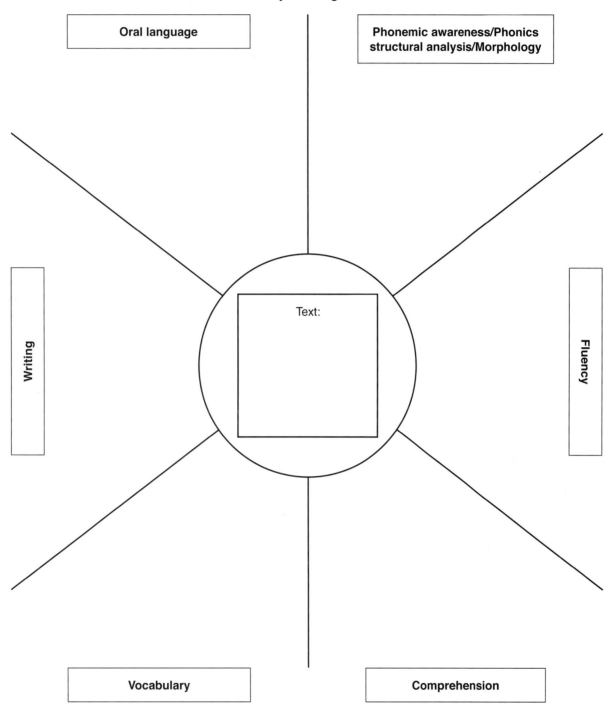

Figure 11.1. Literacy planning wheel.

Date: _____

Developed by: _____

Text(s): _____

Grade(s): _____

Standards: _____

_____

	Oral language	Reading	Writing
Phonemic awareness			
Phonics			
Fluency			
Vocabulary			
Text comprehension			

Figure 11.2.   Literacy planning matrix.

Table 11.1. Selecting texts for instruction

Age level	Examples of choosing text
Elementary (Grades K–5)	*Library Lion, Chicka Chicka Boom Boom, Frog and Toad, Diary of a Wimpy Kid* series, *Stellaluna, The Secret Garden, Number the Stars, The Mysteries of Harris Burdick, Creatures of the Night, So You Want to Be President?*
Middle (Grades 6–8)	Graphic novels, *Hatchet, The Giver, The Diary of Anne Frank, Holes, The Book Thief,* informational web sites, "A Letter on Thomas Jefferson," *Harriet Tubman: Conductor on the Underground Railroad*
High school (Grades 9–12)	*To Kill a Mockingbird, The Wall Street Journal,* the *Twilight* series, *The Catcher in the Rye, The Outsiders,* informational web sites, "The Gettysburg Address," *I Know Why the Caged Bird Sings,* "I Have a Dream" speech, graphic novels
Transition (Grades 12+)	Employee handbook, magazines, cookbooks, cover letters

Any good planning tool should be flexible and modifiable for different classroom situations. The process of planning comprehensive literacy instruction around a text can be greatly enhanced by working collaboratively with colleagues, as appropriate, within a classroom, grade level, content area, and school. In general, to use the literacy planning wheel and literacy planning matrix to create universally designed differentiated units and lessons, the following steps are recommended:

1. *Choose text that is appropriate for the curriculum standards and subject area(s) addressed in the unit.*

   The text that could be used for a language arts unit include a single book, a series of books by one author, textbooks, various works from a particular genre of literature, poetry, plays, graphic novels, environmental print, or newspaper and other media. The literacy planning wheel or matrix can also help teachers integrate literacy instruction into other core subject areas and electives, using text such as books or sets of books, textbooks, historical documents, newspapers, magazines, web sites, instruction books, environmental print, or even lecture notes. The length of the text(s) chosen will vary according to students' grade level and the time available for the unit. Table 11.1 provides an example of what this planning might look like at each level.

2. *Brainstorm ways in which the different areas of literacy instruction (oral language, phonemic awareness/phonics/structural analysis/morphology, fluency, vocabulary, comprehension, and writing) can be addressed using this text.*

   See Figures 11.3 and 11.4 for examples of completed literacy planning wheels—one for elementary school students and one for students preparing to transition out of high school. See Figures 11.5 and 11.6 for examples of completed literacy planning matrixes; these examples use texts and activities appropriate for middle and high school students.

REFLECTION QUESTION 3

Think of ways in which the literacy planning wheel and/or matrix could facilitate collaborative planning between general and special educators, including related service providers. List two ways these tools could be used for this purpose.

3. *Clarify and expand the ideas generated by the brainstorming activity.*

   Look at all of the brainstorming ideas. Which activities address the standards appropriate to grade-level expectations for the students you teach? Which ideas can lead to a series

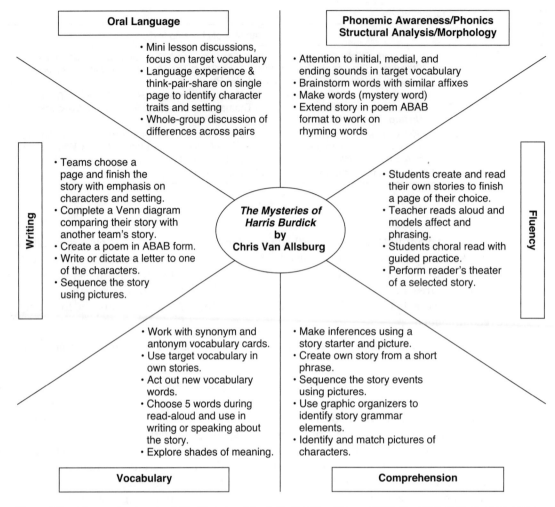

Figure 11.3. Literacy planning wheel: *The Mysteries of Harris Burdick* (Van Allsburg, 1984). *Key:* IEP, individualized education program.

of lessons to provide rigorous instruction—instruction that will allow all students to meet content standards and incorporate their IEP objectives? Can these lessons be made accessible to all students in the classroom through UD-DI? Which aspects of the lessons can be used to assess whether the students have made progress in grade level curriculum and met standards-aligned IEP goals as expected?

Figure 11.7 is an example of a seventh-grade unit plan created from the brainstorming ideas generated in Step 2. After consulting standards, the teacher developed essential questions for the unit. The questions were chosen by reviewing the CCSS for seventh grade to determine what needed to be covered. Ideas were pulled out from the literacy planning matrix that aligned with the essential question of the unit. You will notice that the lessons represent all five federally required components of literacy instruction along with oral language and writing.

4. *Develop lessons that can be realistically implemented in the time frame available. Any lesson planning format will work with the literacy planning wheel or matrix.*

For a sample UD-DI lesson plan template, see Figure 11.8. Figure 11.9 is an example of a sample lesson plan for days seven and eight of the unit plan described previously.

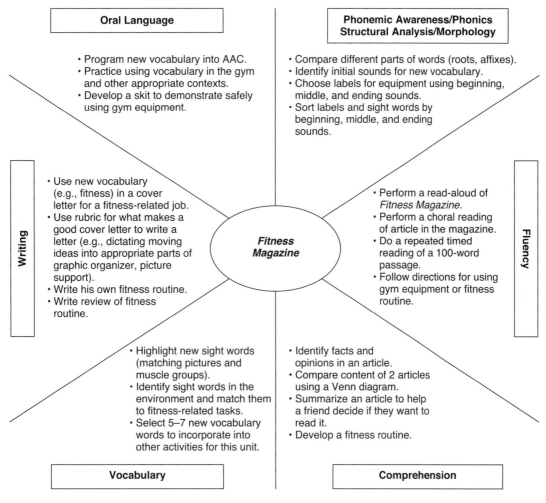

Oral Language

- Program new vocabulary into AAC.
- Practice using vocabulary in the gym and other appropriate contexts.
- Develop a skit to demonstrate safely using gym equipment.

Phonemic Awareness/Phonics Structural Analysis/Morphology

- Compare different parts of words (roots, affixes).
- Identify initial sounds for new vocabulary.
- Choose labels for equipment using beginning, middle, and ending sounds.
- Sort labels and sight words by beginning, middle, and ending sounds.

Writing

- Use new vocabulary (e.g., fitness) in a cover letter for a fitness-related job.
- Use rubric for what makes a good cover letter to write a letter (e.g., dictating moving ideas into appropriate parts of graphic organizer, picture support).
- Write his own fitness routine.
- Write review of fitness routine.

Fitness Magazine

Fluency

- Perform a read-aloud of *Fitness Magazine*.
- Perform a choral reading of article in the magazine.
- Do a repeated timed reading of a 100-word passage.
- Follow directions for using gym equipment or fitness routine.

Vocabulary

- Highlight new sight words (matching pictures and muscle groups).
- Identify sight words in the environment and match them to fitness-related tasks.
- Select 5–7 new vocabulary words to incorporate into other activities for this unit.

Comprehension

- Identify facts and opinions in an article.
- Compare content of 2 articles using a Venn diagram.
- Summarize an article to help a friend decide if they want to read it.
- Develop a fitness routine.

Figure 11.4. Sample literacy planning wheel: *Fitness Magazine. Key:* AAC, alternative and augmentative communication.

5. *Complete an evaluation and reflection of the unit and/or lesson after it is completed.*

It is important to continuously reflect upon and evaluate your own teaching. Examples of questions to ask yourself include the following:

- Was the lesson successful? How do I know?

- Did the students meet lesson objectives?

- Did the assessments accurately capture what students learned?

- If I teach this lesson again, what will I do differently?

- What choices did I give my students?

- Did I embed principles of UDL into my teaching?

- How did I support the students who were struggling with this lesson?

- How did I challenge my students?

- Did the unit allow students the opportunity to make progress in the grade-level curriculum and meet standards-aligned IEP goals as expected?

Text: *Drama: A Graphic Novel*
Level: Middle school

	Oral language	Reading	Writing
Phonemic awareness	Select words that describe characters and that have the same beginning sounds as letters in the character's name to create an acrostic poem. Brainstorm a list of words that rhyme to create a summary in the form of a rap.	Set a focus for reading so that students are listening for words to use to create an acrostic poem.	N/A (Phonemic awareness becomes phonics in written language.)
Phonics	Discuss words that help you read and spell other words (e.g., if I can read the word *thought,* I can read and write the word *bought*).	Listen or look for specific digraphs/blends in words and track for use in a personal dictionary or journal entry (based on individual student needs).	Write an acrostic poem based on a character of choice. Create a rap with rhyming words.
Structural analysis/ morphology	Discuss how knowledge of a particular Greek or Latin root helps to understand deeper meanings of related words.	Use commonly known affixes to help decipher the meaning of new words (*in*justice).	Create a word web with a particular Greek or Latin root and brainstorm other words that contain that root.
Fluency	Students read aloud sections of the story. Students act out a portion of the story.	Students choose a character in the story to represent, and read aloud any text pertaining to that character with a partner.	Student constructs a journal entry using the text as a reference for evidence and spelling.
Vocabulary	Hold class discussions incorporating targeted vocabulary. Students act out the definitions of target vocabulary related to character traits (e.g., cool, annoying).	Find targeted vocabulary within text. Students find synonyms for target vocabulary words and put them in a personal dictionary to use in other writing.	Students create their own narrative based on the story's characters using targeted vocabulary.
Text comprehension	Students discuss character development using conversational moves* and student-generated guiding questions. *Conversational moves provide a structure to support productive student discussion and include phrases like "I agree with . . .," "I disagree with . . .," "I'd like to add to what Tommy says because . . . ."	Focusing on character development, students use sticky notes to mark places in the text that provide evidence for how a character changes throughout the story.	Students write a letter from the perspective of Callie (the main character) to another selected character.

Figure 11.5. Literacy planning matrix: *Drama: A Graphic Novel* (Telgemeier, 2012).

Text: "I Have a Dream" speech by Martin Luther King Jr.
Level: High school

	Oral language	Reading	Writing
Phonemic awareness	Students watch a video of the speech and listen for alliterations.	Students select a sentence or short passage and analyze the syllables and sounds in each word. Students identify patterns in both and think about how these might contribute to flow or clarity of the message.	N/A (Phonemic awareness becomes phonics in written language.)
Phonics	Students construct a rap version of "I Have a Dream."	Students read the speech silently, recording the alliterations in a journal.	Write a poem to convey an emotion (of students' choice) using at least one example of alliteration.
Structural analysis/ morphology	Create a game that uses different forms of particular words as needed to indicate different meanings using different parts of speech (e.g., *definition, define, definitively*).	Use highlighter tape to indicate unknown words in the text and practice using context and knowledge of common roots and affixes to determine the meaning of highlighted words.	Create a Mad Libs-style game using different forms of particular words; peers can use this game to practice using words that are different parts of speech with related meanings (e.g., *definition, define, definitely, definitively*).
Fluency	Students recite their written work with fluency and appropriate emphasis	Students read parts of the speech aloud to a peer or small group and practice emphasizing different words and thinking about how that impacts what meaning is conveyed.	Students will construct a short written piece advocating for a cause that is important to them.
Vocabulary	Students read aloud the "I Have a Dream" speech, with emphasis on the vocabulary words they believe convey emotion and passion.	Students read the speech, listening for words that convey passion. They record these words in a journal.	Students use the vocabulary words they determined conveyed passion in the "I Have a Dream" speech to write their own speech, conveying similar passion.
Text comprehension	Students read aloud their own speech, or King's speech, using passion to relay meaning.	Students find a contemporary speech that powerfully communicates a message and compare/ contrast with "I Have a Dream."	Students choose a social justice issue of importance to them and write a persuasive speech.

Figure 11.6. Sample literacy planning matrix: Martin Luther King, Jr.'s "I Have a Dream" speech.

Unit plan	
Grade level	7
Theme	Understanding Different Perspectives
Standards addressed	CCSS.ELA-Literacy.RL.7.6 Analyze how an author develops and contrasts the points of view of different characters or narrators in a text. CCSS.ELA-Literacy.W.7.3 Write narratives to develop real or imagined experiences or events using effective technique, relevant descriptive details, and well-structured event sequences. CCSS.ELA-Literacy.W.7.10 Write routinely over extended time frames (time for research, reflection, and revision) and shorter time frames (a single sitting or a day or two) for a range of discipline-specific tasks, purposes, and audiences.
Essential questions	*For all students:* What are the different points of view in the graphic novel *Drama* and how do those points of view complement or conflict with each other? *For some students:* How do different points of view impact a character's motivations? *For a few students:* How do characters' points of view develop throughout a story and what external factors contribute to this change?
Summative assessment	Students will have a choice of writing a letter or creating an audiovisual presentation, film, dialogue, or skit that demonstrates understanding of different perspectives and is graded using a rubric.

	Lesson activity	Literacy areas of focus	Lesson objectives	Formative assessment
Day 1	Script read Act 1 with peer.	Phonics Phonemic awareness	Students will compare and contrast different genres of literature.	Class created Venn diagram or comparison chart.
Day 2	Script read Acts 2 and 3 with peer.	Phonics Phonemic awareness Vocabulary	The students will explain orally or in writing three character traits that their selected character possessed.	Students listed character traits.
Day 3	Script read Acts 4 and 5 with peer.	Phonics Phonemic awareness Text comprehension Vocabulary	With a peer, the students will create a Venn diagram comparing and contrasting the character they represented in the previous lesson with their peer's selected character.	Venn diagram
Day 4	Script read Acts 6 and 7.	Phonics Phonemic awareness	The students will create fictional scenarios in which they must represent (in any given modality) an assigned character from the text.	Scenarios
Day 5	Script read Act 8.	Phonics Phonemic awareness Text comprehension	Focusing on character development, students will use sticky notes to mark places in the text that provide evidence for how a character changes throughout the story.	Sticky notes in text
Day 6	Literature discussion: compare and contrast characters	Text comprehension	As a group, the class will compare all the characters and how they developed throughout the text. Students will use evidence from the text to support their answers and illustrate character development.	Literature discussion rubric
Days 7/8	First draft and final copy of letter	Writing Vocabulary Comprehension	The students will create a friendly letter to another character that will communicate a personal perspective.	Friendly letter
Days 9/10	Creation of final product	Vocabulary Text comprehension	Given 2 days, students will demonstrate understanding of different perspectives by constructing a product (i.e., a letter, audiovisual presentation, film, dialogue, or skit) that represents two different characters' perspectives.	Final product rubric

Figure 11.7.   Sample unit plan: *Drama: A Graphic Novel* (Telgemeier, 2012). *Key:* CCSS, Common Core State Standards; ELA, English language arts.

UD-DI Lesson Plan

Unit:	Lesson title:
Unit essential question(s):	

Standards addressed

Lesson components	UD-DI checklist
Goal:	❐ Is the lesson goal aligned to the standard(s)? ❐ Is the lesson goal aligned to the essential question(s)?
Objectives:	❐ Do the lesson objectives support attainment of the lesson goal? ❐ Are the lesson objectives observable and measurable?
Materials:	❐ Are the materials grade appropriate and engaging? ❐ Are the materials accessible for all students? ❐ If not, what adaptations need to be made so materials are accessible to all students? ❐ Do students have a choice of materials to use?

(continued)

Figure 11.8. Universally designed differentiated instruction (UD-DI) lesson plan template. *Key:* CCSS, Common Core State Standards; ELA, English language arts.

Figure 11.8. *(continued)*

Instructional procedures: Time frame: Preparation of the environment: *Grouping:* *Physical classroom changes (e.g., seating):*	❏ Does the time frame allow ample opportunities for modeling, guided practice, and independent practice? ❏ Have I intentionally planned for flexible, responsive grouping formats that provide students choice and supports as needed? ❏ Is the classroom layout accessible for all students?
Introduction to lesson:	❏ Does my introduction grab students' attention? ❏ Do I communicate the learning objectives in a student-friendly way? ❏ Does my introduction activate prior knowledge? ❏ Does my introduction use multiple means of representation so it is accessible to all learners? ❏ Can my students interact with this information in a variety of ways?

Instructional input and modeling:	Do I provide instruction in a way that all students can access and respond to, using:
	   ❏ Multiple means of representation?
	   ❏ Multiple means of engagement?
	   ❏ Multiple means of action and expression?
	❏ Do I model what I want my students to do on their own, using multiple means of representation?
	❏ Do I use grouping formats to allow students to interact with each other as they learn the content?

Independent practice:	Do I provide a variety of options for students to engage with the learning objective(s) through:
	   ❏ Materials?
	   ❏ Content?
	   ❏ Grouping?
	❏ Have I provided scaffolding and support to ensure that students can engage meaningfully with the learning objectives?

Closure:	❏ Have I supported multiple means of expression and ensured that students can demonstrate and share what they've learned? ❏ Does my wrap-up include a review of the lesson objectives?
Assessment:	❏ Does my assessment align to my lesson goal and objective(s)? ❏ Does this assessment align to skills that lead to an understanding of the overarching essential question(s) for the unit? ❏ Have I supported multiple means of expression and engagement to ensure that students can demonstrate what they know?

Unit: Understanding Different Perspectives	Lesson title: Day 7–8: Writing a Friendly Letter to Illustrate Perspective

Unit essential question(s):
For all students: What are the different points of view in the graphic novel *Drama* and how do those points of view complement or conflict with each other? *For some students:* How do different points of view impact a character's motivations? *For a few students:* How do characters' points of view develop throughout a story, and what external factors contribute to this change?

Standards addressed
CCSS.ELA-Literacy.RL.7.6 Analyze how an author develops and contrasts the points of view of different characters or narrators in a text. CCSS.ELA-Literacy.W.7.3 Write narratives to develop real or imagined experiences or events using effective technique, relevant descriptive details, and well-structured event sequences. CCSS.ELA-Literacy.W.7.10 Write routinely over extended time frames (time for research, reflection, and revision) and shorter time frames (a single sitting or a day or two) for a range of discipline-specific tasks, purposes, and audiences.

Lesson components	UD-DI checklist
Goal: The students will understand different perspectives within a text.	❏ Is the lesson goal aligned to the standard(s)? ❏ Is the lesson goal aligned to the essential question(s)?
Objectives: Given the format of their choice (e.g., computer, paper and pencil), the students will construct a letter from the main character's perspective to a character of their choosing.	❏ Do the lesson objectives support attainment of the lesson goal? ❏ Are the lesson objectives observable and measurable?
Materials: The text *Drama* E-book/audio version of *Drama* Word processor Writing utensils Paper	❏ Are the materials grade appropriate and engaging? ❏ Are the materials accessible for all students? ❏ If not, what adaptations need to be made so materials are accessible to all students? ❏ Do students have a choice of materials to use?

(continued)

Figure 11.9. Sample universally designed differentiated instruction (UD-DI) lesson plan: *Drama: A Graphic Novel* (Telgemeier, 2012). *Key:* CCSS, Common Core State Standards; ELA, English language arts.

Figure 11.9. *(continued)*

Instructional procedures: Time frame: Two 45-minute class periods Preparation of the environment: *Grouping:* Whole group for modeling and guided practice; students will have a choice of working independently or in pairs for the independent practice activity. *Physical classroom changes (e.g., seating):* No alterations needed for this lesson.	❏ Does the time frame allow ample opportunities for modeling, guided practice, and independent practice? ❏ Have I intentionally planned for flexible, responsive grouping formats that provide students choice and supports as needed? ❏ Is the classroom layout accessible for all students?
Introduction to lesson: 1. Tell the students that today's lesson will involve different characters in the text *Drama*. 2. Have the students think about/record as many different characters from the text as they can. 3. When they finish, have them compare their list with a peer's. 4. As a whole group, create a master list.	❏ Does my introduction grab students' attention? ❏ Do I communicate the learning objectives in a student-friendly way? ❏ Does my introduction activate prior knowledge? ❏ Does my introduction use multiple means of representation so it is accessible to all learners? ❏ Can my students interact with this information in a variety of ways?

Instructional input and modeling:
1. Ask the students what the term *perspective* means. Write it on the board.
2. Give students the definition. Have students repeat the definition.
3. Have students use the term *perspective* in a sentence. Have them share their sentence with a peer.
4. Have the students imagine they are the main character.
5. Pose questions (to the whole class) they are to answer as if they are the main character. Have students answer the questions while speaking to a peer; then, discuss as a whole class. Tell the class that they are answering the questions from the main character's perspective.
6. Let the students know that today they will be writing letters to different characters in the story, all from the viewpoint of the main character. Go through the list of characters and ask the students to talk about the relationship the main character has with each character and also list reasons why the main character might write a letter to each of the other characters in the story. Record these ideas on the board.
	Do I provide instruction in a way that all students can access and respond to using:
	    ❏ Multiple means of representation?
	    ❏ Multiple means of engagement?
	    ❏ Multiple means of action and expression?
	❏ Do I model what I want my students to do on their own using multiple means of representation?
	❏ Do I use grouping formats to allow students to interact with each other as they learn the content?

Figure 11.9. *(continued)*

Independent practice: 1. Have the students pick one character (from the list on the board). Explain that their job is to create a letter, written from the perspective of the main character and addressing the other character they have chosen. They are free to use the ideas on the board or create their own. 2. Give students time to write letters, providing assistance as needed.	Do I provide a variety of options for students to engage with the learning objective(s) through: ❏ Materials? ❏ Content? ❏ Grouping? ❏ Have I provided scaffolding and support to ensure that students can engage meaningfully with the learning objectives?
Closure: Allow students the opportunity to share their letters (read aloud, text to speech, peer sharing).	❏ Have I supported multiple means of expression so students can demonstrate and share what they've learned? ❏ Does my wrap-up include a review of the lesson objectives?
Assessment: Using a checklist, students will be assessed on their ability to write a letter using the format of their choice (e.g., computer, paper and pencil) that demonstrates an understanding of the perspective of one of the main characters in the graphic novel *Drama*.	❏ Does my assessment align to my lesson goal and objective(s)? ❏ Does this assessment align to skills that lead to an understanding of the overarching essential question(s) for the unit? ❏ Have I supported multiple means of expression and engagement to ensure that students can demonstrate what they know?

(Character Perspective) Friendly Letter Lesson Checklist
Students can identify the perspective of the main character.
Students can identify the perspective of an additional character.
Students can construct an introduction that communicates a purpose for the letter.
Students can construct a body to their letter that includes details from the text to support conversation between characters.
Students can construct a conclusion to their letter that reviews the purpose.
Students use conventional grammar, punctuation, and spelling.

The use of holistic planning tools such as the literacy planning wheel or matrix, along with lesson planning structures like the UD-DI format we have demonstrated, provides students access to a kaleidoscope of literacy opportunities. This can prevent students with complex support needs being stuck on the bottom rung of the literacy ladder (Kliewer et al., 2004).

REFLECTION QUESTION 4

Look back at the case study for Max presented at the beginning of this chapter. Then look back at the sample UD-DI lesson presented in Figure 11.9. How was this lesson universally designed so that students like Max would be able to access the lesson without many additional accommodations and modifications?

Specific Instructional Planning Strategies for Students with Disabilities

UD-DI makes it easier to include students with complex support needs. The conceptual planning tools described previously ensure that all students have access to all areas of literacy instruction and are not trapped at the bottom of the literacy ladder. However, it is not enough for students with complex support needs merely to be present in general education classrooms; they must also be meaningful participants and full members of the classroom. For this reason, additional strategies must be in place to ensure that each student's individual educational needs are being addressed. We describe several useful strategies in the following sections.

Program-at-a-Glance   IDEA 2004 requires that an interdisciplinary team develop goals and objectives for each student with disabilities. (Ideally, the team will include the general and special education teachers and any therapists working with the students. Parental and student involvement in the planning process is also encouraged.) The goals and objectives the team develops are part of a student's IEP. However, although it is essential that special and general education teachers have readily accessible information about students with disabilities and their objectives, the IEP document itself is too overwhelming for many educators to make into a living document. Thus, one role of the special education teacher is to summarize a student's IEP for the general educator(s) and other members of that student's educational team in a way that makes the information accessible and useful. One tool for accomplishing this is the program-at-a-glance (e.g., Janney & Snell, 2006). The program-at-a-glance provides basic information about a student's strengths, objectives, and management needs on one page in straightforward language. Figure 11.10 shows a program-at-a-glance for Max.

Infused Skills Grid   Once a student's program-at-a-glance has been completed, educators need to work together to ensure that the general education classroom provides opportunities for the student to meet his or her IEP objectives. One tool used to achieve this goal is the infused skills grid (see Figure 11.11), which is completed by the educational team (Castagnera, Fisher, Rodifer, & Sax, 1998). The infused skills grid is a matrix that allows the educational team to see how a student's individualized goals can be infused or embedded in general education settings throughout the day. It is important to note that the infused skills grid helps educators examine the needs of the individual students to see how skills can be addressed in general education, rather than asking the student to meet the demands of the general education classroom. Figure 11.12 is an example of an infused skills grid completed for Max.

The infused skills grid achieves several important goals. First, it communicates to the team opportunities for meeting a student's individual goals, including literacy skills, in general education. Second, it ensures that all team members are aware of the student's goals. Third, it reassures the special education teacher, therapists, and parents that the student's individual objectives will be addressed in the general education setting. Finally, the grid identifies any

Program-at-a-Glance

Max's objectives	Max's strengths
Academic • Write 3–4 sentences on a given topic (with correct spelling and grammar) • Increase sight-word recognition • Comprehend when text is read aloud to him • Comprehend multiplication and division facts **Social/communication** • Use assistive technology to communicate with peers and adults • Initiate social interactions • Respond to peers and adults • Increase time spent with peers outside of school **Self-determination** • Advocate for needs • Set goals **Motor** • Move arms and legs • Improve fine motor skills • Use stander	✓ Works hard ✓ Is patient ✓ Cooperates ✓ Works well with peers ✓ Is very responsive ✓ Is friendly ✓ Enjoys school ✓ Understands more than people think ✓ Making gains in communication when provided engaging opportunities ✓ Can write 1–2 sentences ✓ Can answer comprehension questions when text is read aloud ✓ Knows 15 sight words
	Management issues
	• Educational assistant will toilet at approximately 12:30 pm. • Educational assistant will tube feed at 12:45 pm. • Peer buddies can help in class and transitioning between classes.

Figure 11.10. Program-at-a-glance for Max.

Infused Skills Grid

School name: ____________________ School year: ____________________

Student name: ____________________ Course: ____________________

Age: ____________________ Advocate/teacher: ____________________

Grade: ____________________ Parent/guardian: ____________________

Activities/subjects/environments	Infused skills									
Check here if the infused skill was identified by: Family										
Student										
Peers										
School										

Figure 11.11. Blank infused skills grid.

Infused Skills Grid

Subject → / IEP goal ↓	Math	ELA	Science	History	Physical education	Art/music
1. Write 3–4 sentences on a given topic with correct grammar.		✗	✗	✗		
2. Increase sight-word recognition.		✗	✗	✗		
3. Comprehend text when read aloud.	✗	✗	✗	✗		
4. Comprehend multiplication and division.	✗		✗			
5. Use assistive technology to communicate.	✗	✗	✗	✗	✗	✗
6. Initiate conversation and respond to peers.	✗	✗	✗	✗	✗	✗
7. Advocate for needs (including goal setting).	✗	✗	✗	✗	✗	✗
8. Improve range of motion in both right and left arms.					✗	✗

Figure 11.12. Max's infused skills grid. *Key:* ELA, English language arts; IEP, individualized education program.

skills that cannot be addressed in that setting. In those instances, the team may decide that the goal is no longer needed or that the general education environment can be modified so that the skills can be addressed. In rare cases, the student may need to leave the general education classroom to work on a skill.

REFLECTION QUESTION 5

How could you use the program-at-a-glance and infused skills grid to support the inclusion of students with complex support needs with their peers in the classroom, school, and community?

The Principle of Partial Participation

Students with complex support needs are often denied access to quality literacy instruction because they cannot participate in all aspects of a particular program or lesson in the same way as their general education peers. For example, if the student cannot participate in prepacked literacy programs or curriculum, then he or she may be removed from the general education classroom for literacy instruction. Rather than taking this all-or-nothing approach, educators can apply the principle of partial participation.

The *principle of partial participation* is that all students can participate meaningfully in some aspect of an activity, lesson, or program. Instead of asking whether the student can do a particular activity, we can ask what individualized objectives the student can achieve by participating in the activity. Research has demonstrated that when we give students access to partially participate in general education curriculum, they often achieve at higher levels than expected (e.g., Mirenda, 2003; Ryndak, Morrison, & Sommerstein, 1999). For this reason, it is essential to consider the principle of partial participation (Baumgart et al., 1982) when designing literacy instruction for students with complex support needs in general education settings.

Modification Questions

Once opportunities for meeting the needs of a student with complex support needs in the general education classroom have been identified—by considering the principle of partial participation and using program-at-a-glance and infused skills grid—the next step is to determine what specific adaptations need to be designed. Remember that universally designing your classroom, routines, and instruction should minimize the need for additional adaptations and ensure that, if needed, they are not more specialized than necessary. A useful strategy to decide on appropriate modifications is to ask the following curriculum adaptation questions while planning lessons (see Figure 11.13):

1. Can the student participate in this activity in the same way as his or her general education peers?

2. Can the student participate in the same lesson with adaptations in the environment, materials, support, and/or expectations?

3. Can the student partially participate in some aspect of the lesson?

4. Can the student participate in a similar or parallel activity within the same classroom?

5. If the answer to all these questions is *no*, does the student need to leave the general education classroom for an alternate activity? If so, could one or more general education peers also participate in this alternate activity?

In addition to deciding which adaptations are needed, the educational team must also discuss who will provide the necessary adaptations and supports for the student and who will be responsible

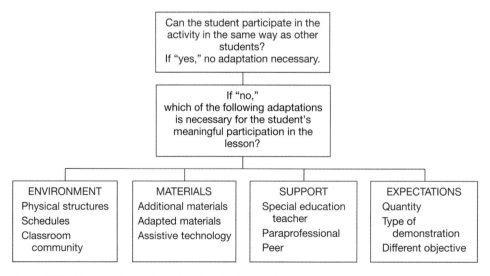

Figure 11.13.   Example of curriculum adaptation planning questions.

for evaluating and documenting the student's progress. This kind of planning requires the establishment of strong collaborative relationships between general and special education educators.

SUMMARY

UD-DI is one way students with complex support needs can access literacy instruction in the context of the general education classroom. These students need to be included in planning from the very beginning. This chapter described routines teachers can establish in their classrooms to create effective UD-DI environments. We have also described in detail the processes involved in planning units and lessons that use accessible texts and address multiple components of literacy; we have provided numerous planning tools that can be used to implement best practices in literacy instruction and inclusive education for students with complex support needs. Tools to ensure that IEP objectives are addressed were included, and the importance of meaningful participation in literacy instruction was stressed. Using these approaches, a teacher can plan units that include appropriate text and that are guided by standards rather than being limited to IEP goals.

RESOURCES

The following resources provide tools you can use to get to know your students—a hallmark of effective UD-DI.

General Surveys

These web sites provide examples of general "getting to know you" surveys.

- **Education World** (http://www.educationworld.com/a_curr/back-to-school-student-survey-questionnaire.shtml)

- **Scholastic** (https://www.scholastic.com/teachers/articles/teaching-content/fit-print-getting-know-you-reproducible-activities)

- **Busy Teachers Café** (http://www.busyteacherscafe.com/worksheets/interviewquest.pdf)

- **Learn NC** (http://www.learnnc.org/lp/pages/1294?ref=search)

Multiple Intelligences and Learning Styles Inventories

The web sites listed here provide multiple intelligences and learning styles inventories. Note that multiple intelligences and learning styles should not be used as an additional way to label students; nor should their results be interpreted as "fixed" or "absolute" information about students. They simply provide information about learning preferences and interests that can be used to inform the UD-DI you implement in your classroom.

Multiple Intelligences Inventories

- Surfaquarium (http://surfaquarium.com/MI/inventory.htm)

- Edutopia (http://www.edutopia.org/multiple-intelligences-assessment)

Learning Styles Inventories

- Georgia Department of Education (https://www.gadoe.org/Curriculum-Instruction-and-Assessment/Special-Education-Services/Documents/IDEAS%202014%20Handouts/LearningStyleInventory.pdf)

- Education Planner (http://www.educationplanner.org/students/self-assessments/learning-styles-quiz.shtml)

REFERENCES

Baumgart, D., Brown, L., Pumpian, I., Nisbet, J., Ford, A., Sweet, M., . . ., Schroeder, J. (1982). Principle of partial participation and individualized adaptations in educational programs for severely handicapped students. *Journal for the Association of Persons with Severe Handicaps, 7*(2), 17–27.

Calculator, S.N., & Black, T. (2009). Validation of an inventory of best practices in the provision of augmentative and alternative communication services to students with severe disabilities in general education classrooms. *American Journal of Speech-Language Pathology, 18,* 329–342.

Castagnera, E., Fisher, D., Rodifer, K., & Sax, C. (1998). *Deciding what to teach and how to teach it: Connecting students through curriculum and instruction.* Colorado Springs, CO: PEAK Parent Center, Inc.

CAST. (2011). *Universal design for learning guidelines version 2.0.* Wakefield, MA: Author.

Every Student Succeeds Act (ESSA) of 2015, S.1177. Retrieved from: https://www.congress.gov/bill/114th-congress/senate-bill/1177/text

Individuals with Disabilities Education Improvement Act (IDEA) of 2004, PL 108-446, 20 U.S.C. §§ 1400 *et seq.*

Janney, R.E., & Snell, M.E. (2006). Modifying schoolwork in inclusive classrooms. *Theory Into Practice, 45*(3), 215–223.

Kearns, J.F., Towles-Reeves, E., Kleinert, H.L., Kleinert, J.O., & Kleine-Kracht Thomas, M. (2011). Characteristics of and implications for students participating in alternate assessments based on alternate academic achievement standards. *Journal of Special Education, 45*(1), 3–14.

Kliewer, C., Fitzgerald, L.M., Meyer-Mork, J., Hartman, P., English-Sand, P., & Raschke, D. (2004). Citizenship for all in the literate community: An ethnography of young children with significant disabilities in inclusive early childhood settings. *Harvard Educational Review, 74,* 373–403.

Marzano, R.J., Gaddy, B.B., & Foseid, M.C. (2006). *A handbook for classroom management that works.* Alexandria, VA: Association for Supervision & Curriculum Development.

Mirenda, P. (2003). "He's not really a reader . . . .": Perspectives on supporting literacy development in individuals with autism. *Topics in Language Disorders, 23,* 271–282.

Ryndak, D.L., Morrison, A.P., & Sommerstein, L. (1999). Literacy before and after inclusion in general education settings: A case study. *Journal for the Association of Persons with Severe Disabilities, 24*(1), 5–22.

Taub, D.A., McCord, J.A., Foster, M.H., & Ruppar, A. (2015, December). *Curriculum alignment to the Common Core State Standards for students with complex support needs.* Breakout session presented at the annual meeting of TASH, Portland, OR.

Telgemeier, R. (2012). *Drama: A graphic novel.* New York, NY: Scholastic/Graphix.

Tomlinson, C.A. (2001). *How to differentiate instruction in mixed-ability classrooms.* Alexandria, VA: Association for Supervision and Curriculum Development.

Udvari-Solner, A., Villa, R.A., & Thousand, J.S. (2002). Access to general education curriculum for all: The universal design process. In J.S. Thousand, R.A. Villa, & A.I. Nevin (Eds.), *Creativity and collaborative learning* (2nd ed.). Baltimore, MD: Paul H. Brookes Publishing Co.

Van Allsburg, C. (1984). *The mysteries of Harris Burdick.* New York, NY: Houghton Mifflin.

Creating Opportunity and Access to Literacy in School and Beyond

CHAPTER 12

Adapting Books and Other Literacy Genres

Laurel Lane and Andrea L. Ruppar

LEARNING OBJECTIVES

By the end of this chapter, readers will

1. Understand how access to texts contributes to effective literacy instruction.
2. Identify and use a decision-making process to decide types of text adaptations for students with complex support needs.
3. Design and implement multiple ways to adapt texts for learners of all ages across all areas of literacy instruction.
4. Understand the ways in which assistive technology can facilitate access to text.

This chapter addresses the adaptation of books and other literacy genres for individuals with complex support needs. Because these adaptations are grounded in our growing understanding of what literacy means for this population, we begin by sharing relevant, exciting research about expanded conceptions of literacy. Following this overview, we provide useable examples of ways books can be adapted, or modified, by educators, family members—and indeed by anyone who cares about someone whose disability interferes with knowing the joys of interacting with text. These adaptation suggestions, useable across age ranges and contexts, address the full range of support needs; we hope they are simple enough to achieve without excessive time demands or financial costs. Finally, we also include numerous resources to assist in the adaptation of texts and other literacy materials that may be used across literacy events, which are considered as opportunities, in any mode or circumstance, and including one or more sensory forms, for communication to occur—bus or train schedules, maps, grocery lists, sales fliers, directions for preparation on food packages, restaurant menus, and recipes are a few examples of other literacy material that may be adapted for use by individuals with complex support needs.

A RATIONALE FOR ADAPTING TEXTS

The importance of literacy in our lives is something we seldom think of consciously as we move through our daily activities, but consider the myriad ways we routinely interact with text in our environments. We make our coffee, tea, or breakfast based on instructions that were, at least initially, read. We may have purchased those items based on nutritional labeling information or the sale price offered in a weekly grocery flier or web site. We may have learned about these products or recipes from conversations with friends or by reading about them online or in a magazine. We read and sign permission slips from our children's teachers. On the way to school or work, we read the instructions on the gas pump and signs on the streets. Later, we check our e-mails and may read and respond to text messages. Once we are at work or school, language demands of us an immediate response. It further demands that we interact with the people around us and in various social contexts. All of these interactions are based in the concept of access to *literacy*.

At its most basic, literacy is reading and writing, but Keefe and Copeland (2011) include an additional component we consider as key to the rationale for this chapter—that literacy is grounded in social interactions with other people. This means that literacy itself is a social concept. We humans are social beings, and if we are deprived of literacy learning, we are deprived of opportunities for social contact with others. These may include, for example, opportunities for education, recreation, independent living, employment, and general functioning in our communities. People with complex support needs are often so deprived because they lack access to meaningful age-appropriate literacy genres.

We propose that interaction with texts and other literacy genres is a critical piece in the literacy puzzle for individuals with complex support needs. This should begin early and continue throughout the life span, just as it does for typically developing individuals. Literacy-rich environments, composed of many examples of print materials and texts that are inviting and meaningful for students, are critical to successful literacy instruction.

These texts, however, are often not accessible to individuals with complex support needs. Examples of individual characteristics and needs for support that may preclude someone from accessing texts and other literacy materials include, but are not limited to:

- Motor impairments that prevent the turning of a page or impede the ability to hold a book steadily

- Intellectual and developmental disability (IDD) that impedes learning generally, and literacy learning specifically

- Sensory impairments that interfere with or prevent someone from seeing printed words or hearing oral language content presented either in person or in an audio format

- Learning disabilities that inhibit appropriate progression in literacy development

- Psychosocial challenges accompanying poverty and other risk factors that impede physical, mental, and emotional development

Language barriers are another challenge that may prevent people from accessing literacy materials. These barriers are not disabilities in the same sense as those originating from medical or traumatic causes, or from social and ecological factors such as poverty. Yet, they are certainly challenging to the extent that individuals who are not functional in the majority language of the culture within which they live are also deprived of the benefits that accompany literacy because it is a socially constructed and lived component of culture.

We believe literacy is critically important for functioning in everyday life and, moreover, that reading should be a joyful experience. With that in mind, we explore research literature on the use of adapted texts to facilitate literacy for learners with complex support needs.

REFLECTION QUESTION 1

Do you believe that conventional literacy competencies are possible for individuals with complex support needs if they are provided with the proper tools and support?

RESEARCH-BASED METHODS FOR ADAPTING TEXTS

There are many reasons why an adult reading role model (reading expert) might adapt text for an individual with complex support needs. These individuals might have difficulty decoding the text, comprehending the information within it, seeing the text, hearing it read aloud, or physically accessing the text. The first step for teachers and other adult role models is to determine whether adaptation of a text or other literacy materials is necessary. Many reading experts have used Bormuth's (1968) visual cloze method—shared as an example in Dyck and Pemberton (2002)—for assessing whether text adaptations are necessary for certain students. In that procedure, the reading expert selects a short reading passage of roughly 250 words from the text; every fifth word is eliminated. The learner is then asked to fill in the missing words. The cloze procedure may be used to assess vocabulary acquisition, or comprehension, and may require either oral or written responses, depending upon the needs or disability attributes of the individual learner being assessed. If he or she is able to fill in the missing words, it may indicate that no textual adaptations are needed. Some learners may not be able to fill in the missing words, indicating a need for more support in accessing the text.

Once it has been decided that an individual does need text adaptations, Dyck's (1999) decision tree (see Figure 12.1) is helpful in determining how best to adapt materials to suit individual needs and the context within which the reading is being done.

Five types of adaptations are suggested by Dyck (1999): bypass reading, decrease reading, support reading, organize reading, and guide reading. These five types of adaptations have been examined in literacy research for learners with complex support needs.

Bypass Reading

In *bypass reading,* the modality of the text is changed, usually by presenting it as a read-aloud led by another person, or as a recording (Dyck, 1999; Dyck & Pemberton, 2002). More recent investigations have used the bypass reading approach during shared reading with learners with complex support needs to increase their engagement and listening comprehension skills (Browder, Lee, & Mims, 2011; Browder, Mims, Spooner, Ahlgrim-Delzell, & Lee, 2008; Hudson, Browder, & Jimenez, 2014; Mims, Browder, Baker, Lee, & Spooner, 2009; Mims, Hudson, & Browder, 2012). Shared reading, as discussed in these studies, describes an adult or proficient peer reading the text aloud to the learner and providing a series of prompts to encourage the learner to engage with the text or answer comprehension questions. These studies indicated that learners with complex support needs showed gains in comprehension and engagement when reading was bypassed.

As Dyck (1999) and Dyck and Pemberton (2002) asserted, several considerations are important when deciding to use bypass reading. First, certain reading goals, such as decoding, cannot be met when reading is bypassed. Thus, gains in the areas of comprehension and engagement may be the only objectives met. In addition, some learners might have difficulty attending to spoken words, so although they may appear to be engaged, their minds may wander during read-alouds or recorded reading, resulting in decreased comprehension. Finally, learners do not have the opportunity to reread parts of passages or search for clues in the text, both common strategies experienced readers use. Thus, bypass reading might interfere with the learner's interaction with the text. Nevertheless, this is a simple, low-cost option for individuals who do not yet read text.

Decrease Reading

Decrease reading is an option for learners who need the amount or complexity of the text reduced (Dyck, 1999; Dyck & Pemberton, 2002). Some studies in which adapted texts have been used for individuals with complex support needs have included text reduced in length or complexity (e.g., Hudson, Browder, & Wakeman, 2013). *Decrease reading* has also been implemented in combination with *bypass reading* and other techniques referenced in Dyck (1999) in studies of literacy for students with significant disabilities; this has been effective in supporting comprehension for learners who require simplified vocabulary and language structure to access the content of text. Hudson and Test (2011), for example, analyzed evidence-based research studies that used shared story read-alouds in combination with other interventions to promote literacy learning among students with complex support needs. Three studies included in their research review that implemented shared story read-alouds along with adapted age-appropriate texts (Browder et al., 2008; Browder, Trela, & Jimenez, 2007; Mims et al., 2009) showed promising

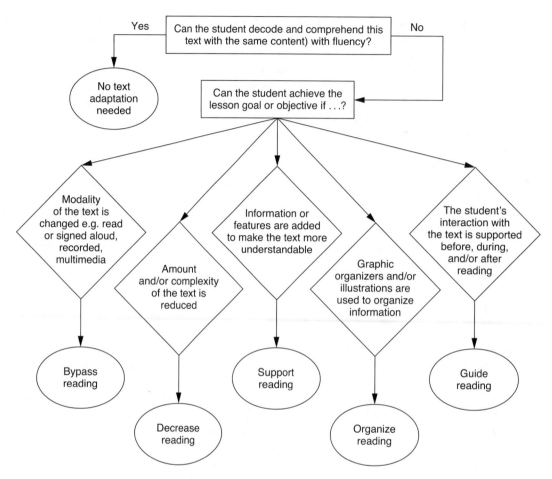

Figure 12.1.　Decision tree for selecting text adaptations for students with complex support needs.

results for students with complex support needs. The results from these studies indicated gains in literacy skills, including early comprehension and response to questions. Browder and colleagues (2007) also combined interactive read-alouds with adapted literature that summarized some passages, used picture symbols to accompany key vocabulary words in the text, and used repeated storylines to teach the concept of main idea. They found that students were more engaged and showed increased comprehension of the text.

Support Reading

Reading experts can *support reading,* according to Dyck (1999) and Dyck and Pemberton (2002), by adding features to make the text more understandable. For example, keywords can be underlined, bolded, or highlighted, and questions can be interspersed throughout (Ruppar, Afacan, Yang, & Pickett, 2017).

　　One common way that text has been supported for learners with complex support needs is through the use of picture symbols. However, Didden, Prinsen, and Sigafoos (2000) suggested caution when determining whether to use picture-enhanced text. Their research has demonstrated that pictures, when paired with text, actually interfere with the individual's learning to read the word. Another consideration surrounds the concern that too much visual information can interfere with learners' attention and comprehension of a word (Glennen & DeCoste, 1996). Similarly, careful assessment is necessary to ensure that the individual can understand the picture without the word being present (Hudson et al., 2013; Ruppar, 2014). Glennen and DeCoste also questioned whether line drawings or photographs are more understandable to the student. It is important to note that research about supporting text with pictures is limited, so teachers and other adult service providers should be systematic and always aware of the evolving needs of the individuals whom they are supporting. Pictorial enhancements of text meet one of the fundamental requirements of universal design for learning (UDL)—the degree of enhancement is readily personalized to learners' individual needs.

Organize Reading

Teachers can also help learners *organize reading,* according to Dyck (1999) and Dyck and Pemberton (2002), through supports such as graphic organizers. Many different types of graphic organizers can be used to assist learners' access to literacy (see Dyck). A few studies have examined the use of graphic organizers to help students with significant disabilities access grade-level content. For example, Schenning, Knight, and Spooner (2013) used graphic organizers to support comprehension of social studies content among students with significant disabilities. Much more research is needed to examine how graphic organizers can support text access for students with significant disabilities, but these recent findings are promising. This topic is addressed in more detail in Chapter 5.

Guide Reading

Finally, Dyck (1999) and Dyck and Pemberton (2002) recommend strategies to help *guide reading* for learners with complex support needs. Adapted study guides can help individuals get more information from the text and maintain their attention to it. Text previews and summaries, fill-in graphic organizers, and frame outlines, which set each component piece in a hierarchy within a frame or box, are recommended. An example of a tool to make appropriate modifications and technological adaptations is CAST's *Book Builder,* which is included in the Resources section at the end of this chapter. Knight, Wood, Spooner, Browder, and O'Brien (2015) discuss ways in which these organizers represent tools that may help students work more independently during reading.

These five types of adaptations—bypass reading, decrease reading, support reading, organize reading, and guide reading—offer opportunities for learners to engage with text across all areas of literacy instruction. We will discuss specific ways to apply these methods later in this chapter. First, however, it is important to note factors that may prevent teachers from using adapted texts with learners who could benefit from them. These factors include feasibility and teacher assumptions.

We found the comprehensive literature review conducted by Scott, Vitale, and Masten (1998) to be particularly relevant to this chapter on literacy adaptations. In this review, the authors sought to understand teachers' perceptions and use of instructional adaptations. These studies included teachers working in inclusive classrooms across all grade levels. In a number of the studies included in the literature review by Scott et al. (Bacon & Schulz, 1991; Bender, Vail, & Scott, 1995; Ellett, 1993; Johnson & Pugach, 1990; Schumm & Vaughn, 1991), teachers responded positively to the *desirability* of many proposed adaptations (to curriculum, planning, and materials) but tended to find many of them less than feasible. Although this literature review is more than 20 years old, our own experiences suggest that it remains relevant and is worthy of inclusion here.

In addition, as noted in Chapter 1, if we are to support literacy development in learners with complex support needs, we must begin by believing that literacy skills can be developed in the first place. This belief is at the heart of what Donnellan (1984) called the *least dangerous assumption.* This presumption of competence is a starting point when considering how to deliver literacy instruction to these learners. We find this to be true for all learners with complex support needs across the life span, regardless of how much previous experience they have with texts or other literacy materials.

REFLECTION QUESTION 2

If you have ever attempted, but failed, to deliver literacy instruction to an individual with complex support needs, what do you think were the reasons that literacy instruction did not result in success for the learner?

OVERVIEW: ACCESSING AGE-APPROPRIATE, CONTENT-SPECIFIC TEXTS AND LITERACY MATERIALS

Access to literacy, as discussed previously, should begin with several objectives in mind. First, regardless of the disability type, support needs, or literacy level of the person for whom text is being adapted, that text should be age appropriate. Too often, especially in school, students are provided literacy materials matched to their reading levels rather than their ages, interests, and life goals. Although a 6-year-old who is not yet a conventional reader may indeed be happy with a book about a bunny family's misadventures, a 15-year-old in the early stages of literacy learning is more likely to be interested in the same topics typically developing 15-year-olds consider relevant to their own lives—a famous singer or celebrity, professional athletes and sports stories, the trials of being a teenager, tales of heroes, stories about love and relationships, informational texts surrounding topics the individual finds interesting, and other culturally relevant literacy materials that are personally meaningful.

A key objective to consider when helping a person with complex support needs to achieve conventional literacy skills involves choosing a text that interests that individual; this often ties directly into age appropriateness, as discussed previously. We can ascertain a learner's personal interests through informal discussion with the individual. Also, teachers can glean useful information by talking with the student's family members and friends about the activities he or she enjoys. Direct observations, interviews, or surveys can also help. The absence of interesting reading material specifically matched to an individual can thwart efforts to instill a love of reading.

Finally, when choosing texts in the school setting, consider specific content and/or genres. Especially at the middle and high school levels, students are often required to engage with nonfiction informational texts, procedural "how-tos" (often referenced as task analyses), or instructions, expository texts that contain complicated ideas or theories, and literary/narrative texts, including fictional stories.

In the next section, we share specific textual adaptations that integrate, singly or in combination, the five types of adaptations suggested by Dyck (1999): bypass reading, decrease reading, support reading, organize reading, and guide reading. We categorize these ideas as low-, mid-, or high-tech, depending on the materials and equipment required.

Although there are slight differences in how low-, mid-, and high-tech adaptations are defined, generally, *low-tech* adaptations use inexpensive materials and equipment—for example, highlighters, magnetic letters, or even something as simple as a pen and a pad of sticky notes—and do not require special training. *Mid-tech* adaptations may be slightly more expensive but are still easy to use—for example, audiobooks and electronic dictionaries. *High-tech* adaptations are more expensive and may require specialized training. They generally require devices such as desktop or laptop computers, tablet computers, or handheld computerized devices (Conderman & Jung, 2014). Note that these three technological categories sometimes overlap; the main focus in this chapter, whenever possible, is on adaptations that are primarily low-tech.

As you read through these suggestions, consider which of Dyck's (1999) adaptations are being implemented; many ideas combine types. Consider also how you can use the decision tree in Figure 12.1 to help you choose an adaptation or combination of adaptations. In doing so, be aware that the ideas we provide may be considered as prompts for your own ideas or supplements for adaptations you are already using. It is important to recognize that it will be critical to tailor any or all of them to the specific needs of your learners and your learning environment.

We will begin by suggesting low-tech adaptations that make literacy materials accessible for learners with complex support needs, along with some activity extension ideas. The suggested adaptations can stand on their own if resources are limited and access to the materials and equipment needed for the extensions is not available. We begin each example by noting the age level of the individual for whom the modification and type of literacy materials described might be most appropriate. Many of the adaptations would benefit learners along a broad continuum in terms of support needs, age levels, and content. Some adaptations are appropriate for all age levels, so we hope that some may be useful for caregivers and other service providers of adults with complex support needs as well.

CREATE ACCESS USING WORDLESS PICTURE BOOKS

We recommend using wordless picture books with all ages and literacy levels, depending on the activity, the wordless book chosen, and the content being taught. Wordless books are an excellent resource to implement adaptations that bypass, decrease, or organize reading, or that combine these approaches. Because wordless books are also engaging and challenging for conventional readers, they are well suited to inclusive learning environments. Their open-ended nature provides plenty of opportunities for challenging and meaningful differentiated instruction. (Resources for finding wordless books are provided at the end of this chapter.)

As a tool for literacy learning, wordless or near-wordless picture books provide pedagogical opportunities for enhancing young readers' language skills, but they are often overlooked when considering older students or adults whose literacy levels are low. Lane, Keefe, Copeland, and Kruger (2015) and Copeland and Keefe (2007) explained that wordless picture books have the following advantages:

- They encourage creativity and imagination.
- They provide a link between an image and its representative word.
- They help develop understanding of story structure (e.g., sequencing).
- They help develop the skills of making predictions or inferences.
- They provide a tool for teachers to learn about students' cultural and linguistic background knowledge.
- They allow students to become more invested in a story.
- They serve as a motivational means to create interest in new content or subject matter.
- They work across grade and content levels.

For people with complex support needs who are preliterate or at a very low literacy level, beautiful images provide a safe, nonthreatening means for introducing literacy across all ages and contexts. We suggest using them in the following ways, and you can also refer to Chapter 6 for more information about using wordless books in literacy instruction.

Create a Narrative

One way to use wordless picture books is to ask an individual, group, or class to provide the text that should accompany each picture—in other words, to create the narrative. This is a great shared reading activity to use for modeling purposes in that an expert reader—a teacher, parent, older sibling, service provider, or caregiver—begins by paging through the book and sharing aloud his or her own perceptions of the pictures. During the first time through the book, the expert reader might think aloud in order to share these observations. In this way, the audience with whom the book is being shared is introduced to the meaning-making process. Next, the expert reader might page through the text while asking the audience participants for suggestions about words to accompany the pictures. At this point, emerging readers might benefit from modeling or from visual or (simple) written prompts. Prompts are especially helpful in developing learners' comprehension of narrative sequencing. Consider using prompts such as *in the beginning, one day, all of a sudden, later, then, finally,* or *in the end.* The expert might write the suggested words on sticky notes and attach them to the pages.

After the pictures have been text-enhanced in these ways, the expert and audience participants reread the book together. The expert then asks questions about whether any changes should be made. Questions may include those surrounding whether the story makes sense, or if there are different words that should be used because of what is happening in the picture. When the story is satisfactory to everyone involved, read through it again, and continue reading it over the course of several days. Repetition is one important element in the development of literacy, and reading the collectively written story aloud may be reinforcing for some learners. When the story is familiar, the activity might be further enhanced through drama or reader's theater. Arts-based activities are discussed further in Chapter 13.

This activity also can be enhanced in mid- and high-tech ways. Assistive technology enhancements include scanning the pages of the book (and printing them, if desired) and adding a caption or text box with the words provided by learners. The teacher can also create an electronic slideshow so the story can be read aloud from a large screen or white board. In addition, instead of using plastic covers, the teacher might laminate them. Captions and text may be handwritten directly on the scanned pages, but for the sake of preserving natural resources, it's better to choose an option that allows the pages to be reused. Collecting a reusable set of scanned wordless book pages will ensure that the materials are always ready when the opportunity for creative storytelling presents itself.

Remember, every learner will see something different in the wordless story, so the goal is to provide a great opportunity for creative storytelling each time. We highly recommend adapting wordless books as a whole-group activity because it provides learners with complex support needs opportunities to shine among their peers—something many of them seldom experience.

Figure 12.2 shows how one teacher used a wordless book (*Flotsam* by David Wiesner [2006]) with her middle school students with autism spectrum disorder (ASD). She asked students to create individual narratives for it by placing sticky notes on each page. Students then typed their narratives and met in small groups to compare and contrast their storylines.

Using and enhancing wordless picture books is not limited to narration of a story. We provide some additional ideas in the pages that follow and encourage you to come up with your own ideas as well.

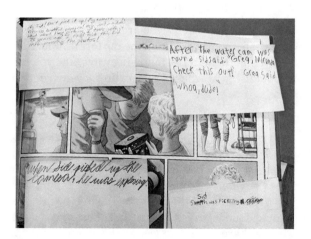

Figure 12.2. Sticky notes used by middle school students to create a narrative for the wordless book *Flotsam*, by David Wiesner (2006).

Write a Poem Together

We sometimes forget that poetry is a viable and engaging form of literacy. We have found that learners are naturally drawn to the rhythmic cadence of a well-constructed poem, and "Using poetry activities and games can help students access... literacy development" (Lane et al., 2015, p. 15). Because poems often contain fewer words than narratives, and because poetic license means the usual rules of chronology, characterization, capitalization, and punctuation do not necessarily apply, we like the idea of allowing learners to enhance pictures with poems. David Wiesner's (1991) book, *Tuesday,* helps us to illustrate a poem's potential for helping learners to access literacy. Here is an example:

The frogs can fly
They move so high
While turtles watch
And fishes sigh

In the previous example, two practices discussed so far in this chapter for adapting books were applied—the use of wordless picture books generally, and enhancing wordless books with poetry. The poem was written by the first author of this chapter as a description of an illustrated page—the book has no page numbers. It serves as an example of one way poetry might be used to create a story from a wordless picture book.

Increase Vocabulary

Wordless picture books can be used to introduce learners to new or recurring vocabulary words by using sticky notes or other methods to label items in the picture so that the link between a word and its visual representation can be made clear.

Another extension activity might include copying the labeled page(s) and then creating a word wall containing targeted vocabulary and placing it where learners can see it. Regular and ongoing exposure to words, as occurs in a literacy-rich environment, is critical in the acquisition and evolution of literacy skills across the life span. (See Chapters 5, 8, and 9 for other ways to incorporate word walls into literacy instruction.)

Support Grammar Instruction

After enhancing the pictures in a wordless book with text, you might use this text to introduce learners to grammar concepts. Label punctuation and different parts of speech using small sticky notes or other methods. As another variation, you might copy the labeled pages, post them, and include related grammatical terms on a nearby word wall.

Teach Writing Dialogue

When enhancing pictures with text, consider adding dialogue spoken by the characters shown in the picture. Figure 12.2, in addition to showing student-created narratives, shows how two middle school students used their sticky notes to create dialogue within their narratives on the page from Wiesner's (2006) *Flotsam.* Dialogue balloons like those in comic books and graphic novels can also be used to make it clear who is speaking. The use of sticky notes, laminated pages, dictation, SMART Boards, and other low-, mid-, and high-tech adaptations can make this activity accessible to all students.

Teach Story Mapping

To teach story mapping using wordless books, start by creating a blank story map with spaces to record information about the title, author, characters, settings, and plot events, including spaces for the story's main problem and its resolution. (Consider making a copy of the blank

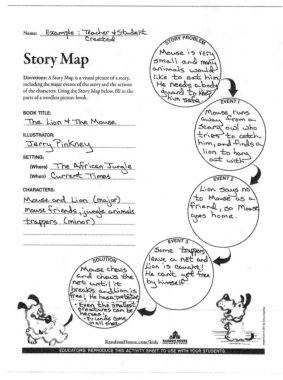

Figure 12.3. Story map for *The Lion & the Mouse*, illustrated by Jerry Pinkney (2009).

story map, perhaps enlarged, and then having it laminated for repeated use with different books.) Figure 12.3 shows how we used a sample story map template from Random House (http://images. randomhouse.com/teachers_guides/9780375858611.pdf). Many other reproducible story map template designs are available online.

We used this story map template for the book, *The Lion & the Mouse,* adapted to wordless picture book format by Jerry Pinkney (2009). Because fables have a moral lesson, the teacher and students added that to the Solution circle. Story maps can be designed for whatever learning goals are taking place, and they may be made genre specific. Please note that although our example in Figure 12.3 maps a wordless book, story maps can be used as text adaptations in many different types of texts. Another extension activity might involve making a copy (perhaps enlarged) of the blank story map and then having it laminated so it can be used repeatedly with different books. (See Chapter 6 for additional ways to use story maps.) An additional extension for individuals who are moving beyond the very early stages of literacy learning, more than one picture displayed side-by-side can be used to teach compare and contrast, cause and effect, or other more advanced literacy concepts.

Enhance Instruction in Specific Content Areas

Many wordless picture books lend themselves to teaching students information specific to a given content area or unit of study. For example, *Why?* by Nikolai Popov (1996) might serve as an introduction to a social studies unit on war, conflict, or the Holocaust. *You Can't Take a Balloon into the Metropolitan Museum,* by Jacqueline Preiss Weitzman and Robin Preiss Glasser (1998), is a book that includes depictions of actual works of fine art on display in New York's Metropolitan Museum amid the drawn illustrations, and it would be a great book to use in an art, art history, or humanities class, all commonly offered at the high school and postsecondary levels of education.

Accessible Versions of Otherwise Inaccessible Texts

Some wordless books—such as Jerry Pinkney's adaptation of the Aesop fable, *The Lion and the Mouse,* described previously—were created as alternate versions of existing texts. If you wish to teach a particular text to a student who is preliterate, check whether a wordless picture book version is available. If so, the student may be able to access lesson objectives by using this version. Wordless picture books can be a great way to present texts that, as originally written, might be inaccessible to individuals with complex support needs.

The use of wordless picture books as a literacy tool for individuals with complex support needs is a sound pedagogical practice limited only by imagination. Although this strategy is highly versatile, however, it is not necessarily appropriate for teaching certain literacy skills; moreover, advanced texts may not be available in picture-book format. With this in mind, we will now address ways educators might adapt complex literacy materials for this student population.

ADAPTING COMPLEX LITERACY MATERIALS: SIMPLIFY AND CLARIFY

In some instances, educators need to simplify and clarify complex literacy materials for a particular student's needs or to provide instruction addressing a particular concept, skill, or text. In the following sections we discuss ways to do so. The literacy materials addressed here are, for the most part, at the opposite end of the complexity continuum from wordless picture books. They include advanced vocabulary or content-specific language that requires higher order understanding of academic English. Students may encounter these texts as they progress to higher grade levels, to postsecondary school settings, and finally, to the adult world beyond school. For them to function well in these contexts, literacy learning across many genres is required. For many learners with complex needs for support, advanced or content-specific literacy materials must be made accessible for learning to occur. We recommend *simplifying* or *clarifying* text for learners who are required to understand more advanced language or concepts.

One way to make complex text accessible is to simplify the content for the reader without losing the "big ideas" that are critical for understanding the text. An example of simplifying textual content is Dyck (1999) and Dyck and Pemberton's (2002) adaptation method of *decrease reading,* described previously. We offer several additional suggestions for simplifying text and note the types of text in which the modifications may be most helpful.

Substitute an Alternate Print Version: Abridged Text, Summaries

Substituting an alternate print version of the text is an option included in Dyck and Pemberton (2002), who suggested that the simplest adaptation requiring the least amount of time and monetary resources to meet curricular objectives and individual student needs should generally be the one selected. We recommend this particular adaptation for individuals who have some literacy skills and may be able to read a simpler version of the original text.

In some instances, specific texts or other literacy materials already exist in adapted formats. Many texts that include complicated vocabulary and literary concepts are available in alternate forms, such as text summaries. These alternate forms allow individuals who are preliterate, or whose literacy levels are far too low to access the original text, to access required curriculum content. If your students need access to a text they cannot read in its original version, we suggest visiting your school or public librarian in order to find out whether a suitable alternative text is available. Many classic texts commonly read by students in the upper grades, such as Mark Twain's *The Adventures of Tom Sawyer* and *The Adventures of Huckleberry Finn,* also exist in alternate versions. These versions, created for younger readers, can provide access to the text for older students with complex support needs.

Substitute an Alternate Print Version: Enhanced Summaries

Some teachers of individuals with complex support needs may find existing summary versions of complex texts a viable alternative—for example, *CliffsNotes* or *SparkNotes.* Note that these summaries can be provided *in lieu of* the original text or *in addition to* the original text, depending on the learner's needs. That is, they can be used as a means of simplifying text (the learner reads the summary version only, a form of decreased reading) or as a means of clarifying text (the learner reads the original text, using the summary version as a support).

CliffsNotes, "booklet"-size versions of the original text, serve primarily as summaries, retaining all of the main ideas and important plot elements. A CliffsNotes version of a given book also provides a study guide and other test preparation materials for that book. Many classic literature texts written for students of all ages, as well as many required texts for students in the upper grades, exist in a CliffsNotes version.

The simplifying features described previously have made CliffsNotes, SparkNotes, and the like the butt of jokes. The stereotypical consumer of these "mini books" is a typically developing student who relies on them to pass English class without having to read lengthy, complicated, possibly boring literary texts. However, these versions can be a valuable instructional resource. It is now understood that CliffsNotes and similar products offer textual access to individuals with complex support needs for whom the lesson objective cannot be met using the text in its original format (Dyck & Pemberton, 2002). This is certainly one of the least labor intensive and most affordable means of providing access to complex literacy genres for learners with complex support needs because these adaptations retain the original text's key ideas, story chronology, and important vocabulary and provide background knowledge.

In their print versions, these summary texts can serve as a valuable low-tech text adaptation. Associated resources potentially allow for mid- and high-tech text adaptations as well. Most CliffsNotes print texts are now available online as free, downloadable audiobook versions that users can download onto a desktop or laptop computer or smartphone—a great option for some individuals with complex support needs and for those who are blind or visually impaired. One thing we love about the 21st-century version of CliffsNotes is that it provides free, downloadable audiobook versions for iPhones and Android devices in addition to the Internet audiobook versions, adding yet another option for accessing text for individuals with complex support needs. We have included the web-site information for Cliffs Notes in the Resources section located at the end of this chapter. The online and app versions of CliffsNotes have features such as "cram plans" that help students with test preparation; there is also a test prep feature for teachers. Summaries and quizzes are also a useful feature for users of the online and app versions of CliffsNotes. Literature reviews are also available for around $2.00 each. Both the web site and apps are easy to navigate.

Create a Summary of the Text

Some researchers suggest rewriting text in a summary version as an adaptation that makes text accessible across content areas and grade levels for learners with complex support needs (Hudson et al., 2013). Summarizing a text retains its key ideas while allowing these learners to gain access to the same stories, poetry, or informational materials read by their peers who are proficient readers. We recommend this adaptation for individuals for whom complex, content-specific textual material as written is inaccessible, and for those who must meet lesson objectives that include comprehension, especially at higher grade levels.

When summarizing a text, regardless of its length, the structure of the original text must be retained. The main ideas, important details, and necessary vocabulary (for all text types) must also be retained, as well as the characters, settings, and plot events (for narrative text). Definitions, callout cues, and additional sidebar information also may be added to either the original or summarized versions of text. We discuss this in the next section on supported reading. We also like the suggestion by Hudson et al. (2013) to use pictures at the beginning of each chapter when summarizing a book-length text, so as to cue students about that chapter's theme or other important material. In-text pictures may also be included at points where a visual representation might make a difficult word, phrase, or concept more comprehensible (as is done in some dictionaries, for example). These pictures can be added to text within any genre, especially content-specific informational text that is complex or comprises new concepts.

Text summaries, especially of narrative and dramatic genres, may not always be appropriate as an end product but instead may sometimes be used as a supplement to support comprehension of the original text. One study (Duke, Caughlan, Juzwick, & Martin, 2012) found that summarizing a narrative or dramatic text may likely change the genre to an informational type. This is why maintaining the original structure of the material being summarized, especially in narrative and dramatic genres, is important. Changing the genre may, in turn, change the purpose for reading the text. For example, most people read a novel not only to learn the sequence of events—information typically found in a summary—but also to experience the language and rhetorical devices, dialogue, structure, pacing, and other embedded literary elements that are all embedded in the literature. Thus, we recommend that you consider carefully how summaries are written and assess the extent to which it is important that the genre's original structure be maintained in order to meet your specific learning objectives before determining whether or not a summary may serve as an end product. Also consider using summaries as a supplement to other literacy activities related to a text, such as listening to an audiobook, watching a film version, or listening to a peer or other expert read the text (Apitz, Ruppar, Roessler, & Pickett, 2017).

Finally, we caution that summarizing longer texts can be cumbersome; it is time consuming and may not be practical for other reasons. For classroom teachers who will use the same texts over many years, the effort may well be worthwhile. However, for texts that may not be used more than once, the parent, teacher, or service provider may wish to consider alternative means besides summarization for making grade-level texts accessible. We offer more low-tech examples for adapting text here.

Create a Supported Version of the Text

In some instances, it is valuable to a teacher not only to summarize a text but also to create a supported version of it. Complex texts become more prevalent in the classroom as students reach higher grade levels. These include informational and expository texts based in scientific or mathematical concepts, texts about important historical periods or unfamiliar geographical territory, or texts based in cultural elements that are unfamiliar and therefore not already present in an individual's stored background knowledge. In addition, at higher grade levels, academic content-specific vocabulary becomes more advanced, literary devices such as figurative language (e.g., metaphor, irony, personification) become more common, and expectations of students become more rigorous in general. For example, students may be expected to formulate hypotheses in science, explain a particular theorem in math, or make inferences in English language arts. Learners with complex support needs should not be deprived of the opportunity to connect with texts just because the concepts being taught are difficult to express in simple terms.

Access to grade-level text can be aided by textual adaptations that involve what Dyck and Pemberton (2002) referenced as *supported reading.* Many low-tech adaptations fall within this realm, such as providing definitions of important words, adding pictures to enhance difficult concepts visually, or using highlighters to indicate importance in the main ideas or to call attention to ideas related to the lesson's main focus. The teacher might also adapt text by placing written questions beside portions of the text, or at the end, to guide reading and aid comprehension or test preparation.

Still another adaptation is to provide the reader with previously agreed-upon cues in the form of symbols or words. For example, a student and teacher may agree in advance that a complex text about trees with unfamiliar names will contain a certain tree symbol accompanying each word that is representative of any referenced specific species of tree in the text. The student is then cued that each word with a tree symbol is an important vocabulary word to learn for this unit of study.

Finally, as noted previously, summaries that are written at an accessible literacy level but retain key ideas can be provided as a supplement to challenging texts.

For many of these augmentations, sticky notes are convenient; they allow for definitions, visual aids, and cues to be placed wherever needed on the page. Because they are easily removed, they may be used with texts or other literacy materials that must be saved or returned intact, such as handouts or nonconsumable workbooks. (We have also discovered glue sticks with a repositionable bond; these can be used to make almost any piece of paper into a sticky note!)

Although highlighters, markers, and pens cannot be used to mark nonconsumable print materials directly, these writing instruments can still be used for underlining or boxing texts, adding marginalia, and so forth. The teacher can provide a photocopy of the text to be marked, or, if this is impossible or impractical, clear plastic sheets can be laid over the page, and dry or wet erase markers or highlighters can then be used freely. These suggestions allow for customizing textual adaptations to meet the needs of individual students with complex support needs who may need different types of adaptations.

As with summarization, we recognize that the steps involved in supported reading as an adaptation may be labor intensive. They may not be practical for a teacher with many students and many needs for supports to address, as is often the case for secondary school teachers. These content-area teachers may see more than 100 students each day, including students with complex support needs—whose presence in those general education classrooms is something we are very happy to see! Again, if a teacher plans to use a given text year after year, the initial effort involved is heavy but well worth it once the adaptations have been made.

We know from our own work that this *can* be done. For example, the first author taught language arts and literature for a number of years in an inclusive secondary school classroom where supplementary texts, including historical novels and memoirs, were used throughout the year. Recognizing that, over time, students needed definitions of many of the same terms, or needed the same ideas highlighted, she saved sticky notes on cardboard sheets, which were then hole-punched and stored in a binder with separate sections for each text or lesson. The sticky notes contained relevant information (e.g., chapter, page number, handout title) penciled in lightly on the corner of each and placed on the cardboard sheets in sequential order for easy access. As the sticky notes became less "sticky," a couple of removable glue dots, or some tacky putty like the kind used to hang student work on walls, ensured continued usability of the sticky notes. With the advent of repositionable glue sticks, however, glue dots and putty may not be necessary.

A mid-tech idea for the previous sticky-notes-in-a-binder suggestion involves putting the sticky notes on the cardboard and then having the entire page (cardboard and sticky notes) laminated. Afterward, the teacher can cut the sticky notes back out and then place the laminated squares on the cardboard sheets in the binder using Velcro, a friend to every educator. Alternatively, the laminated sticky notes could be placed in envelopes within the binder. These envelopes can be labeled with the chapter number and organized by topic (as might be done in math or science), by era (in history, literature, or art history), or by region (in geography or social studies).

Figure 12.4 is an example of a page that has been adapted using some of the supported reading techniques discussed previously. Please know that we would *not* expect anyone to use all of the adaptation techniques on a single page of text; doing so would be overwhelming and unsustainable. We simply wanted to provide as many technique examples as was practical on one page. This example shows adaptations made for Elie Wiesel's (2006) memoir, *Night,* a text that is often required reading in high school. Because few students have background knowledge about the setting in which the events depicted took place, or the surrounding culture, it is difficult reading for most students without guidance and support. It was chosen as a strong example of the type of rigorous reading that may be required of students at the high school and postsecondary levels.

Most written text can be augmented with pictures to enhance meaning for learners with complex support needs; such an adaptation will be considered as "easy-read." Providing

The summer was coming to an end. The Jewish year was almost over. On the eve of *Rosh Hashanah, the last day of that cursed year, the entire camp was agitated and every one of us felt the tension. After all, this was a day unlike all others. The last day of the year. The word "last" had an odd ring to it. What if it really were the last day?

The evening meal was *distributed*, an especially thick soup, but nobody touched it. We wanted to wait until after prayer. On the *Appelplatz, surrounded by electrified barbed wire, thousands of Jews, anguish on their faces, gathered in silence.

Night was falling rapidly. And more and more prisoners kept coming from every block, suddenly able to overcome time and space, to will both into submission.

What are You, my God? I thought angrily. How do You compare to this stricken mass gathered to affirm to You their faith, their anger, their defiance? What does Your *grandeur* mean, Master of this misery? Why do you go on troubling these poor people's wounded minds, their ailing bodies?

POSTREADING QUESTION

How do you think Elie is feeling in this scene? Why?

INTERESTING NOTE

The teacher can use a special color to highlight the Y in the words "You" and "Your" and the M in the word "Master" in the last paragraph, to demonstrate that these letters are capitalized to let the reader know that these words relate to God.

CULTURAL DEFINITIONS

Rosh Hashanah: the Jewish new year
Appelplatz: where roll calls took place in Nazi concentration camps

GENERAL DEFINITIONS

Distributed: handed out
Grandeur: the state of being very important or majestic

VISUAL LEGEND

Stars * are visual cues to the student indicating something to notice.
Underlined words are defined under "Cultural Definitions."
Italicized words are defined under "General Definitions."

NOTES REGARDING THIS SAMPLE

In this example of supported reading, the teacher has matched visual cues (i.e., underlined and italicized words) to the words being defined and their definitions. A teacher can also use coordinating colors and highlight text and match the word and its definition with a like color sticky note. The use of like colors is an additional visual cue to struggling readers. Noting items of interest is also a good practice because it indicates to the student who is struggling that the teacher cares enough to share something that may not be necessary to know but is interesting nonetheless. Highlights, arrows, stars, underlines, or other visual cues can be written on a clear plastic sheet placed over the page if the text is borrowed. The postreading questions may be answered orally, or choose from several possible answers. We would not advise using all of these text supports on one page because it may be overwhelming to students with complex support needs, and it would certainly be overwhelming for the person creating the adaptations, but any of these visual cues are good options.

Figure 12.4. Sample of supported text: Elie Wiesel's (2006) *Night,* p. 66.

easy-read or pictorial enhancements of text is an adaptation recommended for several kinds of learners:

- Individuals of all ages who do not yet understand the functions of print or who decode at a low level

- Learners who respond well to visual prompts

- Individuals who are striving to navigate independently among a variety of literacy contexts in the school and community

Pictorial enhancements can potentially encompass all five of Dyck's (1999) forms of adaptation—bypass reading, decrease reading, support reading, organize reading, and guide reading. Engaging visuals can make literacy activities more enjoyable for any learners.

Although not all text lends itself readily to a complete pictorial translation, most written text, including many nonfiction genres, may be augmented with pictures to enhance meaning for learners with complex support needs. For example, procedural texts that provide instructions are fairly easy to convert to a pictorial rendering by using your own photos, clip art, or photos available online. Figure 12.5 shows a page from a set of easy-read recipe instructions for how to make Rice Krispies Treats, used in a literacy class for adults with IDD. In Figure 12.6, class participant Henry poses in front of the chocolate-covered pretzels he made from an easy-read recipe. These recipes are a literacy genre—visually enhanced procedural text—that we notice more and more frequently on the packaging of various grocery items that require the consumer to follow simple steps for preparation: cakes from a prepackaged mix and microwave popcorn are two examples.

Texts might also be adapted to be easier to read using various in-text supports for comprehension, attention, and self-monitoring. Ruppar et al. (2017) designed an adaptation process for secondary-level English language arts texts. Through their research, they adapted texts used in general education English language arts classes, such as *The Odyssey, Romeo and Juliet,* and *To Kill a Mockingbird.* They recommend these steps for adapting a complex narrative or dramatic text:

1. Outline the story.

2. Identify the key themes of the book.

3. Choose key vocabulary to target for instruction.

4. Identify key events in the story.

5. Write the adapted text.

6. Choose pictures.

Completing these steps is time consuming at first; however, there are templates for adapted versions of these texts that can be used and modified year after year for students enrolled in general education English language arts classes.

In the community, individuals who are navigating among a wide array of literacy events have been shown to derive benefit from adaptation of some genres of literacy when the text was augmented with pictures (Morgan, Moni, & Cuskelly, 2013). These literacy genres included menus, timetables, and displays such as those found in stores or at public venues—museums, zoos, and parks, to name a few.

SUGGESTIONS FOR LOW-TECH ADAPTATIONS ACROSS VARIED SUPPORT NEEDS

Each adaptation, as noted in the following sections, is recommended for individuals with more specific needs for support and is noted as a general guideline. We know you will find these ideas to be applicable to other learners as well.

Ingredients

For the treats: For decorating:

Figure 12.5. A page from an easy-read recipe. (ARCA Career Enhancement Services Literacy Class, December 22nd, 2015.)

Figure 12.6.   Henry, a client at ARCA Career Enhancement Services in Albuquerque, NM (December 22, 2015), shows off the results of his hard work making chocolate-covered pretzel treats. These were given as gifts to family, friends, and staff at Christmas. Easy-read recipes and supported reading were used to support Henry's growing literacy skills.

For individuals who are visually impaired or cannot access traditional written text for other reasons, consider the following:

- Read-alouds/shared reading of the text by a peer or adult

- Adding tactile elements to pages (e.g., a tree branch attached to a page with text about trees)

- Using texts with very large font, when available—try your local library first (they have interlibrary loan services and can access many materials from other libraries); if unsuccessful, try Learning Ally (especially for content specific academic texts)

- Adding glow-in-the-dark paint like Tulip puffy paints to images in wordless picture books to make them tactile because they literally pop off the page

Additional resources for students with visual impairments include audiobooks. These are discussed in sections referencing CliffsNotes and Learning Ally—web-site information for both is included in the Resources section at the end of this chapter. Additional audio adaptations are also discussed in a broad way in the next section, Mid-Tech and High-Tech Text Adaptations.

For individuals who have disabilities involving fine motor control or other physical impairments that make handling traditional text difficult, you may try the following:

- Add "handles" to the edges of pages of books using items like Popsicle-type wooden craft sticks, or use thick sticky tabs for easier page turning.

- Provide a desktop easel to hold a text or other literacy materials (e.g., handouts) in place and for easier reading; ask a peer to assist in turning the pages when it is time.

- Use letter, word, or phrase magnets and provide a metal cookie sheet on which to move them around so that students can practice vocabulary, grammar, sentence structure, and other literacy skills.

For individuals who have difficulty with decoding in general, some of these ideas are known to help:

- Support reading by rewording content, using short sentences, offering sidebars with vocabulary definitions, providing space between lines of text, using large enough font, blocking out unnecessary text that may serve to distract, or circling/underlining/highlighting text on a page that is important and should be read.

- Create story maps with individuals or groups.

- Provide *completed* graphic organizers before, during, and after reading.

- Create a glossary of vocabulary terms that may be used throughout reading.

- Ask comprehension questions throughout the text (sticky notes attached to the page margins are great for this).

- Provide study guides and test reviews.

- Consider giving short, more frequent quizzes throughout a lesson or unit rather than end-of-unit tests that are more comprehensive and may be overwhelming for some learners; quizzes that require simple *yes/no* responses that may be circled may be a good choice for some learners.

- Use color coding for routine practices such as sticky notes with definitions, questions, symbols used as cues (e.g., stars, exclamation points), and main ideas.

- Allow students who respond well to kinesthetic activities to move around the classroom while reading and writing by providing clipboards and agreeing to rules ahead of time.

- Whenever possible, allow students to make choices surrounding texts to be read, responses/homework/projects, and other forms of informal assessment.

REFLECTION QUESTION 3

Are you willing to speak to colleagues, friends, family members, and other community stakeholders about some of the ways that text can be adapted to make it accessible for learners with complex support needs? How might they be able to help you find appropriate ways to modify text for the learners with whom you work?

MID-TECH AND HIGH-TECH TEXT ADAPTATIONS

As noted earlier in this chapter, when we reference mid-tech adaptations, we are referring to those types of adaptations and modifications that require more than paper and pen but are not as complicated (or expensive) as computer equipment or high-end electronic augmentative and alternative communication (AAC) devices such as type-to-speech communicators or voice synthesizers. We have grouped mid-tech and high-tech adaptations together under one subheading because, in some instances, an adaptation may actually be considered as both depending upon the equipment used to access the adapted text, as in the audio adaptations referenced next.

Audio Adaptations of Text

We recommend audio adaptations of text for individuals with complex support needs who are preliterate or who respond well to auditory materials, as well as individuals who are visually impaired and learners with disabilities that prevent comprehension of traditional written text or other literacy genres, which is true for many individuals with complex support needs.

Because the translation of written text to audio format involves the use of equipment to record (if the teacher, parent, or other service provider is making the recording) or equipment to playback prerecorded audiobooks and other literacy genres, we consider it to be generally a mid-tech adaptation despite the fact that many individuals now own smartphones, tablets, or other digital technology. In the past decade, access to audio recordings of texts has expanded greatly. This access may be provided through free apps, web sites like CliffsNotes or Learning Ally, or via other online digital downloads onto a desktop or laptop computer. That said, for those who do not have ready access to technology, there are many organizations that exist for the purpose of not only providing audiobooks but trained staff and volunteers to train individuals in how to understand and use them. As mentioned previously in this chapter, CliffsNotes not only provides thousands of literary texts in summary form, along with study guides and test preparation, but also has available free downloads of many of those texts to apps available on iPhones and Android phones. As well, Learning Ally has tens of thousands of content-specific texts in audio format and thousands of trained volunteers who are available for phone consultations or who can provide information on other services and available training. The web sites for both of these organizations can be found in the Resources section at the end of this chapter.

If an adult reading expert is opting to record written text, there are a few things to keep in mind, according to Dyck and Pemberton (2002)—with some additional notes from us. These include the following:

- Record in a quiet place, free of background/ambient noise.

- Seek help from others (e.g., a same-age peer) with strong reading fluency and a good speaking voice, who may be willing to make an audio recording of written text.

- Provide written text to accompany the audio recording, and mark the text with consistent symbols and cues.

- Provide recorded verbal instructions about pages for additional information.

- Guide the student to visual material like maps and illustrations, and discuss them verbally (on the recording) right after they are mentioned in the text.

- Provide pre- and postreading instructions about items to review in advance of listening to the recording, or questions to consider during or after listening.

YouTube and Other Internet Resources

For those not familiar with YouTube's versatility for educators and parents, we encourage you to check it out. Look for educational resources by simply typing any word or phrase you would like to find more information about in the search box. There are many options to choose from, and many of these may be considered as augmentations to traditional written text that will help individuals with complex support needs, as well as others who love digital media formats, gain access to literacy when used in combination with traditional written text.

REFLECTION QUESTION 4

What suggestions for adapting text or other literacy materials within this chapter do you think you might be willing to try? Why would these adaptations be appropriate for the learners with whom you work?

SUMMARY

For every suggestion we have offered in this chapter, we know there are many more. Many of you who work with people with complex support needs may already be making text adaptations we have not included. For those who do have some experience with adapting text and who would like more specific guidelines for summarizing, identifying key themes, choosing vocabulary and important events, and writing and piloting the resulting adapted text, we recommend the condensed list, "Steps for Adapting Text" (Apitz et al., 2017). However, this list might be overwhelming if you are venturing into a first attempt at text adaptation. In that case, we encourage you to begin with a small step, such as one of the low-tech adaptations discussed previously.

We hope that we have provided some usable ideas for adaptation of texts and other literacy genres that are feasible. We further hope that individuals working with people with complex support needs will attempt at least a few of them, if for no other reason than their belief in the right of all individuals to acquire literacy skills, to the extent each is able, in order to engage with the rich worlds that reveal themselves to readers. We are certainly well aware of the time constraints and budget issues faced by classroom teachers at all levels because we have both spent years in the classroom as well. For these reasons, we have attempted to provide as many low-tech text adaptation ideas as possible. The clear advantage to the low-tech adaptations referenced in this chapter and elsewhere surround the minimum monetary resources required to implement them. That said, we acknowledge that some of these adaptations require considerable time, which is also a valuable commodity among busy parents, teachers, and support personnel who work with individuals with complex support needs.

Although some might argue that the availability of technology diminishes the need for conventional literacy skills that are gleaned from reading and interacting with texts, we agree with Chilton (2013), who described the computer as a mere "digital daze" for individuals who use it but are not literate. When Chilton (a local editorial columnist for the *Albuquerque Journal,* who frequently wrote on education-related issues) interviewed librarians about the accommodations they offered for their patrons with developmental disabilities, he found that librarians did not seek to match books to an individual's reading level but rather to the person's interests, regardless of the disability label or range of support needs. This, we know, is perhaps the most important factor in developing a lifelong love of reading—engagement with text that captures the reader's interest, imagination, and dreams.

In conclusion, it is worth reiterating that individuals with complex support needs are often relegated to lives lacking in opportunities to engage with texts and other literacy genres, merely because they were not provided with opportunities to access literacy in school. We agree with Luckasson (2006): Schools in which individuals with complex support needs are not provided ample opportunity to access literacy are violating the rights of those individuals. Luckasson suggested that we ought not to be able to preclude certain individuals from any foundational human rights, and that among these rights is the right to literacy. With literacy, we are all free to exercise our citizenship—fully participating in and fully contributing to our families, our local communities, and the larger world community.

REFLECTION QUESTION 5

Why are you reading this book? (If it is because you care about someone with complex support needs, and want that person to have a more enriched life through literacy, then we say "thank you" and urge you to never give up on that possibility.)

REFLECTION QUESTION 6

How important is it that our schools mirror society in terms of the inclusion of individuals with disabilities alongside their typically developing peers?

RESOURCES

- **CAST UDL Book Builder** (http://bookbuilder.cast.org/) allows people to create and publish their own digital books; it's a great site to consider for learners who are engaged and motivated by computer activities.

- **Goodreads** (https://www.goodreads.com/shelf/show/wordless-picture-books) is one example of a great resource for finding wordless books for learners of all ages; it provides detailed story synopses and direct links for purchasing online.

- **CliffsNotes** (http://www.cliffsnotes.com/) provides literature notes and summaries, test preparation materials, and study guides for hundreds of literary texts; in addition, the web site now provides free, downloadable audiobooks for smartphone users.

- **Houghton Mifflin Harcourt's Education Place** (https://www.eduplace.com/graphicorganizer/) provides free, reproducible classroom resources, including dozens of graphic organizer templates for an array of literacy contexts, available in both English and Spanish.

- The nonprofit organization **Learning Ally**, formerly **Recordings for the Blind & Dyslexic** (https://go.learningally.org), maintains a library of thousands of audiobooks for people who cannot read standard print. In addition to offering reading materials through digitally recorded or audio app formats, the organization maintains a large volunteer staff trained to assist parents and classroom teachers in using these materials. Learning Ally also provides information on tutors, professional development, and lesson plans.

- **Rewordify** (http://www.rewordify.com/) is a free resource for simplifying a text's complexity level.

- **The "Solved" Mysteries of Harris Burdick** (http://hrsbstaff.ednet.ns.ca/davidc/6c_files/documents/mysteries/divmysteries.htm). Author Chris Van Allsburg provides mysterious images from the Harris Burdick books and invites students to provide captions or to write stories.

- **Tar Heel Reader** (http://tarheelreader.org/) offers "a collection of free, easy-to-read, and accessible books on a wide range of topics," including books for all ages; each available book can be speech enabled. The site even offers opportunities for writing your own books.

- **YALSA, Picture Books for Teens** (http://www.ala.org/yalsa/booklistsawards/booklistsbook), maintained by the Young Adult Library Services Association (YALSA), provides a wide range of wordless picture books for teens and young adults.

- **YouTube** (www.youtube.com) is often overlooked as a literacy resource, but search through the *Education* category and find yourself in a wonderful world of possibilities, no matter what you're teaching. For example, from the Education homepage, type *Wordless Picture Books* in the search box. (Always watch the videos before you show them to your class! Occasionally there is one miscategorized.) David Wiesner's (1991) *Tuesday* has many animated renditions, but the 12:54 version by Michael Grubb (presented by Paul McCartney) is fantastic to supplement with the book for any classroom.

REFERENCES

Apitz, M., Ruppar, A.L., Roessler, K., & Pickett, K. (2017). Planning lessons for students with significant disabilities in high school English classes. *TEACHING Exceptional Children, 49*(3), 168–174.

Bacon, E.H., & Schulz, J.B. (1991). A survey of mainstreaming practices. *Teacher Education and Special Education, 14,* 144–149.

Bender, W.N., Vail, C.O., & Scott, K. (1995). Teachers' attitudes toward increased mainstreaming: Implementing effective instruction for students with learning disabilities. *Journal of Learning Disabilities, 28,* 87–94.

Bormuth, J.R. (1968). The cloze readability procedure. *Elementary English, 45,* 429–436.

Browder, D.M., Lee, A., & Mims, P. (2011). Using shared stories and individual response modes to promote comprehension and engagement in literacy for students with multiple, severe disabilities. *Education and Training in Autism and Developmental Disabilities, 46,* 1–14.

Browder, D.M., Mims, P.J., Spooner, F., Ahlgrim-Delzell, L., & Lee, A. (2008). Teaching elementary students with multiple disabilities to participate in shared stories. *Research and Practice for Persons with Severe Disabilities, 33,* 3–12. http://doi.org/10.2511/rpsd.33.1-2.3

Browder, D.M., Trela, K., & Jimenez, B. (2007). Training teachers to follow a task analysis to engage middle school students with moderate and severe developmental disabilities in grade-appropriate literature. *Focus on Autism and Other Developmental Disabilities, 22,* 206–219.

Chilton, L. (2013, October 7). Why it's vital for disabled kids to read. *The Albuquerque Journal,* pp. C1, C4.

Conderman, G., & Jung, M. (2014). Using technology to support effective instruction in early childhood settings. *Issues in Early Education, 1*(24), 6–19.

Copeland, S.R., & Keefe, E.B. (2007). *Effective literacy instruction for students with moderate or severe disabilities.* Baltimore, MD: Paul H. Brookes Publishing Co.

Didden, R., Prinsen, H., & Sigafoos, J. (2000). The blocking effect of pictorial prompts on sight-word reading. *Journal of Applied Behavior Analysis, 33,* 317–320.

Donnellan, A. (1984). The criterion of the least dangerous assumption. *Behavioral Disorders, 9,* 141–150.

Duke, N.K., Caughlan, S., Juzwick, M., & Martin, N. (2012). Teaching genre with purpose. *Educational Leadership, 69,* 34–39.

Dyck, N. (1999). *How to adapt text for struggling readers.* Lawrence, KS: Curriculum Solutions.

Dyck, N., & Pemberton, J.B. (2002). A model for making decisions about text adaptations. *Intervention in School and Clinic, 38,* 28–35. http://doi.org/10.1177/10534512020380010401

Ellett, L. (1993). Instructional practices in mainstreamed secondary classrooms. *Journal of Learning Disabilities, 26,* 57–64.

Glennen, S.L., & DeCoste, D.C. (1996). *Handbook of augmentative and alternative communication.* New York, NY: Singular.

Hudson, M.E., Browder, D.M., & Jimenez, B.A. (2014). Effects of a peer-delivered system of least prompts intervention and adapted science read-alouds on listening comprehension for participants with moderate intellectual disability. *Education and Training in Autism and Developmental Disabilities, 49*(1), 60–77.

Hudson, M.E., Browder, D., & Wakeman, S. (2013). Helping students with moderate and severe intellectual disability access grade-level text. *TEACHING Exceptional Children, 45,* 14–23.

Hudson, M.E., & Test, D.W. (2011). Evaluating the evidence base of shared story reading to promote literacy for students with extensive support needs. *Research and Practice for Persons with Severe Disabilities, 36,* 34–45.

Johnson, L.J., & Pugach, M.C. (1990). Classroom teachers' views of intervention strategies for learning and behavior problems: Which are reasonable and how frequently are they used? *The Journal of Special Education, 24,* 69–84.

Keefe, E.B., & Copeland, S.R. (2011). What is literacy? The power of a definition. *Research and Practice for Persons with Severe Disabilities, 36,* 92–99.

Knight, V.F., Wood, C.L., Spooner, F., Browder, D.M., & O'Brien, C.P. (2015). An exploratory study using science e-texts with students with autism spectrum disorder. *Focus on Autism and Other Developmental Disabilities, 30,* 86–99. http://doi.org/10.1177/1088357614559214

Lane, L.A., Keefe, E.B., Copeland, S.R., & Kruger, A. (2015). Literacy strategies for all students: Accessing the general education curriculum. In B. Cole & W. Farone (Eds.), a publication of the *Parent Education & Advocacy Leadership (PEAL) Center.*

Luckasson, R. (2006). The human rights basis for personal empowerment in education. In E.B. Keefe, V.M. Moore, & F.R. Duff (Eds.), *Listening to the experts: Students with disabilities speak out* (pp. 11–20). Baltimore, MD: Paul H. Brookes Publishing Co.

Mims, P.J., Browder, D.M., Baker, J.N., Lee, A., & Spooner, F. (2009). Increasing comprehension of students with significant intellectual disabilities and visual impairments during shared stories. *Education and Training in Autism and Developmental Disabilities, 44,* 409–420.

Mims, P.J., Hudson, M.E., & Browder, D.M. (2012). Using read-alouds of grade-level biographies and systematic prompting to promote comprehension for students with moderate and severe developmental disabilities. *Focus on Autism and Other Developmental Disabilities, 27,* 67–80. http://doi.org/10.1177/1088357612446859

Morgan, F.M., Moni, K.B., & Cuskelly, M. (2013). Literacy strategies used by adults with intellectual disability in negotiating their everyday community environments. *Australian Journal of Adult Learning, 53*(3), 411–435.

Pinkney, J. (2009). *The lion & the mouse.* New York, NY: Little, Brown.

Popov, N. (1996). *Why?* New York, NY: North-South Books.

Ruppar, A.L. (2014). Knowledge is power: Reading, writing, and promoting self-determination among adolescents with multiple disabilities. *Perspectives on Augmentative and Alternative Communication, 23,* 192. http://doi.org/10.1044/aac23.4.192

Ruppar, A.L., Afacan, K., Yang, Y.-L., & Pickett, K. (2017). Embedded shared reading to increase literacy in an inclusive English/language arts class: Preliminary efficacy and ecological validity. *Education and Training in Autism and Developmental Disabilities, 52*(1), 51–63.

Schenning, H., Knight, V., & Spooner, F. (2013). Effects of structured inquiry and graphic organizers on social studies comprehension by students with autism spectrum disorders. *Research in Autism Spectrum Disorders, 7,* 526–540. http://doi.org/10.1016/j.rasd.2012.12.007

Schumm, J.S., & Vaughn, S. (1991). Making adaptations for mainstreamed students: General classroom teachers' perspectives. *Remedial and Special Education, 12,* 18–25.

Scott, B.J., Vitale, M.R., & Masten, W.G. (1998). Implementing instructional adaptations for students with disabilities in inclusive classrooms: A literature review. *Remedial and Special Education, 19*(2), 106–119.

Weitzman, J.P., & Glasser, R.P. (1998). *You can't take a balloon into the Metropolitan Museum.* New York, NY: Puffin Books.

Wiesel, E. (2006). *Night.* New York, NY: Hill & Wang.

Wiesner, D. (1991). *Tuesday.* New York, NY: Clarion Books.

Wiesner, D. (2006). *Flotsam.* New York, NY: Clarion Books.

CHAPTER 13

Beyond the Common Core

Art, Music, and Creativity in Literacy Learning

Laurel Lane

LEARNING OBJECTIVES

By the end of this chapter, readers will

1. Understand the rationale, based in the context of education history and research literature, for including arts-based activities in the curriculum for learners with complex support needs.

2. Become familiar with both historical and current examples of the ways in which artistic activity—alone or as a component of conventional literacy instruction—may serve to promote literacy learning among individuals with complex support needs.

3. Learn multiple ways in which the arts can be incorporated into meaningful instruction for individuals with complex support needs.

This chapter addresses the role of the arts-based literacy curricula for individuals with complex support needs. First, this chapter discusses the relationship among creative expression, communication, and literacy, each of which is fundamental to the human experience. Next, I will review the research literature on the use of arts-based activities in providing instruction to individuals with complex support needs, grounding this discussion in historical context. I posit that these activities can and should be included in literacy instruction for this population. The remainder of the chapter discusses how to use these activities as part of multimodal literacy instruction, providing numerous examples.

RATIONALE FOR ARTS-BASED ACTIVITIES IN LITERACY LEARNING

The drive to make art is so strong, so central to what it means to be human, that some individuals, when deprived of artistic media, will create their own. The picture in Figure 13.1, for example, is a cow [ca. 1962], sculpted of compressed breadcrumbs secreted away at mealtimes by an anonymous institutionalized patient with severe schizophrenia (Marinow, 1963) until she had enough to create the cow. This patient would later be encouraged to create *real art*—although it is my opinion that the breadcrumb cow, in its original form, is absolutely art in its own right. She was provided with *real* art materials and supplies for this pursuit, but the fact that she managed to feed her artistic hunger, despite having no external direction or art materials at the onset, speaks to the innate human desire to be creative.

Many literacy experts view conventional reading and writing as the cornerstone we use for defining what it means to be literate and what activities and forms of expression constitute literacy. However, in doing so, people with complex support needs and others whose interactions with

Figure 13.1. Breadcrumb Cow [ca. 1962].

the world around them may not include conventional reading and writing are forever relegated to the illiterate side of the dichotomy that is *literate* on one side, and *illiterate* on the other. Keefe and Copeland (2011) ask that we expand our definitions of what it means to be literate because people with extensive needs for support are excluded when we limit literacy definitions to traditional conventions of reading and writing. As a consequence, these individuals "represent the last group of people routinely denied opportunities for literacy instruction" (Keefe & Copeland, 2011, p. 92).

Furthermore, in denying any person the right to the experience of literacy, we are, in essence, denying them a fundamental human right. Luckasson (2006) maintained that while the United Nations has some 180 human rights documents, there is a truth about human rights that goes to conditionality. We must ask ourselves if we believe in human rights for everyone, or if we believe that conditions impairing intellect and cognition, mental or emotional functioning, or physical capabilities may preclude some people from exercising certain rights. For the purposes of this discussion, we should ask ourselves whether we believe that people with disability attributes severe enough to prevent them from participating in conventional literacy frameworks that incorporate reading and/or writing still have the right to literacy instruction (Lane, 2015). I assert that they do, and I suggest that artistic expression be considered as valid for purposes of discussion alongside other more traditional literacy frameworks.

By broadening our conceptualization of what it means to be literate, we are in essence acknowledging that some people, with or without identified disability attributes, may interact with the world around them using modes of communication other than those contained within conventional literacy frameworks—that is, reading, writing, and otherwise interacting with written text, or engaging with oral language. These modes of communication may be, for some individuals, creative expression in various artistic forms, including the visual and performing arts (i.e., music and drama).

Creative expression may serve as a means of enhancing and broadening current conceptualizations of literacy across school and community settings for people with complex support needs. It may also serve to empower individuals by improving functionality so that they may be contributing and participatory community members in their work, living, and social environments. In addition, the resultant products of artistic endeavors inform us about the background knowledge and cultures of the individuals who created them.

Communication by artistic means contributes to resiliency both among the individuals creating it and those who derive benefit from its existence: it may lead to people flourishing rather than merely surviving—for all members of the community. This is because the arts are not necessarily considered as a requirement for survival, but their existence certainly enhances the world (Lane, 2015).

This chapter proposes the act of making art to be, at its most basic, the act of constructing meaning; this is central to any definition of literacy. By extension, a person's creative expression, as central to the act of meaning-making, must also be considered a fundamental human right for all, just as the right to access conventional literacy is so considered. Engaging in creative activities is also motivational, which is especially important for individuals with complex support needs because, for many, literacy learning is often arduous and sometimes unachievable.

For these individuals, artistic endeavors may provide the means for opening doors previously closed insofar as their communication with the world is concerned.

The learning objectives for this chapter surround artistic expression as the sole or companion component to communication generated or received within conventional literacy frameworks. There is a paucity of research surrounding creative expression as either an alternative to or companion of conventional literacy pedagogy for individuals with complex support needs because throughout most of our history, this population was not considered as potentially creative in the first place. That said, there is evidence that artistic expression is a viable means for promoting and strengthening literacy skills among individuals within this population. Were this not so, the Council for Exceptional Children (CEC) would surely not have been compelled, in recent years, to add the Division of Visual and Performing Arts Education (DARTS). According to the CEC's web site, DARTS is focused not only on including arts education for students with disabilities but also on collaborating with both general and special educators whose work is arts focused, including visual art, music, drama, and dance/movement. Therefore, the following research is offered as such evidence.

REVIEW OF THE RESEARCH LITERATURE

There are some very practical, physiological reasons that conventional literacy may not be achievable or may be functionally limited for individuals with complex support needs. Some of these are explained by Berninger and Richards (2002), who cited the different language systems that must develop in a separate but overlapping fashion in order for the reading and writing aspects of literacy to develop fully. These systems all require interaction with nonlanguage brain structures (e.g., visual systems, memory systems), and, when functioning properly, they continue to develop over time. That something might go amiss, considering the complexities of the brain, might be expected. And when this occurs, especially where learners with complex support needs are concerned, it behooves us to be prepared to teach to a variety of learning needs and using a variety of motivational tools—such as opportunities to participate in arts-based activities—to address them.

Another impediment to literacy learning for a specific subpopulation with complex support needs may involve the unintentional and invisible walls many of us construct to separate ourselves from that which we do not understand and which may be frightening to us for various reasons. This is especially true when we encounter certain disability attributes, such as mental illnesses like schizophrenia, or certain unfamiliar severe physical disabilities. As an aspect of society, this separation of people with disability attributes from individuals who are typically developing serves as the beginning of the social construction of disability. Thus, it can often serve to prevent individuals with these attributes from achieving conventional literacy skills because they are so often not provided an education alongside their typically developing peers.

Regardless of the reasons an individual may not achieve conventional literacy skills, there remains an acute need for every human being to communicate, and creative expression may be the sole or main means for this communication to be achieved. Sacks discussed this in regard to both children and adults living with disabilities, noting as an example the long-held belief among many physicians treating patients living with autism spectrum disorder (ASD)—then called *autism*—that "proficiencies and performances. . . were apparently based on calculation and memory alone, never on anything imaginative or personal. . . . No allowance (was) made for an individual, let alone a creative personality" (1970/2006, p. 219). Sacks, Adamson (1984/1990), and a handful of other enlightened specialists came to recognize, as early as the 1940s and 1950s, that art could sometimes do what words could not for some individuals with complex support needs and others for whom words often serve to confine and relegate with their emphasis on rules and labels. Meaning, then, it has come to be understood, may be formulated without words through art. There is also, now, the understanding that artistic endeavors may eventually lead to words—the speaking to the art, the questioning, the critiquing, the descriptions of it rendered by the artist both verbally and in writing; and that words, in return—as in the generating of ideas, for example—may lead to artistic expression. But, for some, the art *is* the language with which they speak (Lane, 2015). This is true for adults as well as students, and perhaps most especially for the individual with complex support needs who has moved beyond school age and exists in the community within which he does not *fit* and in which he may live a long life of mental, emotional, and, too often, physical segregation.

Adamson's views, in which he described his role in the hospital's art studio as that of a facilitator rather than a director, are similar to the beliefs held by Dewey (1900/2009), Freire (1994), and Vygotsky (1962/2012) whose educational philosophies saw the roles of teachers and other knowledgeable experts and role models as less the *sage on the stage*, than the *guide on the side,* in all aspects of learning regardless of content. These individuals, who contributed greatly to our understandings about meaning-making being constructed within the context of an individual's physical environment, are important to our foundational understandings about the relationships among creative expression and literacy learning for individuals with complex support needs. This is because when we allow individuals to share with us the ways in which they already know the world—their background knowledge of it—through their art, we are facilitating that knowledge by giving it space and time and respect; we are acknowledging their experiences as valid and then using them as the foundation for their literacy learning.

For people with disabilities, the sense of belonging—their *presence*, if you will—within the larger social culture is often missing; for some, this sense of belonging is fed by creative processes and communication. When we do not give due consideration to the potential for creativity among people with disabilities, we dehumanize them. When this happens, it does not matter what laws are in place to protect them, or how much progress we have made in recent decades toward including them in our general education classrooms and our communities beyond school. When individuals are denied acknowledgment as creative, their *presence* is also denied. It is as if they are not present at all (Lane, 2015).

Is there a broad enough framework of literacy that might allow people with complex support needs acknowledgment as literate people even if they cannot read and/or write in the conventional sense? Some conceptualizations of literacy encompass a comprehensive definition that allows for the ways literacy enables participation in one's community. Keefe and Copeland cited as two such examples the literacy definitions from the United Nations Educational, Scientific and Cultural Organization (UNESCO), and the Program for International Student Assessment (PISA), but noted that even these definitions are "problematic for individuals with extensive needs for support who often do not read and write in conventional ways" (2011, p. 93). The best framework for what matters in literacy may be found in the UNICEF Convention on the Rights of the Child (1990), cited in Keefe and Copeland, who referenced Article 13's language. I will quote it in part here: "The child shall have the right to freedom of expression; this right shall include freedom to seek, receive and impart information and ideas *of all kinds* [emphasis added] ... either orally ... *in the form of art* [emphasis added], or through any other media...." (Keefe & Copeland, 2011, pp. 94–95). There it is—art—acknowledged in an official capacity, and at an international level, as one of many ways one may express what one knows (Lane, 2015).

Conceptualizing meaning-making in nontraditional ways, including creative expression, was also proposed by Dewey, who posited that "the needs of daily life have given superior practical importance to one mode of communication, that of speech" (1934, p. 110). This is problematic for those excluded by disability from this mode of communication. Dewey asserted that each separate object of art, created as it was within the framework of a specific medium, "says something that cannot be uttered as well or as completely in any other tongue" (1934, p. 110). Important to a discussion regarding the interrelationship between art and literacy is Dewey's aesthetically oriented philosophy, as posited by Eisner, who discussed Dewey's "attendance to the ways in which qualitative, artistically crafted form can convey meaning" (1998, p. 31). By these standards then, we may envision the student with complex support needs being provided with the freedom to learn, to be creative, to be self-governing, and from these to be prepared, eventually, for active participation and contribution within the larger community—the same hopes one has for all our students and citizens.

Creative Expression and Self-Discovery

Freedom of self-discovery, long recognized as crucial to a person's full development, is often withheld from individuals with complex support needs. Their time and space are filled by necessary services and appointments with professionals, and by the near-constant presence of caregivers and other support staff, who make many decisions about their lives. It is important that each of us be allowed the opportunity to self-discover. Creative expression provides an opportunity for such self-discovery and may be the only means for communication and interaction in the absence of conventional literacy skills for some.

Many teachers of students with complex support needs may feel they do not have the time or resources to provide opportunities for artistic experiences, given budget cuts that often target both arts-based curriculums and special education programs. However, if we are to acknowledge the importance of the allowance for freedom of self-discovery in the face of these hardships, we might look to the work of Friedl Dicker-Brandeis (see Figure 13.2), artist and progressivist art teacher, who was arrested and sent to teach in the Theresienstadt (Terezín) concentration camp during World War II. Because teachers there were also "role models and surrogate parents," they took it upon themselves to guide the children to express themselves and their experiences through "the symbolic language of art" (Dutlinger, 2001, p. 30). Dicker-Brandeis and others

Figure 13.2. Friedl Dicker-Brandeis [ca. 1936].

"facilitated education for life. The children painted and drew freely, using art as an outlet" and thus, "gaining control of their own personal space and time" (Dutlinger, 2001, p. 30).

This control of one's personal space and time does not exist for many individuals with complex support needs, so artistic opportunities are important to their development as fully involved (and fully evolved) community members. Therefore, as educators and role models for these individuals, whether they are children or adults, we are called to heed the wisdom of Friedl Dicker-Brandeis and others. We must provide all learners the freedom to explore, and to express, and we must accept from them whatever creative work they offer us.

Wix shared Dicker-Brandeis' thoughts concerning "children's creative spirits (and) the role of adult mentors" (2010, p. 26), in her excellent text chronicling the artist-teacher's life and work, which was focused on children's artistic expression. Dicker-Brandeis' words, shared here, were originally directed to the mentors of children, but they are applicable to any mentor or facilitator serving individuals with complex support needs and who are being provided opportunities for creative endeavors. Dicker-Brandeis (as cited in Wix, 2010) cautioned adult mentors regarding their inclination to "direct the sparks of children's inspirations" (p. 26), and suggested that "if we want to look at children's drawings with enjoyment and see their usefulness, we must first silence our wishes and demands in regard to form as well as content and expectantly accept what they can offer" (p. 26). Educators are seldom called to do this. What an amazing gift Friedl Dicker-Brandeis and the other teachers at Terezín gave to the children whose lives were so tenuous, whose freedoms so few—this freedom of time, and nurturing encouragement to create. And what amazing gifts the children gave back.

As an artist and art teacher, Friedl Dicker-Brandeis did not address multisensory literacy in her work. However, when a teacher and student engage in creative endeavors, both are participating in what we might call *literacy events,* which are considered as opportunities—in any mode or circumstance, and including one or more sensory forms—for communication to occur. In the case of the teacher and student engaging in creative endeavors, the literacy event would be in the mode of *visual literacy.* Debes (as cited in Seglem & Witte, 2009) considered visual literacy as an ability to distinguish and understand the visual images present in one's environment and to incorporate those as a means of learning and self-expression in a larger sense. As technology has evolved, visual literacy as a concept has evolved as well because learners, including those with complex support needs, now receive constant visual information from many different sources (e.g., the Internet, television, video games, movies); the ability to utilize that input in one's imagination—creating a visual image and expressing that image through opportunities for creativity—becomes more readily available. As to the concept of visual literacy in terms of education and scholarship, it has become more readily accepted as our understandings and definitions of what it means to be literate have become broader. Therefore, it is helpful here to move from a discussion of theory to relevant examples in practice.

How Literacy Learning and Creative Expression Influence One Another

There is no shortage of studies evidencing the interactions between and among literacy events and artistic endeavors (inclusive of music, visual arts, and drama) by individuals with a variety of disability attributes and across many literacy events (Danielsson, 2013; Grocke, Bloch, & Castle, 2009; Hall, 2013; Hermon & Prentice, 2003; Joosa, 2012; Kidd, 2009; Lacey, Layton, Miller, Goldbart, & Lawson, 2007; Miller et al., 1998; Sagan, 2007, 2008, 2011; Wexler, 2002). In addition, the dis-abling impacts resulting when individuals are effectively rendered as conventionally illiterate due to language barriers have also been addressed by and through creative expression (Greenfader, Brouillette, & Farkas, 2014, McLeod & Ricketts, 2013). In each of these studies, art-making was either the focused objective, and the literacy applications were derived from the creative process; or literacy learning was the focus, and because of the modality (e.g., visual, digital, multisensory) the presence of creative expression was an integral component. Only those studies and their outcomes thought to be most relevant to a discussion about the role that creative expression may play in literacy learning for individuals with complex support needs are included in this discussion.

It is always desirable that individuals with complex support needs be provided with the tools and opportunities necessary to acquire conventional literacy skills so that these skills may develop and evolve across the life span. In other words, we should always begin with the presumption of competence. This belief—that literacy skills can be gained, to whatever extent is possible for a given individual and regardless of disability—is the central tenet of *least dangerous assumption* articulated by Donnellan (1984), and reiterated in Lane, Keefe, Copeland, and Kruger (2015a). In this chapter, arts-based activities are discussed in the context of conventional literacy learning. However, it is important to keep in mind that art may, in the end, be the chosen mode of communication with which some individuals are most comfortable and most competent. As Dewey suggested, the pursuit of art, and hence, "the path the work of art pursues. . . , keeps alive the power to experience the common world in its fullness" (1934, p. 138).

Outsider Artists

The drive to participate in creative pursuits is an inherently human one, and in classroom and community settings, it may serve as a great equalizer. No longer does the individual with disability attributes stand out because of what she *cannot* do. If she has engaged in making art, and it is shared with classmates or with the community beyond school, she suddenly finds herself an integral and contributing person in that world. Consider examples of individuals who have come to be known as outsider artists. Some of these individuals were literate in the conventional sense, and others were not. These self-taught artists, many with disability attributes severe enough to result in institutionalization over much of their life spans, were intrinsically motivated to create art (i.e., the Breadcrumb Cow in Fig. 13.1). With few exceptions, this art was not known to people living in the world outside the walls of the institutions in which it was created; much of it was, in fact, tossed away, deemed worthless by the professionals working in their individual capacities with the artists. Over the years, however, scholars and researchers—some focused upon the art-making of these individuals as an instrument of resiliency, others interested in the art itself—unearthed many of these discarded works. As the Outsider Art movement took hold, some of these artists and their work have become known by a larger public audience. In a few cases, their work has become admired and even collectible—for example, Martín Ramirez (1895–1963) and more recently, Stephen Wiltshire (1974–), to name only two. What might we learn from this appreciation of the art of the *outsider*? Do we merely admire the art, or should we seek to understand the motivation to create the art and, by extension, better understand the artist?

Arguably the starkest example of an individual with complex support needs finding her "voice" through artistic expression may be Judith Scott (1943–2005), best known for her elaborate three-dimensional sculptures made of string, yarn, or other forms of fiber and an assortment of found objects. You can see examples of her work and learn more about her national and international permanent exhibitions at http://judithandjoycescott.com. Scott was Deaf, nonverbal, and had Down syndrome; although these disabilities were not likely the sole reason she was driven to create art, they most certainly played a role in that drive because the art was the only means by which Scott could communicate. To know Judith Scott, one had to engage with her artistic creations, most of which remain untitled because she could not assign names to the pieces either verbally or in writing because she possessed no conventional literacy skills. Should we consider Judith Scott illiterate? Are her artistic creations forms of visual literacy? How we answer these questions depends on our personal definition of what it means to be literate.

For Judith Scott, Martín Ramirez, and Stephen Wiltshire, as well as many other individuals with complex support needs unknown to us, creative expression, both in terms of the experience of its making and the end product, may be the only endeavor which allows them to be *heard* during the course of a lifetime of marginalization, and too often filled with instances of *not* measuring up and *not* fitting in by society's measures. For that reason alone, the allowance for creative expression is a worthy pursuit for researchers, parents, teachers, caregivers, and support persons who regularly engage with individuals with complex support needs.

Much of the remainder of this chapter will focus on providing ideas and examples of the ways in which arts-based activities may serve to contribute to literacy acquisition, may augment conventional literacy skills once acquired, or may become a mode for communication (perhaps considered as an alternative form of literacy) unto itself. Consideration is given more to the possibilities for engagement across disability contexts than to specific disabilities. In addition, consideration is also given to the importance of reciprocity between schools and their communities and the ways in which a community's unique culture may serve to enhance literacy pedagogy through arts-based activities; examples from the Nambé Community School, a progressivist experiment in education that took place in northern New Mexico during the years spanning from 1935 to 1942, are included in that discussion.

REFLECTION QUESTION 1

What would your life be like without the presence of arts and creativity—your own or someone else's?

ARTS-BASED ACTIVITIES AS MULTISENSORY FORMATS

The art created by individuals is as unique as the individuals themselves. Therefore, unlike many other literacy activities, the *voice* may be more open to interpretation though that is not to say that there is not intentionality on the part of the person participating in the artistic endeavor, regardless of the medium. Especially for individuals with complex support needs, this malleability of meaning may be a welcome departure from the mandates inherent in conventional literacy, which require adherence to strict rules and guidelines about what is right and wrong.

For students with complex support needs, opportunities to share their worlds with others through creative means often level the educational playing field. A child who does poorly with traditional test formats, who struggles with conventional literacy, and who may lead an isolated life due to disability attributes, poverty, or both, can stand shoulder to shoulder with his typically developing peers when provided the opportunity to make art.

As a starting point for developing a literacy pedagogy for individuals with complex support needs, it is important to develop an understanding of their background knowledge. For example, suppose a student's phonological awareness, vocabulary, spelling, and general comprehension skills preclude his ability (and motivation) to complete a writing assignment about life experiences independently. This student might be included in a class assignment about life experience if the jumping-off point is arts based. With these considerations in mind, we'll consider the ways arts-based activities might be included in literacy instruction. (See the Resources section at the end of this chapter for information about adaptive tools, publications, advocacy groups, and more that will help you to include students with complex support needs in all types of arts-based activities.)

Visual Art: Photography, Illustrations, and Collage

For learners with complex support needs, beginning with a visual image as a basis for reading and writing activities is a great way to create motivation and interest. In contrast, literacy pedagogy based in the written or spoken word, to the exclusion of visual images and collaborative hands-on activities, may intimidate individuals with complex support needs who are just learning the conventions of traditional literacy. In this section, photography, drawing, painting, and collage activities are the basis for literacy pedagogy that acknowledges the potential for artistic visual literacy modes as a beginning point or an augmentation to conventional literacy activities.

Picture Your Life: Using Visual Art to Tell a Story   Background knowledge for any individual is the knowledge that is formed by living life. Individuals with complex support needs can readily participate in sharing their knowledge of the world through visual creations that include drawings, paintings, collages, and photographs representing their lives.

What does this look like in practice? Students might use visual creations to tell *their* stories in any number of ways. For example, you might ask a student who likes to draw to create a drawing of something or someone important in that student's life. Use the drawing as an anchor for a story, either true or fictional, that the student "writes." The telling of the story may be done orally, and then recorded by a teacher or peer, and finally transcribed into writing. If the story is true to life, it may become a language experience story as described in the section that follows. If students are nonverbal, it is a great opportunity to involve family and friends to share their knowledge of the person in the drawing—this is an example of reciprocity between school and community as well. By committing the story to writing, the individual comes to know that oral language is directly connected to written words, which educators understand as the *alphabetic principle*. Read the story back to the author or, better still, share it with the entire class in read-alouds; repeated readings are understood to be important to conventional literacy learning. Have everyone in the class make a drawing of an important individual to be used as the anchor for a story, and then invite families and community members to a storytelling event in which everyone comes to know one another better through the stories.

Another way to help students document their lives is to provide them with a disposable or digital camera (or smartphone, if available) to capture images of people, places, and daily activities they find meaningful. (Communication with adults in the student's life is important here.) You might also ask the student to bring in existing photographs with this kind of significance; a family member might help with this assignment. Once the photographs have been printed, you can use them in a variety of literacy-based activities. Consider making a book of the student's life, school year, or a specific event by enhancing each photograph with a caption or sentences that add written meaning to the photos. Then, use the book frequently as a literacy teaching tool. Learners are motivated when they see themselves in the story. Another activity learners often find engaging is the addition of dialogue balloons to photos of people. Dialogue lessons can address virtually anything in the photo—colors, weather, moods through facial expressions, events occurring. Also, conventional literacy elements present in storytelling such as sequencing, transitions, and beginnings and endings can be taught through ordering the photographs.

Finally, you can provide students with alternative sources for these pictorial representations of their lives (in the form of magazines, or other print sources, which are ideal for collage work). The provision of alternative sources of visual representations is especially important for individuals who may not have access to family photographs for a variety of reasons, including learners who may be living away from their families of origin.

A final note for working with student-created photographs: If necessary, plan to be the person responsible for developing, uploading, copying or scanning, and printing these photos. However, keep in mind that, ideally, learners might benefit from doing so themselves. If they have access to the necessary equipment, learning to work with it would contribute to their evolving literacy skills.

Language Experience Stories   Arts-based activities lend themselves well to the language experience approach in literacy learning. Generally, this approach has three parts: First, students participate in an activity and then answer a related question or describe their experience. Next, the response is recorded by a teacher, other adult, or peer. Finally, individuals perform a writing task, the completion of which should be supported as necessary. Supports may include asking a peer to transcribe an individual's spoken words or recording them in audio format so they can be transcribed. Later, playing the audio recording back at a slower speed and pointing to each word as it is heard is one way to allow individuals with complex support needs to see what a word looks like and hear what it sounds like concurrently, thus drawing a connection between spoken and written words.

Language experience stories are one way to allow individuals with complex support needs to access the general education curriculum. For example, the steps described previously might be incorporated within a classroom art gallery tour (Lane, Keefe, Copeland, & Kruger, 2015b), a great way for individuals with complex support needs to share their personal thoughts about the process and product involved in their own art-making. (This language experience activity begins with individuals making art; no title or written description is done at this point.) This tour activity is not specific to art as a subject area, and it can also be extended to include other literacy activities. In the classroom, the art may be connected to a specific unit of study, or it may serve as a means for individuals to introduce themselves to a new group of which they are a part if asked to depict something that is representative of their daily lives. The finished artworks are displayed around the room in art gallery fashion. Following the language experience approach (with a slight variation as to the first respondent), the following steps are completed:

1. A teacher or adult role model begins by asking a question of the artist or the audience about the artwork. Examples: *What have we learned about Catherine by looking at her painting? Why do you think Henry used so much blue in his painting?*

2. After the artist has heard two or three responses, she shares her own thoughts about what she has created. The teacher/adult role model records the responses of both the artist and the audience.

3. After each artist's work has been discussed, artists use large lined index cards or sticky notes to write a title for the artwork and a brief description of it. Individuals may be supported in this activity by dictating a description verbally, or they may be given choices among several that are created by the recorder, based on the artist's own words.

After the written descriptions are complete, each artist stands or sits near his or her own artwork and shares the title and description from the card, with necessary supports in place as needed. Then the teacher/adult attaches the card to the wall near the artwork.

Several literacy-based activities can also be conducted as extensions of the art gallery tour:

- Individuals can create written descriptions or answer questions about the artwork of others (peers or professionals).

- Words pulled from individual written descriptions may be used as vocabulary words and added to word walls.

- School and community members may be included by displaying the art in public spaces inside or outside of school.

- Community members can be invited to a "meet the artist" event to tour the exhibit (having the teacher dress as a waiter with a "silver tray" of drinks and snacks will add fun to the event).

- Students can take a field trip to a museum or art gallery in the community, and then create *more* language experience stories from the excursion.

An example of how students with complex support needs might complete these steps is provided in Figure 13.3, which describes how the language experience activity, art gallery tour, was completed by Tanya, a student in a supported high school science class in which students are learning about the seasons. Students were asked to create a visual picture of their favorite season of the year. Tanya loves to draw and paint and created the painting of her favorite season, shown in Figure 13.3. She has multiple sclerosis and works with Sam, her peer tutor, who helps her with note-taking and other in-class writing activities.

In the activities depicted within Figure 13.3, the teacher provided students in her supported high school science class with choices within a specific set of parameters, an effective teaching strategy when working with individuals with complex support needs. The limited number of choices—in this case, four seasons—helps to ensure that students can access background knowledge but are not overwhelmed by an endless array of possibilities.

LE Step 1

Teacher, Ms. D. (to class): What is Tanya's favorite season?
Class (in unison): *Winter!*
Ms. D. (to class): Raise your hands, please. Give me three things that make you think this painting is about winter?
Class responses include: *no leaves on trees, snow,* and *it looks cold!*

LE Step 2

Ms. D. (to artist): Tanya, what would you like to share with us about your painting?
Tanya (verbally, while teacher audio records and Sam takes notes about her response): *I love how snow makes everything quiet. I think the moon looks bigger in winter. Blue means cold, so I used a lot of blue.*

LE Step 3

Sam converses with Tanya about possible title ideas. He then uses the sticky note the teacher gave them to write the title and Tanya's dictated description on the note, which he reads back to Tanya to verify correctness. (Next, Tanya helps Sam write the title and description for his painting of fall.) Later, Tanya, Sam, and the other class members will share their titles and descriptions, which Ms. D. then places next to the paintings on the classroom wall.

> *Blue Winter*
>
> *Blue has two meanings. It's a color and it means sad. In winter, some people are blue, but I feel happiest in winter, so I tried to include all the things I love about it in my painting.*
>
> Tanya S.

Figure 13.3. Example of a language experience activity, art gallery tour. *Key:* LE, language experience.

Language experience stories may be created from photographs or other visual images for any number of purposes. Consider using them in procedural text genres to provide instructions, or in content-specific coursework as a means of informally assessing a student's understanding about the material taught; see an example of the latter in Figure 13.4. These stories can also be used in community settings in which an individual is encountering complex new information and must navigate among various literacy events.

Photography as a Multidimensional Literacy Learning Tool   Photography was discussed previously as one means by which students might communicate about their own lives by creating visual media. Photography can also be used to support learning and literacy activities within particular content areas. These types of activities have the added benefits of being quickly completed, if necessary, and being accessible to all students regardless of artistic training or innate talent. The photographs used may be obtained through any of the means described previously or from other source materials on hand in your classroom, such as magazines, catalogs, and the like, or from online sources.

Zach tells Thomas that he wants to find a picture of cranberry sauce. They locate an image that Zach likes online. Thomas then helps Zach to enlarge the font size on the software program used for writing, and Zach types the following excerpt:

Being there without Ma,

Without the baby,

Wouldn't have been so bad,

If I'd just remembered the cranberry sauce.

My father loved Ma's special cranberry sauce.

But she never showed me how to make it.

January 1935

> When questioned by Mr. F. as to why the cranberry sauce represents a big idea from this section of the book, Zach explains that Billie Jo is missing her mom and brother and it's the first Christmas without them.

(From Karen Hesse's *Out of the Dust*, Section "Winter 1935," pp. 97–143: "Christmas Dinner Without the Cranberry Sauce, pp. 100–101)

Figure 13.4. Visual comprehension activity.

Activities that incorporate photography within curriculum-based instruction may serve as the foundation for easy formative assessments (e.g., an exit card) or be used within more complex summative assessments (e.g., curriculum based). These arts-based responses are just as relevant as written ones in assessing understanding, and they have the added benefit of immediacy because the teacher or support person can gauge quickly whether or not the individual has a grasp of new material before moving on.

Photography's potential value in the classroom goes far beyond simply teaching new concepts and skills. As the examples discussed here will illustrate, photography has a lasting impact on students' lives and provides them a means to share their experiences and know what they have shared is valued.

Figure 13.4 is a sample of an exercise in which students were asked to choose an existing photo to illustrate comprehension of a passage of text. Students in a seventh-grade inclusive literature class were reading along to an audiobook version of Karen Hesse's (1997) *Out of the Dust* and had just finished reading the section, "Winter, 1935." Their teacher has asked them to find a picture that represents a big idea for this section of the book in one of the many available visual texts available for arts-based activities in his classroom; they are to cut the picture out, glue it to a sheet of paper, and include a quote of an excerpt from the reading that will explain why the picture they chose is representative of a big idea from this section.

In this example, the student, Zach, worked with a passage about cranberry sauce from Karen Hesse's *Out of the Dust*. The teacher questioned Zach about what he sees in his mind when he thinks about this section of the text. Because Zach has co-occurring disability attributes including visual impairment and dysgraphia, his teacher assigned a class peer, Thomas, to help him use the classroom computer to search online for an image that would complement this passage and that could be enlarged.

In the story, the passage is significant because it illustrates how the family misses Ma, who used to make cranberry sauce for Christmas dinner. Zach explained that he was drawn to the passage because he understood that the story's protagonist, Billie Jo, missed her mom, and it was the family's first Christmas without her. Billie Jo knew her dad loved the cranberry sauce Ma used to make, but she didn't know how to make it herself. In this instance, the student's response to the visual comprehension activity served as a springboard for another classroom project designed to reinforce literacy skills, call upon students' creativity, and connect meaningfully with their personal experiences, described in the "In the Classroom" textbox.

IN THE CLASSROOM

MR. F'S COOKBOOK PROJECT

Zach's work with the passage from *Out of the Dust* gave his teacher, Mr. F., an idea for a class cookbook project that would link to another planned curriculum objective, exploring procedural text genres. (Cookbooks can also be language experience stories because they invite the lives of families, through their cooking traditions, into the learning environment.) Mr. F. asked each student to bring in a treasured family recipe, or one from a friend or mentor for those who may not have access to family recipes. He used these to create a class cookbook, allotting one full page for each student. Students were asked to include their recipes and some accompanying visual artwork that would express their individuality. On the resulting recipe pages, students included photos, drawings, images of favorite celebrities, team logos, candy wrappers, ticket stubs, and the like.

The class cookbook project was very well received by students and their families. It was a great motivator for students as they studied procedural text genres; they internalized the importance of providing accurate and complete steps within procedural writing, because only those recipes that were accurate and complete would be included in the cookbook. That means the student whose recipe for his aunt's turkey instructed it be baked for 10 hours at 2,000 degrees was directed to make the appropriate fixes if he wanted it included. This arts-based activity was used as a motivator in other ways as well. For example, Mr. F. allowed students to work on their cookbook pages only if their other work had been completed satisfactorily and if their recipes had been checked and approved.

Not only was the cookbook project an immediate success, it also had a lasting impact on students' lives and later literacy experiences. Two years after completing the project, Mr. F. got a call from a former student, Josh, who had contributed. Because Josh was in the foster care system, he had initially struggled to come up with a family recipe. A conversation with Mr. F. helped him decide to include a recipe for a fried tomato sandwich like the ones his uncle used to make; he found a similar one online to include in the cookbook. During the phone call, Josh revealed that he still had the cookbook and used it all the time when he cooked for his new foster family. Not only was the cookbook project his favorite school assignment ever, it also helped him settle on a career choice. Josh explained to Mr. F. that he was planning to take a culinary arts class during his sophomore year of high school; he had decided that he wanted to be a chef. This illustrates how arts-based activities, especially those grounded in students' cultures, have the power to inspire.

In an example of the way photography was used to improve literacy skills among English language learners (ELLs), Roswell & Kendrick (2013) asked students in a secondary English class, one of whom also received support/remediation, to become photographers. They were instructed to take photos in a physical environment from their worlds and then to write narrative descriptions to accompany the photos. When learners are provided opportunities to choose the subject of their own photography and then speak to its meaning, multilayered creativity occurs alongside personal and academic growth—in this case, the growth toward English proficiency, in part—for the photographer-learner. This applies to learners with complex support needs across a continuum of diagnoses and circumstances, including language barriers that serve to impede conventional literacy learning.

I recently became acquainted with Kim Gavin, M.A., a graduate of Moore College of Art & Design's one-of-a-kind graduate degree program, *Master of Arts in Art Education with an Emphasis in Special Populations,* and a current adjunct instructor in its Art Education program. (See the Resources section at the end of this chapter for a link to Moore College.) Kim's fifth- and sixth-grade art class was one of six chosen to participate in Moore's then-outreach program, *Learning through Photography.* In the program, all learners, including those with complex support needs, were given opportunities to learn across content areas through photography. In its inaugural year, grant money along with great collaborative efforts among many involved with the graduate program and at the Galleries at Moore resulted in the exhibition, *Seeing Through Young Eyes: Inside the Philadelphia Classroom & Community* (May 25–September 10, 2011). The photos depicting both the art-making processes and student-generated products inclusive of photography and accompanying text are shared in the book, *Learning through Photography at Moore* (Gilly & Lavin, 2011).

Student participants attended grades 5 through 12 at six different Philadelphia-area schools. Teachers and others involved at each of the school sites made their own decisions about focused projects based on the needs of their students. In Kim Gavin's fifth- and sixth-grade art classroom, students were asked to show her their lives through photos. Accompanying written text in various forms illuminated the meaning behind the photos the students created. These photos were a means for Kim to see the world through the eyes of her students, many of whom lived realities that would be difficult for most adults. One photo, "My Rescue Dog," was taken by one of her fifth-grade students (see Figure 13.5). The accompanying text speaks to much more than the dog's rescue, and the visual image and the words together provide us the means to care about the boy who loves the dog and who was compelled to share the dog's story.

Students with complex support needs are often at risk for failure, due to the circumstances of their lives as well as the disabilities attributed to them. For example, another student of Kim's shared a story that accompanied a photograph of her uncle. Her uncle had been killed by drug dealers after reporting them to the police for hiding drugs under her mother's car. The photograph that was the basis for the story showed the student's uncle, smiling while wearing his yellow shirt—an item of clothing referenced in the last line of her story. "I can see the light of heaven when I look at him in his yellow shirt." Still another one of Kim's students also spoke about the presence of drugs in her neighborhood. She photographed a gas cap in the street, and in the circle around the gas cap, she wrote about how local drug dealers often hid their drugs within the gas line under the street. This student titled the piece "Hiding Places."

By providing opportunities to share important personal realities, something as simple as a photograph becomes much more. Learners with complex support needs, including those in at-risk populations living in poverty, are too often provided little or no opportunity for creative expression. The literacy instruction they receive is more likely than not remedial and is totally disconnected from their own cultural experiences and background knowledge, rendering it all but meaningless.

Providing this disconnected, remedial instruction is not the only option we have as educators. As the previous examples illustrate, we can choose to acknowledge our students' voices and

Figure 13.5. My Rescue Dog.

the worlds they share with us. When Freire (1994) posited that an understanding of the *world* must precede an understanding of the *word,* he was, in my view, speaking not only to the learner for whom literacy is in its early stages, but also to the teacher, who must acknowledge the visual world from which a child's words come into existence. This then generates *aesthetic empathy,* a term that is, at its most basic, understood by art therapists as the ability to *feel* what an artist is expressing through a generated piece of work and to acknowledge, in so doing, that we respect their experiences of the world and are grateful for their sharing of them with us. We then become, in this one small moment, *enlightened witnesses* (Miller, 1997/2015) to their experiences. Miller suggested that enlightened witnesses are charged with recognizing the injustices and abuse suffered by others and that allowing them to speak to those injustices in a manner that is respectful helps in their own healing process. The young photographer-writer who shared the visual image and story in "My Rescue Dog" was being provided that respectful allowance of *voice,* as were all the individuals who participated in the program.

REFLECTION QUESTION 2

In what way can creative expression provide opportunities to better understand an individual learner's background knowledge and cultures?

Drawing the Scene   Having students draw or use other means to depict content visually (as in the painting shown in Figure 13.3) provides an instant means for a teacher or support person to informally assess a student's content knowledge. Aside from that, drawing and painting are engaging for most learners across the life span and can be a departure from the often dryly depicted content that accompanies many subjects. There are many ways to incorporate drawing within instruction. Here are a few to consider as a starting point:

- Ask individuals to visually depict a specific scene or passage from a text by creating a drawing that reflects their understanding.

- Expand on the preceding idea by asking learners to create story boards for entire chapters or for complete texts.

- Encourage students to add drawings to notes taken by them, or notes provided by the teacher, and where content-specific new information is being learned.

- Model visual/drawn examples in accompaniment with text being read in class so that learners who struggle with decoding may *see* the context and begin to make connections between the visual image and the words.

- Offer a selection of arts-based menu options for learners to choose from as a component to a project-based, summative assessment. Examples of menu options may include any of the activities discussed in this chapter.

Collages and Photo Montages

For individuals with complex support needs, especially those with physical disability attributes affecting vision or mobility, collages and photo montages may provide a more readily accessible visual art form than drawing or painting.

Resources for completing these activities can include, but need not be limited to, traditional art supplies. For example, you might provide crayons, markers, and paints; rubber stamps, ink rollers, and ink pads in assorted designs and colors; magazines and catalogs as a source of both pictures and textual enhancements; and fabric puffy paints that puff up when dry to add texture. Consider also providing supplies such as an assortment of textured materials and fabric swatches; buttons, beads, tiles, and other small embellishments; wrapping paper, ribbon, raffia, and yarn; and even natural items like twigs, leaves, pebbles, or bark. If necessary, provide old shirts for students to wear as protective smocks over their clothing.

Some students may need support to complete photo montages or collages. Supports you can provide students include tools such as scissors, paint brushes, pencils, and markers that are adapted to be accessible for all manner of support needs. It is also important to provide assistance from a same-age peer or adult, as needed.

These activities provide opportunities for a teacher or support person to assess comprehension in content-specific grade level classes. Alternatively, they may serve as an end in themselves that allows for individuals with complex support needs to enjoy the freedom of self-expression, regardless of whether they have innate artistic abilities or prior training. They are motivating and the end result often instills a sense of fulfillment from the pride of accomplishment and self-determination. Figure 13.6, the Holocaust collage activity, is just one example of how collage may serve as an arts-based enhancement to conventional literacy.

Johnna, the student whose work is shown in Figure 13.6, was in the preliterate stage of reading and writing conventions due to intellectual disability. Her word recognition skills were at a pre-K level, and she was not able to express comprehension of text either orally or in writing. Johnna was learning to write the letters of her name by tracing over broken-line letters created by her teacher and paraeducator, but she was unable to communicate her understanding of text using any conventional literacy formats, including oral language. Despite these limitations, and like many students with complex support needs, Johnna had clear intentionality where her collage was concerned. For example, she could provide her reasoning for choosing the materials she wanted to work with, and she could also verbally provide a title and description of her work. Johnna's ability to verbalize her intentions indicates that she may be able to gain at least some conventional literacy skills when she is motivated by the content of the reading, and that she has some allowance for creative expression. This is because the literature class in which Johnna is

Scenario: Johnna is 11 years old and in Mrs. L.'s social studies class. Johnna has complex support needs inclusive of severe ID and she uses a wheelchair for mobility. Students in the class range from 9 through 14 years old and read at different grade levels. This is a fully inclusive K–8 charter school that is experimenting with multi-age/grade-level electives courses. The class is mixed ability in its make-up, with roughly half of the students having identified disability attributes and the other half considered as typical for their age and grade. Students and their families were chosen by lottery to attend the school, and this class is an elective that is focused entirely on the concept of *conflict* from individual to world perspectives. Students have just spent 6 weeks learning about the Holocaust through the reading of various texts, both fiction and nonfiction. After studying the artwork in the book, *I Never Saw Another Butterfly . . . Children's Drawings and Poems from Terezín Concentration Camp, 1942–1944*, the students were offered choices as to the type of curriculum-based assessment they wanted to complete, and they chose to complete multimedia collages like some of the ones in the text. Mrs. L. supplied all the materials. She worked personally with Johnna and Alex, Johnna's peer tutor, to help her complete her collage. Johnna chose the materials, directed Mrs. L. in the cutting, and did the arrangement and gluing herself. Her decisions were intentional and are shared as well.

Johnna chose the fabric from a large selection. Mrs. L. had always thought of it as having a floral pattern, but Johnna called it "smoke" and pointed to the reddish centers and called it "hot." She told Mrs. L. where to cut the pattern. Johnna also chose to use yellow paper for the angels, which Alex made by folding the paper and cutting half a figure on the fold. Finally, Johnna used feathers for the angels' wings. Using the glue bottle was challenging for Johnna, but she wanted to arrange her collage and glue it herself. She supplied the quote shown on the sticky note.

"My collage is called 'Smoke and Angels.' I think the people who were killed in the Holocaust turned into smoke and then into angels who are in heaven."

—Johnna D.

Figure 13.6. Holocaust collage activity.

included has been studying the Holocaust. Students have been reading a variety of texts, all of which are also accompanied by either audiobooks or teacher read-alouds. Her ability to make decisions about how she will represent her understanding of the material indicates that while conventional literacy skills may not yet be present, Johnna has a grasp of the material. Her collage could be used as an anchor for a number of activities that would support her literacy learning.

Three-Dimensional Art Activities   It is a common misconception that individuals who are blind or severely visually impaired have naturally more enhanced tactile abilities. As with other skills, tactile skills must be learned. Arts-based activities, especially those that result in a three-dimensional product, may provide a great means for individuals who have visual or other physical disability attributes to fine tune these tactile skills (which are an important component in learning the braille system as well). Working with media like clay or sculptural wire not only provides the means for creative activity that does not require keen vision, but it can also help to develop fine motor skills in the process. These media are "forgiving" in that they can be formed, scrunched back into a nondescript blob, and reworked. Of course, many students with complex support needs that do not affect vision would enjoy working with one of these media as well, and they have the added benefit of being fairly affordable and, in the case of modeling clay, easy to prepare. Cost may, however, be prohibitive when working with more than a few students, but there are many recipes for making different kinds of modeling clay (air-drying, baking, homemade playdough, and even Kool-Aid types). The recipes are almost all very affordable, generally involving flour, salt, and water as the major ingredients. The online resources have the advantage that often comments are provided by others who have used the instructions and offer their feedback about strengths and challenges. A great web site that provides multiple recipes for different types of homemade clay is Homeschooling-ideas, included in the Resources section at the end of this chapter.

Clay or other putty-like media, such as playdough, can be modeled into letters of the alphabet and used to help individuals with complex support needs access written literacy. There is certainly more motivation for using letters if individuals make them themselves.

Making the letters of the alphabet out of clay, and then painting and decorating them after they are dry, is a great way to begin the process of familiarizing individuals with the letters' phonological properties. While creating or painting the letters, parents, teachers, and support people can think aloud, helping the individual to hear what the letters sound like in words, and sharing memories in the process. For example: "I love the letter *A* ... some of my favorite things start with *A* ... *apples*, *art*, your sister *Amy*, *alligators* ... and I love the word *anniversary* because that's when your dad takes me out to dinner. Your dad's name is Alan, so he's one of my favorite *A* words too!"

When a student invests time and creative effort in an activity related to literacy, such as creating a clay alphabet, the student may be more motivated to attain literacy skills.

Adaptations to Resources and Environment to Consider for Visual Arts Activities

When conducting arts-based activities in classrooms or community settings for individuals with complex support needs, consider making these adaptations to ensure that the activities are accessible for all students. First, assign everyone in the class, regardless of abilities or disability attributes, an "art partner" with whom they work on all visual arts–based activities. Create art kits that mix a wide variety of supplies, and place one kit at every pair's work station. This way, art-making can begin with less fuss, and creating art—rather than hunting for supplies—can be the focus of everyone's valuable time. Some art materials may need to be stored elsewhere in the room; if so, ensure that all of the most desirable materials can be easily reached by all students—wheelchairs should not be an impediment to getting to the prettiest paper or the best embellishments. Finally, provide adapted art supplies whenever possible. These might include paintbrushes with wide handles and round ends for easier gripping, paint sets with larger wells of color that can be seen more easily, rubber grips that make it easier to handle drawing tools, and rubber-backed nonslip mats to keep supplies in place on tables and desktops.

THE PERFORMING ARTS: MUSIC AND DRAMA IN LITERACY LEARNING

Classroom activities based in the performing arts—playing music, singing, performing in a dramatic skit or play—may support literacy learning across multiple content areas for individuals with complex support needs. For instance, suppose students are reading an assigned literary text; it is important that we bring text to life whenever possible for individuals with complex support needs and, indeed, any students, regardless of ability. This makes music- and drama-based activities a great choice for inclusive classrooms and community settings in which literacy events are taking place—in other words, virtually *anywhere*. This is not to say that walking down the street while belting out the theme song from *The Fresh Prince of Bel Air* may not turn a few heads, but so what!? Playing a musical instrument has also been positively associated with improvements in math learning. The mathematician Pythagoras (as cited in Samuel, n.d.) discussed the vibration and resulting sounds produced by objects in motion; he expanded this idea to the planets, suggesting that as very large bodies in motion, they (the planets) "must also produce a sound. Given that their relative distances were concordant with musical intervals, Pythagoras surmised that the resulting sound must be a harmony—a 'music of the spheres'" and it is well understood that the counting, rhythm, and patterns in music are mathematically based.

Not only do activities based in the performing arts aid in academic learning, they also have emotional and social benefits. Research suggests that singing may make us happy (Hunter, Schellenberg, & Schimmack, 2010; Terwogt & Van Grinsven, 1991), may stabilize symptoms in individuals with severe enduring mental illness (SEMI) (Grocke et al., 2009), and allows for community participation and feelings of belonging for individuals isolated by language deficits (McLeod & Ricketts, 2013). As to the use of dramatic play, it has been understood for decades to be a powerful tool for development of many skills, including social skills (Bailey, 1997; Feiner, 1941; Parker, 1997), as well as motor, language, socioemotional, and personal life skills (Parker, 1997). Reagan (1997) also uses an example of a dramatic activity in which typically developing middle school students have an opportunity to learn more about their peers with disabilities. In addition, programs such as the well-respected Wild Swan Theater in Ann Arbor, Michigan (see the Resources section at the end of this chapter) have as just some of their objectives the development of communication, creativity, imagination, and self-esteem. The organization's outreach programs include summer theater camps and productions that premier in Ann Arbor and tour throughout the Midwest.

I don't pretend to be an expert in the performing arts, but I have been honored to enjoy some amazing musical and dramatic performances by individuals with complex support needs, including students across a range of age levels, disability types and degrees of severity, and literacy status. I have also used music and drama in my own middle school classroom and found these activities to be extremely user-friendly in terms of their adaptability, the excitement they generated for all students, and the ease with which they allow for true inclusion in the classroom. I hope that some of the ideas that follow will help. I know there are many more out there, and I would love to hear them.

Musical Activities as Mnemonic Devices in Literacy Learning

Musical activities can be used as a mnemonic device—that is, a mental "trick" we use to help us memorize related pieces of information, usually in a certain order. Mnemonic devices may employ letters (acronyms), words, phrases, rhymes, or songs. Advertisers have long understood the value of musical mnemonic devices as tools to help them sell their products, according to Parkinson (2008). The author used the example of the "seven fluctuating notes composed by Steve Karmen in 1969 . . . 'Nationwide is on your side'" (p. 114) as an example of catchy, musical simplicity with staying power. It is why mnemonic devices work. The Nationwide jingle is *still* being used to sell insurance more than 45 years after it was originally written for the company.

Lullabies and "nursery songs" use the same kind of simplicity and thus are readily committed to memory. The content of the songs, therefore, can be readily turned into lessons that support phonological awareness, oral language development, and reading fluency, to name just a few. A great example of one such song can be found in the English lullaby, "Twinkle, Twinkle, Little Star." According to Encyclopædia Britannica, the poem was written in the early 19th century by Jane Taylor and published as "The Star," but it is sung to the tune of a mid-18th century French melody, which was later arranged by several composers, including Mozart, with variations on "Ah vous dirai-je, Maman." The poem/song is a simple rhyming couplet and it is a testament to its memorability and longevity that the melody has been replicated at least twice ("The Alphabet Song," and "Baa-Baa Black Sheep"). With that in mind, this song may serve as a musical (hence, arts-based) starting point for any number of basic conventional literacy lessons. Consider (for individuals just becoming familiar with the conventions of language) the following example (to the melody of "Twinkle, Twinkle, Little Star"):

Vowels are a, e, i, o, u,

Sometimes y *is a vowel too!*

OR

Nouns are persons, places, things:

Grandpas, houses, shiny rings.

Verbs show action or just are,

Run, hop, read, sing, *be a star!*

These two examples took only a few minutes to write because of the rhythm and cadence of that simple melody. These are the same reasons it is a good tune to use as a mnemonic device. There are probably other songs that would work just as well. The key elements that make them usable to learners with complex support needs surround the melodies that are (or can easily become) familiar to everyone in the classroom or community setting in which the lesson is being taught—they are simple and they carry a basic message about language that is important to the foundations of conventional literacy.

More Musical Applications for Literacy

Mnemonic devices are, arguably, the simplest musical applications to literacy pedagogy, but there are many other ways that music can be used in classrooms or community settings.

- Invite students to make up song lyrics to wordless melodies played on a musical instrument, on the computer, or on a karaoke machine.

- There's more to YouTube than entertaining kitty and puppy videos (although we all know those are fun, too). Teach some of the basics of oral and written language, such as rhyme, rhythm, sequencing, and repetition, through music. (See the Resources section at the end of the chapter.) There is very likely already a song or piece of instrumental music for almost any lesson you're teaching.

- Include music in a menu of options for project-based activities and assessments. Some of these options may be suggestions included in this chapter, but move in any direction your imagination takes you. Consider working with your school's music teachers. In addition, don't forget to reach out to the often-underused community members, such as community-based music organizations (local choirs, musical ensembles, and music clubs) who may be happy to share their musical talents and suggestions for ways to include students with complex support needs in musically based activities.

- Use song lyrics as a way of providing context clues for vocabulary words.

- Play relaxing music as individuals enter the classroom, home, or community space at the start of the day, or as they reenter following a recess, return from another setting, or arrive after lunch; no talking as they move to their seats; everyone is calmly breathing and listening to the music.

- Play music in the background during work time for projects—the pace of the music sets the tone for the pace of the work.

- Invite individual students or group members in community settings who sing in choirs or play instruments to perform for their classmates during a time set aside to do so—for individuals with complex support needs, a musical performance, either solo or with classmates, can serve to *open the eyes* of peers who may see them as limited.

- Finally, consider keeping a ready supply of simple instruments at hand for impromptu performances. Tambourines, maracas, drums, acoustic guitars or ukuleles, and small battery-operated keyboards are great instruments to have at the ready when a jam session is called for. Remember, *music hath charms...*

Drama (No! Not That Kind of Drama!)

Playing a role that transforms one's own reality into that of another is a gift for both the actor and the audience. Especially for people with complex support needs, the opportunity to be seen as something more than the sum total of one's deficits is a great gift. Many popular actors from stage and screen have their own disability attributes, and learners with complex support needs who are made aware of this may be more likely to want to participate in dramatic activities. Dan Ackroyd, Daryl Hannah, Richard Dreyfus, Harrison Ford, Brooke Shields, Jim Carrey, Ben Stiller, Danny Glover, and Henry Winkler are just a few of the individuals who did not let disability get in the way of their acting success. Playing created roles provides freedom to be someone else and allows the actors to say the things they could never say in *real life*. In the process, they are participating in multisensory literacy activities, even if they did not know that. Some ideas for the rest of us are considered here.

Drama in the Classroom and Beyond   It's often a little surprising when even the quietest person in the group responds with excitement when the teacher first asks everyone what parts people want to play in the dramatized version of... well, almost anything! When students in my inclusive eighth-grade class had just finished reading a modern version of *Cinderella*, I jokingly asked who wanted to play the part of the glass slipper. Almost every girl in the class raised her hand. That surprise led to an animated discussion about what kind of dialogue the glass slipper might speak: *I wish my ugly step-sister had used Cascade when she put me in the dishwasher! That mean prince hurt me, and he KNOWS how fragile I am!* And (after the prince dropped the glass slipper on the stairs) *That man cracks me up!*

Many individuals of all ages and ability levels love to participate in dramatic activities, and it is relatively easy to find dramatic editions of some of the most common/classic texts being read at all grade levels online. Chapter 12 of this book suggests multiple ways to adapt existing texts and other literacy materials; using a summarized version of a play, or another version that decreases the amount of reading for the user, is one way to help make drama accessible for students with complex support needs.

There are also many ideas for dramatic games and activities available online. Two web sites that offer wonderful ideas include Gemma Dilley's Drama for Special Needs on Pinterest, and Our Everyday Life (see the Resources section at the end of this chapter.) These sites provide specific information about adapting dramatic activities to make them accessible to learners with a variety of support needs on a continuum. YouTube is another valuable resource for literally thousands of examples of texts that have been adapted for the stage.

In the preschool stages of development, children role-play the parts of parents, adults in careers they aspire to (e.g., teacher, doctor, construction worker), or characters from favorite movies. As Parker (1997) suggested, we learn much from the way children play, including the development of multiple skill sets. The author provided a wonderful adaptation grid, "Adapting Dramatic Play Activities for IFSP and IEP Goals" (p. 11) for a train unit that was a component of a larger transportation unit to use with children with individualized education programs (IEPs) or individual family service plans (IFSPs). The IFSP/IEP categories included on the grid are comprehensive and include gross motor, fine motor, prereading, concepts, social-emotional, language, and life skills. After consulting this adapted skills grid, it would be difficult, in my view, to dismiss the value of dramatic activities for learners with complex support needs. In fact, the entire issue of *Disability Solutions* in which Parker's work is included also contains Bailey (1997) and Reagan (1997). It is a wonderful reference for anyone interested in including drama games and activities for learners with complex support needs because the issue's entire focus is on using drama, role play, and dramatic play.

More Applications for Drama in Literacy Learning   Learners with complex support needs enjoy dramatic games and activities for the same reasons the rest of us do—they're engaging and fun! Dramatic games and activities also serve as a means to develop or improve a variety of literacy skills. For example, to use drama as a way to aid in the development of fluency, you might have students read a scene chorally or act in a play. You can also adapt a well-known story to create a different, "mixed-up" dramatic version; this can develop learners' understanding of characterization and the role of sequencing in a story. Learners may also write and perform their own plays to build literacy skills across the spectrum. Finally, students can attend plays performed in community venues outside the school setting. These are a great way to help learners with complex support needs to engage with individuals with whom they might not otherwise interact.

There are as many educational objectives that can be met through music and drama as there are educational objectives.

CULTURALLY GROUNDED ARTS-BASED ACTIVITIES AND COMMUNITY RELATIONSHIPS IN LITERACY LEARNING

This section includes what I consider as historical validity where the use of arts-based literacy pedagogy is concerned. It's a snippet of a story from a place few people know about, but it strikes at the heart of our current understandings about the importance of honoring individual cultures in our schools and communities. And every individual culture has some basis in art.

During research for my doctoral dissertation, I sought examples of arts-based activities being used in practice as an intentional component of literacy pedagogy. I hoped for evidence affirming my own classroom experiences in which I found arts-based activities to be motivational and instrumental not only in literacy learning but also in developing student self-determination, especially for students with complex support needs who were present in my middle school language arts classroom. Ultimately, my search led me to the archival collection then known as the *Nambé Community School Teacher Diaries* (1937–1942)—the collection name has since been changed to *Inventory of the Nambé Community School and San José Demonstration School Records and Teacher's Diaries, 1935–1942*. These primary source documents include large, handwritten teacher and administrator diaries documenting school and community interactions for this Depression-era progressive experiment in curricular reform. It was done primarily in order to address disparities in the achievement of students for whom English was the home language as compared to those for whom English was the second language. In addition, the collection includes teacher lesson plans, correspondence with schools outside of the community and state who sought information about the work being done at Nambé, and student work samples.

This collection verified that arts-based activities and literacy pedagogy were not only being practiced but were succeeding in developing conventional literacy skills as well as restoring cultural pride to this small mountain village in Northern New Mexico during the Great Depression in the United States. Textbooks were in short supply, so curricular activities were hands-on and based in community resources. These activities included art lessons shared by local artisans; music taught by teachers and community members; dramatic productions created by teachers and shared by students with the community throughout each school year; after-school classes for students and community members that were based in what was referenced in the diaries as "household arts"—woodworking/furniture-making, sewing, and cooking, for example; and language experience stories used in the classroom curriculum that began with visual depictions rendered by the children, which were supplemented with narrative script as they gained conventional English-language literacy skills. In addition, the reciprocity that existed between members of the community and school personnel served to enhance these arts-based activities and, thus, the learning taking place across contents, as community members contributed their knowledge and talents to the school and the school faculty shared what they knew in return.

The student population at Nambé included all age levels from approximately 3 to 16 years. (Some of the eighth-grade students with disability attributes started school at a later age and stayed longer than is average in a pre-K–8 school.) Because of the extreme poverty in the village, virtually every student in the school presented with, at a minimum, the psychosocial disability attributes commonly resulting from poverty and malnourishment. The school also included students with co-occurring physical, mental, and emotional disabilities of all types and degrees of severity. *All* students were considered to be teachable and to be valuable for their contributions. Despite having no laws in the 1930s mandating the education of children with disabilities, these amazing educators and nurturers figured it out, using their own wits and experience and their willingness to risk failure; and they failed often, generally with humor in the process.

Although it was not the school's main objective to provide the arts-based curriculum it ultimately embraced, creative expression was one of the targeted goals for all students. School personnel (transplanted "city folk" hand-picked by Dr. Loyd Tireman of the University of New Mexico) worked with community members to arrive at an agreement about what and how the students should be taught. The results, several years into the experiment, were a testament to community reciprocity, as was the arts-based curriculum, some of which is described previously. Community members, students, and the school faculty all contributed their knowledge and talents to the planning and ever-evolving curriculum of the school as the needs of the students and the community changed. Bachelor (1991), in fact, noted that some researchers and other individuals familiar with the experiment have credited the school with contributing to the revival of Spanish Colonial art forms in the village; this was during a time in American history when the culture was moving away from any celebration of individual cultures that were different from those understood as *American* and toward the vision of a "melting pot" instead.

Because most of the families at Nambé wanted, as a primary learning objective, to ensure that their children developed conventional literacy in English, educators and other staff worked toward this goal. These educators included the amazing teachers; the wonderful principal, Mary Watson, and the devoted school nurse. The federal agencies and their programs set in place by President Roosevelt's New Deal programs allowed the school and community beyond it to participate in soil conservation efforts, learn new agricultural practices, and find employment through organizations such as the Civilian Conservation Corps (CCC), as just a few examples. Dr. Tireman (supported by myriad faceless politicos from whom he called in favors) also participated in these efforts in order to teach the students to read and write. He helped the teachers work with students to revive the ravaged land with sound land management practices; the students learned life skills that would primarily keep them healthy and strong and later support them as they raised families of their own. Perhaps most important, students discovered their own creative talents hidden within. These talents, one hopes, provided them with a great sense of strength and dignity and perhaps even something resembling joy as the United States moved into the World War II era. Many men from the village left to fight; just like men across the country, they returned home to something different from the life they left behind—if they returned at all.

Fast forward more than 70 years later and I find it fascinating that many of the inclusive practices, the arts-based activities, the culturally relevant pedagogy, and the community engagement evidenced in the Nambé story are what we now recognize as critical to the educational process for learners with complex support needs.

REFLECTION QUESTION 3

How might you enhance one of your current conventional literacy assignments with an arts-based activity?

SUMMARY

That human beings, regardless of the presence or absence of identified disability attributes are drawn, innately, toward self-generated creative expression is well established in research. Miller et al. (1998) found that even individuals with no previous artistic interest or skill sets became visual artists with the onset of frontotemporal dementia (FTD). As their ability to read, write, or converse conventionally deteriorated or disappeared, artistic production became the means for these patients to communicate with the world. To me, this suggests a much deeper and more important relevance to our provision of arts-based opportunities for learners with complex support needs, many of whom are also unable to communicate in conventional ways.

Despite all the evidence, the current race toward some indefinable *better* manifests as an emphasis in our schools on Science, Technology, Engineering, and Math (STEM), often to the exclusion of the arts. This is especially true for individuals with complex support needs whose educations are often remediated in a scripted, rote, letters-based fashion with little or no opportunity for creativity. In addition, myriad standardized tests that presume every student must be college-bound—a presumption that automatically eliminates many learners with complex support needs from consideration—are often the basis for what is taught in the classroom. Teaching to "the test" is very real in far too many classrooms across America. In this educational climate, learners with complex support needs are often excluded from academic success and certainly from finding personal joy within the school setting.

Because it is my belief that the arts can play a key role in helping many learners to achieve conventional literacy objectives, I propose that we incorporate Science, Technology, Engineering, *Arts,* and Math (STEAM) as more inclusive, more evolved, and more humane in terms of educational objectives for all learners. STEAM takes into account the fact that the term *evidence-based* is not just a reference to *some* evidence, but it incorporates much more of the available and relevant educational research than STEM does. If viewed in this way, STEAM becomes an additive model of education for its inclusion of culturally sound, evidence-based research surrounding the role of the arts as important to a well-rounded and complete education. By contrast, then, STEM can be viewed as a deficit model, not only for the arts-focused evidence-based research that is not included in this model, but for the learners with disability attributes that preclude them from participating in many of the rigorous components it includes.

We know that many individuals may never achieve the benefits that come with highly developed conventional literacy skills. Consider just three examples:

- Judith Scott, whose string and fiber art, often described as being reminiscent of a womb, spoke in ways that she could not about her perceptions of the world

- Stephen Wiltshire, whose language manifests in the elaborate panoramic cityscapes for which he is now famous

- Larry Bissonnette, whose desire to make art was so strong, despite being institutionalized for 10 years, that he was often found making art in the middle of the night after breaking into a locked workroom

For these individuals, for the patient-subjects in Miller et al. (1998) whose FTD resulted in artistic abilities that replaced conventional language, and for many learners with complex support needs, the arts become even more important when we consider personal life satisfaction as being of paramount importance to each of us. In the life cycle, many of us will lose some or all of our conventional literacy skills to the ravages of old age or disease. How then might we express ourselves to the world? If we have no words, what language might we speak?

RESOURCES

- **Council for Exceptional Children (CEC), Division of Visual and Performing Arts Education (DARTS)** (http://community.cec.sped.org/darts/home) is a relatively new division of the CEC and to the world of arts and special education. The web site provides information about DARTS, including how to learn more about joining this division.

- **Our Everyday Life** (http://www.oureverydaylife.com) provides step-by-step instructions for adapting dramatic activities for children with special needs. The steps address modifications and accommodations for environment, props, and costumes.

- **Homeschooling-ideas** (http://www.homeschooling-ideas.com) is a web site created for the growing number of parents and other service providers who work with learners who receive their educations at home, either by choice or as recipients of homebound educational services. This free site provides multiple recipes for different types of homemade clay (http://www.homeschooling-ideas.com/how-to-make-clay.html); an e-book for specific clay projects is available for a low cost.

- **Moore College of Art & Design** in Philadelphia, Pennsylvania (http://moore.edu/academics/graduate-studies/ma-art-education) has a one-of-a-kind graduate program, an M.A. in Art Education with Emphasis in Special Populations, designed for educators interested in developing the necessary skills to bring art to all learners, including those with complex support needs. To obtain information about program, use the link above or contact the program director at 215-667-6811.

- Gemma Dilley's **"Drama for Special Needs"** board (https://www.pinterest.com/gem1904/drama-for-special-needs/) has a selection of drama games and activities for learners with complex support needs. Pinterest is a go-to resource for many educators.

- **The VSA: Education page at The John F. Kennedy Center for the Performing Arts** (http://education.kennedy-center.org//education/vsa/resources/adaptive_resources.cfm) [sic] provides a comprehensive list of artist resources, including art supply stores, adaptive art tools and supplies, music and performance-related organizations, publications, and advocacy organizations.

- **VSA Intersections: Arts & Special Education Conference, A Jean Kennedy Smith Arts and Disability Program** (http://education.kennedy-center.org//education/vsa/programs/sec_2017.cfm) [sic] is an annual conference that unites the arts and special education. The link provided here is for the 2017 conference that took place on August 6–7, 2017, in Austin, TX.

- **Wild Swan Theater** (http://www.wildswantheater.org/) works to bring drama productions, camps, and activities to individuals who may not otherwise be provided with opportunities for dramatic engagement, including individuals with disabilities and children from low-income homes. For teachers, this organization has created a package called "Dramatically Able" (http://www.wildswantheater.org/education/dramatically-able/); the kit includes a teacher's handbook and video.

- **YouTube** (www.youtube.com) has become so ubiquitous in our culture that we sometimes forget (or may not be aware yet) that it has many educational applications. Type *education* in the YouTube search box, and then pick your topic.

REFERENCES

Adamson, E. (1984/1990). *Art as healing.* Boston, MA: Coventure.

Bachelor, D.L. (1991). *Educational reform in New Mexico: Tireman, San José, and Nambé.* Albuquerque, NM: University of New Mexico Press.

Bailey, S. (1997). Drama: A powerful tool for social skill development. *Disability Solutions, 2*(1), 1–4.

Berninger, V.W., & Richards, T.L. (2002). *Brain literacy for educators and psychologists.* Amsterdam, Netherlands: Academic Press.

Danielsson, H. (2013). Double perspectives: multimodal degree projects and society. *International Journal of Education through Art, 9*(1), 89–105. doi:10.1386/eta.9.1.89_1

Dewey, J. (1900/2009). *The school and society & the child and the curriculum.* Chicago, IL: University of Chicago Press.

Dewey, J. (1934). *Art as experience.* New York, NY: Penguin Books.

Donnellan, A. (1984). The criterion of the least dangerous assumption. *Behavioral Disorders, 9,* 141–150.

Dutlinger, A.D. (Ed.). (2001). *Art, music and education as strategies for survival: Theresienstadt 1941–1945.* New York, NY: Herodias.

Eisner, E. (1998). *The enlightened eye: Qualitative inquiry and the enhancement of educational practice.* Upper Saddle River, NJ: Prentice Hall.

Feiner, A.L. (1941). Dramatic art in Detroit special education classes. *American Journal of Mental Deficiency, 46*(2), 230–232.

Freire, P. (1994). *Pedagogy of hope.* New York, NY: Continuum.

Gilly, E., & Lavin, G. (Eds.). (2011). *Learning through photography at Moore.* Philadelphia, PA: The Galleries at Moore.

Greenfader, C.M., Brouillette, L., & Farkas, G. (2014). Effect of a performing arts program on the oral language skills of young English learners. *Reading Research Quarterly, 50*(2), 185–203. doi:10.1002/rrq.90

Grocke, D., Bloch, S., & Castle, D. (2009). The effect of group music therapy on quality of life for participants living with a severe and enduring mental illness. *Journal of Music Therapy, 46*(2), 90–104.

Hall, E. (2013). Making and gifting belonging: Creative arts and people with learning disabilities. *Environment and Planning A, 45,* 244–262. doi:10.1068/a44629

Hermon, A., & Prentice, R. (2003). Positively different: Art and design in special education. *JADE, 22*(3), 268–280.

Hesse, K. (1997). *Out of the dust.* New York, NY: Scholastic.

Hunter, P.G., Schellenberg, E.G., & Schimmack, U. (2010). Feelings and perceptions of happiness and sadness induced by music: Similarities, differences, and mixed emotions. *Psychology of Aesthetics, Creativity, and the Arts, 4*(1), 47–56. doi:10.1037/a0016873

Joosa, E. (2012, January). Drama and dreams: Looking through a cultural-historical and semiotic lens at the graphic-dramatic interplay of a young adult with Down syndrome. *Cultural-Historical Psychology, 2012*(1), 26–33.

Keefe, E.B., & Copeland, S.R. (2011). What is literacy? The power of a definition. *Research and Practice for Persons with Severe Disabilities, 36*(3–4), 92–99.

Kidd, S.A. (2009). A lot of us look at life differently: Homeless youths and art on the outside. *Cultural Studies Critical Methodologies, 9*(2), 345–367. https://doi.org/10.1177/1532708608321402

Lacey, P., Layton, L., Miller, C., Goldbart, J., & Lawson, H. (2007). What is literacy for students with severe learning difficulties? Exploring conventional and inclusive literacy. *Journal of Research in Special Education Needs, 7*(3), 149–160. doi:10.1111/j.1471-3802.2007.00092.x

Lane, L.A. (2015). *Reciprocal relationships and creative expression in literacy learning: Ameliorating disability circumstances by empowering individuals* (Unpublished doctoral dissertation). University of New Mexico, Albuquerque, NM.

Lane, L.A., Keefe, E.B., Copeland, S.R., & Kruger, A. (2015a). Literacy strategies for all students: Accessing the general education curriculum. B. Cole & W. Farone (Eds.), a publication of the *Parent Education & Advocacy Leadership (PEAL) Center,* Pittsburgh, PA. Available at https://pealcenter.org/wp-content/uploads/2017/05/Literacy_07-07-2015.pdf

Lane, L.A., Keefe, E.B., Copeland, S.R., & Kruger, A. (2015b). Literacy strategies for all students: Creating literacy-rich environments. Unpublished manuscript, created for the *Parent Education & Advocacy Leadership (PEAL) Center,* Pittsburgh, PA.

Luckasson, R. (2006). The human rights basis for personal empowerment in education. In E.B. Keefe, V.M. Moore, & F.R. Duff (Eds.), *Listening to the experts: Students with disabilities speak out* (pp. 11–20). Baltimore, MD: Paul H. Brookes Publishing Co.

Marinow, A. (1963). Modeling in the treatment of a schizophrenic patient. *Bulletin of Art Therapy, 2*(3), 120–126.

McLeod, H., & Ricketts, K. (2013). 'In between the fireflies': Community art with senior women of Chinese heritage around issues of culture, language and storytelling. *International Journal of Education through Art, 9*(1), 23–39. doi:10.1386/eta.9.1.23_1

Miller, A. (1997/2015, February 6). The essential role of an enlightened witness in society. [Alice Miller Child Abuse and Mistreatment web site]. Retrieved from http://www.alice-miller.com/en/the-essential-role-of-an-enlightened-witness-in-society/

Miller, B.L., Cummings, J., Mishkin, F., Boone, K., Prince, F., Ponton, M., & Cotman, C. (1998). Emergence of artistic talent in frontotemporal dementia. *Neurology, 51,* 978–982.

Nambé Community School Teachers' Diaries (1935–1942). (Collection number MSS 306 BC). Center for Southwest Research, University Libraries, University of New Mexico, Albuquerque, NM.

Parker, B. (1997). All aboard: A look at dramatic play. *Disability Solutions, 2*(1), 9–13.

Parkinson, J. (2008). *i before e (except after c): Old school ways to remember stuff.* Pleasantville, NY: Michael O'Mara Books.

Reagan, T. (1997). A recipe for success: An interactive disability awareness activity. *Disability Solutions, 2*(1), 6–8.

Roswell, J., & Kendrick, M. (2013). Boys' hidden literacies: The critical need for the visual. *Journal of Adolescent & Adult Literacy, 56*(7), 587–599. doi:10.1002/JAAL.184

Sacks, O. (1970/2006). *The man who mistook his wife for a hat: And other clinical tales.* New York, NY: Touchstone.

Sagan, O. (2007). An interplay of learning, creativity and narrative biography in a mental health setting: Bertie's story. *Journal of Social Work Practice, 21*(3), 311–321. doi:10.1080/02650530701553617

Sagan, O. (2008). The loneliness of the long-anxious learner: Mental illness, narrative biography and learning to write. *Psychodynamic Practice, 14*(1), 45–58. doi:10.1080/14753630701768974

Sagan, O. (2011). Interminable knots: Hostage to toxic stories. *Pedagogy, Culture & Society, 19*(1), 97–118. doi:10.1080/14681366.2011.548992

Samuel, D. (n.d.). "The music of the spheres." [Article written for *Sensory Studies,* an online resource.] Concordia University, Portland, OR. Retrieved September 30, 2016, from http://www.sensorystudies.org/picture-gallery/spheres_image/

Seglem, R., & Witte, S. (2009). You gotta see it to believe it: Teaching visual literacy in the English classroom. *Journal of Adolescent & Adult Literacy 56*(3), 216–226. doi:10.1598/JAAL.53.3.3

Terwogt, M.M., & Van Grinsven, F. (1991). Musical expression of moodstates. *Psychology of Music, 19*(2), 99–109. doi:10.1177/0305735691192001

Volavkova, H. (Ed.). (1993). *I never saw another butterfly. Children's drawings and poems from Terezín Concentration Camp, 1942–1944* (2nd ed.). New York, NY: Schocken Books.

Vygotsky, L. (1962/2012). *Thought and language.* Cambridge, MA: MIT Press.

Wexler, A. (2002). Painting their way out: Profiles of adolescent art practice at the Harlem Hospital Horizon Art Studio. *Studies in Art Education, A Journal of Issues and Research, 43*(4), 339–353.

Wix, L. (2010). *Through a narrow window: Friedl Dicker-Brandeis and her Terezín students.* Albuquerque, NM: University of New Mexico Press.

CHAPTER 14

Literacy Beyond High School

Megan M. Griffin, Laurel Lane, Tammy Day, and Elise McMillan

LEARNING OBJECTIVES

By the end of this chapter, readers will

1. Describe issues specific to the transition out of high school and into adulthood that impact literacy for individuals with extensive support needs.

2. Discuss broader definitions of literacy and how these might relate to individuals with extensive support needs.

3. Explain how opportunities for literacy learning and application can be promoted in various contexts after high school: postsecondary education, employment, and community settings.

LEADING A LITERATE LIFE: Maria

Maria is a 26-year-old woman with Down syndrome who is a bit shy until she gets to know unfamiliar people. She loves spending time with her extended family and especially likes to take care of her many nieces and nephews. She lives at home with her parents but will often stay at her older sister's apartment on the weekends. Maria takes the bus to work each day, and on her commute, she listens to audiobooks. Her current obsession is the *Hunger Games* series, and she is almost finished with the third book. She looks forward to the bus ride every day and to finding out what happens next in the story.

Maria's career goal is to work in a preschool or kindergarten classroom someday as a teacher's aide. People say that she has a knack for working with little kids, and she has lots of experience caring for the children of her siblings and cousins. She has picked up some "baby sign language" that her nieces and nephews learned at child care (e.g., the sign for MORE). Knowing that many early childhood centers now use this form of sign language in working with toddlers, Maria's mom suggested that she take an introductory sign language course at the local community college. It has turned out to be a great idea—Maria loves the class because the professor and other students have been very friendly to her. She already knew some signs beforehand, and she has learned many more from the videos that are assigned as homework. She can communicate via sign with her classmates and has taught many new signs to her nieces and nephews who love talking with her in a "secret" language that their parents don't understand.

Maria has taken some additional steps toward her desired career path. With her mom, she has inquired about openings at local child care centers, preschools, and elementary schools. Although she has not found a job as a teacher's aide, she was hired to do part-time office work at an elementary school downtown. Her job involves many different tasks—shredding confidential documents, sorting mail, and entering attendance data. She has also recently been asked to assist with managing the school's recycling center. Her job is to collect recyclables from each classroom and sort them according to type. The secretary who oversees her work created a checklist with pictures of all the rooms in the school where she should collect recyclables. It also included pictures of the different recyclables she would collect—white paper, colored paper, cardboard, plastic bottles—and the category for each.

Even though Maria's current job is not her ideal job, she likes being at the school. She has gotten to know many of the staff members and students. Inspired by her work at the school's recycling center, Maria plans to offer to teach the kindergartners about recycling. She hopes that someday there will be an opening for her to work in that classroom.

Maria's enjoyment of working with young people is also reflected in volunteer activities she does for her community. Her family is very involved in their church, and she had always been a part of the youth group growing up. Now that she is older, she has started to volunteer with the Sunday school. She researches crafts online that she can do with the students. One activity she found was to create an illustrated prayer book. She typed out the words for several prayers and found clip-art that represented the ideas. The kids loved coloring in the pictures, and now she and the other volunteers use the books to teach the children words for different prayers.

In various aspects of her day-to-day life—her job, her continued education, her volunteer work, and her leisure activities—Maria relies upon her literacy skills. She also knows these skills will help her make a difference in the lives of the young people with whom she works.

THE JOY OF A LITERATE LIFE: PROMOTING LIFELONG LITERACY

Literacy pedagogy for older learners with extensive needs for support has traditionally focused on functional skills, such as those necessary for gaining employment and maintaining safety (Copeland, 2007). Although we do not dispute the importance of these goals, we believe that the joy of leading a literate life should also be a priority. For example, we note that Maria is engrossed in *The Hunger Games* in anticipation of watching the movie based on this series; listening to the books brightens her daily commute, and it is an interest she shares with several co-workers and friends. This is just one of many ways that literacy enriches her life; Maria's other day-to-day activities also involve various literacy modes, skills, and supports.

We believe that denying any person the right to lead a literate life denies them a fundamental human right (Luckasson, 2006). With that premise in mind, we provide information in this chapter that is devoted to the *why*, *where*, and *how* of promoting literacy among adolescents and adults with complex support needs who are either in the process of transitioning from high school or who have already moved beyond it. The *who* in this chapter includes individuals with extensive needs for support, such as individuals with intellectual and developmental disabilities, as well as individuals with multiple disabilities. However, we do not limit our discussion to specific disability categories; instead, the *who* in this chapter generally includes any individual who might benefit from the examples provided.

Our goal is to assist educators, family members, service providers, and self-advocates who seek examples of promoting literacy that they can put to immediate, practical use. To that end, we first establish the need for promoting literacy after high school among adolescents and adults with extensive support needs. The remainder of the chapter is devoted to describing context-specific opportunities to promote literacy for this population within postsecondary education (PSE), community, and employment settings.

It is important to point out that there has been less research examining literacy instruction for adults with complex support needs than for younger students, likely because of the issues described previously. The research that has been done has documented that adult learners with complex support needs can acquire literacy skills when provided the opportunity (e.g., Morgan, Moni, & Jobling, 2009), but this is still an emerging area of practice and research. We predict that this will change in the near future, particularly as PSE opportunities proliferate. In the meantime, this chapter highlights practices derived from evidence-based instructional strategies for students with complex support needs.

The Need for Promoting Literacy in the Transition to Adulthood and Beyond

According to Keefe and Copeland, people with extensive needs for support "represent the last group of people routinely denied opportunities for literacy instruction" (2011, p. 92). We suggest that, within this larger category, older individuals are even more frequently denied these opportunities because younger learners are most often the recipients of literacy instruction. As Copeland (2007) noted, experts have traditionally believed that after a certain age, learners with extensive needs for support are incapable of academic growth. Because of this misconception, efforts to teach literacy skills to older learners often were never attempted or were limited exclusively to teaching functional literacy.

This lack of instruction not only deprives adult learners of the pleasure of pursuing literacy activities for their own sake; it can also have a negative impact on other aspects of their lives. As just one example, literacy is a critical skill needed to access health care. Accessing health care is one of the most important among the literacy events that must be negotiated (Morgan, Moni, & Cuskelly, 2013). For those among us who do not have disabilities, the complexities surrounding health care literacy are daunting, to say the least. For individuals with complex support needs, deficiencies in this critical literacy area may mean the difference between living a healthy life or not. There are so many components of health care literacy, from understanding how to make an appointment with the appropriate specialist, to grasping the information that is reported to us after visiting the doctor, to following medication instructions, and finally, to understanding the itemized list of charges in the billing statement. Yet, individuals with extensive support needs can learn health-related knowledge and skills, provided the appropriate instruction and supports—and they can learn literacy skills needed for other facets of adult life as well.

Contrary to traditional conceptions, we recognize that older learners have a distinct advantage in terms of literacy learning: years of background knowledge that comes naturally as the result of having lived a life. Freire (1994) described this background knowledge as the means by which one reads the *world* and considered it a necessary antecedent to any reading of the *word*. We find that this ideology complements what researchers and scholars now understand about literacy learning as a fluid and ongoing process that continues throughout the life span (Copeland & Keefe, 2007).

To that end, we like the term used by Morgan and colleagues (2013)—*everyday literacy*. Everyday literacy means literacy that encompasses the myriad interactions individuals have as they move through their daily lives—from making calls on a cell phone to making purchases to navigating the internet. Everyday literacy is achievable for all people, regardless of types or severity of disability, and despite the amount of time that has elapsed for an individual since leaving high school. That said, for some individuals with complex support needs, it is appropriate to consider literacy in a broader way; for them, literacy is focused on communication and social interaction by means that look different from traditional reading and writing skills and move beyond these skills. For example, literacy might encompass arts-based activities, as discussed in Chapter 13, and multimodal literacy formats, including picture texts, as discussed in Chapter 12.

The Role of Transition Services in Promoting Literacy

For individuals with disabilities, the period when they transition out of high school is a critical time to maximize the skills—including everyday literacy skills—that are necessary to live a full and engaged life in the community. The need for transition services for adolescents and young adults with disabilities is critical, in part because of the apparent difficulties that occur in transferring literacy strategies that are school based, or context specific, to a wide variety of other settings and situations (Hutchison & Auld, 2015; Morgan et al., 2013).

This need for transition services is recognized within current education law. The 2004 reauthorization of the Individuals with Disabilities Education Act (IDEA; PL 108-446) requires that all students age 16 years or older be provided transition services from a coordinated group of service providers; services in which their goals, needs, interests and preferences for life beyond school are addressed. The purpose of these services is to facilitate the transition from high school to students' postschool goals, such as PSE, employment, independent living, and community participation.

The team planning transition services for an individual (including the individual, his or her family, teachers, and related services professionals) must take into account the student's strengths, needs, interests, and preferences. Based on the previous discussion, we would argue that one need common to all students—regardless of disability status—is the need for continued literacy learning after high school and that this need is likely more pronounced for students with disabilities who have extensive support needs. We would further argue that literacy is essential for individuals to realize fully the goals related to their interests and preferences. Individualized education program (IEP) and transition planning teams should consider what particular literacy skills are most important to target and how those skills align with the interests and preferences of the individual. By capitalizing on an individual's strengths, interests, and preferences, teams are more likely to effectively support students in achieving literacy goals.

Thus, literacy is a critical area for consideration in planning for transition services. Central to this discussion is the need for individuals with extensive support needs to evolve in their literacy skills across the life span. This requires thinking beyond skills that are specifically school-based and toward a wider variety of context-specific skill sets so that people with extensive needs for support can navigate the settings that are important to them as individuals. Depending on individual priorities, preferences, and interests, such settings might include college campuses, faith communities, recreation centers, and local businesses. In the following sections, we explore examples of engaging in literacy activities across a variety of contexts: individuals with extensive support needs who are continuing education post–high school, participating in recreational activities, and working in the community.

REFLECTION QUESTION 1

When developing transition goals for individuals with complex support needs, what should IEP teams consider in terms of promoting literacy?

PROMOTING LITERACY IN POSTSECONDARY EDUCATION

PSE programs for students with complex support needs are one means of promoting ongoing literacy development after high school. Because PSE programs vary greatly, we cannot characterize the literacy opportunities in each. Instead, we provide a brief overview of these programs; we then present an exemplar—the Next Steps at Vanderbilt program—and describe the ways in which literacy learning is infused into its activities.

Postsecondary Education Programs for Students With Intellectual and Developmental Disabilities

Until recently, individuals with intellectual and developmental disabilities have had very limited opportunities to continue their education after high school. Most such opportunities were within segregated settings, completely apart from friends and relatives attending college. Over the past decade, however, this has changed dramatically. Today, there are more than 200 college-based programs designed to support students with intellectual and developmental disabilities across the United States (Grigal & Hart, 2010; ThinkCollege, 2017).

Although these programs share a common goal—to afford students with intellectual and developmental disabilities the opportunity to pursue higher education—their ways of achieving this goal differ. For example, some are "dual enrollment" programs in which transition-age students are concurrently enrolled in both high school and college classes (e.g., Rogan, Updike, Chesterfield, & Savage, 2014). Others are programs at 2- or 4-year community colleges and universities. Just as each college and university campus is unique, so too are the PSE programs in these settings.

Next Steps at Vanderbilt University

Next Steps at Vanderbilt is an inclusive 4-year PSE program for students with intellectual disability (ID). Students take one traditional course each semester alongside their typically developing peers. They also participate in classes and activities coordinated by the program staff, such as completing a semester internship to foster employment skills. At the heart of the program is person-centered planning, in which individual goals, strengths, desires, preferences, and needs for support are identified so that the opportunities provided are optimally suited to each individual.

In addition, each student has a "circle of support" composed of other college students who offer support, as needed, to the students with ID as they navigate college life (Griffin, Wendel, Day, & McMillan, 2016). These circles are composed of approximately 8–12 peer supports who are scheduled to meet with the students with ID over the course of their day to share meals, work out together, study together, and just "hang out." The circles of support are critical in promoting inclusive experiences for each student in the program, and they provide individualized support as needed. For example, if a student needs support in organizing notes and handouts from a class, someone in their circle of support could provide this assistance.

Students in the Next Steps at Vanderbilt program engage in literacy learning in numerous ways; for the purposes of this chapter, we have chosen to highlight three: participation in classes, daily journaling, and texting. The support needs of students engaging in these activities vary widely, and supports are therefore highly individualized, as described in the following sections.

Coursework   Students in the Next Steps at Vanderbilt program participate in a wide range of classes related to a career aspiration, a personal interest, or both—for example, past classes have included Presidential Politics: College Students, Social Movements, and Civic Activism; Fundamentals of Theater; Non-profit Organizations and Serving as a Board Member; Oceanography; and Harry Potter and Child Development. At the outset of each semester, the program staff meets with the faculty who are teaching courses in which students are enrolled in order to develop independent learning agreements based on the syllabus. For a sample independent learning agreement (Day, 2016), see Figure 14.1.

Of course, taking any college class involves many literacy skills, such as learning information from assigned readings and from in-class lectures that often use PowerPoint presentations, and completing assessment activities such as writing a paper or preparing a presentation. To assist students in the Next Steps at Vanderbilt program with learning new information, in some cases program staff will identify more accessible texts. In addition, like any other eligible student with a disability in the class, students with ID may receive notes from another student who is reimbursed through the campus Disability Services office. Students can then review notes after class to reinforce key concepts. These supports allow students to better access the course content.

Students are also supported when they draw on their literacy skills to complete course assessments. They may write a paper or prepare a presentation with support from a Next Steps at Vanderbilt staff member or a member of their circle of support. Each student's independent learning agreement for a given course specifies the parameters of a particular assessment, including any accommodations made for the student which are determined to be appropriate jointly by the professor and program staff. These agreements also specify any modifications or accommodations needed for the student to demonstrate knowledge or skills. For example, rather than taking an in-class multiple-choice quiz, the student might meet with the instructor

---

Independent Learning Agreement

EDUC 1690.01

Dead Poets, Mean Girls, & Freedom Writers: Images of Teaching & Learning in Popular Film

The student will be following the regular course syllabus and working to complete the course assignments with the following modifications:

1. **Required Readings:** The student will scan through the readings independently to the best of her ability. She will then again scan through each week's readings with one of her tutors. When there are multiple assigned readings for one week, the student will choose one to focus on.

2. **Tumblr:** The student will post one weekly image, quote, or link representing a mass-media image of teaching or learning. Further explanation of this assignment is in the course syllabus.

3. **Film Viewing & Responses:** The student will view the films and write a one-page response to each film using the questions in the course syllabus as a guide for this paper.

4. **Final multimodal project:** This project is optional for the student; see syllabus for details.

It is understood that the student will not earn a grade for her participation in this course. She will receive feedback on her assignments from the professor and Next Steps Director.

Next Steps Student: _____ Date: _____

Class Professor: _____ Date: _____

Next Steps Director: _____ Date: _____

Figure 14.1. Sample independent learning agreement. (From Day, T. L. [2016]. *Sample independent learning agreement.* Next Steps at Vanderbilt University.)

to answer oral questions about the course content. Finally, students may also review notes and readings with members of their circle in order to study for a quiz or test.

Daily Journaling   To facilitate ongoing development of writing skills, Next Steps at Vanderbilt requires that each student keep a daily journal. Assigned writing topics include details about what they are learning in a class, observations about internships, reflections on time spent with circle members, and weekend plans. In addition, a new and popular journal assignment is to view a TED Talk on any topic, discuss it with a friend, and write about what was learned.

Because students enter the program with varying levels of writing skills, this requirement is individualized. For example, Next Steps at Vanderbilt staff determine the minimum number of sentences required for each student's daily journal entry; some might be required to write two sentences, whereas others are expected to compose a paragraph. Students are expected to use the supports provided by standard word processing software, such as spell-check and grammar-check. Students who need more support with writing will dictate their sentences to a member of their circle, who types them; then, the student types the sentences again, using the model that has been provided. Over time, as students become more fluent in typing and composition, they need fewer and fewer supports.

Texting   Most college students have cell phones and communicate with each other frequently via text messages. Texting, which seems to be a way of life for some, certainly involves many literacy skills, and students in the Next Steps at Vanderbilt program use texting to communicate with program staff, members of their circles of support, and their family and friends. Just as for most college students, texting serves both a social function and a logistical one—allowing students to coordinate meeting up with one another. For those individuals who are not fluent in typing text messages, or who prefer automated supports, most phones come with some built-in technology supports. For example, many have a "predictive text" feature that will suggest words based on what the user has typed and on past writing patterns, which allows the user to simply select the appropriate word rather than typing it out entirely. In addition, many smartphones now have built-in speech-to-text functions. Although these can be very helpful supports, we would caution that students with extensive needs for support will often need to receive direct instruction on these functions and would benefit from modeling and practice in order to use them effectively.

Along these lines, texting is inherently a social behavior, and in our observation, some students with developmental disabilities may need instruction on the social aspects of this medium. For example, they may need help with questions such as, *What is an acceptable number of texts to send to someone who has not responded? Are there times that students should refrain from texting, such as in class or during a conversation with someone else? Are there other times when texting would be inappropriate, such as before or after certain hours?* Program staff members provide this instruction and sometimes involve members of the student's circle of support as well. In our work with college students with intellectual and developmental disabilities, we have found that it is important to explicitly teach students these social norms to help them use the medium successfully; furthermore, often the best instructors on these issues are students' peers. Hearing from peers about behaviors that are appropriate or inappropriate has been a very effective way for students in the program to learn these social skills.

A final word about social media, literacy, and learners with complex support needs: In our informal observations, social media such as YouTube and Facebook are as engaging for people with disability as they are for the public at large. Indeed, technology brings us in contact with one another and makes us all part of an accessible community without our ever having to leave the comfort of our own homes. However, an individual who lacks literacy skills may not be fully participatory in these activities—whether the individual is using social media for entertainment purposes or in an effort to learn. In addition, individuals with complex support needs can be as vulnerable to exploitation and mistreatment in the cyber-world as they are elsewhere (Didden et al., 2009). Thus, as with other context-specific skills, we note the need for instruction in order for individuals with complex support needs to fully and safely use the Internet and social media.

PROMOTING LITERACY IN COMMUNITY SETTINGS

Literacy development for adults with complex support needs can also be facilitated through the supports available in various community settings—for example, public libraries, book clubs, and day habilitation programs designed to address the needs of these individuals. In the next sections, we describe how these programs can provide valuable literacy supports.

Accessing Libraries and Book Clubs

Public libraries provide ready assistance from librarians; access to print books, as well as audiobooks and computers; and a vast array of additional resources, including community activities and classes. Most, if not all, of such services are free to the public. However, accessing libraries can be a challenge due to transportation limitations common among individuals with extensive support needs. We discuss the issue of transportation and travel training in the following section on employment.

Individuals with extensive needs for support, as well as their friends, family, and staff, would benefit from learning what specific services are available at their local libraries. One approach to educate the public about available services is the City Bus Outreach project (Hands & Johnson, 2012). This project proposes that librarians and library supporters ride public buses serving low-income populations within the local community and that during the course of the bus ride, the library consultant would point out library branch locations, educate riders about available resources and services, offer passengers the opportunity to register as library users, and conduct demonstrations with e-books and other interactive technology.

Book clubs are often facilitated by local libraries and are a way many adults engage in reading new books and socializing. Founded in 2002, the Next Chapter Book Club is a program designed for individuals with developmental disabilities to engage in book clubs like their typically developing adult peers. It is the most widely known and documented program addressing this need for individuals with intellectual and developmental disabilities.

The Next Chapter Book Clubs are coordinated by affiliate organizations, such as libraries, advocacy organizations, and literacy groups (Fish & Rabidoux, 2009). Club meetings can be held at any number of host sites, including local bookstores, coffee shops, and community centers. Volunteer facilitators work with club members to select a book—typically, members will nominate selections of interest to them and then vote to choose a book to read. The Next Chapter Book Club has developed a library of books with appropriate reading levels— including many adapted classics—to ensure that selections are accessible to club members. In addition, club-associated authors who have expertise in literacy for people with developmental disabilities have published a volume of short stories of appropriate reading levels that address topics of interest to adolescents and adults (viz., Fish & Ober, 2012).

To facilitate club members' engagement, Next Chapter Book Club offers many helpful suggestions for encouraging literacy learning. Some focus on meeting the needs of emergent readers (Fish & Rabidoux, 2009). For example, one suggested activity is for members to draw a scene from the book and then describe it to the club; this not only fosters participation but also encourages comprehension, builds memory skills, and provides practice in public speaking. Another activity designed for more advanced readers involves different members taking turns reading a sentence from the book (Fish & Rabidoux, 2009). This activity encourages participation as well as reading fluency. The manual, *Next Chapter Book Club: A Model Community Literacy Program for People with Intellectual Disabilities*, describes many other activities—focused on improving comprehension, vocabulary, phonemic awareness, fluency, participation, and social interaction—which can be geared toward readers of all levels.

Figure 14.2 features a member of the Next Chapter Book Club affiliated with the Next Steps at Vanderbilt program.

Figure 14.2. Member of the Next Chapter Book Club associated with the Next Steps at Vanderbilt program at Vanderbilt University.

Ongoing Skills Development

Many individuals with extensive support needs participate in day-habilitation programs as adults. In this section on promoting literacy in the community, we would like to highlight ARCA, a nonprofit serving individuals with developmental disabilities. Founded in 1957, ARCA provides various services in the Albuquerque, New Mexico, community, including employment supports and day-habilitation activities that include opportunities to participate in bowling, service work within the community, and art and cooking classes. ARCA also provides its clients with family-based supported and independent living, and respite. As well, ARCA provides nutrition education that is especially important to clients living with Prader-Willi syndrome, which affects growth, metabolism, appetite, behavior, and development.

We highlight ARCA here because the opportunities for literacy learning it provides individuals with intellectual and developmental disabilities can serve as an exemplar to other adult service agencies. In its literacy classes (offered 3 days per week), individuals expand their skills in a variety of areas, working on both group and individual learning objectives. Participants work with traditional written texts as well as computers and iPads.

ARCA also encourages literacy through its traveling theater troupe, which collectively writes short plays to be performed at local venues. Not only do the theater participants expand their literacy skills, they also serve as ambassadors in the community, showing the possibilities that are present for everyone regardless of the perceived limitations of individuals with ID. Following their performances, which have become ever more popular, the actors and actresses hold question-and-answer sessions with audience members—an opportunity for theater-group participants to build their oral language skills, self-esteem, and confidence.

Beyond these activities that involve literacy in ways that are obvious, ARCA provides a range of other activities that foster everyday literacy, as described previously in this chapter. As we have noted, literacy is necessary for individuals to navigate a wide range of tasks to experience success within their communities—with "success" defined here as opportunities to build independence, establish relationships and natural supports, and enhance self-determination.

For example, one such activity involves grocery shopping and subsequently preparing a meal using the ingredients purchased. In one ARCA class alone, individuals navigate a wide range of literacy skills related to this task, including locating appropriate recipes, creating a pictorial grocery list to identify items accurately, and shopping—which also involves seeking out sales, comparing options, following instructions, and engaging in conversations with community members. The preparation and serving of the meal require work in both literacy and cooperative engagement with others. Arguably the best part of the process comes when everyone sits down to eat the meal together. This activity takes place in a local facility (often a local community center with an available kitchen) and brings together not only the participants in the class and their support staff but also other members of the community who are using the shared space.

REFLECTION QUESTION 2

Think of an individual with extensive support needs whom you know. What "everyday literacy" activities does this person engage in regularly?

PROMOTING LITERACY IN EMPLOYMENT SETTINGS

For many adults with complex support needs, ongoing literacy development occurs not only in PSE programs and community settings but also at work. Employment settings require these adults to use existing literacy skills and also provide opportunities to develop new skills. In the next section, we describe examples of ways in which employment settings can foster literacy in adults with complex support needs.

Getting to Work

Previously, we described how Maria listens to audiobooks to pass the time on her commute to work. What we have not addressed, however, is the critical issue of how she accessed this transportation in the first place. For individuals with complex support needs such as intellectual and developmental disabilities, transportation is critical to independence and participation in the community. Although some drive, the majority access transportation via family members or caregivers or use paratransit services or public transportation.

In Maria's case, taking the city bus to her job downtown was feasible, but she had never ridden the bus before and needed training to travel to and from work independently. For several weeks before Maria started working at the elementary school, her mother rode with her to teach the route and procedures that she would use, and she took pictures of Maria engaging in different component parts of this new skill set. She took pictures of Maria waiting at the bus stop near their house, paying the fare, getting off at the correct stop, and walking to the school. Then, using the pictures, she created a step-by-step list of directions based on the easy-read information sheet described by Ellison (2013). These information sheets are single-page resources that use pictures and minimal text to help individuals with extensive support needs navigate specific community settings or tasks. (For a sample easy-read information sheet for riding the city bus, see Figure 14.3.)

One advantage of these information sheets is that they are very flexible—they can be individualized to reflect specific contexts, tailored to the level of detail needed, and used appropriately across a wide range of settings and activities. In addition, Morgan et al. (2013) found that using visual texts across contexts and settings provided more effective construction of meaning and engagement among young adults with extensive support needs. The authors found that pictures, used alone or as an accompaniment to minimal text, were among the most helpful supports to individuals attempting to navigate and participate in various community settings.

Learning on the Job

Beyond getting to work, many literacy skills are required to learn the skills needed for a new job. The easy-read information sheets described previously can support individuals to learn and complete novel tasks; technology can support this as well. For example, when teaching Maria how to enter students' attendance data, the secretary recorded a short list of directions that Maria could listen to while completing this task. To do so, the secretary first completed a *task analysis*, in which she identified and described each component step of the task (Cooper, Heron, & Heward, 2007). Then, she taught each step to Maria systematically. For example, to teach Maria how to open the data-entry application on her computer, the secretary showed her what to do (modeling) and then asked Maria to do it herself, providing praise for correct attempts and correction for incorrect attempts (guided practice). Finally, the secretary recorded herself listing the component steps so that Maria could listen to the instructions and complete the task independently. Maria liked this because she could always listen to the instructions if she was confused about what to do next; because she often listened to music on her headphones at work, she could easily review recorded instructions without anyone else in the office being aware. In this way, the secretary was very successful in using an audio recording to support Maria's learning of a new skill.

Another evidence-based technological support for learning on the job is the use of video modeling (Bellini & Akullian, 2007; Shipley-Benamou, Lutzker, & Taubman, 2002). Video modeling has been used effectively with high school students and adults with a wide range of support needs (Ayres, Mechling, & Sansosti, 2013; Bellini & Akullian, 2007; Shipley-Benamou et al., 2002). In the previous vignette about Maria learning to enter attendance data, the secretary used modeling to show Maria how to do a part of the task. Video modeling uses this same strategy, but instead of modeling provided by someone in real time, the model is captured on video. This is helpful because the video allows for multiple viewings of a model. Video modeling is supported

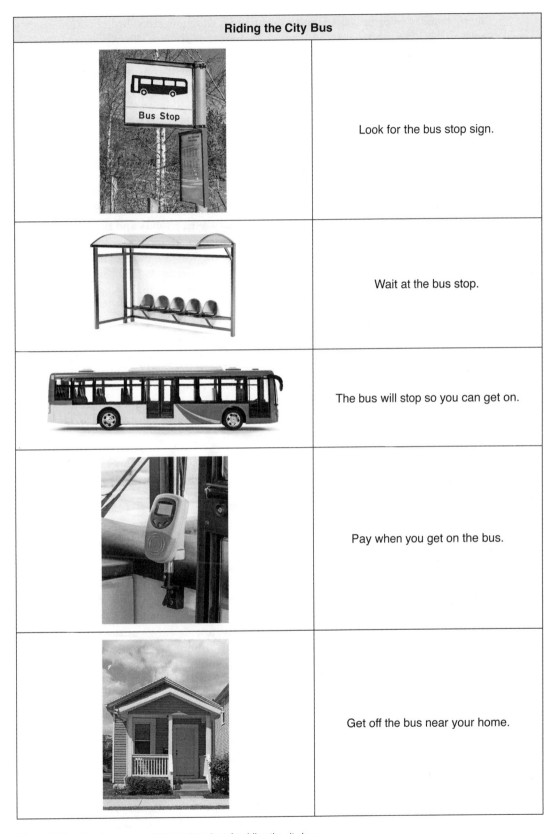

Riding the City Bus

	Look for the bus stop sign.
	Wait at the bus stop.
	The bus will stop so you can get on.
	Pay when you get on the bus.
	Get off the bus near your home.

Figure 14.3. Sample easy-read information sheet for riding the city bus.

by research, and promises to increase the independence and self-determination of individuals with disabilities, both on the job and in various other areas of life (Ayres et al., 2013).

In Maria's case, the secretary found that, when she tried to teach Maria the procedures for shredding documents, providing verbal instructions was confusing to Maria. So the secretary decided to record video of herself completing the different component parts of this task. This allowed her to show Maria in which cabinet the documents were stored, where the key was located, how to turn on the shredder, and how to feed papers into it so that they did not jam. Maria loaded the short video onto her smartphone so it would be available for her to refer to for the first few weeks that she worked on this new task.

Computer Literacy

For individuals with disabilities, being computer literate is important because, beyond providing entertainment and a way to communicate with friends and family, it provides access to employment opportunities. As noted in prior sections, use of technology can support the acquisition of new skills. In many jobs, technology is the way business is done. Assistive technology can allow individuals with extensive needs for support to do jobs that otherwise might not be accessible. And, as for all us of in this digital age, various technologies can make work tasks more efficient.

However, individuals with extensive support needs must be taught how to use and troubleshoot problems with unfamiliar technologies in the first place (Tanis et al., 2012). For example, individuals might need to learn to use Microsoft Word or the specific e-mail application used in their place of employment. Much research has documented the ability of individuals with extensive support needs to learn such skills (e.g., Fajardo-Flores & Contreras-Castillo, 2009). Again, we note that appropriate instruction, modeling, and supports will be needed to help individuals to become fluent in using various technologies.

REFLECTION QUESTION 3

Beyond the examples given in this chapter, how could your community better support the literacy learning and engagement of adults with extensive support needs?

SUMMARY

We believe that literacy skills may be most readily acquired in the context of the "real world" in authentic, community-based settings—and that literacy learning is most successful when it is socially embedded and in a context that is meaningful to the individual. Consider the common activity of texting with a friend, which involves a wide range of reading and writing skills as well as technological literacy. Because texting is inherently social, and because the communication is likely meaningful to the individuals involved, it presents an ideal opportunity for the development of literacy skills.

We also believe reciprocity is an important aspect of literacy learning, and appreciated that the participants in Morgan et al. (2013) were provided with opportunities to be both student and teacher across various literacy contexts. We find that many of the activities in which the clients at ARCA participate also include reciprocity—from participating in the traveling theater troupe to volunteering in the community. These activities provide participants with an opportunity to learn while also contributing to the community.

When individuals are allowed to take on the role of knowledgeable teacher, it not only builds on previously learned literacy skills but also helps them to gain important social skills, build motivation for further learning, and increase self-determination. For example, Maria's sign language class allowed her to teach her nieces and nephews new signs. (Eventually, their parents—her siblings—wanted to learn the signs, as well, to "keep tabs" on their children!) Maria also took on the role of teacher as a volunteer for her church's Sunday school class. Maria's literacy learning allowed her to be successful in these valued social roles, in addition to extending her own learning. As most educators would attest, one of the best ways to learn is to teach.

Literacy events occur in a wide range of contexts and settings in our daily lives (Morgan et al., 2013). In this chapter, we have discussed literacy in inclusive PSE, employment, and community settings. However, we note that our prior examples are not exhaustive—adults with and without disabilities encounter a vast range of literacy events in the community beyond those already described. As we have suggested through this chapter, no one should be excluded from experiencing what is important in his or her own life because of a lack of literacy skills. We all have the right to go shopping for the items we need or want, to make use of public transportation services, to continue our education after high school, and to make informed decisions about our health. These and many other activities all have their own context-specific literacy requirements. Our hope is that individuals with extensive support needs can access the instruction and ongoing supports required to participate fully in these and all aspects of their lives. In short, our hope is that communities see individuals with extensive support needs as they are: adults capable of and empowered by literacy.

RESOURCES

- Fish, T., & Rabidoux, P. (2009). *Next Chapter Book Club: A model community literacy program for people with intellectual disabilities.* Bethesda, MD: Woodbine. This book describes the Next Chapter Book Club's history and structure and provides information for volunteer facilitators.

- **ThinkCollege** (www.thinkcollege.net). This web site is a central resource for students with intellectual disability who want to go to college; it includes many resources, including a searchable database of programs.

- Ellison, E.W. (2013). Reaching out to patients with intellectual disabilities. *Community Eye Health Journal, 26*(81). This article includes information about accessing health care and also describes the easy-read information sheets referenced in this chapter.

REFERENCES

Ayres, K.M., Mechling, L., & Sansosti, F.J. (2013). The use of mobile technologies to assist with life skills/independence of students with moderate/severe intellectual disability and/or autism spectrum disorders: Considerations for the future of school psychology. *Psychology in the Schools, 50*(3), 259–271.

Bellini, S., & Akullian, J. (2007). A meta-analysis of video modeling and video self-modeling interventions for children and adolescents with autism spectrum disorders. *Exceptional Children, 73*(3), 264–287.

Cooper, J.O., Heron, T.E., & Heward, W.L. (2007). *Applied behavior analysis* (2nd ed.). Upper Saddle River, NJ: Pearson.

Copeland, S.R. (2007). Literacy for life. In S.R. Copeland & E.B. Keefe (Eds.), *Effective literacy instruction for students with moderate or severe disabilities* (pp. 157–165). Baltimore, MD: Paul H. Brookes Publishing Co.

Copeland, S.R., & Keefe, E.B. (Eds.). (2007). *Effective literacy instruction for students with moderate or severe disabilities.* Baltimore, MD: Paul H. Brookes Publishing Co.

Day, T.L. (2016). *Next Steps at Vanderbilt: Sample independent learning agreement.* Vanderbilt University, Nashville, TN.

Didden, R., Scholte, R.H., Korzilius, H., De Moor, J.M., Vermeulen, A., O'Reilly, M., . . ., Lancioni, G.E. (2009). Cyberbullying among students with intellectual and developmental disability in special education settings. *Developmental Neurorehabilitation, 12*(3), 146–151.

Ellison, E.W. (2013). Reaching out to patients with intellectual disabilities. *Community Eye Health Journal, 26*(81).

Fajardo-Flores, S.B., & Contreras-Castillo, J. (2009). Training people with disabilities in the use of IT: A community case. *The International Journal of Learning, 16*(7), 577–582.

Fish, T., & Ober, J. (2012). *Lucky dogs, lost hats, and dating don'ts: Hi-lo stories about real life.* Bethesda, MD: Woodbine.

Fish, T., & Rabidoux, P. (2009). *Next Chapter Book Club: A model community literacy program for people with intellectual disabilities.* Bethesda, MD: Woodbine.

Freire, P. (1994). *Pedagogy of hope.* New York, NY: Continuum.

Griffin, M.M., Wendel, K.F., Day, T.L., & McMillan, E.D. (2016). Developing peer supports for college students with intellectual and developmental disabilities. *Journal of Postsecondary Education and Disability, 29*(3), 263–269.

Grigal, M., & Hart, D. (2010). *Think college! Postsecondary education options for students with intellectual disabilities.* Baltimore, MD: Paul H. Brookes Publishing Co.

Hands, A.S., & Johnson, A. (2012, Summer/Fall). Lighting the way: Grant applications showcase range of programming ideas. *Children and Libraries, 10*(2), 56–57.

Hutchison, K., & Auld, G. (2015). Softening the walls between home and school literacies to reimagine connections. *Practically Primary, 20,* 34–36.

Individuals with Disabilities Education Improvement Act (IDEA) of 2004, PL 108-446, 20 U.S.C. §§ 1400 *et seq.*

Keefe, E.B., & Copeland, S.R. (2011). What is literacy? The power of a definition. *Research and Practice for Persons with Severe Disabilities, 36*(3–4), 92–99.

Luckasson, R. (2006). The human rights basis for student personal empowerment in education. In L. Keefe, V. Moore, & F. Duff (Eds.), *Listening to the experts: Students with disabilities speak out about their school experiences* (pp. 11–20). Baltimore, MD: Paul H. Brookes Publishing Co.

Morgan, F.M., Moni, K.B., & Cuskelly, M. (2013). Literacy strategies used by adults with intellectual disability in negotiating their everyday community environments. *Australian Journal of Adult Learning, 53*(3), 411–435.

Morgan, M., Moni, K.B., & Jobling, A. (2009). Who? Where? What? When? Why? How? Question words—What do they mean? *British Journal of Learning Disabilities, 37,* 178–185.

Rogan, P., Updike, J., Chesterfield, G., & Savage, S. (2014). The SITE program at IUPUI: A postsecondary program for individuals with intellectual disabilities. *Journal of Vocational Rehabilitation, 40*(2), 109–116. doi:10.3233/JVR-140673

Shipley-Benamou, R., Lutzker, J.R., & Taubman, M. (2002). Teaching daily living skills to children with autism through instructional video modeling. *Journal of Positive Behavior Interventions, 4*(3), 166–177.

Tanis, E.S., Palmer, S., Wehmeyer, M., Davies, D.K., Stock, S.E., Lobb, K., & Bishop, B. (2012). Self-report computer-based survey of technology use by people with intellectual and developmental disabilities. *Intellectual and Developmental Disabilities, 50*(1), 53–68.

ThinkCollege. (2017). *Find a college.* Institute for Community Inclusion at the University of Massachusetts Boston. Retrieved from http://www.thinkcollege.net/component/programsdatabase/?view=programs database&Itemid=339

CHAPTER 15

Where Do We Go From Here?

Elizabeth B. Keefe, Susan R. Copeland, Ruth Luckasson, and Diane Ryndak

LEARNING OBJECTIVES

By the end of this chapter, readers will

1. Review the major themes of this book and how these themes apply to literacy learning.

2. Examine how information in this book can be applied by people within the following groups to effect positive change in literacy instruction: people with complex support needs, families, educators, educational leaders, community support providers, teacher preparation programs, and policy makers.

As we noted in Chapter 1, individuals with complex support needs represent the last group of people routinely denied opportunities for literacy instruction. Our purpose for writing this book is to provide specific, evidence-based instructional approaches to ensure that there is no longer any excuse to deny effective comprehensive literacy instruction across the life span to any individual with complex needs. Chapter 1 laid the foundation for the approach to literacy instruction for these individuals throughout this book. In this final chapter, we will briefly review four major themes. Then, taking the perspective of several different groups—including people with complex support needs, families, educators, educational leaders, community support providers, educators who teach in teacher preparation programs, and policy makers—we will explore the ways in which this book can be used to welcome everyone into the literate community.

SUMMARY OF MAJOR THEMES

The four major themes we will review are

- Recognizing the power of literacy and need for a broader definition of literacy.

- Acknowledging literacy as a human right through applying the least dangerous assumption and presuming capability.

- Using an evidence-based comprehensive literacy approach.

- Following six important guidelines when designing literacy instruction.

The Power of Literacy—and the Power of Definitions

Literacy is power. As discussed throughout this book, a critical purpose of education is to equip students with knowledge and skills that will lead to increased opportunities, choices, and autonomy; for 21st century students, this includes literacy. Furthermore, literacy is a crucial component of meaningful education and required for full participation in all societies. This is the *power of literacy.*

Throughout this book, we have also discussed the serious consequences individuals with complex support needs might experience when caregivers, teachers, or other practitioners have low expectations of the individuals' potential to become literate citizens. Too often, these low expectations result in limited literacy instruction, or none at all, along with restricted access to the everyday literacy activities and materials that build understanding of both language and literacy. Ultimately, these low expectations result in unfortunate outcomes: adults who lack basic literacy skills and who are thus further excluded from their typical-age peers in school, employment, and community settings. In contrast, acquiring even basic literacy skills can create opportunities to participate more fully in one's community, be less dependent on others, and make individual choices about what one wants to do or learn. In other words, literacy skills contribute to a more engaged, satisfying life.

Definitions are powerful. We believe one of the major reasons for this lack of opportunity is related to how we *define literacy.* It is clear that our definitions of literacy directly affect classroom instruction, community services, and the literacy opportunities offered to students with complex support needs for supports across the life span. In Chapter 1, we rejected any definition of literacy that was based on the assumption that only some people can be literate, because we propose that there is no dichotomy of literate/illiterate individuals (Downing, 2005; Kliewer & Biklen, 2007; Koppenhaver, Pierce, & Yoder, 1995). Instead, our book expands the concept of literacy by applying five core definitional principles to ensure that individuals with complex support needs are never excluded.

1. All people are capable of acquiring literacy.

2. Literacy is a human right and is a fundamental part of the human experience.

3. Literacy is not a trait that is isolated in the individual person. *It is an ever-developing interactive tool and status for mutual engagement between a person and a community and its people, knowledge, and ideas; literacy requires and creates connections (relationships) with others.*

4. Literacy includes observation, communication, social contact, internal connection and incorporation, and the expectation for interaction with all individuals and ideas; *literacy leads to enhanced empowerment.*

5. Acquiring literacy is an individual responsibility of each member of a community as well as a collective responsibility of the whole community; *that is, ensure that every person develops meaning-making with all human modes of communication* in order to exercise their personal and communal responsibilities and opportunities and to transmit and receive information and ideas.

These core literacy definitional principles have grounded our discussion of literacy throughout this text and serve as important guidelines for providing quality literacy instruction.

Literacy Is a Human Right

Throughout this book, we have asserted that literacy is more than an educational right—it is a basic human right. As noted specifically in Chapter 1, future directions in literacy for people with disability will be shaped by past restrictions, current and future law, and contemporary research and practices. People with complex support needs, their families, their friends, and those who work with them need to recognize the context for literacy experiences set by this political, social, and legal history. Each chapter in this book is based on understanding the absolutely critical nature of literacy in the lives of people with disability, improving literacy legal policies and evidence-based practices, assuring effective advocacy for literacy for all, and enhancing the literacy rights of people with complex support needs.

Lunsford, Moglen, and Slevin stated that for all people, "literacy is a right and not a privilege: A right that has been denied an extraordinary number of our citizens" (1990, p. 2). Throughout the history of the United States, some groups have been denied access to literacy, including people of color, women, and the poor. Few first-person accounts exist that describe the deprivation. One exception is Asante. Let's take a moment to revisit his moving account, first cited at the beginning of his book, *Buck: A Memoir:* "Now I see why reading was illegal for black people during slavery. I discover that I think in words. The more words I know, the more things I can think about. Reading was illegal because if you limit someone's vocab, you limit his or her thoughts. They can't even think of freedom because they don't have the language to" (2014, p. 229). Asante understood that literacy is power. Similarly, we note in our fourth core definitional principle, discussed previously, that literacy leads to enhanced empowerment.

Individuals with complex support needs are the last group routinely denied access to literacy instruction. As is the case with other groups denied access to literacy, we do not have many first-person accounts of the impact of this denial of human rights. One exception is the book *Listening to the Experts* (Keefe, Moore, & Duff, 2006), which includes multiple chapters written or dictated by students with and without disabilities sharing their high school experiences. Keefe et al. proposed that the students are the real experts about their educational experiences, and we should listen to their stories. In their concluding chapter, Duff, Keefe, and Moore noted, "The students' message is clear: *All students need to feel as though they belong in the school community*" (2006, p. 209). This includes having access to meaningful literacy instruction, as noted by a student named Elliot Shelton: "The teachers didn't give me the opportunity to show what I could do; they just focused on the things I couldn't do. In school, we just read out of books and did worksheets. Tons of worksheets. I hate worksheets. How can a kid with dyslexia learn anything from worksheet packets?" (2006, p. 7). Although Shelton did not have complex support needs, he gave voice to the experiences of students with disabilities who experienced segregated educational environments in high school.

REFLECTION QUESTION 1

We hope you agree that literacy is a basic human right. How can your actions make this right a reality for individuals with complex support needs?

Evidence-Based, Comprehensive Approaches to Literacy Instruction

Fortunately, there is a renewed interest among researchers and practitioners in examining literacy instruction for individuals with complex support needs. Our book is based on the assumption that all people, including those with complex needs for support, are fully capable of benefiting from evidence-based, comprehensive literacy instruction. Furthermore, we believe our field as a whole could benefit from a more optimistic and inclusive approach to literacy instruction.

Research conducted within the past 10 years has demonstrated positive student outcomes associated with providing what we term *comprehensive literacy instruction* (e.g., Allor, Mathes, Roberts, Cheatham, & Al Otaiba, 2014). This model of literacy instruction differs markedly from the decontextualized instruction of the past that sought to teach discrete skills (Browder, Ahlgrim-Delzell, Courtade, Gibbs, & Flowers, 2008). We define a *comprehensive literacy instructional model* as *integrated instruction that teaches all the components of reading concurrently: early literacy skills such as concepts about print; language development and vocabulary skills; word recognition skills that include both sight-word and phonics knowledge; listening and reading comprehension skills; fluency; and writing.* The chapters in this book, taken together, are designed to help the reader develop and implement the latest evidence-based practices in comprehensive literacy instruction for students with complex support needs.

Always Remember the Guidelines

In Chapter 1, we discussed how our research and review of the research and practitioner literature examining literacy instruction for this population resulted in the development of six general guidelines to use when planning and implementing literacy instruction. We asked you to keep these in mind as you read each chapter. These guidelines are so critical that we are revisiting them briefly in this last chapter as we look to the future.

The first of these guidelines is to *begin instruction with, and maintain, high expectations for students with complex support needs.* Our beliefs about our students' abilities and our definitions of literacy strongly influence what we choose to teach and how we teach it. A disability label alone does not tell us what a given student can learn.

The second guideline is to *combine high expectations for students with provision of individualized, systematic, and sustained instruction.* Students with complex support needs benefit from well-planned, consistent instruction throughout their school years and across the life span (e.g., Allor et al., 2014). It is important to remember that individuals with complex support needs will continue to learn when given high-quality, sustained instruction.

The third guideline is to *provide language and communication interventions and supports from the earliest years of a child's life.* Because language is the foundation on which later literacy develops, it is crucial to support its development beginning at birth, as we discussed in Chapter 2. We must give every child the opportunity to develop their language and communication abilities and always consider a child's home language when planning language/communication and literacy intervention, as discussed in Chapter 3. Relatedly, the fourth guideline is to *begin structured, developmentally appropriate literacy instruction during the preschool years and continue instruction across a student's formal schooling.* As noted in Chapter 14, many individuals with complex support needs attend postsecondary programs or adult education programs where they may continue literacy instruction.

Fifth, *create comprehensive literacy instruction that includes concurrent instruction in all of the core components of reading*—the most effective type of instruction for individuals with complex support needs (e.g., Allor et al., 2014; Browder et al., 2008; Browder, Ahlgrim-Delzell, Flowers, & Baker, 2012). Practitioner preparation programs have a responsibility to teach their students to move beyond highly scripted intervention programs focused narrowly on only one component of literacy and, instead, provide instruction across skill areas using engaging materials and activities. This leads to a sixth guideline: *Students with complex support needs learn to read in a similar manner to typically developing peers and alongside those peers* (e.g., Wise, Sevcik, Romski, & Morris, 2010). This practice uses the natural supports, motivation, and incidental learning opportunities this arrangement provides. The intensive, individualized instruction that students with complex support needs require can be successfully provided within general education contexts (Hudson, Browder, & Wood, 2013; Ryndak, Moore, Orlando, & Delano, 2008/2009; Ryndak, Morrison, & Sommerstein, 1999).

HOW OUR BOOK CAN BE USED

All of us have a responsibility to provide effective, high-quality literacy instruction for individuals with complex support needs. This includes educators, policy makers, researchers, families, adult service providers, and so forth. Society is strengthened when all of its members have the opportunity to become part of the "literate citizenship" Kliewer (2008) described. However, making these opportunities a reality requires substantial changes in how we prepare teachers and other practitioners and in how we conceptualize, implement, and fund supports for this group of learners across the life span.

Here, we examine how the main themes of the book impact the future for the following groups and how these groups can facilitate the needed changes: individuals with complex support needs, families, educators, educational leaders, community support providers, teacher preparation programs, and policy makers. We provide some suggestions on how each group can play its part in implementing the changes necessary to make the themes we have discussed become real—in the lives of individuals with complex needs for support and in the lives of their families, friends, communities, and societies.

People With Complex Support Needs for Supports Across the Life Span

How does our book impact individuals with complex support needs? We propose that recognizing that literacy learning progresses from birth across the life span has significant implications for the types of services and supports provided to these individuals. Throughout this book, we have presented a broader definition of literacy and a more comprehensive understanding of how it develops. This view opens up exciting opportunities for learning that can lead to increased personal empowerment and increased participation in social, school, community, and employment settings for individuals with complex support needs. The presumption of capability and the least dangerous assumption open up opportunities for effective literacy instruction for people with complex support needs. From our perspective, instead of being seen as unable to acquire new knowledge and skills, individuals with complex support needs are viewed as capable and are offered opportunities to develop critical academic skills across the life span.

Students with disabilities—including those with complex support needs—and their typically developing peers have provided insight into their experiences in high school and what can happen when the presumption of capability and the least dangerous assumption are not followed (Keefe et al., 2006). Two student stories will serve to illustrate the key message of this book: *All students need to feel as though they belong in the school community.*

In a very moving description, a student named Farrah Fernton (2006) shares her experiences in school as a student with cerebral palsy. Before she went to school, Fernton remembers, she did not feel different from others, or think much about her disability, "because I was just a little girl. I was more concerned with combing my babydoll's hair" (p. 59). Fernton recalls that this changed when she went to school: "I think that is when I was really forced to realize that no matter how much I wanted to be thought I was like everyone else, I really was going to be looked at as different" (p. 60). She remembers having no interaction with typical peers in elementary school in Texas, being segregated even for lunch, which was brought to the classroom. Fernton movingly describes the difficulties she encountered with her teacher during one year when she was included in a general education fourth-grade class for math:

> I remember one horrible incident vividly. I came to class this particular day, and my homework was not finished. I explained to her that it was because there were too many problems and I did not quite understand how to do it. All of a sudden her face got very red, and she screamed at me, 'I knew you did not belong here. People like you cannot do this kind of work!' I was mortified. I could see the hatred in her eyes. I also heard the other students laughing in the background. (2006, pp. 60–61)

This experience almost made Fernton give up, but her family encouraged her to keep fighting.

Fernton (2006) reports that, throughout her school career, she remained primarily in special education classes. It wasn't until her last year in school that she had a positive and inclusive school experience in a humanities class. Fernton recalls, "For the first time I feel I have been able to sort of become more outgoing and stop being so afraid of how people will react to me because I have a disability" (p. 62). In her final year of high school, Fernton made friends, and after a significant struggle with the school system, she was able to leave campus like any other senior and eat lunch with her friends. As she writes in her chapter, "I, still to this day, cannot understand why keeping a small group of students separated away from their nondisabled peers is supposed to be good for them" (p. 61). Fernton has a lesson for all of us when she concludes: "I have come to realize that I can succeed in the outside world, where there is no different place set aside for people with disabilities. After all, there is no special ed McDonalds" (p. 62).

Farrah Fernton has presented her story in our university classes and local conferences. When asked to name the greatest change that resulted from her being included, Farrah always emotionally thanked her teacher, Ms. Duff, for welcoming her into her general education classroom. As a result of being educated alongside her peers, students now said "hi" to Farrah in the hallway for the first time ever in her time in high school. What kind of literate community can schools provide if we deny some students the opportunity to interact daily with their peers and they live their lives unknown by their typical peers?

What impact does such segregation have on typical peers? One such peer, Michelle Murray (2006), talked about her friendship with Farrah Fernton and the challenges she and other friends encountered when they wanted Farrah to be able to go to lunch off campus just like the other seniors. Describing her senior year of high school, Murray wrote, "I have made a friend who just happens to be in a wheelchair. I had never seen this girl for the 3 previous years that we both attended the same high school" (p. 63). Remembering how Farrah appeared in her humanities class, Murray asks, "Where had she been? I wondered. Her huge electric chair was not easy to miss, especially in the halls of our overcrowded school" (p. 63). Murray reports her outrage that "there was another 'world' behind the main building where a collection of portable classrooms defined the boundaries for many students with disabilities. It was as if she and I had attended school in different hemispheres" (p. 63). Murray, Fernton, and two other friends had to overcome administrative hurdles in order to go with Farrah off campus for lunch. This was quite the learning experience for all of them, as well as the school administration. But it did end well. Murray reflects on the experiences as follows:

> Now that this is all behind us, it seems like a happy story. But if you look at it from a different angle, it seems a little less straightforward. It all started when four girls wanted to go to lunch together, you have to wonder why there was so much red tape. Why were the rules different for a disabled student rather than for typical students? Wasn't this discrimination? . . . The administration thought they were helping her by trying to protect her; . . . in actuality, they were stifling her independence. (2006, pp. 66–67)

Murray and Fernton's stories show what can happen when the least dangerous assumption and presumption of capability are missing in a school setting. The impact on the lives of students both with and without disabilities is significant and unfortunate. If individuals with complex support needs are not part of the literate community, it diminishes life experiences for everyone.

REFLECTION QUESTION 2

In what ways were you a part of, or excluded from, the literate community in the schools you attended?

An increased focus on defining literacy more broadly and encouraging lifelong literacy learning for individuals with complex support needs is illustrated by new research findings showing that effective instructional practices, combined with innovative technology, can provide these individuals with genuine access to literacy learning opportunities. Different chapters in this book specifically demonstrate how evidence-based, comprehensive literacy instruction can be developed and implemented for individuals with complex support needs.

The six guidelines for literacy instruction that we presented previously apply to learners with complex support needs across the life span. Families, advocates, and self-advocates need to ensure that service providers in schools and other community settings follow these guidelines. Individuals with complex support needs must have instruction based on high expectations, the least dangerous assumption, and the presumption of capability. Following these guidelines will ensure that these individuals are contributing, active participants in the literate community.

Families

We often think of literacy as something addressed primarily in school. However, its foundations truly begin in the home and community with families. It is within the family that children first observe and acquire language and communication skills and discover how literacy is used in everyday life. Literacy learning is a social process, learned most effectively in settings where children interact with others. Home provides an ideal context for this learning. How many of us remember cuddling with a parent, sibling, or caregiver while a story was read? Parents and other caregivers engage in many different literacy activities with their children from an early age as they support and facilitate their child's language and communication development. Children might listen to their mother telling family stories, watch their grandmother using a family recipe to cook a favorite meal, observe an older sibling writing his name, discuss the storyline of a favorite movie with a parent, and on and on. All of these daily activities are teaching important "lessons" about how oral and written language are used; they afford rich literacy learning opportunities.

Often, parents and caregivers are in a better position than professionals to support their child's literacy learning, especially because professionals only see a child for limited amounts of time. Parents, who are with their children every day, have a front row seat to observe the ways in which their child uses language or engages with symbols or print. Unfortunately, some families with sons and daughters with complex support needs have reported that their expectations of their children's capability to acquire literacy skills are different from those of teachers or therapists who provide services. This was illustrated in a study in which Spanish-speaking parents of children with complex support needs were interviewed regarding parent expectations for their children's literacy and language development (Copeland & de Valenzuela, 2010). These parents noted that, compared to some of the teachers and therapists who worked with their children, they themselves viewed their children as having greater potential to acquire literacy knowledge and skill. Perhaps because of these lower expectations, some of these professionals provided services that did not allow opportunities for the child to engage in literacy learning.

One of these parents, the mother of Annelise, indicated that "none of them [homebound teachers] really had a vision for her learning how to read" (Copeland & de Valenzuela, 2010, personal communication). It is important to consider that Annelise, although having extensive physical and medical challenges, did not have a cognitive disability. Her teachers and therapists, however, focused on her multiple disabilities and assumed that she would not be able to learn conventional reading skills. Because of this unfounded assumption, they concentrated on teaching her daily living skills. What a missed opportunity! In contrast, consider what the parents of Milagro, whom you read about in Chapter 1, reported: "She watches PBS with her dad, listens to NPR with her mom, is read to and/or listens to bilingual/bicultural audio books that soothe her mind and continue to strengthen her world of literacy. Our assumption is that she can learn, and she does not disappoint" (Avila & Silva, 2013, p. 10).

What can families do to support children's literacy learning? The first step for family members is to seek out and insist that their child have appropriate language and communication intervention from birth. Language is the foundation for later print-based literacy. All children have the right to a reliable means of communication and to any assistance they require from competent specialists to help build their language skills.

Another powerful way families can help to build a child's literacy skills is to read with a child. Sitting down every day and reading together, even for a few minutes, models how important literacy is and helps a child learn how books and print work. It also builds new vocabulary and creates a positive association with reading for the child. Even older children and adolescents enjoy these moments of individual or family time with a parent, caregiver, or sibling. Books written in the language the family uses in their home are best for parent and child read-alouds. As seen in Chapters 5 and 12, simple adaptations to books can enhance a child's access to the story or information in a text. Greater access increases the child's active participation in the reading and, as a result, further strengthens the learning opportunities that reading together provides.

Another important role for families is to help school personnel understand the importance of literacy for their children. Children with complex support needs learn best when parents or other caregivers and school personnel work together (de Graaf, van Hove, & Haveman, 2013). As discussed throughout this book, not all teachers or therapists have training in the most recently developed, evidence-based literacy interventions for students with complex support needs. Parents can advocate for their child's inclusion in appropriate literacy instruction and steer educators to resources on literacy instruction for these students—including the list of myths and facts presented in the supplementary materials to this book, as well as the information on how to teach specific skills found in each chapter.

Schools and Educators

Within schools, educators—including teachers, paraprofessionals, and related service providers—provide context and opportunities for literacy learning that are often critical for students with complex support needs. Despite the research demonstrating that these students can develop literacy skills, low expectations and lack of effective teacher preparation often lead to an absence of evidence-based comprehensive literacy instruction. Educators must consider how they define literacy for these students. Embracing the principles and guidelines proposed in this book will create access to effective literacy instruction using the methods presented throughout.

If educators accept that literacy is a human right, schools will need to change to provide access to literacy instruction for all students. As a result, school mission statements and strategic plans will reflect a commitment to literacy instruction for all. Educators will accept responsibility for all students and will need to work together to provide comprehensive literacy instruction to all.

We know that many educators are not prepared to teach literacy to students with complex support needs. Various myths surrounding literacy instruction for these students result in the denial of literacy learning opportunities. The explosion of these myths provided at the beginning of this book could be part of in-service training in schools. Exploring and learning about standards-based individualized education programs (IEPs) and comprehensive literacy instruction would be other important areas for professional development.

The implications of the six guidelines for literacy instruction will need to be systematically considered by educators within schools. The first of these guidelines is to *begin instruction with, and maintain, high expectations for students with complex support needs.* Educators will need to discuss their beliefs about students' abilities and about the definition and nature of literacy, because these beliefs impact what we choose to teach, how we teach it, and, as a consequence, outcomes for students. Second, *combine high expectations for students with provision of individualized, systematic, and sustained instruction.* As noted previously, sometimes educators have not been prepared to provide effective literacy instruction; they may need continued professional development to be able to do this, so that these individuals continue to learn.

The third guideline is to *begin language and communication interventions and support from the earliest years of a child's life.* Educators must be committed to giving every child the opportunity to develop language and communication abilities, including considering a child's home language when planning intervention. The fourth guideline is to *begin structured, developmentally appropriate literacy instruction during the preschool years and continue instruction across a student's formal schooling.* Educators need to be aware of and support individuals with complex support needs who choose to attend postsecondary programs or adult education programs to continue their literacy instruction.

Fifth, *create comprehensive literacy instruction that includes concurrent instruction in all of the core components of reading.* Educators need to seek out ways to develop the knowledge and skills necessary to move beyond highly scripted intervention programs and instead provide engaging instruction across skill areas. A commitment to inclusive educational practices is central to the sixth guideline: *Students with complex support needs learn to read in a similar manner to typically developing peers and alongside those peers.* Educators must collaborate to effectively provide literacy instruction for students with complex support needs alongside typically developing peers. Professional development may help educators reap the benefits of inclusive education.

Is this all really possible? We have all worked with educators, schools, and districts to support them in implementing systems change consistent with the major themes of this book. It is very difficult for students with complex support needs to be members of the literate community if they do not have access to effective educational services in inclusive general education contexts. We know that it can be done.

Consider the example of Ken and Victor, two middle school students with complex support needs who were initially placed in a self-contained classroom with limited access to general education contexts (Ryndak, 2007). Through the process of school system change, this self-contained placement ended for Ken and Victor because the principal and teachers at the middle school, with support from the district director of special education, decided to provide these students with opportunities to interact with their schoolmates without disabilities. Although this was initially considered "social inclusion," it became clear to the teachers and peer supporters that Ken and Victor could do much more academically than they previously had been asked to do. It was also clear that Ken and Victor's augmentative and alternative communication (AAC) devices were inadequate to reflect their literacy abilities, so they were provided with more complex AAC systems. For the first time in their educational careers, Ken and Victor were provided with a method to communicate their needs, desires, and knowledge of academic content in a meaningful way. They also had AAC systems that enabled them to communicate across activities, contexts, and communication partners when *they* needed or wanted to communicate. The boys were finally able to participate in real middle school experiences simply by being provided with (a) opportunities to interact with other middle school students; (b) access to literacy instruction, situations in which literacy was required, and literacy models; and (c) appropriate AAC systems to demonstrate literacy skills they had developed *in spite of* years of ineffective instruction in self-contained settings.

Students with complex support needs should have access to general education curriculum, as discussed in Chapter 4; as educators, we need to be concerned with, if not outraged by, the current lack of access. These students also must have access to the individualized modifications and accommodations as described in Chapter 11. Finally, a growing research base demonstrates the effectiveness of comprehensive literacy instruction across all areas of literacy in inclusive settings as discussed throughout this book. Ken and Victor's story tells us that this can be implemented successfully.

Adult Services and Supports

As Griffin, Lane, Day, and McMillan pointed out in Chapter 14, literacy learning does not stop at age 18 or 21, when formal schooling for most individuals with complex support needs ends. Literacy skills are associated with improved health and well-being for adults because literacy skills promote active participation in adult life—for example, by opening up new employment opportunities, creating access to participation in civic activities, supporting health and wellness, and enhancing social interaction. These are just a few of the ways in which literacy skills enrich an adult's life. Yet, many adults with complex support needs do not have even basic literacy skills. Indeed, some researchers consider lack of literacy skills to be a secondary condition experienced by most people with developmental disabilities, including those with complex support needs (Koritas & Iacono, 2011). By "secondary conditions," we mean generally preventable conditions that are related in some way to a person's disability and that have negative effects on the individual's health and well-being—such as reducing the individual's access to active participation in the typical activities. Koritas and Iacono (2011) found that lack of literacy skills was the number one secondary condition that negatively affected adults with intellectual disability (ID). They surveyed 659 caregivers of adults with ID; 67% of these caregivers rated lack of reading skills as a significant problem for the adults with ID whom they supported. Their lack of skills increased the adults' dependence on others and restricted their opportunities for active participation in their communities and workplaces. This finding is especially concerning given that secondary conditions are preventable.

The good news is that adults with complex support needs, if offered the opportunity, can continue to learn literacy skills across the life span (e.g., Copeland, McCord, & Kruger, 2016). Literacy learning for adults can take place in various ways through various types of organizations. Postsecondary programs are obvious places where continued literacy instruction can occur (e.g., Hua, Woods-Groves, Kaldenberg, & Scheidecker, 2013). Community literacy programs designed for adults (not specific to disability) offer other opportunities for continuing literacy education. Some adult disability service providers also provide various types of literacy programs for individuals with disabilities, as described in Chapter 14.

Regardless of which type of organization offers literacy instruction, adult learners in general do better when they recognize and make connections between skills they are learning and the ways these skills apply to their everyday lives. Because of this characteristic of adult learning, it is especially important to base adult literacy instruction on the learners' individual goals and interests. Adult learners' motivation to persist and ability to transfer what they are learning to their lives outside of the classroom will be strengthened when staff take time to determine the adult's goal for continuing education and create instruction that helps the individual meet that goal. For example, one adult with complex support needs in our community wanted to improve her literacy skills so that she could read articles and blogs about her favorite professional football team, such as her chosen NFL team; her family enjoyed and participated in many activities related to professional sports, and she wanted to do so as well. Her tutor paid careful attention to this goal and created literacy materials and instruction using information about football. These materials were highly motivating to this individual and thus were effective for her. Her word recognition skills soared and her active participation in her family's favorite activities increased.

As with school-age individuals, adults with complex support needs may find their opportunities for continuing literacy education are negatively influenced by some professionals' low expectations about these adults' literacy capabilities. Frequently, programs for these adults take place in segregated settings where staff may hold very low expectations of their capabilities; some staff also believe that adults should focus exclusively on learning work tasks and not work on developing literacy skills. These beliefs create barriers to providing effective, meaningful literacy instruction.

Related to this potential barrier is a lack of training for individuals providing services and supports to adults with disabilities. Copeland, Kruger, and Keefe (2013) conducted a qualitative study of individuals employed in community agencies who provided some type of literacy instruction for adults with complex support needs. They found that most study participants had neither formal nor even informal training on how to effectively teach literacy skills. These literacy instructors were doing the best they could but had few resources, no relevant experience, and no training in how to teach literacy to anyone, much less individuals with complex support needs. In a related study, McCord, Keefe, and Copeland (2015) found that after only a few professional development sessions focused on basic literacy instruction, direct support staff in sheltered workshop settings improved the quality and quantity of literacy instruction they provided to the individuals with complex support needs they supported. This study's findings document that when appropriate professional training is available to adult service providers, adults with complex support needs can and do continue to develop their literacy skills.

Another solution to these potential problems is to have adults with complex support needs take advantage of the basic education programs available in every state for adults with low literacy levels (see, e.g., New Mexico Higher Education Department, n.d.). Individuals teaching in these programs typically have training and expertise in literacy instruction for adults. With some additional training in how to modify instruction to create access for adults with complex support needs, they can successfully incorporate these adult students into their classes. These adults could benefit from receiving literacy instruction in such programs, which provide age-appropriate instruction within inclusive community settings—thus avoiding the segregated settings in which staff often have low expectations and provide poor-quality instruction. This instructional arrangement would also take advantage of the social nature of literacy learning and likely increase the motivation and persistence of adult learners with complex support needs to continue their education.

Administrators and Other Educational Leaders

Administrators and other educational leaders play a critical role in leading and transforming schools and other settings to ensure meaningful and effective literacy instruction for students with complex support needs. Ensuring literacy instruction for these students is an important change. Meeting the challenges of leading such an important change can be aided by having leaders work within a conceptual framework that includes the focus areas necessary for change. Fullan provided one useful framework for leading in a culture of change. Fullan's framework includes five focus areas: 1) moral purpose, 2) understanding change, 3) relationship building, 4) knowledge creation and sharing, and 5) coherence-making (2001, p. 4).

Following Fullan's (2001) framework, one of a leader's first tasks is to develop and communicate a moral vision of a school in which all students, including those with complex support needs, learn literacy. This vision must be explicit—for example, a clear, prominent statement on the school's web site or in its entry hall. It must also be communicated repeatedly and thoroughly—for example, by referring to it frequently in meetings and by making copies readily available for teachers to include in collaborative planning. It should be obvious to anyone who comes to the school. The vision can be expressed in many different ways so that it is accessible to everyone. For example, consider a catchy wall graphic that could accompany this elementary school vision:

We believe in literacy for all.

Lose the limits on literacy!

The vision must be communicated honestly and broadly to staff, community members, all of the students in the school, and families so that everyone knows that this is the vision for the school. Keeping the vision secret might initially be tempting; a wary leader might think it will engender less pushback if no one knows it exists! But, secrecy or obfuscation will not meet the goal: making true changes to bring the school in line with the vision. Moreover, it would not be fair to the people to whom a leader has responsibilities. The students, teachers, families, and community members have a right to know the leader's vision and expectations.

The leader must also understand change, including the dynamics of change and what is required to help change succeed. Change is not easy to accomplish; the more a leader learns about change, the more likely it is to succeed. The leader must also build relationships with and among all parties who are necessary for the change to succeed and be sustainable. This includes not only maintaining the relationships between the leader and each individual, but also making sure that all the parties involved build mutual relationships with each other. Better relationships yield better results. One example may be the principal who proactively makes sure educational teams have a common planning time scheduled during the school day.

Similarly, the leader in a changing organization must ensure that all the parties in the change effort constantly build the knowledge to implement successful change and share their knowledge. Only in a knowledge-sharing organization can people feel confident sharing what they know and revealing what they need to learn in order to accomplish the moral vision. New knowledge will be an essential part of changing an organization; all parties must be committed to developing and exchanging knowledge, and they must be provided the time to work together to improve knowledge. An example is the district superintendent who seeks feedback from each school regarding professional development needs rather than implementing a one-size-fits-all model.

Finally, a critical role of the leader is to help the people in the changing organization understand what is occurring. In addition, the leader must help them make sense of the big picture of their organization's efforts to change toward the important vision of literacy for students with complex support needs.

The components of the leader's change work are accomplished with hope, enthusiasm, and energy. According to Fullan, this framework will result in external and internal commitment by the members—and as a result, "More good things happen; fewer bad things happen" (2001, p. 4). To summarize, administrators and educational leaders should, with hope, enthusiasm, and energy,

- Develop a moral vision
- Understand change
- Build relationships
- Support knowledge creation and sharing
- Make coherence

Teacher Preparation Programs

Too many young people with complex support needs are leaving school without the basic academic skills they require to find and keep employment or to participate fully in their families and communities (Newman et al., 2011). This is so despite strong legislation and a long history of litigation that has established legal requirements for the educational services to which individuals with complex support needs are entitled. It remains so despite an extensive research base of effective literacy instructional practices for students with complex support needs. We are still not seeing sufficient positive outcomes for these individuals.

We acknowledge that these poor outcomes represent a multifaceted problem. One place to focus our efforts is on changing the beliefs, actions, and behaviors of the *adults*: the educators, therapists, administrators, and adult service providers working with individuals with complex support needs. As has been discussed throughout this book, low expectations, narrow definitions of literacy, and poor instruction are often at the root of why students with complex support needs do not acquire the levels of literacy of which they are capable. Thus, it seems that a logical starting point is concentrating on the ways in which practitioners are prepared, as a means to affect positively the beliefs, knowledge, and skills of these practitioners providing literacy instruction.

We have previously pointed out that students with complex support needs "must have access to the same instructional activities for general education content, the same highly qualified teachers of that content, and the same quality of effective and evidence-based instruction" (Ryndak, 2007, p. xiii) if they are to achieve the outcomes we value for all of our citizens. Moving to a model of novice practitioner preparation that trains educators to teach *all* children well is fundamental to our vision for education. Achieving this vision will require substantial reconsideration and reconfiguration of how teachers and other practitioners, such as related service providers, are prepared for their professional roles. It is time to do away with practitioner preparation models that perpetuate the notion that practitioners must be trained to work only with certain populations; that is, systems that separate educators into those that work solely with typically developing students or special education students or English language learner (ELL) students. Instead, preparation programs must equip preservice practitioners to work effectively with students who have a range of background experiences, abilities, and strengths; it must also equip them with the professional collaborative skills needed to work closely with specialists in multiple areas.

As mentioned in Chapter 1, what teachers, administrators, and other educational professionals believe about children is incredibly powerful because their expectations influence student performance. We must instill in teachers and other educational providers, from the beginning of their preparation programs, the understanding that *all* children can learn. This requires thinking deeply and broadly about how literacy is defined and having the courage to challenge individual assumptions about the learning capability of certain groups of students. It also necessitates that teacher preparation faculty model holding high expectations for all children and provide opportunities for preservice students to see quality instruction in action. This can be accomplished by having preservice practitioners work with students with and without disabilities, including those with complex support needs, right from the beginning of their preparation programs. It is important that students in preparation programs, for example, conduct observations in classrooms or community settings where students with complex support needs are actively engaged with their typical peers, learning alongside them.

Preservice practitioners must also receive up-to-date pedagogical knowledge about how to teach literacy skills and support students' learning. This is addressed by teaching all practitioners powerful instructional strategies to use with all of their students. Every educator or therapist should learn to implement evidence-based instructional and assessment strategies, should have deep knowledge of curricular content, and should understand that all individuals have a right to have access to literacy opportunities; literacy is a legal and human right.

Specifically, preservice practitioners should be equipped with the skills to create lesson and unit plans that are universally designed and that incorporate differentiated instruction for individual student learning needs. They must learn how to provide comprehensive literacy instruction and how to do so in classrooms that include students with wide-ranging knowledge and skills. They need multiple opportunities to observe and interact with practitioners who model effective instructional and assessment practices in classrooms that include individuals with a range of abilities. Many of the strategies painstakingly researched with students with disabilities work well for any student. For example, students do not need special education eligibility to benefit from the teacher breaking down a complex task into a series of smaller, more manageable steps. Conversely, as seen throughout this book, many "general education" instructional strategies work well for students with disabilities with only slight modifications. For example, Wood and colleagues (2015) taught students with ID and their typically developing peers to generate questions about a social studies chapter they were studying in their general education classroom as a means to boost their comprehension of that content knowledge. Providing this kind of instructional knowledge to *all* beginning teachers and related service providers is powerful and will increase the likelihood that any children they work with will be successful.

Any practicing educator or provider of related services knows that it is impossible to be an effective instructor of students with complex support needs without collaborating closely with other educators, staff, and parents. Practitioners typically require specific training in how to engage in effective professional collaboration—it cannot be left to chance. When preservice educators and service providers enrolled in a unified preparation program attend classes and work together on course projects in school classrooms that include students with diverse abilities, they are doing just that: learning how to build relationships with other professionals and co-create powerful instruction for their students. Opportunities for preservice educators to co-teach with each other during their practica and student teaching further builds their instructional and collaborative expertise. Preservice related services practitioners also need opportunities in their field placements to collaborate with educators, administrators, and parents so that they, too, have these crucial skills.

It is also essential that we prepare future educators and service providers to think deeply about the role of education in society, and in this case, literacy education in particular. Preparation programs must be infused with opportunities for students to understand how to create sustainable change that leads to positive outcomes for individuals with complex support needs. This starts at the individual student level, when preservice practitioners learn how to provide quality instruction and to engage in professional collaboration; but it is enhanced when preservice practitioners acquire leadership skills as a part of their formal preparation. With these skills, their ability to implement and sustain positive change can extend across a school building, across a district, and even beyond, to the state and national level. The preservice practitioners we prepare will lead our educational systems and devise policy in the future. It is crucial that they understand the implications of failing to provide quality literacy instruction to any group of students, and crucial that they have the skills and knowledge needed to ensure that this does not happen.

Policy Makers

Policy makers are typically removed from the day-to-day, on-the-ground work of implementing change that administrators and other educational leaders must engage in. Policy makers work on a broader scale that is somewhat distant from this work, and they must address all the foci listed previously along with additional tasks. Policy makers, for example, must identify an important, relevant problem and then propose a policy agenda for solving it, get the agenda adopted, ensure that the resources needed to accomplish the policy agenda are available, implement the solution, and evaluate the results.

In the case of ensuring literacy for students with complex support needs, advocacy with policy makers such as members of state boards of education, secretaries of education, and legislators will be necessary in order to help them identify this problem of lack of access. Many policy makers have not had direct or up-to-date experience related to the needs of students with complex support needs in schools. The policy makers must be educated about the following issues: the power of literacy, a broader definition of literacy than might have existed when they were in school, literacy as a human right for students with complex support needs, and the evidence base for teaching literacy to students with complex support needs. Only when they become aware of these critical issues and potential solutions can they be in a position to

- Identify this lack of access as an important and highly relevant problem for society

- Ensure that an agenda of literacy for all is adopted

- Ensure the resources necessary to fund the policy agenda

- Implement the agenda for a solution

- Evaluate the results

For both administrators and policy makers, it is critical to consider leadership, change, and social justice as a whole package. When all three are present and connected to an important goal, we as a society are more likely to achieve a more just environment, classroom, and world. But when social justice is missing from the equation—even with leadership and change present—unfortunately, a less just environment, classroom, and world will result. Similarly, consider if only leadership and social justice are present with no change. The result would be continuation of the status quo. And, finally, what would happen if change and social justice are present but no leadership? The result would be confusion and random expenditure of efforts.

REFLECTION QUESTION 3

As you think about the major change of making sure that students with complex support needs have access to literacy, what do you need in your particular work or sphere of influence to make all the pieces come together?

WELCOMING EVERYONE TO THE LITERATE COMMUNITY

Society is strengthened when all its members have the opportunity for the "literate citizenship" described by Kliewer (2008). To welcome everyone to the literate community requires change. As a whole, the broader conceptualization of literacy embodied throughout this book assumes capability and opens up opportunities for students with complex support needs to be active participants in the literate community.

What we understand about literacy affects our practices and thus affects the opportunities to learn that we do or do not provide to individuals. So, it is important to discover what we in the field believe literacy to be and how we view its importance across the life span. Our definition of literacy will affect what we teach, to whom we provide instruction, and how long we continue to provide opportunities to participate in the literate community both in school and beyond school. The closely related principles of *least dangerous assumption* and *presumption of capability* are essential to welcoming students with complex support needs into the literate community. Throughout this book, these principles are embodied in our approach to evidence-based comprehensive literacy instruction.

As discussed throughout this chapter, actually making these opportunities a reality for those with complex support needs requires that all members of the community work together to reenvision literacy instruction and commit to providing adequate funding and support for sustained change. We concur with Kliewer et al. (2004), who stated that individuals with complex support needs should be welcomed as citizens who are capable of participating in, and contributing to, the literate community. It is not the individual's responsibility to prove that he or she is eligible to be admitted to this community; rather, it is everyone's responsibility to ensure that this happens. It is our hope that this book will contribute toward this vision.

SUMMARY

We cannot allow people with complex support needs to be denied access to literacy opportunities for even one more day.

This book has not just been about what we teach in a classroom or community today or tomorrow. We envision the future where, working together, we realize the potential of reconceptualizing how we approach literacy for people with complex support needs. Our central goal is that this book will lead to changes in opportunities and outcomes for everyone in the literate community. Think about how life might change for you and individuals with complex support needs who are welcomed into the literate community.

One of the greatest barriers to providing comprehensive literacy instruction to individuals with complex support needs will be moving past centuries of denial of literacy opportunities and the inertia within our educational and community service systems. Achieving this will take the sustained effort of all of the stakeholders we have considered in this final chapter. Whatever your role, we hope you can use this book to reflect on the way you approach literacy instruction for individuals with complex support needs. We hope it will support your efforts to design and implement evidence-based literacy instruction. Most of all, we hope it will inspire you to welcome everyone to the literate community. Increasing literacy opportunities for individuals with complex support needs will result in their being able to participate in our literate society more meaningfully and make a greater contribution to it.

We do not always see the results of our actions, but we know the results of inaction. What we do, how we treat people, how we make people feel, and what we model for others have an impact far beyond the immediate environment. When you look back on your life, how do you want to be remembered? How many people will you have touched? How many lives will you have changed? There is no right way to do the wrong thing and there is no time to wait. The actions you take today will impact the lives of individuals with complex support needs far into the future.

REFERENCES

Allor, J.H., Mathes, P.G., Roberts, J.K., Cheatham, J.P., & Al Otaiba, S. (2014). Is scientifically based reading instruction effective for students with below-average IQs? *Exceptional Children, 80*(3), 287–306.

Asante, M.K. (2013). *Buck: A memoir.* New York, NY: Random House/Spiegel & Grau.

Avila, M., & Silva, L. (2014). Milagro's story: The role of literacy for children with extensive support needs within the context of family life. *TASH Connections, 39*(2), 8–10.

Browder, D.M., Ahlgrim-Delzell, L., Courtade, G., Gibbs, S.L., & Flowers, C. (2008). Evaluation of the effectiveness of an early literacy program for students with significant developmental disabilities. *Exceptional Children, 75*(1) 33–52.

Browder, D.M., Ahlgrim-Delzell, L., Flowers, C., & Baker, J. (2012). An evaluation of a multicomponent early literacy program for students with severe developmental disabilities. *Remedial and Special Education, 33*(4), 237–246.

Copeland, S. R., & de Valenzuela, J. (2010). Home literacy practices of bilingual families of children with severe disabilities. Unpublished manuscript.

Copeland, S.R., Kruger, A., & Keefe, E.B. (2013). *Literacy and adults with developmental disabilities: Expectations, opportunities, and outcomes.* Unpublished manuscript.

Copeland, S.R., McCord, J.A., & Kruger, A. (2016, August). Literacy instruction for adults with extensive needs for supports: A review of the intervention literature. *Journal of Adolescent and Adult Literacy, 60*(2), 173–184.

de Graaf, G., van Hove, G., & Haveman, M. (2013). More academics in regular schools? The effect of regular versus special school placement on academic skills in Dutch primary school students with Down syndrome. *Journal of Intellectual Disability Research, 57,* 21–38.

Downing, J.E. (2005). *Teaching literacy to students with significant disabilities.* Thousand Oaks, CA: Corwin Press.

Duff, F.R., Keefe, E.B., & Moore, V.M. (2006). Imagine the possibilities. In E.B. Keefe, V.M. Moore, & F.R. Duff (Eds.), *Listening to the experts* (pp. 209–211). Baltimore, MD: Paul H. Brookes Publishing Co.

Fernton, F. (2006). Who's that girl? In E.B. Keefe, V.M. Moore, & F.R. Duff (Eds.), *Listening to the experts* (pp. 59–62). Baltimore, MD: Paul H. Brookes Publishing Co.

Fullan, M. (2001). *Leading in a culture of change.* San Francisco, CA: Jossey-Bass.

Hua, Y., Woods-Groves, S., Kaldenberg, E.R., & Scheidecker, B.J. (2013). Effects of vocabulary instruction using constant time delay on expository reading of young adults with intellectual disability. *Focus on Autism and Other Developmental Disabilities, 28*(2), 89–100.

Hudson, M.E., Browder, D.M., & Wood, L.A. (2013). Review of experimental research on academic learning by students with moderate and severe intellectual disability in general education. *Research and Practice for Persons with Severe Disabilities, 38*(1), 17–29.

Keefe, E.B., Moore, V.M., & Duff, F.R. (2006). *Listening to the experts.* Baltimore, MD: Paul H. Brookes Publishing Co.

Kliewer, C. (2008). *Seeing all kids as readers.* Baltimore, MD: Paul H. Brookes Publishing Co.

Kliewer, C., & Biklen, D. (2007). Enacting literacy: Local understanding, significant disability, and a new frame for educational opportunity. *Teachers College Record, 109,* 2579–2600.

Kliewer, C., Fitzgerald, L.M., Meyer-Mork, J., Hartman, P., English-Sand, P., & Raschke, D. (2004). Citizenship for all in the literate community: An ethnography of young children with significant disabilities in inclusive early childhood settings. *Harvard Educational Review, 74,* 373–403.

Koppenhaver, D.A., Pierce, P.L., & Yoder, D.E. (1995). AAC, FC, and the ABCs: Issues and relationships. *American Journal of Speech-Language Pathology, 4,* 5–14.

Koritas, S., & Iacono, T. (2011). Secondary conditions in people with developmental disability. *American Journal on Intellectual and Developmental Disabilities, 116*(1), 36–47.

Lunsford, A.A., Moglen, H., & Slevin, J. (1990). *The right to literacy.* New York, NY: The Modern Language Association of America.

McCord, J.A., Keefe, E.G., & Copeland, S.R. (2015). An investigation of the literacy learning opportunities for adults with intellectual disability and developmental disabilities in two community settings. Unpublished manuscript.

Murray, M. (2006). Taking Farrah to lunch. In E.B. Keefe, V.M. Moore, & F.R. Duff (Eds.), *Listening to the experts* (pp. 63–67). Baltimore, MD: Paul H. Brookes Publishing Co.

New Mexico Higher Education Department. (n.d.). *Adult education division.* Retrieved August 24, 2016, from http://www.hed.state.nm.us/programs/overview-and-contact-information.aspx

Newman, L., Wagner, M., Knokey, A.M., Marder, C., Nagle, K., Shaver, D., . . ., Schwarting, M. (2011). *The post-high school outcomes of young adults with disabilities up to 8 years after high school. A report from the National Longitudinal Transition Study-2 (NLTS2).* Menlo Park, CA: SRI International.

Ryndak, D.L. (2007). Foreword. In S.R. Copeland & E.B. Keefe (Eds.), *Effective literacy instruction for students with moderate or severe disabilities* (pp. xi–xv). Baltimore, MD: Paul H. Brookes Publishing Co.

Ryndak, D.L., Moore, M.A., Orlando, A.M., & Delano, M. (2008/2009). Access to general education: The mandate and role of context in research-based practices for students with extensive support needs. *Research and Practice for Persons with Severe Disabilities, 33–34,* 199–213.

Ryndak, D.L., Morrison, A., & Sommerstein, L. (1999). Literacy before and after inclusion in general education settings. *The Journal of the Association for Persons with Severe Handicaps, 24,* 5–22.

Shelton, E. (2006). Why can't they figure this out? In E.B. Keefe, V.M. Moore, & F.R. Duff (Eds.), *Listening to the experts* (pp. 3–7). Baltimore, MD: Paul H. Brookes Publishing Co.

Wise, J.C., Sevcik, R.A., Romski, M.A., & Morris, R.D. (2010). The relationship between phonological processing skills and word and nonword identification performance in children with mild intellectual disabilities. *Research in Developmental Disabilities, 31,* 1170–1175.

Wood, L., Browder, D.M., & Flynn, L. (2015). Teaching students with intellectual disability to use a self-questioning strategy to comprehend social studies text for an inclusive setting. *Research and Practice for Persons with Severe Disabilities, 40*(4), 275–293.

Supplementary Materials

Myths and Facts

Incorrect Myths and Unfounded Opinions	Facts
"The daily lives of students with complex support needs do not benefit from literacy instruction, and their acquisition of literacy is irrelevant to the good of society."	Literacy adds richness and expanded opportunities, friendships, improved thinking, imagination, communication, participation, and enjoyment to the lives of students with complex support needs (e.g., Forts & Luckasson, 2011; United Nations General Assembly, 2006). Increased education and literacy for all has been documented to improve economic and social development in all societies (e.g., Annan, 1997; Sen, 2002)
"Because the learning needs and capabilities of students with complex support needs are so different from their typically developing peers, they require segregated instruction provided in separate settings, primarily in one-to-one or very small group formats."	Students with complex support needs learn best when learning alongside their typically developing peers. Doing so provides strong literacy models and takes advantage of the social nature of literacy learning to increase motivation and persistence (e.g., de Graaf & van Hove, 2015; Kleinert et al., 2015).
"Many people with complex support needs are not able to communicate."	Everyone communicates. A few people may not yet have *intentional* communication, but everyone communicates. There are many levels of communication. We should respond to all attempts to communicate in order to respect the human interaction and support people to further develop their communication abilities (Beukelman & Mirenda, 2013).
"Students with complex support needs cannot be bilingual. Trying to make them so will confuse them. Therefore, they should be taught only in English and their families should be told to only speak English to them."	There is consistent evidence that children with complex support needs can become bilingual and that exposure to more than one language does not hold back their overall language development (e.g., Kay-Raining Bird, 2016; Kay-Raining Bird, Genesee, & Verhoeven, 2016; Marinova-Todd & Mirenda, 2016). Bilingualism is important for students and their families, and it can lead to increased opportunities for learning, meaningful relationships, and rich opportunities.

Incorrect Myths and Unfounded Opinions	Facts
"Individual education programs (IEPs) for students and individual family service plans (IFSPs) for adults with complex support needs should focus only on functional skills that will increase their independence and lead to finding and keeping a job."	Federal law mandates that students ages 3–21 have access to the general curriculum (IDEA 2004; PL 108-446), and this includes academic instruction. The poor employment outcomes documented for adults with complex support needs shows that a sole focus on "functional skills" is not producing positive outcomes (e.g., Newman et al., 2011). More recent thinking (and research) demonstrates that better postschool outcomes are associated with inclusive educational opportunities that include authentic access to the general curriculum. (There does not have to be an either/or approach: students with complex support needs can acquire academic skills such as literacy skills and learn key functional skills embedded within academic and social routines.)
"Literacy instruction for students with complex support needs should focus on simple sight-word recognition. These individuals only use literacy for daily living activities like cooking or reading signs, so the need is to focus on words that help them with those daily tasks. Many of the components of literacy are not relevant for them (e.g., fluency or comprehending long sections of text). Teaching these other skills will only confuse them and take time away from instruction on tasks crucial for daily routines."	Students with complex support needs should receive comprehensive literacy instruction. We cannot determine which students will acquire conventional literacy skills simply by their eligibility label, so disability labels should not dictate the type of instruction they receive. There is strong support for providing sustained, comprehensive literacy instruction that includes all the components of instruction associated with improved reading skills (Allor, Mathes, Roberts, Cheatham, & Al Otaiba, 2014).
"Students with complex support needs should learn to write their name, if possible, and basic information. They should not spend valuable instructional time working on writing skills (learning to compose text)."	Writing is important; it is a means of self-expression and social communication and is even a job skill. Technology and use of effective strategy instruction have proven highly effective in teaching individuals with complex support needs to write for a variety of purposes (Cannella-Malone, Konrad, & Pennington, 2015).
"Some students with complex support needs like to read books for younger students, such as *Frozen* or *Thomas the Tank Engine*. They could never understand grade-level books like Lois Lowry's *The Giver*. Adapting books and other grade-level literacy materials is a waste of time."	There is both a legal mandate that all students must have access to the general curriculum (IDEA 2004) and a research base that supports providing age-appropriate instruction for students with complex support needs. Depriving a student of access to age-appropriate materials creates segregation; artificially limits the student's academic, leisure, and emotional growth; and jeopardizes that student's ongoing relationships with all their age-peers who share with each other the experiences of daily and yearly engagement with grade-level materials.
"Postsecondary education is a waste of time for individuals with complex support needs. They will end up working in sheltered work settings; they should be prepared for this type of employment."	Research and practice strongly support the lifelong learning potential of individuals with disabilities. Literacy is an important life skill, both for its functional value and for the joy it brings to our lives. Postsecondary programs provide rich opportunities for continuing to explore new ideas and build on fundamental (functional) skills. The social and academic learning that takes place in these programs equips young adults with complex support needs to be successful in the workforce and to be active members of their communities (Moni & Jobling, 2014).

REFERENCES

Allor, J.H., Mathes, P.G., Roberts, J.K., Cheatham, J.P., & Al Otaiba, S. (2014). Is scientifically based reading instruction effective for students with below-average IQs? *Exceptional Children, 80*(3), 287–306.

Annan, K. (1997, September 4). Secretary-General stresses need for political will and resources to meet challenge of fight against illiteracy. Retrieved from http://www.un.org/press/en/1997/19970904.SGSM6316.html

Beukelman, D.R., & Mirenda, P. (2013). *Augmentative and alternative communication: Supporting children and adults with complex communication needs* (4th ed.). Baltimore, MD: Paul H. Brookes Publishing Co.

Cannella-Malone, H.I., Konrad, M., & Pennington, R.C. (2015). ACCESS! Teaching writing skills to students with intellectual disability. *TEACHING Exceptional Children, 47*(5), 272–280.

de Graaf, G., & van Hove, G. (2015). Learning to read in regular and special schools: A follow-up study of students with Down syndrome. *Life Span and Disability, 1*, 7–39.

Forts, A.M., & Luckasson, R. (2011). Reading, writing, and friendship: Adult implications of effective literacy instruction for students with intellectual disability. *Research and Practice for Persons with Severe Disabilities (RPSD), 36*(3–4), 121–125.

Individuals with Disabilities Education Improvement Act (IDEA) of 2004, PL 108-446, 20 U.S.C. §§ 1400 *et seq.*

Kay-Raining Bird, E. (2016). Bilingualism and children with Down syndrome. In J.L. Patterson & B.L. Rodríguez (Eds.), *Multilingual perspectives on child language development* (pp. 49–73). Bristol, England: Multilingual Matters.

Kay-Raining Bird, E., Genesee, F., & Verhoeven, L. (2016, September–October). Bilingualism in children with developmental disorders: A narrative review. *Journal of Communication Disorders, 63*, 1–14.

Kleinert, H., Towles-Reeves, E., Quenemoen, R., Thurlow, M., Fluegge, L., Weseman, L., & Kerbel, A. (2015). Where students with the most significant cognitive disabilities are taught: Implications for general curriculum access. *Exceptional Children, 8*(3), 312–328.

Marinova-Todd, S., & Mirenda, P. (2016). Language and communication abilities of bilingual children with autism spectrum disorders. In J.L. Patterson & B.L. Rodríguez (Eds.), *Multilingual perspectives on child language development* (pp. 31–48). Bristol, England: Multilingual Matters.

Moni, K.B., & Jobling, A. (2014). Challenging literate invisibility: Continuing literacy education for young adults and adults with Down syndrome. In R. Faragher & B. Clarke (Eds.), *Educating learners with Down syndrome: Research, theory, and practice with children and adolescents* (pp. 221–237). New York, NY: Routledge.

Newman, L., Wagner, M., Knokey, A.-M., Marder, C., Nagle, K., Shaver, D., ... Schwarting, M. (2011). *The post-high school outcomes of young adults with disabilities up to 8 years after high school. A report from the National Longitudinal Transition Study-2 (NLTS2).* Menlo Park, CA: SRI International.

Sen, A. (2002, May 27). To build a country, build a schoolhouse. *The New York Times*, p. A17.

United Nations General Assembly. (2006). *Convention on the rights of persons with disabilities.* A/RES/61/106, Annex 1. Retrieved from http://www.refworld.org/docid/4680cd212.html

Case Studies

Heather DiLuzio with contributions from Sharon L. Head, Elizabeth B. Keefe, and Susan R. Copeland

This section contains three case studies describing individuals with complex support needs: one an elementary school student, one a middle school student transitioning to high school, and one an adult. The case studies are composites based on actual individuals and do not include "answers." Instead, they are deliberately left open-ended so that readers can use them for a variety of purposes. Sample activities are included after each case description, but readers can create different uses for them, as needed. For example, college instructors in literacy methods courses can assign their students activities based on the case studies, or practitioners using the book for self-study can use the case studies for discussion and exploration of the topics, concepts, and ideas contained in the book's chapters. Each case study contains a general description of each individual followed by more detailed information on the individual's literacy and/or communication skills.

CASE STUDY 1: ELEMENTARY SCHOOL STUDENT

Steven

Steven is an 11-year-old student in fifth grade who has autism spectrum disorder (ASD). Steven attends a specialized program for students with ASD, which is provided by his local school district. Steven's parents are divorced; his primary caregiver is his mother. Steven has one older brother who is typically developing and one younger stepbrother who has developmental delays. Steven received a medical diagnosis of ASD at the age of 3 years from a local medical center.

Educational History

After his diagnosis, Steven was referred for early intervention services through his local public school system. From age 3 until his transition into kindergarten, he attended a preschool program specifically designed to meet the educational needs of students with ASD. He also received private speech and language therapy as well as occupational therapy during this time. Steven transitioned to kindergarten at age 5. His educational team decided at that time that Steven continued to require intensive supports in the areas of communication, behavioral self-regulation, social skills, and academics. The team determined that a self-contained autism-specific classroom for students with emerging communication skills would best meet his needs. Steven was not successful in the program in which he was initially placed because of aggressive behaviors. He was moved to another autism-specific classroom in September of his kindergarten year and remained in this setting until the summer after second grade.

From the time of his placement in the second classroom until the end of second grade, Steven received special education services for 6 hours per day (the entire school day). These services were provided in both a general education classroom and within his self-contained special education classroom. During this time period, Steven attended lunch, recess, physical education (PE), music, art, and computer class with a general education class of same-age peers. In addition, Steven also participated in literacy instruction within the general education classroom for

30–45 minutes, four times per week. Instruction within the general education classroom consisted of literacy instruction using the Wilson Fundations program (Wilson, 2002). This program emphasizes instruction in phonemic awareness, phonics, high-frequency words, reading fluency, vocabulary, handwriting, and spelling. Teachers in his special education classroom were also using this program. They pretaught skills needed for Steven to actively participate in the general education setting. In addition, during this time, Steven's literacy curriculum included the use of discrete trial training (DTT) to teach high-frequency sight words, repeated storybook reading instruction, vocabulary instruction, and the use of high-interest reading materials specific to Steven's particular interests.

At the end of second grade, Steven's individualized education program (IEP) team determined that because of the growth Steven had demonstrated in both his communication skills and his behavioral regulation skills, a less restrictive placement in an autism-specific program for students with independent communication skills would benefit him. At the time, this program was not available at his school site, and thus at the end of the summer, he started third grade at a new school. This placement was not successful, and in November of his third-grade year, his IEP team moved him to a third school. He was again placed in an emerging communication program for the duration of third grade. He began fourth grade at the same school site and in the same program but with a new educational staff. Again, Steven's problem behaviors interfered with his success, and in October of his fourth-grade year, he was moved back to the program he had been in from kindergarten through second grade. This proved to be a good match for his learning and behavioral needs, and he began to make steady progress academically and socially.

Steven currently receives services both within a self-contained autism-specific classroom and within a general education classroom with one-on-one support by staff from his special education classroom. Steven currently attends art, computer, library, and PE with his typically developing peers. He also participates in vocabulary instruction within the general education setting for 20–30 minutes, three times per week.

Steven also receives speech and language therapy for 1.5 hours per week, occupational therapy for 1 hour per week, and music therapy for 1 hour per week. Services are provided in both a small-group and one-on-one format. In addition, Steven has a behavior intervention plan (BIP) to address behavioral challenges that are interfering with his ability to learn and that are dangerous to both himself and those around him. These behaviors include self-aggression (biting self) as well as aggression to others, both peers and adults, when frustrated or upset. His current BIP has decreased the occurrences of these behaviors to near zero levels. Given his academic and behavioral progress, his IEP team is now considering having him spend more time in the general education classroom receiving instruction with his typically developing peers. Specifically, they are planning to provide his literacy and math instruction within the general education classroom.

Steven's communication skills have significantly improved from the time of his initial diagnosis. He is currently using a voice-output augmentative and alternative communication (AAC) device. This device is used to support his language development and is accessed throughout his school day. Teachers in the classroom also use a device to model more complex language and language usage throughout the day.

ASSESSMENT INFORMATION

Developmental Reading Assessment

Steven's current independent reading level and instructional reading level were established through the use of the Developmental Reading Assessment, Second Edition (DRA2; Beaver & Carter, 2011-2012). Based on this assessment, his current independent reading level is a level A (beginning to middle of kindergarten level) and his instructional reading level is a level 4 (end of kindergarten level). However, due to Steven's expressive and receptive language delays, the DRA2 may not provide an accurate representation of his reading abilities. The instructional reading level was established when Steven dropped below criteria in all three assessment areas: reading engagement, oral reading, and print concepts/comprehension.

Riverside Interim Assessment

In addition to the DRA2, Steven was given the Riverside Interim Assessment (Riverside Publishing, 2012) on which he scored in the "needs improvement" range with a scaled score of 121 for language arts. On the state-administered standards-based assessment given to all third-through fifth-grade students, Steven scored in the beginning steps range in the area of reading with a scaled score of 403.

Unique Learning Curriculum

Within Steven's self-contained classroom, the Unique Learning Curriculum (Unique Learning System [ULS]) is used. This curriculum has yearly benchmark assessments given in the areas of reading, writing, and mathematics. On this assessment, Steven scored as followed:

- Errorless Writing: Mastery (18/18 points). This task had Steven select an icon from a field of three to complete a written sentence.

- Rhyming Words: Emerging (7/18 points). This task had Steven select a word that rhymed with a word given orally from a field of three icons.

- Expressive Identification of Uppercase and Lowercase Letters: Mastery (17/18 points uppercase; 18/18 points lowercase). This task had Steven identify letters expressively. For this task, Steven used verbal language rather than his AAC device.

- Phonemic Awareness and Phoneme Blending: Instructional Range (11/18 points). For this task, the teacher verbally presented a word broken down into its individual phonemes, and the student was asked to identify the word by selecting the correct icon from a field of three.

- Initial Letters: Instructional Range (10/18 points). This task presents the student with an icon of a familiar thing and a field of three letters. The icon is verbally labeled for the student, and the student is then asked to select the initial letter(s) of the word.

- Word Rimes: Mastery (18/18 points). This task presents the student with an icon of an object and a spoken sentence cue. The student is then asked to select the target word from a field of three words.

- Word Recognition List 1: Mastery (18/18 points). The student is presented with a single word and asked to identify the word expressively. For this task, the student used verbal language and his AAC device to expressively read words.

- Word Recognition List 2: Mastery (16/18 points). The student is presented with a single word and asked to identify the word expressively. For this task, the student used verbal language and his AAC device to expressively read words.

- Word Recognition List 3: Instructional Range (12/18 points). The student is presented with a single word and asked to identify the word expressively. For this task, the student used verbal language and his AAC device to expressively read words.

- Final Letter: Review/Revise (0/18 points). This task presents the student with an icon of a familiar object and a field of three letters. The icon is verbally labeled for the student and the student is then asked to select the final letter(s) of the word.

- Reading Fluency & Comprehension: Steven was assessed using the ULS Benchmark Reading Fluency and Comprehension assessment. Steven was given both the nonverbal and verbal assessments. The nonverbal assessment is presented in a maze format that requires the student to indicate the correct word to fill in the blank with a sentence from a field of three words. The comprehension for the nonverbal assessment presents a question and the student selects the answer from a field of three icons. The verbal assessment is conducted in a standard running record format. The comprehension assessment requires the student to provide an expressive answer (e.g., verbal, AAC, sign) to a spoken question.

- Level A (DRA Level A-1): Book: *I Eat*

    Verbal: Accuracy 96% (Independent) Comprehension 4/5 (Fair)

    Nonverbal: Accuracy 100% (Independent) Comprehension 5/5 (Good)

- Level B (DRA Level 2): Book: *Many Colors*

    Verbal: Accuracy 97% (Independent) Comprehension 4/5 (Fair)

    Nonverbal: Accuracy 89% (Frustration) Comprehension 4/5 (Fair)

- Level C (DRA Level 3–4): Book: *What Is Bigger?*

    Verbal: Accuracy 98% (Independent) Comprehension 1/5 (Poor)

    Nonverbal: Accuracy 50% (Frustration) Comprehension 0/5 (Poor)

- Scoring Guide for ULS:

    - 18–15: Mastery. This indicates that the student should apply the current skills into higher-level reading strategies.

    - 14–10: Instructional. Incorporate routine skill instruction to strengthen this reading skill area.

    - 9–6: Emerging. Emerging reading skills in this skill area may be developed through structured learning tasks.

    - 5-0: Review/Revise. Review the student's present level and revise goals to more appropriately address learning potential.

PCI Reading Program

Steven also receives daily one-on-one or small-group instruction using the PCI Reading Program (PRO-ED, 2007). This program teaches high-frequency Dolch and Fry sight words in addition to real-world words. PCI uses a highly structured instructional sequence that focuses on sight-word instruction for Levels 1 and 2. In Level 3, instruction expands into scaffolded phonics instruction through the use of word analysis, word building, and decoding strategies.

PCI Reading Program Level 1:

Initial Assessment: Expressive Verbal, 131/140; AAC Identification: 54/90

2nd Assessment: Expressive Verbal, 138/140; AAC Identification: 81/140

Basic Skills Checklist

The following data include information gathered using the Basic Skills Checklists (Breitenbach, 2000).

Reading

- Steven is currently able to identify 89 of 220 of the Dolch high-frequency sight words expressively when presented in isolation and asked, "What word?" (29/40 preprimer, 14/52 primer, 18/41 first grade, 10/46 second grade, 18/41 third grade).

- Steven is currently able to demonstrate the following concepts of print: book orientation, title, beginning of text, left to right, and return sweep. Steven is unable to perform the following directions when assessing for concepts of print: "Show me the front cover," "Show me the back cover," "Point to the part that tells the story," "Point to where you start reading," and "Show me how you read."

Alphabet Skills

- Steven is currently able to expressively identify 25 of 26 uppercase letters when presented with a letter and asked, "What letter?" Steven was unable to identify the uppercase letter *I* during assessment.

- Steven is currently able to expressively identify 26 of 26 lowercase letters when presented with a letter and asked, "What letter?"

- Currently, Steven is able to receptively identify the following short vowel and consonant sounds, long vowel sounds, vowel teams, welded sounds, and digraphs from the Fundations curriculum.

  - Short Vowel and Consonant Sounds: A–Z

  - Long Vowel Sounds: a-safe, a-acorn, o-home, o-no, u-rule, u-pupil, i-pine, i-hi, e-pete, e-me, y-cry

  - Vowel Teams: ow-plow, oe, ey, oo, oa, er, oy, ay, ue-rescue, ee, ou-trout, ai, oi

  - Welded Sounds: old, ind, am, ive, ild, ost, ing, ang, onk, ank

  - Digraphs: ch, sh, ck, wh, th

Dictionary and Book Skills

- Places Letters in Alphabetical Order: When given all 26 letters of the alphabet, Steven is currently able to place the letters in alphabetical order with no more than one additional prompt to stay on task.

- Places Words in Alphabetical Order by First Letter: When given 26 words, each starting with a different letter of the alphabet, Steven is currently able to place 26 of 26 words in alphabetical order.

- Places Words in Alphabetical Order by Second Letter: Steven is currently not able to demonstrate this skill.

- Locates Words in Dictionary: Steven is currently not able to demonstrate this skill.

- Locates Table of Contents: Steven is not able to demonstrate this skill.

Written Language
Capitalization and Punctuation

- Capitalize: Steven is able to independently demonstrate the following skills: capitalize the beginning of a sentence, days of the week, and months and capitalize the first letter of his first and last names. Steven is currently not able to capitalize the following items without additional prompting: people's names, holidays, cities, countries, and titles of books.

- Punctuation: Steven is able to demonstrate the following skills: place a period at the end of a sentence and place a comma between date and year. Currently, Steven is not able to demonstrate the following skills: place a comma between city and state, use an exclamation point appropriately, use a question mark appropriately, or use an apostrophe appropriately.

Writing

- Writes Letters from Dictation: Steven is currently able to write 25 of 26 letters when dictated to him. He wrote *s* for *z*.

- Writes Numbers from Dictation: Steven is currently able to write the following numbers when dictated to him: 0, 1, 2, 3, 4, 6, 7, 8, 9, 10, 16, 17, 18, 19, and 20.

- Writes Name: Steven is currently able to write both his first and last names from memory when given the direction "write your name." Steven is also able to write his name across all school settings during appropriate activities.

SAMPLE CASE STUDY ACTIVITIES

1. Role-play an IEP team meeting for Steven, with different people taking on different roles (e.g., Steven's mother, fifth-grade general education teacher, special education teacher, administrator, speech-language pathologist, behavior specialist, Steven, district ASD specialist). The team is reviewing Steven's current assessment and monitoring his progress data. They are considering moving Steven into the general education setting for most of his instruction.

   a. What questions might each of these team members ask? What plans would need to be put in place? What natural and paid supports would ensure Steven's success—that is, when might he need support from a paraeducator or his special education teacher (paid supports) and when might peers (natural supports) provide assistance? What organizational tools might be helpful in creating effective instructional plans for Steven?

   b. Write standards-based goals/objectives for Steven related to literacy. Use information from the case study to support answers, or provide a rationale for recommendations and decisions as well as information from relevant chapters in the book.

2. The case study mentions that some of the assessments used might not have accurately assessed what Steven actually knows/can do regarding literacy skills. What are some suggestions for changing the assessment process or adapting specific items? Use what you know about Steven and information on how to adjust assessment for students with complex support needs that you read about in the book.

3. Using the assessment data information in the case study and the description of Steven's communication system, develop at least three detailed lesson plans, to be implemented within the general education classroom, which will build on his current literacy skills. Plans should include learning objectives (what you want him to know and be able to do at the end of the lesson) and a plan for assessing his performance on lesson objectives. Include a detailed description of how his AAC device will be used during the instruction and assessment portions of the lesson.

4. How might age-appropriate literacy materials be adapted to provide access for Steven? What adaptations and commonly available assistive technology could be explored?

5. Consider strategies and supports that would help not only Steven but peers who also have learning needs or who need opportunity for enrichment in general education settings. What information is needed about Steven's peers in general education? How can collaboration time with special and general education staff be used to design and implement learning opportunities that are academically and social effective for all learners in Steven's classrooms?

CASE STUDY 2: MIDDLE–HIGH SCHOOL

Michelle

Michelle is a 14-year-old female student with intellectual disability (ID). Michelle is an only child; her father is her primary caregiver. Michelle's mother left the family shortly after Michelle was born and has not been in contact with her child since that time. Michelle's father works a full-time job in addition to caring for Michelle, but he is an active participant on Michelle's educational team.

Michelle began receiving intervention services at the age of 2 for a developmental delay after being referred for evaluation by her pediatrician. Her language and communication skills were significantly delayed. She also struggled with motor tasks that required fine motor control, such as feeding herself. Her early intervention services were provided by a local agency and included speech-language therapy, occupational therapy, developmental instruction, and social work. These services were provided in the home.

Educational History

At the age of 3 years, Michelle transitioned into her local public school system and continued to receive early educational services within a special education preschool classroom, based on her significant developmental delay. From ages 3 to 5, Michelle attended this preschool program and continued to receive speech-language therapy, occupational therapy, and social work to support her development. These services were provided within her preschool classroom. Michelle's primary mode of communication was verbal speech. She had limited vocabulary and articulation problems but made progress in both areas during her preschool years. She enjoyed story time in preschool but received little systematic literacy instruction beyond small-group instruction on identifying the letters of the alphabet.

At the age of 5, Michelle transitioned into kindergarten. For elementary school, Michelle attended her neighborhood school and was included in the general education setting throughout her day. During this time, she continued to receive occupational therapy, speech-language therapy, and social work. At the age of 6, Michelle was reevaluated, and it was determined that she met the criteria to qualify for special education services under the eligibility ID. Throughout her time in elementary school, Michelle was provided special education services within the general education classroom. She was an active member of her school and classroom community and enjoyed attending school. She had friends in and out of school.

By the end of elementary school, Michelle was able to expressively identify most of the uppercase letters and a few of the lowercase letters. She was able to identify her first and last names when written and was able to write the first three letters of her name independently when asked to write her name. She could type her first name correctly using an adapted keyboard. Michelle was able to trace all 26 uppercase letters and a few lowercase letters when writing.

Michelle's sight-word vocabulary at the end of elementary school consisted of 100 words (high-frequency words, words needed to participate in academic instruction, and some words related to her particular interests). She knew the initial sounds for four consonants (/b/, /m/, /t/, /p/) but had not mastered any short vowel sounds. She increased her vocabulary during these years, particularly in picking up content words in social studies and science as well as other academic vocabulary. Her listening comprehension was at a second-grade level; her reading comprehension at a preprimer level. Michelle developed a keen interest in maps during this time and enjoyed spending time looking at maps and talking to others about maps. Her general education teacher included "map words" in the sight-word instruction that Michelle received so that she could expand her participation in these activities.

Michelle transitioned into middle school at the age of 11. She attended her neighborhood middle school with many of the same students from her elementary school. Although Michelle had been provided special education supports in an inclusive setting throughout elementary school, she was placed in a self-contained special education classroom in middle school. During middle school, Michelle received all of her reading, mathematics, and written language instruction within the self-contained classroom. One time per week, she attended an elective class, art, with her typically developing peers.

During middle school, Michelle was able to maintain few of the friendships she had developed with her peers during elementary school. Because of her limited access to the general education environment, most of her relationships faded throughout middle school as she saw her peers less often. In addition, Michelle made little progress academically during middle school. In some areas, her skills actually decreased. Her academic IEP goals throughout middle school remained the same as in elementary school; they continued to focus on alphabet identification, writing words from dictation, and sight-word identification. The special education teacher used the PCI Reading Program to teach sight words, primarily through the computerized version. There was no attempt to teach words outside of those in the PCI curriculum. Throughout her middle school experience, Michelle maintained her fondness for maps. During this time, she also began to enjoy traveling and planning vacations with her father. They frequently took road trips on the weekends, and Michelle was always excited to talk to others about her trips.

At the age of 14, Michelle transitioned to her neighborhood high school. Frustrated by her lack of progress and limited enthusiasm around school, Michelle's father advocated for more inclusion opportunities for Michelle in high school. As a result, Michelle's educational team was tasked with planning for Michelle to participate in the general education setting. Michelle currently receives a full day of special education supports. In addition, she receives occupational therapy to address her fine motor delays and speech-language therapy to support her articulation and communication skills.

ASSESSMENT INFORMATION

PCI Reading Program

This program teaches high-frequency Dolch and Fry sight words in addition to real-world words. PCI uses a highly structured instructional sequence that focuses on sight-word instruction for Levels 1 and 2. In Level 3, instruction expands into scaffolded phonics instruction through the use of word analysis, word building, and decoding strategies.

Michelle is still on PCI Reading Program Level 1 after 3 years of instruction. She can expressively (verbally) identify 30 of 140 words and 45 of 140 receptively (selecting a word from an array of three).

Basic Skills Checklists

The following data include information gathered using the Basic Skills Checklists.

Matching

- Identical: Michelle is currently able to demonstrate the following skills:
  - Object-to-Object
  - Picture-to-Picture (object)
  - Picture-to-Picture (action)
  - Picture-to-Object
  - Object-to-Picture
  - Colors: red, blue, yellow, green, orange, purple, brown, black, white, grey, pink
  - Shapes: circle, square, triangle, rectangle, oval, star, diamond, heart, hexagon

- Numbers 1–20 (Field of Three)
- Community Signs (Field of Three): go, stop, in, out, men's, women's, restroom, enter, exit, ladies, gentlemen, walk, poison, caution, danger

- Michelle is not able to demonstrate the following skills:
  - Object-to-Outline
  - Words

- With extensive prompts, Michelle is able to match the written word for colors, shapes, and community signs.

Alphabet Skills

- Michelle is currently able to expressively identify 25 of 26 uppercase letters when presented with a letter and asked, "What letter?"

- Michelle is currently able to expressively identify 23 out of 26 lowercase letters when presented with a letter and asked "What letter?"

SAMPLE CASE STUDY ACTIVITIES

1. Role-play working with educational team members to develop a program-at-a-glance and infused skills grid for Michelle for one or more class periods.

2. Write two age-appropriate standards-based IEP goals that incorporate literacy. How would you assess these goals?

3. Develop two lesson plans that address literacy across content areas that would address standards-based IEP goals as part of instruction.

4. Choose a content area and explore how access could be provided to content in this area without the need for grade-level decoding skills. Are there activities and materials that could be differentiated so that they would be appropriate to Michelle and her typical peers? Develop a 2-week unit around a content area topic or concept.

5. Envision a plan for inclusion that begins with Michelle's strong interest in maps. Brainstorm ways to incorporate this interest into instruction across content areas. What could literacy instruction look like for Michelle if her strongest interests were put at the center of reading and writing activities? How can this instructional approach be broadened once Michelle is more engaged and better able to access content in her general education classes?

CASE STUDY 3: ADULT

Mary

Mary is a 25-year-old female who has multiple disabilities, including ID and cerebral palsy. At times, she engages in challenging behavior that consists of throwing objects on the floor (not at people) or hitting her head forcefully with her hand. She currently has a BIP in place that appears to be helping her and has had zero incidents of problem behavior in the past month.

Mary was typically developing until the age of 10 when she contracted bacterial meningitis and became severely ill. She went into a coma and was in the pediatric intensive care unit for a considerable length of time. After her illness, Mary experienced a variety of learning challenges including the loss of her ability to read. She also experienced damage to the motor cortex of the brain with the result that she was diagnosed with spastic cerebral palsy, which requires her to use a wheelchair. She does have use of her arms and hands but struggles with fine motor tasks.

Educational History

Mary uses speech to communicate but speaks slowly with some articulation errors, especially when she is tired. Although Mary received intensive direct instruction throughout the duration of elementary school, she never regained the ability to read beyond the preprimer level. Mary was able to learn how to write her name and the names of familiar people and to identify simple familiar words. Once Mary moved on to middle and high school, the vast majority of her instruction concentrated on "functional or vocational skills" rather than academic content. She had very limited opportunities to use any form of technology while in school. Mary transitioned out of her local public education system at the age of 21.

Mary currently lives in a group home setting with three other women and participates in a day habilitation program that is designed to increase her participation in the community. Her days vary but include a variety of activities including physical fitness classes at the local YMCA, arts and crafts at her group home, and community outings to various locations such as the local park. Mary participates in the faith community where her family has attended since her childhood. She sees her parents weekly when they go out to a favorite restaurant but has no other regular social activities outside of what is offered through the agency providing her adult services.

Mary is currently employed part time at a garden center. She works there three afternoons per week, repotting and watering plants. She recently expressed an interest in learning how to read better so she can learn more about the flowers and plants with which she works.

Mary's case manager, John, followed up on Mary's comment about wanting to improve her reading skills. John began by conducting the Student Interview, Grades 5–12 portion of the Critical Reading Inventory (CRI; Applegate, Quinn, & Applegate, 2008) with Mary to find out more about her interests and motivations as a way to improve her literacy skills.

He modified the questions to reflect the fact that Mary is an adult and is no longer in a school setting. During the interview, Mary expressed an interest in gardening, talking to friends, and taking Zumba classes. When probed about her reading habits, Mary indicated that she enjoys looking through magazines about gardening and often saves pictures of flowers or plants that she likes. When asked what was the hardest part of reading, she indicated that she wanted to be able to read about the different types of plants and that she found the names of plants and flowers "confusing." When asked how she felt about writing, she stated that she wanted to write so that she would be able to write letters to her sister who lives in another state. Mary also expressed interest in advancing her reading and writing skills so that she would be able to contribute to a monthly gardening newsletter published by her employer.

John then used the CRI to assess Mary's current literacy skills to determine where to begin her instructional program. John went over the results of the CRI assessment at the next meeting of her individual support planning (ISP) team. (Mary and her mother are members of the team.) The team began a discussion of how they could support Mary's goal of improving her literacy skills to meet the specific goals she had identified. They were also interested in finding other opportunities for Mary to engage in community activities based on her interests. The behavior support consultant, in particular, expressed that he thought Mary was often bored at her group home and had noticed that problem behaviors were more likely to occur when this was the case.

ASSESSMENT INFORMATION

Critical Reading Inventory

CRI is a developmental reading inventory designed to assess a range of reading skills from preschool through approximately ninth grade. Following are Mary's scores on this assessment.

Oral Reading Fluency Rubric

- Oral Reading: 1
- Intonation: 2
- Punctuation: 3
- Pacing: 3
- Total score: 9 = Inadequate

Word Recognition: Preprimer Word List   The student identifies single words from a graded list.

- Flash (identified immediately): 12 (60%)
- Untimed (identified): 14 (70%)

Preprimer Narrative Passage 1   The student reads a passage written at a particular grade level.

- Reading Accuracy Index: 88% (13 Scoreable Miscues)
- Meaning Making Index: 90% (11/13 Scoreable Miscues were meaning violating)

Comprehension

- Oral Comprehension: 7% (0.5/7)
- Retelling: 0.5 (able to identify main characters)
- Text-Based Questions: 0.5 of 3
- Inference Questions: 0 of 3
- Critical Response Questions: 0 of 2

Listening Comprehension   This is administered 1 week after initial assessment using the same passage as for the reading comprehension assessment.

- Retelling: 1 of 5
- Text-Based Questions: 2 of 3
- Inference Questions: 0.5 of 3
- Critical Response Questions: 0 of 2

SAMPLE CASE STUDY ACTIVITIES

1. Discuss what next steps Mary's ISP team should take to make her literacy goals a reality. What community organizations might be able to assist or where else might she find literacy instruction? What additional professional expertise might be needed on her team to make her goals a reality? Is there a possible mentor (a natural support) at Mary's worksite who would work with her on vocabulary related to her strong interest in gardening?

2. Design a series of three to five lesson plans based on the assessment information provided, Mary's interests, and Mary's goals. Be sure to consider how to make them engaging and age appropriate for an adult.

3. How could literacy become part of Mary's everyday environment? What vocabulary words could be targeted? How could these words be used in connected text?

4. What online and technology resources could be used to provide access to literacy activities around Mary's interest areas? For example, Mary has a strong interest in plants/gardening and an equally strong desire to communicate with others. She could learn to use any number of accessibility tools commonly found in Microsoft Office, Google Apps, or other programs to develop articles, presentations, and so forth, to share with an audience.

5. What literacy-based activities could be designed and/or planned by residents and staff at Mary's group home? Mary's need for connection and challenge (expressed by her behavior at times) is likely a community need. Reflect on the possibility that Mary's need for connection with others may provide her with an opportunity to serve fellow residents and the neighborhood/world at large.

REFERENCES

Applegate, M.D., Quinn, K.B., & Applegate, A.J. (2008). *Critical Reading Inventory* (2nd ed.). Pearson College Division.

Beaver, J., & Carter, M. (2011-2012). *Developmental Reading Assessment, Second Edition.* Pearson Assessment Division.

Breitenbach, M. (2000). *Basic Skills Checklists: Teacher-friendly assessment for students with autism or special needs.* Arlington, TX: Future Horizons.

PCI Reading Program. (2007). Austin, TX: PRO-ED.

Riverside Interim Assessment (2012). Rolling Meadows, IL: Riverside Publishing Company, Houghton Mifflin Harcourt.

Wilson, B. (2002). *Fundations.* Oxford, MA: Wilson Language Training.

Index

References to tables and figures are indicated with a *t* and *f* respectively.